MAGILL'S
SURVEY
OF
CINEMA

MAGILL'S SURVEY OF CINEMA

Foreign Language Films

VOLUME 4
INS-MEL

Edited by

FRANK N. MAGILL

Associate Editors

PATRICIA KING HANSON

KAREN JAEHNE

SALEM PRESS
Englewood Cliffs, N.J.

Library of Congress Cataloging-in-Publication Data
Magill's survey of cinema, foreign language films.
    Includes index.
    1. Moving-pictures—Plots, themes, etc.—Dictionaries.
I. Magill, Frank Northen, 1907-
PN1993.45.M34   1986   791.43'75   85-18241
ISBN 0-89356-243-2 (set)
ISBN 0-89356-247-5 (volume 4)

FIRST PRINTING

PRINTED IN THE UNITED STATES OF AMERICA

LIST OF TITLES IN VOLUME FOUR

LIST OF TITLES IN VOLUME FOUR

MAGILL'S
SURVEY
OF
CINEMA

THE INSECT WOMAN
(NIPPON KONCHUKI)

Origin: Japan
Released: 1963
Released in U.S.: 1964
Production: Nikkatsu
Direction: Shohei Imamura
Screenplay: Keiji Hasebe and Shohei Imamura
Cinematography: Shinsaku Himeda
Editing: Mutsuo Tanji
Art direction: Kimihiko Nakamura
Music: Toshiro Mayuzumi
Running time: 123 minutes

> *Principal characters:*
> Tome .... Sachiko Hidari
> Nobuko .... Jitsuko Yoshimura
> Karasawa .... Seizaburo Kawazu
> Chuji.......................... Kazuo Kitamura
> Matsunami...................... Hiroyuki Nagato
> En .... Sumie Sasaki
> Onagawa .... Shoichi Kuwayama
> Midori........................ Masumi Harukawa
> Suma.......................... Tanie Kitabayashi
> Midwife .... Tanie Kitabayashi
> Honda .... Shoichi Tsuyuguchi
> Yoshiji Kamibayashi............. Daizaburo Hirata

Since about 1920, when the Japanese cinema began using actresses to portray the female roles (*oyama*, the male actors trained in women's parts, were previously used, as in the traditional theater), women have occupied a significant role on Japan's screens. It is believed that perhaps no major national cinema has produced a more substantial body of work about women than Japan. Within this cinematic tradition of focusing on women, two directors stand out for their sympathetic treatment and cinematic brilliance: Kenji Mizoguchi and Shohei Imamura.

To the Japanese, Mizoguchi and Imamura are *feminisutos* (from the Japanese pronunciation of "feminists"), male directors who idealize and worship women for their ability to suffer uncomplainingly with courage, endurance, and virtue. Although this is hardly what the West considers genuinely feminist, in the films of both directors can be found an orientation toward examining women in social contexts, thus pointing the way toward explicit or (as is mostly the case with Mizoguchi) implicit political statements.

On first viewing, Imamura seems to share little with Mizoguchi. Where Mizoguchi is aesthetically elegant, Imamura is earthy; where Mizoguchi is discreet, Imamura is positively bawdy. Yet for both filmmakers, women are superior, idealized beings. For Mizoguchi, women represent the religious, transcendental ideals of traditional Japanese high culture; for Imamura, women represent the ancient, prehistoric essence of folk belief. The essence of Imamura's cinema can be found in *The Insect Woman*, his first important film devoted to the image of the Japanese woman.

The Insect Woman begins in rural Tohoku, several years before World War II. Tome (Sachiko Hidari), the insect woman of the title, lives with her mother, En (Sumie Sasaki), and her father, Chuji (Kazuo Kitamura). Chuji is slightly retarded, as well as poor. It turns out that Chuji is not Tome's real father, for En had taken a lover, Onagawa (Shoichi Kuwayama). In fact, En and Onagawa virtually live together; when Tome was six, she had seen them making love and had asked Chuji if En and Onagawa were really husband and wife, and, if so, could she and Chuji be considered husband and wife since they sleep together.

Soon after the start of the war, Tome takes a job in a textile factory, where she becomes the lover of her boss, Matsunami (Hiroyuki Nagato). En wants Tome to marry Honda (Shoichi Tsuyuguchi), the son of a wealthy landowner in Tohoku. Tome is raped by Honda and bears a daughter. The midwife (Tanie Kitabayashi) asks Tome whether to allow the little girl to live; Tome says she will keep the child. Tome, however, leaves home again and returns to work in the factory and continues her relationship with Matsunami. Tome also becomes quite active in union organizing when the war is over, but she is accused of being a Communist when the Cold War ideology finds its way to American-occupied Japan.

Tome then goes to work in Tokyo as a maid for Midori (Masumi Harukawa), who lives as the mistress of an American soldier. Tome soon leaves that job to work as a maid at an inn run by Suma (Tanie Kitabayashi, in a dual role as she also plays the midwife). Suma is also the madam of a bordello that operates at the inn. Suma schemes to have Tome raped by one of her clients so that Tome can be persuaded to become a prostitute. Tome does become a prostitute and becomes a favorite of Karasawa (Seizaburo Kawazu), a well-to-do fabric wholesaler, who is also something of a *yakuza* (gangster). When Suma is arrested, Tome becomes the madam and buys the inn. Tome is a cruel mistress to her girls, but she gets her comeuppance when she is robbed by her patron and framed for a crime. While Tome is in prison, her daughter, Nobuko (Jitsuko Yoshimura), returns to Tokyo to earn money for farm machinery. She wants to marry Yoshiji Kamibayashi (Daizaburo Hirata), a boy from their village who wants to start a communal farm. To get the money, Nobuko has an affair with Karasawa. She steals a large quantity of money from him and returns to her village.

Tome is released from prison, broke and abandoned. Karasawa offers her a lot of money if Tome will return to Tohoku and tell Yoshiji what Nobuko has done. Nobuko, meanwhile, is pregnant with Karasawa's child, but Yoshiji seems not to care in the least. Tome leaves Tokyo to return to Tohoku.

For Imamura, Tome, the insect woman, represents all Japanese life, a life whose roots lie in the traditional heart of Japan: the countryside. Tome is vital, alive, strong, at one with her sexuality, uncorrupted so long as she remains in the village. Even the incestuous aspects of Tome's relationship with her stepfather are shown to be innocent, and the adulterous nature of her mother, while never condoned, is also not destructive. Tome becomes corrupted only when she must leave her native village behind, only, that is, when she moves to the city. Then she becomes corrupted, a victimizer as well as a victim. Her sexuality, far from naturally expressing itself, becomes something to be bartered, sold in a marketplace along with other desirable goods.

In the cities of this new, postwar Japan, Tome learns about power—economic, political, and sexual power. Tome also learns how even good ideas, such as unionizing and working for economic and political gain, become corrupted by power. Most important, she learns that her sexuality, too, can be a source of power. In a society in which men control political and economic power, women can learn to seize a part of it by using their sexual power. Imamura shows the viewer that Tome's life as a prostitute and a madam is a far cry from her life in rural Japan.

Because Tome stands for the essence of Japanese life, her experiences in the film stand as a microcosm for all Japan in its modern era. Tome begins life in a farming village and as a member of a family. Economic changes, as well as the moral changes such "advances" bring about, force Tome to depart from her family. Tome goes to work in a factory, a movement that directly corresponds to the changes in modern Japan in its shift from a primarily agricultural, rural society to an industrial, urban culture. Tome's union activities represent the promise of the postwar society under the influence of the American occupation. Tome's decision to work for a woman who lives with an American shows the betrayal of the postwar promise and the prostitution of Japan to the United States. Tome literalizes this metaphorical prostitution when she actually becomes a prostitute. Moreover, the corruption that begins to infect postwar society is mirrored by Tome's becoming a madam, a cruel, exploitive madam. (This vision of postwar Japanese society, especially in its relationship to the United States, is also on view in Imamura's darkly comic, political satire *Pigs and Battleships*, 1961.) Tome's progress away from her life in the countryside is a continual progress away from her true roots. The film shows the audience how Tome, like Japan, becomes ever increasingly driven by economic forces. At the film's end, however, Tome returns to the village, thus indicating that there is a chance to break out of the economic trap, a chance to return to some more essential part of one's being.

The idea of one's essential being, and the idea of the essence of the nation and its people, is an indication that Imamura is as much an anthropologist as a filmmaker, and *The Insect Woman* is one of the best examples of his anthropological leanings. The title itself indicates that the central figure is under examination, like a specimen in a laboratory or out in the field. In the best anthropological investigative tradition, Imamura refrains from too close an identification with his subject, and he certainly refrains from romanticizing her. Indeed, one could find few films, especially in the Japanese cinema, in which a director is so clearly dispassionate toward his female lead. Tome is presented with all her faults intact, from the terrible poetry she writes in her diary to the cruelty she inflicts upon her girls in the bordello. Yet she is also presented as a fully realized being, one whose motives derive from a specific sociocultural context. That is what is most central to Imamura's conception of the insect woman—her roots in culture and her transcendence of that culture.

What one also sees in *The Insect Woman* is a Japanese woman, a strong, courageous survivor. Through hardship such as poverty, rape, economic exploitation in the factory and in the house of prostitution, Tome survives. She may not come out on top, but she endures. What is it that makes her endure? It is, according to Imamura, her nature as a woman, as a primitive, sexual being. It is no coincidence that Imamura concentrates his film on Tome's early life, her exposure to sex as a natural part of existence and her innocent "incest" with her stepfather, Chuji, before showing Tome's corruption in the city. It is as if, in these early sections, Tome lives a premodern existence: She lives during a time before economics and politics, before, even, psychology. It is a woman's nature, a nature at some very deep level that is incorruptible, that tenaciously holds on to its roots in this premodern civilization, that enables Tome to endure.

Tome's nature corresponds to the essence of the Japanese spirit, and Imamura finds that it extends back to the ancient priestesses (*miko*) of Japanese village life before the dawn of history. The image of the priestess is fundamental to the native Japanese tradition known as Shinto, an animistic religion with roots in Japanese mythology. In this Shinto mythology, which, Imamura is quick to point out, has many remnants in today's Japan, women occupy a central place in the pantheon of gods, which are ruled over by the sun-goddess, Amaterasu. Each tribe in ancient Japan had its own *miko*; for Imamura, the *miko* survives in essence in that tribe known as the family. At some very deep mythic levels, the Japanese conceive of themselves as one large family, an image aided by the relative homogeneity of the Japanese people. In some sense then, Imamura would have it, the concept of incest is foreign to the native Japanese spirit. Thus, not only does the audience find the motif of incest in *The Insect Woman*, but the idea also reappears in another extremely important work in Imamura's canon, *Kamigami no Fukaki Yokubo* (1968; *The Profound Desire of the Gods*, also called *Kuragejima: Tales from a Southern Island*), a work devoted to showing the primitive spirit within the soul of modern Japan. In *The Insect Woman*, this essential spirit keeps Tome alive and even offers her a glimmer of hope, if only she can return to the village from which she derives her essence.

The links between Tome and the ancient goddesses and priestesses of the folk belief is further reinforced in the film because of its cyclical structure. Tome leaves the village of her birth to venture forth into the larger world, only to return to the village at the film's end. Tome thus experiences something like the mythic cycle of life-death-rebirth when she is born into the village, undergoes something like a death in the outside world, and is to be understood as being reborn upon her return. The idea of a mythic, never-ending cycle is also to be understood as occurring not only in terms of Tome, but also in terms of all women. Tome's experiences are precisely mirrored by her daughter, Nobuko. Nobuko, too, is born in the rural village, experiences life in the outside world, becoming a prostitute, like her mother, only to return to the seat of true life back in the village. Both Tome and Nobuko journey from innocence to sophistication, to decadence, and then back to innocence, a journey to be understood as characteristic of all women who mystically maintain their tribal, Japanese essence. While the men either remain innocent all of their lives, like Chuji, or become decadent, like Karasawa, the women have the ability to pass through these stages, to transcend them.

Thus, one is brought back full circle to Mizoguchi. These two great *feminisutos* ultimately share a vision of women that finds them superior to men in their ability to transcend the social and historical forces that seek to oppress them. For Mizoguchi, women are something like the bodhisattvas of the Buddhist canon, would-be Buddhas who choose to remain on Earth to help men; for Imamura, women are the ancient *miko*, the priestess-shamanesses of the tribal village who intercede for man with the gods. Operating at the folk level of belief, unlike Mizoguchi, who is more comfortable in the high, aristocratic culture, Imamura sees women as maintaining deep within their inexhaustible natures the true essence of the Japanese people.

David Desser

INSIANG

Origin: Philippines
Released: 1976
Released in U.S.: 1979
Production: Ruby Tiong Tan for CineManila
Direction: Lino Brocka
Screenplay: Mario O'Hara and Lamberto E. Antonio; based on the story by
  Mario O'Hara
Cinematography: Conrado Baltazar
Editing: Augusto Salvador
Art direction: Fiel Zabat
Music: Minda D. Azarcon
MPAA rating: no listing
Running time: 95 minutes

> *Principal characters:*
> Insiang . . . . Hilda Koronel
> Tonya. . . . . Mona Lisa
> Dado. . . . . Ruel Vernal
> Bebot . . . . Rez Cortéz

Although perhaps not Lino Brocka's most important work—critical consensus points to his earlier *Maynila, sa mga kuko ng liwanag* (1975; *Maynila: In the Claws of Neon*)—*Insiang* is the film that first gained for him international recognition through its screening in the prestigious Directors' Fortnight at the Cannes International Film Festival 1978. It was, in fact, the first commercially produced Philippine film to be shown at a major European film festival since Manuel Conde's celebrated breakthrough with *Genghis Khan* (1950) at the Venice International Film Festival in 1952.

Like Brocka's *Bona* (1980), *Insiang* first appeared in a television version (1974), which in an interview he called "more virulent" than the final film, primarily in its franker handling of the theme of sexual relations in the slums. The television film caused such a scandal that the master tape eventually had to be destroyed.

Both versions are based on a story by actor, director, and writer Mario O'Hara, a longtime associate of Brocka, who collaborated on the screenplay with Lamberto E. Antonio. The sparse dialogue is entirely in Tagalog or Pilipino, the principal dialect of the Philippines.

Insiang incorporates elements of the melodrama but Brocka's film transcends these conventions through its almost classic symmetry of time, place, and action. Set in Tondo, Manila's most notorious slum, *Insiang* is first a study of an adolescent girl reared in miserable surroundings. The girl, Insiang (Hilda Koronel), who gives the film its title, serves as a reflection of the violence engendered in the subproletariat of an urban milieu. The film demonstrates the destruction of a human being and the loss of human dignity provoked by the physical and social environment of the slums. It is a film about the girl's futile attempt to break out of her bleak world and the brutal transformation evoked by her defeat and loss of identity.

Although the setting could be transferred to other conditions—Brocka had originally planned to treat the story of a girl who had been moved into a modern urban housing unit—and despite the fact that the film can be seen and enjoyed as a tale of love and revenge completely detached from its political and social significance, Brocka, as the major moral force of the Philippine film industry and one of the leading members of the political opposition, never tires of stressing the fact that *Insiang* is designed to underline the necessity of changing the living conditions that it portrays.

The melodramatic core of *Insiang* is a triangular love-hate relationship among the adolescent girl Insiang (one can imagine her to be about seventeen years of age), her mother, Tonya (Mona Lisa), and her mother's lover Dado (Ruel Vernal), a neighborhood tough some fifteen years younger than Tonya. Like a Jacobean revenge tragedy, it depicts the devastating vengeance of a girl violated by her enemy, oppressed through her environment, and robbed of her hopes and dreams.

With extreme economy of means, Brocka sets the scene for the drama. The opening shots show Dado at work in a slaughterhouse. He is a so-called Matador, the man whose job it is to slash the throats of the pigs that are being processed. There is little time for the blatant symbolism of this opening to dawn on the viewer—an act of violence committed by a man accustomed to killing—for over the credits the camera follows Insiang as she walks through her slum area toward the shack that she inhabits together with numerous relatives. The camera scans over sleeping children and finally lands on Insiang's mother, Tonya, who complains that there is no more sugar. Only one sentence has been uttered and the viewer has already been introduced to the latent violence, to the street that dominates the daily affairs of the slum dwellers, to the complete lack of privacy and to the constant deprivation inherent to life in Tondo.

Insiang's first encounter with Dado on the street as she delivers laundry to her customers anticipates their conflict. After she has rejected his flirtatious offer of help, one of Dado's cronies mockingly asks him which one he is after, mother or daughter—or both?

Family life consists of a number of confrontations. Tonya, a shrewish fishmonger, treats her daughter Insiang cruelly, since she reminds her of her husband, who has left her to live with another woman. She is further annoyed by her husband's sister's family, whom she supports and puts up in her house.

A seemingly minor incident brings the conflict to a head. While drinking beer with other boys at the local store, Insiang's cousin grabs the breasts of the young storekeeper on a dare. This act of violation foreshadows the rape of Insiang's innocence. It also gives Tonya an excuse to throw the whole family of in-laws out of the house, some of the children being forced to leave naked because their clothes were bought by Tonya. This is a woman with no pity and in the end one feels little pity for her.

The sister-in-law's final insult prepares the scene for the remainder of the film: Tonya only wants to be rid of them so that her lover can move in.

In many of his films, Brocka uses imagery as a leitmotif. In *Insiang*, the key image implying a kind of sexual promiscuity is the dripping of a faucet into a large metal drum, an image drawn from the actual slum practice of turning on a faucet (or a loud radio) to drown out the sound of amorous diversions. When her mother orders her to "draw her bath" she really means that she will be making love with Dado.

The scenes of the faucet dripping at night (accompanied by Minda D. Azarcon's haunting theme music) give a false sense of peace. In reality they reveal the shame that Insiang feels about her mother's affair. There are no secrets in the community, and Dado has the reputation of being a brute, a bully, and a gigolo.

As Brocka has explained, Dado is a kind of "godfather" in this area: the man who gives the orders and sets the tone. This is demonstrated in his relation to Bebot (Rez Cortéz), Insiang's young boyfriend. At a pool hall, Dado teases Bebot about his earring and throws him out. Bebot echoes his behavior by bullying one of his workmates at the garage. Brocka demonstrates a system.

In keeping with his economy of means, and further proof of his reputation as an actor's director and skillful cinematographer, Lino Brocka is able to tell whole stories through the glance of an eye, a brief change of facial expression, or the exchange of looks behind the back of a third person. This "eye-talk" is particularly pronounced in the relation between Insiang and Dado, who pass through the entire gamut of emotions during the film, but hardly exchange a word with each other, perhaps a reflection of their brutish interrelationship.

Hilda Koronel is extremely apt at conveying her emotions through her eyes. When Insiang returns home to find Dado emerging from the washroom, she returns his mockingly flirtatious smile with a look of disdain. Later, soon before the rape scene, she shows a mixture of hatred and fear, then the horror of a frightened rabbit, until she is finally able to savor her revenge with a cold, unmoving, and at the same time fascinated look of revulsion.

Brocka discovered Hilda Koronel when she was fourteen, giving her the role of a deaf-mute in *Santiago* (1970), his second film, for which she received the FAMAS Best Supporting Actress Award in Manila. Thereafter, she played leading parts in some ten of Brocka's fourteen films prior to *Insiang*. He devoted a television feature to his young protégée in 1972.

Another cinematic method employed by Brocka is the symbolic blocking of characters in the frame. At one point, for example, Brocka shows Tonya and Dado bickering and flirting in the foreground when Insiang enters a door in the background, thus completing the triangle. Their roles are reversed later when Dado is making advances to Insiang, and Tonya enters through the same door.

The love-hate relationship moves toward its inevitable end. Dado, a notorious ladies' man, cannot help but be attracted to the blossoming adolescent. When Tonya scolds Insiang for not giving her the entire earnings from her washwork, Dado defends her (and turns around and scolds Tonya for not giving him enough money). From day to day, Tonya becomes increasingly jealous of the attention that Dado pays to Insiang.

Finally, an incident allows Dado to take the initiative. Bebot, who has been stood up by Insiang after having pawed her at the movies, comes to Insiang's house at night and persuades her to let him in. Nothing happens between them, but Dado sees them and tells Tonya about it. The next morning, Tonya slaps Insiang and calls her a whore. Meanwhile, Dado meets Bebot and tells him to stay away from Insiang.

Sensing the danger, Insiang seeks Bebot's support, but he has been completely intimidated by Dado. Insiang is now alone and defenseless. Dado makes his move.

When Insiang confronts Dado, he starts to fondle her. At this moment, Tonya enters and interrupts his scheme. It is significant in this world without communication and understanding that Insiang is unable to utter a word of explanation.

As Insiang sleeps peacefully on her cot the camera focuses on the dripping faucet, the calm before the storm. In the dark, Dado suddenly appears at her bedside and holds her mouth shut to prevent her from screaming. He hits her brutally and she passes out.

Once again, Brocka is able to depict the whole scene cinematographically, without a word being spoken. The rape itself is not shown; Dado is seen carrying the inert body away. Without doubt, the strict Philippine censorship would not allow a rape to appear on the screen, but it is also characteristic of Brocka's methods to suggest rather than display sexual encounters. The violation becomes evident the next morning when Insiang bursts into tears in her mother's arms, the only scene in which Tonya demonstrates any tenderness toward her.

Before Insiang can formulate a plan of revenge, she must suffer further humiliations. It appears to be the law of the slums that the downtrodden can always fall even further. Like Poldo, the slum-kid in *Jaguar* (1979), and

Julio in *Maynila*, Insiang is so completely destroyed and degraded by her experiences that her character is transformed and in a sense she goes mad.

First of all, Dado convinces Tonya that Insiang has provoked him to his deed and that she was having an affair with Bebot, for which Tonya again slaps her and calls her a whore. This reiterated curse functions as a self-fulfilling prophecy: Insiang, like Julio and other Brocka slum characters, is finally forced to prostitute herself before she can find revenge. She is further humiliated by Bebot, her last hope, who takes her to a hotel, sleeps with her, and then disappears at dawn. To add insult to injury, he did not have enough money for the room and she was forced to contribute eight pesos.

Soon, Dado's affair with mother and daughter is common knowledge. The storekeeper's brother, one of the few who will ever make it out of the slum, declares his love to Insiang, but it is too late. She has other plans.

Dado, now apparently in love with Insiang, fulfills her first plan for revenge. She has him beat up Bebot, a sordid scene on the waterfront at the base of a dump. Insiang encourages her hated lover to come to her at night and thus gains power over him. He promises to get a job in a far-off province and take her there as his wife. Insiang is now ready to take on her mother. When confronted, she admits to her affair. When her mother slaps her, she slaps her mother back, taunting her by saying that Dado is disgusted by her withered body. With deliberate cunning she sets up the scene that follows.

Unaware that Tonya knows of the affair and has concealed herself in the back room, Dado returns to the house and tells Insiang that he has found a job in Cebu. She is to join him there. At this moment, Tonya rushes at him from the back room and stabs him to death while Insiang looks on in cold fascination.

Brocka takes the film one step beyond this melodramatic climax. Again, with great efficiency, he shifts the scene to the prison where Insiang visits her mother. She seems to be trying to purge herself, yearning for forgiveness and understanding. She admits that she had planned her vengeance and had lied about Dado's feelings for her, but Tonya remains cold. Only after Insiang leaves without her blessing is Tonya able to shed tears, perhaps in the realization that she has lost her daughter forever and has herself been guilty of Insiang's downfall.

Insiang is a film of rich cinematic texture. Its weaknesses and inconsistencies lie in its hasty production—the filming was completed in fourteen days—and its low budget, which gives it, however, a feeling of almost documentary realism, reminiscent of the Italian neorealists of the 1950's and 1960's. The acting is excellent throughout, and the editing shows a highly developed sense of rhythm and timing.

There is no need to make excuses for Lino Brocka as being simply another Third World filmmaker, or to see *Insiang* as some kind of exotic picture book of oriental customs. Brocka is a highly sophisticated and skill-ful director and is well acquainted with the history of Western cinema. He is most at home dealing with topics arising from this particular social milieu in the Philippines and from the character traits of his own people. *Insiang* is a document of lasting interest and a tribute to the humanity with which Lino Brocka approaches his characters, victims of an oppressive society, but still very much responsible for their own behavior.

Stephen Locke

INTERMEZZO

Origin: Sweden
Released: 1936
Released in U.S.: 1937
Production: Svensk Filmindustri
Direction: Gustaf Molander
Screenplay: Gustaf Molander and Gösta Stevens; based on a story by
  Molander
Cinematography: Åke Dahlqvist
Editing: Oscar Rosander
Art direction: Årne Akermark
Music: Heinz Provost
Song: Heinz Provost, "Intermezzo"
Running time: 88 minutes

> *Principal characters:*
> Anita Hoffman . . . . Ingrid Bergman
> Holger Brandt . . . . Gosta Ekman
> Margit Brandt . . . . Inga Tidblad
> Greta . . . . Emma Meissner
> Ake . . . . Hasse Ekman
> Ann-Marie . . . . Britt Hagman
> Thomas Stenborg . . . . Hugo Bjorne
> Charles Moller . . . . Erik Berglund

The career of Swedish director Gustaf Molander spanned and connected all the great names in Swedish film. He began his career as an actor in Stockholm in 1911. During the silent period, he wrote screenplays for Mauritz Stiller and Victor Sjöstrom. He directed a comedy, *Malarpirater* (1923), and two films by Selma Lagerlöf, *Ingmarsarvet* (1925; *The Ingmar Inheritance*) and *Till Österland* (1926; *To the Orient*). Both featured Lars Hanson in the cast, and the former also starred Conrad Veidt. Molander directed *Synd* (1928; *Sin*), which was based on August Strindberg's play *Brott och brott* (1912; *Crime and Crime*). It was coproduced by England and Sweden and starred Lars Hanson and Elissa Landi.

At the end of the silent era, Molander went to the Soviet Union to study film with Sergei Eisenstein, the master innovator of the film montage. As a result, Molander created *En Natt* (1931; *One Night*), which has been called the most important Swedish film of the 1930's. Although he directed many comedies in Sweden, he is best remembered for his bittersweet love story *Intermezzo*, which introduced Ingrid Bergman to the international film world. Toward the end of his career, he encouraged the young scriptwriter

Ingmar Bergman. He had the opportunity to direct Ingrid Bergman in "The Necklace," an episode in *Stimulantia* (1967), toward the end of his career. Unfortunately this film was not released in the United States. *Intermezzo* was not the first film in which Molander directed Ingrid Bergman, but all the other films in which she appeared under his direction pale compared to *Intermezzo*, a touching love story told with great restraint and good taste. Although most film viewers are more familiar with the Hollywood version, produced by David O. Selznick and directed by Gregory Ratoff in 1939, the Swedish version offers a subtler account of essentially the same script.

The Swedish film begins as a ship called *The Kungsholm* reaches Vinga lighthouse near Gothenburg. A medium shot shows Professor Holger Brandt (Gosta Ekman), thin, sensitive-looking, and forty-six years old. He arrives in his home in Stockholm, reunited with his wife, Margit (Inga Tidblad), his son, Ake (Hasse Ekman), who is twenty-one, and his daughter, Ann-Marie (Britt Hagman), who is seven.

After two years of living as an international celebrity, giving violin recitals all over the world, Holger finds his middle-class home life to be boring and confining. He asks his wife to join him on his next tour, but she decides that she must stay home and take care of the children. His accompanist, Thomas Stenborg (Hugo Bjorne), introduces Holger to his best pupil, Anita Hoffman (Ingrid Bergman), who also happens to be Ann-Marie's teacher. When Anita plays the piano at a party, Holger is fascinated by her artistry, and he begins to accompany her on the violin.

By chance, they meet and go to a restaurant together. Holger falls in love with Anita. She tries to leave him but is obviously attracted to him. He confesses his love for Anita to his wife and persuades Anita to accompany him on a tour of Europe, serving as his new accompanist.

They are extremely happy until Anita sees that Holger misses his young daughter and the secure life that he once thought was dull. Even though Anita still loves Holger, she decides to leave him to continue her career without him. It is an act of personal sacrifice.

When Holger arrives home in Sweden, his wife and daughter greet him from the other side of a busy street. Ann-Marie, as soon as she sees her father, rushes to greet him. She is knocked down by a truck. In the hospital, the Brandts learn that Ann-Marie may die. While waiting for additional news, they share the experience of being parents together. Finally, they learn that she will recover, and the happy news serves to unite them again as a couple. The final image shows Holger holding his wife in his arms, surrounded by their clinging children.

The reviews were highly favorable in Sweden and in the United States. Molander was praised for the care in which he framed each shot. He was criticized for not shooting on location in Sweden and the Alps and for relying too much on studio setups. The careful lighting on the bridge sequence, however, the most praised shot in the film, would not have been possible on location.

In addition to the direction, the music was highly praised, and the title song became an international hit. The music gives continuity to the film as it carries the viewer from one shot to the next. Also praised was the acting. Gosta Ekman was a stiff actor who could reveal a range of feelings when he relaxed. He died in 1938, and the film thus represents the culmination of his career. The most important person in the film, however, is Ingrid Bergman. For her it represented a beginning. As a result of this film, she moved to Hollywood as a house guest of David O. Selznick and Irene Selznick for the remake. The Swedish press praised her performance, and *Variety* predicted her stardom. Although her five previous Swedish films had shown a development in her career, this film made her famous. She was very reluctant to give up her career in Sweden, but she became a celebrated actress in her thirteen American feature films during the 1940's. Nominated for Best Actress in *For Whom the Bell Tolls* (1943), she won her first Academy Award for Best Actress in *Gaslight* (1944); she received the award a second time for her role in *Anastasia* (1956). She won Best Supporting Actress for *Murder on the Orient Express* (1974). She died on her birthday at the age of sixty-seven on August 29, 1982.

Although sometimes dismissed as a small film, *Intermezzo* reveals a subtle artistry which is powerfully effective in moving an audience. The audience is caught up in the various stages of the love story and cares about what happens to these people.

Michael Porte

INTIMATE LIGHTING
(INTIMNÍ OSVĚTLENÍ)

Origin: Czechoslovakia
Released: 1965
Released in U.S.: 1969
Production: František Sandr for Barrandov Film Studios
Direction: Ivan Passer
Assistant direction: Jiři Ružička
Screenplay: Jaroslav Papoušek, Václav Šašek, and Ivan Passer
Cinematography: Miroslav Ondříček and Josef Střecha
Editing: Jiřina Lukešová
Art direction: Karel Černý
Sound: Adolf Böhm
Music: Oldřich Korte and Josef Hart
MPAA rating: no listing
Running time: 72 minutes

Principal characters:
Stepa	Věra Křesadlová
Peter	Zdeněk Bezušek
Grandpa	Jan Vostrčil
Grandma	Vlastimila Vlková
Bambas	Karel Blažek
Marie	Jaroslava Štedra
Pharmacist	Karel Uhlík
Kaja	Miroslav Cvrk
Young Marie	Dagmar Ředinová

Like Miloš Forman and Jaroslav Papoušek, the two directors with whom he is most closely associated, Ivan Passer was an important figure of the Czechoslovakian "New Wave" of the 1960's. Passer collaborated on the screenplays of several important New Wave films, including Forman's *Loves of a Blonde* (1965); in *Intimate Lighting*, Forman's wife, Věra Křesadlová, plays the part of Stepa. Like several of the New Wave directors who went abroad after the Soviet invasion in 1968 ended the "Prague Spring" of Czechoslovakian cinema—including Miloš Forman, Ján Kadár (*The Shop on Main Street*, 1965), and Vojtěch Jasný (*All My Good Countrymen*, 1968), who is considered the father of the Czech New Wave—Passer now lives in the United States.

Even among the fragmented, dislocated stories of his generation of exiles, Passer's career has been particularly quirky. *Intimate Lighting* was widely recognized as a masterpiece; in 1970, following its belated release in the

United States, it won the New York Critics' Prize. Nevertheless, it was not until 1971—six years after *Intimate Lighting*—that Passer made another film, *Born to Win* (1971). This film, his first American feature, was both a critical and a box-office failure.

While the hiatus between Passer's first and second film can in part be attributed to the exigencies of exile and readjustment, it must also (and probably in larger part) be attributed to his idiosyncratic sensibility. Later in the 1970's, he completed a black comedy starring Omar Sharif, but the film was shelved and has never received a commercial release. Passer's next film—as usual, utterly different from anything he had done before—was *Cutter and Bone* (1980, rereleased in 1981 as *Cutter's Way*). Although this film failed on its original release, it has enjoyed some success on the revival circuit. It is a powerful and extraordinary work, interweaving a mystery-story plot involving California-style corporate corruption with a personal drama centering on a brilliant, crippled and embittered Vietnam veteran. Passer continued his unpredictable course with *Creator* (1985), starring Peter O'Toole as a Nobel Prize-winning scientist who seeks to re-create his dead wife.

Intimate Lighting is a masterfully controlled little comedy of subtle ironies, deadpan humor, and hidden seriousness. Deceptively little happens in the film: All of its charm, pathos, and humor are revealed almost as if by accident, in small, casual incident and in visual and verbal *non sequiturs*. Nothing much happens that could be called plot in the traditional sense, for Passer's camera, in the spirit of the film's title (the literal translation of which would be "intimate aspect"), conveys the impression that it "just happens to be there," observing unscripted reality—the day and night when Peter (Zdeněk Bezušek) comes from Prague with his young and pretty girlfriend Stepa (Věra Křesadlová) to visit his old schoolmate Bambas (Karel Blažek) in the country.

Bambas and Peter studied music together at the local conservatory ten years before, and while Peter has gone on to become a cellist with the Prague Symphony, Bambas now heads the village conservatory and is conductor of the local amateur orchestra. Bambas has invited Peter to perform at one of their town concerts (which we never see), and the main thrust of what follows is the revelation in small details of Bambas' home life with his wife, two small children, and parents-in-law, and his nostalgia for whatever it is Peter represents—bachelorhood, perhaps, and the rewards of a musical career in the big city.

Peter is rather impressed by what Bambas has achieved—first, the house. It has taken seven years to build, and to Peter it is magnificent. Grandpa, Bambas' father-in-law (Jan Vostrčil), tells Peter that the family has been paying for it in kind: eight bricks per shot of rum, and bricks as payment for playing at funerals. Peter does a quick mental calculation and concludes that the house has probably cost eight hundred drinks so far. There is a funeral taking place that afternoon, as chance would have it, and Grandpa promptly invites Peter along. When Peter looks apprehensive, Grandpa assures him that there will be music, too. "And it's good music. You'll see— once we start playing everybody cries, even the relatives. But what's really important is that we plant one stiff and two hundred bricks grow."

Stepa, in the meantime, is playing with the children. Her introduction to them is not very successful, since the boy starts crying as soon as she asks him his name, and the girl hides behind her father in a fit of shyness. The boy (Kaja, named after his father) then scampers off with surreal resolution to slosh around in a tub containing a large live fish. There is more screaming when the fish bites (or the child imagines it has bitten) him, and Bambas, an already slightly frantic host, attempts to calm the child with a promise to fry the fish as punishment.

When Bambas opens the garage door, the chicken that he claims is still trying to "hatch" the car is standing on the car's roof. He calls his mother-in-law, Grandma (Vlastimila Vlková), to remove the hen, but tries to shoo it away himself. Grandma implores Bambas not to act violently or he will scare the chicken to death. (The viewer sees the unhappy hen's point of view from beneath the car.) A bizarre scene of rising hilarity follows when the hen's hysterics attract a dozen other chickens to the garage. The hen mayhem that ensues reminds one briefly of scenes in Alfred Hitchcock's *The Birds* (1963), although throughout, Grandma and Bambas are bickering about the cost of the car. Bambas is yelling about how the garage has turned into a henhouse and he is always stepping into something. "Big deal!" she says. The car is not exclusively his; she and Grandpa contributed plenty. He, she reminds him ("I have to keep reminding you. You forget very fast"), "came with a bare ass." Besides, the chicken lays eggs once in a while. One here, one there: They add up.

In a frenzy of frustration, Bambas leaps into the front seat of the car and drives out blindly, through and over all the squawking, witless birds. One is killed, and just when the film's joke seems to have been pulled up short, an egg rolls across the pavement and comes to rest beside the dead chicken, which makes the joke even darker.

The next shot depicts a funeral procession that seems, for a moment, to be for the chicken. Then Passer cuts to the interior of the car in which Bambas, Grandpa, Peter, and Stepa are following the procession, and the emphasis turns to Grandpa's reflections on music, happiness, and tears. People always prefer a good cry to a good laugh, he tells the others, and one sad song is enough to go around the world. "Now, if this [he taps the dashboard of the car] ran on tears!"

While the funeral takes place in the local church and Stepa wanders off by herself, Grandpa remarks on how beautifully Peter's girl walks. She is not just nice—she is fabulous. In an effort perhaps to change the subject, Bambas asks Peter if he has heard about the parachutist whose parachute failed to open and who dropped ten thousand feet and landed on a pile of cotton, suffering not a scratch in the experience. Grandpa, in his free-associating manner, tells of the time he "fell . . . er, jumped" from the second story of a building and landed on a concrete floor. Oh, what a bloody mess. And how about his boots? Bambas asks. His boots came out of it just fine, because he was holding them in his hand. One expects Passer to end the tale there, but Grandpa goes on to tell how he wore the boots when he walked from Budajovice to Vienna, and how he decided to do the return trip by train. When he reached home, his father asked him if his boots were new. He told him that they were the old ones.

While Stepa is at the funeral, Bambas and Grandpa (with Peter) wait in the nearby wheat field for someone at the church to give them the sign to play their instruments—to create the effect of music floating across the fields, like an answer or call from nature itself, as the body is interred. Six or seven men in black coats emerge from the church and in a row, simultaneously, urinate on the cemetery wall facing the field. One of them breaks away from the others to investigate something in the field. It turns out to be a young woman in a bathing suit, enjoying the sun. At his approach, she sullenly rouses herself and walks away. Witnessing this, Grandpa again makes one of his odd connections, to which Bambas, as the straight man, gives an unintentionally humorous touch. "Yes. That was Smetana," Grandpa sighs. "He was deaf, but he heard with his heart. You know [he turns to Peter], once in a field of rye like this I laid a girl like that. And she cried, too. She cried." Peter does not know what to say. Bambas says, "Except that this isn't rye, Grandpa." "So what?" Grandpa says.

The funeral proceeds. They play first in the field, then indoors, where the mourners dance and drink their grief away. Stepa is back in the car, waiting, where she finds herself submitting to the frankly curious stares of a dozen ancient women, who file past her on their way home after a day raking in the fields. At this moment she looks very much like the bored, urban creature she is. Back at the house, after the funeral, Grandpa tells the women how everybody at the funeral was crying tears "the size of marbles." Who cares? Bambas wants to know.

Dinner that night is rendered somewhat farcically. The chicken that was killed in the fowl fiasco has been roasted, but it provides only two drumsticks, hardly enough for six adults and two children. Stepa gives her chicken leg to a squealing child, which prompts Marie (Jaroslava Štedra) to give Stepa hers; then Grandma gives her portion to Marie, and around and around the pieces of chicken go in a choreography of reaching hands and proffered plates. The unamusing fact is that there is not enough food, and when the original drumstick, now somewhat battered by its recent travels, lands accidentally on the tablecloth, Stepa breaks into hysterical laughter. She staggers from the table, gasping for breath and reaching for the radiator for support. To compound the hidden theme, the pharmacist (Karel Uhlík), who has come to join Bambas, Grandpa, and Peter in playing informal after-dinner chamber music, appears at the door bearing the liquor that it was arranged he would bring.

While the four men play, Bambas and Grandpa bicker across their music stands without missing a note. The women—Grandma, Marie, and Stepa—are tiptoeing among the sleeping children upstairs. Later, when the men are still playing, Grandma tells Stepa how Grandpa kidnaped her three days after they met and how they eloped to France. It is amusing to look back on those days now, she says, but at the time she felt bad for her mother, who was no doubt worried sick. Grandma shows Stepa how to do the exercises she used to do before her back started to give her trouble, and how to dance like Mirna Ray, who was her friend. It is one of the most poignantly humorous moments in the film—as poignant as the pharmacist screeching through a movement on his violin, muttering "Gentlemen, I love this movement. I love it passionately!" Stepa, generally bored with rural amusements, wanders off again and comes across the village idiot. He is obviously a real idiot, but Passer handles the scene with delicacy. The grinning, ugly fellow calls her Věra (the actress' name), and he is confused when she says no, her name is Stepa. He has never seen a girl as pretty as she. Won't she come for a walk with him? "But where would we go?" she asks, laughing gently. She teases him with mock offers of the apple she is eating. The scene could be judged as exploitive of the man and exemplary of Passer's treatment of the country folk in the film generally, but this does not seem to be the case.

Passer is deeply fond of all of his characters, because of and despite (or, neither because of nor despite) their foibles. The characters in *Intimate Lighting* are not as in touch with "nature" and the country as melodrama's country-city paradigm conditions us to expect, and the members of Bambas' family are neither country bumpkins nor simple folk rooted to the soil who offer peasant wisdom against urban rationality and sophistication. Much of Passer's sly but generous humor springs from a quiet subversion of stereotypes that the viewer does not realize he generally uses when watching films.

When everybody has gone to bed (Grandma's last words to Grandpa before the lights go out are "So, we'll get a divorce over some eggnog,"), Peter and Bambas drink and reminisce about old times. They listen to some music on the radio, lapse into silences, and drink and smoke some more. The two also listen to the concert of snores from the sleeping household—something which amuses Peter much more (since he does not have to live with it) than it does Bambas. They decide (now quite drunk) to run off together, with a vague plan to play music for people who really care about music. Off into the night they go, musical instruments in hand, Peter in his pajamas. Their hitchhiking attempts are unsuccessful, and the next morning at the breakfast table on the terrace, only Grandpa and Stepa are in good spirits: Marie has a toothache, Bambas has a hangover, and Peter is stifling irrepressible yawns. Grandma comments, "It's a little thick, but good." Stepa responds, "Yes, I like eggnog." Grandpa says, "It's nauseating."

An alarm clock goes off. It is twenty-five years old, Grandma tell Stepa. If she does not wind it, she cannot sleep, even though it rings arbitrarily— sometimes two hours late, depending on the weather. "She's not interested in your clock," Bambas says. "I'm not talking about clocks—but about habits," Grandma says. The same thing can be said of *Intimate Lighting* in general. Passer is not talking about clocks (the happenings of plot) but about habits. Grandpa proposes a toast—to their health, the concert, and to pretty women. When he asks if there is anything else anyone would like to toast to, Bambas says, "Who gives a damn!" They raise their glasses and tilt back their heads to drink to Grandpa's toast, but the eggnog is so thick that it will not budge from the glasses. "With a little patience it'll taste good," Grandma says. In this absurd pose, Passer leaves them, heads back, waiting for the eggnog to slide to their lips. "Oh, these Sundays," Grandpa sighs.

Passer's control is exquisite, although his strategy is more carefully conceived than the film's appearance of accidental charm would suggest. Much of the film's wit is purely cinematic—in shot juxtapositions that seem to capture reactions that are actual, that is, of nonactors unfamiliar with Hollywood codifications of gesture. Yet the dialogue, too, is comic. Like Stan Mack's "Real Life Funnies" in *The Village Voice* ("All Dialogue Guaranteed Verbatim"), the conversations in *Intimate Lighting* offer the illusion that although they have been selected (by the director), they are in fact real—plucked from life and put into this film, which explains why they are fragmentary and why they often have the hilarity, or seem to contain the special insight, of something overheard. The viewer's awareness of the director's controlling vision is effaced to produce a slice-of-life effect that is far from the reality in Hollywood films, which Hitchcock, describing his own films, called "slices of cake." For a long time, Czechoslovakian filmmakers (during various periods since World War II) have had to disguise their political beliefs and make films that do not appear to criticize the State in any way, and in *Intimate Lighting* one sees the core of disillusionment that, beneath the film's lightweight story and absurdist comedy, probably speaks keenly to native Czechs living in the oppressive shadow of the Soviet Union. That Passer could make a comedy that succeeds on several levels of interpretation and is as much a delight to watch now as it was in 1965 is a kind of proof of the talent of this filmmaker.

Robert Lang

INVESTIGATION OF A CITIZEN ABOVE SUSPICION (INDAGINE SU UN CITTADINO AL DI SOPRA DI OGNI SOSPETTO)

Origin: Italy
Released: 1970
Released in U.S.: 1970
Production: Daniele Senatore for Vera Film (AA)
Direction: Elio Petri
Assistant direction: Antonio Gabrielli
Screenplay: Ugo Pirro and Elio Petri; based on a story by Pirro and Petri
Cinematography: Luigi Kuveiller
Editing: Ruggero Mastroianni
Art direction: Carlo Egidi
Makeup: Franco Corridoni
Costume design: Angela Sammaciccia
Sound: Mario Bramonti
Music: Ennio Morricone
MPAA rating: R
Running time: 112 minutes

Principal characters:
Police Inspector . . . . Gian Maria Volonté
Augusta Terzi. . . . . Florinda Bolkan
Plumber . . . . Salvo Randone
Police commissioner. . . . . Gianni Santuccio
Mangani. . . . . Arturo Dominici
Biglia . . . . Orazio Orlando
Antonio Pace . . . . Sergio Tramonti
Augusta's husband . . . . Massimo Foschi
Homicide functionary. . . . . Aldo Rendine

During the late 1960's and early 1970's, quite a few films about Fascism were released. Constantin Costa-Gavras' *Z* (1969) and *L'Aveu* (1970; *The Confession*), Bernardo Bertolucci's *Il conformista* (1970; *The Conformist*), Luchino Visconti's *La caduta degli dei* (1969; *The Damned*), and other films addressed the phenomenon of dictatorial authority. It is thus no surprise that Elio Petri, one of the world's major political filmmakers during his short career, should have made *Investigation of a Citizen Above Suspicion*, a story about a police inspector obsessed with power. The film was a commercial and critical success, in part because of Petri's courage in making it. At the time, expressing "contempt" for authority was a punishable offense under Italian law. Yet *Investigation of a Citizen Above Suspicion* is not mere polemics. On the contrary, Petri, as in all of his films, moves the intense drama along with adept pacing and dazzling camera work. The politics are almost secondary. The film contains no specific references, and the hero is never even given a name. The film has a clear political message, but it is contained within an entertaining and suspenseful plot.

Petri manages the delicate balance between political program and narrative pleasure by structuring *Investigation of a Citizen Above Suspicion* around two separate but related stories. The first is about the Police Inspector (Gian Maria Volonté) and his attempts to demonstrate his authority; the second concerns the police department's crackdown on student activists. Petri weaves these two plots together. In the film's opening scene, the Inspector kills his girlfriend, Augusta Terzi (Florinda Bolkan), and deliberately plants clues which implicate him in the crime. His intention, as he later says, is to prove that he is entirely above suspicion. While his bizarre and perverse relationship with Augusta is being outlined in a series of flashbacks, the Inspector's tenure as chief of political intelligence is described in present time. In the end, the Inspector confesses to the murder, but the film concludes before revealing his ultimate fate.

Throughout the film, Petri's attitude toward the Inspector is highly ambiguous. The audience is asked alternately to involve themselves with his actions and to stand back from them in order to judge him. This dichotomy is established in the very first scene, when the Inspector goes to Augusta's apartment and slashes her throat. The film begins with a tracking shot of the Inspector walking toward Augusta's building. Petri then cuts to a camera position which approximates the Inspector's point of view, as Augusta is seen through billowing window curtains. Then, an image of his face as he looks up at the building is followed by a point-of-view shot which reveals what he sees. The Inspector enters the building and looks up into the stairwell; Petri cuts again to the Inspector's point of view. This editing pattern, which alternates shots of the Inspector with his point of view, so characteristic of Alfred Hitchcock's powerful, subjective technique, immediately involves the viewer with the Inspector. He is the visual entrance into the film. The rest of the opening scene contains several examples of another classic involvement technique: the close-up. Petri understands that by focusing viewers' attention on an important detail, a close-up can make them participants in a character's behavior. After the Inspector has killed his girlfriend, the action is seen mostly in tight close-ups. He leaves a thread from his blue tie on Augusta's fingernail, a wad of money on her dresser, and his fingerprints and footprints throughout her apartment. Petri's use of music also asks the viewer to ally himself with the Inspector. The film's theme is obsessive and slightly perverse and perfectly mirrors the Inspector's personality.

Yet at the same time, Petri employs distancing devices which serve to remove the viewer from any easy alliance with the hero. In the opening scene, Petri uses long, telescopic lenses, which emphasize the audience's status as viewers of and not participants in the action. In addition, Petri sets up several compositions so that the audience's vision is partially obstructed, further distancing them from the characters. Immediately before the Inspector is about to kill Augusta, the audience sees them in long-shot, with various objects from her cluttered apartment in the frame. The actual murder is seen in another long-shot from about the same angle. Augusta sits up and moans. On first viewing, the audience probably imagines the couple to be making love, but as Augusta rolls over and the bloodied Inspector stands up, it becomes clear that he has murdered her. He walks behind a stained-glass window into the bathroom to wash off the blood. The confusion in the audience's mind, together with Petri's compositional strategy and use of long-shots, alienates the audience and removes them from the action. The dichotomy of long-shot and close-up reflects the attitude that Petri wants the viewer to take toward the Inspector. The audience is supposed to identify with him, to wonder whether he will get caught, to be emotionally involved in his situation and, simultaneously, to stand back from him, to see his obsession with power, and to criticize his behavior. Significantly, as the film progresses, Petri's involvement of the audience in the film's action grows weaker, as the Inspector's megalomania becomes more obvious.

The Inspector's authority is illustrated by Petri's use of camera movement. In the film's opening frame, the Inspector looks into the camera, which then tracks toward him, as if beckoned. The Inspector is linked to the camera in an indication of his power. The camera follows him as he approaches Augusta's apartment. It tracks behind him as he enters the apartment. In the first scene at the police station, the intricate and elegant camera movements are virtually choreographed to his actions. Petri's camera shows a character who, at least during the first half of the film, is powerful and in control. The Inspector's plan has worked perfectly. At the scene of the crime, all of the clues that he has left are found and yet he is not suspected. He is above suspicion.

Yet as the new chief of homicide, Mangani (Arturo Dominici), shows the Inspector some photographs that he has found in Augusta's apartment, the audience begins to see another side to the enigmatic Inspector. For one of the first times in the film, the camera moves dramatically without direct motivation from the Inspector's activity. The camera entraps the Inspector against a wall as he looks at the pictures. Augusta's voice is heard, and Petri flashes back to the Inspector photographing her in reenactments of various murder cases. Petri moves to the past not through a slow, hazy dissolve but in a hard cut, perfectly illustrating the continuity between past and present and the influence that the Inspector's perversions have on his behavior as chief of political intelligence.

After this first glimpse of the past, successive flashbacks are organized in chronological order, gradually filling in the nature of the Inspector's relationship with Augusta and suggesting the reasons for his pathological obsession with power. As the Inspector rests at home after visiting the scene of the crime, four alienating and fairly rapid cuts bring the audience from long-shot to a close-up of his tired face. Augusta's voice is heard, and again the audience is thrown back into the past. Augusta makes a series of anonymous and teasing telephone calls to the Inspector, who eventually traces them to her apartment. On the phone, she has begged him to interrogate her, and it becomes clear that she will play masochist to his sadist. This flashback is immediately followed by the Inspector's speech to the entire political intelligence department, of which he has recently been named head. The backward-moving camera as the Inspector approaches the podium illustrates, as before, his authority. The speech concerns the moral equivalence of the criminal and the political activist and is marked by Petri's camera moving amid the appreciative crowd. The speech culminates in a close, low-angle shot of the Inspector, speaking animatedly. This camera position makes him appear as the Fascist dictator whom he would undoubtedly like to be. As the policemen break into thunderous applause, the Inspector exits, and the camera again follows him. The placement of this speech immediately after the flashback to the couple's first meeting suggests a connection between the Inspector's bizarre sex life and his delusions of grandeur, a connection that Petri continues to explore in the rest of the film.

At the Inspector's insistence, Augusta's husband (Massimo Foschi) is arrested for the murder and interrogated by the police. As the Inspector watches the questioning, the film's musical theme returns, and another flashback begins. This flashback (again introduced by a hard cut), is preceded by an optical effect which resembles a rapid, downward camera tilt; the frame seems to be lost only to reappear. This effect illustrates the Inspector's uncertain grip on reality, as he sinks deeper into his obsession. From this point onward, the flashbacks are longer and appear more often. In this scene, the Inspector and Augusta play roles: He is the interrogator, and she is the suspect. At the conclusion of their game, she casually mentions that he is really nothing more than a child. He becomes livid with rage, and, with his hands around her throat, he corrects her. He is authority, the unassailable father; it is the suspects who are the children. The connection between the Inspector's feelings of inadequacy and his desire to exercise power is now made clear. His motives for killing Augusta are also laid bare. In both the flashback and in a later one, she tells him of his childishness. She says that he makes love like a little boy, that he is a baby, a sexual incompetent. In a symbolic castration, she cuts off his tie with a large pair of scissors. He has killed her because she has exposed him to himself, and to compensate, he has reasserted his power by proving that he will not be caught for her murder.

As the film progresses, the Inspector becomes afraid that he is not being considered a viable suspect, so he plants more clues. He sends the murder weapon, the stolen jewelry, and one of the shoes that he wore during the murder to the homicide department. He forces a plumber (Salvo Randone) whom he finds on the street to look at his face, urging the man to go to the police and identify him as the killer. Later, after a group of students have been rounded up in connection with a series of bomb explosions, the Inspector interrogates one of the activists, Antonio Pace (Sergio Tramonti). Pace, a former lover of Augusta, has lived in her building and has seen the Inspector leave it on the day of the murder. On the verge of complete breakdown, the Inspector begs Pace to turn him in. Pace refuses. Ultimately, the Inspector simply hands Mangani his written confession, saying that his actions demonstrate the glorious power of authority. The Inspector is placed under house arrest.

As the Inspector sits on his bed, Biglia (Orazio Orlando) tells him—in a scene which is probably, but not unambiguously, a fantasy—that the others are waiting. The scene is difficult to read clearly because the distinction between reality and fantasy has almost totally disintegrated by this point. The Inspector walks out into the den and is confronted by the police commissioner (Gianni Santuccio) and his staff. They want him, for the good of the department, to profess his innocence. Fruitlessly, the Inspector insists that he is guilty, but each bit of evidence that he advances to prove his case is rejected by the commissioner, and, in an ironic twist, he is eventually beaten and humiliated into signing a confession of his innocence. Petri then cuts back to the present, as the Inspector gets off his bed and welcomes the police staff into his house. He lowers the curtain in his sparsely furnished den, walks to the commissioner, and bows slightly. In a final distancing device, Petri points his camera at the characters through the falling curtain, partially obscuring the viewer's vision, and then freezes on the final image. Petri allows the viewer to decide the Inspector's fate.

It is clear that, while the Inspector's situation is extraordinary, it is merely an exaggeration of the norm. Petri, in two rather similar scenes, shows the audience the police department's obsession with power. After the Inspector has been named chief of political intelligence, he is taken to the archives on political activists. The camera, almost with a life of its own, tracks quickly past the rows of files, pausing only to pan slightly to the right to show the enormous depth of the room. Later in the film, the Inspector goes to a wiretapping room. In a shot paralleling the earlier one, the camera tracks down the scores of personnel monitoring tape recordings of telephone conversations. In these two scenes—as well as during the brutal police interrogations—Petri generalizes from the Inspector's case and accuses the entire department of an overzealous application of their authority. Petri's film, in addition to being an insightful dissection of the pathological exercise of power, is a courageous condemnation of the Italian police system of the time.

David Rivel

IRACEMA

Origin: Brazil
Released: 1975
Released in U.S.: 1982
Production: Wolf Gauer and Jorge Bodanzky for Stopfilm/ZDF
Direction: Jorge Bodanzky and Wolf Gauer
Screenplay: Orlando Senna
Cinematography: Jorge Bodanzky and Wolf Gauer
Editing: Eva Grundmann and Jorge Bodanzky
Art direction: no listing
Sound: Achim Tappen
Music: no listing
MPAA rating: no listing
Running time: 90 minutes

Principal characters:
Iracema.........................Edna de Cassia
Tião ....Paulo César Peréio

Jorge Bodanzky's semidocumentary *Iracema*, made with the assistance of West German director Wolf Gauer, employs a vigorous, rough style that points up the tawdry quality of dreams of progress and development and the cruel disillusionment they can bring. Through careful attention to detail, it captures the sometimes hallucinatory ironies of daily life on the cutting edge of progress.

Iracema is a political fable structured by one person's voyage into the interior of the Amazon basin. In 1975, the controversial Transamazonica highway had finally cut through the forest. Vast acres of trees had been replaced by dusty flatlands studded with stumps. Huge ranches, farms, factories, and lumber projects were well under way, bringing with them a floating population of migrant workers, prostitutes, con artists, and officials.

The lead characters of *Iracema* exemplify two social types that are sacrificed in this forced march of progress: the Indian and the Brazilian worker. Iracema (Edna de Cassia) is an Indian girl whose family members work as fruit pickers in the forest, selling their produce at shamefully low prices to a local middleman. She escapes this nineteenth century-style subjection, fleeing to the Amazon port city Belém, where she becomes a prostitute. Quickly learning the language of rootless discontent, she hustles a ride out of town with a trucker.

The trucker (Paulo César Peréio) is an independent operator who calls himself "Tião Brasil Grande" (Joe Big Brazil). He seems to have swallowed whole every jingle, slogan, and sticker that the military government's media campaign pumped out in the early 1970's—phrases such as "Brazil, love it or leave it," "No one can hold us back," "Forward, Brazil!" and "Count on me, my country!" For him, the government-issue T-shirts boasting about Amazonian development speak only the literal truth. Amazonian development is, quite simply, Brazil's future—and his own.

Tião takes Iracema along on a run that he makes to a dismal lumber-mill settlement, and he leaves her there, standing in the road in her brand-new, Coca-Cola-emblazoned hot pants. "What am I gonna do?" she yells at him. "Trust in the future!" he yells back.

Iracema blunders from one bad deal and misbegotten settlement to the next. One day, she meets Tião again, at a small storefront shed on the road, where she and a handful of other prostitutes sit in wait for the occasional traveler. Drunk, despairing, missing a tooth, she is at the end of her road at sixteen. Tião, however, blearier than before but ever optimistic, is on his way to the newest frontier to the West, Acre. He proudly hails it as being on the way to "a sea, I think it's called the Pacific or something." Tião is always willing to look around the next corner for the wonders of the future. Caught up in the current romance with technological progress as an answer to all social problems, he barely notices that he is only a pawn in a big game.

Iracema, on the other hand, is an antiromantic heroine. Her name, an anagram of "America," is drawn from a romantic novel by nineteenth century writer José de Alencar, in which the Indian princess Iracema symbolizes the higher spirituality of the Indian in contrast to that of the literal-minded Christian whites. The novel was written at the height of the Brazilian romance with an imaginary, indigenous heritage, more a native's defense against European culture than an homage to any genuine Indian culture. The modern romance, however, is not with Hiawatha but with hydroelectric power, and Iracema, searching haplessly for the good life, becomes an easy victim.

Working from a sketchy script, the filmmakers made enthusiastic use of *cinéma vérité* techniques. The only experienced actor in the film is Paulo César Peréio; almost everyone else plays himself: a peasant complaining that the land reform agency sold his land to a developer, a prostitute hilariously enjoying her moment of glory in front of the camera, a labor broker who sells workers off of pickup trucks as though they were slaves, road workers and beaten-down mothers who cook on outdoor fires for dispirited, malnourished children. Much of the dialogue was improvised, and the people's conversations have an authentic ring to them.

Bodanzky's camera eye wanders from face to face in the restaurants, on the docks, on dirt airstrips, and on the porches of sheds. The movement is often slow and horizontal—the view from the ground of this empire built on air. It is a view that takes in the flies, the sweat-beaded mugs of beer, the huge signs forbidding almost everything, and, crucially, the facial expressions of the people, who are usually merely in the background of such scenes. Bodanzky's camera travels thoughtfully and relentlessly, moving from face to face of the exhausted workers who sit on their "parrot's perch" in the labor broker's pickup truck. All in all, it is a devastating group portrait.

The tenor of daily life for the working poor dictates the look of the film, and the perspective of the man and woman on the street becomes the camera angle. It is not clear for several minutes into the film who the main characters will be. Iracema is only one of a horde of hopeful newcomers and hustling residents of the port city.

If the film has an unfinished, raw-edged look to it, it bears a close resemblance to the unfinished-yet-already-decaying look of a pioneer town, especially one in the tropics. Indeed, the film was too real, it seems, for Brazil in 1975. The government film agency Embrafilme disqualified it for distribution, ostensibly because the film was funded in part by German television and because foreigners worked on it. This rationale obscured the fact that the film touched an economic nerve. The results on the military's much-touted Economic Miracle (luring foreign investment with easy cash flow and a cheap, controlled labor supply) had come in, and they were not good. Most workers' real wages had fallen, some by as much as sixty-five percent; infant mortality had soared, while the health budget had been cut by more than half; the economy was sickly as well, with foreign companies dominating the economy without investing in it.

The Amazon development was the last resort for a government desperate for new dreams of economic growth. *Iracema* cut through the rhetoric with evidence from days in the lives of the dreamers: No wonder it took until 1980 for the government to allow Brazilians to look at the film. Unfortunately, by that time the initiative had been taken in the Amazon. Other Brazilian filmmakers were busy with a Brazilian populist film style with a higher gloss than that to which *Iracema* aspired. Neither populace nor critics were eager to celebrate a cinema of underdevelopment.

Yet *Iracema* holds its interest as a film quite apart from its specifically Brazilian concerns. It reveals the way a social issue unfolds in daily life, and it submits it frankly—even with humor—to the audience's judgment. This is a travelogue of one way to Hell, and it ought to ring true to those who know the scenes around Alaskan pipelines, Arabian development projects, hydroelectric schemes in Africa—wherever visions of technological progress are being realized. The film is also testimony to the dramatic potential of daily life when captured by a patient filmmaker with an eye for irony.

Pat Aufderheide

THE ISLAND
(HADAKA NO SHIMA)

Origin: Japan
Released: 1961
Released in U.S.: 1962
Production: Kaneto Shindo and Eisaku Matsura for Kindai Elga Kyokai
Direction: Kaneto Shindo
Screenplay: Kaneto Shindo
Cinematography: Kiyoshi Kuroda
Editing: Toshio Enoki
Art direction: no listing
Music: Hikaru Hayashi
Running time: 92 minutes

> *Principal characters:*
> Toyo .... Nobuko Otowa
> Senta........................... Taiji Tonoyama
> Taro .... Shinji Tanaka
> Jiro .... Masanori Horimoto

Although *The Island* has virtually no dialogue, it does have a haunting musical score by Hikaru Hayashi and all the sounds of nature that accompany the protagonists as they struggle with the unyielding elements. Only occasionally does one hear a human sound, and that is but a child's laughter or a woman's sob. Only a simple story could be told in this fashion, and *The Island* is exactly that.

The island is a tiny bit of barren rock that sits in the harbor of Mihara City on Japan's inland sea. Nothing grows there naturally, and only through constant toil is the peasant family able to sustain a meager crop of yams. The film's writer and director, Kaneto Shindo, found the tiny island he needed two years before the picture was shot. Shindo rented the island from the hermit who lived there for a few bags of rice. For the next year or so, Shindo made many trips to the island with materials to build the humble house in which his filmic family would live. For the project, Shindo used all of his own money, money he had saved from twenty-seven previous years behind the camera.

When the time came for Shindo to assemble his four-person cast, he chose two professional actors to portray the parents but promised them no wages, only a part of the profits and living expenses. The same offer was made to the film crew. The total cost of making the film came to only fifteen thousand dollars.

Kaneto Shindo had been a director since 1951. His first film, *Aaisai monogatari* (1951; *The Story of a Beloved Wife*), was both a popular and artistic success. It had a realistic look that the studio-bound films of most Japanese films lacked. The story dealt with wives as individuals, an unusual perspective in the male-dominated society of Japan. Like most of his subsequent films, Shindo's first feature was criticized for its excessive sentimentality.

Shindo had another success with *Shukuzu* (1953; *Epitome*) an exposé of geishas. Also in 1953, the Japanese teachers' union asked him to make a film of the novel, *Genbaku no ko* (1952; *Children of Hiroshima*). It was a wonderful picture, but the union was displeased with Shindo's humane vision and had another version made by a filmmaker who showed callous American tourists buying as souvenirs the bones of people killed in the explosion, something that Shindo would never have considered doing in his work.

The Island opens before the sun has even risen above the water. A man and woman are ladling water from a spring into large wooden buckets that are attached by a yoke. They struggle under the weight as they carry the buckets down to their primitive boat. The man, Senta (Taiji Tonoyama), carefully pushes off, and they begin their arduous row back to their island. Carrying the buckets up the stony slopes proves to be a tremendous task. Footing is difficult, but they are cautious and do not spill a drop. Then, when they have finally reached the small field of parched-looking yams, they carefully measure out a cupful of water to each tenacious plant. That is the routine of their day, over and over again, except the woman, Toyo (Nobuko Otowa), must also cook for her husband and their two sons, Taro (Shinji Tanaka) and Jiro (Masanori Horimoto), row her eldest boy to school each morning, and return for him in the afternoon.

One day, as the man and woman trudge up the slope, she trips and spills one of her buckets. She freezes in fear as her husband carefully sets down his load and walks over to watch the precious liquid being sucked into the rocky dirt. He turns to her, slaps her face, and then they continue as before.

Occasionally, the water is poured into the family bathtub to be used for the plants after bathing. The father and the two sons use the water first, and finally the woman is allowed to use the gray water.

One day the eldest boy catches a large fish, and the family sells it and uses the money to take a day's excursion in the city. They have a restaurant meal, which the woman luxuriates in, and the boys are fascinated by the sight of a television set in a store window.

On another day the eldest son complains of feeling ill, so he stays home from school. When his parents return home from their day of toil, they find the boy in a worsened condition. The father rows over to the city and borrows a bicycle to ride to the doctor's house. The doctor returns with the husband to the island, but it is too late; the boy has died.

The father takes the doctor back to the mainland, and then with his life's savings, he buys a small coffin and carries it down to the boat. The eldest son is buried on the island under a blazing sun. When the last shovelful of dirt has been piled on the grave, they pick up their buckets and walk to the boat. Again, the whole painful routine is performed, but as the plants are being watered, the woman deliberately turns over her bucket. This time the husband only looks with pity at the woman. Then she gets down and begins to tear the plants out of the ground, and again the husband merely looks at her. When she has stopped and is sobbing on the wilting pile of vegetation, he goes back to ladling the water carefully onto the yams.

The Island naturally reminds one of Robert J. Flaherty's 1934 documentary, *Man of Aran*. That film is about a rocky island off the coast of northern Ireland. The icy wind is that island's particular problem, not a lack of water. All day long the farmers on Aran drag seaweed from the shore to fertilize their poor soil. The men brave the rugged sea to catch a few fish in the frigid water. Likewise, there is no dialogue in Flaherty's film. In addition to the combat with nature found in *Man of Aran*, *The Island* also has psychological insight into the question of man's purpose in life. The woman's story fully develops Shindo's thesis: One struggles, one loses, one grieves, and one goes on.

Shindo's next film, *Onibaba* (1964), dealt with two women struggling to survive during wartime. They kill dying soldiers so that they can strip the bodies of armor and exchange it for food. Later, Shindo became more commercial, and made films with titles that echoed their vulgarity—*Lost Sex* (1966), *Libido* (1967), and *Nineteen-Year-Old Misfit* (1970). Better is *Heat Wave Island* (1969), an interesting account of how a family similar to that in *The Island* is shaped differently by their city environment.

Many critics were harsh in reviewing *The Island*, calling it boring and repetitive. *The Island* will not appeal to every taste, but it remains a unique and important film.

Larry Lee Holland

IVAN

Origin: U.S.S.R.
Released: 1932
Released in U.S.: 1933
Production: Kiev Film Studio
Direction: Alexander Dovzhenko
Screenplay: Alexander Dovzhenko
Cinematography: Danylo Demutsky, Yuri Yekelchik, and Mikhail Glider
Editing: no listing
Art direction: Yuri Khomaza
Music: Igor Belza, Yuli Meitus, and Boris Lyatoshinsky
Running time: 85 minutes

Principal characters:
Ivan	Pytor Masokha
Ivan's father	Semyon Shagaida
Ivan's uncle	D. Golubinsky
Guba	Stepan Shkurat
Clerk	G. Yura

Ivan was Soviet director Alexander Dovzhenko's first sound film. Dovzhenko's early silent films brought him favorable attention from his contemporaries, who considered his filmmaking talent equal to that of Vsevolod Pudovkin and Sergei Eisenstein. Dovzhenko's films, with their lyric sequences and interwoven themes of nature and the inevitable cycles of life, growth, and death, celebrate the beauties of his native Ukraine. Films such as *Zvenigora* (1928), *Arsenal* (1929), and *Zemlya* (1930; *Earth*), considered to be his masterpiece, assure for Dovzhenko a place in the annals of great Russian filmmakers. With *Earth*, Dovzhenko achieved worldwide fame for his innovations in the medium and for his powerful, poetic images. Official Soviet critics denounced the work as counterrevolutionary, however, and his later films tended to be more favorable to the regime.

Always inclined toward huge themes, Dovzhenko, with *Ivan*, turned his attention to portraying the transformation of the Soviet Union from an agrarian to an industrialized society, exemplified filmically in the construction of the Dnieper hydroelectric works undertaken in the 1930's.

Juxtaposed to the crashing noise and frenetic activity of that grandiose project is a simple peasant, Ivan (Pytor Masokha), from the countryside. In this cauldron, Ivan's old-fashioned peasant mentality is reshaped and tempered into the "progressive collectivist" mentality of the ideal Soviet worker, as he gradually attains the revolutionary attitude toward work and the socialistic way of life. Dovzhenko's Ivan is neither an overachiever nor a leader; rather, he is an "unheroic hero" who, directed and reformed by the harsh realities of the Soviet work setting, becomes a conscious, aware proletarian.

The film's plot is almost primitively simple, reflecting Dovzhenko's uncanny ability to address the fundamental questions of life, touching on them at their most common roots and in an original, sincere, poetic language of metaphor, symbol, and allegory. It was, perhaps, the originality of Dovzhenko's filmic language that complicated his relationship to his audience. Often, contemporary critics and viewers were puzzled by his unorthodox approaches and nonnaturalistic techniques.

The film opens on the majestically flowing Dnieper, calm and mighty, a suitable symbol for the Ukraine. An icebreaker floats through the water, intensifying the beauty of the open sky and endless expanses. Quietly and gently, the notes of a Ukrainian folk song waft through the air. Suddenly, all grows quiet; the rhythm is interrupted and accelerated, until it establishes a new tempo with the voices of oarsmen: "And one, and two!..." Together with the oarsmen, the viewer sees the edge where the waters of the Dnieper are foaming and rushing. It is the same river which, moments earlier, was flowing so peacefully, yet one can hear explosions, crashing noises which shake the seemingly eternal peace of the surrounding countryside. The viewer can hear the construction site, the grand view of which will presently loom.

The scene shifts to a small village, where Ivan's father (Semyon Shagaida) is trying to persuade the village peasants to volunteer their labor at the construction site. The reactions to his arguments are as varied as the individuals, but eventually, the wide Ukrainian steppe is filled with a mass of people, moving toward the site, keeping pace with a song that rings clearly and then fades as they disappear.

After Ivan arrives at the site, there is a series of alternating episodes which do not follow a normal cause-and-effect plot line. Dovzhenko often deviated from sharp plot lines, preferring to use attention-getting devices, such as sharp shifts in mood, to keep the viewer interested. This elliptical style, in which the logical connectives must be supplied by the viewer, is one of the more innovative and interesting techniques used by Dovzhenko. Since the true protagonist of the film is actually the project, symbolic of the changes taking place in the country itself, this deemphasis of plot is appropriate.

Indeed, the characters in *Ivan* have no special character traits; rather, they are presented as universal images and symbols for a whole class of people. The name "Ivan" itself has special significance in the film. Besides the main character, there are two other Ivans in the story. One of them is a "Udarnik" worker who dies in an accident at the construction site; the other, a Komsomol (a member of a Russian Communist youth organization), is at the point of entering into adult life. Thus, there is the Ivan who is sacrificed to the larger project, the Ivan who comes to an understanding of his place in the total scheme of Soviet life, and the young Ivan, who represents the future. There are also other characters—a truant, Guba (Stepan Shkurat), a clerk (G. Yura), and a demagogue—all symbolizing the various social and cultural groups that constitute the collective portrait of the population. Thus, the construction of the plant symbolizes the re-creation of a new life, the rebuilding of Soviet society.

The power of Dovzhenko's cinematographic aesthetic is evident in the film's rhythmic and spatial characteristics. When, for example, the mother of Ivan the Udarnik finds out about the death of her son, her despair is expressed not so much by acting technique as by the setting, through the background of the construction site and its appearance, which changes before the viewer's eyes. She freezes in shock before the body of their son. Then she tears away and runs through the site, which visually overshadows her, as though piling all of its monstrous machines, all of its soulless technology, on top of her. The noise becomes gradually more frightening, and the abundance of faces—which seem distorted and all-devouring—intolerable. A brief, precise series of images demonstrates the psychological distance of this simple woman from that momentous and suddenly opposing force which runs the whole site: Throwing open the door, she runs into a room, as though searching for someone responsible for her son's death—this action acquiring symbolic power as she repeatedly and futilely attempts to open the door.

The Dnieper construction site takes on a kind of dramatic complexity. Symbolic of the momentous changes being undergone in Soviet society, it is also shown to extract its toll—there can be no change, no growth, without sacrifice. Some will die, some will be changed. Dovzhenko's intention was to make the site of the plant the dramatic center of the story. He had the camera rails laid along the dam and shot with the camera in motion, producing the effect of the viewer being present, of immersing the viewer totally in the atmosphere of an industrial scene. This is without doubt the first industrial stage set in cinema history that lived, sounded, and beat with a pulse and rhythm all its own. Dovzhenko had concluded that only in sound film could the conditions for producing real silence on the screen be appropriate, since in silent films, the viewer would assume the presence of sound. The quiet of the countryside is made more tangible against the noise of the site.

The film is thus a study in contrasts. It exhibits the opposition of rural to industrial existence, exemplified in the beauty and peace of the countryside—the quiet, open spaces—in contrast with the loud, frenetic, claustrophobic interiors of the plant. Another contrast is the more subtle depiction of the dual nature of a single entity: The plant is at once heroic and villainous—representing the progress of mankind, but not without its price in lives. Duality is again seen in the use of water, which is often associated with gradual, inexorable change, with the slow but grandiose sculpture of the landscape, here opposed to the more rapid, sudden change imposed on the landscape by man, again through water, also a vehicle of villainy and hope.

Dovzhenko was criticized for portraying heroes who lived on a level above the common, typical characters with whom the masses might more easily identify. He was also criticized for his nonrealistic techniques. Dovzhenko, however, believed in showing the extraordinary in the ordinary, the greatness in the smallest of men. To the criticism that his films were too severe, too sparse and dry, he responded that the aim of film is not primarily to amuse and to entertain but to bring the art of filmmaking to the highest level possible.

There is no denying the beauty of Dovzhenko's images, the power of his effects, and the idealism of his worldview. Although a product of its time and the political and economic circumtances under which it was conceived, *Ivan*, like all of Alexander Dovzhenko's work, will stand, ultimately, on its own merits: the poetry of its scenes, its fascinating elliptical style, and the beauty of its images.

Olga Surkova-Spaans

IVAN THE TERRIBLE I AND II
(IVAN GROZNY)

Origin: U.S.S.R.
Released: 1945 (Part I), 1958 (Part II)
Released in U.S.: 1946 (Part I), 1959-1960 (Part II)
Production: Alma-Ata Film Studio (Part I), Mosfilm Studio (Part II)
Direction: Sergei Eisenstein
Screenplay: Sergei Eisenstein
Cinematography: Éduard Tissé and Andrei Moskvin
Editing: Sergei Eisenstein
Art direction: Yosip Spinel
Costume design: Leonid Naumova
Music: Sergei Prokofiev
Running time: 99 minutes (Part I), 90 minutes (Part II)

Principal characters:
Ivan the Terrible	Nikolai Cherkasov
Anastasia Romanovna	Ludmila Tselikovskaya
Efrosinia Staritsky	Serafima Birman
Vladimir Staritsky	Pavel Kadochnikov
Prince Andrei Kurbsky	Mikhail Nazvanov
Fyodor Kolychev (Philip)	Andrei Abrikosov
Pimen	Alexander Mgebrov
Pyotyr Volynets	Vladimir Balachov
Malyuta Skuratov	Mikhail Zharov
Fyodor Basmanov	Mikhail Kusnetsov
Young Ivan	Eric Pyriev

The history of Russian cinema is dominated by the genius of Sergei Eisenstein. As a director, he was only able to complete seven feature films before his death at the age of fifty. Nevertheless, those seven films—and in particular, *Bronenosets Potyomkin* (1925; *Potemkin*) and *Ivan the Terrible*—along with his theoretical writings on film constitute a monumental achievement. Eisenstein had native talent as an artist and received early training in architecture, qualities which would manifest themselves in his "visionary" sketches for the production of *Ivan the Terrible* (indeed, the sketches served as the film's shooting script). He became interested in theater while still in his teens, but the direction of his life was altered by the Russian Revolution, during which Eisenstein served in the Red Army. After the war, his first job was in theater, as a set designer. He began study at the School for State Direction, and after having directed several plays, made his debut as a film director with *Strachka* (1925; *Strike*), the story of a strike in a metalworks in

1912 czarist Russia. *Potemkin*, universally acknowledged as one of the masterpieces of cinema, deals with the mutiny aboard the *Potemkin* in 1905 and the brutal slaughter of the crew by czarist forces. This point in his career dates the beginning of official criticism which would track Eisenstein throughout the remainder of his professional life. Difficulties with official powers stimulated his interest in working abroad, and in 1930, Eisenstein arrived in Hollywood. His stay in the United States was a failure, but his subsequent attempt to make an epic film in Mexico was a veritable disaster. With the encouragement of Mexican painter Diego Rivera and Charles Chaplin and the financial backing of American novelist Upton Sinclair's wife, Mary Kimbrough, Eisenstein set out for Mexico to begin work on a vast undertaking involving the very life and history of the country. As time passed, Eisenstein went over budget, and Sinclair withdrew his support, stranding Eisenstein in Mexico temporarily. *Que viva Mexico* was never finished as Eisenstein had conceived it, and much of the film that had been shot was badly mutilated. Upon his return to Russia, Eisenstein managed to survive more intense criticism of his work and went on to achieve the success of *Alexander Nevsky* (1938). It was in 1941 that Eisenstein began to devote serious thought to *Ivan the Terrible*, beginning, characteristically, with notes and numerous sketches of scenes. It is the extraordinary visual sense of Eisenstein, which will be expressed in terms of great attention to composition within the frame, in stylized gestures of the characters, in close supervision of lighting and costume, in a strange kind of operatic grandeur, that will provide the viewer with a unique cinematic experience.

Eisenstein's interest in Ivan IV was both patriotic and personal. Evidently he identified with the czar's tragic struggle against established authority and his will to assert himself amid betrayal, but Eisenstein also sought to glorify the ruler who unified Russia in the sixteenth century. The film was projected in two parts, and the filming of Part I, most of it under trying conditions in Russian central Asia, took more than two years to complete. Nevertheless, Part I was an immediate success and received a Stalin Prize. The reception accorded Part II, however, was quite different: Premier Joseph Stalin apparently strongly disapproved of the film, and it was censured by the Communist Party for its unflattering (in the Party's view) depiction of Ivan's bodyguard, the Oprichniki, and of Ivan's own moments of indecision. Part II was banned and not released until 1958. Oddly enough, Stalin gave Eisenstein permission to begin work on a third part of *Ivan the Terrible*, but Eisenstein did not live to complete even the shooting script.

Even though each part can stand alone, Part I, having its own closure, it is more instructive to consider the two parts as a whole. The structure of the film divides itself nicely into well-defined episodes, most often bracketed by fades. Part I presents the coronation of Ivan (Nikolai Cherkasov) as czar; the wedding feast of Ivan and Anastasia (Ludmila Tselikovskaya) and the manifestation of the conspiracy by Efrosinia (Serafima Birman) against Ivan; the people's revolt against Boyar corruption, the arrival of the envoys from Kazan and the threat they pose to Ivan's ideal of unity; the battle for Kazan; Ivan's illness and "miraculous" recovery; the poisoning of Anastasia by Efrosinia and Anastasia's subsequent death; Ivan's decision to withdraw from Moscow to Alexandrov; and Ivan's declaration that he will return to Moscow, having been recalled by the people. Part II includes the betrayal of Kurbsky (Mikhail Nazvanov) and the conspiracy of Poland against Ivan's Russia; Ivan's confrontation, having returned to Moscow, with his Boyar enemies (this episode contains a flashback sequence in which the viewer sees the young Ivan [Eric Pyriev], after the poisoning of his mother, finally assert his authority against the Boyars); the success of Malyuta (Mikhail Zharov) in persuading Ivan to deal harshly with the Boyars (Malyuta subsequently carries out the executions); a brief transition scene: the outrage of Pimen (Alexander Mgebrov), Efrosinia, and Philip (Andrei Abrikosov) against the executions of the Boyars; the "Fiery Furnace" play, ending in Ivan's ultimate acceptance of Efrosinia's role in Anastasia's death; the hatching of the plot by Efrosinia to have Ivan killed and to elevate her son Vladimir (Pavel Kadochnikov) to the czar's throne; the banquet scene and the murder of Vladimir; and a short epilogue: Ivan expresses his sense of triumph.

The substance of the plot of *Ivan the Terrible* is the struggle of the czar to unify his country and to open communications with the West. He is opposed from within by the Boyars (Part II is subtitled "The Boyars' Plot"), the hereditary aristocratic caste headed by Efrosinia and by the Church in league with the Boyars, represented by Pimen and Philip, and, rather briefly, by the Tartars. Ivan is menaced from without by other territorial powers, principally Poland, who wish to keep Russia in her place, divided and weak. Much to Ivan's chagrin, he is betrayed by his trusted Kurbsky, who is jealous of Ivan's power and in love with Anastasia, and who thus, near the end of Part I, transfers his allegiance to Poland. In addition, Ivan is beset by doubts and fears. Anastasia's death is particularly painful for him because he sees her as his only real friend and ally. After she dies, he wonders aloud if Anastasia has been taken from him by God as punishment for wrongdoing, and he even begins to doubt the validity of his goals. Ivan suddenly snaps out of his wavering as he kneels beside Anastasia's coffin in the Kremlin cathedral, and his sense of mission is confirmed at the end of the first part as he glories in the public demonstration of his people's loyalty.

In Part II, Ivan hesitates before the prospect of violence against the Boyars, but, with the help of Malyuta (the now faithful servant who had been a member of the mob which had stormed the cathedral early in Part I and who was converted by the czar's charisma), Ivan comprehends, reluctantly, that it was Efrosinia who poisoned his wife. His resolve for vengeance is thus confirmed. In fact, it is at the point that he realizes what Efrosinia has done and the extent of the Boyars' plot against him that he announces that he will play the role which has been forced upon him by necessity: He will become "Ivan *grozny*"—Ivan the formidable, awesome, "terrible." At the end of Part II, Ivan is firmly convinced that justice has been done, that he has been right in acting as judge and seeing that sentences have been carried out. Having now taken care of internal strife, Ivan looks to defend against external forces which threaten the greatness of his country. With the end of the film is resolved the "tragic" dilemma of Ivan the Terrible as Eisenstein saw it: the tragic nature of Ivan's personal struggle and of the awful loneliness of a great and powerful head of state.

The film does indeed possess much of the grandeur and theatrical trappings which one is accustomed to associate with the tradition of Greek tragedy—a chorus which punctuates and comments upon the action, elaborate costuming and makeup, a scenario written in verse, acting which features exaggerated gestures and tableaux of groups of characters, and a cast of "gods," in the shape of wall paintings, who look down impassively upon the creatures playing out their parts. Moreover, the major characters, with the exception of Anastasia and Efrosinia, cannot be categorized as simply black or white, good or evil. In Part II, one even feels a certain sympathy for the dim-witted Vladimir, who begins to show some moral sense and who becomes the victim of his mother's lust for power. Malyuta and Fyodor Basmanov (Mikhail Kusnetsov), the czar's loyal henchmen, who, according to Eisenstein's plan, would betray Ivan in Part III, derive a certain pleasure from violence, and the Oprichniki are indeed a frightening crew. Ivan himself, even though he does what he has to do in order to protect himself and the country, begins to act, in Part II, more and more like a man on the edge of madness.

Eisenstein wished to refurbish the image of Ivan IV, whose insane cruelty had become legendary and virtually eclipsed the good which he had done for Russia. The director even takes liberty with historical fact in order to make the viewer feel more sympathetic toward Ivan. It should not, therefore, surprise the viewer to see Ivan presented in the film as a god unto himself and a Christ figure, victim of unjust persecution. After the battle for Kazan has been won, Ivan proclaims himself truly the czar of all the Russias, and the film viewer sees him in a low-angle medium close-up, arms outstretched. Clouds of smoke pass behind his head and emphasize his majesty. This shot fades out as a bell tolls. The viewer hears a bell again as there is a fade into the next shot: a medium close-up of a head of Christ on a wall in the Kremlin. The shot of Christ's image is the first shot of a scene in which Efrosinia attempts to undermine Kurbsky's fidelity to Ivan. The czar is the father of his people, sings the chorus at the end of Part I, and Ivan, rather ironically, speaks to Philip in Part II of creating the Oprichniki in his own image, as God created Man. Through his people he hears the voice of God and does His will, and God Himself, in the form of a painting on the ceiling in Ivan's banquet hall, watches from a cloud the wild dancing of the Oprichniki and the murder of Vladimir. Beneath a painting of the Last Judgment, Ivan, in the last scene of the film, says that he, as czar, metes out rewards for the good and just punishment for the wicked.

God's eye is the keenest, but the motif of vision is of evident importance throughout the film. In the first sequence of Part I, the coronation of Ivan, several minutes pass before one sees the czar's face; a sense of anticipation is created as one is shown his hands and his head, upon which the crown is placed. Finally, Ivan turns to face the people and the camera, and his eyes dart swiftly and menacingly about him as he seeks to control those before him with his powerful presence. Most of the action of *Ivan the Terrible* takes place indoors, much of it beneath low ceilings and doorways, which require the characters to bend low in order to pass through them. Extraordinarily frequent low-angle shots of the characters silhouetted against the ceilings not only often render grotesque facial features but also convey a sense of claustrophobia, a feeling that the action takes place underground, in the labyrinths of the human spirit. In such an oppressive atmosphere, it is important for conspirators and potential victims alike to be ever alert, vigilant, and circumspect, ever careful to see before being seen. Power is all; to see is to know, and to know is to control. So important were the eyes of his characters to Eisenstein that Serafima Birman, who plays Efrosinia, had to endure extremely painful makeup procedures which involved drawing up her eyelids at the desired angle.

On one level, the intrigue of *Ivan the Terrible* is a struggle of looks between Ivan and Efrosinia, of hide-and-seek, of illusion and mistaken identity. Ivan fails to prevent the murder of Anastasia because he does not see Efrosinia lurking in the shadows below him as he gives his wife the goblet poisoned by his aunt. The czar is finally completely sure that Efrosinia was responsible for Anastasia's death only when she, at the end of the "Fiery Furnace" play sequence, cannot look him in the eye, and Ivan succeeds in avenging Anastasia's death because neither Efrosinia nor Pyotyr Volynets (Vladimir Balachov), the assassin, recognize Vladimir, dressed in the czar's regalia. Ivan's glance is withering, but, in his absence, Malyuta serves as "the czar's eye." In an unforgettable scene in Part I, when Ivan lies gravely ill and Efrosinia is attempting to entice Kurbsky away from Ivan, the viewer is shown Malyuta's black shadow, distorted to resemble that of a malicious bird of prey, descending a nearby stairway. Malyuta himself appears at the bottom of the steps, stops and stares at the camera in close-up. Moments later, Efrosinia is with Kurbsky again, beseeching him to swear allegiance to Vladimir as the future czar. The viewer hears the sound of a door opening: Again, it is Malyuta, possessed of an uncanny sense for conspiracy. The face of Malyuta appears; he raises one of his eyelids with a finger as he stares at

Efrosinia and Kurbsky, daring them to do anything unseemly. The two traitors are suitably apprehensive. Christ's eye, as a giant image on the wall of the Kremlin chapel, is witness to Kurbsky's vacillation and ultimate decision; in fact, Kurbsky looks up at the image more than once, as though it were a living presence in which he could find direction. Finally, discovering that Ivan is not, as he had thought, dead, Kurbsky swears allegiance to Ivan's infant son, Dmitri.

Even if one might call *Ivan the Terrible* a great historical epic, it will be obvious to all who see the film for the first time that Eisenstein did not intend to produce a realistic costume picture: In *Ivan the Terrible*, the image is not simply a register of a reality to which dialogue can be attached. Eisenstein clearly thought of the frame as an area within which to arrange all elements—scene, actors, and objects—in order to achieve the maximum artistic and expressionistic effect, to create mood and emotion. Each shot of the film can be considered as a work of art and judged on its own merits. While the ideas for *Ivan the Terrible* were germinating in Eisenstein's mind in the early 1940's, he was at the same time working on an article on the painter El Greco, a master of expressionistic distortion. One can surely see a similarity in the tortured poses of figures in El Greco's paintings and the attitudes which Eisenstein forces his actors to strike. Cherkasov in fact complained of the great discomfort which he experienced in making his body conform to the positions which the director had imagined in his sketches. For Eisenstein, the actor becomes a thing like any other, subject to the requirements of the desired compositional effect. A notable example of such a telling arrangement of figures is seen in Part I, at the point when Kurbsky must choose between Anastasia and Efrosinia. Kurbsky and Anastasia are at Ivan's bedside, Kurbsky leaning over Ivan, Anastasia standing. Anastasia looks down into Kurbsky's eyes. This is followed by a shot of the two of them in profile. Efrosinia's head comes into the shot from the left; she looks down at Kurbsky also, disturbing the complicity between Kurbsky and Anastasia. Both Anastasia and Kurbsky look up at Efrosinia, the intruder; both feel threatened by her. Kurbsky looks down and away, then sideways up at Anastasia while she and Efrosinia look each other in the eye over Kurbsky's head. There is a long-shot of the three: Kurbsky is between the two women, head bowed, considering the course which he ought to take—to side with Efrosinia and thereby open his way to the throne or give in to his love of Anastasia. The antagonism between Efrosinia (dressed in black) and Anastasia (always in white), what they each want from Kurbsky, and Kurbsky's own dilemma have been neatly expressed without a word of dialogue. Attention is nearly always focused throughout the film on the center of the frame. There are very few vertical thrusts in the composition; instead, diagonals, either in the form of architectural shapes or patterns of light and darkness, dominate. The arch is a repeated form, and there are many instances in both parts of the film where an arch effectively frames characters within the shot and draws the eye to the center. Of all such shots perhaps those where architecture and figure most obviously combine to create a stunning almost three-dimensional composition arrive at the end of Part I, as Ivan looks out of the Alexandrov Palace upon the serpentine shape (itself a visual echo of the long-shots from the Kazan episode) of the procession of followers who have come to recall him to Moscow. Ivan is apparently looking down at the procession, but in separate shots he is in profile, despite the fact that the crowd is still some distance away: Ivan's posture could not possibly permit him to see the crowd. He is framed looking right, then left in one of the arches along a stairway. These poses are held for several seconds, signaling the fact that Eisenstein wants to allow the viewer adequate time to appreciate the structures within the frame.

Some reference has already been made to the superb use of lighting and shadows in order to enhance characterization. Low-angle lighting is often used to cast gigantic shadows on the walls of rooms and therefore to add another dimension to the action, sending the viewer a message concerning the true nature of what is taking place. Late in Part II, as Vladimir is about to be murdered (as he senses only too well), lighting from below casts ominous shadows of pillars and moving figures: The drama is played out on two visual levels at the same time. In Part I, just after Efrosinia has suggested her plan to kill Anastasia, Ivan is in his stateroom with his ambassador to Queen Elizabeth of England. Ivan is explaining the necessity of establishing an alliance with England, and on his desk are maps and an astrolabe. High on the wall are enormous shadows of Ivan's head and the metal globe, thus juxtaposing symbolically the power of the czar and his passion to free his country from isolation.

One cannot discuss *Ivan the Terrible* without commenting upon the roles of Sergei Prokofiev's score and the color passages of Part II. Prokofiev's contribution to the film is much more than traditional background music. The important part played by the chorus in providing a kind of commentary and narrative, has been mentioned earlier. Prokofiev's leitmotifs, themes which accompany certain characters, such as Ivan's "terrible" theme, and specific sequences, such as the poisoning of Anastasia, constitute a major element of the impact of the film. The leitmotifs facilitate transitions between episodes, and, when they are in fact repeated, identify similarities in significance between sequences. The scene involving Ivan and Nepeya opens with the strains of "The Tents of Ivan," initially heard before the battle for Kazan. Thus the viewer is encouraged to understand the resemblance between what is at stake in this scene, where Ivan expresses his longing to break out into the world, and his first conquest. The scene closes as the viewer hears the music for "Anastasia's Illness," effecting the movement from this episode to the next.

Eisenstein was at first antagonistic toward the use of color in film. In 1945, however, having seen a color documentary on the Potsdam Conference, his attitude changed. He had not yet filmed the banquet scene and the dance of the Oprichniki, and he decided to try color himself. The colors which prevail in Part II of *Ivan the Terrible* are in fact the red, gold, and black which impressed Eisenstein the most in the film which he had seen. Once again, however, Eisenstein's interest lay in the emotional impact, in the moods and emotions which the colors could evoke. The psychological associations of red, gold, and black—fire, passion, blood, death—are certainly appropriate for a sequence which begins with the frenzied dance of the Oprichniki, increases to a frantic tempo, and leads to the scene of Vladimir's murder. A fourth color, blue, shocks the viewer at a critical moment: as Vladimir, in the cathedral, understands what is about to befall him, a blue light heightens the terror of his expression. Unfortunately, the Agfacolor film, captured from the Germans, which Eisenstein used, was inferior in quality, and the intensity of the colors is generally disappointing.

Although the acting in *Ivan the Terrible*, because of its "operatic" nature—the broad gestures, the wild-eyed looks between characters, the tableaux of figures—may often appear quaint to the contemporary viewer, careful consideration will convince the attentive and sensitive spectator that he is witnessing remarkable talent. Nikolai Cherkasov, who also had the title role in *Alexander Nevsky*, was unhappy with the demands made of him, but the role of Ivan, as one might expect, is a virtuoso performance. Serafima Birman was justifiably proud of her work as Efrosinia, and the doglike Malyuta, in the person of Mikhail Zharov, is a great supporting part. Note should be taken of the very effective performance, in a minor role, of Eric Pyriev, as the young Ivan, who, in one shot sits upon the throne, legs dangling, and not long after, suddenly gives notice that he will rule as his own man.

Gordon Walters

IVAN'S CHILDHOOD
(IVANOVO DETSTVO)

Origin: U.S.S.R.
Released: 1962
Released in U.S.: 1963
Production: Mosfilm Studio
Direction: Andrei Tarkovsky
Screenplay: Vladimir Bogomolov and Michael Papava; based on a story by Bogomolov
Cinematography: Vadim Yusov
Editing: L. Feyginova
Art direction: Ye. Chernayev
Music: Vyacheslav Ovchinnikov
Running time: 95 minutes
Also known as: My Name Is Ivan

> *Principal characters:*
> Ivan .... Kolya Burlyayev
> Ivan's mother .... I. Tarkovskaya
> Captain Kholin .... Valentin Zubkov
> Lieutenant Galtsev .... Ye. Zharikov
> Masha .... V. Malyavtina
> Old man .... D. Milyutenko
> Colonel Grygznov .... Nikolai Grinko

For a first feature, Andrei Tarkovsky's *Ivan's Childhood* made an outstanding impact on cinema both in the Soviet Union and abroad. This taut, emotive film about the searing impact of war on a young boy was hailed throughout the world not only as a sign of the renaissance of the Soviet cinema but also as a major innovation in the use of film language itself. It received the Golden Lion at the 1962 Venice International Film Festival (sharing First Prize with the Italian film *Cronaca Familiare*, 1962; *A Family Chronicle*), the Grand Prize at San Francisco, the Grand Prize and a diploma for "poetic direction condemning war" at a festival in Acapulco, and the Selznick Prize for "a film contributing powerfully to peace." Tarkovsky's film is more than an ordinary story of a boy brought prematurely to manhood through his experience of and involvement in World War II; it is also a startlingly visual integration of images, drawn from dreams and reality, and memories and visions, which elucidate Ivan's experiences.

The story is taken from a simple, almost prosaic story by Vladimir Bogomolov which tells of the horrors of war as seen through the eyes of a young child. The incidents that Bogomolov relates have many real-life parallels with the involvement of children in the war. The father of Ivan (Kolya Burlyayev) is killed on the first day of war, his town is overrun by the Germans, his mother is shot, and his sister is killed, in his arms, by a bomb. Ivan is only twelve. Alone and friendless, he becomes a self-appointed spy for the Soviet army, creeping behind enemy lines to gain useful military information. His comrades try to persuade him to accept evacuation and return to school, but Ivan refuses, preferring to remain actively involved in the war. During his missions, Ivan often remembers a more peaceful time, when there was no war, but he remains committed to fighting the Nazis. One day he sets out on a dangerous mission to penetrate enemy lines and to remain there for a fortnight, gathering intelligence. Years later, in the last days of the war, his comrades find a reference to him among the stacks of documents and files about people arrested and tortured by the Germans. A brief note attached to his file explains that he is thought to have been executed.

Through this simple story, Tarkovsky presents a powerful indictment of war and, in particular, of the effects on the people who fight it, thus making one of the first Soviet war films to portray the hero as a victim of war. At the same time, he manages to convey the beauty of a world without war.

In part, the unusual impact of the film can be attributed to the acting of Kolya Burlyayev, the youngster who plays Ivan. This was his second film to win international honors; his first—a short, *Malchik i golub* (1962; *The Boy and the Dove*)—was awarded a Bronze Lion at the 1962 festival of children's films held at the Venice International Film Festival. Burlyayev brings Ivan to life, at times looking like a frail and hungry child but at other moments exuding the confident air of a professional, expert spy. His face, capable of numerous changes, is equally able to suggest a childlike hunger for affection or a burning adult anger focused on the Germans. Ivan's single-minded determination to carry on the fight is an effort to give meaning to an existence that has been irrevocably transformed by the horrors of war.

The primary source of the film's power, however, is Tarkovsky's unique style, which he already handles with assurance in this, his first feature. Tarkovsky has himself argued that music is the highest art form, expressing pure emotion through total abstraction, and his films are a constant, restless search for a cinematic version of that ideal. Thus, his narrative resembles a stream of consciousness drawn from a variety of sources: the story, representing reality itself; the mind, utilizing memories, dreams and visions, and cultural references from music, art, religion, and poetry. (These latter are often steeped in a Russian tradition that often makes his films difficult—sometimes to the point of obscurity—for Westerners to understand fully.) This style, seen at its most developed in his semiautobiographical *Zerkalo* (1975; *The Mirror*), is present in embryo in *Ivan's Childhood*, as memories of Ivan's prewar life with his parents and fantasies of peaceful pastures jostle unnervingly with the harsh imagery of war. Tarkovsky rarely makes any visual differentiation between the present and the past or between reality and fantasy, and so Ivan's mother (I. Tarkovskaya) can appear long after she is dead in a way that prefigures the more complex interweaving of tenses in his science-fiction fantasy *Solaris* (1972). The whole composes a rich, many-sided elaboration of the main character, presented in a highly personal way. It is a style that Jean-Paul Sartre, borrowing a phrase from the poet Andrei Voznesensky, dubbed "socialist surrealism."

Tarkovsky, who studied film at the State Institute for Cinema under Mikhail Romm, first worked with his cinematographer, Vadim Yusov, and composer Vyacheslav Ovchinnikov on his graduation short *Katok i skripka* (1960; *The Roller and the Violin*). Together they have created a powerful cinematic style which makes unusual, and often startling, use of light and shade to create resonant images which add to the more obvious references. There is a scene in *Ivan's Childhood* in which Ivan and his comrades are sitting around a table in a hut not far from the front line, discussing Ivan's future. The light above the table swings back and forth with the sound of shellfire, forming a shadow on the wall, the shape of which resembles that of a censer. This conjuring up of religious imagery is prevalent in all of Tarkovsky's work, always with a deliberately Russian flavor. It is this omnipresent theme in Tarkovsky's work that has led many critics to associate Tarkovsky with the dissident trend of Soviet intellectuals, while others have argued that his is a conscious search for the rehabilitation of prerevolutionary traditions within the contemporary social structure. This critical debate lost much of its relevance, however, when, in 1984, Tarkovsky sought political asylum in the West.

Tarkovsky's images are never one-dimensional. They resonate with meanings, some cultural, some autobiographical, and some (in his later work) referring back to his own earlier films. Further, the same themes recur time and time again. An idealized, loving mother figure—perhaps taken from his own family (or his own wishes), perhaps representing Mother Russia, or perhaps both at once—haunts his work. Ivan remembers her fondly at times of great stress, dreaming about the idyllic life that he might have led if the war had not happened. Another recurrent image is a painterly, watery landscape: In *Solaris*, green leaves ripple below the surface; in *Stalker* (1979), the flotsam of civilization defiles a stream; and in *Ivan's Childhood*, the reflections of stark leafless trees in a lake appear as bleak crosses, recalling the victims of the war. Tarkovsky's use of water is typical of his use of imagery generally. Water, which is so often seen as a peaceful, natural metaphor, is here used to disquieting effect. Beneath the calm surface, there lingers a harsh reminder of something else—a testament to man's destructiveness.

Through this very conscious weaving of plot and imagery, Tarkovsky's own philosophy of humanity surfaces, as consistent in his first film as in his later ones. His films bemoan the loss of innocence, idealizing a past before man's corruption (though by what is never clear). This approach, posed at its sharpest in *Stalker* in the dilemma of the three men facing the room where every desire is fulfilled, is evident in the character of Ivan, the child whose loss of innocence through war leads inexorably to his death. For Tarkovsky, innocence is the state to be desired, the condition of man in which great achievements can be accomplished. In his films, it is children—the beings nearest to that state—who can do the most remarkable things: In *Andrei Rublev* (1966, released 1969), it is a child who, without training or experience, manages to cast a beautiful bell; in *Stalker*, a crippled child has telekinetic powers to move a glass along a table; and in *Ivan's Childhood*, it is again a child who can literally go into areas forbidden to adults.

Alongside this, Tarkovsky introduces the pantheistic notion of man as part of nature. This concept, more fully developed later, when his camera often lovingly lingers on the natural movements of insects, fishes, or leaves, can be seen in his earlier work. Ivan, with his weasel-like face and frightened eyes, moves like an animal between the barbed-wire-filled no-man's-land that separates the enemy lines. Tarkovsky's poetic glorification of nature is often sharply contrasted with the destructive tendencies of a "civilized," technological world. In *Ivan's Childhood*, it is this underlying philosophy that sharpens Tarkovsky's abhorrence of war and his plea for peace.

Sally Hibbin

THE JACKAL OF NAHUELTORO
(EL CHACAL DE NAHUELTORO)

Origin: Chile
Released: 1970
Released in U.S.: 1983
Production: Luis Cornejo and Luis Alarcón for Cine Experimental de la
  Universidad de Chile and Cinematográfica Tercer Mundo
Direction: Miguel Littín
Screenplay: Miguel Littín
Cinematography: Héctor Ríos
Editing: Pedro Chaskel
Art direction: no listing
Music: Sergio Ortega
MPAA rating: no listing
Running time: 95 minutes

> *Principal characters:*
> José (the Jackal of Nahueltoro)......Nelson Villagra
> Rosa ....Shenda Román
> Journalist ....Marcelo Romo
> Chaplain ....Héctor Noguera
> Judge............................Luis Alarcón
> Captain of firing squad..............Pedro Villagra
> Mayor................................Luis Melo
> Corporal Campos................Rubén Sotoconil
> Warden.......................Rafael Benavente
> Prison director ....Roberto Navarrete

The diverse movement known as the New Latin American Cinema appeared in the late 1950's and the early 1960's. Most filmmakers associated
with this movement are Leftists, acutely aware of the underdevelopment and
neocolonial status characterizing Latin America. Recognizing Latin America's cultural dependency, these filmmakers have called for the "decoloniza-
tion" of filmmaking practices, and they have rejected the escapist themes
and the aesthetics of Hollywood as well as the highly technical and industrialized Hollywood production model. Most of the New Latin American
Cinema films are low-budget, nonindustrial productions made without
elaborate technical and financial support. The New Latin American Cinema
filmmakers view cinema not as a profit-making activity or as mere entertainment, but rather as a tool in political or ideological struggles. Consequently,
their films examine specific socioeconomic, historical, or political problems
of Latin American countries. In Chile, the New Latin American Cinema

flourished in the late 1960's and the early 1970's, before and during the presidency (1970–1973) of the Marxist-Socialist Salvador Allende. Miguel Littín, the Chilean director of *The Jackal of Nahueltoro*, is one of the principal figures in this film movement.

The Jackal of Nahueltoro is one of the finest and most typical films of the New Latin American Cinema movement. An intensely researched, documentary re-creation, this film explores the problem of Chilean marginality (*marginalidad*)—the exclusion of vast numbers of citizens from the socioeconomic and political mainstream of the nation. The film was financed with funds provided by friends of director Miguel Littín. Littín, a Marxist,. conceived of his film as a pretext for discussion of pressing Chilean social problems such as land ownership and agrarian reform, the moral values governing national education, and the marginal population. Littín had a specific political intention in making his film: to denounce the injustice of the Chilean socioeconomic system and to bring middle-class Chileans face-to-face with that injustice.

In *The Jackal of Nahueltoro*, Littín crosscuts between present time and past time to reconstruct the life of a real Chilean farm laborer, known by several sobriquets and by various names, such as Jorge and José (Nelson Villagra). This lack of a single name to call his own symbolizes the protagonist's marginal status in Chilean society; he is a landless, homeless peasant, without access to education, permanent employment, political representation, or other sociopolitical benefits and guarantees. In the film, the ignominious tag, "the Jackal of Nahueltoro" is used by Chile's sensationalist media to refer to the protagonist after he serially murdered his female companion and her five children on the Island of Nahueltoro in 1960.

The film commences *in medias res* with an untitled sequence in which the shackled, bedraggled José is led through a jeering crowd to a waiting police van. José's blank countenance and submissive demeanor contrast with the crowd's bloodthirsty taunts and suggest that the prisoner is the uncomprehending victim of an oppressive social system. Littín will investigate that social system and José's past life in the five formal parts of the film, which are all introduced by insert titles.

"José's Childhood" blends the adult José's voice-over with flashbacks of his childhood to narrate the major events in his life after leaving home at age eight. "José's Travels" shows the protagonist working as a farmhand, becoming a down-and-out alcoholic, establishing a common-law marriage with Rosa (Shenda Román), and—in a drunken stupor—murdering Rosa and her children. "Pursuit and Arrest of José" depicts the protagonist's flight and his capture while "Education and Taming" shows the socialization process he undergoes in prison. In the final section, "José's Death," an unnamed journalist (Marcelo Romo) becomes a key figure as he conducts numerous interviews with José and others in order to elucidate the criminal's background and deeds as well as the Chilean legal process. The film concludes with José's execution by firing squad.

Irony is the most prominent trait of this narrative. The overarching irony is that the socioeconomic system makes socialization, education, and training available to a man only after he is incarcerated and condemned to death. It is as a condemned prisoner that José internalizes society's dominant values of patriotism, the importance of hard work, the value of property, and Catholicism. Many lesser ironies mark José's socialization in prison. José becomes literate in order to read and sign the official document condemning him to death. A chaplain (Héctor Noguera) teaches the convict to be a good Catholic in time to die within the faith but too late to live a fruitful religious life among his brethren.

Stylistic diversity characterizes *The Jackal of Nahueltoro*; the different styles generally mesh well with the particular themes being explored by the filmmaker. The shooting and editing styles vary from fast-paced montage sequences to sequence-shots. An effective montage technique is seen in the brothel sequence in "José's Travels." This sequence features many brief shots of prostitutes and clients dancing, musicians playing, the madame and José observing the scene, and the vulgar decor of the whorehouse. The shots are edited to the beat of a popular tune heard on the sound track; the sequence ends as the music does—at which time José is thrown out of the brothel. This sequence is a success because the rapid-fire editing style and the music immerse viewers in the atmosphere of the brothel and also succinctly depict a typical event in José's life.

The use of long-takes and sequence-shots (in which one sequence consists of a single, long-duration shot) is more frequent and of greater importance than the montage sequences. Long-takes and sequence-shots are particularly important in the first three parts of the film, where they are effectively employed as an investigative device to explore realistically José's relation to his environment and to other persons. The finest sequence-shot is the brilliantly conceived sequence in which José and Rosa first meet. This long sequence commences as a close-up of an ax descending on firewood (Rosa is chopping); the sequence ends with a close-up of Rosa and the sound of wood being chopped offscreen (now José is chopping). In this sequence, the carefully planned *mise en scène* orchestrates a nonsubjective, traveling camera, the complicated movements of several characters, and offscreen dialogue and actions within a framework of uninterrupted chronological time in order to probe Rosa's poverty-stricken life-style and to depict the approach-avoidance psychological conflict which grips her when she sees José. Furthermore, the chopping motif in this sequence foreshadows both José's integration into the family unit and the manner in which Rosa and four of her children will be murdered.

The traveling camera is a key stylistic device in Littín's attempt to investigate José's place in the socioeconomic structure—that of victim in a victimizing society. In the opening sequence (and other similar sequences), an agitated, hand-held camera roams the jeering crowd of onlookers; the violent camera movement directly reflects the violence and fury aimed at the prisoner. During the murder scenes, subjective-camera, traveling shots from the viewpoint of the intoxicated and staggering José graphically install viewers within the man's alienated and distorted vision. A masterful subjective-camera, traveling shot depicts José's entry into prison: As doors swing open before the prisoner's eyes, his slowly advancing field of vision takes in the walls and bars which will now mark the boundaries of his physical world.

In order to reconstruct José's life, Littín structures much of his film around the use of flashbacks and crosscutting between past and present. This crosscutting technique is prominent in "José's Travels," in sequences depicting the reconstruction of the murders. In the present time, the prisoner is on the Island of Nahueltoro, accompanied by a judge (Luis Alarcón), the police, other officials, and onlookers in order to explain to the judge the manner in which Rosa and her children were murdered. Littín frequently crosscuts from the present (the judge's questions, the crowd's fury) to the past (flashbacks of the killing of the six victims). The effect of this crosscutting is to interrelate two instances of victimization—José's brutal acts and the State's unrelenting persecution of one of its uncomprehending, marginal citizens.

Another significant feature of *The Jackal of Nahueltoro* is its innovative use of voice-over narration. The transitions from present to past time are often clarified by the skillful introduction of voice-over narration. For example, the sequence in which José drinks from a jug before killing Rosa is introduced by the protagonist's voice-over narration, which establishes the time of day and the fact that Rosa had obtained three liters of wine. Voice-over commentary by the adult José is an important device of characterization, because it serves as the unmediated oral expression of a marginal existence. At times, voice-over narrators provide a concurrent commentary on the images, as when the radio announcer describes in a sensationalist manner the search for the murderer while the images depict the mundane reality of José's flight. The legalistic and bureaucratic jargon characterizing the actuary's voice-over narration reminds viewers that José is but a cog in the impersonal machinery of the legal system.

The Jackal of Nahueltoro is an outstanding example of the documentary re-creation genre in part because of the historical authenticity that the film achieves. To achieve this authenticity, Littín shot his film on location, used some nonprofessional actors, including inhabitants of Nahueltoro and convicts in Chillán Prison, and based some of the dialogue directly on journalists' recorded interviews with the historical Jackal of Nahueltoro and others involved with the case. The song heard in certain prison sequences (concerning a Chillán convict sentenced to be shot) was actually composed by the real-life Jackal of Nahueltoro.

To understand fully *The Jackal of Nahueltoro*, viewers must grasp the significance of certain Chilean themes and motifs. Alcoholism has long been a major social problem in Chile. It is worth noting that José is not the only character affected by alcoholism: Rosa's first husband was murdered when he was inebriated, and the mayor (Luis Melo) insists on serving Corporal Campos (Rubén Sotoconil) two large glasses of wine. The debilitating physical effects of alcoholism on José and others are briefly glimpsed in the montage sequence set in a bar in "José's Travels." The history lecture delivered to José and other inmates centers on the brave deeds of the famous Chilean naval hero Arturo Prat, who gave his life while valiantly defending his country in the nineteenth century War of the Pacific. During the lecture sequence, several shots show a painting of Prat's glorious resistance against unequal odds. Littín uses the heroic figure of Prat to symbolize the textbookish notion of patriotism that is being inculcated in the prisoners. The Spanish in the film is very Chilean, and lead actor Nelson Villagra's vocabulary, pronunciation, and grammar create a faithful linguistic portrait of an uneducated Chilean peasant. While marginality is not a problem unique to Chile, this topic was in the 1960's and early 1970's the subject of great debate among Chilean intellectuals and politicians. *The Jackal of Nahueltoro*, a unique and powerful portrayal of a marginal Chilean, was released in the midst of this national debate.

Critics have correctly noted that *The Jackal of Nahueltoro* has weaknesses. A well-rounded psychological portrait of José never emerges; viewers never learn, for example, the protagonist's psychological motivation in placing stones on the cadavers of his victims. The shooting and editing styles of the last two parts of the film are frequently rather conventional. In spite of such defects, *The Jackal of Nahueltoro* proved a great success from the viewpoint of Littíns's intention to use the film to stimulate discussion of Chilean socioeconomic realities. The controversial film was shown in thirty-five millimeter in commercial theaters and in sixteen millimeter in jails, shantytowns, and meetings of workers and peasants. The filmmakers themselves often organized sixteen-millimeter showings, and they held debates on the film in both the commercial cinemas and the sixteen-millimeter facilities. A national forum on the class bias of Chilean justice featured a screening of the film. *The Jackal of Nahueltoro* became the most widely seen and debated film in the history of Chilean cinema and a classic of the New Latin American Cinema movement.

Dennis West

JAIL BAIT
(WILDWECHSEL)

Origin: West Germany
Released: 1972
Released in U.S.: no listing
Production: Gerhard Freud for Intertel (for Sender Freies Berlin)
Direction: Rainer Werner Fassbinder
Screenplay: Rainer Werner Fassbinder; based on a play by Franz Xaver Kroetz
Cinematography: Dietrich Lohmann
Editing: Thea Eymèsz
Art direction: Kurt Raab
Music: Ludwig van Beethoven and Paul Anka
MPAA rating: no listing
Running time: 102 minutes
Also known as: Game Pass and *Wild Game*

Principal characters:
Erwin	Jörg von Liebenfels
Hilda	Ruth Drexel
Hanni	Eva Mattes
Franz	Harry Baer
Dieter	Rudolf Waldemar Brem
Ärtzen	Hanna Schygulla
Boss	Kurt Raab
Policemen	Karl Scheydt/Klaus Löwitsch
Prison guards	Irm Hermann/Marquard Bohm
Friend	Heli Ben Salem

The late Rainer Werner Fassbinder is acknowledged as one of the most innovative and original directors to have emerged from the movement known as the New German Cinema. At his death in 1982, at the age of forty-six, Fassbinder left a legacy of more than forty films and numerous stage plays and television productions. His prolific output is unmatched in recent film history, and the highly personalized nature of his work inspired the ideals of the movement in which he was a leader.

New German Cinema (*Das neue Kino*) began in 1962, with the Oberhausen Manifesto that called for an alternative to the vested commercial interests and conventionalized filmmaking that dominated German cinema in the 1950's. To these filmmakers, a new film had to be created as both a process and a style. New forms, new artistic honesty, and, at its most ambitious, a new cinematic language, formed the goals of the movement. The result was a new kind of German cinema which reflected the cultural realities of the postwar existence.

While recognition on the Continent came quickly for such filmmakers as Volker Schlöndorff, Alexander Kluge, Wim Wenders, and Fassbinder, international recognition—especially in the United States, was slow to arrive. Fassbinder's *Der Händler der vier Jahreszeiten* (1972; *The Merchant of Four Seasons*) was shown at the New York Film Festival in 1972, but not until the 1973 festival screening of *Die bitteren Tränen der Petra von Kant* (1972; *The Bitter Tears of Petra von Kant*), was Fassbinder's reputation among American critics assured.

Jail Bait, coming on the heels of the masterful *The Bitter Tears of Petra von Kant*, is a film that has been critically neglected. It is neither one of Fassbinder's most popular films nor one of his most critically praised, but as a "lesser" film it still demonstrates the breadth of Fassbinder's talent and his daring exploration of the relationship between politics, sex, and violence.

Jail Bait was adapted by Fassbinder from a play by Franz Xaver Kroetz, who later denounced the film version of his work as pornography. Kroetz's denunciation is in some respects correct: The film might be called pornographic, but it is not because of the generous amount of screen time spent displaying the lovers in the act of copulating or lounging around in the nude. Fassbinder's film views its subject with an objectivity that suggests that he finds certain aspects of power relations (in society in general as well as in sex) repellent or degrading, yet the film itself cannot be dismissed as such. The spectator is not allowed the kind of unmediated voyeurism expected from explicitly pornographic media. Instead, Fassbinder's film demystifies sex and demands a different, more complex viewer response.

In *Jail Bait*, as in a number of his films, Fassbinder relies on genre conventions to generate suspense but turns the familiar sentimental tale of outlaw lovers on its head. *Jail Bait* tells the story of a fourteen-year-old German schoolgirl who takes up with a motorcycle riding nineteen-year-old who sports a slicked-back ducktail hairdo and tough-guy pretensions. Before they are finished, they kill her father. The basic plot forms a striking parallel to the infamous American case of Nebraska murderer Charles Starkweather and his fourteen-year-old lover, Carol Ann Fugate. After killing Fugate's father (among others), the couple went on an interstate murder spree that left almost two dozen people dead. Starkweather was executed, Fugate left to serve a prison term. This notorious case served as the direct inspiration for Terence Malick's *Badlands* (1973). In Malick's film, narration is provided by the girl, whose adolescent romanticism and flatly intoned amorality make the story a tale of innocence gone inexplicably bad. The lovers are likable; they intersperse killing with dancing to the car radio in the moonlight. The film becomes an ironic celebration of America's vast landscape and the childish naïveté of American violence.

Fassbinder's *Jail Bait* uses similar material to make a very different point about sexuality, violence, and a specific ideological context—postwar West Germany. *Jail Bait* is a deeply ironic examination of German mores, the German family, and the predilection for violence. It is not romance but carnality that dominates its portrait of adolescent crime. The film opens with a bleak panorama of an unidentified German city. Hilda (Ruth Drexel), a plump, middle-age German housewife, gets dressed to start the day. In her slip, her sagging flesh suggests a sexuality that is discounted by her part in the remainder of the film, in which she functions solely as a mother. Once dressed, her sexuality is muted. She attempts to rouse her fourteen-year-old daughter, Hanni (Eva Mattes), from bed. Hanni is running late for school. Hanni appears as a youthful version of her mother: plump, coarsely sensual, not particularly attractive but possessed of a knowing look beyond her years. Hanni's tight, childishly cut jumper dress and her pigtails seem oddly incongruent with her facial expression and her body language. Her mother waits on her slavishly but informs Hanni that if she wants a ride to school she will have to convince her father to give her one. Hanni's seductive manner toward her father, Erwin (Jörg von Liebenfels), and his response uncomfortably suggest the interaction of lovers rather than father and daughter. The sexualized quality to their relationship immediately overturns the notion of the patriarchal family unit as the source of all stability in the capitalistic economy. The Oedipal undertones to the relationship become explicit, as though Fassbinder is forcing his audience to confront the psychosexual dangers in what is regarded as the normal structure for living. There is also the suggestion that the utter banal mediocrity of this family unit—father the truck driver, mother the *Hausfrau*, and child, demonstrates the predictability of the violence and sexual rivalry that occurs. The family members represent the interlinking of the personal with the social. They are both victims of the structures under which they live (family, work, political powers) and perpetrators of the corruption that ensures the survival of destructive and irrational emotional forces.

The family unit of Erwin, Hilda, and Hanni also represents the proletarian aspiration to middle-classness. Order, duty, and a good family name dominate their values. Underneath the façade of order lies chaotic violence, not only because of the lovers' destructive passion, but also, Fassbinder suggests, in the passion that the mediocre have for order. Erwin extols the Nazis' ability to maintain order. Unwittingly, the talent for order and the talent for killing become synonymous, both in Germany's history and in its present as represented by Hanni and Franz (Harry Baer).

On her way home from school, Hanni meets Franz and the two ride off on his motorcycle. They make love in a barn. For Hanni, losing her virginity is more a painful than a pleasurable experience. Both Hanni and Franz are curiously diffident about the entire experience. When they meet again and go to a bar with some of Franz's coworkers at a chicken-processing plant,

Hanni displays herself with hip-swinging abandon. When she breaks into the conversation between the men, she is quickly put in her place: Franz spits on her. She gets up, goes to the ladies' room, then returns without a change of expression or a protest. The demands of the relationship include a clearly established tolerance for self-abasement at the hands of the loved one, a theme which runs throughout Fassbinder's films.

When her father discovers that Hanni and Franz are lovers, he has Franz arrested for rape. The police pick up Franz at the chicken-processing plant, but not before Fassbinder lingers over each step of the butchering process with his camera. The expressions of the workers and the gory repulsiveness of the chopping, shredding, and pulling apart of the chickens suggests that the workers are inured to the slaughter. Fassbinder offers a similar sequence in his later film, *In einem Jahr mit 13 Monden* (1978; *In a Year with 13 Moons*). The autobiographical source of such scenes may be found in the fact that one of Fassbinder's lovers worked as a butcher. Critics have speculated that Fassbinder sees the workers' conditioning to slaughter reflected in their relations outside work, in aggressive behavior toward others, and perhaps self-annihilation.

Franz is sentenced to prison but paroled after several months. His parole is conditional: He cannot see Hanni. On the day of his release, he appears at the school. Once again, he is astride his motorcycle, but his James Dean-like look is gone: Prison pallor and a closely cropped hairstyle compromise his wild look. He and Hanni begin meeting clandestinely. In one of those coincidences typical of Fassbinder's ironic plays on melodramatic convention, Hanni's father happens to spot the lovers sitting under a bridge. When Erwin confronts Hanni with this, she smoothly lies and says her meeting with Franz was chance and only a brief farewell exchange rather than a resumption of their affair. Erwin is hysterical; the good name of the family has been sullied by the affair and the trial. He warns her against seeing Franz. He promises to tell the judge and have Franz thrown in jail if she disobeys. Hanni dutifully swears she will never see Franz again.

The lovers become bold. They even make love in Hanni's room (cluttered with dolls and cuddly animals) when her parents are at the cinema. The power relations between the two begin to shift. When Hanni discovers that she is pregnant, she is eager to promote the solution: They must kill her father to keep him from sending Franz to prison. Hanni takes the active role in planning the murder. She tells her father that Franz wishes to reconcile with him. A meeting is set.

Hanni and Franz wait in a forest clearing for Erwin. It is Franz who appears most nervous. Erwin rides up on a bicycle. Fassbinder draws out the suspense by photographing with a telephoto lens the father's zigzag, arduous movement through the rough thicket. Erwin's progress through the woods toward Franz and Hanni seems interminable. Finally, Franz shoots him. In a grotesque effect, the father will not be killed; he keeps moving. Franz shoots him again and again. Hanni screams and runs over to the body. She convulses with strangely gleeful cries of "Papa." Her response is virtually orgiastic. Daughter and father have their relationship consummated in patricide, in a rite of violence, rather than incest.

When the police arrive at the house, it is apparent that weeks have passed. Hilda is confused. Her husband has been gone for several weeks. She initially thought that he was out on a haul in his truck. The police inform her that he is dead. Innocently, Hanni asks whether he was in an automobile accident. The police say no.

A daring ellipsis in time robs the audience of the opportunity to savor the melodramatic climax of the killing. Hilda's reaction to her discovery that her daughter has murdered Erwin is never shown. Franz and Hanni's trial is not shown. Instead, Fassbinder cuts to a scene in which a very pregnant Hanni is being examined by a woman prison doctor (Hanna Schygulla). Then he cuts to a scene in a hallway. In handcuffs, Franz meets with Hanni. They speak in maudlin clichés about their relationship and their dashed hopes for the future. Hanni talks of their baby boy, who was born deformed and died. Franz sentimentalizes over the baby and its death. The scene outrageously counters the entire portrait of the two lovers offered previously in the film. Their passion is spent, the death wish faded, and the daring extremity of their cruelty gone. The scene is unbelievable, and no doubt Fassbinder intends it that way. Hanni and Franz mouth the simpleminded responses of melodrama's heroes and heroines, but neither their sentiments, nor the film itself should be taken as real. As with so many other of his films, Fassbinder is slyly reminding the viewer that Hanni and Franz are creations; their actions may be emblematic of a time, a place, and a people, but they are not real. For Fassbinder, it is only through the dramatic license of unreality, through exaggeration and distance, that one confronts what is hidden in the everyday and the mundane. Although not a masterpiece of filmmaking, *Jail Bait* is an interesting working out of the Fassbinder philosophy.

Gaylyn Studlar

A JAPANESE TRAGEDY
(NIHON NO HIGEKI)

Origin: Japan
Released: 1953
Released in U.S.: 1979
Production: Takashi Koide and Ryotaro Kuwata for Shochiku
Direction: Keisuke Kinoshita
Assistant direction: Yoshio Kawazu
Screenplay: Keisuke Kinoshita
Cinematography: Hiroshi Kusuda
Editing: no listing
Art direction: Kimihiko Nakamura
Music: Chuji Kinoshita
MPAA rating: no listing
Running time: 116 minutes

Principal characters:

Haruko Inoue	Yuko Mochizuki
Utako	Yoko Katsuragi
Seiichi	Masami Taura
Tatsuya	Keiji Sata
Akazawa	Ken Uehara
Mrs. Akazawa	Sanae Takasugi
Wakamaru	Keiko Awaji

Keisuke Kinoshita is one of Japan's greatest postwar directors. Although little known in the West, he is beloved by the Japanese filmgoing public. After working his way up through the ranks at Shochiku (he began in the film processing lab in 1933), and before turning to television in the 1960's, Kinoshita made more than seventy films. He shares with his friend and contemporary, Akira Kurosawa, a preoccupation with socially relevant subjects, and, like the great Kenji Mizoguchi, Kinoshita is one of the truly authentic stylists of all Japanese cinema.

A Japanese Tragedy is Kinoshita's tragic masterpiece. It contains the director's central theme, that external social forces have a corrupting effect on the essential goodness of ordinary people. Despite this rather dark view, Kinoshita is no pessimist; rather, he is a serious artist who values the lives of simple people, whom he portrays as transcending their suffering. The Kinoshita hero always represents what is best in life, even if he or she is called upon to pay for that goodness through death. Most often, it is the heroine of a Kinoshita film whose life is built on sacrifice and whose purity comes into conflict with an unfeeling society.

As a director, Kinoshita excelled at virtually every film genre. His first film, *Hana saku minato* (1943; *The Blossoming Port*), was a tour de force of social satire—a rarity in Japan. The story of two country bumpkins who try to defraud each other, it ranks as one of Japan's great wartime comedies. The equally unpredictable *Karumen kokyo ni Kaeru* (1951; *Carmen Comes Home*) is a bizarre story of a Tokyo stripper who returns to her hometown to scandalize the local residents. The tables are turned when she and her friend raise money for the local school, and the film is famous for showing the effects of Japanese provincialism at its worst. The attention to detail that Kinoshita brought to these films also characterizes his romances and tragedies. Each is informed by an artistic vision as complete and mature as that of any consummate artist.

The subject matter of Kinoshita's films varied throughout his career, and his style changed often from picture to picture. To a handful of Japanese critics, this eclecticism has made Kinoshita less of an auteur; to others, it is the stuff of genius. Like Mizoguchi and Teinosuke Kinugasa, Kinoshita saw every film as a chance to experiment with film style. In *Narayamabushi-ko* (1958; *The Ballad of Narayama*), for example, he uses a host of theatrical conventions associated with the Kabuki theater, even to the extent of changing the sets during a take. For *Fuefukigawa* (1960; *The River Fuefuki*), he had artists hand paint the filmstrip to duplicate the effects of Japanese picture scrolls. *A Japanese Tragedy* is no exception. Here, he borrows conventions from the genre of the tendency film (*keiko eiga*), including documentary footage of news events in order to situate his screen story in reality. This technique gives Kinoshita's fictional subject a social dimension unusual outside the European avant-garde.

A Japanese Tragedy is often called a *haha-mono* or mother picture—an extremely popular genre in Japanese cinema. The central character is Haruko Inoue (Yuko Mochizuki), who, like many women in Japan, has lost her husband in the war and must rear two children alone. Her daughter Utako (Yoko Katsuragi) works as a seamstress while studying English, and her son Seiichi (Masami Taura) is in medical school in Tokyo. The drama is set in motion by a documentary preface. Labor strikes, assassination attempts, the war crimes trial, mob violence—all set the tone of Kinoshita's postwar tale. Within this chaos, Haruko makes her meager living in the resort town of Atami, catering to businessmen in need of female companionship.

Haruko sacrifices her own personal happiness for her children, but they misunderstand and grow into cold and avaricious people. Through flashbacks, it is seen that the children think that their mother is neglecting them when in fact she is away from home working only for their benefit. Thinking of their best interests, Haruko puts the children in the care of her brother-in-law, but his wife reinforces the children's hatred of their mother. As an adolescent, Utako was raped, and she harbors a deep resentment against men, especially those on whom her mother is dependent. The ungrateful daughter flirts with her English teacher, Akazawa (Ken Uehara), and decides to run away with him. When the man's wife (Sanae Takasugi) confronts Utako, she insults the older woman and flees home. Haruko is horrified and reluctantly travels to Tokyo to seek her son's advice. He is full of his own plans—he hopes to be adopted by a wealthy man whose son has died—and in the face of Haruko's grief, all he can talk of is changing the family records. Burdened by her son's final rejection, the mother heads back to Atami. She thinks back on her life and her sacrifices—all in vain. In despair, she hurls herself in front of an oncoming train. Back in Atami, Tatsuya (Keiji Sata), a street musician, and Wakamaru (Keiko Awaji), a geisha, Haruko's only friends, sing of her memory.

Like all of Kinoshita's major films, *A Japanese Tragedy* uses a tight cause-effect structure to show the interrelationship between the social environment and the behavior of the characters. The economic hardships of the postwar period are shown to be the cause of Haruko's extreme burdens, and she must resort to any means in order to support her children. In Japan, she thus honors her dead husband and his family. In the present chaos, however, her children are blind to the older traditional values that Haruko upholds. Kinoshita makes clear that her children are part of the new Japan that is too unfamiliar with democratic principles to see beyond their own selfish interests. They become cold and greedy, unaware of their mother's sacrifice. Haruko is left alone with her suffering in a world in which young people no longer feel an obligation to care for their parents. This, then, is the interpretation that the narrative chain forces on the viewer, built up as it is out of the documentary context and the fictional drama.

The majority of Kinoshita's films have women as the central characters, and Haruko is typical of the director's heroines. Self-sacrificing and pure in heart by nature, they are misunderstood by their loved ones and abused by an unfeeling society. This film tradition of the long-suffering Japanese woman was spawned in the films studios of Shochiku, and Kinoshita is one of its best postwar directors. He made films with the Ofuna flavor, as these Shochiku productions were called, and he used heroines of this type in both his modern stories and the period films, in his comedies and in the darker tragedies. His work is often like that of Mizoguchi, whose women can represent all those dispossessed in Japan, all those Japanese who are made vulnerable either by poverty or by the social pretentions of others less pure in heart.

The scenes in *A Japanese Tragedy* which take place in the present are shot in a realistic style. Deep-focus photography and the long-take give the drama its just-lived quality. In contrast, the flashbacks are cut into the narrative with such dynamic speed that the film's largely conservative view takes on a very modern character. This kind of juxtaposition is characteristic of directors such as Tadashi Imai, to whom Kinoshita is often compared. In *A Japanese Tragedy*, such a contrast adds to the film's rhetorical quality.

The fast cutting between past and present is used to show the events that have shaped the lives of the characters. In one episode, the brother and sister demand more money from Haruko as they sit together eating. Immediately, Kinoshita cuts in a scene from the past that shows the mother desperately negotiating to buy rice on the black market. Juxtapositions such as this are continually intercut with the documentary footage to emphasize the lack of social morality that underlies the children's demands. The viewer comes to understand their estrangement from the point of view of the film itself, which is carefully constructed with this end in mind. Kinoshita's aim here is to place Haruko in her goodness against the children's evil, which becomes an extention of that of society at large.

This type of film style is one example of the direction that postwar realism took in the hands of a director such as Kinoshita. *A Japanese Tragedy* is a film of the *shomin-geki* genre or films which celebrated the common people. This genre flourished as a realistic form in the hands of men such as Yasujiro Shimazu, who was Kinoshita's mentor. The prototype for such films are those by Yasujiro Ozu. In films such as *Hitori musuko* (1936; *The Only Son*), *Higanbana* (1958; *Equinox Flower*), and *Samma no aji* (1962; *An Autumn Afternoon*), it is said that life is depicted as it is lived. This view supposes a balance in the narrative's point of view toward the characters. Questions about their morality are raised, for example, but they are left with no definitive answer. Kinoshita's films, however, are seldom inconclusive. Their themes are more provocative, and at their best, the characters are extreme examples of everyday people made extraordinary by the social events around them.

Unflattering critics are always attuned to the sentimentality never far away from any Kinoshita film. Most often it arises when the antagonist is not fully developed or when evil forces go unexplored. The characterization of Haruko is kept from sentimentality because the viewer understands her children and their unfortunate point of view. In like manner, the film remains a powerful indictment of postwar Japan because the social background is clearly a living context for the characters.

In Kinoshita's famous film *Nijushi no hitomi* (1954; *Twenty-Four Eyes*), the situation is less satisfying. The film is about a schoolteacher who protests against the government's censorship of books during the prewar years and during World War II. She resigns from teaching rather than abide by the government's edict, and she watches passively as her young students go off to war. The film is called a five-handkerchief picture in Japan because of its extreme poignancy. What makes it overly sentimental is that the war effort is never questioned, and the repressive government measures of the time are never explored. Unlike *A Japanese Tragedy*, the evils are rendered as a faceless abstraction against which the heroine is never shown to be a worthy adversary.

Kinoshita's brand of drama became less popular during the 1960's, as new directors came to the front whose more explicit realism embraced a modern view of sexuality and politics. The Japanese New Wave, associated with the work of Nagisa Oshima, supplanted the dramas of pathos made so expertly by Kinoshita. Nevertheless, many younger directors have paid their respects to this great artist. His prolific output of comedies, tragedies, and social satire places him on a level by himself, and few directors in all of Japanese cinema have been honored as much as Kinoshita.

Robert N. Cohen

JITSUROKO ABE SADA

Origin: Japan
Released: 1975
Released in U.S.: no listing
Production: Ryoki Yuki for Nikkatsu
Direction: Noboru Tanaka
Assistant direction: Sanji Tobikawa
Screenplay: Akio Ido
Cinematography: Masaru Mori
Editing: Shinji Yamada
Art direction: Gunji Kawasaki
Sound: Eiji Kimura
Music: Koichi Sakata
MPAA rating: no listing
Running time: 76 minutes
Also Known as: A Woman Named Abe Sada

> *Principal characters:*
> Sada Abe .... Junko Miyashita
> Kichi .... Hideaki Ekaku
> Principal .... Naganori Sakamoto
> Geisha .... Genshu Hanayagi

The genre known as *roman poruno*—romantic pornographic films—was introduced by the Nikkatsu Corporation in 1972. A creative response to Japan's slumping box office, which had forced another of Japan's five major production companies into bankruptcy, this new genre saved Japan's oldest studio. Using respectable budgets, expressive and innovative camera angles, excellent acting, and strong plots, several "roman porno" productions quickly won acclaim for their high quality, fervor, social relevancy, and open approaches to a broad range of mature topics. Several, including Noboru Tanaka's *Jitsuroko Abe Sada* received important film awards in Japan and have been presented at international film festivals abroad.

With the dawn of roman porno, a number of young directors were given opportunities to demonstrate their talents. They faced restrictions not operative in much of the West: Japan's Motion Picture Code of Ethics Committee prohibits exposure of the genitals or the pubic regions, so their sex scenes cannot be nearly as explicit (they would be considered soft core by American standards). Yet a unique type of eroticism has been a driving force in Japanese art. Roman porno allows an original Japanese response to this. Eros and voyeurism are frequently key components in these films; sadomasochism and bondage are not uncommon. They often feature violence but at the same time are much more realistic than their Western counterparts. Japan's rigid censorship laws may have prevented routinely made hard-core pornography, but they stimulated films which were considerably more erotic and ecstatic.

"Pink films," as soft-core pornographic films are called in Japan, were not uncommon before 1972. They possessed minimal routine plots (if any), crude production values, and were made on miniscule budgets. Although Nikkatsu's production expenditures are not as great as those for important works of other major studios, they are considerably greater than those of the "pink films." The French word "roman" was included in the genre's name to give it special class, "pornographic novels" being elevated above previous works. In fact, roman porno has a following among students and intellectuals as well as blue-collar workers.

Its initial success attracted considerable attention. *Koi no karyudo* (1972; *Love Hunter*) and *Ol nikki, mesuneko no nioi* (*The Smell of the Wildcat*) passed the Ethics Committee's screening board in 1973; however, the police department seized the prints. In a famous obscenity case, the courts ruled that they could be shown, virtually guaranteeing their audiences. Nikkatsu has carefully worked around such laws since then, seeking to avoid expensive court cases.

Like any popular genre, roman porno has its own set of acclaimed directors and stars. Noboru Tanaka merges harsh worlds and expressive images with a very poetic lyricism and a sense of surrealism; he will be discussed further later. Tatsumi Kumashiro is known for his special efforts to depict pure sensual pleasure. His *Yojohan fusuma no urabari* (*The World of Geisha*; literally, "the backpaper four-and-a-half mat room's sliding door") accurately re-creates geisha and teahouse life in Tokyo's gay quarters in 1918. Using the small tatami mat room as a symbol of closed-space sex, this playful and witty film features sensual photography through a mosquito net on a sweltering summer night. Kumashiro's *Monzetsu-donden gaeshi* (*The Peculiar Triangle*) humorously depicts the twisted relationship between a foppish University of Tokyo graduate (Japan's Harvard with even more prestige) who discovers that he is gay, a *yakuza* (gangster), and a bar hostess who brings home her customers. Kumashiro also satirizes his breed of filmmaker searching for loopholes in *Kuro-bara shoten* (*Professional Specialists*), a comedy with erotic moments.

In *Hana to hebi* (*Flowers and Serpents*) director Masaru Konuma transforms bondage and torture into ecstasy while making a black comedy much more bizarre than Kon Ichikawa's classic *Kagi* (1959; *Odd Obsession*). Konuma's unusual works also contain a fine sense of lyricism; unfortunately, he has been forced to accept a number of studio assignments in order to make his specialty films. On the other hand, Koyu Obara takes torture and sadomasochism quite seriously in *Ori no naka no yosei* (*Trapped*), which depicts atrocities of military police during World War II, and *Shin jitsuroku onna-kanbetsusho rengoku* (*The Inside Story of a Women's Prison*). In the tongue-in-cheek *Sengoku rokku hayate no onnatachi* (1973; *The Naked Seven*), director Yasuharu Hasebe uses a group of beautiful Amazon warriors to recall a famous samurai classic.

The talented Junko Miyashita, the star of *Jitsuroko Abe Sada*, became Nikkatsu's queen of roman porno. Beautiful Naomi Tani, a frequent star in films by Konuma and Obara as well as *Monzetsu-donden gaeshi*, completely threw herself into her work to reign as the "queen of bondage" until she retired in 1979. Hiroko Isayama won *Kinema Jumpo's* 1972 Best Actress Award (Japan's Academy Award equivalent) for her portrayal of a thrill-seeking girl turned pickpocket in Toru Murakawa's *Shiroi yubi no tawamure* (*White Fingers of Ecstasy*).

The most acclaimed roman porno films thus far were made in the initial years of this era. In the early 1980's, coupled with falling box-office receipts, there have been complaints that new films are too formulaic and repetitious. Several directors, including Tanaka and Kumashiro, have worked for other productions companies, desiring larger production budgets and a greater diversity of topics. Konuma has had difficulty in receiving approval for his scripts. Several younger assistants were promoted into the directoral ranks, but none have established a reputation for originality thus far. Since they are still relatively inexpensive to produce and promote, however, roman porno films are likely to remain Nikkatsu's staple for some time.

Jitsuroko Abe Sada is one of the best Nikkatsu roman pornos. The true story of Sada Abe (Japanese convention gives surname first; Sada is the first name), also told in Nagisa Oshima's *Ai no koriida* (1976; *In the Realm of the Senses*) caused a nationwide sensation in 1936, and Sada became a Japanese celebrity. Numerous artists, novelists, and philosophers have been haunted by her myth. Many Japanese critics consider Tanaka's exploration of a radical form of sex and love to be superior to *In the Realm of the Senses*, and find Junko Miyashita to be a more realistic Sada. This film was made first, and Oshima is known to have been impressed by several films by Tanaka and Kumashiro.

Jitsuroko Abe Sada begins with a black screen and Sada narrating that she was using a pseudonym when she was arrested in Tokyo. After she enumerates several of her aliases, the words "Kichi Sada 2" appear. Japanese, familiar with her story, immediately know that these are the words Sada Abe inscribed in blood on her lover Kichi's body. Newspaper headlines then report "Document—Abe Sada," the Japanese title for this film. The passionate lovers Sada Abe (Junko Miyashita) and Kichi (Hideaki Ekaku) are then introduced against a rural background, where Kichi exclaims that he will become a skeleton shortly if they continue their violent lovemaking. Soldiers are marching by as the couple reach an inn. The year is 1936, which marks the dawn of the prewar Japanese military buildup. Sada and Kichi, however, remain oblivious to the soldiers. Instead, they go inside, and Kichi predicts his death. Their ecstasy begins immediately, as Sada licks Kichi's fingers, then instructs him to bite her firmly until she becomes senseless. Sada, the mistress, requests that he abandon his wife and children. As they make love, she vows to follow Kichi to Hell.

Kichi leaves for a shave. When he returns, Sada wields a knife at him. He is late, Sada believes, because he took advantage of his barbershop appointment to "commit adultery" with his wife. After several wild slashes, they joke. Sada, however, further foreshadows the future by predicting that she will kill him and chop off his instrument to prevent him from fornicating with anyone else. Kichi refuses to take her threat seriously. As they eat, they continue their revelry in front of a shocked geisha (Genshu Hanayagi), who sings a popular song about longing. Kichi pretends to pluck Sada's nipples with his chopsticks and eat them. They continue making love, and Sada binds Kichi with her pink kimono band. They are still at it the next morning when a maid brings sake. The words "Kichi Sada 2" reappear on the screen.

Sada wishes to buy a knife, fearing Kichi's capricious nature. In response to her jealousy, Kichi vehemently tugs her hair and asks her about her first affair. Partially through flashbacks, Sada relates her experiences with the school principal (Naganori Sakamoto) who trained her and has taken care of her for several years. The couple then indulge in some raw foreplay. Sada seems to enjoy the pain, but Kichi complains when she bites his penis. When they are finally sleeping, a maid tries to air their room out, but Sada awakens and orders her to stop so the smell of Kichi will not go away.

There are more shots of soldiers. Everybody listens to the radio reporting the "2.26 Incident," a famous revolt of the young officers. Yet Sada and Kichi, who briefly join the crowd, are more interested in each other and return to their room. Sada grabs the knife again, and flashes it in Kichi's face, accusing him of thinking of his wife. Their mad passion is unleashed once more. They drink sake while making love. Later they strangle each other with the sash rope. When they stop, Kichi's neck is hot. A red ring is quite noticeable there when they bathe together.

After they eat sushi, Sada gets her lover a doctor. Kichi is placed on a liquid diet; his complete recovery is expected after two months. He declares his intention to return home for the couple's future financial happiness; however, Sada refuses to share him with anyone. Upset, she accidentally spills all of Kichi's medicine in his soup. Knowing how much pleasure Sada had derived from playfully strangling him earlier, Kichi invites her to do it again, he asks Sada not to stop in the middle of the act this time—it would be too painful for him afterward. When Kichi falls asleep, Sada realizes that she cannot bear to allow her lover to return to his wife and uses her kimono band to do what her emotions tell her is necessary.

When he is dead, Sada affectionately kisses him, rubs her breasts against his face, and tries to feed him beer. Apologetically, she then spreads his legs and castrates him with her familiar knife. She wraps his organ in a napkin and places it next to her body. Then she cuts herself. She writes "Kichi Sada 2" with her blood on his naked body, thinking of only the two of them, alone; in her mind true love can only come once for each person. During this scene juxtaposed flashbacks relate her personal history. The daughter of a wealthy tatami mat-maker in Tokyo, she was raped when she was young. After that she was degraded several times. She served as a barmaid and a prostitute, wandering all over Japan. When she was thirty-one, she became a maid at the inn that Kichi operated, and found true affection for the first time.

After Sada leaves the inn and her crime is discovered, she wanders around Tokyo for three days. Meanwhile, newspapers report rumors that she has been seen all over the country. All Japan discusses the event, including a masseur who is treating her. Not revealing her identity, she tells the man that Sada must have loved Kichi very much, since she wanted everybody to know about the two. The film ends with a police report after her eventual arrest.

According to the case history, although not depicted in *Jitsuroko Abe Sada*, Sada received a prison term of several years. When she was released, she returned to her job as a maid at Kichi's inn and worked with Kichi's wife. She then disappeared, but her legend continues.

Comparisons with Oshima's *In the Realm of the Senses*, made the following year, are unavoidable. Tanaka's film focuses entirely upon the intensity of the relationship between the lovers, building upon a confined space and a limited period of time. Although restricted to the tiny inn room, he strengthened his material by employing a greater variety of camera angles. Unlike Oshima's detached coldness toward his principals, *Jitsuroko Abe Sada* offers more personal warmth and compassion toward both Sada and Kichi. Tanaka intended his film primarily for a Japanese audience and faced no censorship restrictions. Oshima, on the other hand, sought international attention; several hard-core scenes were air brushed in Japan. Both films ranked among Japan's ten best films for their respective release years.

Born in 1937 to a landlord family, director Noboru Tanaka majored in French literature at Meiji University (Tokyo). Several of his classmates, including novelist Yumiko Kurahashi, later became writers. During his senior year Tanaka served as a production assistant on Akira Kurosawa's *Yojimbo* (1961). He became enchanted by the film image's poetic inspiration and entered the Nikkatsu Studio as an assistant director following his graduation. He served under several directors, including Seijun Suzuki—*Shurpuden (The Story of a Spring Woman)*—and Shohei Imamura—*Jinruigaku nyumon* (1966; *The Pornographers*)—Nikkatsu's best at that time; both possessed interests similar to his. *Kaben no shizuku* (*Dewdrops on the Petals*), his first film, was made in 1972 and helped to usher in roman porno. Exploring a frigid woman's motivations and fears, it is set against a background of postwar history. His films quickly established a reputation for their colorful, aesthetic images appearing in a brutal world muted by his poetic, often surrealistic, expression. Through *Maruhi joro semejigoku* (*The Ill-Fated Courtesan*; literally "the secret: whore-torturing Hell") he won the 1973 New Director Award from the Japan Society of Film Directors. His 1974 *Maruhi: shikijo mesu ichiba* (*The Oldest Profession*; literally, "the secret: market of nymphomaniac females"), still one of his favorites, explores prostitution long after the passage of the Anti-Prostitution Law for which his colleague film director Kenji Mizoguchi labored; his views of the strong women of Kamagasaki, Osaka's biggest slum, are completely opposite those of the late master. *Jitsuroko Abe Sada* is less surreal than most of his work, but his fascination with blood comes through strongly. *Yaneura no sanposha* (*The Stroller in the Attic*), his 1976 adaptation of a bizarre Rampo Edogawa novel which also features Junko Miyashita, is a frenzied fantasy treat. Seeking to expand his talents, Tanaka has worked with other studios. His 1983 Shochiku production *Ushimitsu no mura* (*Village of Doom*), for example, incorporates his aesthetic eroticism into a harsh story of a despondent village youth whom Japan's prewar army rejected.

Star actress Junko Miyashita, who was born in 1949, was waitressing in a coffeehouse when she was recruited into the adult-film business in 1971. Already relatively mature (most pornography stars begin before they are twenty), she quickly gained a following for her traditional, pure, Japanese manner, her relatively plain appearance combined with a subtle beauty, and her talented, vigorous acting. When Kazuko Shirakawa retired in 1973, Miyashita became her successor as queen of roman porno. Her best-known films are *Jitsuroko Abe Sada*, *The Stroller in the Attic*, *Yojohan fusuma no urabari*, and its sequel, *Akasen tamanoi, nukeraremasu* (*Red Light District, Tamanoi*, which also goes under the title *Street of Joy*), and *Akaikami no onna* (*The Red Haired Girl*). She now freelances, rather than working under a studio contract like most Japanese actors and actresses. Extremely gifted, she has crossed over to act on the stage and on television as well as in legitimate films for other studios. She won a prestigious Blue Ribbon Award for Supporting Actress in Hideo Gosha's *Kumokiri nizaemon* (*Bandits vs. Samurai Squad*), which starred Tatsuya Nakadai. Occasionally she returns to roman porno, where she still reigns as its queen despite her age.

Bill Thompson

JOM
(JOM: OU, L'HISTOIRE D'UN PEUPLE)

Origin: Senegal
Released: 1982
Released in U.S.: 1983
Production: Baobab Films and Zweites Deutschen Fernsehen
Direction: Ababacar Samb Makharam
Screenplay: Ababacar Samb Makharam and Babacar Sine
Cinematography: Peter Chappell and Orlando Lopez
Editing: Alix Régis
Art direction: no listing
Music: Lamine Konté
MPAA rating: no listing
Running time: 80 minutes

Principal characters:
Khaly	Oumar Gueye
Madjeumbe	Amadou Lamine Camara
Diop	Zator Sarr
N'Dougoutte	Abou Camara
Diéri	Oumar Seck
Koura	Oumi Sene

Since World II the presentation of Africa in narrative films has undergone a curious evolution. At first, with filmmaking in the hands of Westerners, Africa and its peoples provided little more than local color, a backdrop for familiar dramas involving Europeans and Americans, such as *Stanley and Livingstone* (1939) or *The African Queen* (1951). Here and there a few filmmakers did begin to focus on Africans but still within the context of the colonial culture, as in *Men of Two Worlds* (1946) or *Cry the Beloved Country* (1951). Meanwhile, Western ethnographers were making nonfiction films that undertook to reveal the Africans' own culture. A link with narrative film was provided by Jean Rouch, whose *Cocorico Monsieur Poulet* (1977; *Cock-a-doodle-do, Mister Chicken!*), made in Niger with local collaborators, featured what he called the African storytelling device of presenting each major incident three times. Yet this French attempt to convey the style as well as the substance of African culture is likely to strike the Western viewer as rambling and incoherent. Ironically but understandably, most of the French-speaking African filmmakers who have emerged in the past decade or so have turned Rouch's approach inside out. They have studied in Europe and mastered an eclectic style of filmmaking; at the same time, they have chosen themes that are rooted in their nations' culture and history.

Typical of such films is *Jom: Ou, L'Histoire d'un peuple*, by Ababacar Samb Makharam. Because Senegal has accounted for a disproportionately large number of black African films, and also because *Jom* refers to events in Senegalese history, some background notes on the country may be helpful. Located on the western bulge of Africa, Senegal, in the early 1980's, had more than six million people, of whom the largest group (just over one-third) is the Wolof. During their known history, the Wolof have had to contend with two major outside influences. One was that of Islam, which diffused across the Sahara: By the fifteenth century, the small Wolof empire was Muslim. By that time, too, the other major influence was arriving: that of Europeans, for whom the western bulge of Africa was a convenient place to begin their pursuit of the continent's wealth. French contacts with the area now known as Senegal began in the sixteenth century and gradually increased during the next three hundred years. France's interests were primarily economic and limited to the coast and major waterways; the slave trade was of minor importance in the area, and there were educational opportunities for a handful of Africans. In the 1880's, as the European powers began their competitive scramble for Africa, France used military power to extend its political rule over vast areas of the hinterland, including all of Senegal. In 1960, Senegal gained political independence, but its economy still depends heavily on France.

French cultural influence on Senegal has lasted longer and has probably been more extensive than on any other sub-Saharan territory. At the same time, many Senegalese have used French culture as a channel for expressing their own outlook on the world. Thus Léopold Senghor, the president of Senegal, has written in French to promote the concept of *negritude* (blackness), while Ousmane Sembène, the best-known Senegalese filmmaker, first made his name with French-language novels on the African experience. Ababacar Samb, born in 1934, studied drama in Paris and filmmaking in Rome; he also acted on the stage and in films and worked in radio and television production in Paris before returning to Senegal. *Jom* is his third film.

The Wolof word that serves as the film's title is said to be untranslatable, but the film enables the non-Wolof-speaking viewer to acquire a good idea of its meaning: self-respect, integrity, strength of mind. The film is set in the present but also moves freely back into the past. The workers at a factory have gone on strike, and the manager, Diop (Zator Sarr), tries to win the leaders over by bribery. Some, led by N'Dougoutte (Abou Camara), are willing to accept. Others, led by Madjeumbe (Amadou Lamine Camara), insist on holding out until all workers are offered gains. Khaly (Oumar Gueye), the local *griot*—a kind of sage who is the keeper of the people's history and traditions—shows where *jom* lies by presenting two examples of it from the past. For Madjeumbe, Khaly evokes a prince named Diéri (Oumar Seck) who resisted the French colonizers at the turn of the century even though he was to be hunted down and killed by a collaborating kins-man. For Diop, Khaly tells the story of three women who left their village in a time of drought to seek work in a city. They became servants to tyrannical women who were acting as hosts to a famous visiting dancer named Koura (Oumi Sene). When Koura gave her performance, however, it was the ser-vants she celebrated. Back in the present, N'Dougoutte's group persuades many of the workers to break through the picket line of Madjeumbe's group. Khaly, however, brings along the strikebreakers' wives, and they force their husbands to return home.

At first sight, *Jom* might seem to be a complement to Ousmane Sem-bène's *Ceddo* (1976), which focuses critically on the Islamic influence on Senegal. Samb does indeed show the direct and indirect influence of France: the colonization of Senegal and the development of class and eco-nomic distinctions among the Senegalese. His primary concern, however, is not to explore sociopolitical conditions. He paints the three main conflicts in the film with such broad brush strokes that it is quite clear from start to fin-ish which side is good and which is bad. Yet *Jom* is not at all a belaboring of the obvious. What interests Samb is the way individuals act and react within the given conditions: Do they, or do they not, have *jom*. Behind the simple events of the film, Samb works out this inner drama with both subtlety and control.

First, the structure of the film binds its apparently scattered elements together and gives them cumulative power. The film opens with three wives bawling out their husbands for various shortcomings. This largely comic se-quence may appear to be inserted for local color, but it prepares the viewer for the film's denouement, in which it is the women who save the strike. Before telling the story of Prince Diéri, Khaly offers extensive praise of the meal that the group has just eaten; in the flashback, Khaly himself is seen gatecrashing the governor's garden party in order to seize food from the ta-ble, saying that he is only taking back what the French have stolen. On a deeper level, by comparing the strikers' resistance to the factory's manage-ment with Diéri's resistance to French colonizers, Samb may be hinting at Senegal's continued economic dependence: the telex messages that urge Diop to break the strike may be coming from a white business leader. When Diéri confronts a French officer, the latter speaks French, but the prince speaks to him only in Wolof; similarly, when Diop meets with the strike leaders and tries to bribe them, he speaks in French but Madjeumbe retorts in Wolof. Before the second flashback, concerning the tyrannized maids, the viewer sees Diop's wife delivering a tirade against *her* maid, who has been trying on her mistress' clothes. Then Khaly arrives, summoned by Diop, who plans to give a traditional party and wants Khaly to sing his praises at it. Khaly says that he sings only for those who have *jom*, and the flashback shows Koura singing for the maids, not the mistresses. At the end, when the strikebreakers have been driven from the factory, Khaly turns to Madjeumbe and his supporters and says, "I sing your praise."

Over and above all these individual links between different sequences of the film, there is the recurring presence of Khaly, who is at once observer, commentator, and participant. Appearing not only in the present scenes but also in the flashbacks, Khaly becomes the embodiment of both the real and the mythic. In present and past scenes alike he enters upon the scene casually, wearing the same red and black headdress, a creature of flesh and blood, jovial rather than solemn or ascetic; at the same time, he continually talks of *jom* and of great deeds of the past, exhorts people to behave well, and praises them when they do. To appreciate the power and complexity of Khaly's role, one can compare the climaxes of the two flashback sequences.

In the first, the attackers are under orders to take Diéri alive; but when all of his supporters, including Khaly, have been struck down, Diéri stabs himself. After the victors leave, Diéri's widow arrives and has his body covered; then she too leaves. The camera looks down on the bodies scattered on the dusty earth among huge baobab trees. Then Khaly rises to his feet, takes the cover from Diéri's body, and walks out of the frame; as he does so, his voice (in the present) says: "I defy time and death. . . . Time has no hold over me. . . . I am an actor on the theater of eternity. . . ." With its stillness and visual restraint, this scene has an intensity that recalls the resurrection of Inger in Carl Theodor Dreyer's *Ordet* (1955).

The second flashback sequence reaches its climax during Koura's performance. To begin, Khaly is seated on the ground at the edge of the outdoor area in which Koura is dancing. Then he is on his feet and moving around with her, acting like an enthusiastic coach or master of ceremonies, and for a time, he actually carries her, dancing for her as she continues singing. Here, as in the first flashback, Khaly may be said to come to life, but the mood is completely different—exhilarated and exhilarating, bursting with sound and motion.

Yet even amid this exhilaration, Khaly does not abandon himself to any trancelike state. He remains an observer, smilingly aware, always in control. Samb too retains his control: there are no blurred camera movements or flash cuts. At the height of the dance, he inserts a lengthy continuous scene in which the camera follows Koura and Khaly all the way around the edge of the arena, keeping the action in sharp focus from start to finish.

This kind of control can be found throughout the film. At first sight the photography seems transparent, as if Samb's camera is simply recording the action from a good vantage point. Nevertheless, patterns emerge here, as well. In one example, the few obviously composed shots call attention more to the bad characters than to the good: in the first flashback, Senegalese in Western dress stroll elegantly toward the French governor's garden party, and the brightly costumed band of attackers form a colorful design as they move in on Diéri; in the present, the camera lingers on a low-angle view of the orange-painted luxury high rise where Diop lives and also pans slowly over the gleaming walls of his factory. It is as if these people and places have been drained of life and exist only as surfaces. Another example can be seen in the second flashback, which takes place in a time of drought and contains no interior scenes. Nearly every shot in that sequence tacitly reminds the viewer of the parched earth.

Perhaps the most effective use of control is found in the transitions between present and past. Except for a fleeting dissolve that leads into the second flashback, Samb avoids any devices that would set up a contrast between the two periods of time: there are no changes of image tone, tempo, or sound. The incidental music that bridges the transitions manages to suggest both a traditional African ensemble and a New Wave rock group, drawing past and present together. As illustrated above, Khaly looks and behaves the same at all periods of time. He also sounds the same, sometimes talking in a conversational tone and sometimes exhorting people in brief, half-chanted phrases that are punctuated with exclamations of assent from his listeners.

The fascination of *Jom* derives largely from its fusion of the real and the mythic. Samb avoids adding mystery and portentousness to the scenes in the present but, rather, extends their clarity and immediacy to the scenes evoked by Khaly. This clarity makes the film particularly rewarding for non-African viewers, since it neither conceals nor exaggerates the differences of the African cultural world. Thanks to Samb's eclectic style, the strangeness of the characters and events becomes familiar.

William Johnson

JONAH WHO WILL BE 25 IN THE YEAR 2000
(JONAS QUI AURA 25 ANS EN L'AN 2000)

Origin: Switzerland and France
Released: 1976
Released in U.S.: 1976
Production: Yves Gasser and Yves Peyrot
Direction: Alain Tanner
Screenplay: John Berger and Alain Tanner
Cinematography: Renato Berta
Editing: Brigitte Sousselier and Marc Blavet
Art direction: Yanko Hodjis
Makeup: Michele Pissanchi
Music: Jean-Marie Senia
MPAA rating: no listing
Running time: 110 minutes

Principal characters:
Max	Jean-Luc Bideau
Mathilde	Myriam Boyer
Marco	Jacques Denis
Marcel	Roger Jendly
Marguerite	Dominique Labourier
Madeleine	Myriam Mezière
Marie	Miou-Miou
Mathieu	Rufus
Charles	Raymond Bussières

Alain Tanner's 1976 film is the culmination of a series of films that he has made, often with the collaboration of John Berger, about the mesh between political concerns and everyday life in a modern, industrialized, Western European society. With a story and plot line literally broken into seventy scenes, or 150 shots, which follow the lives of eight major characters, the film combines several elements introduced in the earlier films *La Salamandre* (1971), *La Rétour d'Afrique* (1973; *Return from Africa*), and *Le Milieu du monde* (1974; *The Middle of the World*). Tanner examines the lives of those on the margin of Swiss society—respectable, but poor; dissident, but pacific; articulate, but highly self-ironic—exploring the ways in which they cope with the problems of making a living, maintaining a romantic, but equal, relationship with a spouse, and rearing a family. He also uses a number of innovative cinematic devices to focus attention on the passage of real time and to distance his audience from his characters. As a result, he has earned for his films, and for the growing Swiss cinema, a wide audience and critical acclaim. The socially minded are pleased by his jokes at the expense of the rich and powerful; the formalists enjoy his mobile camera and offscreen narrators, while all are drawn by the gentle humor and endearing characterizations in his films.

Jonah Who Will Be 25 in the Year 2000 is a film that is in large measure about education; not only is one of the major characters a high school teacher when the film opens, but also another becomes a teacher for a short time. One of the opening shots is a lateral track by the camera, in black and white, of a statue of Jean-Jacques Rousseau, whose metaphorical work about education, *Émile* (1762), is cited by an offscreen narrator. The audience is then quickly introduced to the most explicitly political character in the film, Max (Jean-Luc Bideau), who complains to a shopgirl about the new, higher price for the cigarettes that he is constantly smoking. A very similar scene will, in fact, close the film, introducing the element of anticipation with which many of Tanner's films end. The first character shown at length in a number of punctuated scenes is Mathieu (Rufus), an unemployed typesetter who must care for his three children while his wife, Mathilde (Myriam Boyer), works in a factory. Intercut into the scenes of the characters' daily life in color is a black-and-white sequence that depicts the fantasies in the characters' lives. In Mathilde's case, it is the ability to talk with the foreman whom the audience sees clocking her movements at a machine. In other cases, the black-and-white sequences illustrate part of the dialogue, recall some historic event, or comment visually on the action.

Mathieu applies for a job as a farmhand on an organic farmstead run by Marguerite (Dominique Labourier) and Marcel (Roger Jendly). While apparently a typical married couple with children, Marcel and Marguerite are the oddest pair to be matched in the film. Marguerite is the more practical of the two and actually manages the farm. She hires Mathieu, while Marcel is content to lecture him on the mystery of whales. Marcel is a recluse who is interested primarily in the animals that he photographs and sketches. The laconic discussion between Mathieu and Marguerite about his duties as a farmhand is punctuated by one of the fantasy scenes in black and white, in which she agrees to show him her account books—the representative of capital demonstrating her fairness to the representative of labor, following the pattern of their introductions to each other.

Another eccentric introduction occurs in a Geneva high school class, where Marco (Jacques Denis) presents his first lecture on the nature of time and history with the aid of a metronome and a huge length of sausage. While his students are amused, fascinated, and, finally, excited by Marco's innovative techniques, the film's audience is drawn in by a more cinematic device, the fleshing out of Max, a character introduced at the film's start. Max is the most stereotyped person in the film; above his bed is a poster of Vladimir Ilich Lenin, and next to it is a pile of books and magazines. Even

Max's fantasies are rather typical; he imagines blasting his alarm clock with a revolver hidden in his dresser drawer. Marco, too, is obsessed with the end of time and brings his lecture to a raucous end by leading the class in beating on their desks to the rapid click of the metronome. Later, the audience is shown how the class reacts to an equally radical, if stylistically more traditional, lecture by Mathieu.

Max soon finds an outlet for his frustrated radicalism through sheer accident. He meets an old schoolmate in a fancy gambling salon and learns of a scheme to erect housing in the city's agricultural suburbs. He also meets Madeleine (Myriam Mezière), a temporary secretary, obviously entranced by the disheveled Max rather than by her elegantly clad employer. Her obsession is Tantric Buddhism, and the audience sees her imagining Tantric rites while busy at her typewriter. She is pleased at Max's visit, although his interest is more practical; he wants the names of those owners whose property the speculators covet. Max simply plans to inform them in advance and watch the resulting difficulty for the bank. On the other hand, Madeleine is far more interested in Max than in his small conspiracy, and the camera pans from one to the other, catching the flickers of romantic interest between them. Max's scheme also acts as the structure which incorporates all the characters in the film.

Marco, the teacher, learns of the bankers' interest in the farm, since he has stopped by to purchase some vegetables and stays to share a meal. This dinner sequence (the film has several) signals the beginning of approximately two years in the life of a small, informal communal group—the veterans of the storms of the 1960's that swept across American campuses and urban Europe with an odd mixture of delusion and illusion, high hopes and deep fury. This initial dinner also highlights the gap between Marcel and Marguerite, since she has a lover among the Italians, Greeks, and Turks who live in the nearby "guest worker" barracks. Although two unnamed farmhands gloat over her perceived promiscuity, it is clearly a misconception, and there are several still photographs depicting the solitude and desolation of these workers' lives. Although this is a brief sequence, it is a subject which Tanner and Berger treated previously in *The Middle of the World* and which Berger treated in his book *A Seventh Man: Migrant Workers in Europe* (1975). When Max tells the diners of the speculators' plans, Marguerite, ever practical, asks if he is "in politics." In response, Max says that politics are dead now, and in the black-and-white insert, Swiss and Soviet troops and missiles are shown on parade.

The final "M" in Tanner and Berger's modern fable is Marie (Miou-Miou), a supermarket clerk who intentionally undercharges the pensioners who dutifully line up at her cash register. A youthful blonde, Marie is a modern Robin Hood who robs from the supermarket to give extra discounts both to the poor elderly and to those who simply strike her fancy, such as

Marco, with his head full of dark curls and a bottle of whiskey in his shopping cart. She is again an expression of the screenwriters' interest in migrant workers, since Marie lives on the French side of the border between France and Switzerland. It is through Marie that Marco meets her elderly neighbor, a retired locomotive engineer, Charles (Raymond Bussières), for whom she does the shopping, since he has a bad leg. Charles tells her stories about his adventures, and they playfully act them out when he is not warning her about the shoplifting that she does for him. "Engine House Charlie" also encourages Marco's growing interest in older people and in the times through which they have lived. The strongest hint of this growing concern on Marco's part is his fantasy of how his high school students will look in forty or fifty years.

Commenting on the measurement of history against a human lifetime, Madeleine probes the roots of Max's disillusionment with politics as they walk together along the banks of the Rhone. In their barbed conversation, Max is consistently critical and disparaging about himself and others. He describes 1968 as the literal apogee of a downward curve and states that he now simply proofreads for a newspaper rather than writing for it. Nevertheless, Madeleine tells him how disruptive his sabotage has been for the bank and takes him to a local carnival. Max's profound pessimism—he predicts war and Fascism—affects his relationship with Madeleine. The tension between her Tantric yoga and his Marxist perceptions often erupts in his sarcasm, and, pointedly, the childish wall mural that depicts all eight characters shows Max with downcast face, embracing all of them within his grasp, but with Madeleine barely within reach.

That mural is drawn by the farm children when all eight major characters, "the little prophets" as Tanner and Berger have called them in the published English translation of their screenplay, meet for the first time. Their shared fantasy is that they, like the children, could play in the mud, doing somersaults and getting their clothes dirty. The closest realization of a fantasy is accomplished by Mathieu, who does indeed become a teacher at an alternative kindergarten that he establishes in an unused greenhouse on the farm, for his own and for Marcel's and Marguerite's children. He is shown asking the students questions both as part of an insert and in the color portion of the film, which represents reality.

Marco's unusual teaching methods at the high school—he grades his students on the basis of the questions that they ask Marie about her work and life, has Mathieu deliver a Marxist lecture on economics, and tells the class about his secret sexual desires—culminates in his being fired. He tells Max and Mathieu about his leaving the school while they prepare a communal dinner at Marcel and Marguerite's house. In the conversation that follows, Max is condescending, while Mathieu is practical, but the visual scene is enriched by the pans from face to face as they trade quips and ripostes while crying from the onions that they are preparing for dinner.

At the actual dinner, marked by Marie's absence, since she has been arrested for her continuing discounts for elderly pensioners, Mathilde announces that she is pregnant with a fourth child. In the discussion over the proper name for the child, Max suggests that eminently political name, Leon. Angered by the negative reaction, Max lashes out at Madeleine's suggested Shiva. They finally settle on Marcel's Jonah, a reference to his fascination with whales. They sing a song about Jonah and the whales, invoking a reference to the year 2000, which, Mathieu has said in a class lecture, may be a year of crisis.

Economic crisis comes much sooner to Marcel and Marguerite; they cannot afford to let Mathieu continue his alternative school. In an argument with them, Mathieu is even offered a look at the account books, a reference to one of the first fantasy sequences. Mathieu must get another job. He is last seen in the film on his motorbike, during a cold morning, on his way to a factory for his work shift. Mathieu, in a voice-over, addresses both the audience and his fellow "prophets" in a monologue directed to his son, Jonah. Like Max, he envisions a political crisis in the future, "when the police and the army fire on thousands like you." There is even a segment of newsreel footage depicting such a scene in Geneva in 1932. Mathieu asks, "Will things be better for you?"

The film's closing scenes are part of the cyclical nature of the fable; the audience sees Max in the tobacconist's shop, where he learns that the price of his cigarettes has risen another ten percent, as it had in the opening sequence. This also serves as a playful comment on the passage of time, since Jonah is now a toddler. The audience hears Mathilde calling for him while the camera draws nearer to him. Jonah stands in front of the wall that is still decorated with the mural of the "little prophets." Wearing a red jumper with a black sweater, Jonah is busily scrawling on the figure representing Max. He does not run to his mother's voice but instead grins impishly at the audience.

Lenny Rubenstein

JOUR DE FÊTE

Origin: France
Released: 1949
Released in U.S.: 1952
Production: Fred Orain for Cady-Films
Direction: Jacques Tati
Screenplay: Jacques Tati, Henri Marquet, and René Wheeler
Cinematography: Jacques Mercanton and Marcel Franchi
Editing: Marcel Moreau
Art direction: René Moulaert
Music: Jean Yatove and Henri Marquet
Running time: 90 minutes
Running time in U.S.: 74 minutes
Also known as: The Big Day, The Big Night, and *The Village Fair*

Principal characters:
François .... Jacques Tati
Roger .... Guy Decomble
Marcel........................... Paul Frankeur
Roger's wife........................ Santa Relli
Jeannette .... Maine Vallée
Barber .... Roger Rafal
Café owner .... Beauvais
Cinema operator...................... Delcassan

Writer-director-actor Jacques Tati confessed that he was strongly influenced by American silent film comics Buster Keaton, Harold Lloyd, Harry Langdon, Mack Sennett, and, most especially, Charles Chaplin. Like Chaplin, Tati was fascinated with machines, gadgets, and new technology and was both amused and appalled by the way industrial mechanization and labor-saving devices depersonalized human beings and often complicated rather than simplified their lives. Chaplinesque themes of Old World versus New, Man versus Machine, Traditional Craftsmanship versus High-Tech Production are common in all Tati's shorts and feature films, but they are most subtly utilized in *Jour de fête.* This film was Tati's first feature production, had a relatively modest budget of thirty thousand dollars, and involved six months of carefully paced location shooting in the little village of Sainte-Sévère-sur-Indre. Though Tati's comic genius was consistently original throughout all of his films, *Jour de fête* is the most subtle and appealing vehicle for his brand of humor—comedy that lampooned life and the human condition with sight gags, gentle satire, and physical humor that stopped just short of being farcical or cartoonlike.

Jour de fête also contains some comic and "human observation" themes that are unique to Tati films: the status of leisure activities in the modern world, humorous public drunkenness, and a surfeit of sustained long-shots. Besides marking Tati's first venture into feature films, *Jour de fête* also provided his backers with the best return on their investment, for despite critical acclaim, subsequent Tati films had production budgets that became so overblown that they led to the filmmaker's commercial undoing.

Jour de fête opens with a number of idyllic establishing shots of the meadows and farmland around the quaint village of Sainte-Sévère-sur-Indre, then focuses upon an intrusive van trundling along the cow path. The van bears the wooden horses and unassembled parts of a carnival merry-go-round. At the wheel is Roger (Guy Decomble), and as he heads his truck into the town square, he is escorted by a little boy with jug-handle ears. When Roger pulls to a stop, he is greeted by the glad-handing mayor, who has arranged for his participation at the town's annual carnival. An old woman, doubled over with age and blessed with a face that seems right out of a painting by Hieronymous Bosch, lends a cynical tone to the scene as the mayor sits down with Roger at the café to negotiate terms (and fouls his clothes on the freshly painted chairs). The woman provides a witty and waspish commentary about the town merchants and other participants who are trickling into the square: the self-seeking café owner (Beauvais); the handsome ex-soldier who is now an artist; the attractive woman, Jeannette (Maine Valée), who catches Roger's wandering eye; Roger's shrewish wife (Santa Relli); and the nosy shopkeepers. Children pour into the square and help Roger and his assistant Marcel (Paul Frankeur) assemble the carousel. A number of men from the village vainly struggle with a huge pole bearing the French tricolor; their struggle resembles a Keystone Cops routine.

Amid this flurry of pratfalls and sight gags enters the hero of the story: François (Jacques Tati), the bicycle-borne village postman. Immediately after François rides into the square, he is almost killed by the collapsing flagpole. The postman sees that the flag-raising effort is in need of some supervision and sets about directing the men. A number of gags follow, many of them cleverly physical (like those of Harold Lloyd), or marginally cartoonlike (resembling Max Fleisher's "Popeye" stunts), or simply silly (in the manner of Jerry Lewis). The task completed, François resumes his mail delivery and boasts of his accomplishment during the course of his leisurely rounds. This allows Tati the opportunity to set up and deliver a number of wonderfully amusing gags and gives the viewer an understanding of how casually François pursues his duties—often interrupting his delivery schedule for a glass of wine at the café. When attention shifts away from François' rounds back to the carnival activities in the square, colors appear (however, color was added only in the 1961 rerelease and subsequent prints) on balloons, Chinese lanterns, bunting, and merry-go-round horse collars.

The carnival activity increases as the number of happy revelers increases. Soon, even François is unable to resist participating, and he commits a number of gaffs while playing at the various booths and games of chance.

Once again lured into the café, François becomes inebriated and performs a number of amusing dances, pratfalls, and gags. A friend drags the tipsy postman from the saloon to see a documentary film being shown in a carnival tent. The film is about the high-tech methods of delivery employed by the United States Postal Service: high-speed sorting machines, helicopters, airplanes, and the like are featured. As the drunken François watches, he becomes increasingly inspired and agitated. Hours later, the postman is seen staggering through the deserted square while grumbling about his American counterparts. Passing within sight of Roger (who has just watched Jeannette undress for bed), François seeks refuge in a railway car and falls asleep.

Morning comes to the village and the Bosch-like old woman hobbles around the square providing cynical commentary about the hung-over citizens who are facing the cruel light of day. François is rudely awakened by the bump of a switching engine, and he resolves to spend the day delivering the mail like his colleagues in the United States. Roger and Marcel add fuel to the postman's hyperkinetic fire by giving him a few pointers on how to mount and dismount his bicycle more efficiently. Riding around the village on his bicycle, François performs a number of increasingly frantic gags, culminating in his driving himself into a canal. The old woman helps the hapless postman out of the water and consoles the poor man by saying that no matter what the method of delivery, or how good or bad the news, it gets to people "soon enough." The film concludes with François stopping to help a farmer thresh his wheat. The jug-eared boy who appeared at the beginning of the film offers to resume François' delivery duties and provides an escort to Roger's loaded merry-go-round van as it leaves the empty village square and departs down the same road from which it arrived.

The basic statement made by all Jacques Tati's films is that the fast pace and routine of the modern world is ruinous to the human soul; it not only makes one's life in the workplace miserable, but it also destroys all the joy that can be derived from one's leisure time. This contempt for the "assembly line" life-style also extended into the way that Tati produced films: His production schedules were slowly paced, and the budgets of his later films became increasingly unwieldy. *Jour de fête* provides Tati with only an indirect means to comment upon assembly line activities (workmanship) versus slow, efficient activity (craftsmanship). *Trafic* (1971; *Traffic*) offers a scornful picture of the automobile assembly line, and in *Mon Oncle* (1958) Tati directly mocks industrialized society with a scene involving a plastic tubing assembly line, while simultaneously paying homage to Charlie Chaplin's *Modern Times* (1936).

Tati's films not only satirize the way modern society has allowed itself to be overwhelmed by the frenetic pace of the workplace, but also mock the way humans make use of their free time. Clearly, Tati believes that all the negative and soul-killing aspects of the assembly line have spilled over into the way people go about their leisure activities: The Hôtel de la Plage in *Les Vacances de Monsieur Hulot* (1953; *Mr. Hulot's Holiday*) is operated with all the joy and efficiency of a factory; the hapless vacationers sharing M. Hulot's grand tour in *Playtime* (1967) might as well be objects traveling on a tourist conveyor belt; *Traffic* deals with the absurd mechanics of a "recreational vehicle"; the viewer sees the protagonist in *Mon Oncle* leading a pitifully structured homelife that is virtually ruled by restrictive timetables and oppressive technology.

Tati's commentary upon craftsmanship versus workmanship extends to his theories on filmmaking. *Jour de fête* drives this point home when it satirizes the Hollywood Western, in a scene in which the carnival tent show screens a tritely written sagebrush melodrama entitled "The Rivals of Arizona Jim" (a joking allusion to Jean Renoir's film *Le Crime de Monsieur Lange*, 1936). Similarly, the frantic pacing and montage cutting of the documentary on the United States Postal Service stand in contrast to Tati's typically leisurely pacing and extended long-shots, developed under the influence of Jean Renoir.

Thematic content and social commentary aside, *Jour de fête* (like all Tati's films) owes much of its style and humor to films by Buster Keaton, Harold Lloyd, Charles Chaplin, and René Clair. Tati's training as a vaudeville mime was also responsible for the subtlety of his comedy. In like manner, certain contemporary filmmakers owe Tati a debt for the ground broken by his films—Yves Robert, for example, in *The Tall Blond Man with One Black Shoe* (1972).

Born on October 9, 1908, in the Parisian suburb of Le Pecq, Jacques Tati (Tatischeff) was groomed to enter the family's long-standing picture-framing business (past clients allegedly included Toulouse-Lautrec and Vincent van Gogh). Tati's preparation for this career included attendance at the Lycée de Saint-Germain-en-Laye and the Hanley Professional School at Choisy-le-Roi. During his apprenticeship in England, Tati put his skills as an impressionist and mime to use in some amateur variety shows and decided that vaudeville was his true calling. Success and recognition did not come immediately, and for a number of years Tati was given low billing in provincial theaters and third-rate cabarets. By 1931, he was playing with the likes of Maurice Chevalier and was asked by a film producer to perform his famous "tennis sports" mime routine before a motion-picture camera. *Oscar, Champion de Tennis* (1932; *Oscar the Tennis Champion*) was the uncompleted short that resulted.

Subsequently, Tati appeared in a number of other shorts, and soon was also writing and directing them. *L'École des facteurs* (1937; *School for Post-*

men) was the eighteen-minute Tati vehicle that inspired the feature-length *Jour de fête*. By a happy accident, Tati was chosen to direct, and his efforts were well received by critics and audiences.

The profits from *Jour de fête* enabled Tati to write and direct *Mr. Hulot's Holiday*. Produced in Brittany over an eight-month period at a cost of $215,000, the film was an immediate box-office hit. Tati provided a reprise for Hulot in *Mon Oncle* and earned for himself an Academy Award for Best Foreign-Language Film of 1959. In 1961, Tati fulfilled an artistic dream when he released *Jour de fête* as he had originally envisioned it. Instead of the Thomson-Color process, which had been botched in the laboratory, thus losing the color negative forever, he had colors stenciled onto the print. The result was a crude effect reminiscent of "color" films made during the nickelodeon era. Tati's American promotional tour for *Mon Oncle* allowed him to fulfill another dream: He was able to meet confessed idols Harold Lloyd, Buster Keaton, Stan Laurel, and Mack Sennett. During this time, Tati even attempted to acquire the European distribution rights to the Sennett films.

Playtime, another Monsieur Hulot vehicle, was Tati's next project, and, with this film, his budget got out of hand: The ultimate price tag for his ultramodern urban set built on the back lot was $800,000, and the total budget for this commercial failure was three million dollars. It put Tati into bankruptcy, and placed all the rights to his previous films in the hands of creditors. Despite this financial setback, Tati sprang back in 1971, with the ill-fated *Traffic*. Soon after, Tati agreed to write, direct, and appear in a program for Swedish television that dealt with clowns. Entitled *Parade* (1974), this videotaped program was eventually transferred to film and received limited distribution. In 1974, a Paris film distribution company paid off Tati's old creditors and once again enabled the public to see and appreciate *Jour de fête*, *Mr. Hulot's Holiday*, *Mon Oncle*, and *Playtime*. Encouraged, Tati began a new project entitled "Confusion"; a pulmonary embolism prevented him from beginning production, however, and Tati died on November 5, 1982, at the age of seventy-five.

Tim Kennedy

LE JOUR SE LÈVE

Origin: France
Released: 1939
Released in U.S.: 1940
Production: Sigma
Direction: Marcel Carné
Screenplay: Jacques Prévert; based on a screen story by Jacques Viot
Cinematography: Curt Courant
Editing: René Le Hénaff
Art direction: Alexandre Trauner
Costume design: Boris Bilinsky
Sound: Armand Petitjean
Music: Maurice Jaubert
Running time: 85 minutes
Also known as: Daybreak

Principal characters:
François	Jean Gabin
Françoise	Jacqueline Laurent
M. Valentin	Jules Berry
Clara	Arletty
Concierge	René Génin
Concierge's wife	Mady Berry
Gaston	Bernard Blier
Paulo	Marcel Pérès
Inspector	Jacques Baumer
Café proprietor	René Bergeron
Old woman on the stairs	Gabrielle Fontan
M. Gerbois	Arthur Devère
Blind man	Georges Douking

Le Jour se lève is an excellent example of what has come to be known by students of French cinema as poetic realism. "Poetic realism" describes a somber pessimism which coexists, in certain French films of the mid to late 1930's, with lyric, metaphorical, and even metaphysical dimensions. The style is exemplified by works of Jacques Feyder (*Le Grand Jeu,* 1934, *The Great Game; La Kermesse héroïque,* 1935, *Carnival in Flanders*), Julien Duvivier (*Pépé le Moko,* 1937), Jean Renoir (*La Bête humaine,* 1938; *La Règle du jeu,* 1939, *The Rules of the Game*), and Marcel Carné (in addition to *Le Jour se lève, Quai des brumes,* 1938, and *Les Enfants du paradis,* 1945, *Children of Paradise*). Carné had been an assistant of Feyder, and he and Prévert, a renowned poet in his own right, collaborated on several other films, including *Jenny* (1936), *Quai des brumes*, and *Children of Paradise*. It is certainly noteworthy that of these films cited as representative of poetic realism, Jean Gabin, the star of *Le Jour se lève*, heads the casts of *Pépé le Moko*, *Quai des brumes*, and *La Bête humaine* as well.

Le Jour se lève is an expression of the tragedy which results from the confrontation of harsh reality and the limits of existence, on the one hand, and on the other, the hope of escape, dreams of love and freedom, and destructive fantasy. The title (in English, *Daybreak*) of the film itself is ironic, for the dawn of a new day brings with it, not rebirth and hope, but the suicide of the protagonist, François (Jean Gabin). Even before the credits have appeared on the screen, a brief title appears and informs the viewer that a man has been killed, and that the killer (whom the viewer soon discovers to be François) is alone in his room, considering the circumstances which have made of him a murderer. The point of view articulated here is important: François is to some degree relieved of the responsibility for his act in that he himself has been the victim of conditions and events.

Behind the credits, when they appear, dawn is breaking over Paris. Soon follows a shot of a working-class neighborhood (constructed in the studio according to the needs of Carné), dominated by a multistory apartment building, windows on the front, blind on one side, where an advertisement for Dubonnet covers the entire wall. The camera work and the action of the first few minutes of the film are important, not only for the progress of the narrative, but also because they establish a metaphorical context and present crucial visual motifs. The viewer is immediately struck by an extreme high-angle shot of the stairwell of the building. A blind man (Georges Douking) is on the first floor and begins slowly to make his way up the stairs. A noise and finally a gunshot are heard. Shortly thereafter, Valentin (Jules Berry) appears from the door of a room on the top floor, his hands clutching his stomach. He tumbles down the stairs, finally arriving at the feet of the blind man, who is stunned and disquieted by what he thinks is the occurrence of an accident. The blind man appears later in the film, again nervously asking what has happened, never finding the answer. He is, indeed, a representation of all people, asking similar questions and receiving the same lack of response. Nevertheless, the viewer does discover that François has just killed Valentin, for he emerges from his room, pistol in hand. The high-angle shot of the stairwell, the medium low-angle shots of Valentin seen through the posts which support the bannisters, the strong diagonals and verticals which are provided by shadows and the decor of François' room provide the accurate impression that François already inhabits a prison-labyrinth. In fact, his room will become for him a cell, a fortress besieged by the police several times, and, ultimately, his tomb.

The camera eventually takes the viewer into François' room. The background music is dominated by the irregular rhythm of timpani which creates an atmosphere of foreboding and tension. Two policemen have attempted to gain entrance to François' room, but have retreated upon hearing François' threats to shoot through the door. The viewer subsequently sees François in his cluttered one-room flat, holding the gun; the viewer observes the furnishings of his room—an enormous armoire which he will use as a barricade, a mirror, a mantle upon which lie, among other things, a woman's brooch and a stuffed toy bear. The essentials of François' situation have thus been set forth: He is a murderer and a fugitive, a classic case of the normal man gone berserk, as his neighbors' comments imply, and he has no intention of surrendering to the authorities. Through a series of wonderfully orchestrated flashbacks triggered by slow dissolves, the audience will review with François the events which have determined his predicament and the significance of those objects in his room which appear incongruous in a workingman's apartment.

The movements from the present to the past and back tell the story of François' disillusionment, in the fundamental sense of the word. Indeed, it is in his anger, pain, and frustration, having seen his hopes of a better life dashed, that he kills Valentin. François works a dreary dehumanized job as a sandblaster in a factory, and falls in love with Françoise (Jacqueline Laurent), a girl who delivers flowers to the factory one day by mistake. Much to his chagrin however, François discovers that Françoise is apparently maintaining a liaison with a small-time animal trainer, Valentin, who is performing in a local café-music hall. François, in his dejection, turns to Clara (Arletty), Valentin's former assistant. He still loves Françoise, as Clara well knows, but is stunned when, during a conversation one afternoon, Valentin claims to be Françoise's father. When he confronts Françoise with this news, she reveals that this tale is simply one of the many fantasies which Valentin is in the habit of concocting. Still, she confesses her attachment to Valentin, the only person other than François who has seemed to care for her. She does finally express her love for François and agrees to stop seeing Valentin. Valentin, even though he does not love Françoise, is intent upon discouraging François' pursuit of her. One day, he comes to the worker's apartment, armed with a pistol, intending to kill him. Instead, Valentin and François argue until, unable to stand further mockery and the revelation of sordid details of Valentin's relationship with Françoise, François picks up Valentin's pistol in a sudden fit of rage and fatally wounds him. It is at this point in the story that the action of the film begins. Eventually, with the coming of dawn a police gas assault begins. François, alone in his room and offscreen, shoots himself. The film ends as, in a long take, the light of day streams through the window of François' demolished room; the brutal irony of the arrival of a new day as the protagonist lies dead is emphasized in the score by final chords of triumph sounded by full orchestra.

The dark side of French poetic realism has been variously explained as the expression of disillusionment with a government apparently moving toward Fascism, as an example of the influence of American thrillers and gangster films, as the cinematic equivalent of the bleak outlook of French naturalist novelists such as Émile Zola. Whatever their ideological or philosophical inspiration may have been, it is clear that Carné and Prévert intended to make a statement, with *Le Jour se lève* of their vision of man as the victim of forces which he cannot control and prey to longings which he can never realize. In French literature, "realism" and its extreme form, "naturalism," especially as seen in the works of Zola and in Gustave Flaubert's master-piece, *Madame Bovary* (1857), feature characters, usually bourgeois or pro-letarian, trapped by the cruel banality of everyday life (or worse, in the case of Zola's characters, by the determinism of heredity) who are humiliated and destroyed by their own weaknesses or by a terrible concatenation of events for which they are not totally responsible. Writers such as Flaubert and Zola pay close attention to the importance of physical description of people and things, but they do not neglect symbolic motifs, the beauties of style, and the multiple dimensions of metaphor—in short, they subject real-ity to poetic interpretation. Prévert's script for *Le Jour se lève* provides the story, its sociological force, and the symbolic configurations; the collabora-tion of Carné, Curt Courant, and Alexandre Trauner contribute further to give a poetic quality to the realistic surface of things.

François' story does seem to be in the realist-naturalist tradition. In fact, the film was banned as demoralizing by the French military censor in September of 1939. François is approaching middle age, doomed, it appears, to an early death because of the dust which he has inhaled over the years on the job. He has been a drifter, a worker in various hazardous and humdrum occupations; he thinks of life in terms of a long series of street-cars in which there has been no room for him and which, therefore, have passed him by. Yet he is fortunate enough to meet Françoise.

It is not to confuse the viewer of *Le Jour se lève* that the hero and heroine of the film were given the masculine and feminine forms of the same name. The characters represent two sides of human nature—the beaten, tired, and discouraged; the naïve, imaginative, and hopeful. François and Françoise meet on their "name day," the Feast of Saint Francis, a saint who was him-self a poet and is traditionally associated with the joy of nature. They find that they have more than similar names in common: They were both or-phans, brought up as wards of the state. It is not for nothing that Françoise works for a florist: In a memorable scene, she brings flowers to the factory, but the flowers wilt during her brief stay because of the polluted air in which François must work every day. Jacqueline Laurent brings a delicate, doll-like beauty to the role of Françoise, and Françoise's fragile vulnerability and the escape from his drab existence which she represents for François constitute a strong attraction. Nevertheless, she is also under the spell cast by the tales of faraway places (the flowering mimosas of Nice, for example) spun by the elegant but evil Valentin.

Valentin seduced her, and as a souvenir, gave her a cheap brooch—emblazoned with a floral motif. She has continued to see Valentin because he brings her presents from his trips and sends her picture postcards. In her childish simplicity, Françoise gives this same brooch, one of her treasured possessions (as is the stuffed bear, "Bolop," a childhood memento which François lovingly adopts), to François as a token of her love for him. Unfortunately, later in the film, Clara, in her pique at losing François to Françoise, reveals to him that Valentin makes a practice of giving identical trinkets to all of the women whom he sleeps with; she herself has such a brooch, and moreover, she shows to François a cardboard, which she took from Valentin, to which are pinned several other brooches, destined for future victims of his deception. Françoise too wants to escape from unhappiness (when reality is grim, dreams help), from the hothouse flowers which she tends, to the country, where there are real flowers, and in response to the dream of mimosas with which Valentin had stimulated her imagination, François counters with a promise to take her to pick lilacs after Easter—a time of celebration of rebirth. Indeed, in a moving passage at the end of the film, just before François shoots himself—in the heart, which is only logical—the viewer hears the voice-over of Françoise, reminding him of his promise.

The floral motif, indicative of Françoise's delicacy and the possibility of renascence, is cleverly used in other instances as well. François and Françoise confess their love to each other in the soft light of a greenhouse, surrounded by flowering plants—as well as, ominously, by the long dark diagonals of the window frames, which remind the viewer of the "bars" of François' "prison," seen at the beginning of the film, and which foreshadow visually what the viewer already knows, that this love will come to a bad end. Later, when François is in his room, surrounded by the police, Françoise runs into the crowd in the street and falls and hits her head. She is carried to Clara's apartment across the street, where Clara tends her in her delirium (her dreams of love and happiness have turned out to be only that—delirium). As Françoise lies in bed, half-conscious and restlessly protesting her love for François, the viewer sees Clara hovering over her, clad, ironically, in a blouse with a floral print.

Meanwhile, in François' room, Bolop, the teddy bear, a talisman of François' hope, has already fallen victim to the shots fired into the room by the police. In his despair, François smashes Françoise's brooch against the wall, and, pondering his own image in the bullet-riddled mirror above his mantle, in anger at what he has become and the real life which the glass only too faithfully reflects, François shatters the mirror with a chair. In one sense, François will kill himself because, as he says, he is alone; in another, he is done in by life, the tortuous grind, the slow death which he has breathed in each day, like the sand at the factory, and from which love has provided no escape. After François fires the fatal shot, his alarm clock sounds; it is dawn—time to get up, time to go to work, time to take one's place on the treadmill to oblivion.

The acting of the principals, particularly that of Jean Gabin and Jules Berry, is outstanding. Gabin was probably the greatest star in the history of the French cinema. His screen presence, which expresses physical strength coupled with gentleness, his features, which at the same time suggest toughness and vulnerability, will perhaps remind American viewers of Humphrey Bogart, Spencer Tracy, and even John Wayne, although Gabin lacks the physical bulk and often annoying mannerisms of the latter. Gabin continued acting in films until his death in 1976 and retained an immense popularity, but his best work is represented by the great films which he made in the 1930's. Jules Berry is extraordinarily effective as the mesmerizing Valentin, beneath whose suave exterior lies the brutality of a man who tortures dogs in order to get them to do his bidding and who uses women in an equally bestial and amoral fashion. Berry has a most expressive face, and low-angle medium close-ups show off his artful use of gesture. Arletty, although cast in the film in a supporting role, gives a touching performance as the bruised woman of the world who retains a heart of gold and can be hurt by a man whom she loves. She starred in Carné's *Children of Paradise*, *Hôtel du nord* (1938), and *Les Visiteurs du soir* (1942; *The Devil's Own Envoy*) and had a long and distinguished career in films.

Le Jour se lève was one of the films which represented France at the Venice International Festival in 1939, but because of prewar turmoil no prizes were given. *Children of Paradise* remains one of the most highly esteemed French films, but Marcel Carné's reputation began to decline after World War II. *Le Jour se lève* is typical of his remarkable style, however, in the evicence that it offers of his gift for composition and expressionistic use of lighting. The work of Alexandre Trauner, who designed the sets (witness, in particular, the importance of the stark isolation of François' apartment building, which symbolizes the alienation of the protagonist), and of Maurice Jaubert, who wrote the score, cannot be ignored. Carné manipulated all of these elements—lighting, decor, and music—in order to achieve a most memorable fusion of symbolism and realism.

Gordon Walters

JUD SÜSS

Origin: Germany
Released: 1940
Released in U.S.: no listing
Production: Otto Lehmann for Terra Filmkunst
Direction: Veit Harlan
Assistant direction: Wolfgang Schleif and Alfred Braun
Screenplay: Ludwig Metzger, Wolfgang Eberhard Möller, and Veit Harlan
Cinematography: Bruno Mondi
Editing: Friedrich Carl von Puttkammer and Wolfgang Schleif
Art direction: Otto Hunte and Karl Vollbrecht
Costume design: Ludwig Hornsteiner
Choreography: Sabine Ress
Sound: Gustav Bellers
Music: Wolfgang Zeller
Song: "All mein Gedanken," from the *Lochheimer Liederbuch* of 1452
Running time: 97 minutes
Also Known as: Jew Süss

Principal characters:
Josef Süss-Oppenheimer	Ferdinand Marian
Duke Karl Alexander	Heinrich George
Levy/Rabbi Loew	Werner Krauss
Councillor Sturm	Eugen Klöpfer
Dorothea Sturm	Kristina Söderbaum
Christian "Kali" Faber	Malte Jaeger
Von Remchingen	Theodor Loos
Duchess	Hilde von Stolz
Colonel von Röder	Albert Florath
Luziana	Else Elster
Hans Bogner	Emil Hess
Prima ballerina	Ursula Deinert
Master of the blacksmith's guild	Erich Dunskus
President of the court	Otto Henning

Jud Süss is a film which never should have been made. This infamous work, the best-known and most successful of all propaganda films from the Third Reich, was ordered to be made by Joseph Goebbels, Reich Minister for Popular Enlightenment and Propaganda, in order to create and intensify anti-Semitic sentiments among the people in Germany and in areas occupied by the German army and to prepare them for the National Socialist government's planned "final solution to the Jewish problem." The film claims to be an accurate reenactment of Josef Süss-Oppenheimer's rise and fall at the court of Württemberg in the eighteenth century. In reality, the film proves to be an ideological interpretation and distortion of history, whose sole purpose was to present a negative and repulsive image of the Jewish people and their faith.

Born in 1692, the historical Josef Süss-Oppenheimer went to the court of Prince Karl Alexander of Württemberg in 1732. When Karl Alexander became Duke of Württemberg in 1733, Süss-Oppenheimer was appointed to be his financial adviser. Süss was authorized to collect taxes to pay off the state's debts, a duty which did not ingratiate him with the people and which enabled him to enrich himself. The Protestant population began to feel threatened by the Catholic duke, fearing that they would be forced to convert to Catholicism, and the Diet of Württemberg objected to the financial measures imposed by Süss as well as to the duke's plan to make himself head of a military autocracy. When representatives from the diet presented their demands to the duke on December 3, 1737, he suffered a stroke and died. Süss was arrested, accused of various crimes, including high treason, and after a lengthy trial he was executed on February 4, 1738.

These relatively obscure historical events became the subject of literary adaptations, all entitled *Jud Süss*, by various German authors. Of these, the most important is Lion Feuchtwanger's novel (1925), which was enormously popular in Germany until it was banned in 1933 along with his other works. In 1926 it appeared in English translation as *Power* and became an international success. In the novel both the duke and Süss are portrayed as equally lecherous and power hungry. Süss turns against the duke after his daughter Naemi kills herself while fleeing from the amorous advances of the duke. Süss offers himself as a scapegoat to those who conspired against the duke and is condemned to death as a result of anti-Semitic mass hysteria. Before his death he refuses to reveal the fact that his father was a Christian nobleman, which would save his life, and he accepts and finds consolation in the Jewish faith. Feuchtwanger's penetrating psychological study of Süss's self-destruction draws many parallels between Germany in the eighteenth century and the early twentieth century.

This philosemitic novel became the basis for the British film *Jew Süss* (1934) by the Jewish director Lothar Mendes with Conrad Veidt playing the role of Süss. Goebbels considered editing this British film for release in Germany but then decided to turn a German production of the life of Süss-Oppenheimer into one of his pet projects.

In 1938, Goebbels requested that all German film companies make anti-Semitic films in order to "enlighten" the population about the economic and sexual threats of international Jewry. The three major anti-Semitic films were all released in 1940: *Die Rothschild Aktien von Waterloo* (1940; *The Rothschilds' Shares in Waterloo*) on July 17, *Jud Süss* on September 24, and

Der ewige Jude (1940; *The Eternal Jew*) on November 24. The release of these three films within approximately five months was consciously orchestrated to prepare the German people for the expulsion of the Jewish population. The Nuremberg Laws of 1935 deprived the German Jews of citizenship and forbade intermarriage. On October 12, 1939, the deportation of Jews from Austria and Czechoslovakia to Poland began, and by February, 1940, German Jews were also being deported to Poland. In the last months of 1941, the first gassing camps were set up in Eastern Europe to provide the "final solution to the Jewish problem."

Veit Harlan was chosen to direct *Jud Süss* not because he was known to be a fervent nationalist but because he had gained a reputation for making quality pictures cheaply and under production deadlines. (Most of the films by Harlan which had been released in the United States between 1937 and 1940 had received positive reviews in *The New York Times*.) According to statements made by Harlan and others after the war, almost no one involved with the film wanted to make it, and many tried in vain to get out of the project. The casting was largely influenced by Goebbels, who reportedly insisted that Werner Krauss, Ferdinand Marian and Harlan's Swedish wife Kristina Söderbaum (who had become the filmic incarnation of the Nordic heroine) play specific roles. In preparation for the film Harlan visited the Lublin ghetto in Poland and brought back 120 Jews for different parts in the film, but this was forbidden to be mentioned in the press. According to statements made by Harlan after the war, all the actors performed under duress, representatives of the Propaganda Ministry and the Gestapo were on the set, and he tried to minimize the more vicious scenes in the film. These remarks contradict the prerelease publicity for the film which clearly revealed the intentions of the scriptwriters to present Nazi ideology through historical parallels. On January 20, 1940, Harlan stated that "the film keeps strictly to historical fact," and he compared Süss's crime of miscegenation with the Nuremberg Laws. Harlan also stated that Werner Krauss was cast to play Rabbi Loew, Levy, and several minor characters not in order to present "a bravura performance by a great actor" but in order "to show how all these different temperaments and characters—the pious patriarch, the wily swindler, the penny-pinching merchant and so on—are ultimately derived from the same roots."

The film begins with the coronation of Prince Karl Alexander (Heinrich George) as Duke of Württemberg in 1733 as he swears to rule according to the constitution and together with the Württemberg Diet. The city of Stuttgart celebrates the event, and the new duke is cheered by the citizens as he rides through the streets.

Von Remchingen (Theodor Loos), an emissary of the duke, visits Süss (Ferdinand Marian) in Frankfurt's ghetto in order to purchase a gift for the duchess (Hilde von Stolz). Süss will sell a string of pearls for one-fifth of its value and bring it to the duke personally in return for a pass to enter the city of Stuttgart from which all Jews are banned. He will shave off his beard and exchange his caftan for more standard attire in order to be able to enter the city. Here Süss is supposed to represent "the Jew in disguise," the Jew who can assimilate, put on European clothes, and go about unnoticed.

On the way to Stuttgart Süss's coach overturns, and he meets Dorothea Sturm (Kristina Söderbaum), the daughter of Councillor Sturm (Eugen Klöpfer), who drives him into the city. Their conversation along the way is intended to reveal the rootlessness of the Jews and the ubiquitous menace of international Jewry. Dorothea is impressed when Süss tells her that he has been to London, Vienna, Rome, Madrid, Lisbon and that his home is the world. She asks if there is not one place where he has felt happiest, and he responds that he has never been as happy in his whole life as he is now near her. Süss's interest in the innocent "Gretchen" figure Dorothea was to be interpreted by the audiences in 1940 as an example of the sexual contamination by the Jews which threatened Aryan women.

The provincial diet denies the duke's request for a regiment of bodyguards, an opera, and a ballet. Süss offers to lend him money to finance his projects, stating that he only wants to be a loyal servant of his sovereign lord. Süss not only helps Karl Alexander financially but also encourages his dissolute life-style by devising new ways for the duke to chase after and humiliate the young women of Württemberg. In exchange for the loans, Süss is appointed Minister of Finance and authorized to administer the roads and bridges for ten years. With the help of his secretary Levy (Werner Krauss) he increases tolls and road taxes, an action which brings about inflation and severe hardships to the people. The irate blacksmith Hans Bogner (Emil Hess) attacks Süss with a hammer after Süss has half of Bogner's house torn down. Süss manages to obtain the duke's permission to have Bogner hanged.

Süss persuades Karl Alexander to revoke the ban against Jews which results in the arrival of thousands of Jews in Stuttgart. They are presented as an ugly, ragged caravan as they come into the city. Süss also requests a carte blanche from the duke which would state that all of his actions were in the name of the duke. The people and the diet become more and more discontented with Süss's policies, the inflation, and the presence of the Jews in the city. Representatives of the diet visit the duke and ask him to revoke the decree which permitted the Jews to enter Stuttgart. Karl Alexander will not dismiss Süss because he would be poor and powerless without him. Süss advises him to dissolve the diet, declare himself absolute ruler of Württemberg, and set up a ministry of advisers composed of loyal subjects.

Rabbi Loew (also Werner Krauss) warns Süss against overextending his power, stating that the Lord wants His people to serve in sackcloth and ashes, to remain hidden and thus rule over the people of the earth. Loew tells Süss to control the Gentiles' money but to stay out of the duke's conflicts because the duke may be pardoned but the Jew will be hanged. Süss explains that he wants to turn Württemberg into the promised land of milk and honey for Israel. (This scene alludes to the so-called Jewish conspiracy to rule the world and purports to depict the two types of Jews: the Jew in disguise and the real or archetypal Jew, Rabbi Loew with his beard, yarmulke, prayer shawl, and caftan. Regardless of their appearances and methods, both are portrayed as having the same goal: the exploitation and domination of the Gentiles.) The duke is reluctant to dissolve the diet until Rabbi Loew, at the instigation of Süss, interprets the stars for the duke and prophesies that the stars will obey "him who dares."

Chief Councillor Sturm rejects Süss's offer to preside over the new ministry, saying that he has taken an oath of loyalty to the Württemberg Diet. Süss reveals to Sturm his desire to marry Dorothea. To prevent this, Sturm has her marry her fiancé Faber (Malte Jaeger) that same night. When Süss visits Sturm the following morning to renew both offers, Sturm throws him out of the house. Because of this insult, Süss has Sturm falsely accused of treason and arrested. This is more than the people can endure, and under the leadership of von Röder (Albert Florath) and Faber they plan a revolt to have the Jews expelled from the city. The duke dissolves the diet, breaking the vow he made when he was sworn into office. Süss convinces Karl Alexander to borrow troops from Würzburg, which would intimidate the people and prevent a violent revolt. The Jewish community which had been permitted to enter the city will pay for the foreign troops. As the threat of revolution increases, the duke regrets having followed the course of actions set by Süss, but it is too late. He travels to Ludwigsburg and gives Süss a free hand to crush the rebellion.

Dorothea's husband, Faber, is arrested as he tries to leave the city with secret orders for the planned revolt. Dorothea comes to Süss with a petition for the duke which Süss tears up. She hears Faber's screams while he is being tortured in a cellar across the courtyard from Süss's house. Süss tells her that she can save Faber by submitting to him and proceeds to rape her. Filled with grief and shame, she runs away and drowns herself. Faber, who has been released, carries her body through the streets, which becomes a signal for the people to revolt.

In a drunken state, Karl Alexander has one of his few moments of insight and asks Süss (who has also come to Ludwigsburg) to take off his last mask. When the men from Stuttgart arrive to present the duke with their demands, he dies of a stroke. Süss is captured and convicted of a litany of crimes: extortion, usury, fornication, profiteering, procuring, and high treason, but his greatest crime is the shame and suffering he caused the people of Württemberg.

In the courtroom scene Süss appears without his disguise: He now has a beard and speaks with a Yiddish accent as he protests that he is on trial for having been "a loyal servant of his master"—words which uncannily fore-shadow the position of justification adopted by many Nazi criminals during the postwar trials. The president of the court (Otto Henning) asks Sturm to speak, since he has suffered the most. Sturm states that he does not ask for retribution but only for what is right; he refers to the old criminal code of the empire where it is written that "if a Jew should unite physically with a Christian woman then he is to be put to death by the rope." These words are repeated as the scene changes to the town square where the execution of Süss takes place. The guild of blacksmiths has built a special gallows for him, higher than the one from which the blacksmith Hans Bogner was hanged. Süss is placed into an iron cage which is hauled into the air above the square. He pleads for his life, promising to make up for everything, but his screams suddenly stop when the floor of the cage opens and his feet fall out and become limp. Sturm addresses the people who have witnessed the execution, proclaiming that all Jews must leave the city within three days. He hopes that future generations will "hold on to this law so that they may be preserved from suffering and harm to their lives, property, and to the blood of their children and their children's children."

The parallels between 1738 and 1940 could not have been missed by the audiences. The message was clear: The German women must be protected from the vicious and lecherous Jews. The sexual threat which Süss repre-sented was perceived as being more dangerous than his criminal nature. The final scene is a justification for the measures already taken by the Nazi re-gime and for the expulsion and genocide which were to come.

Jud Süss premiered in Venice on September 5, 1940, and German critics called it an "unqualified success." (It must be noted here that film reviews printed in Germany at this time are not very reliable because Goebbels had issued a decree requiring all reviews of films to be merely descriptive and positive.) Before its Berlin premiere, newspaper critics were told how they were to interpret the film. They were to stress the criminal nature of all Jews and "the message that every Jew has only his well-being and that of his racial brothers in mind, even when he pretends generous motives." On the day after the Berlin premiere on September 24, 1940, *Jud Süss* was praised as "the decisive breakthrough in creating cinematic art out of our National Socialist ideology." Critics especially praised the acting and the faithfulness of the film to historical sources.

The film became a great box-office success: In November, 1940, approxi-mately 700,000 people had seen the film, at the end of December, 1940, it was being shown in sixty-six theaters in Berlin alone, and after fifteen months the box-office receipts totaled 5.97 million reichsmarks (compared to production costs of approximately two million reichsmarks). These statis-tics are somewhat deceptive, however, when one considers that a great amount of social pressure existed among the population to see the film and that, for example, women's and youth organizations had to see the film in groups. The film received the *Prädikate* (merit awards) "politically and artistically especially valuable"—the highest designation available until 1941—and "valuable for youth." Because of the overpowering emotional impact the film would have on children, it was officially banned for viewers under fourteen.

Already on September 30, 1940, Heinrich Himmler ordered the SS and the police to see *Jud Süss* during the coming winter months. The film's horrifying effects in contributing to the extermination of European Jews cannot be measured. At Auschwitz, the film was shown in order to instigate mistreatment of prisoners. In the occupied Eastern territories, the film was shown to the "Aryan" population before an evacuation or liquidation of a ghetto was to take place in order to desensitize and incense them against the Jews.

Jud Süss fulfills Goebbels' requirement that propaganda be presented in an artistic manner. The film is technically well made: The melodramatic script is well constructed, although contemporary audiences may find the scenes of domesticity mawkish; the sets and costumes appear authentic; the musical sound track consists of a moving blend of Hebrew hymns, the melody of a German folk song ("All mein Gedanken") and full orchestration; the acting is excellent, that is, convincing in its 1940, stylized, melodramatic manner; the night scenes are very dramatic; the crowd scenes are well edited, cutting from the masses to close-ups of people in the crowd, and the parallel editing of the torture and rape scenes successfully builds up suspense. Yet the film's artistic accomplishments cannot be separated from its propagandistic intentions and effects. In the experiences of the characters on the screen the audience was to see a microcosmic representation of its own situation. In order to present Süss as the prototype of the criminal Jew, he and the other Jews are depicted as stereotypes who are contrasted with Aryan stereotypes. This black-and-white representation of good and evil proved to be very effective. Except when Süss is "in disguise," all the Jews are portrayed as dirty, hook-nosed, and repellent; the citizens of Württemberg on the other hand are Nordic prototypes: the beautiful and innocent child-bride Dorothea, the incorruptible Sturm, and the ascetic fiancé Faber; only the members of the court are depicted as decadent. The loud foreign sounds of the Purim service in the synagogue are contrasted with Dorothea singing a simple German folk song. The contrasting structure made the film's message easily accessible. It appealed to the emotions, not to the intellect. The maliciousness of *Jud Süss* is perhaps only surpassed by Fritz Hippler's *The Eternal Jew*, which purports to be a documentary about European Jews. The montage technique in *The Eternal Jew* compares the poor Jews of a Polish ghetto with rats, and a narration underscores the images to demonstrate the necessity of driving such people out of civilized societies everywhere.

With the success of *Jud Süss*, Veit Harlan became one of the Third Reich's star directors. He made six more films before the end of the war, including *Der grosse König* (1942; *The Great King*), the last in a series of films about Frederick the Great, and *Kolberg* (1945), an epic set during the Napoleonic Wars which was intended to rival the grandeur of *Gone with the Wind* (1939). His wife Kristina Söderbaum acted in five of these films. Ferdinand Marian, who was already a matinee idol, received much more fan mail from women than before the film. Werner Krauss went on to play a notorious Shylock on the stage.

After the war, Veit Harlan was blacklisted and twice tried (1949 and 1950) for crimes against humanity for having directed and coscripted *Jud Süss*, but he was acquitted both times for lack of evidence. A series of character witnesses appeared at the trial and testified to his having helped many out-of-work and persecuted Jews during the Third Reich (in 1933 Jews had been banned from working in the film industry). Between 1950 and 1958, Harlan directed nine films in West Germany. An attempted boycott of his first postwar film *Unsterbliche Geliebte* (1950; *Immortal Beloved*), failed. Kristina Söderbaum acted in most of his films after the war and later appeared along with other leading figures of the Nazi cinema in Hans-Jürgen Syberberg's *Karl May* (1974). Wolfgang Staudte, who played a minor role in *Jud Süss* and was widely criticized for this, became one of the most important directors in postwar Germany. Staudte first made socially committed films for DEFA (the East German production company), including *Die Mörder sind unter uns* (1946; *The Murderers Are Among Us*), the first film made in Germany after the war, and later he directed films in West Germany. Werner Krauss was blacklisted, and an attempted return to the stage in Switzerland resulted in street riots; he eventually returned to the stage and acted in a few films. Heinrich George died in the Russian concentration camp Sachsenhausen in 1946. Ferdinand Marian apparently committed suicide in a car accident in 1950 as a result of his guilt feelings for having played the role of Süss, and his widow was later found drowned in Hamburg.

Harlan was ordered by the court to destroy what was believed to be the only remaining negative of *Jud Süss*. He reportedly did this, but another negative existed in East Germany from which prints were made and openly distributed in the Middle East by Sovexport. These Arabic-dubbed prints of the film were very successful in the 1950's and 1960's, when they were used as propaganda against the new nation of Israel.

Franz A. Birgel

JUDEX

Origin: France and Italy
Released: 1964
Released in U.S.: 1966
Production: Robert de Nesle for Comptoir Français du Film and Filmes Cinematografica
Direction: Georges Franju
Screenplay: Jacques Champreux and Francis Lacassin; based on the original film by Arthur Bernède and Louis Feuillade
Cinematography: Marcel Fradetal
Editing: Gilbert Natot
Art direction: Robert Giordani
Costume design: Christiane Courcelles
Music: Maurice Jarre
Running time: 100 minutes

Principal characters:
Judex (Vallières)	Channing Pollock
Diane Monti (Marie Verdier)	Francine Bergé
Jacqueline Favraux	Edith Scob
Favraux	Michel Vitold
Cocantin	Jacques Jouanneau
Daisy	Sylva Koscina
Moralès	Théo Sarapo
Réglisse	Benjamin Boda
Pierre Kerjean	René Génin

Georges Franju, the director of *Judex*, is as unique as his films. Born in 1912 in Brittany, France, he fell between the French Old Guard directors, such as Marcel Carné and Jean Renoir, and the New Wave directors, such as François Truffaut and Jean-Luc Godard. Franju's best films have the silky smooth technique of the former group and the subversive imagery associated with the latter. As a boy, Franju read the pulp thriller upon which *Judex* is based, as well as reading works by Sigmund Freud, Karl Marx, and the Marquis de Sade—a volatile mixture which laid the basis for his Surrealist viewpoint.

Franju's first films were short documentaries, of which *Le Sang des bêtes* (1949; *Blood of the Beasts*) remains the most famous. The first image is a rubbish heap. A dress dummy sticks up at an angle. Alongside some furniture, an electric lamp hangs from the branches of a tree. As a train goes by in the distance, a voice announces that junkyards are the attics of the poor. It looks like a canvas by Georgio De Chirico, the Italian Surrealist painter, or perhaps by the man most influenced by him, the Belgian Surrealist painter René Magritte.

The second image is a Parisian slaughterhouse, shot in such a way as to resemble a painting; flat and two-dimensional. Later in the film, nuns with their great seagull-like headdresses walk along a cobblestoned alleyway running with the slaughtered animal's blood. On the sound track the audience hears the Charles Trenet song "La Mer" (the sea).

These are all seeming contradictions: open-air attics, a real building that looks like a stage set, and blood in cramped quarters juxtaposed with the open freshness of the sea. The nuns, who turn up later in *Judex*, are more normally associated with the divine blood of Christ. All of this forms the core of Surrealism. The collision of opposites is meant to dislocate the senses so that genuine mystery may penetrate the consciousness. What distinguishes the master from the apprentice Surrealist is the choice of opposites, the nature of their opposition and the way in which they are juxtaposed. At this game, Franju is a master.

Franju's short documentaries are mood pieces, all texture and atmosphere with an antidramatic bias. This basically poetic sensibility carries over into his features and is not always successful. At times, he was like a poet straining to write a novel.

His only other features that strike a satisfactory balance between style and story are *Thomas l'Imposteur* (1964) and *Les Yeux sans visage* (1959; *Eyes Without a Face*, also called *The Horror Chamber of Dr. Faustus* in a dubbed version). The first is from the Jean Cocteau novel of the same title set during World War I and shortly after the time of *Judex*. The central metaphor is that war equals a stage play and the title character dies while pretending to be dead so that the enemy will stop shooting at him. There are two fantastic scenes in the film. In one, fire licks sensuously over the furnishings, tapestries, and paintings of a château, and, in the other, a horse with a flaming mane appears in a war-torn village and jumps over a nurse.

Eyes Without a Face is closer to *Judex*, but instead of being a film on the marvelous, it is a Gothic horror story. The iconographical elements of the horror genre—mad doctor, sinister house, physical disfigurements—are transformed through Franju's ruthlessly calm viewpoint. As in *Judex*, it is this antimelodramatic quality that gives the lurid plot its magical resonances.

The first *Judex* was made as a serial by pioneer French director Louis Feuillade in 1917. Its title character was a superhero created to rival the popularity of the French pulp character Fantômas, master criminal. Feuillade had made *Fantômas* in 1913 and 1914: The success of these and other Feuillade serials, such as *Les Vampires* (1915-1916) and *La Nouvelle Mission de Judex* (1917), had both immediate and far-reaching influences. In an attempt to emulate the Feuillade productions, the New York branch of Pathé created the Pearl White serials, which in turn gave birth to every

American pop serial right through to the present day and even up to the seriallike *Raiders of the Lost Ark* (1981).

When the originals appeared in 1917, they were seen by a number of the then-emerging Surrealists, who took the style and subject matter of the serials to heart. Most obviously influenced was Magritte; like Franju, he read the adventures, saw the films, and finally painted Fantômas and characters from that world. His dreamlike oils featuring expressionless, bowler-hatted men derive their disturbing power from their flat, matter-of-fact rendering—a style similar to that of Feuillade's unblinking camera, which records simple master-shots of masked figures in black tights creeping over tiled rooftops, stage shows of bat-costumed women framed by potted palms, and conservative terrorists blowing up distant bell towers with cannons concealed in their comfortable studies. *Les Vampires* contains all these images as well as one of a bowler-hatted man riding a giant wheeled bicycle along a twisting high-walled street. The shot is in one take, with the camera framing the man head on as it pulls back at the same rate as he advances. A mysterious monotony is set up, broken only by cut-aways to the frantic table-top party of a criminal gang. The deadpan lack of affect that characterizes these serials stands in marked contrast to the tone of the classic German Expressionist films of the 1920's—most notably the convulsive-paranoiac fantasies of Fritz Lang. Franju's *Judex* is not only credited as a homage to Feuillade but also the screenplay is based on the original.

Judex begins at the peaceful country estate of the unscrupulous banker Favraux (Michel Vitold) and his widowed daughter, Jacqueline played by Edith Scob, an actress Franju had used in *Eyes Without a Face* to represent an ethereal, birdlike purity and goodness. She is cast to portray these qualities here. Also on the premises are Favraux's aged, dignified servant Vallières (Channing Pollock) and Marie (Francine Bergé), the provocative governess. A private detective, the bumbling Cocantin (Jacques Jouanneau), has been called in by Favraux to discover who has written several threatening letters which demand that the banker make restitution to the people he has ruined. This is to be done on the eve of Jacqueline's engagement ball. The penalty for not complying with the letters' orders is death. They are signed "Judex."

Outside the house, an old beggar named Kerjean (René Génin) accuses Favraux of having ruined him. Vallières leads the beggar away, and later Favraux runs him over in his motor car.

Outside Favraux's mansion on the night of the ball, the strains of an elegant waltz are heard. Through a columned walkway a pair of shoes can be seen. Slowly, the camera glides upward, revealing a male figure in formal wear who holds an inert white dove in his hands. The man wears a huge crow's head, imperious and commanding. At once he turns and makes his way into the crowded ballroom where the dancers make way for him. They are all masked as well. Jacqueline wears the head of a duck, Favraux wears the head of a vulture.

The crow man steps up on a dais, passes his hand over the dove and watches as it flies away to the stilled crowd's astonishment. He turns to Favraux and whips a handkerchief off his palm, revealing a glass of liqueur. The banker drinks it. The crow man gives the dais over to Favraux who begins to make an engagement announcement. The clock begins to chime midnight; as soon as it is done, Favraux pitches forward senseless. A doctor rushes up and pronounces him dead.

The next day, Vallières tells Jacqueline that the charges in Judex's letters were accurate. Her father's fortune had its beginnings with the Panama Scandal of the early 1890's. Jacqueline decides to sell the estate and have the money distributed among her father's victims.

Meanwhile, caped men disinter the body of Favraux and take him to Judex's hideout in a ruined castle on a hillside. Here the drug that was administered to him wears off. He is to be imprisoned for life.

Back at the Favraux mansion, Marie, the governess returns with her lover Moralès (Théo Sarapo). Jacqueline discovers them as they attempt to steal some documents, and they chloroform her. As they carry her up to the iron gates, German shepherds appear and growl menacingly. The pair lay her down and slip out. A tall, caped figure in a broad-brimmed hat steps out of the shadows, carries her back to the house, and departs, leaving her with a white dove in a cage. She is to release the bird whenever she is in trouble. Jacqueline takes up residence in a plain boardinghouse. Here, she accidentally discovers that Vallières and Judex are the same.

Marie sends a member of her underworld gang to steal the papers in the boardinghouse room. When Jacqueline returns, the thief tries to hide on the window balcony but falls to his death, inadvertently releasing the white dove.

As Judex receives the dove, Jacqueline arrives by train in the country where she has been lured by a message from Marie. Outside the station, Marie, dressed as a nun, rushes up to Jacqueline and plunges a hypodermic needle into her back. Marie and Moralès put Jacqueline into their car, drive her to a bridge, and throw her over the railing into the stream below. A little boy, Réglisse (Benjamin Boda), spots her floating by and signals some fishermen. They carry her to a small house in a neighboring village. Marie and Moralès arrive in a stolen ambulance and take Jacqueline away to an old mill.

The little boy rushes to Cocantin, who is reading a Fantômas thriller, and tells him that the nun is Marie. Cocantin follows the ambulance but the villains ambush him and steal his car. The little boy has hidden in the trunk, however, and, after escaping, leads Judex and Kerjean, whose life Judex has saved, to the mill.

They arrive just in time to stop Marie from killing Jacqueline with a hat pin. Marie barricades herself in an adjoining room, slowly strips off her nun's habit until she is wearing only a slinky black leotard and then plunges through a hole in the floor to the rushing waters below. (This scene caused a protest against its blasphemy in France and resulted in a delayed release in that country.)

Favraux escapes from Judex's hideout and joins Marie and Moralès in the top floor of an abandoned house in some outlying suburb. Judex arrives with Cocantin and the little boy. Judex pursues the villains, Cocantin alerts his men, and then solicits the aid of an old love, Daisy (Sylva Koscina). Apprised of the situation, she doffs her cape and follows Judex, wearing her circus tights.

Judex enters the top floor through the window and is knocked unconscious before being tied to a wooden pillar. Marie sends Moralès to check on Favraux in another room. She then encourages Judex to join forces with her. She tries to kiss him, but he turns his head away. Enraged, she spits in his face and puts a hood on him. She then goes to Favraux's bedside, tenderly asking him to sleep. She returns to Judex and stabs him with a bone-handled knife. Judex appears in back of her. She pulls off the hood of the corpse and sees that it is Moralès. She flees onto the rooftops, Daisy in pursuit. Favraux emerges from his room, sees Judex, runs back, and, locking himself in, shoots himself.

Marie and Daisy fight on a steep roof. Marie loses her balance, slides down the roof, and grabs onto an eave. Judex's men try to pull her to safety, but she slips from their grip and falls to her death in the weeds below—her expression is one of shock at her own mortality. The little boy stands next to her dead body, looking down with tears in his eyes.

The film dissolves to a sunny beach. Judex and Jacqueline stroll along the sea's edge. He produces a dove for her. They kiss. A title appears announcing that all this happened before 1914 and that it is a souvenir of a happier time.

Thus, the film ends with a title card that not only fixes it in time but also reminds the viewer that what has been seen is in the spirit of the silent films. The silent-film techniques are numerous. There are the short scenes that fade to black, analogous to the one-sentence paragraph of early pulp fiction. Half of the action is played in long master-shots before a motionless camera. The other half are done in velvety tracking shots that are very well integrated. The dialogue, although spoken, is, in most cases, more utilitarian and compressed than actual old title cards—many of which are very flowery. For the non-French-speaking viewer, the effect of watching a silent film is enhanced by the subtitles.

Another inheritance from the silents is the wealth of preposterous cliffhanger incidents and Victorian coincidences. Such a Dickensian narrative propulsion acts as a strong current. Franju's contemplative temperament is not allowed to stagnate because, no matter how slight, the story is always in movement.

As in most dreams and myths, the characters in *Judex* are archetypes, devoid of any individuated psychology. Each stands out starkly against the various backdrops. *Judex*, unlike the average superhero film or comic book, reflects Franju's ability to invest his characters with the power to get below the consciousness of the audience until they are like figures from dreams.

This is accomplished in two ways. First, every principal in the film starts out as one thing and subtly becomes something else. Jacqueline, although always pure and good, changes from a pawn of her father and becomes a self-willed woman. Favraux loses his prideful arrogance and craves anonymity and finally death. Marie turns from an icy calculating temptress into a spurned vulnerable girl. Judex himself, starting as an omnipotent bird-god with Jules Verne machines and faceless minions, becomes, through his love for Jacqueline, a decent man who needs to be rescued from his blunders. Franju's gradual humanization of his stylized characters loosens their puppetlike rigidity and lends them a rhythm as inexorable as the film itself.

Second, underneath surface relationships, the main figures appear to be parts of one whole, or family, held in a curious magnetic tension. Judex and Marie, with their dark good looks, elegant movements, black clothing, and independent feline spirits are like twins. Marie is the lustful, destroying negative alter ego of Judex. It is she who assaults Jacqueline three times, twice with phallic stabbings: She wishes to destroy the higher self to which Judex aspires. Her nun disguise is almost a mocking echo of Judex's monastic life in his castle.

Although Favraux asks Marie to marry him in the beginning of the film, her strangely compassionate treatment of him at the end suggests more of a father-daughter relationship than anything else. Kerjean, who turns out to be Moralès' father, seems to adopt Judex as his son. Cocantin, the childlike adult and the little boy, the adultlike child, can be likened to the integration of child and adult in the viewer, an integration necessary for any appreciation of the film.

Judex opened in America in 1966, the time of Batman and camp taste. Instead of a farcical satire, audiences encountered an oddly measured art nouveau poem. The occasional laughs died out to puzzled silence. The film has become no more accessible over time; it remains a cult film for the cognoscenti.

Indeed later, the pulp melodrama became a highly commercial genre, but personal, poetic treatments of it are, as always, anathema. Franju, that spiritual dandy of the *faux naïf*, made *Judex*, like all of his films, full of disturbing contradictions—something that angers the basic black-and-white of the adolescent mind. His sensibility may be an acquired taste, but it is nevertheless a lasting one. As D. H. Lawrence remarked with regard to the writing of the esoteric novelist Baron Corvo: "It may be caviar but at least it comes from the belly of a live fish."

Dick Blackburn

JULES AND JIM
(JULES ET JIM)

Origin: France
Released: 1962
Released in U.S.: 1962
Production: Marcel Berbert for Les Films du Carosse and Société
d'Exploitation et de Distribution de Films
Direction: François Truffaut
Assistant direction: Georges Pellegrin and Rober Bober
Screenplay: François Truffaut and Jean Gruault; based on the novel by Henri-
Pierre Roché
Cinematography: Raoul Coutard
Editing: Claudine Bouché
Narration: Michel Subor
Art direction: no listing
Music: Georges Delerue
Song: Boris Bassiak, "Le Torbillon"; sung by Jeanne Moreau
Running time: 105 minutes

Principal characters:
Catherine	Jeanne Moreau
Jules	Oskar Werner
Jim	Henri Serre
Gilberte	Vanna Urbino
Albert	Boris Bassiak
Sabine	Sabine Haudepin
Thérèse	Marie Dubois
First customer	Jean-Louis Richard
Second customer	Michel Varesano
Drunkard	Pierre Fabre
Albert's friend	Danielle Bassiak
Merlin	Bernard Largemains
Mathilde	Elen Bober

It now seems clear that *Jules and Jim* is both the quintessential New Wave film and its director's masterpiece. Based on an autobiographical novel by Henri-Pierre Roché, the man who supposedly introduced Gertrude Stein to Pablo Picasso, it combines the celebration of human freedom and the sheer joy in filmmaking that characterized the New Wave with the themes of obsessive, destructive love and personal morality that marked the oeuvre of François Truffaut. Like the enigmatic, smiling face of the woman sculpted in stone that first transfixes its heroes and then initiates their mythic quest,

Jules and Jim remains an ever-elusive, ever-seductive image of the need to preserve love and friendship against the erosion of time and doubt.

The story begins in 1912 with a rapid montage sequence while the narrator, Michel Subor, introduces the viewer to the pair of carefree young writers, Jim (Henri Serre), a tall, dark Parisian, and Jules (Oskar Werner), a rather short German and a stranger to Paris. "Everyone called them Don Quixote and Sancho Panza." While viewing slides at the home of an acquaintance, Albert (Boris Bassiak), the two friends become enraptured by the mysterious image of a woman's head carved in stone. They immediately visit the open-air museum in the Adriatic to gaze at her disdainful, yet beautiful smile, which Truffaut presents through a dramatic series of zooms, pans, and tracking shots circling around the stone figure. Not long after, Jules invites Jim to meet three girls visiting Paris, one of whom bears an uncanny resemblance—reinforced by Truffaut's repetition of the montage—to the statue. The sculpture-come-to-life is Catherine (Jeanne Moreau), and she infatuates them both. Jules, who has been unlucky in love while away from home, begins to court her—with his friend's blessing. Catherine's independence, which Jules attributes to her mixed parentage (her father was a French aristocrat, her mother, a lower-class Englishwoman), fascinates Jim and rather overwhelms Jules with her freedom and spontaneity. At her whim, they set up residence in the French countryside; when she decides that she misses Paris, they instantly return. The moment the men ignore her, she rebels—either playfully, as when she slaps Jules for not responding to her jokes, or more disturbingly, as when she suddenly leaps into the Seine to protest their disparaging remarks about women following an August Strindberg play. Jules is frightened by this strange, ominous act; Jim admires it, and draws it from memory the next day. In time, Jules's innocent charm and tolerance of Catherine's impulsiveness win her over, and she accepts his proposal of marriage shortly before the outbreak of World War I. "You haven't known a lot of women, but I have known many men," she tells Jules. "It balances out, so perhaps we'd make a good couple."

The war—presented in a stunning montage of archival footage, much of it stretched to Scope dimensions—divides the film and separates the two friends, whose greatest concern is to avoid killing each other. Jules writes beautiful, erotic love letters to Catherine; Jim stays with his patient girlfriend, Gilberte (Vanna Urbino), while home on leave. "Jules's country lost the war, Jim's had won it," the narrator informs the viewer. "But the real victory was that they were both alive." In a poignant reunion at Jules and Catherine's rustic chalet on the Rhine, the men resume their friendship. Yet things have changed. Though she has given Jules a daughter, Sabine (Sabine Haudepin), Catherine has not been domesticated: She has had several lovers, including Albert, the singer who first showed them the statue and who now lives nearby. Jules fears losing her, but blames neither Catherine nor Albert. Jim is filled with sadness for Jules, but he is not surprised. When Catherine leads him on a long midnight walk through the woods and tells her side of the story, Jim finds himself inescapably drawn to her. "Was she deliberately seducing him? Jim was not sure. Catherine only revealed what she wanted once she had it in hand." Out of loyalty to their friendship and a desire to remain in her presence, Jules renounces his claims on Catherine and tells Jim to marry her. Once more the three set up living together, but this time Jim sleeps with Catherine.

The new arrangement seems to work for a while—Truffaut creating an idyllic sequence of bicycle rides, songs, and games of dominoes—but the relationships inevitably become strained: Jim feels guilty that their friendship suffers, then jealous when Catherine seduces Jules one evening; Catherine resents the fact that Jim is younger than she and that he returns to Paris to say farewell to Gilberte. Only Jules remains stoic, loving them both. After a series of separations, infidelities, and reconciliations, the love affair finally is broken when Catherine suffers a miscarriage and Jim resolves to marry Gilberte. In a deliberately melodramatic sequence, Catherine draws a gun on Jim and threatens to shoot him, whereupon he escapes through an open window. Some time later, Jules and Catherine accidentally meet Jim at the Cinéma des Ursulines (a favorite haunt of the New Wave group), where the newsreel records the Nazis burning books. Though it is now 1934, Jules and Jim have hardly aged in twenty-two years; Catherine bears all the burden of time in the film. As the two friends discuss the collapse of their world at an open-air café beside the river, Catherine, with a mischievous look in her eye, invites Jim to take a ride in the car with her and tells her husband to watch. She then drives off the edge of a broken bridge, killing them both. For Jules, Catherine's death brings a great wave of relief. "His friendship with Jim had no equivalent in love," the narrator says.

Truffaut's dazzling mixture of cinematic styles in *Jules and Jim*—from slapstick and comedy of manners in the first half of the film to the documentary footage that structures and divides the narrative, to the melodrama that pervades the final reel—goes beyond merely rehearsing the New Wave's enthusiasm for the myriad possibilities of the medium. Instead, these special effects and shifts of mood reinforce the story at every stage. For example, the rapid cutting in the opening sequences reflects the joie de vivre of Bohemian Paris before the Great War, the energy that Jules and Jim invest in their friendship, their writing, and their goddess of love. Similarly, such techniques as mounting the cameras on bicycles to follow the group on their jaunts in the countryside and the aerial tracking shots that link the separated lovers serve to suggest the vitality of their relationship and their efforts to transcend the limits of social conventions and historical events. As in the famous concluding shot to *Les Quatre Cents Coups* (1959; *The 400 Blows*), Truffaut again utilizes the freeze-frame, but with much different effect. The series of stop-action shots of Catherine early in the film identify her with the statue that Jules and Jim had first seen in slide projection; at the same time, it captures her smile at its apex of influence and glory. The almost subliminal single freeze-frame of the men reunited after the war is even more compelling, preserving the ideal of friendship at the very moment that it seems most precarious. Ultimately, the stylistic eclecticism of *Jules and Jim*, like that of Jean Renoir's *La Règle du jeu* (1939; *Rules of the Game*), expresses a vision of human experience in all of its complexity and ambiguity—a lyric appreciation of life itself.

More than a dictionary of cinematic styles or an entertaining variation on the familiar themes of *l'amour fou* and the femme fatale that mark the mainstream of Truffaut's work, *Jules and Jim* is a meditation on art and history, social convention and private morality, love and friendship. In one sense, the film describes the continuous efforts of the central characters— sometimes heroic, sometimes perverse—to make art out of life, and thereby to overcome the impositions of history. Indeed, the passage of time in *Jules and Jim* is seen through a chronological succession of Picassos as well as the insertion of documentary footage. Catherine is linked to the enduring appeal of art through her identification with the ancient statue, although in the later stages of the film—when she dons spectacles or, in a profoundly expressive long take, slowly wipes cold cream from her face in front of the dressing table mirror—she paradoxically comes to represent both timelessness and mutability. Jules and Jim, who first meet on their way to the Quatres Arts Ball, write novels (Jim reads from his tale about two friends named Jacques and Julien; after the war, Jules describes a novel he is planning—a love story with insects as characters), translate each other's work, discuss William Shakespeare, August Strindberg, Charles Baudelaire, and Johann Wolfgang von Goethe. Catherine, however, remains their greatest creation, their eternal muse. When the men meet for the last time, they lament the book burnings that signify not only the destruction of the culture that they have worshiped but also their own failure as artists to sustain their vital illusion. Perhaps it is because Catherine alone acknowledges this failure, or perhaps because she alone has remained an unregenerate Bohemian, true to the spirit that once bound them together, that she decides to save what she can by destroying the triangle, preserving the memory of the community that they had once been.

Like a true goddess ("une vraie femme," Jules calls her), Catherine works in mysterious ways. To interpret *Jules and Jim* requires an understanding of her character, and Truffaut willfully precludes the possibility of definitive judgment. Catherine can be described as neurotic, tyrannical, morally insane; she is also a victim of biology, patriarchy, and history. Undoubtedly, she stands as one of the greatest female characters in all of cinema, in large measure because of Jeanne Moreau's remarkable performance. Truffaut deserves much credit as well for the risk involved in such a script. "The gamble for me," he said, "was to make the woman moving (without being melodramatic) and not a tart, and to prevent her husband from seeming ridiculous." He succeeded by remaining sympathetic to all of his characters while at the same time maintaining an awareness of the impossibility of their quest for absolute freedom.

The pervasive ambiguity of *Jules and Jim* may be illustrated by two of its most emotionally moving moments: when Jim first kisses Catherine, and when Catherine returns to her husband's room after quarreling with Jim. In each case, the content of the scene—consummation, reconciliation—is subtly complicated, even subverted, by the cinematic presentation. From the time very early in the film when Jules invites Jim to visit him and Catherine but pleads, "Not this one, Jim," the narrative has been leading to this climax when Jim's desire for Catherine overcomes his loyalty to Jules. Truffaut prepares the viewer with several romantic codes: a midnight tryst, Georges Delerue's lush music, soft focus and low-key lighting. As Jim enters the chalet to return Catherine's copy of Goethe's *Elective Affinities*, Catherine leads him to a window where he traces her silhouetted profile, reaches her mouth, and raises it. The close-up reveals a small insect crawling across the windowpane, and as Jim bends to kiss her, the fly appears to enter her uplifted lips. In a single astonishing stroke, Truffaut has poisoned the kiss and, by association with his occupation as an entomologist, signified Jules' presence in this dark moment of intimacy.

Another extraordinary example of the film's visual complexity occurs soon after when Catherine crosses the hall to her husband's room to complain about Jim. After he calmly defends his friend and she accuses him of despising her, Jules replies, "No, Catherine. I have never despised you. I shall always love you, whatever you do, whatever happens." To this point, the sequence has been entirely composed of alternating shots of the two characters, but now, as they embrace and Catherine tearfully recalls their happy moments together, Truffaut includes them both in a tight close-up. This scene balances in intimacy the earlier one with Jim, and again the direction brilliantly undercuts the shot's apparent meaning, for as Catherine kisses Jules, her face fills the screen, threatening to push him off the left edge of the frame. Even at the moment when she appears most vulnerable and affectionate, Catherine needs to dominate.

In the end, however, Catherine's wishes are defeated by the same destiny that overcomes all human beings. She had wanted her ashes cast to the winds, the narrator relates, "but it was not permitted." *Jules and Jim* remains a paean to those who dream of living in total freedom, who dare to defy existing rules, and who, in failing, affirm the wonder of all human aspiration.

Lloyd Michaels

JULIET OF THE SPIRITS
(GIULIETTA DEGLI SPIRITI)

Origin: Italy
Released: 1965
Released in U.S.: 1965
Production: Angelo Rizzoli
Direction: Federico Fellini
Screenplay: Federico Fellini, Tullio Pinelli, Ennio Flaiano, and Brunello
  Rondi
Cinematography: Gianni Di Venanzo
Editing: Ruggero Mastroianni
Art direction: Piero Gherardi
Music: Nino Rota
Running time: 137 minutes

Principal characters:
Juliet	Giulietta Masina
Giorgio	Mario Pisu
Susy/Fanny/Iris	Sandra Milo
Mother	Caterina Boratto
Adele	Luisa Della Noce
Sylva	Sylva Koscina
Grandfather	Lou Gilbert
Valentina	Valentina Cortese
Bhishma	Waleska Gert
Lynx-Eyes	Alberto Plebani
Juliet (as a child)	Alba Cancellieri
Medium	Genius
Oriental lover	Raffaele Guida

When Federico Fellini's *Juliet of the Spirits* was released in 1965, it was
generally viewed as the feminine side of *Otto e mezzo* (1963; *8½*), the film
Fellini had made two years before. In both films, the protagonist is in a
quandary about life and marriage, and in both, fantasies and memories play
a major role. In *8½* the protagonist is the husband, who is, like Fellini, a
film director, while in *Juliet of the Spirits*, the protagonist is the wife, who is
played by Fellini's real wife, Giulietta Masina, although none of the characters in the film is involved in filmmaking. Both films received mixed
reviews. In general, those who did not like *8½* also did not like *Juliet of the
Spirits*, and those who did like *8½* thought that *Juliet of the Spirits* was not
as good as its predecessor.
Despite its two-hour-and-seventeen-minute length, its large cast of

outlandish characters, and its plentiful supply of curious events, *Juliet of the Spirits* has a relatively simple plot. A middle-aged woman, Juliet, feels neglected by her husband, Giorgio (Mario Pisu), and then suspects that he is having an affair. She receives advice from many people as well as from the voices of spirits. Also influencing her feelings and actions are memories and fantasies from her past. After Lynx-Eyes (Alberto Plebani), a private detective whom she has hired, provides conclusive evidence of her husband's affair, Juliet tries to confront Gabriella, the other woman, but she is not at home. Returning to her own home, Juliet finds that Giorgio is leaving on what he describes as a business trip, but Juliet knows that he is going with Gabriella. After Giorgio leaves, various visions pass through the mind of Juliet, but she faces her situation and conquers the spirits that have plagued her, causing them to disappear.

Fellini has described how he wants the conclusion to be seen. He stated that the ending "should mean the discovery of an individuality." Juliet, he says, finds that the departure of her husband is a "gift of Providence," not a catastrophe, and she feels grateful because Giorgio and the other characters—"even those who seemed the most fearful enemies—helped the process of her liberation. In the end, Juliet's real life begins when she comes out of the shadow of Giorgio."

The spirits referred to in the title can be seen as three different types: There is a spirit named Iris (Sandra Milo) who is invoked by a medium; there are a number of characters, from Bhishma (Waleska Gert)—a disgusting-looking person of indeterminate sex who is regarded as an oracle—to Juliet's mother (Caterina Boratto), who freely gives her advice; and there are her memories from her childhood that continue to inhibit her until the film's end.

Most of the characters are introduced in the first sequence. Because it is their wedding anniversary, Juliet plans an intimate candlelight dinner, but when Giorgio arrives, he has not only forgotten the anniversary but also has brought a number of friends with him. These include Valentina (Valentina Cortese), one of the many attractive, extravagantly clothed but superficial women in the film, and the Medium (Genius), the man who conducts the séance and makes contact with Iris. The next long sequence introduces the other main characters: Juliet's sisters, Adele (Luisa Della Noce) and Sylva (Silva Koscina), their mother, and Susy (Sandra Milo), Juliet's neighbor. All of these women are costumed fancifully, which emphasizes the difference between them and Juliet, whose clothing and manner are always restrained. Indeed, her mother tells Juliet that she should wear more makeup.

It is Susy who provides the most contrast to Juliet. Susy is, in fact, so different from Juliet that critic Suzanne Budgen suggests that Susy is "an unrestrained and extravagant version" of Juliet. Susy lives in the house next to that of Juliet and Giorgio. Outside, one sees such adornments as a white peacock and a statue with the head of a hawk but the breasts of a woman. Inside, the decoration is somewhere between ornate and garish, and the people are somewhere between chic and decadent. The centerpiece of the house is Susy's bedroom. It features a large, sumptuous bed with an overhead mirror and a slide that leads to a swimming pool.

Juliet first visits Susy's house to return a cat. She is somewhat intrigued by the outlandish environment—so different from her own. Susy is also interested in Juliet, apparently thinking that Juliet needs a taste of a less inhibited life-style. Susy, in fact, arranges for Juliet to meet, in Susy's bedroom, a young man (Raffaele Guida) who wants to make love to her. Juliet likes the idea at first, but a vision from her religious upbringing quickly changes her mind and she rushes from the room.

Juliet's memories from her past center upon two events: a religious pageant in her school, and her grandfather (Lou Gilbert) running away with a beautiful circus performer, Fanny (Sandra Milo, who also plays Susy and Iris). In the pageant the child Juliet (Alba Cancellieri) plays the part of a Christian martyr. She is placed on a metal grill with crepe paper flames and then raised above the stage by a rope attached to a winch turned by nuns. This is to represent the martyr being burned alive and ascending to heaven. As Juliet begins to rise, however, her grandfather arises in the audience and angrily demands that the performance be stopped because it is a travesty. After this incident, the grandfather calls Juliet a little beefsteak because of her being on the grill. The grandfather's running away with Fanny is always envisioned by Juliet as the two of them taking off in a theatrical airplane used by the circus. This image occurs several times in the film.

The principal image of Juliet's liberation at the end of the film is the mature Juliet going to the young Juliet tied to the grill and—with great effort—untying her, thus setting herself free of her repressive upbringing.

Juliet of the Spirits was made by the same creative team that made *8½*. In addition to Fellini as director and coscenarist, the other writers, the set and costume designer, the cinematographer, and the composer of the music were the same for both films. The great difference, between the films, in addition to the woman protagonist, is that *Juliet of the Spirits* was photographed in color. Since many of the scenes and characters are fanciful or deliberately outrageous, the color is seldom subtle. The opinions on Fellini's use of color ranged from "astonishing" to that of critic John Simon: "brilliant, precise, and tasteless."

Juliet of the Spirits is an interesting film that is almost experimental in its use of color and the occult. Although it is not a masterpiece, it is often dazzling and exciting, which is what one expects from Federico Fellini, one of world cinema's greatest talents.

Timothy W. Johnson

KAGEMUSHA
The Shadow Warrior

Origin: Japan
Released: 1980
Released in U.S.: 1980
Production: Akira Kurosawa and Tomoyuki Tanaka for Toho/Kurosawa
  Productions
Direction: Akira Kurosawa
Screenplay: Akira Kurosawa and Masato Ide
Cinematography: Takao Saito, Masaharu Ueda, Kazuo Miyagawa, and
  Asaichi Nakai
Editing: Keisuke Iwatani
Art direction: Yoshiro Muraki
Costume design: Seiichiro Momosawa
Music: Shinichiro Ikebe
MPAA rating: PG
Running time: 179 minutes
Running time in U.S.: 159 minutes

> *Principal characters:*
> Shingen Takeda/Kagemusha . . . . Tatsuya Nakadai
> Nobukado Takeda . . . . Tsutomo Yamazaki
> Nobunaga Oda . . . . Daisuke Ryu
> Ieyasu Tokugawa . . . . Masayuki Yui
> Takemaru Takeda . . . . Kota Yui
> Katsuyori Takeda . . . . Kenichi Hagiwara

In a career spanning several decades, Japanese film director Akira Kurosawa has put his name on nearly thirty films, about half of them with modern subjects, half of them *jidai-geki*, or period films. Only about half of his films have been distributed on the international art-film circuit, but here the percentage is rather different, with the *jidai-geki* outnumbering the modern films by three to one. The tendency of foreign critics to associate Kurosawa mainly with Samurai films is, therefore, a rather misplaced one: He has devoted as much of his career to analyzing the tensions and pressures of modern Japan as he has to depicting the intricacies of the country's past. *Kagemusha: The Shadow Warrior*, which was set up with the financial help and endorsement of American filmmakers George Lucas and Francis Ford Coppola, is a film which is at once the purest of all of his *jidai-geki*, and, since it is set at a time of total change, the period film which can most easily be seen as a detached reflection on modern Japan.

The film is set during the *sengoku jedai*, the "period of the country at war" which closed the sixteenth century in Japan and which began the two-hundred-and-fifty-year Tokugawa shogunate. This shogunate—"rule of the shoguns"—is the period most closely and obviously associated with the Samurai films, since it was two and a half centuries in which history was arrested. Traditional notions of honor, courage, and duty ruled Japanese court life at Kyoto, while the Tokugawa dynasty ruled the country with as absolute a power as any tyranny has ever exercised. The climax of *Kagemusha: The Shadow Warrior* and the thing toward which the whole film irresistibly tends, is the Battle of Nagashino in May, 1575, at which the Tokugawa wiped out their rivals, the Takeda, using rifles against their opponents' swords and arrows. The paradox of the Battle of Nagashino is that it was the Takeda, with their archaic weapons, who were the ones most likely to introduce change and progress into a country which had effectively kept itself untouched by outside influences since the ninth century. Under the Tokugawa, Japan would remain entirely self-contained for another 250 years. It is, perhaps, this point which most closely relates *Kagemusha: The Shadow Warrior* to Kurosawa's modern films, since it touches on a problem that is important in all of them: the tendency of Japan's ruling classes to acquire such elements of Western civilization as enable them to maintain their power (in this case, the rifles), while rigorously keeping any of the attendant benefits of Western-style progress from the population at large. This flirtation with the West, Kurosawa suggests, has accounted for many of Japan's strengths and weaknesses.

Kurosawa's own relationship to the Samurai period is a complex one: He seems both to admire its style and the Samurai's steely sense of identity and to deplore their authoritarianism and violence. *Kagemusha: The Shadow Warrior* is, accordingly, both violent and beautiful, a simultaneous celebration and criticism of the values of feudal Japan. The comparison between Kurosawa and the American director John Ford has often been made, and Kurosawa himself has openly acknowledged the influence of Ford on his masterpiece, *Shichinin no samurai* (1954; *Seven Samurai*). The quality that Kurosawa shares most obviously with Ford is an ambiguous relationship to a key period of his country's history: For Kurosawa, this period is the Tokugawa *shogūnate*; for Ford, it was the period of the American frontier. *Kagemusha: The Shadow Warrior* could be seen as Kurosawa's *Cheyenne Autumn* (1964)—an elegant and eloquent farewell to an era about which he has made some of his finest films.

The focus of *Kagemusha: The Shadow Warrior* is the Takeda clan. Shingen Takeda (Tatsuya Nakadai) is mortally wounded at the start of the film during the siege of Noda Castle. In order to conceal his death from their rivals—and prevent Shingen's impulsive son, Katsuyori (Kenichi Hagiwara) taking over the clan—Shingen's brother Nobukado (Tsutomo Yamazaki reprieves a condemned thief (Tatsuya Nakadai) from crucifixion because of his resemblance to the dead clan leader (both parts are played by the same actor), and coaches him as a *kagemusha*, or shadow warrior—a tradition quite common among Japanese ruling families, since it relieved the leader of certain of his more onerous official duties. Nobukado had previously fulfilled the role, helped by the formality of Japanese court dress and traditions, but his resemblance to his brother is not close enough to carry off so total an impersonation. The *kagemusha* is at first inept and strongly resistant to the loss of his own identity. As time goes by, and especially at the fierce battle around the supposedly impregnable Takatenjin Castle, he begins to adopt many of the habits and skills of Shingen, especially the latter's tendency to remain staunchly and fiercely immobile during battle.

The *kagemusha* manages to carry off a particularly difficult aspect of the deception by the ingenious device of joking with the royal concubines (who are, after all, more likely to notice the difference than anybody else) that he is indulging himself in the fantasy of pretending to be an impostor. Yet he strikes up a close relationship with young Takemaru Takeda (Kota Yui), Shingen's grandson, who comes to idolize him. Gradually, the hauntings by Shingen's ghost that the *kagemusha* experiences fade away, and his old identity becomes all but forgotten. It is this which leads to his downfall. The adoring Takemaru persuades him to ride Shingen's horse, an animal which no one else has ever been able to tame. He is thrown, and in the process of tending him, the concubines notice the absence of Shingen's battle scars.

Now that his imposture has become public knowledge, the *kagemusha* is no longer of any use to the clan, and they peremptorily eject him from the castle. Shingen is finally buried in state, and his impetuous son, Katsuyori, succeeds him. Observed by the *kagemusha* from a bush on the battlefield, Katsuyori leads the Takeda against the Tokugawa at Nagashino, and the clan is wiped out. Appalled, the *kagemusha* comes out of his hiding place and is mortally wounded. As his final act, he walks out to his death in the misty lake in which his noble double had previously been buried. The Takeda are finished and the *kagemusha*, now as much a ghost as the man whom he had impersonated, goes to join them.

Kagemusha: The Shadow Warrior is Kurosawa's late masterpiece, a somber, stately, reflective film with all the complexity of William Shakespeare's *The Tempest* (1611). The slightly shortened "international version," though, distributed in the United States by Twentieth Century-Fox, makes the opening sequences particularly difficult to follow. This is to a certain extent built into Kurosawa's treatment of the material, since not only is he dealing with a period whose basic outlines would have been as familiar to Japanese audiences as the Civil War to Americans, but he is also not concerned so much with the history of the period as with the myths that have grown out of it which link it to modern Japan. The film was reputed to be the most expensive ever made in Japan, and the wide-screen array of authentically armor-clad soldiers is, during the battle scenes, breathtaking. Many other of the set-piece scenes are also extremely beautiful, especially those with Katsuyori in the bare, sharply lit lakeside house, and the burial of Shingen. Almost all the scenes in the film compare with the best compositions that Kurosawa, who is also an accomplished oil painter, has ever achieved on the screen.

The film's elegiac tone, combined with its formal perfection, tends to make *Kagemusha: The Shadow Warrior* beautiful but cold, an exercise in form and symmetry which lacks the rough edges of energy that have brought other Kurosawa epics such as *Seven Samurai, Kumonosu-jo* (1957; *Throne of Blood*), and *Sanjuro* (1962) suddenly and unforgettably to life. *Kagemusha: The Shadow Warrior* is, in every sense of the word, an epic, and, like many epics, it is often more to be admired than enjoyed.

As a summation of Kurosawa's film career, though, it is technically and thematically flawless. The battle scenes are shot with the same telephoto lenses which, in *Seven Samurai*, thrust the viewer directly into the midst of the action, before pulling back to reveal the overall pattern. The effect is riveting, since it enables the viewer simultaneously to appreciate the strategy and to be caught up in the visceral excitement and danger of the battle. The pacing of the film as a whole is along the lines evolved by Kurosawa throughout his career, in both the *jidai-geki* and the modern films: long periods of static tension, broken by brief flurries of action—as when the messenger, seen from above, descends flight after flight of steps and, in so doing, awakens the whole army—a sequence which closely echoes the opening one in *Kakushi toride no san-akunin* (1958; *The Hidden Fortress*). The color, too, is controlled and enhanced rather than real, as it was in Kurosawa's bizarre and underrated experimental color film *Dodeskaden* (1970), with the battle scenes taking on a stately and somewhat nightmarish beauty. Finally, the moment at which the *kagemusha* is obliged to say goodbye to his adopted grandson Takemaru, who is staring back helplessly at him from outside the bars of the castle gate, is one which recalls Kurosawa's modern masterpiece *Ikiru* (1952) in its ability suddenly to inject a moment of pure and overwhelming emotion into what had previously seemed a detached and slightly unfeeling film.

Nick Roddick

KAMERADSCHAFT

Origin: Germany
Released: 1931
Released in U.S.: 1932
Production: Seymour Nebenzahl for Nero Films, Gaumont, and Franco-Film-Aubert
Direction: G. W. Pabst
Assistant direction: Herbert Rappoport
Screenplay: Karl Otten, Peter Martin Lampel, and Ladislaus Vajda
Cinematography: Fritz Arno Wagner and Robert Baberske
Editing: Hans Oser
Art direction: Erno Metzner and Karl Vollbrecht
Music: no listing
Running time: 93 minutes
Also known as: Comradeship

> *Principal characters:*
> Wilderer . . . . Fritz Kampers
> Kaplan . . . . Gustav Püttjer
> Kaspers . . . . Alexander Granach
> Françoise . . . . Andrée Ducret
> Jean . . . . Georges Charlia
> Wittkopp . . . . Ernst Busch
> Émile . . . . Daniel Mandaille
> Georges . . . . Pierre Louis
> Grandfather . . . . Alex Bernard

Because of its location at the confluence of Germany's two main aesthetic orientations of the 1920's and 1930's—Expressionism and realism—G. W. Pabst's film legacy has frequently proved problematic to those critics seeking clearly defined boundaries between the two. Fluent in both styles, Pabst tempered his efforts in either with elements of the other, but his most lasting contributions were to the realist cinema. His early explorations of realism in *Die freudlose Gasse* (1925; *The Street of Sorrow*) signaled the start of a movement in film that would witness the creation of masterpieces such as Walter Ruttmann's *Berlin—Die Symphonie einer Grosstadt* (1927; *Berlin—Symphony of a Big City*) and Robert Siodmak and Edgar G. Ulmer's *Menschen am Sonntag* (1929; *People on Sunday*). By the start of the 1930's, particularly in *Westfront 1918* (1930) and *Kameradschaft*, Pabst's own realist film style reached its highest state of refinement.

Like *Westfront 1918*, *Kameradschaft* is a plea for international understanding and pacifism presented through the experiences of ordinary characters, this time through the story of a disaster in the French portion of a coal mine that runs underneath the French-German border and is jointly mined by both countries. By examining different kinds of relationships—fraternal solidarity within and between the French and German miners, the romantic bond between a miner and his fiancée, and the family tie between a man and his grandson—Pabst examines the complex influences that produce nationalism and suggests forces that can overcome it.

Kameradschaft's subject, treatment, and production design provide strong examples of Pabst's multivalent realism. The characters are drawn from the working-class milieu of the French and German mining communities, and are presented in an unglamorized way. The exteriors were filmed mostly on location at the Gelsenkirchen and Betugne mines, and the interiors were designed by Erno Metzner with compelling authenticity. Pabst's selection of cameramen, however, tempered this manifest realism. Robert Baberske (who photographed Ruttmann's documentary *Berlin—Symphony of a Big City*) and Fritz Arno Wagner (renowned for his expressive use of moving camera techniques) joined forces to create an almost documentary realism that was nevertheless evocative and expressive. Although both styles are evident in the film, the recurrent imagery of the elements—earth, fire, water, and air (smoke)—unifies its visual structure.

Kameradschaft was based on a 1906 French mine disaster in which more than one thousand men died. In order to relate the film to the growing problem of German nationalism, and particularly the ill feelings about the terms of the Versailles Treaty, Pabst set the story in the Lorraine area on the French-German border in the period just after the war. Located at this controversial juncture, his themes of pacifism and brotherhood reverberate with pronounced clarity. This attempt to deal with contemporary social and political conditions is an important dimension of Pabst's realism and an index of his artistic integrity. Although idealistic and perhaps even naïve in its views, *Kameradschaft* was one of the last nonpolitically aligned feature-film appeals for pacifism and reason before the rise to power of the National Socialists.

Pabst's reputation as a director rests mainly on his power as a visual dramatist. In *Kameradschaft*, sound, dialogue, and acting serve secondary functions in what is primarily an imagistically conceived narrative. The film is structured on spatial boundaries—above the ground or below it, on the French side of the border or the German—and it is within these visual sectors that sound and language play a supporting role. The first three scenes in the film form a prelude to the narrative and provide an example of one of Pabst's addictive visual strategies.

As the film opens, two small boys, one French, one German, are playing marbles near the border. Several German workers approach, and as they pass the German checkpoint, a guard remarks that they will probably be denied entrance into France in their attempt to find work. The men are indeed turned away, but the emotional tension of the scene is expressed through the boys, whose game suddenly erupts in a quarrel. Pabst cuts to the interior of the German part of the mine, and this suggestion of tension takes on a more ominous tone. One of the miners notes with concern that a fire is burning in the French sector, and in the French tunnel, an inspector observes increasing gas levels and orders the reinforcement of a wall to contain the fire. The confining, smoke-filled tunnels and the camera's tracking movements toward the fire create a sense of smoldering danger.

This prelude introduces the central conflicts of the film—that is, the national border problem and the danger in the mine—before the introduction of the main characters. Moreover, it establishes the divisions that will permeate and motivate the film: national territory, language, and identity, both above and below the ground.

These elements combine as the plot begins to take form in a smoky French dance hall. Three German miners, Wilderer (Fritz Kampers), Kaplan (Gustav Püttjer), and Kaspers (Alexander Granach), venture into the milieu of their French counterparts for the evening. Pabst maintains the use of two languages not only to enhance the realism of the scene but also to express the miners' isolation and underscore the divisions of nationality. The tension established in the prelude intensifies when one of the Germans approaches Françoise (Andrée Ducret), who, unknown to him, is accompanied by her fiancé, Jean (Georges Charlia). Her curt refusal to dance and her abusive remarks nearly provoke a fight, and finally the infuriated Germans leave.

Just as this scene provides a verbal edge to the national division, the subsequent scenes articulate the tensions between above- and below-ground. Françoise refuses to sacrifice her future to the evident dangers of Jean's occupation as a miner, arguing that if their planned marriage fails to encourage Jean to seek better working conditions, it is best called off. She leaves him, and the intensity of their argument is visually reinforced as the dreaded explosion rips through the mine. The disaster, which traps Jean among many others, motivates the exploration of the film's two main divisions through other relationships. Françoise's anger and reluctance to sacrifice, which disappears when she learns of the disaster, is counterpointed by the unselfish love of an old man (Alex Bernard) who steals into the mine to save his grandson, Georges (Pierre Louis). These two relationships suggest a strategy of balance in the creation, division, and articulation of the narrative, enabling Pabst to portray the emotional complexities of an otherwise abstract set of issues.

In a rapidly cut montage, the frenzied townspeople rush to the mine entrance to learn the fate of the workers. Shifting from scenes of the anguished families above ground as they push against the mine's gates, to scenes of the miners below-ground in their struggle for survival, Pabst enhances the formal paralleling previously established with the border.

Meanwhile, Pabst uses a shift change in the German mines to modulate the dominant visual elements established to this point. The fire and smoke of the mine tunnels and the sweaty faces of the surging French crowd are contrasted by the German shower room, rich with images of water, reflections, steam, and a sensuality absent from the previous scenes. As is often the case in Pabst's films, textures, light, and compositional elements are as fully expressive as the narrative they support. In *Kameradschaft*, Pabst uses these elements as images to reinforce and interconnect the dualities that pervade the film and to unify visually an otherwise disparate set of experiences.

The above-ground romantic and familial bonds are themselves balanced by two sets of underground relationships. One of the German miners, Wittkopp (Ernst Busch), pleads for solidarity and urges his comrades to help their trapped French brothers. He forms a rescue team, and they head for the French mine. This view is balanced by the three miners who had experienced the problem in the French dance hall, who voice their nationalist sentiments and refuse to join. Plot symmetry is enhanced, however, when these three, like Françoise earlier, have a change of heart and decide to become involved. One of them, Kaspers, knows a shortcut that will enable them to bypass collapsed portions of the mine, and they set off on their own rescue mission. When they reach the 1919 underground border, they destroy it to reach the French. Again, Pabst parallels the events above ground, where Wittkopp and his team ignore the commands of the French border guards and break through the checkpoint.

The themes of nationalism and the lingering trauma of war which smolder throughout the film become explicit in a dramatic departure from the documentary realism that dominates the film to this point. A German rescue worker, in gas mask and helmet, finds a French miner partially overcome by gas. When he hears his rescuer's language, the French miner thinks that he is in the war and under attack. Pabst relies on an advanced form of the psychological realism developed earlier, in his *Geheimnisse einer Seele* (1926; *Secrets of a Soul*), forcefully depicting the miner's battle hallucinations in scenes that recall *Westfront 1918*, made the previous year.

This dramatic expression of the film's theme is sustained, albeit on a more mundane verbal level, following the successful rescue of the trapped miners. In a ceremony at the border checkpoint, the German representative recalls the problems of the Versailles Treaty but points to the moral obligations that transcend nationality and the underlying human bonds that unite workers of both countries. The French representative, thanking the Germans, points out that their common enemies are gas and war. Although moving, this verbal reiteration of the film's dramatic and visual substance is redundant and ultimately weak. Some versions of the film (not those usually available in the United States) have an epilogue, in which the French and German officials meet to reestablish the underground barrier. This ending, however, largely subverts the meaning of the earlier scene in which Kaspers and his comrades destroy the gate, and it emphasizes official division despite the solidarity of the workers.

Kameradschaft remains an essentially visual narrative, even with the verbal excesses of the closing scenes. The themes and their connection to contemporary social problems are enhanced by the film's realist visual style. Thus, Pabst's characters, their setting and depiction, form a tightly woven fabric that stands as one of the high points of prewar German realism. The components of this style and orientation strongly influenced subsequent documentary production and reaffirm the integrity of Pabst's artistic vision.

William Uricchio

KAMIKAZE 1989

Origin: West Germany
Released: 1982
Released in U.S.: 1983
Production: Regina Ziegler Filmproduktion/Trio Film/Oase Filmproduktion
Direction: Wolf Gremm
Screenplay: Wolf Gremm and Robert Katz; based on the novel *Murder on the 31st Floor*, by Per Wahlöö
Cinematography: Xaver Schwarzenberger
Editing: Thorsten Näter
Art direction: Horst Furcht
Makeup: Barbara Naujok
Costume design: Barbara Naujok
Music: Edgar Froese of Tangerine Dream
MPAA rating: no listing
Running time: 106 minutes

Principal characters:
Inspector Jansen .... Rainer Werner Fassbinder
Anton .... Günther Kaufmann
"Blue Panther" .... Boy Gobert
Police Chief .... Arnold Marquis
Barbara .... Nicole Heesters
Elena .... Petra Jokisch
Personnel director .... Brigitte Mira
Nephew .... Richy Müller
Vice-president .... Jörg Holm
Zerling...................... Hans Wyprächtiger
Weiss .... Franco Nero

Kamikaze 1989 stars the late Rainer Werner Fassbinder in a bizarre detective story set in the near future. Fassbinder plays Jansen, a detective with a perfect crime-solving record, on a case that pits him against the all-engulfing pop-media conglomerate known as the Combine. A bomb threat forces the "Blue Panther" (Boy Gobert), as the Combine president is known, to evacuate thirty floors of the Combine's skyscraper headquarters. Jansen sets out to find out who sent the threat.

The work is hard, but the Combine suddenly makes it harder. The Combine president's own nephew (Richy Müller) disingenuously confesses to the crime and, when this does not throw off Jansen, tries to run him off the road. As he does, the nephew calls himself Krysmopompos (the name combines two Greek words meaning "anointed guide"), a spirit of evil from one of the Combine's most popular comic books.

Yet Jansen doggedly tracks suspects through the heroin joints, slums, warehouses, mansions, and corporate headquarters of an industrial world collapsing under the weight of its own corruption. His only clue is a fragment of the bomb threat linking its author to previous employment at the Combine. His last suspect turns out to be the bomber. He confesses that he worked as a house intellectual there for eight years, on a secret thirty-first floor, before realizing that the division was a kind of prison of creativity; nothing that the group did ever saw the light of day. His bomb threat was a nihilistic attempt to revenge himself on the Combine.

Jansen rushes back to the skyscraper, where another bomb threat is in process. All thirty floors are evacuated. Jansen knows the Combine's secret—that there is a thirty-first floor full of troublesome intellectuals who have not been told. He is too late to save them. Not only has he lost the case, but also he has lost his position. When he returns to the office, they are moving his furniture out, leaving him the cold promise symbolized by his poster of Neil Armstrong standing on the moon.

The story has a hectic, action-packed pace, but it may be the least important part of the film. (The screenplay is drawn from a much more spare 1964 crime thriller, the novel *Murder on the 31st Floor*, by Swedish writer Per Wahlöö.) The plot is a clothesline on which the director hangs a vision of a future—indeed a present—at once authoritarian and permissive.

Authoritarianism asserts itself in the workplace, especially in the ruthless and peremptory hierarchy of the Combine. It is reflected in architecture that is inhumane on a Fascist scale but coated with a steel-and-glass modernity; it is also found in the ever-present police surveillance and casual brutality. Personal style, however, is wildly permissive. Coldly cruel top executives dress in bright yellow jumpsuits with shiny spangles; a neon sign flashing a picture of a hypodermic adorns the bar next to police headquarters; police badges are gaudy buttons; streetwear comes in a profusion of mannerist complementary colors. Fashion is everything—the rich indulge in nouveau-riche splendor while the poor live in corners littered with gaudy junk and dye their hair in pink and blue stripes. *Kamikaze 1989* is reminiscent of *Diva* (1980) in its visual inventiveness and playfulness, and like it too in making wit take the place of money—the film was made for approximately one million dollars and shot on a marathon, twenty-five-day shoot.

The contradictions of this society are on a collision course, and the police seem to be at the intersection. At one point an underling complains to the always cynical Jansen, as the police shovel drunks out of vans, that the police first prohibit alcohol, then create a society where people have to drink themselves silly, and then arrest and beat them. Irrationality and hyperrationality come to the same thing. As the Combine's secretary expresses it when she speculates that the Combine itself may have planted the bomb to collect the insurance and build even bigger headquarters, business may not be good, but that does not stop the Combine from growing.

The tawdry pop look of the film is a constant comment on the terms of this society's collapse. One of the symptoms of the general social illness is the cancerous overproduction of meaningless information. The disinformation of daily life has become an addictive anesthetic, a drug on which the Combine has built a media empire. Everywhere, even in elevators, television sets are tuned in to the Combine's biggest hit show—a laughing contest. Beautiful, seminude young women in disco cages laugh for hours and even days, the edge of insanity in their voices unnoticed by those who watch with a blank narcotized look. Occasionally the show breaks away for "happy talk" weather: In 1989, the weather is always fine.

Electronic distraction has ceased to be novel. The sound of videogames pongs off the walls in the background sound track, while modernistic jukeboxes provide for the 1989 citizen who is temporarily without white noise. As in *Blade Runner* (1982), much of this machinery is in decay. Jansen's home microwave, for example, is as dispirited as the sandwich that he puts into it.

The information addiction goes beyond consumption. The videocamera has become as ubiquitous as the Instamatic is today. It is a world where people record their casual interactions and then play them back, as if the real stuff of life were in the video replay of it. At one point, Jansen and a suspect show each other their recordings of the same moment. Even the police's third degree has a postmodern, high-tech touch: Torture is executed on a mixing board.

Wolf Gremm's heady use of popular culture comes from a complicated attitude toward it. He celebrates its energy but is also appalled by its capacity to be manipulated by an elite, whether corporate or political. The cheap popular culture of *Kamikaze 1989* is not a critique of modern mass culture but a comment on the dangers of having mass culture controlled from the top. The point is made when the corporate head picks up a telephone in the shape of Superman, and again when a glimpse into a slum room shows a magazine photographer at work making an accident fatality look sexy and fashionable. (Sex is all fashion, no passion in this film; some of the costumes are sadomasochistically kinky, but no one has an intimate relationship.)

In the midst of this brain-clouding excess of information, Jansen has a curt motto: "Avoid unnecessary remarks." He is a truthseeker, although not necessarily a good man. Jansen is not one of Raymond Chandler's heroes, no last honest man in a corrupt world. His integrity is all in his egotism. Cruel to his subordinates, casually brutal to his suspects, and settled into a disheveled, lonely personal life, he only goes up against the Combine because he will not let a mere worldwide conspiracy stand in the way of his unblemished record.

The differences between the book and film suggest that Gremm's vision may yet come true. Wahlöö used his thin plot to make a sharp criticism of the affluent welfare state, charging it with creating alienation by pacifying dissidents rather than by encouraging social control of production and real control over one's life. He has one of the suspects say, in the English translation of the book, "We were so dazzled by our own excellence, so filled with confidence with the results of so-called practical politics . . . that socialism became in itself superfluous. . . . The problems were lied away. They were smothered by the constantly rising material standard of living, or clouded by meaniningless talk which was pumped out via the radio and television. . . . Reaction in the individual was first confusion and then gradually indifference. At the root of all this lay this indefinite fear."

By 1982, when *Kamikaze 1989* was released, Gremm's near future, reflecting the jerry-rigged quality of modern, short-term economic solutions was all too evident. The dependence of the Scandinavian welfare state on an economic boom had become uncomfortably apparent and was the subject of the Swedish film *Sally och Friheten* (1982; *Sally and Freedom*), directed by Gunnell Lindblom. The process that Wahlöö charted in 1964 is boldly accelerated in Gremm's adaptation. Where Wahlöö's agent of disinformation is the comic book, Gremm's is electronic media. The cathode-ray tube dominates the landscape and penetrates the senses in a way that no Batman comic could.

It comes as no surprise that the film does not end happily. It is appropriate that the film should be more about appearances and style, reflecting a tactile sensibility, than about plot and character. Like the world it describes, the film is overwhelmed by its own gimmickry.

Pat Aufderheide

KANAŁ

Origin: Poland
Released: 1957
Released in U.S.: 1961
Production: Stanisław Adler for Film Polski
Direction: Andrzej Wajda
Screenplay: Jerzy Stefan Stawiński; based on his play
Cinematography: Jerzy Lipman
Editing: Halina Nawrocka
Art direction: Roman Mann
Music: Jan Krenz
Running time: 96 minutes
Also known as: Canal and *They Loved Life*

Principal characters:
Daisy . . . . Teresa Iżewska
Korab . . . . Tadeusz Janczar
Zadra. . . . . Wieńczyław Gliński
Madry . . . . Emil Karewicz
Composer . . . . Władysław Sheybal
Kula. . . . . Tadeusz Gwiazdowski
Smukly . . . . Stanizław Mikulski
Halinka. . . . . Teresa Berezowska

Since the end of World War II, Andrzej Wajda has been Poland's preeminent director. In film after film, he has taken on controversial subjects in a variety of styles that mirror the tumultuous changes in his country's politics and culture. His own peculiar blend of realism and romanticism, and of history and myth, makes it difficult for critics to agree on the nature and the quality of his achievement. Like all Central European filmmakers, he has also had to contend with state censorship, so that audiences in Poland and elsewhere have been prone to "read between the lines" and to attribute an allegorical significance to his films that he has often, as in the case of his *Danton* (1982), denied. However one ranks Wajda, his influence on Polish artists and on world cinema is widespread. Outside Poland, he is perhaps best known in France, where his blending of the symbolic and the documentary modes has been well received notwithstanding the largely negative response to *Danton*, which was made there.

Kanał is a representative Wajda film. It is set in late September, 1944, just after the Warsaw Uprising in August. Warsaw is nearly leveled to the ground by the Nazis, and three groups of Poles try to find a way out of the city through its sewers (*kanaly*). The film spares no effort in portraying, in documentary fashion, the foul underground environment in which the escapees, who have fought valiantly for their nation, struggle to survive. Roman Mann's sets superbly convey the claustrophobia experienced by a people driven literally to the depths of despair. All that is left is the will to imagine a better world above—one in which the sun still shines, as one character notes.

It is virtually impossible to contest the authenticity of Wajda's film, which is measurably enhanced by Jerzy Stawiński's screenplay, based on his own experiences during the Warsaw Uprising as a Home Army officer. Inevitably, however, *Kanał's* subversive political implications have to be considered, since the film's characters are not Communists. Indeed, they represent the remnants of the Home Army, loyal to the government in exile in London, the very government that Poland's Communist rulers replaced after the war. *Kanał*, moreover, reflects (without deliberately trying to do so) a period in Polish politics in which a much more candid view of the war years was emerging in public discussion.

Indeed, it is remarkable that such a somber motion picture should appear in a country that officially celebrates the Communist triumph over Fascism, the country's "liberation" by the Soviet Union, and tries to ridicule the Home Army's contribution to Poland's defense. To many Poles, however, the very act of confronting without illusions their wretched defeat in the unrelenting grimness of *Kanał* was liberating after many years of the postwar goverment's emphasis on showing the positive or balanced picture of society. Many American reviewers missed this essential point when complaining about *Kanał's* heavy-handed approach to the depiction of suffering. The film's prologue employs camera pans, long tracking shots, and close-ups of characters—accompanied by the foreboding language of a voice-over narrator—to establish simultaneously the utter individuality of each person's agony and the collective tragedy of the "last hours of their lives." There are no plots to follow in the film; what is left is the horrendous journey through the sewers. Madry (Emil Karewicz), a romantic in the traditional self-destructive Polish way, actually finds a route out of the dim sewers only to fall dazedly into the grips of the expectant German soldiers. Daisy (Teresa Iżewska) and Korab (Tadeusz Janczar), on the other hand, are sentimentalists who linger over long conversations about love and reach an opening to the river that is cut off by an iron grille. Zadra (Wieńczyław Gliński), a Home Army officer, is the least certain of all these characters that there is a way out of the sewers or out of the irrationality of Polish history—the commitment to lost causes—which has defeated reason so many times. He is *Kanał's* skeptic, yet his service in the Home Army makes him, in many ways, the film's most committed character.

As Bolesław Michałek puts it, *Kanał* "is a singular blend of the affirmative and the critical." As such, the film puzzles viewers who are not certain whether Wajda is dealing in ambiguities that enrich his handling of complex viewpoints or is caught in a confusion over how to respond to the conflicts his characters express over romantic and realistic modes of perception. Zadra, for example, is hardly unreasonable in his rejection of the Polish tendency to sacrifice everything for a hopeless cause—whether that cause is the Warsaw Uprising or the earlier insurrections in the eighteenth and nineteenth centuries against the foreign rulers of Poland. There is a histrionic side to Wajda's characters—even the realists such as Zadra—that is itself, perhaps, a form of romanticism. Zadra's vehemence is understandable, but as a result of Gliński's declamatory acting style, the character's considerable integrity never quite prevails over the very fanaticism that he deplores.

One way of interpreting *Kanał* is to call it a Polish *No Exit*, and there is merit in an analysis that would stress the Dantesque quality of the hellish experience of a trapped people facing the final end of their illusions. Opposed to this metaphysical view would be the political argument that *Kanał* is an allegory about a country crumbling under the massive weight of the Soviet Union, which did not come to the aid of the Home Army during the Warsaw Uprising. With Poland's well-developed underground, a whole subculture, in fact, which counters the government's official versions of history, it is not difficult to regard a film set in the sewers of Warsaw as a symbolic statement about a populace barely holding on to its dreams of a faraway freedom.

Because the director and screenwriter are so careful to demonstrate what individuals do to themselves—as well as what history makes them do—it is not fair to treat *Kanał* in exclusive terms. In other words, it is neither a symbolic morality play nor a political drama, although the film veers toward both and causes viewers to look for a consistent approach, a way of uniting the different levels of meaning. Wajda and Stawiński may be striving, however, to put a question that cannot be satisfactorily answered: How can humanity survive a descent into the sewers and the aftermath of a holocaust? Two reviewers, for example, were particularly struck by the scene in which Halinka (Teresa Berezowska) commits suicide after learning from Madry, with whom she has been flirting, that he has a wife and child. He shows her a picture of his family, of another world, in truth, from which she is exiled. The flirtation made the sewers just bearable for her, but the illusions which she has entertained about her relationship with Madry are her undoing. She has expected too much of him. Still, the alternative is worse: Expecting too little makes life hardly worth living at all. Disillusionment is difficult to face, but to have no illusions at all would truly flatten life to the level of the sewer. What is most heartening about *Kanał* is that there are survivors as well as suicides. It is beside the point to call the film pessimistic or overly grim, as some reviewers have done, for the images of sunlight filtered through a sewer grating are the only glimpses of hope that can be justified in a world so close to oblivion.

Carl E. Rollyson, Jr.

KEETJE TIPPEL

Origin: The Netherlands
Released: 1975
Released in U.S.: 1976
Production: Rob Houwer for Rob Houwer Film
Direction: Paul Verhoeven
Screenplay: Gerard Soeteman; based on stories by Neel Doff
Cinematography: Jan de Bont
Editing: Jane Sperr
Art direction: Roland de Groot and Dik Schillemans
Music: Rogier van Otterloo
MPAA rating: no listing
Running time: 101 minutes

> *Principal characters:*
> Keetje . . . . Monique van de Ven
> Eitel . . . . Rutger Hauer
> André . . . . Eddie Brugman
> Mina . . . . Hannah de Leeuwe
> Keetje's mother . . . . Andrea Domburg
> Keetje's father . . . . Jan Blaaser
> Painter . . . . Peter Faber

During the 1970's, a new wave of big-budget "commercial" productions marked the history of Dutch cinema. Rob Houwer, who in that period became an influential producer, took some calculated risks invariably and courageously involving his own money and started to collaborate with director Paul Verhoeven and scriptwriter Gerard Soeteman. This team embarked on a series of feature films that collectively have earned more money than could ever have been imagined on the Dutch market. The financial success of *Wat zien ik?* (1971) and *Turks Fruit* (1972; *Turkish Delight*) cleared the way for more expensive productions, such as *Keetje Tippel* and *Soldaat van Oranje* (1977; *Soldier of Orange*). Paul Verhoeven has distinguished himself more by his striking idiosyncratic style than by his choice of subject, which, in fact, has proved to be extremely varied: from a comedic report of the prostitution industry in modern Amsterdam (*Wat zien ik?*) to the serious and tragic story of a romance (*Turkish Delight*), from the realistic account of the hard conditions of working-class life in nineteenth century Amsterdam (*Keetje Tippel*) to the epic screen version of a historical novel concerning the Netherlands in wartime (*Soldier of Orange*). Verhoeven may be criticized by his intellectual contemporaries, yet he has established a rapport with the Dutch public of which any director might be proud. His plain treatment of any subject whatsoever, together with his interest in the social behavior of the individual, apparently appeals to the sober and matter-of-fact mentality of the Dutch. He does not wish to impose on his audience a personal view on life or society at the expense of representing people and facts credibly and realistically.

It had always been Verhoeven's ambition to work on important historic subjects, particularly on the role that outstanding men play in history—the influence certain people are able to exercise over their surroundings so as to obtain power over the masses. Verhoeven wished to present characters thrust into extreme situations, such as revolution, war, or catastrophe, as a matrix for the rise of personalities such as Napoleon and Adolf Hitler. In short, Verhoeven wished to examine the interaction of group and individual in a historical context.

Although these processes fascinated Verhoeven, he could not allow himself to start on such an ambitious project as soon as he would have liked, because the costs of a costume film with crowd scenes were prohibitive. After *Turkish Delight*, however, he could partly realize his ambitions by making *Keetje Tippel*. In contrast with the closed "microworld" of the former film, in which relatively little attention is paid to the description of the social background of the two protagonists, there is considerable widening of perspective in the latter. In *Keetje Tippel*, daily street life and the contact between different classes of people have taken on greater importance. In fact, at one point, producer Rob Houwer had to interfere with the script, because Verhoeven and Soeteman were so attracted by the idea of representing the historic Eel Revolt of 1886 (when the poor disobeyed an official regulation in Amsterdam, and the consequent riots were put down with much bloodshed by the army) that they digressed from the real story of Keetje Tippel.

Keetje Tippel is composed of a number of autobiographical stories by Neel Doff (1858-1942), who, when she was a rich Belgian widow, wrote about her former misadventures. The separate, independent stories lacked a consistent dramatical composition; the principle of the chronological order in Keetje Tippel's life had to compensate for the want of structure.

When the film opens, Keetje Oldeman (Monique van de Ven)—the surname Oldeman will give way to the nickname Tippel, alluding to the prostitution to which she was driven—and her family are waiting to sail for Amsterdam. (By the end of the nineteenth century, many impoverished workers had moved from the country to the urban centers in the hope of finding work and riches.) The Oldeman family is leaving Stavoren, a fishing village in the northern province of Friesland. The year is 1881; Keetje is still an adolescent girl (Neel Doff would have been about twenty-three years old). The first few shots anticipate in a minor key the great difficulties they are likely to encounter: the very large family, all of them wrapped in rags, is sheltering from the heavy rain, which delays the ship's departure. Keetje is being sent by her mother to look for her father (Jan Blaaser). She finds him in a nearby public house. She watches through the window at the humiliation that he has to endure in order to get a free drink. Then, for a few seconds, the point of view shifts, and the face of Keetje can be seen from inside: It shows a blank expression, but the raindrops that keep falling on the glass of the window intensify the emotional effect more than tears could do.

The weather clears, and the ocean crossing begins. The family has not been allowed to enter the cabin; lacking sufficient money, they are obliged to make the passage in the ship's hold. In bird's-eye view, the camera slowly moves in circles around the proud three-mast sailing ship, which in its picturesque splendor seems to emphasize the contrast between illusion and reality. The following scene, still on the ship, portrays the different members of the family. An embittered mother (Andrea Domberg) confronts her guilty husband; the small-fry fight over a puppy dog; Keetje finds temporary distraction in reading; Mina (Hannah de Leeuwe), the elder sister, sells herself for a piece of bread. After their arrival in Amsterdam, they hardly manage to earn a living. Keetje finds work as a washerwoman in a factory but is sent away after a quarrel with the other women workers. Father is dismissed very soon, and Mina has to leave her "job" at the brothel as well. Working at a milliner's, Keetje for the first time becomes acquainted with the world of the middle class. She is impressed by its riches and is attached to her job. Disastrously, the employer rapes her after closing time, and she is again unemployed. One evening she is forced by her mother into prostitution. Keetje reluctantly obeys and carries out her instructions, while her mother is admiring the meats displayed in the window of the butcher's shop. Keetje, however, is a strong personality. Her pride and sense of justice help her to overcome even the most difficult times. By chance, Keetje meets a Socialist painter (Peter Faber), who asks her to sit for a large painting representing a revolt led by a woman. He introduces her to his friends, who take the open and spontaneous girl to their hearts. One of them, Eitel (Rutger Hauer), a bank clerk, falls in love with Keetje, and they start to live together. She adjusts herself very quickly to her new standard of life and assists Eitel in his work. Later, he betrays her devotion to him by becoming engaged to the manager's daughter. Disheartened by this act of hypocritical conformity, she leaves his house at once. Joining a fortuitously passing protest-march of Socialists, she is able to express all her rage and disillusionment in a confrontation with the police. Many people are killed, but Keetje is saved by the painter and his friend André (Eddie Brugman), who, as they are running away, is wounded by a bullet. Keetje takes care of him and accompanies him home. André lives in a beautiful country house and is a wealthy man. As Keetje sits next to him and caresses him, the film freezes; an explanatory "post-scriptum" informs the audience of their eventual marriage.

The script left out, quite rightly, the episode of the romance between André and Keetje. A second love story in the film would have been, dramatically speaking, a failure, just as the original Eel Revolt version had been a mistake. Indeed, the final scene compresses the most important aspects of the film in a climax: The antithesis between the peaceful luxury of the rich and the violent revolt of the poor and, on the other hand, Keetje's willingness to put up with any kind of injustice, in combination with her unselfish love for her fellowman, are entwined throughout the film.

Keetje's resoluteness heroically manifests itself more than once: In the factory, she faces the women workers' anger, as she ingenuously sings her father's favorite Socialist song and is consequently punished; on the king's birthday, she assaults a baker's cart and is seriously hurt during the police charge; she throws a stone through the milliner's shop-window, avenging herself on her treacherous employer. In the end, her perseverance is rewarded, for in Keetje's rise to luxury and some measure of prominence, there would seem to be optimism. Man's dignity depends not upon wealth but upon his character, according to the fundamental moral of the story. Keetje comments to André that money turns people into rats, and the decadent *fin de siècle* theme song "Money Lies About the Streets" ironically confirms that. Verhoeven's approach, however, avoids drawing such an explicit conclusion: He prefers to show rather than to explain. In his filming, Verhoeven anxiously tries to keep his distance with regard to his subject, and *Keetje Tippel* reflects this. The scene in which Eitel hints to Keetje that she has to leave, for example, shows Eitel, in front, covering Keetje's face partly with his shoulder, so that only her puzzled eyes are visible. Verhoeven uses the presence of Eitel to screen Keetje's direct emotions, but the resulting effect is even stronger. In this case, it is the result not only of the acting but also of the arrangement of the scene as a whole. Another illustration of well-considered *mise en scène* can be observed in the way Verhoeven presents sex: In the milliner's shop, Keetje is wholly absorbed in the shadow play she has invented, and her fancy world is rudely intruded on by the shadow of a man's penis—the metaphor speaks for itself. A similar scene takes place in the brothel: While a customer puts his hand under Keetje's skirt, she herself shyly looks at the ceiling, where a mirror reflects the insolent image of her sister Mina masturbating on the couch. This device of indirect display seems to draw a line between Keetje and her hostile surroundings.

In the acting in *Keetje Tippel*, one can see the effects of a condition that arises in smaller countries: In contradistinction to the situation that prevails in other European countries, where actors tend to specialize in cinema or television or the theater, in the Netherlands the same actors are likely to be found working in all three of these areas; moreover, while the number of theater actors is relatively high, few of them can stand up to a confrontation with the cameras—their theatrical voices and gestures betray the fact that they belong to the stage. Hence, in the Netherlands, the same actors must often appear in many different roles. In *Keetje Tippel*, leading actors Monique van de Ven and Rutger Hauer were familiar to audiences as the leads in Verhoeven's earlier *Turkish Delight*, and, given the situation described above, *Keetje Tippel* is not exempt from the problem of theatrical acting, particularly histrionic delivery of the dialogue. Keetje's father, for example, is supposed to be a countryman, but actor Jan Blaaser speaks his lines in proper, unaccented Dutch. Andrea Domburg, as Keetje's mother, was not appropriately cast to portray a convincingly vulgar woman. As a result, their conversation resembles a schoolboy's recitation by rote.

The part of Mina, on the other hand, is successfully interpreted by Hannah de Leeuwe. It is, however, the acting of Monique van de Ven that undoubtedly carries the film. She meticulously characterizes the process of Keetje's development and the ambivalent traits in her personality. In like manner, Rutger Hauer succeeds in his interpretation of Eitel. He plays the role of a rather snobbish clerk, who furbishes his petty-minded mentality with romantic gestures.

Verhoeven and Soeteman were thorough in their research for this production. The visually attractive scenes seem to grasp the very atmosphere of the epoch: the park, with its string-band playing waltzes; the feast in honor of the king's birthday; the *café chantant*, and its decadent ambience; the stylish brothel—all of these scenes and details combine to create a convincing *mise en scène*. Furthermore, the overdose of color and gaiety reveals the futile endeavor of the upper class to conceal and ignore the simultaneously existing gray world of misery. It is no accident that Verhoeven's human document deals precisely with a period in which increasing industrialization and migration to the city augured inevitable and radical changes in the organization of society.

The lighting is used to advantage to support these striking contrasts: the hovel in which the family lives is dark; shadows loom during the frightful experience at the millinery; Keetje becomes a prostitute in the evening; the political demonstration takes place at night. All represent the negative but relatively realistic side of life. In this respect, the splendid country house and the rising sun not only symbolize the happy future in store for Keetje, but also embody, analogously, the optimistic point of view of the filmmaker.

Arjen Uijterlinde

KING LEAR
(KOROL LIR)

Origin: U.S.S.R.
Released: 1971
Released in U.S.: 1975
Production: Lenfilm Studios
Direction: Grigori Kozintsev
Screenplay: Grigori Kozintsev; based on the play by William Shakespeare
Cinematography: Jonas Gricius
Editing: Boris Slutsky
Art direction: Evgeni Enei; set decoration, Vsevolod Ulitko
Costume design: Suliko Virsaladze
Sound: E. Vanunts
Music: Dmitri Shostakovich
MPAA rating: no listing
Running time: 140 minutes

> *Principal characters:*
> King Lear . . . . Yuri Yarvet
> Goneril . . . . Elsa Radzin
> Regan . . . . Galina Volchek
> Cordelia . . . . Valentina Shendrikova
> Fool . . . . Oleg Dal
> Earl of Gloucester . . . . Karl Cebric
> Edgar. . . . . : . . . . . . Leonard Merzin
> Edmund. . . . . Regimantas Adomaitis
> Earl of Kent . . . . Vladimir Emelyanov
> Duke of Cornwall . . . . Aleksandr Vakach
> Duke of Albany . . . . Donatas Banionis
> Oswald. . . . . A. Petrenko
> King of France . . . . I. Budraitis

King Lear opens with a moving band of paupers slowly filtering their way along stark mountain paths to converge at the palace of the king. Lines of guards with swords and poles patrol the gates separating the people from the intrigues of the court. The film ends with another group of peasants putting out the fires that destroyed their village as a result of these intrigues. Edgar (Leonard Merzin), the legitimate son of the Earl of Gloucester (Karl Cebric), and one of only three surviving protagonists, watches them, looks straight at the camera, and then moves off. These scenes exemplify the prominent concerns that director Grigori Kozintsev felt in translating the play to film. The effects of the actions of the protagonists on the larger world pervade the film from beginning to end. The situating of the characters in movement opens the text to include the spatial, visual world of the people as well as that of their rulers. The play becomes an eerie document of man's creation of hell on earth through its images of wastelands and starving masses, challenging the audience to connect the situation of the play with such historical tragedies as the explosions of the atom bombs over Japan, the rise to power of the Nazi regime, and the effects of war on populations in Southeast Asia occurring at the time that the film was being made.

King Lear tells the story of an aging king of Britain (Yuri Yarvet) who wants to step down from power gracefully by dividing his kingdom among his two married daughters, Goneril (Elsa Radzin) and Regan (Galina Volchek), and his youngest, Cordelia (Valentina Shendrikova), for whom a suitor is being sought. At his urgings, the two eldest spout gushing testaments of their love for their father, while Cordelia refrains from expressing her feelings. Lear is outraged. He sends Cordelia off without a dowry and vows to spend the rest of his days with his two "faithful" daughters. Lear never returns to his place of honor within his family, and only after he is driven insane with disillusionment by his two eldest daughters is he able to appreciate life without its trappings and reconcile himself with his beloved Cordelia. His spiritual victory over his oppressors leads to their downfall, but also tragically to Cordelia's and his own death.

The first scene of the play, the ceremony in which Lear proposes to divide his kingdom among his offspring, introduces all the characters, symbols, themes, and motivations that remain throughout the drama. Kozintsev approaches the scene by contrasting the wandering peasants on the outside with the clans of the courts who have come to Lear's castle to take away part of his kingdom. The followers of Regan's husband, the Duke of Cornwall (Aleksandr Vakach), are thugs masquerading as respectable society, since this is the path to power. The followers of the Duke of Albany (Donatas Banionis), Goneril's husband, are clever automatons who serve their mistress, since the duke is too passive to care. Goneril shows a disdain for her husband, Albany, and both elder sisters have trouble hiding their envies and jealousies toward each other.

Lear and Cordelia provide a contrast to these characters. Cordelia's close-ups indicate a sensitivity to truth and a devotion to her father that, while he does not see it, is apparent to all who view her. Her eyes express her own self-honesty so well that the voice-over which expresses her thoughts seems superfluous. Lear is not a regal king, but instead a spoiled prankster who spreads a map before his daughters to make them go through verbal hoops, competing with one another to please him. He enters the silent room full of waiting personages playing a masquerade game with his Fool (Oleg Dal). Bored by the speeches of Goneril and Regan, Lear sits by the fire warming his hands and playing with the fool. He has his servant read his decree and only comes alive when he asks Cordelia to tell him of her love. When she refuses to give in to him, he rips apart the map. The game is over, since Cordelia will not play by his rules.

Kozintsev situates the action in relation to the map and the fire. The map for Lear is the game board. The land that it represents brings power to the winner of the game, but the game itself invariably brings sorrow and turmoil to the peasants who inhabit the land. The battles for the land which consume the strength, intelligence, and courage of the aristocracy are for Lear unfelt until he becomes an outsider like the peasants he rules and can then appreciate the land in its harshness and beauty.

Fire is Lear's comfort. It is the hearth and heart of his world. As the ceremonies take place to effect a transference of his rule to his daughters, he gravitates toward the fire for warmth and security. Yet the fire quickly gets out of control and in succeeding scenes is used during the struggles for power to engulf the land and burn villages. Kozintsev, in his diary on the making of the film, says that he was greatly moved by the Hiroshima museum, which begins the story of the atom bomb with an exhibit showing the discovery of fire.

By the end of this introductory scene, the harmony of the ceremonial gathering is broken, as each protagonist moves in directions fitting his own needs and at odds with the others. Kozintsev and cinematographer Jonas Gricius create illustrating images of power and poetry, contrasting Cordelia's back-lit wedding to the King of France (I. Budraitis) on a cliff overlooking the sea with Lear's pronouncement from the top of his castle to the kneeling masses below, cursing his "sometime daughter." Lear is seen from below, his unkempt white hair flailing in the wind with smoke cumulating in the background.

In the film's second part, Lear finds that he is no longer accorded the respect and esteem to which he is accustomed and that he believes is his due. Goneril's servant Oswald (A. Petrenko) insults him, his own fool teases and taunts him, and Goneril and Regan verbally abuse him and threaten to get rid of his personal attendants. Lear curses them as he did Cordelia, but they seem unaffected. At the end of this part, Lear literally has the door slammed shut in his face by his daughter's servant. He thinks that he will go mad as he leaves without a place to go.

It is in this second part that the subplot involving the machinations of Edmund (Regimantas Adomaitis), the illegitimate son of Gloucester, takes form. Upset at being a social and political outcast because of his father's meanderings, he tricks Gloucester into believing that his brother Edgar (Leonard Merzin) is planning a rebellion. Edgar is forced to flee society in a situation that mirrors Lear's. Edgar finds his own safety in the anonymity of a wandering band of madmen. He rips off his clothes, covers himself with mud, and then joins them.

In Kozintsev's interpretation, Edmund's rise to power results not so much from evil in his character as from his yielding to the temptation to take advantage of a confused political situation. His dissatisfaction with his station in life leads him to plan deceitfully to improve that position after the division of the kingdom occurs and the previous moral authority is undone. Edmund is able to manipulate the situation to his own purposes in much the same way the Nazi Party in Germany was able to assume power, and this parallel is made explicit when the Duke of Cornwall accepts Edmund's offer of service and Edmund clicks his heels together, raising his hand in a salute reminiscent of the Nazis. Later, when Edmund leads the army, his troops chant his name in a deification ritual common to militaristic autocrats.

Reference to the Nazi menace is also apparent in Kozintsev's choice to make Lear's Fool a boy with tormented eyes and a shaven head. This Fool is not foolish, but a jester who points out other people's foolishness. He is a needler who laughs at others and makes others laugh at the truths about themselves. He is not tolerated in the new regime.

Although the Fool confronts issues with humor, taunting, and wordplay, he does at least confront them, forcing others to look and think also. His taunting is a contribution both to Lear's madness and to his awakening from a lifetime of madness. As a teenager, Kozintsev formed a theater group with two friends, Sergei Yutkevich and Leonid Trauberg (who both became major Soviet film directors) to confront audiences with humor, inventiveness, and play in performing stories from real life. Named FEX for Factory of the Eccentric Actor, the group borrowed from vaudeville, puppet shows, acrobatics, the circus, and American serials and slapstick films. The Fool in his taunting uses songs, sayings, jokes, riddles, and ribald stories to make his points. Kozintsev's sympathies with the Fool are apparent in that he parts from William Shakespeare by having the Fool play the pipes that, with Cordelia's kiss, wake Lear from his madness. Though the Fool is not hanged in the film as he is in the end of the play, he is kicked by one of the casket bearers as a reminder that, although Lear had a triumphal moment and Edmund was defeated, things will probably go on much the same as they did before.

Kozintsev's personal touch is evidenced in the choice of sets, costumes, location, and actors. He has stated that he wanted to keep the decor and costumes from attracting interest for their own sake. He refused to shoot in color since he did not want to draw unnecessary attention to the environment. He wanted a minimum of historical detail since this, too, would divert attention from the drama. Yet he also wanted to make a statement concerning the time and place of the story with his choice of sets, costumes, and locations. The film is set in the distant past, but there are strong images reminiscent of the recent past and others that can be imagined to look similar to scenes after a nuclear holocaust. Without committing himself to any one specific place and time, Kozintsev succeeded in placing the film, in his own words, "in that past which can become the future." He found locations with which to do this on the Crimean steppes at Point Kazantip, the gorges of Daghestan, the towers and fortress built during the reign of Ivan the Terrible near Ivangorod, and in Siberia.

In the next part of the film, Lear is caught in a vast storm as he loses his reason. He is taken by his loyal follower the Earl of Kent (Vladimir Emelyanov) to a hovel inhabited by the wandering band of wretches and madmen that Edgar had earlier joined. Lear for the first time realizes the suffering that as king he had ignored. He decides to expose himself to feel what they feel. He observes Edgar, who appears to be the worst of the lot, eating straw, rolling his eyes, and crawling along the ground without clothes. Lear asks "Is man no more than this?" In his mad state Lear realizes that he sees "unaccommodated man" and begins to rip off his clothes to become such himself. He gestures to his head and expresses the desire to "unbutton here" his whole way of thinking. Lear then conducts a mock trial of his elder daughters and cannot understand why nature should make hearts as hard as theirs. The experience is too much for him, and he falls asleep.

It took Kozintsev more than a year to find an actor whom he recognized as Lear. Kozintsev knew what he was looking for. He had directed *King Lear* in a stage production at the Gorki Theatre in Leningrad in 1941 and had written a long essay on the play in his book *Nash sovremennik Vil'iam Shekspir* (1962; *Shakespeare: Time and Conscience*, 1966). After the film *King Lear* was released, Kozintsev's diary of the planning and production of the film, *Prostrantstvo tragedii* (1973; *King Lear: The Space of Tragedy*, 1977) was published. Kozintsev had auditioned, rehearsed, made up, and tested countless actors for the role, but none had, in his words, "the bitter irony, born of suffering, or the wisdom, arising out of madness" that had to be part of Lear.

In Yuri Yarvet, Kozintsev found a man with a slight build, soft voice, and lively, sympathetic eyes that convey innocence, sorrow, madness, disillusionment, and finally joy and deep despair. Yarvet's acting is so accomplished that one can experience the subtleties of Shakespeare's poetry in his intonations, gestures, and expressions without understanding the Russian that he is speaking. Yarvet, an Estonian, did not speak Russian before the film, but he insisted on learning to speak the Russian verse of Boris Pasternak rather than use a translation prepared for him in his native Estonian.

In this part of the film, Kozintsev shows the first death within the film. Gloucester receives a message from the King of France that he is coming to Lear's aid. He is betrayed by Edmund and suffers having both his eyes torn out by the Duke of Cornwall for collaborating with Lear. Cornwall dies when a servant rises up to stop the violence done to Gloucester. In the play,

Cornwall dies offstage, but Kozintsev shows him fall so that he can also show Regan back away. A trumpet sounds as he faces his death and looks in her face. She coldly stands over him and walks away. She enters Edmund's room, where he is dressing to ride with Goneril back to her castle, and roughly pulls off his coat and embraces him. She then goes to the body of her husband and kisses his mouth. Regan's release of her animalistic desires form a strong parallel to the life that Lear has seen among the madmen in his hovel. Kozintsev is hinting at an outbreak of collective madness that is engulfing both the peasants outside and the members of the court. Suspicion, fear, and the absence of a responsible leader will make Edmund's accession to power nearly unstoppable.

Gloucester encounters the disguised Edgar and confesses that when he had eyes he was unable to see what really was going on. Cordelia lands ashore with the forces of France but cannot find her father since he has now become indistinguishable from the other beggars. Lear emerges from a bed of flowers and grasses with new compassion for humanity. He says that no one offends him. He no longer speaks like a king.

Cordelia's soldiers find Lear and bring him to her. He is sleeping but wakes when the Fool plays his pipes and Cordelia kisses him. He vows to forget and forgive, and the two wander together amid crowds of refugees leaving their homes to escape the war raging between Edmund's forces and those of France. Edmund is burning villages as his armies move on.

The last part of the film shows Cordelia and Lear as prisoners of Edmund but walking triumphantly past him, like conquerors, because they have each other. In a scene which was not in the play, Gloucester dies after discovering that the "madman" who has helped him was indeed his son Edgar. Albany discovers that Edmund has planned to get rid of him and marry Goneril, so he sends him out to do battle with a helmeted Edgar. Edgar mortally wounds Edmund, who before he dies learns that Goneril has poisoned Regan because of jealousy, and Goneril had taken her own life because of Edmund's defeat. Before he dies, Edmund tries to revoke his order to have Cordelia and Lear hanged, but it is too late for Cordelia. Lear sees her hanging from a noose and emits a piercing howl that echoes over the cliff where she hangs. Lear dies soon after and is carried with Cordelia on a bed of straw through the town, followed by the bodies of Goneril and Regan.

This was Kozintsev's final film. His career survived five decades of being at the front of Russian film creation. *King Lear* was the culmination of a lifetime of experiments dedicated to expressively creating works of deep social and human significance. He tried in *King Lear* to pose the question, "What does man live for?" The film offers no easy answers. Kozintsev in his diary explained that he hoped his film would stay with an audience after its viewing so that the question would continue to be asked: "The problem is to ensure that the inner action, the intense exploration of life, should not explode at the end of the film but should continue on in the spiritual world of the audience. One should not demonstrate, but provoke."

Alan Gevinson

KING OF HEARTS
(LE ROI DE CŒUR)

Origin: France and Italy
Released: 1966
Released in U.S.: 1967
Production: Philippe de Broca for Fildebroc/Les Productions Artistes
  Associés/Compagnia Cinematografica Montoro
Direction: Philippe de Broca
Screenplay: Daniel Boulanger; based on an original idea by Maurice Bessy
Cinematography: Pierre L'Homme
Editing: Françoise Javet
Art direction: François de Lamothe; set decoration by Robert Christides
Costume design: Jacques Fonteray
Music: Georges Delerue
Running time: 110 minutes
Running time in U.S.: 102 minutes

Principal characters:
Private Charles Plumpick . . . . Alan Bates
General Geranium . . . . Pierre Brasseur
Duke of Clubs . . . . Jean-Claude Brialy
Coquelicot (Columbine) . . . . Geneviève Bujold
Colonel Alexander MacBibenbrook. . . . . . Adolfo Celi
Mme Eglantine . . . . Micheline Presle
Duchess . . . . Françoise Christophe
Bishop Hollyhocks . . . . Julien Guiomar
M. Marcel . . . . Michel Serrault
Lieutenant Hamburger. . . . . Marc Dudicourt
Colonel Helmut von Krack . . . . Daniel Boulanger

King of Hearts is undoubtedly the best and the best-known film of French director Philippe de Broca. Although it was a commercial failure and received mixed reviews when it was first released, *King of Hearts* became a cult classic. Audiences took it to heart, returning to see it again and again at revival cinemas; the film reportedly played for several years at one theater in Cambridge, Massachusetts, and became a similar favorite in Seattle and Portland.

The antiwar sentiments of de Broca's World War I parable certainly contributed to the film's popularity at the time of the United States' disillusionment with Vietnam, but these sentiments do not entirely explain it. The appeal of *King of Hearts* has transcended contemporary vogue or passing political trends, touching a chord in the hearts and minds of those who have fallen under its spell and enduring through the years.

The genesis of *King of Hearts* can be traced to de Broca's own military experience, when he served as an army newsreel cameraman. He claimed that it was Algeria that shifted his interest to comedy, after which he decided that the real world was simply too ugly. The actual idea for *King of Hearts* came from a brief news article about fifty French mental patients who had been killed by the Germans during World War I after their hospital had been bombed. They had dressed themselves in the uniforms of dead American soldiers and were wandering through the countryside when the Germans shot them by mistake.

As with many of his films, de Broca spins an enchanting story from the slightest of premises. The opening credits of this film appear over the sounds and dark shapes of clockwork gears, as the titles synchronously wind into view in a clever visual design. The dimly lit, ominous figure of a knight in armor is recognizable in the shadows and strikes the hour with its mace, thereby planting a clue at the outset about the solution of the mystery which runs through the film.

It is October, 1918, in a small town in France. At dawn, several German soldiers finish running a line of wire from the clock tower in the village square, under the paving stones, to a concrete bunker in the center, in which several huge bombs are visible before the blockhouse is sealed with cement.

In an apartment nearby, the bald, monocled, mustachioed Prussian General von Krack (played by de Broca's screenwriter, Daniel Boulanger) is having his head shaved by the local barber while he confides his strategy to his adjutant, Lieutenant Hamburger (Marc Dudicourt). The Germans plan to evacuate the town, leaving it mined with munitions, then blow it sky-high when the advancing allies arrive to occupy it. "Sir Lancelot chimes at midnight," they gloat secretively as they prepare to leave. (A young Private Adolf Hitler appears briefly, shouting, "Shall we burn the town, sir?" "Later, Adolf, later," the general replies, much to Hitler's disappointment.)

The barber, who has overheard the plans, spreads word among the townspeople of the danger, telling them to flee. Returning to his shop, the barber, who is a spy for the Resistance, uses a concealed wireless to contact the Allies. Using the code phrase, "Why don't mackerels like potatoes?" he communicates part of the message, including the warning, "Sir Lancelot chimes at midnight," before he is discovered and shot by the retreating German soldiers.

The commander of the Scottish regiment, who receives the warning, Colonel MacBibenbrook (Adolfo Celi), who is a red-haired, blundering, tea-sipping parody of a British officer, decides to send a scout to ascertain the situation, find the explosives, and disarm them. He chooses shy Private Plumpick (Alan Bates), an ornithologist who reads the works of William

Shakespeare to his carrier pigeons.

Carrying a cage with two pigeons, Private Plumpick approaches the nearly abandoned village. He is spotted by a few remaining German soldiers and chased to an insane asylum, where Plumpick disguises himself as one of the inmates, who have been left behind by the villagers. Taking refuge behind a magnificent house of cards built by two patients who identify themselves as Bishop Hollyhocks (Julien Guiomar) and the Duke of Clubs (Jean-Claude Brialy), Plumpick tells the Germans that he is the "King of Hearts." The inmates instantly accept his word and proclaim to the others that the King has returned.

The Germans leave in fear, as though insanity were contagious, and Plumpick cautiously follows. The lunatics discover that the gates to the asylum have been left open and wander into the town as gleefully as children escaping from school, their wooden shoes clattering excitedly over the cobblestones. Georges Delerue's beautiful, haunting music begins as a wondrous transformation takes place. Bishop Hollyhocks enters a cathedral, finding the scarlet robes and miters in the sacristy. Another inmate, a wan, disheveled woman, Mme Eglantine (Micheline Presle), brushes the dust from a vanity mirror in a bombed-out building, peers at her face, and uses makeup from a drawer to paint her lips and eyes, magically becoming a seductive courtesan. A third invalid, clutching a naked doll whose hairless pate he had compulsively combed in the ward, goes into the abandoned barber's shop, dons a white smock and pompadour wig, and assumes his role. Another becomes a "general" in a circus ringmaster's uniform and opens the animal cages, setting the occupants free (just as he has been liberated). The "Duke of Clubs," elegantly attired in morning coat, top hat, and carrying a cane, escorts his lovely "duchess" (Françoise Christophe), shaded by a parasol (the two momentarily posing in one of de Broca's wonted still-life tableaux before strolling off together like an animated Impressionist painting). The music builds to a crescendo of rapture over several aerial shots of the tranquil town whose sunlit splendor makes it seem enchanted.

Plumpick finds the streets filled with peculiar inhabitants, including a dancing girl in circus costume, an aviator, vintage gendarmes, and an albino camel. Puzzled, he makes his way to the barber shop, where he assumes that the proprietor, M. Marcel (Michel Serrault), is the Resistance agent and gives him the code phrase, "Why don't mackerels like potatoes?" The crazy barber replies with equal logic that he would bet that some of them do. Plumpick finds it odd that the barber pays his customers and is told that he hates to see the shop empty. When Plumpick surreptitiously asks where the Germans are, the barber answers that he does not know, and shouts helpfully, "Any Germans here?" Plumpick shushes him, but the barber offers the fool's wisdom that "if one talks loud enough, no one ever listens."

Seeking more information about the hidden munitions, Plumpick finds

General Geranium (Pierre Brasseur) at the circus, but fares no better in another nonsensical conversation. Plumpick gravely inquires what "Sir Lancelot strikes at midnight" signifies. The general strokes his beard and informs him that midnight is the middle of the night. Plumpick suddenly notices that the lion's cage is open and that one of the big cats is lounging inside, and he hurriedly slams the door shut. It is only then that the lion attacks, trying to get out as Plumpick locks the bolt in the nick of time. The general, however, (like all the lunatics in the town) remains blissfully unaware of any danger, protected by his perfect innocence—a theme reminiscent of Marcel Carné's *Les Enfants du paradis* (1945; *Children of Paradise*), when the wife of the mime Baptiste says that he is like a dreamer sleepwalking on the rooftops. If one calls to him and awakens him, he will fall, but leaving him alone will ensure that he returns home safe and sound.

Plumpick soon realizes that all the town's inhabitants are strange dreamers, and sends two messages back to headquarters via his carrier pigeons. The first, describing what he has found, sounds like gibberish to the Scottish colonel, who believes that his campaign is now in the hands of a lunatic. The second message is intercepted by the Germans. They are alarmed to learn that the bunker has disappeared, and return to have a look.

In the village, Plumpick sees the men sneaking into Mme Eglantine's bordello and follows them. He tries to warn the courtesan of their danger, but she, too, is unfazed. She tells him that "all they have is the present, and there is nothing else to own." She offers Plumpick a young virgin, Columbine (Geneviève Bujold), to whom he is attracted. She asks him what he desires, and he replies, "A simple loss of memory." Columbine smiles and leads him upstairs, but before she can grant his wish, the King of Hearts is whisked away to the cathedral for his coronation, conveyed in a carriage that is festooned with ostrich plumes and drawn by a white camel.

The Germans arrive during this bizarre processional and are greeted with cheers and confetti. While the bordello whores sing in the cathedral choir for the coronation, Plumpick watches the soldiers, following them to the square where they check the tower and camouflaged bunker.

Meanwhile, the barber and the general hijack two of the German armored vehicles and race around the village, chasing each other. Plumpick watches from the tower as the soldiers take flight, then rings the carillon bells like Salvatore Quasimodo, laughing madly and descending to the ground on a rope. When he tries to break into the bunker and defuse the explosives, the blockhouse remains impenetrable. The lunatics gather to watch his futile efforts, and the king chastises them, yelling that they are all going to die unless he can find the clock wired to the fuse. His subjects dutifully bring him a vast array of antique timepieces, setting them at his feet.

With no other recourse, Plumpick, seated astride a white horse, tries to lead the inhabitants away from the doomed town. As they reach the city gates, Delerue's musical theme stops, replaced by the distant thunder of war, and the inmates shrink back, urging the king to stay with them. They warn him that the countryside is full of wild beasts, and that "there is murder in their hearts." Plumpick wants to leave, but cannot; the sight of the pitiful figures on the village walls causes him to return. "Long live the king, on my word as a duke!" the duke proclaims. "Who made you a duke?" Plumpick asks querulously. "Who made you a king?" the duke answers evenly. "But my poor friend, you were all in the nuthouse only a few hours ago," Plumpick continues, ruefully trying to pierce their complacency. "Jealous?" the duke inquires, "And where were you yesterday?" The logic of the lunatics is unassailable.

Unable to save them or abandon them, Plumpick resigns himself to enjoying the remaining time with Columbine in a bedroom before a crackling fireplace. The others promenade across the lawns in the setting sunlight, while the duke and duchess rest contentedly on a park bench. As midnight approaches, Plumpick sighs that he has only three minutes left to live. Columbine's face lights up at the wonder of such a precious gift. Then by chance she happens to tell him about the knight inside the clock who will strike the hour. Plumpick suddenly divines the mystery of Sir Lancelot and hurriedly climbs the tower. Struggling with the mechanical knight, he stops the fateful blow with his head and averts the catastrophe at the last moment.

The Scottish soldiers watching the town see midnight pass with no explosion and enter the village as victors, celebrating with a dazzling display of fireworks. The retreating Germans spot the skyrockets, and, believing that their plan has succeeded, also return.

At dawn, the Germans march into the square as the Scots move out, almost missing each other. Then Columbine tosses a fateful bouquet which draw the attention of both sides. They quickly form up and shoot at one another, down to the two commanders, whose horses peacefully gallop off together. The general remarks that they seem to be overdoing it a bit.

Wearying of the game, and with more Allied forces approaching, the inmates return to the asylum, shedding their costumes along the way. The town is reoccupied and the townspeople take up their normal places again. Private Plumpick, the sole survivor of the massacre, is awarded a medal and sent back into action immediately. The Germans are holding another village, he is told by a new commanding officer, and they are going to blow it sky high.

This final irony is the last straw for Plumpick, who deserts from a troop truck. Shedding his uniform, as the inmates did their clothing, he rings for admission at the gates of the asylum, standing naked before the startled nuns and holding only his caged pigeon. Between the gentle insanities of those within and the horrifyingly real ones without, he prefers the former.

King of Hearts has a gemlike quality, a poetic fragility as beautiful and evanescent as the elaborate house of cards the inmates build. De Broca's lunatics are harmless dreamers who are more eccentric than seriously disturbed. Like Shakespeare's wise fools, they possess a greater understanding of life than those who are supposedly sane. Their calm acceptance of impending death and their refusal to share Plumpick's fear demonstrate a nobility of soul. They cheerfully renounce the mortal obsession with tomorrow in favor of enjoying the moment. Unwilling to face a world which terrifies and confuses them, they retreat instead to the realm of the imagination, where they can be whoever and whatever they want.

De Broca artfully and cinematically differentiates their universe from the "real" one. Unlike the individualistic free spirits of the mental patients, the soldiers of both armies are bound by rigid conformity, following orders blindly, against their wishes and against common sense. Their drab uniforms and barren surroundings are photographed in dark, monochromatic tones as opposed to the colorful costumes and profusion of lavish *fin de siècle* ornamentation which surrounds the lunatics. Even the frenetic behavior of the military is counterpointed by the leisurely, florid nature and lilting poetic speeches of the mad. Plumpick, the man in between, who has found a doomed paradise, is both tender and whimsical, delightful and melancholy at the same time. This bittersweet contrast is a de Broca trademark, giving an unusual resonance to his pictures.

The film is built from a series of brief vignettes and episodes, approaching the story from every angle rather than attempting to tell a larger story on a broader scale. As with most of de Broca's works, the slender premise of *King of Hearts* is deceptively simple. The fragments are strung together in chains of irony and humor, whose cumulative effect remains memorable as an epiphany in the mind of the viewer.

Steve Greenberg

KINGS OF THE ROAD
(IM LAUF DER ZEIT)

Origin: West Germany
Released: 1976
Released in U.S.: 1976
Production: Michael Wiedemann for Wim Wenders Produktion
Direction: Wim Wenders
Assistant direction: Martin Hennig
Screenplay: Wim Wenders
Cinematography: Robby Müller and Martin Schäfer
Editing: Peter Przygodda
Art direction: Heidi Lüdi and Bernd Hirskorn
Sound: Martin Müller, Bruno Bollhalder, and Paul Schöler
Music: Improved Sound Limited, Axel Linstädt
MPAA rating: no listing
Running time: 176 minutes

Principal characters:
Bruno Winter	Rüdiger Vogler
Robert Lander	Hanns Zischler
Pauline	Lisa Kreuzer
Robert's father	Rudolf Schündler
Man whose wife committed suicide	Marquard Bohm
Paul	Dieter Traier
Young boy at train station	Patrick Kreuzer

West German filmmaker Wim Wenders has said that there was no script for his fifth commercial feature, only an itinerary. Yet for that itinerary, he chose a potent representation of the film's key metaphor—the borderline. As an opening title announces, *Kings of the Road* was filmed along the border between East and West Germany, from Lüneberg to Hof. The film describes the sense of separation, isolation, and detachment indicated by this metaphor.

With little urgency of plot to propel its progress, *Kings of the Road*, or *Im Lauf der Zeit* (in the course of time), its original and more apt German title, frequently lingers over the details which usually are relegated to the background of a film. Its crisp black-and-white images are eloquent in their evocation of time passing, rich in references that call on cinema history and that spotlight the plight of the contemporary German film industry.

The film's story can be described quite briefly. Robert (Hanns Zischler), a German linguist fleeing his family and home in Italy, crashes his Volkswagen into the river where Bruno (Rüdiger Vogler), an itinerant film-projector repairman, has parked his van. With little verbal exchange, Bruno offers Robert a ride, and they continue along the repair circuit. After a brief separation when Robert visits his father (Rudolf Schündler), who lives near the route, the two rejoin, traveling together for six days and finally parting at the border near Hof.

The metaphor of the borderline is introduced graphically, early in the film. As Robert plunges his Volkswagen into a river in a spontaneous, suicidal act that earns for him the nickname Kamikaze, a watchtower of the East German border guard overlooks the spectacle from the far bank. This is the Elbe River, on the borderline between the separated Germanys.

Borderlines, not all as clearly delineated, pervade the film, forming barriers between people. Nearly everyone is living alone. The Germany on the screen is populated with isolated people. The only groups are of children and the impersonal grouping of people in the dark for the porno films that dominate the cinemas. The landscapes that pass the windows of the van are empty. Buildings are deserted.

The concept of the borderline taken to the individual level becomes the problem of communication barriers, a familiar theme. While Bruno has entrenched himself in the truck, which Robert calls his bunker, no longer trying to cross the barriers, Robert is constantly trying to break through. Symbolically, he crashes the barrier of the Elbe when he plunges into it with his Volkswagen. He is constantly trying to get through to his wife by telephone.

Toward the end of the film, Robert discusses his profession while the two companions spend the night in an American bunker on the West German frontier. Robert says that he works on the borderline between linguistics and pediatrics. He studies the way that children use language before habits are formed that inhibit free expression. Adult language, then, is seen as a barrier between people; Robert turns to children and his own childhood to experience freedom from such barriers. When Bruno leaves in the morning, one clearly sees the watchtower again, right behind a sign that reads "Border Land."

At the beginning of the film, Robert has fled the responsibilities of his marriage and his work. After his half-comic flirtation with suicide, he begins a search for the roots of his problem along a route that leads him back to the setting of his childhood. In the van, Robert is constantly shot from the angle of the driver, so that the backward movement of the road in the rearview mirror beside him conflicts with the direction of movement seen through the window behind him. On the road, his behavior continually exposes his retreat to childhood. Bruno watches him riding in unsteady circles on a bicycle. Robert tries out a Hula-Hoop that he finds in one of the theaters.

Kings of the Road is also a film about borderlines, or barriers, on a different level. The implied barrier of the Nazi era to a historical continuity in German cinema is coupled in the film with a resistance to personal history as a barrier to a continuous, unalienated view of oneself. The film assembles artifacts and images recalling childhood with recollections and invocations of the history of cinema. Each of these facets of the theme is reflected against the background of the other.

Wenders pulls these two threads of theme into close convergence in a scene that begins with the installation of a new sound system in one of the small-town theaters on Bruno's route. The theater is packed with children, restlessly awaiting the film, while behind the screen, Robert, equally restless and waiting for Bruno to finish the job, searches for a light to speed the task. He blasts a spotlight in Bruno's direction. The image switches to a view from the audience so that one can see the shadow show that this creates. Bruno and Robert's clowning in silhouette to Robert's unskillful piano accompaniment conjures up both silent slapstick comedy and the shadow shows that predate the cinema. The delight of the young audience and the childish antics of the performers align childhood itself with the early days, or childhood, of the cinema.

Eventually, Robert confronts his father, whom he accuses of a selfishness that contributed to his mother's early death and to Robert's problems with his own wife. In rejecting his father, however, Robert has rejected his own history.

Robert's past blends with Bruno's when they borrow a motorcycle from one of Robert's childhood friends and set off for the island home where Bruno grew up with his mother. There, along with the abandoned house, Bruno discovers a box containing trinkets of his youth that he had stashed away as a child. The sense of insularity and separateness extends even to this childhood spent on an island, alone with his mother. Bruno says that his father was lost in the war. Later, Bruno expresses the insight that this excursion inspired—that, for the first time, he has seen himself as someone who had gone through a certain time and that this time is his history.

This, then, is another connection with the history of German cinema. The search for a personal history—lost or rejected long ago—is reflected against references to Fritz Lang, whose work spanned forty years of film history. In the first scene of the film, a former Nazi, a theater owner, remembers playing the accompaniment for Lang's Nibelungen films, *Siegfried* (1924) and *Kriemhilds Rache* (1924; *Kriemhild's Revenge*). Later, Robert leafs through a cinema program, stopping at a picture of Lang from Jean-Luc Godard's *Le Mépris* (1963; *Contempt*). In the final scene of the film, another cinema owner quotes her "father," saying that film is the art of seeing, while Lang's picture on the wall behind her gives authority to her words.

In a sense, *Kings of the Road* reclaims early German cinema history—

represented by Lang—rejected for years, tainted by the intervening Nazi period. Wenders acknowledges in this film, as his character Bruno does for his own history, the problem that German cinema of the 1970's is cut off from any sense of its own history.

Fritz Lang, the filmmaker in exile, also evokes the sense of homelessness that Bruno and Robert feel. When asked where his home is, Bruno can only answer that the van is registered in Munich. The home from which Robert has run away is in Italy. Even at home, Robert has been a stranger. Wenders' cinema has been filled with characters away from home, either traveling around Germany or, as in *Alice in den Stüdten* (1974; *Alice in the Cities*) and *Der amerikanische Freund* (1977; *The American Friend*), outside the borders of Germany.

No reading of *Kings of the Road* can be complete that neglects the beauty and clarity of its images. Throughout the film, the wide-screen frame of a black-and-white image always in sharp focus captures a sense of time in the variation of light quality, from the intensity of midday to luminous dusk and moonlight or gray dawn.

A dominant dimension of the construction of any Wenders film is the pace at which it moves. The slowness with which the themes emerge and the limited action that unfolds build up a sense of duration that embodies the quality of the lives of the protagonists. While such a description of the film might indicate a rather tedious viewing experience, this is not the case. The somberness of the themes is lightened by a sprinkling of humor that is more generous than in other Wenders films.

Kings of the Road devotes much time to depicting the movement which is at its core—the dissolving image of spinning tires, an icon of the road film, or the camera catapulting along a winding road, following the movements of a motorcycle. Accompanied by a lyric country-rock sound track, gloating patterns of dark and reflected light toll by the van's windows, intercut with the matching movement in traveling shots of passing landscape.

Like *Alice in the Cities*, this film fills up the sound track with music, both music written for the film and the rock and roll that Bruno plays on his portable record player. In spite of reinforcing an isolation from the world outside the van, the music that the record player produces allows the two traveling companions to recognize a common language. In the scene that expresses this best, Robert and Bruno sing along to the English words of "Just Like Eddie." The words themselves mean nothing, but their joyful rendition provides one of the brighter moments in the film.

Wenders' use of English-language rock-and-roll music points to an ambiguous attitude toward the United States in this and in others of his films. The concept of the Americanization of West Germany is made explicit during the bunker scene, when Bruno's story about English lyrics popping into his head even before he is conscious of their appropriateness elicits

Robert's remark that the Yanks have colonized their subconscious. For Wenders and his characters' generation in Germany, American culture has filled the gap left by a deep distrust of their German heritage. The ambiguity of the treatment of American rock in *Kings of the Road* arises from a conflict between its value as a catalyst for interpersonal communication and its role as an emblem of a generation cut off from its past.

The sense of separateness and detachment present in other forms in the film emerges in aspects of the editing style. Although Wenders' cinema makes use of both subjective shots and point-of-view construction, it is seldom pointedly psychological. Cuts to the objects of a character's point of view are often not followed by meaningful reaction shots. The viewer is also kept at a distance by the acting style of Rüdiger Vogler and Hanns Zischler. At intervals, Wenders pulls the viewer entirely out of the narrative by a cut to an extreme, high-angle shot or a zoom out to an aerial shot. Sometimes the movement is more gradual, the camera drifting away from the protagonist to some formal element of the composition. At one point the camera leaves Bruno sitting in the cab of the truck, pouring water for his coffee, to move up and out to a longer shot and then glide away, following the telephone wires overhead. At times Wenders cuts to empty, still shots, especially night shots, when the characters are offscreen or sleeping. All of these devices tend to disengage the viewer from any intense identification with the protagonists.

Robert's search for his past leads to Bruno's rediscovery of his own. In the final shot, Bruno tears up the itinerary that has kept him traveling alone from cinema to cinema with his van as a refuge. While this ending suggests the possibility of change for Bruno, it is not so optimistic for the future of film in Germany. The theaters that Wenders shows in this film survive only by exhibiting pornography. The small-town proprietors have little control over the program offered by major distributors. The last film-house owner whom Bruno encounters is closing her theater, waiting for a change in the industry, but at least no longer complacent enough to show whatever she is given.

Ann Harris

KNIFE IN THE HEAD
(MESSER IM KOPF)

Origin: West Germany
Released: 1978
Released in U.S.: 1980
Production: Eberhard Junkersdorf for Bioskop Film/Hallelujah
  Film/Westdeutscher Rundfunk
Direction: Reinhard Hauff
Screenplay: Peter Schneider
Cinematography: Frank Brühne
Editing: Peter Przygodda
Art direction: Heidi Lüdi
Makeup: Evelyn Döhring
Costume design: Monika Altmann
Sound: Vladimir Vizner
Music: Irmin Schmidt
MPAA rating: no listing
Running time: 108 minutes

Principal characters:
Bertolt Hoffmann	Bruno Ganz
Ann Hoffmann	Angela Winkler
Anleitner	Hans Christian Blech
Volker Kohler	Heinz Hönig
Scholz	Hans Brenner
Schurig	Udo Samel
Angelika	Carla Egerer

Knife in the Head centers on a search for the truth—a search conducted by a man with a crippled memory. The protagonist, Bertolt Hoffmann (Bruno Ganz), is a biogeneticist at the Traut Institute; the viewer first sees him as a lone, lab-coated individual looking out through the window of his well-equipped laboratory. He seems worried and writes in his diary that if he were an American he would probably have started shooting from the window by now. Roaming through the nighttime streets of a city that seems new but barren, crowded but hostile, Hoffmann is looking for someone; he makes a call from a phone booth, with no result. Eventually, he nears a youth center, a squat, plain building adorned with slogans and patterns of very loud, acrylic colors. Hoffmann arrives in time to witness a police raid; ignoring the policemen's warnings, he rushes into the building, followed by the police. There is the sound of a single gunshot and the frame freezes on a scene of blurred action. Only now do the film's credits appear; the police raid has served as the mystery around which Hoffmann's life will revolve for the rest of the film.

Head swathed in bandages, a tube in his nostril, Hoffmann must be taken to the hospital for an emergency operation—he has a bullet in his brain. Accompanying him, almost into the operating room, is a police inspector, Scholz (Hans Brenner), who wears a perpetual sneer. Scholz believes that Hoffmann knifed or tried to knife the policeman who shot him in the head. Cunning and ruthless, Scholz lets no opportunity go by without trying to extract a confession from Hoffmann, even as he lies dazed and ashen-faced in the recovery room. Hoffmann has other visitors as well—most significantly his estranged wife, Ann (Angela Winkler), who is accompanied by her boyfriend, Volker Kohler (Heinz Hönig). A militant leftist with a black leather jacket, Volker is more upset by the newspaper's account of the incident, which describes Hoffmann as a terrorist, than he is by Hoffmann's appalling condition. Hoffmann can barely speak and seems to have lost control of his right arm and leg. There has been so much brain damage that he will have to relearn many things. He also has trouble with his vision—a condition that the surgeon can explain only by the possibility of a police beating, in addition to the gunshot. The only person to respond normally to Hoffmann is a lawyer, Anleitner (Hans Christian Blech), who good-humoredly tells him that since most people have such wretched brains, his is still better even with a bullet in it.

Hoffmann is not totally helpless; he learns to avoid taking his medication when he chooses and has attracted the friendly attention of one of the nurses on the floor. The police who are watching him are also aware of his speedy recovery, and Scholz takes advantage of the doctor's absence to try to bully a confession out of him. Scholz constantly asks about the knife which, he claims, Hoffmann used to attack the policeman, even speaking in Italian when he thinks Hoffmann may have remembered that language better than his native German. Confined to his wheelchair, Hoffmann starts to tremble; he has also developed a tendency toward epilepsy since the attack. Thus, Scholz's plan to get Hoffmann transferred to a prison hospital is thwarted for the time being.

Visually, the hospital in which Hoffmann is treated is very stylized; it is never seen clearly from the outside except at night, and it seems cavernous, like some metropolitan underground intersection. At one point people are seen bicycling along its wide, dimly lit corridors, and the policeman who guards Hoffmann's ward enhances this feeling of captivity. Still, the hospital is not run by the police; Hoffmann is soon seen walking along, despite a limp, and chatting with the nurses and other patients. He is even something of a celebrity, with his photograph in the newspapers, either as a suspected terrorist or a mild-mannered scientist who is an amateur violinist. One of the hospital orderlies asks for his autograph, while a patient comments on his status as a man with his picture in the papers. Ann and Volker are also having their troubles with the police: They run afoul of a police roadblock, and Volker's police record attracts their attention when it appears on their video-screen terminal. With his surly manner and wisecracking attitude, Volker is a representative example of the young West German leftists and it is clear that he is characterized as unlikable despite the accuracy of his remarks about the police. Volker is arrested briefly as a result of the trouble at the roadblock.

Anleitner has also been visiting Hoffmann and helping him to relearn his vocabulary, but there is a strange difficulty with the word "knife," and Hoffmann is confused when shown pictures of a knife and a file: The pictures, as the viewer later learns, trigger a disturbing memory. Throughout his recovery, Hoffmann is obsessed with the idea of his knife and the fact that he is accused of having stabbed a policeman. Hoffmann is even confronted by Scholz with the victim, Schurig (Udo Samel), but he has no recollection whatsoever of the man. Hoffmann recovers enough to be able to leave the hospital secretly. His hair has grown back, so with commendable skill he dons a doctor's gown and stethoscope and saunters out onto the street to catch a cab to the Traut Institute. Hoffmann even discovers that he has made allies; one nurse waves to him encouragingly, and an associate at the Institute not only clues him in as to the new identity cards but also supports what he thinks are Hoffmann's radical politics. Hoffmann also slyly insults the institute director, who is affably condescending, before going on to meet Ann.

In what may be the only idyllic scene in the film, Hoffmann and Ann drive to their country house, where they discuss his problems and their broken marriage. Hoffmann dons Volker's jacket and plays with his Jew's harp—the only likable thing about Volker, Hoffmann quips. Their idyll is broken by Hoffmann's pent-up fury at her infidelity and the arrival of Anleitner, who warns that he must return to the hospital. Canny as ever, Anleitner calls for an ambulance only minutes before Scholz and his team, armed with submachine guns, surround the house. The presence of a lawyer, the imminent arrival of the ambulance, and Hoffmann's epileptic seizure save him from a year in prison; he is seen later back in his hospital ward chatting with one of the friendly nurses, Angelika (Carla Egerer). Soon thereafter, Hoffmann is released from the hospital, and, accompanied by Anleitner, he trades questions with the newsmen who surround him.

Hoffmann's peculiar quest for the truth about himself has also led him to discover some things about Ann and Volker. He finally realizes that his marriage has ended and that Volker must envisage him as a foolish victim, if not simply a cuckolded husband. When Hoffmann insists on knowing where his knife is and Volker berates him, saying the knife is in his imagination, the part-time violinist lunges at him with a carving knife from the kitchen table. In one more effort to win back Ann, Hoffmann goes to the youth center, again just in time to witness a police raid. This time, however, the police are interested only in Volker, leaving Hoffmann to pursue his own personal demon. He does.

Having trailed Schurig, he confronts the young policeman in his home. He demands to know the truth, especially after seeing the supposed knife wound, a long scratch under an adhesive plaster. They admit to each other that they were scared when the shooting happened, and they begin to reenact the events with their roles reversed. Hoffmann has an automatic pistol aimed at the policeman, who lies on the floor; in front of the prone man lie a knife and a file. Each tells the other to drop his weapon, and the frame freezes with Hoffmann taking a bead on the policeman.

Born in 1939, director Reinhard Hauff belongs to that generation which has made a New German Cinema internationally known and respected. Hauff is interested in the plight of isolated and marginal persons; his first national success came with his third feature, *Paule Pauländer* (1975), which focuses on the life of a country lad and his brutal father. This film was broadcast over Westdeutscher Rundfunk (WDR) and made use of nonprofessional performers. Ironically, Hauff's next film, *Der Hauptdarsteller* (1977; *The Main Actor*), concerned the dilemma of a young boy's identity crisis brought on by instant celebrity as the star of a successful film. The interaction between personality and expected reactions as revealed in the glare of publicity continues in *Knife in the Head*, with a background of the era of radical politics and official suppression that culminated in the early 1970's.

Many Germans believed that domestic politics increasingly resembled a vipers' nest in the 1970's. On the far Right were former Nazis, extreme conservatives, and a popular press that often reverted to diatribe; on the far Left were hippies and various strains of Marxist ideologues, including those willing to use bombs, such as the notorious Rote Armee Faktion (Red Army Faction). Complicating the issue was a tradition of old-fashioned political repression that dates back to the Wilhelminian era and a police force that is only one generation removed from the horrors of Adolf Hitler's Reich and Heinrich Himmler's SS. In *Knife in the Head*, Hauff does not flinch from showing the ruthlessness of the police in their effort to secure an indictment or from showing how inexorable a police force armed with the latest in technology could be.

Aside from the political theme in this film, Hauff examines the role played by convention, routine, and perception in an individual's personality. Except for Scholz, who is convinced of Hoffmann's guilt, everyone assures Hoffmann that he could not possibly have tried to stab the young policeman who shot him in the head. Hoffmann himself, however, believes that their view of him is wrong, that he is capable of more than he has been given credit for, especially by his estranged wife and her young lover—and that includes a capability for violence. Not only must Hoffmann relearn to speak and to feed himself with his left hand (he had been right-handed), but also he takes the opportunity to refashion his own personality, to become more assertive or abrasive. In his diary entry at the beginning of the film, Hoffmann refers to the urge for random violence and brands it as specifically American, yet by the film's close, it is clear that this urge is universal.

There may be something allegorical in this subject, for West Germany has been plagued with the onerous task of redefining itself since 1945, when the Third Reich collapsed. An apolitical man, a biogeneticist, Hoffmann could be a symbol for the typical German as that people's self-definition has it; obsessed with his scientific speciality, he blunders onto a political battlefield. That Hoffmann unblinkingly reconstructs his mind and personality before trying to understand what did happen is both a marvel of acting by Ganz and an object lesson to his German-speaking audience. It is Hauff's singular accomplishment to have made this search for the truth visually and dramatically convincing: The themes of the film grow out of the action rather than being imposed on it.

Lenny Rubenstein

KNIFE IN THE WATER
(NÓŻ W WODZIE)

Origin: Poland
Released: 1962
Released in U.S.: 1963
Production: Stanisław Zylewicz for Zespóly Realizatorów Filmowych Kamera
  Film Unit
Direction: Roman Polanski
Screenplay: Jerzy Skolimowski, Jakub Goldberg, and Roman Polanski
Cinematography: Jerzy Lipman
Editing: Halina Prugar
Art direction: no listing
Music: Krzysztof Komeda
Running time: 94 minutes

Principal characters:
Andrzej .... Leon Niemczyk
Christine .... Jolanta Umecka
Young man .... Zygmunt Malanowicz

Although Roman Polanski has become known throughout the world both for his sometimes sensational films, such as *Rosemary's Baby* (1968), and for his sometimes sensational private life, he began his film career rather quietly with a few short films that he made while studying at the noted Polish Film School at Lodz. One of those shorts, *Two Men and a Wardrobe* (1959), won five international awards and is still shown at screenings of short or experimental films.

His first feature film, *Knife in the Water*, also lacks the concern with violence, horror, and aberrant behavior that have become Polanski trademarks. Instead, the film is a proficient work in which the effects are often subtle, with little of the self-indulgence that so often mars the works of young directors. The action of the film takes less than twenty-four hours and involves only three characters and one major location—a sailboat. A great strength of *Knife in the Water* is the fact that Polanski was able to work within these budget-imposed limitations without drawing undue attention to his virtuosity in doing so.

The film opens with a middle-aged man, Andrzej (Leon Niemczyk), and his wife, Christine (Jolanta Umecka), driving down a road in Poland. A young hitchhiker (Zygmunt Malanowicz) stands in the middle of the road to force them to stop. Andrzej, who is driving, does not stop until the last moment, but he does stop and he does offer the young man (who is never named) a ride. This action, although the viewer does not realize it at the time, sets the tone for the entire film and for the relationship between the two men. The two continually test each other, and neither of them will stop the game, although the older man, especially, has several opportunities to do so.

Andrzej is a successful sportswriter; the young man is a footloose hiker; each feels the need to justify his own style of life to the other. When Andrzej says that he and his wife are going sailing until the next morning, the young man says that hiking is better than sailing, but Andrzej asks him to join them and the young man accepts, saying that he knew he would be invited because "you want to carry on the game." This comment is the first explicit statement of the contest that the two carry on throughout the film.

Once all three are on the boat, the contest centers on each man trying to show his proficiency in a skill that the other cannot match. Chief among these are Andrzej's ability with a sailboat and the young man's with a knife, a large switchblade that he carries with him at all times. Christine observes the contest, but she does not really become involved until near the end. The climax of the action is precipitated by Andrzej's throwing the young man's knife into the water. This act causes a skirmish in which Andrzej pushes the young man into the water. Since the young man has previously said that he cannot swim, Andrzej and Christine both fear that he may drown, although both suspect that he may have been lying about his inability to swim. Both dive into the water to try to find him, but they cannot; so Andrzej swims to shore ostensibly to notify the police. After Andrzej leaves, the young man— who can swim and had been hiding behind a buoy—returns. Christine slaps him and says to him, "You're like [Andrzej]—only half his age, weaker, and more stupid." Nevertheless she lets the young man seduce her, perhaps out of relief that he is safe or perhaps out of disgust with her husband's juvenile behavior.

Christine then sails the boat back to land and lets the young man off before she reaches the pier where Andrzej waits. He has not gone to the police and what Christine tells him leaves him in a dilemma. She says that the young man is safe and that she was unfaithful. He must decide whether she is telling the truth or whether she is trying to make him feel better (by telling him that the young man is safe) or worse (by telling him that she was unfaithful). They drive away from the pier and reach the point where he must turn one way to go to the police station or another to go back to the city where they live. The film stops at the moment before the car goes in either direction.

A key to the quality of *Knife in the Water* is the comment of critic Stanley Kauffmann, who wrote that the drama in the film is a small "system of tensions rooted in character." Polanski does not merely put three characters together and then have something happen *to* them; he has them come together because of what they are and come into conflict, again, because of what they are. The young man tells Andrzej at the very beginning of the film that he takes chances because life would be flat if he did not. This remark defines his character to a great extent and also constitutes a certain challenge to Andrzej. Later in the film, an outgrowth of this same contrast between the two men is seen. The young man laughs when he sees a device Andrzej uses to carry a hot saucepan as they prepare to eat. Andrzej sees this as a challenge to his way of life, an indication that he is too cautious, so he returns the challenge by telling the young man to try holding the pan in his bare hand if he finds the device amusing. The young man cannot pass up the challenge and holds the pan although it burns his hands. In this all too realistic manner, the characters react to each other. There is no need for any such theatrical devices as murder or even a bloody fight.

The screenplay of *Knife in the Water* was written by Jerzy Skolimowski (who was to go on to be a noted director himself), Jakub Goldberg, and Polanski. Although it is a bit long, it is carefully constructed so that the plot dynamics are slowly but convincingly developed. Polanski is masterful in his direction of both the camera and the cast. The composition of individual images is artful without being showy, and the acting performances are evocative but not overly emotional. The action is also well supported by a spare, jazzy score by Krzysztof Komeda. *Knife in the Water* is, in short, a first-rate small film.

Timothy W. Johnson

KÜHLE WAMPE
(KÜHLE WAMPE: ODER, WEM GEHÖRT DIE WELT?)

Origin: Germany
Released: 1932
Released in U.S.: 1933
Production: Georg M. Höllering and Robert Scharfenberg for Praesens Film
Direction: Slatan Dudow
Screenplay: Bertolt Brecht and Ernst Ottwald
Cinematography: Günther Krampf
Editing: no listing
Art direction: Robert Scharfenberg and C. P. Haacker
Music direction: Josef Schmid
Music: Hanns Eisler
Songs: Helene Weigel and Ernst Busch
Running time: 71 minutes

> *Principal characters:*
> Anni .... Hertha Thiele
> Gerda............................. Martha Wolter
> Mrs. Bönike....................... Lilli Schönborn
> Fritz .... Ernst Busch
> Kurt .... Adolf Fischer
> Mr. Bönike....................... Max Sablotzki

Released after considerable censorship problems in 1932, *Kühle Wampe* was a unique experiment in several respects: in the way that the production was organized, as a political film, and as an example of the intelligent mixing of cinematic styles and modes that was the strength of the Weimar cinema. Although most often associated with Bertolt Brecht, the film was a collaborative effort on the part of writers Brecht and Ernst Ottwald, composer Hanns Eisler, and director Slatan Dudow. Immediately before beginning this film in 1931, Brecht had lost a highly publicized lawsuit against the producer of the film version of *Die Dreigroschenoper* (1931; *The Threepenny Opera*) over the fidelity of the screenplay to the spirit of Brecht's play. The law agreed with the producer that Brecht had sold the rights to his play and had been paid to write a screenplay. He was not at liberty to write the screenplay he wanted. This was an experience that Brecht did not intend to repeat. According to an unusual "Collective Presentation" released at the same time as *Kühle Wampe*, the legal contract for the film set a precedent in guaranteeing those who had actually made the film the right of authorship over the final product. Freedom of expression became an issue only after the film was finished, when it was rejected twice by state censors. The filmmakers argued collectively on behalf of the film's artistic integrity. After a number of cuts and a significant delay, *Kühle Wampe* was approved.

The objective of strength through principled teamwork was also at the heart of the film's political project. Made at a crucial time of economic instability in Germany, when the middle class had been practically eliminated by spiraling inflation and unemployment, *Kühle Wampe* is a militant call to young, unemployed workers for survival through left-wing education and organization. The threat posed by ultraconservative groups, specifically the Nazis, is never mentioned. The enemy is economic and transcends nationalism: It is international capitalism. This position is in keeping with the German Communist Party orientation of the filmmakers but quickly proved to be shortsighted. Within another year, these filmmakers were forced, along with hundreds of other political and intellectual exiles, to leave Germany because of the Fascist takeover.

Although *Kühle Wampe* was designed to be a political and didactic film, it is by no means simple propaganda. *Kühle Wampe* is an important cinematic achievement that manages to combine sophisticated montage techniques with an unstudied documentary look. Its presentation of contemporary events, or its method of realism, owes as much to Fritz Lang and G. W. Pabst as it does to influential Soviet imports, such as films by Sergei Eisenstein or Dziga Vertov. *Kühle Wampe* is a highly self-conscious film aesthetically, in the sense of modernist experimentation. Several important traditions in German cinema are imaginatively brought together so that, in retrospect, the film can be studied as a point of culmination and synthesis of film tradition: the city film, internationally popular throughout the Weimar period, taking avant-garde and documentary forms and exemplified by such films as *Berlin—Die Symphonie einer Grosstadt* (1927; *Berlin—Symphony of a City*), and *Chelovek kinoapparatom* (1929; *The Man with a Movie Camera*); the educational documentary (particularly the *Kulturfilm*, emphasizing youth, health, and nature); montage sequences, stemming from a decade of experimentation in German films or from the influence of Soviet films; the *Neue Sachlichkeit* (new objectivity) movement, from studio-shot fiction films with a contemporary, realistic tone to the documentary impulse to use real locations and include nonprofessional actors; left-wing, proletarian films released as full-length dramatic films for a general audience, such as Phil Jutzi's *Mutter Krausens Fahrt ins Glück* (1929; *Mother Krause's Journey to Happiness*), the best-known example after *Kühle Wampe*.

The film is divided into four parts. The first section begins with the title "One Less Unemployed." An elaborate montage sequence of newspaper headlines reveals an alarming rise in unemployment figures and news of government cuts in welfare subsidies. Young men gather to look for jobs, bicycle from place to place, and return with nothing. One young man goes to his family's apartment for the midday meal. His father (Max Sablotzki) and mother (Lillie Schönborn) derisively accuse him of not trying hard enough to find work. His sister, Anni (Hertha Thiele), defends him, saying that there are not any jobs. He sits silently, head bowed, until each of them leaves. Then he quietly moves toward the window, opens it carefully, places his wristwatch neatly to one side, and jumps to his death. Neighbors gather below and comment on the waste of a young life.

In the next section, the Bönike family is evicted for not paying the rent. They end up going to live with Anni's boyfriend, Fritz (Ernst Busch), in a tent camp called Kühle Wampe on the outskirts of Berlin. The lyrics of a ballad describe young love during a montage sequence of Anni and Fritz walking among the trees, intercut with a dissolving series of idyllic, summery, landscape shots. Anni becomes pregnant. Fritz does not want to be tied down, but he finally makes an agreement with Anni's father. After a quarrel on the night of their engagement party, Anni leaves Fritz and her family, who choose to remain with him. She goes to live with her friend Gerda (Martha Wolter).

In the third section, Gerda and her boyfriend Kurt (Adolf Fischer) help prepare banners for a big athletics event for young workers. Their involvement with politics carries over from work to leisure and educational activities. Anni appears to be thriving in this environment; Fritz, who comes back to look for her after losing his job, is skeptical. Yet at the sunny, open-air festival, with the optimism of thousands of participants palpable (3000 worker-athletes organized by the Communist sports leagues), Fritz seems to become less rigid in his ideas. The couple is together again, although their future is left unresolved. They watch a theater group act out an eviction scene that retells the story of the Bönike family; it is presented as a typical case of injustice, but the details are specific to the eviction seen in realistic form earlier. There are suggestions that things will work out for Anni and Fritz. Throughout this section, a militant song of workers' unity, the "Solidarity Song," is heard intermittently; after the sports events are over, everyone sings it in unison. It has replaced the military marches that the older generation was listening to on the radio as the Bönike family moved into Kühle Wampe.

The final section takes place on a crowded train returning from the festival to Berlin. Nearly everyone enters into a discussion arising from a newspaper item reporting that Brazil burned twenty-four million pounds of coffee. The young workers point out to the older generation on the train, in particular one well-dressed man siding with the interests of the capitalists, that overproduction brings prices down all over the world. This explains why the coffee had to be burned—to keep prices up. The high price of coffee is an issue to which everyone on the train can relate, from comical figures such as the housewives who give one another advice on how to make it, to strong images of youth and determination, best exemplified by Gerda, who speaks directly into the camera as she replies to the sleepy man who does not intend to change the world and, indirectly, to the question posed by the film's subtitle (who does the world belong to?): Who will change the world? Those who are not happy with it. Anni and Fritz listen and then join in with the young people explaining this economic puzzle. The film ends on the "Solidarity Song" as people file out of the train toward the street.

Thus, the film ends in Brechtian fashion on a visual and thematic bridge between the fictional world (the film itself) and the real world that the spectator is about to see again after the film is over (like the world into which the people from the train are about to walk). The political problems that the film raises are likewise left with no specific solution, because they remain problems to be solved in the contemporary spectator's society. Similarly, there is no resolution of the conflict between Anni and Fritz over the type of family organization that they will choose—more or less collective, more or less bourgeois, like that of their parents. Although structurally the film leaves the elder Bönikes after the second section, Kühle Wampe appears to be a temporary refuge for them. Not only are these important conflicts left open by the dramatic structure of *Kühle Wampe*, but also stylistically the film is characterized by suggestion rather than direct statement—through editing, sound, and the use of ellipsis in visual style.

One of the problems with which any political film must contend is how to show a convincing relationship between a particular case of injustice and a general social situation. Central to Brecht's view of realism, which was at the core of his theoretical interest in political art, is the belief that the typical must be understood through the individual case. Yet the individual should exemplify the social origin of his situation through significant details of gesture, speech, and costume. Brechtian theory illuminates important aspects of *Kühle Wampe*, but does not account for cinematic style and the elegant system of variation in the film. This is why *Kühle Wampe* has suffered somewhat from the honor of Brecht's imprimatur; it has become difficult to see beyond the typical themes and dramatic strategies associated with Brecht. The film, however, follows the tradition of the best Weimar dramatic cinema in leading the spectator to believe what has not really been established except by inference based largely on cinematic convention.

That Anni's brother takes off his watch to protect it before committing suicide is a gesture that both individuates his action (it is not simply a suicide) and refers to the economic and social causes for it: He despairs of finding work; work has been equated with self-worth; his absence will mean one less mouth to feed; the watch is an item of value, unlike his life, and thus he leaves it behind for his family. This reasoning is not explicit in the film, in contrast to the argument about coffee prices in the final sequence. The scene is also shot in a different style: While the train debate is shot from many angles that divide the space and group the passengers in a variety of ways, the emphasis is on speaking participants who are shown completely. The suicide, in contrast, is enacted in silence. Vision is directed toward objects shown in detail, or parts of the young man's body, often with dramatically important areas offscreen. He is shown fully as he moves to the window, but then the camera tracks in to hold his watch. There is a detail shot of his watch (not his face) as he takes it off and arranges it, and a detail shot of a plant which he moves to open the window. When the young man climbs onto the ledge, the viewer can see only his legs, as the fast-moving legs of the bicycle riders were earlier used metonymically to suggest the group of young men looking for work. From his legs, intercut with his unsuspecting mother coming back up the stairs outside the apartment, there is a cut to a single hand gripping a horizontal bar. The hand lets go, and a scream breaks the silence. A series of silent shots follows, which is strikingly close to the way that the first sequence of Lang's *M* (1931) represents the death of Elsie Beckmann: another close-up of the plant; another close-up of the watch; a repeat shot of the bicycle wheels and churning legs of the boys; the young Bönike's bicycle (wheels only) hanging motionless; an overhead shot of the body covered with a sheet, surrounded by people. The camera then returns to face level among people in the crowd; there is some dialogue with a small amount of information indicating both the individuality of the case and its typicality—one woman looks directly into the camera and says, "one unemployed less," echoing the opening title of the sequence.

The montage technique used here, in other words, is not simply a juxtaposition of shots but rather the incorporation of a principle of ellipsis that increases dramatic involvement by omitting certain kinds of narrative, visual, and aural information. This technique is continued throughout the film, but in a highly varied manner so that in retrospect only certain key scenes tend to be remembered as montage sequences. The partial shots of the bicycles at the beginning of the film, changing screen direction frequently to indicate temporal ellipsis and a series of races against time for work, are not different in principle from the partial views of the athletic events in the third section, which somehow seem more realistic.

After the first sequence, the film begins to move away from the melodramatic family conflict in which the unemployment question has been dramatically couched, with the tragedy of the suicide. The terrain shifts to a more public arena through the character of Anni, and from her to Gerda and the other young workers, and to problems which are more obviously social, rather than private. Thus, the film attempts to break new ground in relating domestic and public questions, and also in relating dramatic, melodramatic forms with documents of alternative modes of living and direct address to the spectator. The media, especially the newspaper, is a unifying source throughout the film that brings the public sphere into private lives, while on a stylistic level, music, narration, and montage techniques suggest the many connections between the two realms. *Kühle Wampe* is an important film to understand for historical reasons, but equally for aesthetic, and political aesthetic, reasons—to study how conventions familiar to different traditions of filmmaking can come together in an innovative sense that speaks to a particular moment in time.

Janet Bergstrom

KWAIDAN
(KAIDAN)

Origin: Japan
Released: 1964
Released in U.S.: 1965
Production: Shigeru Watasuki for Bungei Production-Ninjin Club; released by Toho
Direction: Masaki Kobayashi
Screenplay: Yoko Mizuki; based on short stories by Lafcadio Hearn (Keisumi Yakumo)
Cinematography: Yoshio Miyajima
Editing: no listing
Art direction: Shigemasa Toda
Sound effects: Hideo Nishizaki
Music: Toru Takemitsu
Running time: 164 minutes
Running time in U.S.: 164 minutes and 125 minutes

> *Principal characters:*
> **Black Hair**
> Samurai .... Rentaro Mikuni
> First wife .... Michiyo Aratama
> Second wife .... Misako Watanabe
> **The Woman of the Snow**
> Yuki................................ Keiko Kishi
> Snow woman .... Keiko Kishi
> Minokichi....................... Tatsuya Nakadai
> Minokichi's mother .... Mariko Okada
> **Hoichi, the Earless**
> Hoichi .... Katsuo Nakamura
> Samurai spirit.................... Rentaro Mikuni
> Head priest .... Ganjiro Nakamura
> Priest........................... Takashi Shimura
> Yoshitsune........................ Tetsuro Tamba
> Attendant .... Joichi Hayashi
> **In a Cup of Tea**
> Kannai .... Ganemon Nakamura
> Heinai .... Noburu Nakaya

The Japanese view ghosts and the supernatural very differently from westerners. Each region has its own beliefs and tales, which are generally based in the Shintō concept of ancestor worship as well as local folklore.

The ancient Japanese, like the ancient Greeks, believed that the welfare of the living depended upon the welfare of the dead. Primitive Japanese did not believe in ideas of Heaven and Hell. The advance of Buddhism, and its doctrine of rebirth, necessitated a special reconciliation of such beliefs, wherein the dead lived in an unseen world duplicating the visible one, but they were still dependent upon the living for their happiness and prosperity.

A ghost is identified with the soul or spirit of the dead and possesses a shadowy likeness of the departed. The spirits of those who experience natural deaths and then receive the necessary traditional rites join with the spirits of their ancestors after a special ceremony celebrating the thirty-third anniversary of their death, completely losing their individual identities. Those who suffer violent or unnatural deaths or who die in misery are condemned to wander indefinitely. Occasionally, these *yurei* will reappear before their relatives or transgressors. Appearances of other types of apparitions (*yōkai*) may be tied to a particular location or time. Many Japanese are both Shintō and Buddhist simultaneously, and obediently follow traditional customs that are based in their religions.

The film *Kwaidan*, released in 1964, is based on a series of four sketches of meetings between the visible and the invisible. These ghostly short stories were originally published by Lafcadio Hearn in several haunting collections at the beginning of the twentieth century. These, in turn, were based on folklore and ballads, some of which had been passed on for centuries. "Kaidan" means "weird tales," and Hearn's collection of short stories entitled *Kwaidan* is subtitled "Stories and Studies of Strange Things." Perhaps the stories are fictional, but they possess a haunting sense of spiritual reality.

Kwaidan was highly acclaimed for exquisite photography and vivid atmosphere of an exotic macabre. Its eerie stories transcend convention through director Masaki Kobayashi's personal vision of Hearn's work. The sketches, like those of Edgar Allan Poe or Franz Kafka, may puzzle many viewers who try to read too much into them.

The first of the four episodes is called "Black Hair." A young samurai (Rentaro Mikuni) leaves his home in old Kyoto because he is unable to tolerate his poverty and sees no opportunity for advancement. Not understanding the meaning of love, he divorces his loving wife (Michiyo Aratama), who pleads with him not to go. He remarries into the family of a wealthy governor, but discovers that his new wife (Misako Watanabe) is selfish and callous. The samurai continually recalls memories of his beautiful former wife—her patience, her smiles—and he realizes how unjust he had been.

When his official term has expired years later, he divorces again to return to his first wife. As he arrives late at night, Kyoto is as silent as a tomb. The light shines in his old home, and his wife is still working at her spinning wheel. Welcoming him back and expressing her unworthiness in typical Japanese fashion, she still appears as young and fair as ever. Even her shiny, fragrant dark hair remains as he remembers it. They spend the night together in the room that had served as their bridal chamber much earlier; it is still as clean and immaculate as ever.

The sun is shining when he awakens the next morning. He observes a long stream of black hair trailing over his wife's covers. His idyllic return quickly explodes into terror: When he affectionately lifts the covers, he discovers his wife's decrepit, gruesomely decomposed skeleton with its jet-black hair now snowy white. "Black Hair" concludes with a harrowing scene depicting the samurai's reaction to the knowledge that he spent the night with a revenge-seeking ghost. The immaculate room is now falling apart and ruined. The black hair floats in midair and attacks him. Age grips his body as he goes berserk.

"The Woman of the Snow," the second and most beautiful episode, was regrettably excised from many prints of *Kwaidan* in the United States and Great Britain. As it begins, two woodcutters, old Mosaku and Minokichi (Tatsuya Nakadai), his eighteen-year-old apprentice, live in a village in Musashi province. One cold evening, they are overtaken by a snowstorm on their way home. The ferryman had left his boat on the other shore, so they must seek shelter in his small hut. Both fall asleep in the cold shack.

The door blows open, and Minokichi, in a dreamlike state, appears to awaken. He thinks that he sees a beautiful snow maiden (Keiko Kishi), white-faced and dressed in white, enter the room. She blows her icy breath upon the old woodcutter. Then she bends over Minokichi and begins to blow on him; he begins to become numb. Taking pity on the handsome youth, she suddenly smiles and whispers in a ghostly voice that she will not hurt him now. If, however, he should tell anyone about this incident, she promises to kill him.

The ferryman finds the two the next morning. Mosaku is frozen stiff, as if all his blood had been drained. Minokichi is senseless but still alive. His mother (Mariko Okada) nurses him back to health, but he refuses to tell her what had happened on that fateful night.

A year later, Minokichi overtakes a beautiful girl (Keiko Kishi) on his way home. She tells him that her parents have died, and that she is looking for work as a maid. Her name is Yuki, a common Japanese name which means "snow." Charmed, Minokichi invites her home for dinner. His mother immediately takes a fancy to her and invites her to stay. Eventually the two marry.

Several years later, old women gossip about her. She has borne her husband three handsome children and proved to be a good wife. Even her mother-in-law praised her as she died, something very rare. Yet she never seemed to age.

Minokichi makes sandals for his family for the holiday season. He gives Yuki red thongs to match her complexion and smiles contentedly while she sews. Suddenly, as he looks, her gaze appears identical to the one he saw on the terrible night. He relates his story of the snow maiden, now believing it to have been a fantasy. Yuki, however, responds that it was not a dream—it was really her, and that he has just betrayed her by revealing it. Flinging down her sewing, she shrieks that she will not kill Minokichi because of the children. As she screams, she runs outside and melts into the mist. Only the bright red sandals remain to comfort the sad woodcutter.

"Hoichi, the Earless" begins with a Nō-like recapitulation of the defeat of the Heike, or Taira, clan at the battle of Dan-no-ura, a famous sea battle that occurred on March 24, 1185. Director Kenji Mizoguchi depicted early confrontations between the Genji and a victorious Heike clan in *Shin Heike monogatari* (1955; *New Tales of the Taira Clan*). Several battles later the Heike perished under the rule of a child emperor. This defeat is frequently repeated in Japanese legend. According to the tale, Noritsune, the bravest Heike warrior, wished to fight Yoshitsune, the Genji general. Trapped by the Genji and with arrows sticking in him, he remained fierce, but his body finally succumbed. High waves prevented the Genji from escaping to the shore. Lady Nii saw the end of the battle. Holding the small emperor in her arms, she decided to escort him personally into the next world. All of their brave followers joined their heroic plunge into the water to their deaths. The sea and shore there have remained haunted by restless Heike spirits since then.

The strangest tale about this restless clan concerns Hoichi (Katsuo Nakamura), a blind player of the biwa (a four-stringed lute usually played with a horn plectrum). He was particularly known for his skillful recitations of Heike clan history, whose complete story includes twenty-four secret songs and takes many nights to perform. Because of his great talent, the head priest (Ganjiro Nakamura) at Amidaji Temple invited him to live there. Although it was near the site of the battle, the priests decide not to warn him of the strange occurrences in that area.

One night shortly after his arrival, the head priest is called away. As Hoichi practices his biwa, a shadowy warrior (Rentaro Mikuni) appears in front of him. The samurai announces that his lord is visiting this historic area incognito and wishes to hear Hoichi's celebrated performance. Taking Hoichi by the hand, he leads him away through the heavy mist.

It is very late when the blind biwa player returns, and he spends much of the day sleeping. This strange pattern, which recurs over several consecutive days, is noted at the temple. As Hoichi grows more pale, the head priest questions him; following the warrior's instructions, he simply answers that he was tending to private business. That night, a particularly stormy and thundery evening, the priest sends servants to follow him. They find him playing before an assembly of the spirits of the Heike emperor and his nobles. The area is so spooky that even the flames rush out of their lamps to dance about. Under the priest's orders, the servants immediately bring the blind biwa player, Hoichi, back.

Informing Hoichi that he has been playing before the tombs of the Heike, the high priest warns him that if he obeys the spirits once more, they will possess him and tear him to pieces. He then has another priest (Takashi Shimura) take a brush and write sacred text over Hoichi's entire body—his face, his eyelashes, and so on. The priest, however, neglects to cover Hoichi's ears. Hoichi is instructed to sit and wait to be called, but not to respond. When the samurai ghost returns, only Hoichi's ears are visible to him, so he rips them off the poor biwa player to present to his lord as proof that his will was obeyed.

When this story was told, many people came to hear Hoichi perform with his biwa, and he became wealthy. Now that the danger from the ghosts was over, he continued to play, hoping to console their sorrowful spirits so that they could rest in peace.

"In a Cup of Tea" concludes *Kwaidan*. Lord Nakagara paid a New Year's visit to the village of Hogo in 1679. Kannai (Ganemon Nakamura), one of his guards there, sees the reflection of a man's face in a cup of tea. The liquid shimmers, and the reflection disappears. It reappears two more times. Finally, the reckless samurai throws out the liquid. After the cup has been refilled, he continues to see the other warrior's face smiling at him, so again he tosses away the liquid, now even breaking the cup. When this image recurs in a new cup, he finally drinks the tea, thus ingesting the soul of the man who had possessed that face long ago.

Alone on guard duty that night, Kannai chants to himself. When a cup is overturned, he sees the man (Noboru Nakaya) whose reflection he had observed earlier. After Heinai introduces himself, Kannai thrusts his sword at him. The intruder vanishes, but reappears in another part of the room. After several unsuccessful slashes, Kannai finally wounds him, but he leaps through a wall and disappears. Kannei rouses the off-duty guards, but they only laugh, thinking that he had had a nightmare.

He is off duty the next day, but three men mysteriously appear at midnight and introduce themselves as Heinai's retainers. When they inform him that their master will return during the middle of the next month, the fearless Kannai once again draws his sword and starts slashing. The ghostly visitors vanish and then reappear as had their master. Finally, he seemingly kills all three. Yet they return once again. Kannai laughs hysterically as they surround him.

The narrative breaks here, leaving open the question of punishment for swallowing a soul. "In a Cup of Tea" has been told in flashback, as written by a historian many years later. The writer's publisher arrives, looking for a manuscript that was due. He and the elderly housekeeper, however, are unable to locate the author. Suddenly the old lady is startled: the man's image appears in a huge water bucket, trying to escape.

Although *Kwaidan*'s four episodes vary in mood, style, and period, they work together extremely well. A decade of planning went into this film, which won the Special Jury Prize at the 1965 Cannes Film Festival and finished second in the *Kinema Jumpo* annual poll, whose awards are the Japanese equivalent of the American Oscar. *Kwaidan* became the most expensive Japanese production at the time that it was completed, although its record budget has been topped many times since then. Particular attention was paid to accuracy in period details. Whenever possible, genuine fabrics and accessories, some considered national treasures, were used. Most of Toho's leading actors at that time were included in the cast.

Kwaidan often incorporates a lacquered theatricality, enhancing its highly artificial staging. Its beauty—sets, delicate coloration, and sheer compositions—is omnipresent and enhances its atmosphere of strangeness. Its success must be credited to two men, Lafcadio Hearn, who recorded the stories several decades ago, and Masaki Kobayashi, who gave them a vibrant visual rendering.

Lafcadio Hearn's background touched several countries before he settled in Japan and became its penetrating interpreter to the West. The son of a Greek mother and an Anglo-Irish surgeon major serving in the British army, he was born on a Greek island in 1850. When his parents' marriage dissolved, he was brought up by an aunt in Dublin, but studied in England and France. An accident blinded his left eye and scarred him psychologically. In 1869, he came to the United States, where he worked as a journalist for two decades, leaving for and settling in Japan in 1890. He married a Japanese woman and took her family name (Yakumo), and he became a Japanese citizen. His *Japan: An Attempt at an Interpretation* (1904) is generally considered the most informative and insightful depiction of that country written in its time. He also wrote several collections of short stories and miscellanies about Japan. He died in 1904, bitterly disappointed that the western materialism that he had been attempting to escape was already embracing Japan.

In "The Supernatural Horror in Literature," H.P. Lovecraft stated that Hearn had crystallized the eerie lore and whispered legends of Japan with matchless skill and delicacy. *Kwaidan* and his other collections are mainly taken from old Japanese books. "The Woman of the Snow," according to Hearn, comes from a native legend in Musashi province and may not have been previously recorded. In Japan, a storyteller reshapes and recolors tales into his own form, so there is no question of his authorship.

Born in 1916, Masaki Kobayashi emerged as one of Japan's leading filmmakers in the 1950's and 1960's. Although a student of philosophy, he spent much time studying Oriental art while in college. He was scarred by his war experiences, and *Ninjin no joken* (1959–1961; *The Human Con-*

dition), reflects his opposition to the cruelty of Japan's rigid army system. These criticisms are voiced in documentary form in *Tokyo saiban* (1983; *The Tokyo Trial*), a four-hour, thirty-seven-minute depiction of the trials of Japanese war criminals. His *Kabe atsuki heya* (1953; *Room with Thick Walls*), scripted by Kōbō Abe, was an early attack of Japanese war atrocities (although he limits his criticism of the American occupation in this work). In the internationally acclaimed *Seppuku* (1962; *Harakiri*) and *Joiuchi* (1967; *Rebellion*), Kobayashi uses period action to advance his antiauthoritarian themes.

Several of his early films tackle other topics. *Kono hiroi sora no dokoka ni* (1954; *Somewhere Beneath the Wide Sky*), an uplifting lower middle-class melodrama about a handicapped girl and a shop boy, contains many earmarks of the melodramas made by Keisuke Kinoshita, his mentor. The charming *Uruwashiki saigetsu* (1955; *Beautiful Days*), centers on the relationship between a young girl and three friends of her dead brother. In the later *Kaseki* (1975; literally, "fossil"), he focuses on an elderly executive who has a spiritual awakening while touring France.

Kobayashi's films have always been noted for their brilliant compositions. *Kwaidan*, however, is his only film noted for serenity and a complete fictionalization of the exotica of Japanese folklore.

Bill Thompson

THE LACEMAKER
(LA DENTELLIÈRE)

Origin: France
Released: 1977
Released in U.S.: 1977
Production: Yves Peyrot and Yves Gasser for Citel Films, Action Films, and Filmproduktion Janus
Direction: Claude Goretta
Screenplay: Claude Goretta and Pascal Lainé; based on the novel by Lainé
Cinematography: Jean Boffety
Editing: Joëlle Van Effenterre
Art direction: no listing
Music: Pierre Jansen
MPAA rating: no listing
Running time: 108 minutes

Principal characters:

Béatrice (Pomme)	Isabelle Huppert
François	Yves Beneyton
Marylène	Florence Giorgetti
Pomme's mother	Anne Marie Düringer
Marianne	Renata Schroeter
Painter	Michel de Ré
François' mother	Monique Chaumette
François' father	Jean Obé

Swiss director Claude Goretta's third feature, *The Lacemaker*, his first made in France, is a beautifully crafted "little" film, rich in feeling and understanding. The film synthesizes several potentially sentimental genres— *Bildungsroman*, pastoral, seduction story, poor-meets-rich romance—and manages to evoke fresh responses to its own particular time and place. This is partly because Goretta has filtered his contemporary morality tale, reminiscent in some ways of director Eric Rohmer's films, such as *L'Amour, l'après-midi* (1972; *Chloé in the Afternoon*), through the political consciousness of May, 1968; more important, he has drawn upon the humanist tradition reflected in the seventeenth century genre paintings from which the film derives its title. The result, like the heroine's face, is deceptively simple, redolent with meaning, though its expression is shifting and ultimately bittersweet.

The heroine is Béatrice (Isabelle Huppert), nicknamed "Pomme," a shy young shop girl in a Paris beauty parlor. The story depicts her first romance with a well-bred Sorbonne student named François (Yves Beneyton), who meets her while on vacation in Normandy and rejects her some months later, bringing on an emotional and physical collapse. As the seasons shift from spring to late autumn and the scenery, from seacoast resort to the crowded Parisian streets, the film seemingly invites interpretation as a modern parable of lost innocence, a Marxist allegory on the plight of the working class, or even a clinical study of mental breakdown. Goretta's concerns, however, are less moralistic than Rohmer's, less political than Jean-Luc Godard's or Alain Tanner's, and less intellectual than Alain Resnais'. His deepest interest—and sympathy—lies with Béatrice herself, what she has lost and, possibly, what she has gained.

The film begins with a slow tracking shot through the beauty salon and first explores the friendship between Pomme and Marylène (Florence Giorgetti), a slightly older and far more experienced beautician. Like her illustrious namesake, Marilyn Monroe, whose poster adorns a wall in her high-rise apartment, Marylène is blonde, restless, and seductive, a compulsive poser. Pomme seems her complete opposite: small, quiet, unworldly, utterly guileless. In the opening sequences Marylène acts almost as an older sister, bringing Pomme home for dinner after work, giving her a sweater for her eighteenth birthday, inviting Pomme to join her on her vacation at the beach. Though her extroverted personality, sensuousness, and superior position in the shop clearly present her as a foil, Marylène is shown to be no less vulnerable to men than Pomme will be. Early in the film her married boyfriend of three years calls her at work to inform her that he is breaking off their affair. That night Marylène takes Pomme home for dinner and weeps bitterly over the phone to her lover. After he hangs up on her, she seems bent on jumping off the balcony, but instead throws her white teddy bear over the balustrade. At a loss to help her friend, Pomme can only offer to retrieve the bear from the street, but Marylène tells her to forget it.

This opening movement of *The Lacemaker*, concentrating on the friendship between the women and Marylène's unhappy affair, establishes both the essentially passive quality of Béatrice's character and the motif of abandonment associated with her life. Before she came to Paris, her father had left their home in the country, forcing her and her mother to move in order to find work. In the film's second movement, Marylène will move out of their double room at the hotel to take up with another man; in the end, François will also abandon her.

Marylène decides to forget her troubles by taking a vacation in Cabourg. Pomme will be good company until she can pick up a new man. At the disco, Marylène gyrates provocatively in her see-through blouse; when Pomme is finally asked to dance, she declines—she does not know how. Marylène soon meets someone and returns one morning to move out her things. Pomme acquiesces silently, setting forth for the beach alone and seeming to enjoy the ambience of the peaceful resort town. While eating an ice cream at an outdoor café, she meets François, who introduces himself as a brilliant student of literature from Paris. Goretta departs from his customary unobtrusive cinematic style in the following scene, with a beautiful sequence of long tracking shots and crosscutting to depict François and Pomme looking for each other the next day. The distance between them in the panoramic vistas and the high-angle camera placements suggest both the separate worlds that they inhabit and the fate that draws them together. When they finally meet on the boardwalk, Pomme wears a white dress and François a dark T-shirt and jeans, visually underscoring their differences the very moment their romance begins.

Pomme is attracted by what she calls his considerateness. François shows her the town, invites her for coffee on the sea wall, takes her on a picnic where a local artist secretly sketches her, fetches her shawl when she shivers in the night air, drives her to the soldier's cemetery where she marks a single white cross with a stone. There they meet Marylène and her new boyfriend. She tells François, "Take good care of her. She's fragile." Goretta symbolizes their growing relationship in a game of blindman's buff they play on a steep cliff overlooking the channel. François leads her to the very edge, but Pomme follows his commands without ever opening her eyes. When she finally does, he has to grab her to keep her from falling with fright. Soon after this strangely disturbing interlude, Pomme agrees to sleep with him, her first time with a man.

Goretta cuts abruptly from the bucolic courtship in Cabourg to the domestic arrangements back in Paris. Béatrice leaves her mother's flat, taking one last look at her scrapbook, and moves into François' walk-up. While he goes to classes, she paints his apartment. After an evening listening to an intellectual discussion among his friends about bourgeois society, she asks François what "dialectical" means. When he suggests that she look for a more interesting job, she says that she hopes one day to become a hair stylist. Almost imperceptibly through such scenes, Goretta traces the erosion of their relationship. Though his allegiance is clearly with Béatrice, the director never caricatures those who ignore or undervalue her, nor does he turn his story into a strident feminist tract. Marylène, though a trifle vulgar and superficial, is also a victim of society's illusions; François, though self-absorbed and finally no less shallow than Marylène, is always courteous and genuinely well-meaning. His life with Béatrice seems epitomized in a scene where she tries to eat an apple silently (her nickname, "pomme," means "apple") without disturbing his studies, and he becomes bothered not so much by the sound as her effort at self-effacement.

The pivotal scene occurs during the couple's visit with François' parents. The drive to the country is cold and rainy. When the dinner conversation turns to news about François' successful young friends, Béatrice is overcome by a violent fit of choking. Once she has recovered, François' mother

(Monique Chaumette) asks about the American writer who died that way. If François' mother is insensitive toward Béatrice, his father (Jean Obé) is quite caring. In a tender scene, he takes her out back to see the family kennels. Asked if she is scared by the dogs, Béatrice replies that they seem very nice. Her trusting nature here recalls her role in the game of blindman's buff. The danger for Béatrice in both cases remains muted, imperfectly repressed.

Somber chamber music accompanies the couple's return to Paris, and without a single argument, their romance declines. In a high-angle long-shot foreshadowing their parting and mirroring the panoramic views of Cabourg, François rushes across a city boulevard, leaving Béatrice stranded on a traffic island. Goretta then crosscuts between François at home rehearsing a speech calling off the affair and Béatrice walking back from work, the editing again reinforcing their separation. Béatrice silently accepts the news, washing lettuce while he explains how breaking up will be best for both of them.

Goretta has employed a slow narrative pace throughout *The Lacemaker*, but now events lead quickly to the film's powerful denouement. Béatrice becomes physically ill and severely depressed (the critic Gillian Parker assumes that she is pregnant, but this point is never made explicit). François describes their parting to one of his Marxist friends (Renata Schroeter), who chastises him for ignoring Béatrice's virtues and treating her "like an employer." One day, Béatrice collapses in the middle of a busy intersection.

The final sequence takes place four months later in a sanatorium where Béatrice has been convalescing. François decides to pay a visit, but only after persuading his two friends to keep him company on the drive. When Béatrice walks down a long corridor of the institution to greet him, her appearance is profoundly disquieting. She wears a shapeless black dress like a shroud; she moves and speaks mechanically, drained of all of her former charm. They pass the time together in a park filled with fallen yellow leaves, François filling the gap between them with small talk. When he asks what she has been doing since they parted, Béatrice tonelessly describes a trip to Greece with someone she met. François seems relieved to learn that she has taken new lovers, and they say goodbye with smiles. In the car before rejoining his friends, however, François weeps over the change that has come over her. In the closing shot, the camera tracks in on the therapy room where Béatrice sits alone in a corner knitting in front of a bright poster of Mykonos. Her foreign travel was an illusion, both a deception and a farewell gift for François. As the truth dawns, she turns to the camera with a chilling expression which Goretta then freezes. The closing title appears, with its reference to the anonymous working women—seamstresses, watergirls, lacemakers—of the old paintings: "He will have passed her by without really noticing her. . . . She is one of those who leave no clues, one of those who are difficult to fathom, who require close questioning to come at their meaning." Béatrice's face as she stares into the camera is indeed ambiguous. Is it the face of madness, a solitary soul broken by society's injustice? Or is it the look of defiance and recrimination born of inarticulate rebellion? Goretta leaves it for the audience to judge. Perhaps her expression may best be read as the shock of recognition that follows knowledge of the world.

The Lacemaker is marked by the economy, compassion, and close observation of its director and the virtuoso performance of its star, Isabelle Huppert. Goretta captures Pomme's essential innocence through the many images of white associated with her: the uniform she wears at work, the dress she wears when she first meets François, the sheets she folds while visiting his relatives, the walls she paints in his apartment, even the yarn she knits in the final scene. Similarly, he identifies François with the conventions of his bourgeois class: his 2CV, the *Le Monde* he buys when he meets Pomme, the Gallimard editions that line his walls. Huppert, who appears in nearly every scene, appears to age a full generation from the plump and freckled girl who splashes carelessly in the sea to the wasted woman whose stare haunts the viewer long after the film's closing credits. Along with her performance as the murderous Violette Nozière in her next film, Claude Chabrol's *Violette* (1978), Huppert has created two of the definitive roles in French cinema of the 1970's.

Lloyd Michaels

LACOMBE, LUCIEN

Origin: France, Italy, and West Germany
Released: 1974
Released in U.S.: 1974
Production: Louis Malle for Nouvelles Éditions de Films/UPF/Vides
Films/Hallelujah Films
Direction: Louis Malle
Screenplay: Louis Malle and Patrick Modiano
Cinematography: Tonino Delli Colli
Editing: Suzanne Baron
Art direction: Ghislain Uhry
Music: Django Reinhardt
MPAA rating: R
Running time: 136 minutes
Running time in U.S.: 114 minutes

> *Principal characters:*
> Lucien . . . . Pierre Blaise
> France . . . . Aurore Clément
> Albert Horn . . . . Holger Lowenadler
> Bella Horn . . . . Thérèse Giehse
> Jean-Bernard de Boisin . . . . Stéphane Bouy
> Betty Beaulieu . . . . Loumi Iacobesco
> Mme Lacombe . . . . Gilberte Rivet
> M. Laborit . . . . Jacques Rispal

One of the most inspiring stories to come out of the experience of World
War II is the heroic legend of the Resistance organizations which operated
in the countries occupied by the Nazis. Of all the European nations to be
invaded, the one whose underground force has been most celebrated is that
of France, whose Maquis has come to symbolize the spirit and courage of
democratic defiance. The detention of Klaus Barbie, the accused murderer
of Jean Moulin, leader of the Maquis, underscores the ongoing interest in
bringing before the bar of justice all of those who are guilty of crimes
against this organization of patriots. Understandably, most Frenchmen
would like to believe that the majority of the population of France during
World War II either belonged to or supported the Maquis, but as is usually
the case, historical reality is somewhat more complex.

Nearly thirty years after the end of the war, Louis Malle wrote, produced,
and directed *Lacombe, Lucien,* a film designed to grasp some aspects of the
reality of life for the French during the German Occupation. It was a film,
Malle claimed, which would "show ordinary Fascism" and "tell about the

obscure, mediocre people who are not in the history books." The four-hour documentary *Le Chagrin et la pitié* (1971; *The Sorrow and the Pity*), by Marcel Ophüls, "opened the way to tackling the subject," according to Malle, and his childhood memories of four Jewish boys hidden in a convent, who were sent to their deaths along with their protector priest when they were betrayed, gave him his inspiration. Although *Lacombe, Lucien* is not based directly on any specific incident, Malle says that he has invented nothing, that his reading in books and Occupation newspapers and his discussions with thousands of people underlie the details of the film.

Lucien Lacombe (played by Pierre Blaise, a woodsman who had never acted before) is an uneducated seventeen-year-old country boy living in Southwest France in June, 1944. His father is a prisoner of war, and his mother is living with the landlord of their farm. He scrubs floors in the hospital in Figeac, a small provincial city, and he hunts for diversion and for the necessity of adding some meat (mostly rabbit) to his menu. His involvement with the occupying forces is a part of a chain of circumstance that defies volition and suggests that many "decisions" are actually a product of proximity and reaction. Bored with his work, irritated with his mother, and directionless in the absence of any kind of guidance, he tries to join the local Resistance cell. When they turn him away because of his youth, he is frustrated and his pride is wounded. His anger increases when his bicycle develops a flat tire on the way back to town, and he joins the German police when the opportunity occurs. Their tasks give him an outlet for his energy, and his new power over his neighbors gives him a kind of stature in his own eyes. The consequences of his actions are never an issue because he is living in a kind of permanent present, in which no action is judged for its consequences. His initial delight in his uniform, his gun, and his association with people who seem in control demonstrates the basic, mindless appeal of a Fascist organization to a person who has not developed that crucial quality of human maturity—that is, the capacity for moral understanding. The fact that it is obvious to nearly everyone that Germany's time is up makes his blindness even more bizarre.

The film is structured according to two basic conflicts which Malle uses to coordinate the sequences of the narrative. They are the timeless struggle of freedom against enclosure and the timely (even trendy) contrast between style and substance. Because Malle does not want the audience to be able to identify too easily with his protagonist, or even to like him particularly, Lacombe does not learn very much during the course of the film, nor does he grow toward the kind of humane maturity that is a part of the implied ideological basis for the film. He does, however, come to understand some of the conditions that should compel a choice made on moral grounds. His gradually expanding awareness of the necessities for action based on morality occurs as the two basic conflicts are developed. Lacombe is attracted to the swaggering Nazis with their fancy suits and flashy cars because he has always lived on the surface of existence. He has never doubted or reflected on his freedom of action because it has never been challenged, and because it is essentially a freedom to be bored. The complication in the action which enriches and entangles his life occurs in a typically random fashion when he accidentally becomes involved with a family of Jewish refugees attempting to remain invisible until the Nazis are defeated.

These people are, at first glance, drab and trapped; their apartment is dense with clutter, a realm of limits, photographed at slanting angles to emphasize the boundaries that did not exist for Lacombe in the open countryside. The family includes a once prominent master tailor, Albert Horn (Holger Lowenadler), his lovely teenaged daughter France (Aurore Clément), and his aged mother (Thérèse Giehse). Withdrawn, reserved, unfathomable, they are photographed in subdued, mixed light, underscoring the lines on their faces—unlike the Nazis, who are seen in glistening brilliance, all hard edge and high contrast. Drawn to this family at first by curiosity and by a desire to impress these strangers of another class with his new authority, Lacombe begins to fall in love with the young girl. Their relationship is a parody of conventional courtship because she is attracted by his power to pull her into the horrors of a world that she has been trained to avoid, and he is fascinated by her ability to charm him into an attempt to master the ways of a culture that he has been taught to ignore or despise. On a more primal level, there is an instinctive sensual reaction between them that overcomes or contradicts ideology and upbringing, which serves to reinforce the essentially human element which is at the core of all positive action in the film.

As Lacombe enters their world and begins to learn about the Horns' desperate life, his own perspective broadens subtly. The tailor is both the father of his girlfriend and an unusual version of the father he cannot turn to now for guidance. He admires the man's attempts to maintain some semblance of dignity while complying with the demands of the Nazi officials for custom-crafted suits, and as he watches Horn struggling to retain his integrity, Lacombe begins to see the actual cost of the worldly pleasures that the Nazis offer. It becomes important for Lacombe to earn some measure of respect from the tailor, and he grasps, in his ignorance, for some way to impress the man. In a superb scene, when Lacombe chides Horn for not appreciating his daughter, the old man looks at him with eyes as old as time and rebukes him wearily, "We're both fragile." No connection is really made, but Lacombe has been exposed to a world infinitely vaster than his.

Similarly, Lacombe's love for the girl enables him to feel her confinement (but not her shame) and permits him to begin to understand the true value of freedom. His previous carefree life in the country now seems less ordinary and more interesting, since he can imagine the possibility of sharing it with another person. Lacombe begins to sense also (and the audience sees this very clearly) that the jailers, the collaborators he was dazzled by, are in a jail also, and their opulent headquarters is shown as the fancy dungeon it is when Malle's camera moves through its long corridors, slowly past its security control points, and amid its garish salons, where people out of George Grosz caricatures feign gaiety in rooms illuminated by ghastly green and purple lights.

Because Malle is interested in exploring the ways in which the myths and slogans of both the Right and the Left are really convenient pretexts for avoiding the actuality of the experience, Lacombe's ability to respond to what he sees is limited in a way which is calculated to frustrate the expectations and even the desires of the audience. He never becomes an appropriate lover for France (the irony of her name is unavoidable), a real champion for the tailor and his mother, or a man capable of indignation about what the Nazis have done. When Lacombe flees the chaos of the final collapse of the collaborationist regime, his short stay in the country with France is predictably idyllic, but this episode, too, must be temporary. His "story" as a series of succeeding presents is concluded, without any possibility of a future, when the local Resistance fighters track him down. The film concludes with the printed information that he has been executed, a kind of justice that is understandable for one who has betrayed his neighbors and watched unaffected while they were tortured. Still, he hardly seems like a traitor or even much of a villain. In a sense, Lacombe is simply another casualty of war.

Malle maintains that he interviewed more than one thousand boys before he found Blaise, and the young man's roughly handsome, brooding, and often impassive face reflects the character of Lacombe with an almost uncanny precision. His lack of acting experience removes any sense of reflection from his performance, and this suits the character superbly. Lowenadler has a look of resignation and gravity that seems to have been evolved through centuries of European intrigue, and Clément, conversely, has a freshness about her than makes her degradation especially sorrowful. Yet while acknowledging that the setting and acting are excellent, some critics have maintained that the film is not totally successful because it is so difficult for the audience to become involved with Lacombe that one can be "interested, but never implicated." Perhaps this is part of Malle's point. At the beginning of the film, Lacombe is totally absorbed in himself. Then, when he falls in love with France, he becomes interested in her, and gradually he begins to develop a genuine concern for her, to care for her as a separate human being. He then repeats this process with her father, moving again from an interest in a person who can do something for him to an emerging interest in the person as a recognizable and separate human creature. Throughout the film, however, he is very self-centered and unable to sustain his sense of "an other" for very long. In addition, he can never see the humanity in a person he does not know directly. This flaw, finally, is what condemns him to be merely prey for the Fascist lure.

Where Malle's film is at its most demanding is in its appeal to the viewer to care about Lacombe, to see him as more than simply a name on an official list. Lacombe is certainly an unlikely subject for the sympathy of the kind of viewer for whom this film was made, the serious, reflective, intellectual person who is very concerned with the morality of all action. Yet in *Lacombe, Lucien*, it is that kind of person whom Malle challenges: Malle asks this viewer to try to understand, to accept, even to sympathize with this uneducated, self-centered peasant. This is the kind of compassion, ultimately, that, were it widespread enough, would make totalitarianism impossible. It is from this perspective that Malle can comment in sorrow and pity on the French who were collaborators.

Leon Lewis

LAND IN ANGUISH
(TERRA EM TRANSE)

Origin: Brazil
Released: 1967
Released in U.S.: 1970
Production: Mapa Filmes and Difilme
Direction: Glauber Rocha
Screenplay: Glauber Rocha
Cinematography: Dib Lufti
Editing: Eduardo Escorel
Art direction: Paulo Gil Soares
Music: Sérgio Ricardo
Running time: 115 minutes
Also known as: Earth Entranced and *Land in a Trance*

Principal characters:
Paulo Martins	Jardel Filho
Porfírio Díaz	Paulo Autran
Felipe Vieira	José Lewgoy
Sara	Glauce Rocha
Júlio Fuentes	Paulo Gracindo
Álvaro	Hugo Carvana
Sílvia	Danuza Leão
Padre Gil	Jofre Soares
Senator	Modesto de Sousa
Man of the People	Flávio Migliaccio
Woman of the People	Telma Reston
Chief of Security	Mário Lago
Jerônimo	José Marinho
Aldo	Francisco Milani
Felício	Emanuel Cavalcânti

Glauber Rocha was the undisputed leader of the Brazilian *Cinema Novo* movement, which arose in the early 1960's. At least in its initial phase (1960-1964), *Cinema Novo* called for an alternative form of cinematic practice that would combat the illusionism of what was called the "dominant" cinema (Hollywood) and at the same time participate in the process of national liberation. *Cinema Novo* attempted to portray what its participants saw as the true face of Brazil's underdevelopment as a means of creating a critical consciousness in the Brazilian people. Rocha's films, borrowing from the political tradition of Sergei Eisenstein, Bertolt Brecht, and the Italian neorealists, are complex discussions of Third World politics and aesthetics.

Land in Anguish is the major film of *Cinema Novo*'s second phase, which ranges from 1964 to 1968, from the military *coup d'état* of 1964, which overthrew the populist regime of João Goulart to the military's declaration of the Fifth Institutional Act (1968), which initiated a period of extremely repressive military rule. During this period, in which there was still limited space for political debate, the focus of *Cinema Novo* shifted from rural to urban Brazil, as filmmakers turned their cameras, so to speak, on themselves in an attempt to understand the failure of the Left in 1964. Rocha's film is an anguished dissection of the "populist pact" that characterized the Goulart years and a brilliantly complex analysis of the relationship between art and politics in Latin America. Many critics place *Land in Anguish* among the finest political films ever made.

In terms of its narrative construction, *Land in Anguish* is the agonizing death-poem of Paulo Martins (Jardel Filho), whose life passes before him in his final moments. The film is circular in structure. It begins and ends with Paulo Martins' armed flight and dying moments. The events immediately preceding his flight are presented in a brief prologue that sets the tone and stage for the discourse to follow. The film's narration is mediated through the subjectivity of poet Paulo Martins in a sort of delirious flashback composed of Paulo's recollections of the political and personal events that have led to his failure and impending death.

Rocha's film, however, deals not only with Brazil but also with the tradition of politics and relationships of power throughout the Ibero-American world, set in a quasi-mythical context. The film's action takes place in the imaginary country of Eldorado, a name that recalls the Spanish conquistadors' dream of the promised land filled with gold. One of its protagonists, a right-wing political leader, is Porfírio Díaz (Paulo Autran), the name of the Mexican dictator prior to the Mexican Revolution. Eldorado's president, who never actually appears in the film, is named Fernández, and the country's major press and media magnate is Júlio Fuentes (Paulo Gracindo), both of whom have Spanish, not Portuguese, surnames.

The province of Eldorado where much of the action occurs is Alecrim, a name that recalls Brazil's Lusitanian roots. At one point Brazil's discovery is allegorically represented, with Díaz, a priest, a Portuguese conquistador, and an Indian surrounding a cross on an otherwise deserted beach. The film presents Eldoradó as little more than a series of governmental palaces set against an undefined tropical background. There is little realistic development of cinematic space, thus providing the film with a level of abstraction that a more traditional approach might have rendered impossible.

In the prologue, Felipe Vieira (José Lewgoy), populist governor of Alecrim, is reluctant to resist an order from Fernández to resign as governor. He knows that if he resists there will be widespread bloodshed, but that if he does not Porfírio Díaz will come to power in a coup. After an angry discussion in which Vieira rejects Paulo Martins' entreaties to take up arms, Paulo flees the governor's palace with Sara (Glauce Rocha), a Communist militant who serves as Vieira's secretary. In his car, Paulo breaks through a police barricade and is mortally wounded.

Through his death-poem, the viewer learns that four years earlier Paulo Martins had been a dedicated follower of Porfírio Díaz, who had been elected senator. Paulo himself was in line for election to federal deputy in the next elections. Disillusioned with Díaz, desirous of freedom to make his own decisions, and interested in exploring a new, more political form of poetry, Paulo leaves Díaz and goes to Alecrim, where he joins Sara in Vieira's gubernatorial campaign. Vieira wins the election, but the elitist, ultimately authoritarian nature of his populist politics is soon revealed, and Paulo realizes that he has become a tool in the hands of political interests much larger than himself. Again disillusioned, Paulo begins a life of decadent bourgeois orgies and existential anguish in the company of Júlio Fuentes, a "progressive" national industrialist and press magnate. Fuentes asks Paulo to direct his newspaper and television chains.

Sara later reappears and convinces Paulo to make a television report to destroy Díaz, now allied with EXPLINT, the Company of International Exploitation. The film within the film, *Biography of an Adventurer*, exposes Díaz' successive political betrayals. Angrily denounced as a traitor by his former mentor Díaz, Paulo once again joins Vieira, this time in his presidential campaign. Yet the Right is already preparing its coup, and although Vieira's campaign gains momentum in the carnival of national politics (ironically emphasized as such in a sequence depicting a rally in which the masses and a senator dance the samba), it is doomed to failure. The narrative returns to the film's starting point as the viewer sees Paulo offer Vieira a gun, which he refuses. He prefers to dictate a "noble" statement of national conciliation and unity. Paulo's dying moments and silhouetted, uplifted machine gun alternate in the final sequence with shots of Díaz' imagined coronation.

Paulo Martins oscillates between two apparently opposite extremes—the Rightist Díaz and the Leftist Vieira—before striking out on what is ultimately a suicidal and individualistic mission of armed struggle. *Land in Anguish* is a graph of his consciousness as he vacillates between a personal desire for change and transformation and a political praxis that does little but reinforce the existing power structure. Paulo lives an unresolvable contradiction between the personal and the political, between art and politics. His life is informed by the impossibility of reconciling his personal life and history, by the great distance between his desires and anxieties and the possibility of achieving or resolving them.

In *Land in Anguish*, Glauber Rocha employs the complex character-types that characterize all of his films. There exists no simple division between good and evil, for Rocha's characters are good and evil at the same time; they carry their contradiction with them. At the same time, they represent historical forces much larger than themselves. Paulo Martins is not simply a poet involved in politics, he is *the* Latin American intellectual-artist faced with unresolvable choices. Díaz is not simply a right-wing zealot who uses an ultimately Fascist religious discourse; he is *the* authoritarian Ibero-American dictator. In this sense, *Land in Anguish* is a total denunciation of all the various elements that make up the political "trance" of Latin America.

Vieira is the Populist leader who gives his followers the illusion of being in power through him. His true allegiance, however, is to the established order rather than to the people. When forced to choose between his electoral promises and the interests of the powerful, he chooses the latter. In an ultimately authoritarian gesture, he expropriates the people's voice for his own benefit. When the people attempt to use their own voice, as in the scenes involving the Man of the People (Flávio Migliaccio) and Felício (Emanuel Cavalcânti), he unleashes, or at least does not restrain, the forces of repression. It is precisely Vieira's refusal to order the arrest of the Man of the People's murderer that leads Paulo Martins to abandon him and join Fuentes.

The highly individual camera work, the ultimately baroque *mise en scène*, and the experimental montage, which uses frequent mismatches and Eisensteinian jump cuts, emphasize and demystify the hesitantly ambivalent and ultimately conservative nature of Vieira's politics. Vieira normally appears on the veranda of his palace, that is, on the periphery of the symbolic center of power. Díaz, on the other hand, normally appears inside his palace. Vieira thus never really exercises power, while Díaz never ceases to do so. Vieira's political and personal style—his unaffected manner of dress and informal manner—is designed to reinforce the illusion that he is "people." The music that frequently accompanies him—samba and Afro-Brazilian rhythms—also emphasizes a link with the masses; nevertheless, his aloofness in the few sequences in which he appears face-to-face with the people, undercuts and demystifies the illusion.

Through Vieira, Rocha denounces not only the process of Populism and the fraudulence of leadership but also the ambivalence and indecision of a society whose development has stagnated in the hands of corrupt leaders. He denounces as well the tactics of Communist militants such as Sara and Aldo (Francisco Milani) in their support of men like Vieira, support that has its historical basis in the Brazilian Communist Party's support of figures such as Juscelino Kubitschek, Jânio Quadros, and João Goulart in the period before the coup. At the same time, Sara is the only person given a coherent political consciousness. It is she who constantly brings Paulo back to reality from his sometimes romantic political beliefs.

Paulo's television documentary, *Biography of an Adventurer*, demystifies

Díaz, the other side of the political coin. Rocha's use of the film-within-the-film recalls the "News on the March" newsreel in Orson Welles's *Citizen Kane* (1941). Both "News on the March" and Paulo's documentary trace the lives of powerful, arrogant, and often treacherous men. Just as "News on the March" is intended to destroy Kane, so, too, does Paulo's film-within-the-film propose to destroy Díaz. Yet at the same time, *Biography of an Adventurer* encapsulates *Land in Anguish* as a whole, for Paulo, too, is an adventurer of sorts, whose own career is marked by his successive betrayals of his political leaders.

Díaz, the prototype Ibero-American despot, personifies the imperial origins of Brazil and imagines himself being crowned emperor. As if to reinforce his imperial quality, the music that accompanies him is not the samba of Vieira's campaigns, but, rather, operatic excerpts from Carlos Gomes and Giuseppe Verdi. Yet the central image of Díaz, and the one that concentrates and encapsulates his historical and political background, is his initial appearance in the film as he rides in an open car, framed against the sky and carrying the cross of the Portuguese navigators and the black flag of the Inquisition.

Vieira and Díaz represent apparently opposite poles of Eldorado's political spectrum. Díaz is linked to imperialism (EXPLINT) while Vieira has the support of the Communists. Yet both are bourgeois politicians who ultimately represent and support the status quo. Their ultimate identity is revealed through the parallel montage of their respective presidential campaigns. Paulo's disenchantment with all-bourgeois leaders—expressed at one point in his derision of Vieira as "our great leader"—is revealed fully in his agonizing poem-scream which is repeated in both the prologue and epilogue, saying, in essence, that this self-congratulatory mode of political practice is no longer acceptable.

Stylistically speaking, the influence of Eisenstein pervades the film. The scene at the political rally where Felício is killed recalls the sequence from *Potemkin* (1925) in which Doctor Smirnov uses his glasses as a sort of magnifying glass to examine maggot-covered meat. Rocha's senator uses his glasses in a similar fashion to examine Felício's body while praising the "perfect" society of Eldorado. His words complete the analogy with *Potemkin*, as corrupt members of the ruling class deny the existence of even the most evident social problems.

As in earlier films, Rocha is concerned with the resurrection of a new society from the old, a concern with clearly religious overtones. What interests him is the moment of "trance," the moment of crisis, the moment of revolution. He neither outlines political programs nor maps a political future. He denies the established order and the established solutions (Populism and Fascism), which are dead ends and forms of alienation that must be destroyed for humanity to take control of its own destiny. Whereas on the one hand *Land in Anguish* is indeed an anguished cry of political defeat, on the other, its creator's vision of a new society rising from the ruins is implicit.

Land in Anguish, however, is much more than a cry of defeat. It is a reflection on the relationship between art and politics. Paulo Martins is a poet. He makes a film and it is a poem that sums up the dialectic. Poetry and politics are in conflict. Art may be out of place in a "land in a trance," but ultimately, art transcends not only politics but also death. Although Paulo Martins—one poet—may die, art, the film itself, remains. *Land in Anguish*, through frenetic camera movements and baroque *mise en scène* and discontinuous montage, negates the static, negates a privileged, univocal vision of reality. It negates, in other words, death itself. Paulo Martins may die, but the film's final image, with him and his uplifted machine gun silhouetted against the sky and accompanied by sounds of battle, indicates that the struggle continues.

Randal Johnson

LAND WITHOUT BREAD
(LAS HURDES)

Origin: Spain
Released: 1933
Released in U.S.: no listing
Production: Ramón Acin
Direction: Luis Buñuel
Assistant direction: Rafael Sanchez Ventura and Pierre Unik
Screenplay: Luis Buñuel; based on a book by Maurice Legendre
Cinematography: Eli Lotar
Editing: Luis Buñuel
Narration: Luis Buñuel and Pierre Unlik; read by Abel Jacquin
Art direction: no listing
Music: Johannes Brahms
Running time: 27 minutes
Also known as: Tierra sin pan

Principal characters: no listing

Land Without Bread is, strictly speaking, a documentary film about a group of small, remote villages isolated in a mountainous region of Spain. Yet its subject, the time at which it was made, and the motives of its director, Luis Buñuel, are such that to call it simply a documentary does not accurately describe the film—indeed, is misleading. It may be best to examine first the forces which shaped *Land Without Bread* in order to arrive at a fair understanding of the film.

Central to a grasp of the film is a knowledge of the early life of its director. Buñuel was born in 1900, in Calanda, Spain, into a wealthy family. He was well educated and reared as a devout Catholic. Alfonso XIII was king at the time; his was a corrupt monarchy that openly repressed the landless peasants and working classes, who nevertheless continually attempted to revolt. After enduring several uprisings and attempts to reform the government, the monarchy finally collapsed and the ruling classes lost power. Ultimately, Primo de Rivera took over rule in a military dictatorship. For Buñuel, the insulation of bourgeois life, the hierarchies of class, the urgencies of class struggle, and the rigid constraints of religion were major influences.

Added to these were his strong family relationships, which encouraged Buñuel's ironic sense of humor and taste for the enigmatic, and his genuine feeling for humanity. By the time he was enrolled at the University of Madrid, an urge to revolt against the organizing forces of society was fully aroused, and he spent much of the remainder of his life in active revolution against the complacency of "civilization."

Buñuel was not alone in his efforts during the 1920's and 1930's to awaken a complacent public. He shared his views with the Surrealists of Paris, where he moved after completing his degree at the university (switching from the study of natural science to philosophy and letters). The Surrealists were fighting not only the rationalizing, repressive forces of society but also the avant-garde movement in French art, whose concerns in their view were superficial, romantic, and trite. Buñuel has said that the Surrealists were not making works of art and did not wish to be remembered by art historians but rather were genuinely interested in changing the world.

The principles of the Surrealists were based in part on the work of Sigmund Freud. His influence was felt broadly in literature and art, as elsewhere, but although many artists of the period sought to explore the workings of the unconscious, the Surrealists thought that they were missing the point, providing only a semblance—usually romanticized—of such an exploration. The Surrealists attempted to apply the methods of unconscious thought, of dreams, directly to reality, creating associations which jarred viewers or readers into a new awareness.

Buñuel himself was interested in the manner in which film approached the structure and sense of thoughts and dreams. He collaborated with Salvador Dalí in making what has been acknowledged as the first truly Surrealist film, *Un Chien andalou* (1928; *An Andalusian Dog*), which Buñuel's biographer Francisco Aranda has called something of a text of the language of dreams and unconscious thinking. Buñuel's first exposure to Freud was reading *The Psychopathology of Everyday Life* (1904) in 1921, and Buñuel asserts in his autobiography that Freud's theories, particularly of the unconscious, were most important to him. Freud's influence is certainly clear: Buñuel described *Un Chien andalou* not as a work of art but rather as "a desperate appeal to murder."

Un Chien andalou was followed by *L'Âge d'or* (1930), which began as another collaboration with Dalí but which, after a falling out between the two men, evolved entirely as Buñuel's work. If the earlier film left any doubt in viewers' minds about the political and social views of its director, its sequel forever banished them. *L'Âge d'or* again used the patterns of unconscious thought as a model for its structure and yet managed to allow for greater naturalism (not really a contradiction) than that found in the more highly contrived sequences of *Un Chien andalou*. Herein lies a key to *Land Without Bread*: As unconscious thought does not so much distort elements of experience as create associations with other aspects of experience, so *L'Âge d'or* lifts elements of reality intact, placing them in new associations which produce a concussive impact. Aranda explains that Buñuel's interest in things arises from their intrinsic contradictions, the ironies that are naturally present.

In the part of Spain known as Las Hurdes, Buñuel found a subject in which surprise and contradiction were inherent to such an extreme that it seemed more surreal than any scenario that he could have devised, and his film of the region is seen by many as the completing work of a Surrealist trilogy which includes his two earlier films. By the time that he made *Land Without Bread*, however, Buñuel had become dissatisfied with the Surrealists and their self-proclaimed intellectual supremacy, which had made them into an ineffectual elite. He was interested in Las Hurdes because it presented an enigma: How could people endure such miserable poverty and hardship? Why did they not leave their hostile environment for one more suitable? Why was the region ignored by the world, especially the Spanish government, and no assistance offered to it? And why, in the midst of its backward, almost barbaric culture were fundamental religious codes upheld? Buñuel decided to make "an objective document, a sort of human geographical study" of the area.

The exposition of the film is very straightforward. There are three elements: the imagery, which was shot simply, with little camera movement and no artificial lighting (reflectors were used for fill and to illuminate house interiors); the narration, which is almost clinical in its dry, unemotional description of the characteristics of the community; and background music, which consists of Johannes Brahms's Fourth Symphony running throughout the film.

Two introductory titles explain that Las Hurdes was almost unknown to the world (and Spain) until the first road there was built in 1922, and that it is a place where the battle for survival is waged continually. The film opens in the village of La Alberca, which lies on the approach to Las Hurdes. The villagers participate in an annual ceremony for newlywed men: Riding on horseback, they must pull off the head of a rooster which has been suspended above the street. When they succeed, they offer wine to all the villagers. With that introduction, bizarre in itself, the film moves on to address its subject, the misery of the Hurdanos.

Their misery is absolute. Conditions of terrain and climate make subsistence all but impossible, and what little hope there is is often confounded by the Hurdanos' ignorance and superstition. Bread, for example, is an almost unknown commodity in this impoverished region, and when the schoolteacher brings some to his starving students, he must be sure that they eat it in his sight—otherwise their mistrustful parents will take it from them and throw it away. There is practically no topsoil on the rocky terrain, so villagers must transport bags of humus to small, rock terraces, hand-built beside the river for gardening. Whenever the river floods, as it frequently does, the product of this arduous labor is washed away in minutes. The soil in these small plots is fertile for one season, then it becomes exhausted; since there is too little livestock for manure, villagers must walk barefoot over rocky paths to collect special leaves which they spread on the floors of their homes, to be lived among by humans and animals until they rot and can be used as fertilizer. While collecting the leaves, the Hurdanos are sometimes bitten by adders; the bite of the snakes is not usually fatal, but the remedies which the Hurdanos apply cause infections which are fatal. The inventory of hardship is relentless, and nothing in the film suggests that there is any cause for optimism whatsoever.

This abject pessimism is perhaps the most pronounced quality of the film and makes it very disturbing to watch. Buñuel has said that it is very important to him to present to audiences the indisputable truth that the world is not the "best of all possible worlds," a message that is unmistakably clear in *Land Without Bread*. The wisdom of taking this stance becomes clearer when *Land Without Bread* is compared with a celebrated documentary film of the same period, Robert J. Flaherty's *Nanook of the North* (1922), which purports to chronicle the everyday life of an Eskimo and his family, who—like the Hurdanos—struggle with primitive means to survive against the forces of nature. In Flaherty's film, however, Nanook and his family are presented almost as characters in a story, and the events which are documented were in many cases re-created for the camera in order to allow the film to be shot in narrative sequences. Nanook's struggles are great, but he always prevails; he becomes something of a hero and takes on the qualities of the "noble savage" who lives in harmony with his environment. Flaherty's is a romantic view, and in spite of the great hardships and tests of endurance that Nanook and his family face, the film always gives the impression—apparently derived from Flaherty's own cultural biases—that they will triumph. Audiences that see *Nanook of the North* may feel gladdened, reassured at what they sense is a kind of natural harmony, and confident that Nanook will continue to win his battles for survival. What those audiences seldom learn, though, is that only a few years after the film was made, Nanook died of starvation.

Which of the two films is a more truthful document of reality or more useful in serving its subject? In Buñuel's view, a film such as *Nanook of the North* represses in a Freudian sense some of the very fundamental truths of existence. Although *Land Without Bread* did not please audiences (not surprisingly, it was banned in Spain for a period), it was nevertheless instrumental in calling attention to Las Hurdes: An improved road was built to the area not long after the film was made, and conditions there have slowly improved.

Finally, however, it must be said that *Land Without Bread* is not truly an objective document. In spite of its unobtrusive camera work, its unemotional narration, and the distant (and hence impartial) stance that the film takes, there are several aspects of the work which directly contradict its objectivity. The most pointed is a sequence in which the narrator says that goat meat is eaten only when an animal dies accidentally, which sometimes occurs where the terrain is steep and the footing uncertain. Immediately following is a shot of a goat standing on a precipice, and as an unmistakable puff of smoke appears in the lower, right-hand corner of the frame, the goat suddenly falls off the cliff. Then there is a cut on the motion of the goat falling to a shot taken from above where the goat stood, and the goat's fall is seen to its completion. Obviously this sequence was staged and the goat killed by gunfire; otherwise two cameras would have had to be already in place, both filming the goat when it "accidentally" fell to its death, a miraculous coincidence at the very least. The intent to deceive seems deliberate.

The background music, also, presents an ironic contrast to the other elements of the film. Brahms's Fourth Symphony is highly emotive and full of romantic pathos and cannot but comment upon the cold objectivity of the imagery, making its roughness truly brutal. The narration, also, is too aloof. The image of a baby wearing many necklaces elicits the comment that while the pendants are religious tokens, they can only be likened to the "barbaric" customs of more primitive cultures. Children are shown in school, and the narrator explains that although they are starving, the teacher nevertheless informs them that the sum of the angles of a triangle equals two right angles. One bright student can write on the blackboard something that he memorized from a book on morality: "Respect the property of others." Then there is the discovery on the wall of a "shocking" picture. It is an illustration of a woman dressed in an elaborate gown of the eighteenth century, and the narrator asks simply, "Why is this picture here?" The narrative does not always serve the purposes of the imagery. Sometimes it belies a cultural chauvinism that passes judgment on the Hurdanos (on, for example, their "barbaric" religious charms), and at other times, it steps into the realm of the absurd ("respect the property of others"). In spite of its cool, rational tone, its meaning is often highly ambiguous.

Land Without Bread is a film that defies neat categorization. It is a documentary film, but one in which inconsistency and manipulation call into question the whole notion of objectivity in film. It is a social commentary, but one which reveals anger not only at the society that allowed such inequity to occur and persist but also at the Hurdanos themselves for stupidly enduring their own hardship. It is a film which claims not to be a work of art and yet which employs methods—like the methods of the Surrealists— that call attention to its own form, and therefore (whether the director intended it) comment upon form in all films. These qualities are not inconsistent with Buñuel's intentions, though, for he is a director who is fascinated by ambiguity, irony, and the inexplicable. He is not one to look for simple responses to a complex world.

Land Without Bread received no awards and was not shown widely after its release. Buñuel's next film of note (after several minor works) was *Los olvidados* (1950), which is a feature-length narrative film, made in Mexico, about the violent life of homeless adolescent boys in Mexico City. Although the style and form of *Los olvidados* is completely different from *Land Without Bread*, its basis in true events and real characters, and its insistence on painting a vividly real—if bleak—picture of its subject recall the motives of the earlier work.

Rebecca Abbott

LANDSCAPE AFTER BATTLE
(KRAJOBRAZ PO BITWIE)

Origin: Poland
Released: 1970
Released in U.S.: 1978
Production: Film Polski
Direction: Andrzej Wajda
Screenplay: Andrzej Wajda and Andrzej Brzozowski; based on stories by
   Tadeusz Borowski
Cinematography: Zygmunt Samosiuk
Editing: no listing
Art direction: Jerzy Szeski
Music: Zygmunt Konieczny, Antonio Vivaldi, and Frédéric Chopin
MPAA rating: no listing
Running time: 109 minutes
Running time in U.S.: 110 minutes

> *Principal characters:*
> Tadeusz, "105" .... Daniel Olbrychski
> Charles .... Tadeusz Janczar
> Aspriant .... Mieczysław Stoor
> Nina........................... Stanislawa Celinska
> American camp commandant .... Jerzy Zelnik
> Priest .... Zygmunt Malanowicz

Andrzej Wajda has a deeply ironic understanding of the plight of Poland in modern history. Born into a military family, Wajda has often probed the prewar psyche of this class in *Lotna* (1959) and *The Girls of Wilko* (1979), as well as its devastation during the war in *Kanał* (1957) and *Popiół i diament* (1958; *Ashes and Diamonds*). His 1970 film, *Landscape After Battle*, is concerned with the plight of another typical Polish figure, the disenchanted intellectual, but in a truly harrowing situation: the displaced persons' camps of liberated Europe. Whether former officers, Communist Party organizers, or intellectuals such as the main character, the former concentration camp inmates must decide how to resume their broken lives. Based on a collection of short stories, *This Way to the Gas, Ladies and Gentlemen, and Other Stories* (1967), by Tadeusz Borowski, this feature film is one of the few to depict the psychological damage done to the former camp inmates. The screenplay, coauthored by Wajda, also emphasizes the social and political hatreds which, eclipsed by the war, flared up again in the postwar years and have continued to shape events in Eastern Europe.

The opening scene on the screen (the credits come much later) is very familiar: the arched concrete posts supporting the tiers of barbed wire, the watchtowers, and the wooden barracks of a Nazi concentration camp, while the sound track carries the sounds of battle, the bark of rifles and the stacatto of machine guns. The Allies, in this case American troops, have liberated the camp. Running toward the camera and the strands of barbed wire come the prisoners in their striped suits and caps, on their uniforms and arms their camp numbers and the telltale triangle that announced their crime and nationality to the SS guards. Most of the inmates wear the red triangle of political offenders with a "P" in its center, identifying them as Polish. They approach the wire but stay a few feet before it, in accordance with the camp rule that to approach the wire was to risk being shot. One inmate, however, dares to get closer, and he actually grabs hold of it to see if the electric current is still on. It is not and they all join in tearing a gap in the wire that separates their world from the outside, a snowy landscape through which they run to meet the oncoming American troops. To the strains of music by Antonio Vivaldi the inmates are shown rushing along the camp's perimeter. Some raid the food supplies and eat themselves sick, while others are simply too weak, and still others burn their striped uniforms and put on German uniforms from which they have torn the Nazi insignia. A few others chase a camp trusty, a *Kapo*. Meanwhile inmate number "105" Tadeusz (Daniel Olbrychski), is content to save a few books from a fire, books from which he is seldom separated.

While the Western European inmates return home in trucks festooned with their national flags, the Polish prisoners must content themselves with violin concerts and speeches about law and order made by the young American commander (Jerzy Zelnik). They good-naturedly cheer the American and his interpreter but hide their Kapo prisoner whom they later trample in the marsh when the American leaves. Tadeusz looks on casually as he clutches his books to his chest and devours a piece of bread. The camp mentality of casual death and personal survival has marked them, and this becomes clear as the inmates take on individual personalities in the next part of the film. A narrator's voice explains that they have been moved from the camp site to a former SS barracks, and the mark of the SS is still on their flesh and even in their sense of humor. The Communist, Charles (Tadeusz Janczar), sneaks up behind Tadeusz and yells, "Hände hoch," (Hands up!), and laughs uproariously as the bespectacled fellow quickly raises his arms. When he realizes what has happened, Tadeusz laughs coarsely in Charles's face. Enraged, Charles is about to strike him, but stops in midstroke.

Now, dressed in civilian clothes and discarded uniforms, the former concentration camp inmates must try to readjust to normal life, despite the petty tyrannies of displaced persons' camp society and the real question of Poland's political future. Some try to establish the *statu quo ante bellum* of

1939, including the inmate who had tested the camp wire. He is now revealed as a Polish army sublieutenant (Mieczysław Stoor), who tries to dominate the others and has a running feud with the Communist, Charles, over the political situation in Poland. Tadeusz is openly contemptuous of the Polish military, now clothed in discarded uniforms with hand-made Polish insignia. He comments acidly on how proud they must be to march in columns of four led by their own officers rather than in columns of five watched over by Germans. He takes no part in their drill and in one scene, stands in the middle of the barracks square, his arms clasped around himself as the serried ranks pass him. More immediate are the complaints about poor food and the petty corruption of institutional life. Tadeusz cooks on the sly and is forced into solitary confinement by an officious underling. In near parody of the war years, Tadeusz raises his hands above his head, but for him, solitary is a kind of luxury since he can read and write in privacy, removed from the disputes about food and politics.

Prewar Polish politics revolved around the twin pillars of authority, the Catholic Church and the army. In the displaced persons' camp the officers and men line up to be reviewed by the archbishop, who himself wears an army greatcoat and cap to take their salute. The Catholic High Mass is a pivotal sequence in the film, since as an acolyte Tadeusz first meets Nina (Stanislawa Celinska), a recent arrival at the camp. Charles, by contrast, scornfully watches the ceremony from his perch on a windowsill. Although from the dialogue it is clear that he had helped people survive in the concentration camp, as a Communist, Charles is excluded from the life of the camp. Charles is the sole person to protect a German woman from the wrath of the crowd when she is discovered with a camp cook who had given her food in exchange for sex. The pair are brought before the archbishop, but it is apparent that the cook is exonerated; he leaves, stroking his hands contentedly. The nearly naked girl is thrown to the crowd, and only Charles is willing to escort her out of the camp, even giving her his jacket. Tadeusz' relationship to the former enemy is more complex. Haunted by the memory of a Gestapo secretary whose blonde hair had a distinctive scent, he approaches one German girl in a small church to see if her hair has the same smell. It does not, and he seems disappointed.

The low number, "105," tattooed on Tadeusz' arm, indicates how long he had been in the camp, which has caused an obsession with the experiences of concentration camp life. It cannot help but affect his relationship with Nina. During a stroll away from the camp and in a wooded park, he is fascinated by a German dustman's soft, perfect, and polite speech and demonstrates roughly on Nina how a simple cane could be used to abuse inmates. Nina, too, symbolizes the complexities of postwar life. Although born Jewish, she has been posing as a Catholic and is as reluctant to return to Poland as to go to Palestine. She is the one who makes the first sexual move toward

Tadeusz; she reminds him that he must forget his years in the concentration camp if he is to have any life in the future. Later, as he ironically describes a life of exile in Paris, she grows angry, and the dilemma of where to settle is highlighted by the appearance of Charles, who has decided to leave for Poland. The ironies in their brief romance are obvious: she, a Jew who has been spared a cruel fate; he, a Polish Catholic intellectual who has been petrified by the experience of the war. The irony extends especially to the visual accompaniment to their idyll. They meet near an American armored vehicle and pass slag heaps and abandoned trenches until they come to a highway still littered with the remnants of battle. The wooded park is awash with fallen leaves, and in the small chapel where Tadeusz spies the blonde German girl, the memorial crosses carry small photographs of mourned SS soldiers. Most bleakly ironic, however, is Nina's accidental death at the hands of a nervous American soldier with a loaded gun. The reactions in the camp vary from horror on the part of the soldiers to a mild curiosity on the part of a young girl who peers at the blood. Tadeusz reverts to his old manner and coolly tells the American commander that such deaths are common in Europe.

Even if he returns to his old habits of voracious reading and compulsive eating, Tadeusz' emotional rebirth has been prodded by Nina. The climax to his emotional revival and to the film comes in the pantomime performance of the "Battle of Gruneberg" arranged for the pleasure of the archbishop and his military friends. Against a white scrim, suitably dressed performers act out a living tableau of the fifteenth century battle in which the Poles defeated the Teutonic knights. There is something sadly comic about the display of national colors and ancient savagery, especially since Wajda's camera picks out the smug faces of the Polish officers and the faintly sarcastic smile on the face of the American commander. The event, however, has been oversubscribed, and the waiting crowd quickly becomes angry and charges into the makeshift theater. A very real fistfight displaces the pantomime of national gallantry. This sequence, which some critics regarded as an insult to Poland's national honor, provoked considerable controversy.

The midwife to Tadeusz' rebirth is the intellectual priest (Zygmunt Malanowicz) who has repeatedly tried to talk to him; it is the priest who brings him to Nina's corpse. In the other man's presence, Tadeusz is still the sarcastic intellectual who tells a grim story of concentration camp cannibalism (drawn from one of Borowski's stories). When the priest leaves, however, and he is alone with his dead lover, Tadeusz literally cowers in the niche set below the marble slab on which she rests. The bathhouse location gives the scene the air of both the mortuary and the gas chamber. His anguished face is filmed looking up at her body with her makeshift mezuzah dangling in front of his eyes. His grief-stricken cry is the first he has made since the film began, back in the liberated concentration camp, and this explosion of human feeling is the climax to which the film has led. In the next sequence, he is seen pulling a small wagon loaded with books and a small kerosene cooker out through the camp gate. Tadeusz is going home to Poland.

In the film's closing sequence, Tadeusz joins hundreds of other returning Poles on a flag-bestrewn train. On the boxcars that serve as passenger trains, the film's credits are boldly painted in red and white, Poland's colors, in the broad italic style that "Solidarity" posters have made familiar.

Despite some strong criticism and the suggestion that the film not be shown outside Poland, *Landscape After Battle* had its supporters, who applauded Wajda enthusiastically, and the film was awarded a Golden Globe at the Third International Film Festival at Milan in 1971.

Lenny Rubenstein

THE LAST CHANCE
(DIE LETZTE CHANCE)

Origin: Switzerland
Released: 1945
Released in U.S.: 1945
Production: Lazar Wechsler for Praesens
Direction: Leopold Lindtberg
Screenplay: Richard Schweizer, with additional dialogue by Elizabeth Scott
  Montagu and Alberto Barberis; based on Schweizer's book
Cinematography: Emil Berna
Editing: Hermann Haller
Art direction: Robert Furrer
Costume design: Robert Gamma
Music: Robert Blum
Running time: 105 minutes

Principal characters:

Major Telford	Ewart G. Morrison
Lieutenant John Halliday	John Hoy
Sergeant James R. Braddock	Ray Reagan
Tonina	Luisa Rossi
Innkeeper	Odeardo Masini
Carrier	Giuseppe Galeati
Priest	Romano Calo
Brunner	Leopold Biberti
Frau Wittels	Thérèse Giehse
Bernhard Wittels	Robert Schwarz
Muzio	Tino Erler
Mme Monnier	Germaine Tournier
Hiller Sokolowski	Maurice Sakhnowsky
Chanele	Berthe Sakhnowsky
Professor	Rudolf Kämpf
Dutch man	Jean Martin
Dutch woman	Gertruden Cate
Yugoslav worker	Carlo Romatko
Giuseppe's mother	Renata Italiani
Military doctor	Sigfrit Steiner
Frontier guard	Emil Gerber

Leopold Lindtberg's career spans the world of theater and opera as well as that of film and television. Born in Vienna in 1902, he studied drama and began his career as an actor in Berlin. Lindtberg was strongly influenced by the Marxist stage director Erwin Piscator and by Bertolt Brecht, whom he knew personally. While working on an Expressionist play by Ernst Toller in 1933, Lindtberg discovered the potential of film, but he had no time to explore this medium any further; soon after the takeover of power by Adolf Hitler, he left Germany for Switzerland. There, together with a large number of other German refugees from the world of theater, he established himself as a leading stage director. Between 1935 and 1953, he also directed twelve films—a remarkable figure, given the fact that he had to work with very small budgets and on a number of occasions against considerable prejudice on the part of the Swiss authorities. Lindtberg could not have succeeded had it not been for the steadfast support of the production company for which he worked, and in particular from its head, Lazar Wechsler. Among other things, Wechsler had convinced Sergei Eisenstein to supervise a film on abortion, *Frauennot-Frauenglück* (1930), by Edward Tisse, and had also financed, through his Berlin subsidiary, Slatan Düdow and Bertolt Brecht's *Kühle Wampe* (1932; *Whither Germany?*).

The production history of *The Last Chance* is an excellent illustration of the attitudes toward refugees displayed by the Swiss government during World War II. In 1938, Switzerland was already host to twelve thousand refugees, and the authorities felt that "the boat was full." This metaphor was later used by Markus Imhoof as title for his film *Das Boot ist voll* (1981; *The Boat Is Full*) in which he critically examined this much disputed period in Swiss history. Many attempts were made to discourage the Jews in particular from trying to enter the country. In 1942, Switzerland was completely surrounded by Fascist troops, and only promises of strict political neutrality stopped the planned invasion by the Germans. The border was closed to all but the strictly "political" refugees; "racial" refugees such as the Jews were excluded. In late 1943, a new German front in Italy brought even more pressure upon Switzerland. More than twenty thousand Italians and eight thousand prisoners of war of the Allied Forces wanted to enter the neutral country. In spite of strict orders, many of those guarding the border, customs officers and military alike, were torn between their conscience and the official rules and regulations. For the government, the survival of a tiny neutral country surrounded by enemies was at stake. Those guarding the border were confronted with hitherto unknown human misery. Occasionally, compassion prevailed: In the face of suffering, the term "neutrality" had become ambiguous.

In this atmosphere, the idea for the script of *The Last Chance* was born. It was finished by Richard Schweizer by May, 1944, and filming was scheduled to begin on November 2, after a six-month-long fight against the authorities, who, for fear of public discussion of their policies, refused to cooperate, withholding filming permissions and imposing secrecy regulations.

The film is set in Italy in the summer of 1943, several weeks after Marshal

Pietro Badoglio has taken over the Italian government. The people hope for peace, but the war drags on. The Allied Forces have landed in Southern Italy. Allied prisoners of war are being transferred to camps in Germany. One such convoy is attacked, and the English lieutenant Halliday (John Hoy) and the American sergeant Braddock (Ray Reagan) escape under heavy machine-gun fire. They spend the night in a barn, where a farmer finds them and organizes ways and means to get them to the Swiss border, where they hope to rejoin their units. A carrier (Giuseppe Galeati) hides them under bags of flour and prevents the military police from searching the hiding place. They arrive at Lake Maggiore, where Halliday surprises Tonina (Luisa Rossi), a local girl who is doing her washing. They begin to talk, and it becomes clear that the soldiers will have to make a night crossing of the lake which forms the border between Italy and Switzerland. Halliday and Braddock begin their journey when suddenly they hear Tonina shouting "armistice!" She has heard on the radio that Badoglio has announced an armistice. The Englishman and the American return to the village with Tonina, but there a sad surprise is waiting for them: The village is deserted. Hitler's forces have moved in from the North, and the population is hiding in fright. The two soldiers manage to change into civilian clothing and get on a goods train. When the train stops suddenly during the night, the two witness how civilian refugees are being separated by the German SS in order to be sent to death camps.

The following day, Halliday and Braddock continue their escape on foot until they are stopped at the edge of a village and handed over to the local priest (Romano Calo), who speaks English. He introduces them to Major Telford (Ewart G. Morrison), also an Englishman, whom he has allowed to hide in the church, since the local innkeeper (Ordeardo Masini) is a Fascist. The village is situated on the way to the Swiss border, and more than twenty refugees are being sheltered in the inn. Among them are Sokolowski (Maurice Sakhnowsky), an old Jewish tailor from Russia, his niece, Chanele (Berthe Sakhnowsky), workers from Belgrade, and a university professor (Rudolf Kämpf), who carries the draft for a book on "European minorities" on which he has worked for more than thirty years. There is also Frau Wittels (Thérèse Giehse), an old German lady accompanied by her son, Bernhard (Robert Schwarz), who had been separated from her husband by the SS on the train station. Some of these people have been waiting for years to find a place and a guide to cross the border into Switzerland: their "last chance." Most of them know that the Swiss authorities refuse entrance to civilians. Their hopes lie with the Swiss civilians: If they can cross the border and reach the first village, people might take pity on them and protect them. The three army men get together with a local guide and prepare their expedition.

During the night of September 12, 1944, Benito Mussolini's liberation is announced on the radio. The innkeeper, who so far has kept a low profile, alerts the SS, who attack the village. The inhabitants flee, as do Braddock, Telford, and Halliday, but the refugees are disorganized. The priest and all men of the village, including the guide, have been shot. The three soldiers lead those who have managed to get away toward the mountains. A team spirit develops, and everybody helps to keep the group moving. During a snowstorm, the group finds refuge in a hut. A discussion of war, peace, and human understanding climaxes in singing a song, the tune of which is known to all; each individual sings in his or her own language. A German patrol approaches the hut but moves away toward the border: An escape now seems impossible. The soldiers develop a plan which would involve diverting the Germans' attention. The march then continues, and the group reaches a pass. Having picked up the soldiers' idea, Frau Wittels' son Bernhard suddenly runs away, beginning to gesticulate so as to attract the Germans' attention. They open fire and kill him. The group runs; the professor loses his manuscript, and the Russian tailor dies while Halliday tries to rescue him. Halliday himself is severely injured in the process. The remainder of the group reaches the Swiss border. The soldiers argue fiercely with the Swiss border guards, asking that the group be accepted as political refugees. A Swiss officer spends a long time on the phone trying to convince the authorities that this is a special case. Halliday is dying; he has hoped to see Tonina again, but, more important, he wants to see the group saved. Finally, permission to enter Switzerland is granted. Halliday dies on the carriage which is taking him to the hospital. A long line of refugees is seen crossing a snowed-in pass to Switzerland. In a final dialogue between Braddock and Telford a hopeful note resounds: "Perhaps some day they'll go back . . . yes, they'll go back."

It had been the producer's intention to make *The Last Chance* a film of resistance, but, as a result of the frustrating delays imposed by the Swiss government, events overtook the process of filmmaking. On May 8, 1945, Germany capitulated. Editing of the film was finished at the end of May, and the film premiered in Zürich on May 26, 1945. The accompanying short was the first English documentary on the opening of the concentration camps in Dachau and Auschwitz. Swiss authorities remained cool about the film. Some ministers later apologized to the producer for their obstructionist attitudes; others remained adamant that by making *The Last Chance* he had endangered the existence of the country. The public, however, appreciated the film.

In October, 1945, Lazar Wechsler left for the United States, where he sold the North and South American, as well as the English, rights to the film to Metro-Goldwyn-Mayer. Louis B. Mayer was particularly impressed with the film's visual style, the daring technique of using several languages, and the location shooting. The American opening took place on November 27, 1945, at Loew's Criterion in New York. *The Last Chance* was hailed by figures as diverse as Sinclair Lewis, Ben Hecht, and Cardinal Francis Spellman, and General McLure urged the American government to have the film shown in the American zone in Germany and to have monies so earned distributed among the victims of the concentration camps. At the end of 1945, *The Last Chance* received the National Board of Review Award and the Golden Globe of the Hollywood Foreign Correspondents' Association. In October, 1946, the film received the International Peace Award at the Cannes International Film Festival. Leopold Lindtberg has openly admitted that without Jean Renoir's *La Grande Illusion* (1937), there would not have been *The Last Chance*. Renoir may have provided inspiration, but *The Last Chance* is entirely based on the experiences of the likes of Lindtberg and his friends. Stylistically, he worked in a manner reminiscent of the Italian neorealists. All outdoor scenes were shot on location in Switzerland, and many of the characters in the film play, to some extent, themselves and their history.

Ewart G. Morrison (Major Telford) had been imprisoned in Italy and escaped from there in a way similar to that presented in the film. He even brought his uniform with him and into the film. John Hoy (Lieutenant Halliday) also came via an Italian prisoner-of-war camp to Switzerland. Ray Reagan, the American, had joined the United States Air Force as an engineer. Returning from an air raid over Germany, his plane had been forced to land in Switzerland, where he was interned. The Russian Jewish tailor was played by an amateur actor living in Switzerland, a Jewish tailor who had fled Russia. Each of the actors in *The Last Chance* speaks his or her mother tongue: German, Swiss dialect, English (which makes for sixty percent of the dialogue), Italian, French, Dutch, Yugoslav, Russian, and Yiddish. This documentary quality occasionally contrasts strangely with some of the emotionalism in the film. The flirtation between Tonina and Halliday is by no means integrated into the plot, and Bernhard Mittels' death, as well as Halliday's sacrifice, are both easily predictable—but such conflicts are trademarks of the neorealist tradition. Roberto Rossellini used similar dramatic techniques in *Roma, città aperta* (1945; *Rome, Open City*), as did Vittorio De Sica, Luchino Visconti, and Federico Fellini.

Lindtberg was an excellent director of a cast which ranged from first-class actress to inexperienced layman, working toward a sober and subdued style which only seldom gives way to strong emotional outbursts such as Frau Wittels' desperate chase after the train in which her husband is being led to his death, or the activity shaking the village after it has become clear that the SS is on its way. Similarly, the cinematography changes from poetic passages along the shores of Lake Maggiore, to the harsh, realistic setting of a cramped inn and on to the brilliant alpine scenery where a race against death is set against the peaceful snowcapped mountains.

Lindtberg's approach to a topic which inherently carries all elements of cruelty, torture, and killing is one of restraint. Hardship, fear, and anger are more implied in the atmosphere and the acting than openly shown. Emotional shock is experienced more through the montage on the sound track than through the exposition of disconcerting images. There are no heroic actions in this film. It is the pressure of desperation which forces the refugees, military or civilian, to go on. The visual metaphors are trains, carriages, boats, tracks in deep snow, skis; the mountains are portrayed as the ultimate cruel obstacle: Only those who manage to get across have a chance for freedom, and such a crossing demands extraordinary endurance. The escape from Fascism turns into a purgatory for the refugees, a message which was bound to shake the conscience of many a Swiss.

The exceptional feature of Lindtberg's neorealism is his ability to transcend purely national conflicts, problems, and emotions. *The Last Chance* is a truly "international" film, as was Lindtberg's *Die Vier im Jeep* (1951; *Four in a Jeep*), which was first shown in Zürich in the midst of the Cold War. Again, a set of "international" characters, an American, a Russian, a Frenchman, and an Englishman, are thrown together, having to handle human problems while on patrol with the International Control Patrol in Vienna. Never again, however, did Lindtberg manage to create an appeal for human dignity and understanding as powerful as *The Last Chance*.

Leopold Lindtberg continued to make films until 1953. He worked also on various television projects until 1977, but he spent most of his time directing stage plays in the German-speaking world. Despite all that he had done for Swiss theater and film, he himself had to wait until 1951 before he was granted Swiss citizenship.

Peter Gerdes

THE LAST MÉTRO
(LE DERNIER MÉTRO)

Origin: France
Released: 1980
Released in U.S.: 1980
Production: Marcel Berbert for Les Films du Carrosse/SEDIF/TF1/Société
Française de Production
Direction: François Truffaut
Screenplay: François Truffaut, Suzanne Schiffman, and Jean-Claude
Grumberg
Cinematography: Nestor Almendros
Editing: Martine Barraque, Marie-Aimée Debril, and Jean-François Gire
Art direction: Jean-Pierre Kohut-Svelko
Music: Georges Delerue
MPAA rating: PG
Running time: 133 minutes

Principal characters:

Marion Steiner	Catherine Deneuve
Bernard Granger	Gérard Depardieu
Lucas Steiner	Heinz Bennent
Jean-Loup Cottins	Jean Poiret
Arlette Guillaume	Andrea Ferréol
Nadine Marsac	Sabine Haudepin
Germaine Fabre	Paulette Dubost
Daxiat	Jean-Louis Richard
Raymond	Maurice Risch
Christian	Jean-Pierre Klein

The period of the German Occupation in France has been a source of great pride and great shame to the French, with stories of Resistance heroes and Nazi collaborators providing the basis for such films as Louis Malle's *Lacombe, Lucien* (1974) and Marcel Ophüls' shattering documentary *Le Chagrin et la pitié* (1971; *The Sorrow and the Pity*). François Truffaut's *The Last Métro* also takes the Occupation as its setting, yet the tone of its story is quite different from that of other films which deal with the era. Truffaut's subject is the daily life of the French people under German rule—in particular, the life of a theatrical company as it continues to perform throughout the war while its members react to, and are affected by, the presence of the Nazis in their homeland.

The theater enjoyed considerable popularity in France during the Occupation, although the companies themselves, as well as the works they performed, were monitored closely by the Nazis to prevent the presentation of controversial material. The film's title is derived from the fact that although the nightlife of Paris continued, the strict curfews imposed by the Nazis made it necessary for theater curtains to fall in time for audiences to catch the last métro of the evening to their homes. In the smallest details of his story, Truffaut captures the atmosphere of life lived under the constraints of a foreign power's rule and the ways in which the German presence affected each thread of the fabric of daily existence.

The film opens in the Paris of 1942 as Bernard Granger (Gérard Depardieu), an actor recently hired by the popular Théâtre Montmartre, arrives at the theater to begin rehearsals for a new play. Lucas Steiner (Heinz Bennent), the company's German-Jewish manager and director, has been forced to flee the country, leaving behind his beautiful wife, Marion (Catherine Deneuve), the theater's star, to act as manager in his absence. Taking over for Steiner as director is Jean-Loup Cottins (Jean Poiret), a homosexual who is himself not safe from Nazi persecution. The company's ingenue, Nadine Marsac (Sabine Haudepin, who played Jeanne Moreau's daughter in Truffaut's 1962 *Jules et Jim*), is an ambitious young woman who will take any job that offers exposure and a chance at stardom, while its stage manager, Raymond (Maurice Risch), is an ingenious, much-put-upon jack-of-all-trades with a friend who supplies the theater with black-market goods. The company also includes Marion's dresser, Germaine Fabre (Paulette Dubost), and the set and costume designer, Arlette Guillaume (Andrea Ferréol), whom Bernard pursues earnestly until he learns that she is having an affair with Nadine.

As rehearsals for the play begin, one discovers that Lucas Steiner has not left France, as the company believes, but is hiding in the cellar beneath the theater, which he and Marion have transformed into a small apartment using spare props. Marion visits Lucas nightly after the rest of the company has left, and the two enjoy a warm and loving relationship, although the strain of their situation sometimes surfaces. Lucas soon discovers that he can listen to the rehearsals through the heating vents and he occupies his days making notes on the production for Marion.

As the rehearsals progress, so does a growing attraction between Marion and Bernard, a situation which neither acknowledges. Bernard, too, has a secret life after rehearsals end—as a Resistance fighter. He successfully plants a bomb with the help of his friend, Christian (Jean-Pierre Klein), who is later captured by the Nazis as Bernard watches helplessly. The play comes to the attention of Daxiat (Jean-Louis Richard), a much-feared, anti-Semitic drama critic who has used the presence of the Nazis to further his own influence in French theater. Daxiat visits the Théâtre Montmartre and later expresses to Marion his regret that Lucas has left the country, hypocritically lamenting the loss of a man of such talent. The emptiness of his words is amply demonstrated in his review when the play opens, as he harshly condemns what he labels the production's "Jewish nihilism," and he later attempts to seize control of the theater by proving that the title has been illegally reregistered in Marion's name.

After the play's opening and Daxiat's scathing review, the members of the company encounter the critic in a restaurant. Bernard angrily challenges him to a fight and demands that he apologize to Marion, who accuses Bernard of endangering the theater by his impetuous outburst. The two quarrel bitterly and Marion vows that she will have no further contact with Bernard offstage. Several days later, the theater receives a surprise visit from officials who insist upon inspecting the building's cellar. Marion quickly takes Bernard into her confidence and together they manage to hide Lucas and disguise the fact that he has been living in the basement.

Bernard has informed Marion after his friend's capture that he must leave the company and is in his dressing room packing when she arrives to say good-bye. There, the two admit their true feelings for each other and make love for the first time. The story flashes forward briefly to reveal that Nadine will indeed become a famous actress, Arlette will serve as art director on her first important film, Jean-Loup will be arrested, released, and rearrested before the war ends, and Daxiat will become a hated fugitive. The film ends in the summer of 1944, with Marion visiting a hospital where Bernard is a badly wounded patient. The scene is revealed to be the end of a play, and as the two take their bows, the audience recognizes Lucas seated in a side box, freed from his long sojourn in the cellar now that the war is nearly over. He joins Marion and Bernard onstage, and the three join hands to the applause of the crowd.

Truffaut stated in interviews at the time of *The Last Métro*'s release that the film fulfilled three of his longtime ambitions: to re-create on film the climate of the Occupation, to show the backstage life of a theater, and to provide Catherine Deneuve with the role of a responsible woman. Indeed, it is these three aspects of the film that are most prominent.

In the film's opening moments, the mood of the time is clearly established as a German soldier pats a small French boy on the head and he is promptly dragged indoors by his mother for a thorough scrubbing. Each character's reaction to the Nazis is central to his or her personality. For Lucas, driven into hiding and fearing for his life, it is the vicious anti-Semitism that draws his strongest response. On radio broadcasts, in newspaper and magazine articles, even in children's crossword puzzles, the Nazi propaganda against the Jews reaches Lucas in his tiny cellar. Marion, too, hates the Germans, yet she maintains a measure of civility toward them in order to safeguard her theater and, more important, her husband's life. Her ability to disguise her dislike is an outgrowth of her calm, practical approach to the difficult situation in which she finds herself. Bernard's response to the Germans is fierce but secret opposition in the form of Resistance work. He uses his clowning skills as a former member of the Grand Guignol to avoid shaking hands with Daxiat and berates Marion for her preoccupation with the theater when many of her countrymen are in prisons. Nadine, on the other hand, does not shrink from fraternizing with the Nazis or playing up to Daxiat in hopes of furthering her career, while Jean-Loup treads a careful line between maintaining his self-respect and cultivating cordial relationships with those whose patronage will be useful to the theater. From the black-market goods which supplement daily necessities to the evening curfews and the yellow star worn by the theater's young Jewish seamstress, the lives of all the film's characters are permeated by the presence of the Germans.

Yet the underlying theme of *The Last Métro* is that life continues even in the face of these hardships. Restaurants and nightclubs remain open, women without silk stockings paint seams on their bare legs, the theaters flourish, and the people of France struggle to maintain some sense of normality in their lives, although the world they knew has been thrown into chaos.

Truffaut's second ambition—to portray backstage life in the theater—provides the film with both its technical style and its warm sense of camaraderie. Just as *La Nuit américaine* (1973; *Day for Night*), Truffaut's Academy Award-winning look at the world of filmmaking, makes use of a wide variety of cinematic techniques to tell its story, so *The Last Métro* eschews those techniques in favor of a far more static style. While the film itself, photographed by respected cinematographer Nestor Almendros, has the look of the features made during the 1940's, one is constantly aware of a feeling of confinement, a device which refers to both the story's theatrical setting and Lucas' long stay in the cellar. Only the lingering close-ups with which Truffaut sometimes ends a scene and the flash-forward which concludes the picture break this tone.

As he did in *Day for Night*, Truffaut captures the interplay among individuals thrown together and committed to a shared goal—a spirit symbolized here by Raymond, whose constant improvisations keep the theater functioning through blackouts and supply shortages. Although each character has his or her own life to lead outside the theater, there is a strong sense of community among its members. Like nearly all Truffaut's films, *The Last Métro* is a film of relationships, with the shifting terrain of human interaction one of the story's principal concerns. The central emotional thread throughout the story is the triangle created by Marion, Lucas, and Bernard. Marion's relationship with each man is quite different. With her husband, there is a warm bond of affection and mutual respect. The two bicker occasionally and speak together in the tones of casual familiarity that come only from years of shared experience. In one quiet scene, Marion gives Lucas a haircut, snipping away with her scissors as the two talk in a moment of comfortable domestic intimacy. Marion's relationship with Bernard, on the other hand, is charged with an emotional content that seems lacking in her marriage. The two are at first stiff and formal with each other, gradually becoming friendlier as the rehearsals continue until the awakening attraction they feel causes an explosive friction between them as Marion maintains a forced emotional distance. After the pair have at last confessed their true feelings and made love, the film's ambiguous ending leaves open the question of which man Marion will eventually choose.

The remarkable aspect of what should be the plot's chief romantic interest is that it is barely a love story at all, and this, too, is an outgrowth of the effects of the Occupation. Had Marion and Bernard met in the years before the war, the initial spark between them would doubtless have ignited much sooner. With her husband and their theater dependent on her actions, however, Marion cannot afford the luxury of giving free rein to her feelings, nor can she withdraw her emotional support from her husband while she remains his only source of companionship. Her decision to suppress her own feelings, then, becomes an unselfish act dictated by her response to the extraordinary circumstances at hand.

The relationships among the film's other characters are equally revealing. When the company learns that Arlette and Nadine are having an affair, it is to Jean-Loup, himself a homosexual, that Arlette turns for comfort as her words reveal that she is secretly in love with Marion. Bernard's reaction is one of anxious sympathy and concern for her distress, while Nadine emerges from the episode unruffled, with the relationship, on her side, clearly a case of taking her pleasures where she finds them. Their colleagues' casual acceptance of the affair—and indeed, of both Arlette's and Jean-Loup's homosexuality—is indicative of the tolerance which typifies Truffaut's work as a whole. With a strong cast and vividly delineated personalities, he creates a group of fully developed individuals whom he embraces with affection. Only the odious Daxiat falls outside his favor, emerging as one of the few pure villains in Truffaut's body of work, a position he occupies as a man capable only of twisted hatred and self-serving greed.

In the last of Truffaut's three objectives—to provide Catherine Deneuve with the role of a responsible woman—the director succeeds admirably. The character of Marion Steiner is remarkable in its maturity and dimension, and Deneuve, whose roles in American films have by and large been decorative and undemanding, responds with a performance of immense charm and subtlety. Marion is a woman who has had unexpected responsibility thrust suddenly upon her, and she rises to meet its demands without complaint. Her strength of character is revealed in her resourceful concealment of Lucas, her levelheaded management of the theater, and her consistent willingness to keep her own emotions in perspective. On the play's opening night, she visits Lucas in the cellar and meets his own fears with an outward

show of calm, giving in to her own nervousness only after she leaves him—
and becomes promptly sick to her stomach. She remains a capable, serene
figure throughout the film, a woman of intelligence, humor, and great
courage.

Yet Marion is not perfect. At one point in the film, she spends the night
with a man she has met only moments before, driven by frustration to break
free of the tight hold she keeps on her emotions, and her attraction to Bernard occasionally explodes in uncharacteristic moments of anger. Yet in
these same falls from grace lies the key to Truffaut's approach to his characters. As the film eloquently demonstrates, even the best of human beings
is flawed; indeed, it is our flaws that make us human. Truffaut's recognition
of this fact and the gentle tolerance he displays for the ways in which each
of his characters copes with a difficult, often dangerous, situation infuses
The Last Métro with humanistic insight and understanding. For Truffaut,
wartime heroics are not confined to the battlefield; they can also be found
in the simple actions of daily life.

Janet E. Lorenz

THE LAST STAGE
(OSTATNI ETAP)

Origin: Poland
Released: 1948
Released in U.S.: 1949
Production: Film Polski
Direction: Wanda Jakubowska
Screenplay: Wanda Jakubowska and Gerda Schneider
Cinematography: Borys Monastyrski
Editing: R. Pstrokowska
Art direction: Roman Mann and C. Piaskowski
Music: Roman Palester
Running time: 110 minutes
Also known as: The Last Stop

Principal characters:
Michèle..........................Huguette Faget
Helena........................Wanda Bartówna
Eugenia ....Tatiana Górecka
Anna........................Antonina Górecka
Nadia..........................M. Winogradowa
Marta Weiss ....Barbara Drapińska
Agnes ....Barbara Fijewska

Two years after World War II ended, Wanda Jakubowska made *The Last Stage*, a film which dramatized the events that took place in Auschwitz during the war, bringing home the horrific truth about the concentration camps to people around the world. It was shown in some forty-five countries and reached an estimated twenty million people outside Poland, placing on record some of the crimes that the Nazis had committed. When the Allies entered Germany, the newsreel footage taken at Belsen and other places alerted people to the depths to which the Nazis had plunged, but Jakubowska's more personalized account, based on her own experiences at Auschwitz, shocked in another way.

The recent past was the subject at the center of attention in most Polish literature of the period. During the war, Warsaw had been almost completely reduced to rubble, and whole sections of the population had been wiped out. Poland had had a very large Jewish population and had therefore suffered badly at the hands of the Nazis. As Poland started on the long task of reconstruction, the Polish people had also to come to terms with the terrible events of the war. The German concentration camp at Auschwitz, where an estimated four-and-a-half million men, women, and children met their deaths, was the starkest example of the brutal methods of the Nazis. *The Last Stage*, one of the first Polish postwar films, dealt with this particular horror.

Many films have centered on Auschwitz since then, most notably Alain Resnais' *Nuit et brouillard* (1956; *Night and Fog*) and Andrzej Munk's *Pasażerka* (1963; *The Passenger*), but none has had the immediate impact of *The Last Stage*. Written by Jakubowska and her German colleague, Gerda Schneider, both of whom were themselves inmates of the camp, *The Last Stage* was made and distributed with the support of the United Nations Organization. Filmed at Auschwitz in a compelling documentary style, it was acclaimed at the Venice International Film Festival in 1948 and won the Grand Prix of the International Film Festival at Mananska Lazne in the same year; Jakubowska was awarded an International Peace Prize for her achievement.

Some people who had no personal experience of Auschwitz accused Jakubowska of exaggerating; others, who had firsthand experience of the camps and survived, have suggested that, if anything, she did not portray the whole truth. Nevertheless, this powerful film shook the conscience of the world. The film's force comes from its documentary-style reconstruction of the day-to-day life in the concentration camp. Narrated in an almost cold and objective manner, the film has an impact far beyond any ordinary dramatization. It portrays the cruelty and inhumanity that millions of people suffered, without wallowing in degradation or indulging in sentimentality.

The opening of *The Last Stage* is unforgettable and has become perhaps the single most enduring screen image of the concentration camp, an almost obligatory scene in most films made on the subject since. On a muddy parade ground, row upon row of silent women stand with bare feet and shaved heads, wearing the striped prison gowns characteristic of Auschwitz. One woman sways as if to fall: She is pregnant. A guard steps forward and threatens to add her to the next batch of prisoners to go to the ovens. The camera pulls back and up to reveal, behind the rows of huts and the electrified fence, four chimneys belching out vast amounts of black smoke. The film needs to be no more explicit as the horror of mass extermination is forcibly felt.

The film proceeds as an episodic outline of life in Auschwitz, showing a routine whose reason for existence is imminent death. The arrival of thousands of new inmates, bewildered and confused: Their mood soon changes to hysteria as families are forcibly separated with no hope of ever being reunited. The checking in of the women: Stripped, shaved, and tattooed with their prison number, they emerge with the same look of despair that bedevils the longer-term residents. The birth of a baby: Having started to breathe, he is quickly dispatched by an SS doctor with a hypodermic syringe. The film quickly builds within the audience an acute awareness of the inhuman conditions of the camp.

Other incidents portrayed give a sense of hope, showing that even in these degrading surroundings life continues to exist. In the filthy, crowded huts (shot so realistically that one can almost smell the stench of death), a young Russian woman, Nadia (M. Winogradowa), starts to dance. When asked how she can be happy, she explains that she has just learned that the Germans have been defeated at Stalingrad. The other prisoners join in.

Angela arrives at the camp with her dying sister Ursula. There is not enough medication to go around, and Nadia disobeys the doctor's orders, relieving a mother in pain rather than giving the drug to Ursula. Nadia blames herself when Ursula dies, but Angela is understanding and the two women quickly become friends.

A Red Cross commission visits the camp, and the huts are spruced up with sheets and pillows to create a better impression. One woman, Eugenia (Tatiana Górecka), a prison doctor, runs forward and shouts out the truth about the real conditions of the camp. Later, the Germans take her away to a torture chamber.

It is not these incidents, however, that leave the greatest impression: It is the small, almost incidental, details that cause revulsion in the audience— the piles of clothing or the groups of trusting children entering the chambers. The prison orchestra strikes up, playing the music of Richard Strauss or Franz Lehár as the selection of prisoners to go to the gas chambers takes place. Only the Nazis could have thought up such an exquisitely cruel idea. The portable steps in each truck that transports the prisoners to the chambers, speak more eloquently of the German's single-minded genocide than any number of film deaths.

The main action takes place at the "hospital" in Birkenau, the women's section, and tells the story of Marta Weiss (Barbara Drapińska), a prisoner who serves as an interpreter in the camp. When news reaches Auschwitz that the Gestapo plans to kill all the inmates before they can be rescued, Marta escapes with a prisoner of the male camp to spread the information to the Underground. She is recaptured and taken back to Auschwitz, where she is tortured. Later, the prisoners are assembled on the parade ground. In the middle there is a scaffold which Marta mounts, but just as the noose is placed around her neck, a Soviet air raid disperses the Nazis and Marta is saved.

Jakubowska studied art history at Warsaw University. She began directing documentaries in the 1930's, but she had previously been the production manager of The Society of the Devotees of the Artistic Film (START), which she cofounded with Eugeniusz Cekalsi and Stanisław Wohl and which was later joined by Aleksander Ford, whose *Legion ulicy* (*Legion of the Streets*), about young newspaper vendors in Warsaw, was the most popular film of 1932. START's aim was to establish a more serious and artistic trend of cinema to act as an alternative to the commercial industry. In its activities, and those of its successor, the Co-operative of Film Authors (SAF), founded in 1937, can be seen as the theoretical basis of the New Wave Polish cinema of the 1950's and 1960's.

Polish cinema was transformed during the war. Its legitimate cinema was destroyed under Occupation (the negative of Jakubowska's first feature film, *Nad Niemnem*, 1939; *On the Niemen River*, was burned during the siege of Warsaw), but underground newsreel directors established a practical basis for filmmaking and managed to shoot documentary footage of the war, including the Warsaw uprising. At the same time, film units were organized in the Polish military detachments in Great Britain, France, the Near East, and the Soviet Union. When the war ended, Polish cinema quickly reasserted itself.

The Last Stage, Leonard Buczkowski's *Zakazane piosenki* (1947; *Forbidden Songs*), a chronicle of everyday life under Nazi Occupation built around several songs of the Resistance, and Aleksander Ford's *Ulica graniczna* (1948; *Border Street*), which depicts the effects on a group of children of the last days of the Warsaw Ghetto, were the first films to come out of postwar Poland. Together, they form a riveting picture of the war-torn country, a fascinating, if also shocking testament to the Nazi Occupation.

The film also acted as a training school for several directors who worked on the film in one capacity or another. Jakubowska herself continued to work in the Polish film industry, directing several features which tackle topical issues of contemporary life in her characteristically detailed and realistic way. In 1964, she returned to the theme of the concentration camp to make *Koniec naszego świata* (*The End of Our World*), which contrasts the modern museum at Auschwitz with its horrendous past.

Later films about this subject, such as *The Passenger*, Lina Wertmüller's *Pasqualino settebellezze* (1976; *Seven Beauties*), Liliana Cavani's *Il portiere di notte* (1974; *The Night Porter*), and even Alan J. Pakula's *Sophie's Choice* (1982), take a more complex view, focusing on the inverted and bizarre relationships that were formed in the camps. Jakubowska's film, with its straightforward reportage, remains an outstanding testament to a bleak and shameful episode of human history.

Sally Hibbin

THE LAST SUPPER
(LA ÚLTIMA CENA)

Origin: Cuba
Released: 1976
Released in U.S.: 1978
Production: Santiago Llapur and Camilo Vives for Instituto Cubano del Arte e Industria Cinematográficos
Direction: Tomás Gutierrez Alea
Screenplay: Tomás González, María Eugenia Haya, and Tomás Gutierrez Alea
Cinematography: Mario García Joya
Editing: Nelson Rodríguez
Art direction: Carlos Arditti
Music: Leo Brower
MPAA rating: no listing
Running time: 120 minutes

> *Principal character:*
> Count .... Nelson Villagra

Director Tomás Gutierrez Alea is a committed revolutionary filmmaker associated with the Instituto Cubano del Arte e Industria Cinematográficos, or ICAIC, Cuba's government-supported national film institute, which combines the functions of a film school and a film production facility. Given Gutierrez Alea's political commitment to Cuba's socialist revolution, it is not surprising that the theme of revolution figures prominently in his greatest films. The narrative approaches, structure, and style of these films have varied widely—from the use of self-reflective devices to subvert and question conventional film strategies in *Memorias del subdesarrollo* (1968; *Memories of Underdevelopment*) to the more conventional realistic style and the chronological development of *The Last Supper*.

The Last Supper is set in Cuba in the late eighteenth century, when the collapse of the Haitian sugar industry and the growing international demand for sugar caused Cuban plantation owners to attempt to increase productivity by working their black slaves even harder. The film opens with the visit of an unnamed count (Nelson Villagra) to his sugar plantation during Holy Week. The count, in order to exercise Christian humility, ceremonially washes the feet of twelve of his slaves and invites them to share a dinner with him on Maundy Thursday. The bondmen infer that they are not required to work on Good Friday, and they revolt and set fire to the sugar mill when the brutal slave driver attempts to force them to labor. Shocked by the slaves' rebellion, the count orders the rebels hunted down and murdered. Inside a semicircle of poles topped by the heads of his decapitated dinner guests, the count dedicates a church to Christianity's triumph over savagery and to his overseer, who was killed by the slaves. Yet one stake remains bare because the most rebellious slave, Sebastián, has escaped to freedom. The film's plot is based on a historical incident recorded in historian Manuel Moreno Fraginals' *El ingenio: El complejo económico social cubano del azúcar* (1964); Fraginals also served the filmmakers as an adviser.

Insert-titles are used to mark the chronological progression of events from Holy Wednesday to Easter Sunday. Scriptwriters Gutierrez Alea, María Eugenia Haya, and Tomás González have not simply imposed the Holy Week chronology and the Passion of Christ as a facile symbolic framework; rather, much of the thematic and ideological complexity of the film grows out of the many rich contrasts and comparisons among the film's characters, actions, and motifs and their original Christian counterparts. Though the count speaks of Christ and consciously and conspicuously imitates Him, *The Last Supper* is best read as a symbolic re-creation of the Passion of Christ from a black slave perspective. The suffering bondmen assume the Christ role, and they are figuratively and literally crucified by the count, the representative of the oppressive slaveholding class. The dinner with their white lord is the slaves' "last supper" before their persecution and death. Though the count identifies Sebastián as his Judas, from a black perspective the Judas role is played by the traitorous slaveholder, who invited the slaves to his bountiful table, who described for them Paradise and the glories of Heaven, who even granted freedom to one—only to ordain their murder hours later. On Easter Sunday, the beheaded are figuratively resurrected in the figure of Sebastián, who magically incarnates their collective will to freedom and their indomitable spirit.

The set piece and dramatic core of *The Last Supper* is the approximately fifty-minute banquet sequence; this sequence gives the film its name and provides for the lengthy face-to-face confrontation of two cultures—that of the oppressor and that of the oppressed. The seating arrangement at the banquet (the count at the center of the table flanked by slaves) physically positions both the count-Christ and his slave-apostles in their roles as perceived by the nobleman. In using this banquet device, Gutierrez Alea draws on a literary tradition dating back to the classical symposium. The Cuban director is not the first filmmaker to employ the last-supper motif; Spanish director Luis Buñuel's parody of Leonardo da Vinci's "Last Supper" in *Viridiana* (1961) is one of the most blasphemous moments in cinema history.

Gutierrez Alea's dinner-table subversion, though less spectacular than Buñuel's, is nevertheless thoroughly damning: In expounding the planter-class ideology, the count reveals the racism and religious hypocrisy that underpin a brutally repressive and exploitative socioeconomic system. The inherent racism of the slaveholding society is revealed in the tired clichés—such as that blacks are uniquely endowed to cut cane—which the count trots out. The master's explanation of Christianity to his bondmen emphasizes the Passion of Christ as an example for slaves to emulate. Happiness, according to the count, is not freedom, as the blacks might have surmised, but rather suffering and humble submission to divine punishment. The reward for resigned sufferers is admission to the Christian Heaven, where there are no masters, slaves, or even any work to do. In short, the count preaches an exploitative, racist Christianity that serves to reconcile slaves to a life of bondage and thereby support the socioeconomic status quo.

Gutierrez Alea effectively uses the banquet sequence to develop the individual characterizations of his black personages. While the nobleman spins a web of oppressive religious mystification, his slaves display a vital concern with their immediate earthly problems. Antonio requests a lighter work assignment, and old Pascual asks for manumission. When the count elucidates the dogma of transubstantiation, his ravenous listeners detect references to cannibalism, and they respond with comments on the anthropophagous Carabali tribe. After hearing the count's Christian version of Genesis and the Fall, Sebastián counters with a black myth of creation. In this myth, Deceit decapitates Truth and then uses the head in order to disguise itself as Truth. Sebastián's recounting of this myth and his symbolic use of a grotesque pig's head suggest that this insightful slave understands that the master's Christian "truths" are in reality deceits that serve a socioeconomic system by monstrously perverting humanitarian values. Near the end of this sequence, Sebastián blows a white powder—emblematic of his supernatural transformative and protective powers—onto his sleeping host; this action foreshadows the black hero's magical escape to freedom.

The success of the last-supper sequence stems in large part from the director's capable work with his actors. Though the lead, Nelson Villagra (the count), is one of Latin America's finest and most versatile actors, some of the black actors are nonprofessionals. Gutierrez Alea rehearsed this sequence as a theatrical piece and stimulated actors to find their own solutions to dramatic problems. Black speech patterns reflect the distinctive accents and rhythms of colonial Afro-Cuban Spanish. Mario García Joya's unobtrusive cinematography uses creeping pans to create a slow tempo; certain lighting (candlelight) and color effects (the predominance of ocher) underscore the painterliness of the banquet scene.

Don Gaspar, the *maestro de azúcar* (that is, the master-technician of the sugar-refining process), merits special attention as a member of a class between the slaves and their owners. He is an enlightened Frenchman who serves the count as a salaried employee. Don Gaspar ingeniously adapts European technology to the New World setting: He incorporates chicken excrement into the sugar refining process, and, when local wood supplies are exhausted, he heats boiling-room caldrons with cast-off bagasse. The Frenchman demonstrates his sympathy for the slaves when he hides the fugitive Sebastián from a slave-hunter. Nevertheless, Don Gaspar has no serious commitment to the French Revolution's rights of man; when open rebellion and savage retribution sweep the plantation, he simply rides off. Like the priest, Don Gaspar cannot significantly help the blacks in their struggle for liberation; black liberation must be self-generating and self-sustained.

Composer Leo Brower's fine score allows for both the conceptual and the structural use of music. Musical motifs often underscore dramatic moments or set the tone in opening or closing a scene. As the opening credits pass, the camera roams the Christian imagery of a colonial painting, and a solemn chant is intoned. Throughout the film, similar religious-musical motifs (especially organ music) are associated with Christian rites, symbols, and teaching—and their manipulation by the planter class. Afro-Cuban instruments, chants, and rhythms are initially heard during the blacks' participation in the last-supper sequence. Later, Afro-Cuban musical elements become more predominant, and black voices and percussion instruments build to a dramatic crescendo during Sebastián's final race to freedom. Brouwer's use of Afro-Cuban musical motifs reflects the authenticity of the black struggle.

The most striking shot of the film depicts events on Easter Sunday. In a single, sweeping movement, the camera pulls back and up (from blacks raising a wooden cross) in a revelatory crane shot showing, for the first time, the head-bearing poles. This high-angle long-shot from an omniscient "God's eye" point of view links a symbol (the cross) of the dominant class's ideology to the macabre fruits it reaps (the severed heads). The camera then approaches the tip of the headless stake; then there is a cut to the final montage sequence in which shots of Sebastián running are intercut with images of a bird in flight, flowing water, falling rocks, and galloping horses.

Gutierrez Alea's treatment of Sebastián's destiny is influenced by the Spanish-American literary tradition of Magic Realism (*realismo mágico*). Magic Realism values the indigenous or "primitive" *Weltanschauung*—in which magic figures as a natural, accepted phenomenon—over the modern Westernized worldview, which does not admit magic elements. Sebastián's magic powder is more potent than Don Gaspar's powder, which is merely the product of European science. The final montage sequence and the camera's previous insistence on the headless stake prove the effectiveness of the black rebel-hero's magic powers and also symbolize the historical inevitability of both the triumph of the slaves' struggle and the coming of the socialist revolution.

Gutierrez Alea is not the only director at ICAIC to recognize the historical significance of the revolutionary actions of the Afro-Cubans of colonial times. In the period 1975-1979, black director Sergio Giral made three features that depict black resistance to nineteenth century Cuban slavery. *The Last Supper* and Giral's *El otro Francisco* (1975; *The Other Francisco*), on which Gutierrez Alea worked in an advisory capacity, are the two most important of these films on slavery because of their outstanding aesthetic qualities and the depth achieved in the treatment of the slavery theme. *The Last Supper* has won several international awards, including the Gold Hugo Grand Prix at the 1977 Chicago International Film Festival.

ICAIC has backed these Giral and Gutierrez Alea films because the institute seeks to reexamine and reassess Cuban history and thereby discover the modern nation's revolutionary roots. Afro-Cuban slavery merits cinematic treatment because of the vital black tradition of resistance first to the institution of slavery and then to the Spanish colonial powers during the wars of independence. These black struggles represent significant but little-known contributions to the formation of today's socialist Cuba, a country whose social goals proclaim an end to the oppressive legacy of colonialism and to all forms of domination.

Dennis West

LAST TANGO IN PARIS
(ULTIMA TANGO A PARIGI)

Origin: Italy and France
Released: 1972
Released in U.S.: 1973
Production: Alberto Grimaldi for PEA/Cinematografica/Les Artistes
Associés
Direction: Bernardo Bertolucci
Screenplay: Bernardo Bertolucci and Franco Arcalli
Cinematography: Vittorio Storaro
Editing: Franco Arcalli
Art direction: Maria Paola Maino
Music: Gato Barbieri
MPAA rating: X
Running time: 130 minutes

Principal characters:
Paul	Marlon Brando
Jeanne	Maria Schneider
Tom	Jean-Pierre Léaud
Rosa's mother	Maria Michi
Marcel	Massimo Girotti
Jeanne's mother	Gitt Magrini
Rosa	Veronica Lazare

If the book we are reading does not wake us, as with a fist hammering on our skull, why then do we read it? So that it shall make us happy? Good God, we would also be happy if we had no books, and such books as make us happy we could, if need be, write ourselves. But what we must have are those books which come upon us like ill-fortune, and distress us deeply, like the death of one we love better than ourselves, like suicide. A book must be an ice-axe to break the sea frozen inside us.

What Franz Kafka said about books must be said about *Last Tango in Paris*. It is not a happy film but a deeply disturbing film—a film that strikes the viewer like a fist hammering on his skull. It was a fist when it first hit audiences in 1972, when it made the cover of *Time* and *Newsweek*, when it incited Pauline Kael to extravagant praise: "a film that has made the strongest impression on me in almost twenty years of reviewing." In the years since then, *Last Tango in Paris* has lost none of its power to disturb, to incite anger and disgust, to provoke endless argument and debate. It is still an ice ax breaking the frozen sea inside us.

The film wastes no time in giving the audience an emotional jolt. It opens with a high-angle shot of a man (Marlon Brando) standing under a Metro bridge. With a quick, fluid movement, the camera sweeps down upon him; in a dramatic close-up he is seen to cover his ears with his hands and scream an obscenity, a curse against God, into the noise of the Metro passing overhead. The camera pulls back and he is seen stumbling along the sidewalk in a daze. A young woman (Maria Schneider) suddenly walks by and stares at him, who, lost in himself, does not notice her. The camera follows her as she stops to check out an apartment-for-rent sign, goes to make a telephone call, and sees the strange man again in the telephone booth. Again, no contact is made between the two, as he leaves without seeing her. Off she goes to look at the apartment. She enters the dark apartment, throws open the blinds, and there he is, huddled against the wall.

As the girl is recovering from the shock of the man's presence, the viewer senses that the apartment is a fantasy world, a self-contained realm. The viewer feels himself to be in that apartment with a man and a woman, who are suddenly isolated, alone, face-to-face. They carry on polite conversation, they calmly look at each other, and then they suddenly explode into wonderfully wild, fierce sex. They collapse in ecstasy, slowly recover from delightful exhaustion, quietly dress, and leave the apartment without speaking. Bernardo Bertolucci has scored a hit to the solar plexus. He has exposed the viewer to a primal human fantasy—a pure, direct sexual encounter between total strangers.

The camera follows the girl out of the apartment as she rushes through a train station. She meets a young man who hugs and kisses her; suddenly, a film crew surrounds them and captures their embrace on film. The girl is shocked by her fiancé's deception, even though he tells her that he is making a film about her, a *cinéma vérité* film entitled "Portrait of a Girl." Tom (Jean-Pierre Léaud) naïvely thinks that he is capturing the "real" Jeanne with his hovering camera. When he asks Jeanne what she has been doing while he was away, she gives him the worst of clichés: "I thought about you day and night, and I cried. Darling, I can't live without you." Tom, the cineast of *vérité*, gets all of this "truth" on his film and yells: "Cut! Fantastic!"

There is a sudden cut to a pan shot of a bloody cloth and cleaning bucket which slowly reveals a young woman cleaning up a blood splattered bathroom. As she talks to someone off camera, the viewer gradually realizes that a woman has committed suicide in the bathtub with a razor and that the person to whom the maid is speaking, but who does not answer, is the woman's husband. The camera surveys the bloody bathtub and slowly pans past the glass partition to reveal the husband—the stranger from the apartment. Bertolucci has masterfully allowed his camera, like a detective, to examine each clue of this grotesque world until the viewer registers the full shock that the man whose wife's blood is still covering the bathroom is the man just seen in an intense sexual encounter.

The apartment door opens and Jeanne comes slinking in like a cat. The apartment is empty, but suddenly the door bursts open and some furniture movers initiate a comic sequence of moving in furniture. The man (Paul) enters as the workmen leave. When they are alone, face-to-face again, she offers the key, starts to leave, but suddenly asks his name. He rejects her desire to know his name and says he does not want to know her name or anything about her. He then defines the significance of the apartment: "You and I are going to meet here without knowing anything that goes on outside here. We are going to forget everything we knew—everything—all the people, all that we do, all that we—wherever we live. We are going to forget that everything—everything."

Finally, Bertolucci reveals to the viewer what is happening. He is enacting a powerful fantasy that haunts modern culture: the romantic dream of the recovery of innocence, of the rebirth of new selves that drives men and women to ignore economic status, race, culture, educational differences, age, and social class, confident that love—the naked meeting of two selves—can break through any barrier. Here in the private world of their apartment, a man and a woman will strip off all the clothes of family, society, and history and meet as naked selves—Adam and Eve again in the garden. Bertolucci made this Edenic dream explicit in the screenplay in a piece of dialogue that he omitted from the film. Jeanne says, "Adam and Eve didn't know anything about each other," and Paul replies, "We're like them in reverse. They saw they were naked and were ashamed. We saw we had clothes and came here to be naked."

As the film unfolds in its jarring juxtapositions of inner and outer worlds, the viewer gradually pieces together an understanding of these two strangers and the histories that they bring to their encounter. Paul brings to the apartment his traumatic experience of his wife's suicide. Only when the viewer finally discovers the fact of her death does he understand the significance of the opening shot of the film. Paul's screaming obscenity is an expression of his rage at an event that has shattered his life. Any death is traumatic, but especially suicide, because it exposes one's fundamental ignorance of others and reveals the abyss of irrationality that surrounds one's life. The self-destruction of Rosa (Veronica Lazare) calls into question Paul's life, whose meaning had been built on this relationship of trust and communication. All the incidents of his life outside the apartment explore the meaning of her suicide.

Paul is left in absolute ignorance as to why Rosa killed herself, but he is gradually led into an even more devastating awareness about Rosa. Paul had known about Rosa's lover, Marcel (Massino Girotti), but when he goes to visit him, presumably to find out what Marcel might know about her suicide, he discovers a truth for which he had not been looking. When he enters the room, he is startled to see Marcel dressed in a bathrobe identical to his. As the two talk, Marcel reveals that Rosa had created a life with him that was in many ways a duplicate of her life with Paul. This revelation of her bizarre secret life with Marcel only further confirms for Paul the agonizing truth of her suicide—that he did not know her.

Paul's struggle to come to terms with the suicide climaxes in his confrontation with the dead Rosa, who has been restored to a beautiful innocence in her coffin by her mother (Gitt Magrini). Paul addresses her as though she were alive. After mocking the way her mother has disguised the grotesque fact of death, he expresses his deepest, most powerful insight into the meaning of her suicide: "Even if the husband lives two hundred ... years he's never going to be able to discover his wife's real nature. I mean, I might be able to comprehend the universe but I'll never discover the truth about you, never. I mean, who the hell were you?" This is his anguished and unsettling realization—at the deepest level, all persons are strangers to one another; in any relationship, one is always left with the unanswerable question, "Who are you?"

After expressing this frightening insight, Paul releases his pent-up hurt and anger against Rosa, venting his rage against her death in a string of obscenities. Suddenly he breaks down crying in a tender confession of his love for her. Completely broken by her death, he lays his shattered self before her: "Rosa, my love ... forgive me ... I don't know why you did it. I'd do it too if I knew how." This deeply wounded self, filled with anger and grief, bitterness and hurt, Paul brings to the apartment.

Jeanne brings her innocence. Twenty years old, from a stable bourgeois family, she has had an idyllic childhood and now is about to be married. She has led a perfectly conventional, happy life untouched by the complexities of relationships, by any of the powerful, unsettling realities that lie beneath the surface of existence. Bertolucci creates this picture of Jeanne through the brilliant device of making a film within his film. Most of the scenes involving Jeanne outside the apartment are scenes in which Tom is filming her—a portrait of a young girl from her childhood through romance to marriage. The irony of this spontaneous, unrehearsed documentary of her life is that it is a perfect stereotype. Tom, filming her childhood, captures only an idealized version of her relationships with her dominating father and with her first love, Paul. Jeanne's romance with Tom, which he plays out before his camera, is a Hollywood B-picture in which they mouth the conventional words of romantic love—but remain distanced from each other, untouched by any depth of feeling or involvement.

Two radically different worlds collide in the apartment: Paul's world of death and alienation and Jeanne's world of conventional surface life. In their first return to the apartment after deciding to meet there as anonymous selves, they are naked together, tenderly embracing, playfully enjoying their bodies and emotional closeness as they try to "come without touching."

Jeanne suggests inventing a name for him, but he rejects all names and begins grunting like an animal. Jeanne joins in the play and responds with her own animal sounds. Their attempt at rebirth has begun—with literal and symbolic nakedness. In their initial sexual encounter they remained clothed, essentially hidden, strangers; now they uncover themselves and touch their nakedness. Paul rejects names because names are the essence of social definition. He rejects language itself, attempting to get free of its defining, confining power, down to some primal form of communication of selves through touching and primitive sounds.

Yet all is not tenderness and openness in their Garden of Eden. The way to new life involves the death of the old selves. The longer they are together in the apartment, the more intense the struggle becomes to break through. Smashing the inhibitions and getting down to the deepest level of raw feelings reaches shocking intensity in the controversial sodomy scene. Paul violates Jeanne using her as an object to release his own rage and the hurt he feels for Rosa. Yet the action is not a simple sexual violation, because Paul invests his physical action with the symbolic meaning of an attack on the bourgeois family that rigidly controls its children, teaching them to repress their inner feelings, forcing them into superficial lives of social conformity. From the beginning of their encounter, Paul has been attacking Jeanne's family for being precisely this kind of oppressive family. Everything known about her outside the apartment confirms the truth of Paul's assertion. Thus, Paul's violating act is also intended as an act of liberation. Jeanne consents and does join in the ritual attack on the family. She expresses her anger and hurt when she shocks him with a short in the record player—but she stays with him.

The drama of their rebirth reaches its climax when Jeanne runs away from Tom and back to the apartment, clothed in her wedding dress. She confronts Paul in the elevator and confesses her ambivalence: "I wanted to leave you and I couldn't." They enact a classic romantic scene as he carries his bride over the threshold and puts her in their marriage bed. This gesture is ironic because Jeanne discovers a dead rat in the bed, which shatters the romantic illusion. Paul taunts her with the rat, making morbid jokes that ridicule her conventional feelings. Jeanne cannot handle the assault, desperately trying to escape Paul and the apartment. As she is about to leave, she stops at the door and says: "I forgot to tell you something. I fell in love with somebody."

With brilliant dramatic irony, Bertolucci misleads both Paul and the film viewer. Both Paul and the viewer believe that Jeanne is giving him a parting shot; she is going to tell him about falling in love with someone else (whom the viewer thinks is Tom). In a witty and tender scene, as he gives her a bath before she leaves, Jeanne taunts Paul with the wonderful mysteries of her lover. Paul bitterly attacks what he takes to be a conventional love affair, asserting that she is alone and has to face it; her man can only be a false refuge. Then Jeanne says: "But I've found this man. He's you. You're that man!" Jeanne is not running away; she has broken through to love.

Yet now comes another jolt—there is to be no warm and tender embrace expressing true love. Instead, Paul engages in another shocking, violent act that wrenches the emotions. There can be no rebirth of the self in love unless it faces death. Paul had just criticized any relationship that becomes a refuge from individual loneliness—"foxhole" love. Thus, in a dramatic symbolic act of confronting death, he has Jeanne shove her fingers in his anus in a reversal of the roles of the sodomy scene, as he asks her to engage in sexual acts with a dying pig as a pledge of her love to him. Jeanne joins him in an ecstasy of obscenity and vows "more than that. And worse. And worse than before." Bertolucci hammers the audience again with a repulsive scene that assaults their sensibilities. Here is the final exposure of the self that rips off the pious clothes of sentimental love.

When Jeanne returns to the apartment again, instead of finding her true love waiting, she finds the apartment empty; Paul is gone. Jeanne is devastated; this final trauma is too much, and she cracks. She summons Tom to the apartment, desperately hoping that they might enact the drama of rebirth that she had experienced with Paul. Her hysterical fantasy of contact with Tom, however, is quickly shattered by his categorical rejection of the apartment as a place where they could "live."

Jeanne closes up the apartment and enters the outside world again. Suddenly, Paul is walking behind her. They finally meet outside the apartment for the first time since their paths crossed at that very spot on the day they entered the apartment as strangers. Will the reborn Adam and Eve come out of their garden to love in the world and to live happily ever after? This is the ending Paul has written for the film: "We left the apartment, and now we begin again with love and all the rest of it." This is the reborn Paul's dream, but she does not share it. Jeanne, in a state of total shock and confusion, says: "I don't understand anything any more."

As they walk along the street, Paul ignores Jeanne's reality and tells her who he is, reciting the startling facts of his life as though they were trivial. Ironically, he does not see that each word is a hammer blow to Jeanne, smashing her into emotional pieces. They wind up in a shabby bar where a tango dance contest is in progress. The dancers glide through their intricately synchronized gestures—two moving as one yet frozen in a formal relationship like graceful puppets, without emotion or personal contact. Like the dancers, Paul and Jeanne are physically close but emotionally distant. When he says, "I love you and I want to live with you," Jeanne sarcastically replies, "In your flophouse?" He still does not perceive her alienation and replies in the language of the traditional lover: "What the hell difference does it make if I have a flophouse or a hotel or a castle? I love you!"

To the shattered Jeanne, that statement now makes all the difference. They dance a drunken parody of the tango, crazily moving around the dance floor, no more in touch than the dancers they mock. When they return to their table, Jeanne finally gathers the courage to tell Paul what he is too blind to see: "It's finished." In an ultimate act of noncommunication and rejection, she masturbates the bewildered, uncomprehending Paul and runs away.

Paul chases her through the streets into her apartment building, where he finally confronts her in her apartment. Totally unaware of the great gulf that separates them, he cannot see the uncomprehending fear that stares out of Jeanne's eyes. Paul is ready to act out the final reconciliation scene of his imaginary Hollywood film. In a flourish of romantic hyperbole, he confesses his love: "You ran through Africa and Asia and Indonesia. Now I've found you. And I love you. I want to know your name." Paul's romantic comedy suddenly turns into tragedy. As the terrified, alienated Jeanne gives her name, she shoots and kills him. Paul staggers out to the balcony to die while the stunned Jeanne rehearses her speech to the police: "I don't know him. I don't know who he is. He's a madman. I don't know his name."

Bertolucci swings the final ice ax right between the eyes. The great dream of rebirth ends in death. Paul and Jeanne are finally unable to reconcile the inner world of naked contact with the outer world of their past selves. The terrible irony is that after the catharsis of the apartment, Paul and Jeanne emerge into the world still strangers. Paul, projecting his fantasy of beginning again with love and all the rest onto Jeanne, never sees her reality outside the apartment. Jeanne, torn out of her surface world of external relations by the traumatic descent into the self, cannot finally handle Paul's extreme claims and retreats back into her safe, superficial world. Even after the intense encounter of the apartment, the man she knew in such nakedness, she did not know at all. Jeanne does not lie when she says, "I don't know who he is."

Last Tango in Paris is a masterpiece in which all the elements of the filmmaker's art are perfectly integrated in an artistic whole. Bertolucci brilliantly structures his film as a montage of narrative fragments which constantly shift between three stories: his, hers, and theirs. This fractured narrative line creates constant visual surprise as the film moves back and forth between fragments of the three worlds. Bertolucci's daring use of jump cutting creates the dramatic clash of these incongruous worlds as the viewers experience the shock of seeing Jeanne's and Paul's radically different lives suddenly juxtaposed to each other. The most powerful jump cut in the film occurs when Jeanne and Tom embrace in the train station as he films their "true" love story. The viewer is visually stunned by a jump cut to a shot of a bloody cloth which suddenly ushers in the shocking reality of a suicide. There is another beautifully timed jump cut when Paul says that in the apartment they will forget everything in the outside world. Suddenly, the viewer is puzzled by a close-up of a hand searching in a closet—a brilliant shift to Paul's world, where the viewer will follow that hand groping for a sign until it confronts the harsh reality Paul thinks he can forget: Rosa's suicide.

The artistic element that stands out above all others in *Last Tango in Paris* is the acting. An interior drama exploring the powerful forces of the inner life and the complexity of personal relationships, its successful realization depends largely upon the actors. Bertolucci's casting was exceptional: Maria Schneider, with her unself-conscious sexuality yet open and innocent baby face, is exactly right as Jeanne. Jean-Pierre Léaud, the star of many New Wave films, is a wonderfully ironic choice to portray a caricature of *cinéma vérité* filmmakers. The star, however, is Marlon Brando, who gives a tour de force performance. Brando is brilliant, but much of the credit must go to Bertolucci's direction, which called forth from Brando a range and depth of feeling and expression that no other role, not even that of Stanley Kowalski in *A Streetcar Named Desire* (1951), had demanded of him. The extraordinary technique that Bertolucci used to create Paul was to integrate Brando's real life into the fictional character, blurring the lines between fiction and reality. He gave Paul part of Brando's personal and film identity. In the scene in which the audience discovers that the stranger in the apartment is the husband of the dead woman, it hears the maid recite his history: a boxer, an actor, a racketeer on the waterfront in New York—all allusions to Brando's personal life as well as to his roles in other films. More important, Bertolucci subtly directs Brando's improvisational acting style. Paul's central speeches, his touching memories of his childhood on the farm, his powerful diatribe against foxhole love, and his eloquent dialogue with the dead Rosa are all improvised—improvised out of Brando's personal life. This brilliant collaboration of the director and the actor transmutes aspects of Brando's life into an extraordinary fictional character who powerfully expresses some of the deepest feelings and desires of his audience.

Franz Kafka said that books that disturb and upset are needed—not happy books, which "we could, if need be, write ourselves." Such films are also needed—films such as *Last Tango in Paris*, which continues to explode sentimental ideas about love and relationships, which haunts its audience with the pathos of its closing refrain: "I don't know him. I don't know who he is," reminding viewers again and again of the permanent strangeness of one to another.

John Hartzog

LAST YEAR AT MARIENBAD
(L'ANNÉE DERNIÈRE À MARIENBAD)

Origin: France and Italy
Released: 1961
Released in U.S.: 1962
Production: Pierre Courau for Précitel and Raymond Froment for Terra Films
Direction: Alain Resnais
Screenplay: Alain Robbe-Grillet
Cinematography: Sacha Vierny
Editing: Henri Colpi and Jasmine Chasney
Art direction: Jacques Saulnier; set decoration, Georges Glon, André Piltant, and Jean-Jacques Fabre
Music: Francis Seyrig
Running time: 93 minutes

Principal characters:
A .... Delphine Seyrig
X .... Giorgio Albertazzi
M................................ Sacha Pitoeff

French director Alain Resnais first came to the attention of world of cinema critics with his 1956 documentary film *Nuit et brouillard* (*Night and Fog*), a moving and evocative study of World War II concentration camps. Although the film is technically a documentary, its use of the moving camera and other sophisticated filmic techniques, including some concern with the use of time in film, made it obvious that Resnais was an imaginative director. The promise of *Night and Fog* was fully realized in the first feature film directed by Resnais, *Hiroshima mon amour* (1959). Through the story of a love affair between a Japanese architect and a French actress, the film explored many themes, including the experiences of both Japan and France in World War II. With his next film, *Last Year at Marienbad*, Resnais took his previous excursions into time and filmic techniques to an extreme never seen before in a major feature film. Indeed, its release in 1961 was a major event in the film world, and its influence was felt for at least a decade afterward.

Even a brief description of *Last Year at Marienbad* reveals that it is nothing like a conventional narrative feature. There are three principal characters, none of whom is ever named in the film, but who are identified in the published screenplay by letters of the alphabet. Not only are the characters not named, but also the events that take place on the screen are a mixture of the real (both in the present and in the past) and the imagined (both in the future and in the past). In addition, there is little to tell the audience whether the particular scene on-screen is real or imaginary, present or past. *Last Year at Marienbad* is, in fact, so puzzling that critics have disagreed considerably in their interpretations of the film. Its two main creators, director Resnais and screenwriter Alain Robbe-Grillet, in such public statements as the introduction to the published screenplay, have not given any interpretation of the events on-screen but have instead stated that they decided to trust the audience, to allow it "to come to terms with pure subjectivities."

Many of the techniques used in *Last Year at Marienbad* are more closely related to the literary device called stream of consciousness than they are to conventional cinematic devices. There are, in fact, literary critics who view stream of consciousness as a transfer of filmic technique to the printed page. At any rate, the term "stream of consciousness," as used in literary criticism, refers to the use of words to describe what is going through the mind of a character, in all its complexity and lack of conventional logical relationships. In this connection, Robbe-Grillet has written that human consciousness is like "an interior film continually projected in our own minds." Resnais and Robbe-Grillet and writers who use the stream of consciousness technique attempt to reproduce this "interior film," either on the screen or on paper.

The three principal characters in *Last Year at Marienbad* are a fashionable woman denoted in the script as A (Delphine Seyrig), a handsome man denoted as X (Giorgio Albertazzi), and a thin man with piercing eyes and a strange, haunting face, denoted as M (Sacha Pitoeff). The relationship between A and M is never defined. X refers to M as the man who is "perhaps" the husband of A, and one can see that he is to some degree protective of her, but the viewer does not learn more than that. The action of the film is set in one or more luxurious resort hotels in Europe, and much of the sound track consists of the off-screen voice of M. Sometimes he appears to be talking to himself; at other times he is addressing A. Certain words and phrases recur in his speech, including his opening description of the resort hotel, which he describes as "enormous, luxurious, baroque, lugubrious."

The essential question of *Last Year at Marienbad* is reflected in its title. Throughout most of the film, X tries to convince A that they had met the year before and that she had promised to go away with him but had asked him to wait one year. He says that he is not sure where they met, but it could have been at the same (unnamed) resort where they now are or it could have been at Marienbad. A protests that she has not seen him before, but this denial might be her attempt to escape her commitment to him. As he describes their previous meetings, including one in which they discussed a statue of a man and a woman, these scenes are shown on-screen. Again, however, there is no indication of whether these scenes are remembered or merely imagined.

In one scene, the viewer sees A drop a glass. Critic John Francis Kreidl, in his book *Alain Resnais*, details four possible interpretations of that simple scene: A imagined that she dropped the glass; X imagined that A dropped the glass because she was upset; A actually did drop the glass; or A became insane at that moment. This sort of multiple possible interpretations is also true of many other scenes. In fact, Resnais has said that only fifty percent of the film is on the screen; the other half comes from "the reactions and the participation of the spectator."

Two other seemingly important episodes also invite speculation. In one, M shoots X with a pistol. Does this actually happen or is it merely a representation of the fears of either X or A or both? The rest of the film suggests that it is an imagined event. In another episode, it is suggested that X raped A, but X's voice immediately says that it was not by force. Is this an actual event or imagined, and if it is imagined, by whom and why? Although most interpretations of the film agree that X and A do go away together at the end, the same questions apply to the ending.

Two elements of *Last Year at Marienbad* tend to remain in the memory of most viewers of the film regardless of whether any significance is attached to them. One is a characteristic pose of A, in which she stands or sits touching the hollow of her shoulder with her hand. It is seen frequently, and X remarks about it. The other memorable element is a game that M plays with various guests at the hotel, including X. It uses a simple arrangement of sixteen cards, matches, or dominoes, and M wins every game, even though it is equally possible for either player to win.

Probably the most important element in the film, besides the three principal human characters, is the hotel itself. The camera seems to be moving constantly through long corridors adorned with rich draperies and paintings, and it also occasionally moves outside to show large formal gardens. The extreme stylization of everything in the film is carried out in all details, from the appearance of the hotel to the clothing of all the characters (particularly A and the other women at the hotel) to the movements of the characters. The effect is both ornate and lifeless.

Last Year at Marienbad began with a meeting between Resnais and Robbe-Grillet, the famous French novelist. The two recognized that they shared many characteristics in both style and subject matter and agreed that Robbe-Grillet would write a screenplay for Resnais to direct. This is the way Resnais usually works. He does not write his own scripts and he does not film adaptations of literary works such as novels, but he does find important novelists to write his screenplays. Robbe-Grillet wrote an especially detailed screenplay with almost no guidance from Resnais, and Resnais then filmed the screenplay with almost no changes. Because Robbe-Grillet knew the work of Resnais and because Resnais is a distinctive stylist, the resulting film received its final interpretation by the director, Resnais, whose style over the years has gone through many transformations but has retained as its central concern an experimental approach to time.

Since *Last Year at Marienbad* concentrates almost exclusively upon mental space and time, several elements are missing from it that one expects from a feature film. The main missing element is a clear, definite narrative, but also missing are characters that the audience can come to know and care about. The acting in the film has justly been called mere posing. Critic Eric Rhode wrote that the film is little more than an "exercise in which camera movements and editing conspire to create a splendid mystification," and critic Pauline Kael was especially displeased with the lack of fully developed characters. For many years after *Last Year at Marienbad* was released, she complained about other films showing the influences of "creeping Marienbadism." One must, however, realize that *Last Year at Marienbad* is an experiment in taking one of the possibilities of film almost to its limit—the depiction of psychological space and time as immediate and real. In so doing, it does not suggest that its technique is the only valid one in cinema.

Last Year at Marienbad shares with some twentieth century poetry the freedom from a presentation that is objective and chronological. Indeed, the shots in the film are related to one another in much the same manner that the segments of T. S. Eliot's famous poem "The Love Song of J. Alfred Prufrock" are related to one another. *Last Year at Marienbad*, then, stands as the masterpiece of the career of Alain Resnais, an experiment with film and subjectivity that will remain one of the landmarks of world cinema.

Timothy W. Johnson

LATE AUTUMN
(AKIBIYORI)

Origin: Japan
Released: 1960
Released in U.S.: 1973
Production: Shizuo Yamanuchi for Shochiku/Ofuna
Direction: Yasujiro Ozu
Assistant direction: Masahiro Shinoda
Screenplay: Kogo Noda and Yasujiro Ozu; based on a novel by Ton Satomi
Cinematography: Yuharu Atsuta
Editing: no listing
Art direction: Tatsuo Hamada
Music: Takanobu Saito
MPAA rating: no listing
Running time: 127 minutes

Principal characters:

Akiko Miwa	Setsuko Hara
Ayako Miwa (Aya)	Yoko Tsukasa
Yuriko	Mariko Okada
Goto	Keiji Sada
Mr. Mamiya	Shin Saburi
Fumiko	Sadako Sawamura
Michiko	Miyuki Kuwano
Mr. Taguchi	Nobuo Nakamura
Nobuko	Kuniko Miyake
Yoko	Yuriko Tashiro
Mr. Hirayama	Ryuji Kita
Koichi	Shinichiro Mikami
Uncle Miwa	Chishu Ryu
Masao	Masahiko Shimazu
Kazuo	Koji Shidara
Sugiyama	Fumio Watanabe
Yuriko's mother	Mutsuko Sakura

Late Autumn belongs to the final stage of distillation in the development of a style already distinguished by its extreme purity and refinement. Yasujiro Ozu's films have strong minimalist qualities: a concern for stripping down the elements of one's art to the basics and then building works of art on different permutations of those basic elements, given small but significant variations and rendered in a very spare, rigorous style.

On the level of subject matter, Ozu conventionalized his material to a degree that was extreme even by the standards of the *shomin-geki* genre (dramas of ordinary middle-class life) in which he usually worked. Ozu's films are nearly all stories of domestic life and family relationships—especially those between parents and children. In addition, from 1949 onward, most of Ozu's films contain the same basic plot element: the problems experienced by a family when the daughter is to be married, with special emphasis on the father's sense of loss. The paradigm for this plot is Ozu's 1949 masterpiece, *Banshun* (*Late Spring*).

Late Autumn represents a variation on the basic *Late Spring* formula in one main respect: It is about a mother, not a father, losing her daughter to marriage. As the film opens, Akiko Miwa (Setsuko Hara), a still attractive widow in her forties, has just lost her husband. After the funeral, Akiko is discussed by three friends of the family, Mr. Mamiya (Shin Saburi), Mr. Taguchi (Nobuo Nakamura), and Mr. Hirayama (Ryuji Kita)—middle-aged men who all had loved Akiko in their youth. They decide that it is about time Akiko's only child, eighteen-year-old Aya (Yoko Tsukasa), got married, and that it is up to them to find a suitable prospect for her.

The choice falls on Goto (Keiji Sada), a young man who works for Mamiya's firm. Akiko seems to support the idea, but Aya flatly rejects it, declaring that she is perfectly happy living with her mother. Aya begins dating Goto but resists pressure, mainly from Mamiya, to declare for marriage. Miffed, the three self-appointed matchmakers decide that Aya's uncooperativeness is based on her reluctance to leave her mother living alone. The solution, they conclude, is for Akiko to get married. Hirayama, a widower, is selected for the honor, but his suit is fumbled by his two friends.

Unwilling to give up, Mamiya hints to Aya that Akiko is planning to remarry. Feeling angry and betrayed, Aya bitterly denounces her mother. Akiko, unaware of these latest machinations, is completely confused. Yuriko (Mariko Okada), a spirited young woman who is Aya's coworker and best friend, takes it upon herself to untangle this mess, expediting the engagement of Akiko and Hirayama and thus clearing the way for that of Aya and Goto.

Now reconciled, Akiko and Aya take a final vacation together to a lakeside inn. There Akiko announces that she has decided not to remarry after all. After Aya's wedding, Akiko sits alone in the darkened apartment and prepares for her first night of solitude.

Late Autumn contains most of the characteristic restrictions of Ozu's late style: no camera movement of any kind (a feature of all Ozu films after 1956); the majority of shots taken from the same, slightly low angle; scenes built almost entirely upon the sustained repetition of the same four or five camera set-ups; no fades or dissolves between scenes. Yet Ozu's well-known "transitional shots" (between-scenes shots of dramatically empty spaces whose relation to the main narrative is either inscrutable, extremely tangential, or initially unclear) are unusually scarce here. They are used occasionally (most notably the series of empty spaces linking the opening scenes of the film), but for the most part transitions cut directly either to the action of the next scene or to introductory spaces which are more like those of conventional establishing shots.

Late Autumn demonstrates the distinctive color style developed by Ozu after 1958 (the date of his first color film). For the most part, Ozu's colors are very muted, even drab—brown, gray, beige, black. Against this bland ground, small, well-defined bits of brighter or richer colors—a glass filled with golden beer, a red ashtray, a blue-striped peanut can—will resolve the frame into a carefully arranged, almost two-dimensional formal pattern.

Late Autumn's color scheme is even more subdued and somber than usual for Ozu. The stark blacks and whites that dominate the opening funeral scenes set the pattern for the entire film. In the nighttime restaurant scene between Aya and Mamiya, for example, the backgrounds of the single-shots of each character are dominated by the waiters in white jacket and black tie. Later, when Mamiya lies to Aya about her mother's supposed remarriage plans, Ozu cuts to a previously unseen space featuring a black table and a white cup in the foreground. The trauma of separation and loss associated with the funeral is recalled by these prominent white and black objects and related to the idea of marriage—a connection which is very forcefully carried through in the final wedding-related scenes, whose colors, settings, and compositions explicitly parallel those of the funeral which began the film.

Late Autumn is one of Ozu's most richly comic films and also one of his most melancholy. It is this extremely sharp definition of contrasting yet well-integrated tones that gives the film much of its distinctive character and ranks it among Ozu's finest achievements. The machinations of the three meddling matchmakers, the misunderstandings that develop, the phantom courtship of the randy widower Hirayama (whose nervous excitement sends him dashing to the toilet whenever the prospect of marriage is broached), the spunky candor of Aya's friend Yuriko—these provide a sustained, near farcical tone usually found only in Ozu's more overtly comic projects.

At the same time, however, the film treats the possibilities for love, marriage, friendship, happiness, permanence, and free choice as tenuous at best, and there is always a sense of deep shadow despite the film's good humor. Aya, the central character, is wrested out of a secure and happy existence with her mother and half-coerced, half-duped into a marriage which seems based more on tolerability than passion. Although several other Ozu films concern daughters nudged into nonromantic unions and parents left alone with their mortality at the end, never has the point been driven home so starkly as it is in *Late Autumn*, with its powerfully symmetrical structure paralleling the funeral at the beginning with the wedding at the end. Indeed, it is in many respects difficult to make a strong distinction between the two events: The funeral does not seem a particularly solemn occasion, nor the wedding a particularly festive one.

The shift in the basic *Late Spring* formula from a father-daughter to a mother-daughter relationship in *Late Autumn* has the effect of accentuating the gulf between the sexes as well as the one between the generations. Rather than a father and an aunt working together to have the daughter wed (as in *Late Spring*), *Late Autumn* presents a mother and daughter living harmoniously together, and three men working to get the daughter married. The central exchange of the plot takes the daughter not from an older man (her father) to a younger man (her husband), but from a woman (her mother) to a man (her husband). Although Ozu's films always develop both generational and sexual conflicts, in *Late Autumn* the central conflict is aligned more strongly along a male/female axis.

In the opening scene, the viewer first sees the three men, Mamiya, Taguchi, and Hirayama, sitting together and talking. After a few minutes, a cut reveals Akiko and Aya, previously unseen, on the other side of the screen, where they have been sitting quietly all the while. This opening configuration sets forth both the central separation of men and women and the properly subservient position of women in the arrangement. Subsequent scenes confirm these implications, at several points by actually removing the women from sight—that is, by framing the shot so that the woman is hidden behind a partition while the man remains in view. At one point, Mamiya, in a restaurant, claps his hands and calls to the waitress for a drink. This is followed by a direct cut to Mamiya's home, where one sees his daughter Michiko (Miyuki Kuwano) bringing him a drink on a tray. Women, in Mamiya's view, are expected to serve and to defer. Aya's refusal to cooperate in his grand design represents an irksome disruption of the order of things.

One of the most remarkable scenes in *Late Autumn* is also (not uncharacteristically for Ozu) one of the most incidental. At one point about midway through the film, Mamiya is seen by himself in a sporting-goods store, trying out golf clubs. After a few minutes, he leaves and goes into a restaurant directly across the street. This scene has no apparent narrative function in the film. It takes on an almost mysterious presence by virtue of its seeming irrelevance and its atypicality—a character alone, at leisure, doing "nothing," in a setting other than an office, a home, or a "public house." The scene's incongruous prominence serves to give added weight to Mamiya's importance in the scheme of the film.

With a single exception, this is the only scene in the film that does not take place in one of the three types of settings listed above. That exception involves Aya, who goes on a hiking trip down a country road with a group of her friends. The identification of Mamiya and Aya with these strikingly atypical environments underscores the fact that these two characters are the central antagonists in the film. The main conflict in *Late Autumn* is not between the mother and daughter, but between the daughter and her older, male antagonist. The fact that Mamiya is not Aya's father adds a strong sexual undertone to their struggle—it seems likely that Mamiya's excessive, even bullying concern with getting Aya married stems from his own unacknowledged frustration over never having married her mother, whom he is now attempting to possess via the alternate route of making her daughter (surrogate for Akiko) marry his candidate (surrogate for Mamiya).

A remarkably large number of *Late Autumn*'s scenes are set in what could be called "public houses"; restaurants, bars, and inns. Ozu is usually fond of such locations, but in *Late Autumn* their predominance is extreme: Scenes set in them constitute the major portion of the film. These settings work to emphasize both an underlying formality in all relationships (especially male-female ones) and a certain devaluation of domestic environments. "Home" does not seem to be an especially strong or meaningful concept for the characters in the film—it is merely a functional place to which one can retire at the end of the day. Akiko and Aya live in a rather meager apartment with a sterile-looking corridor outside the door. Mamiya, Taguchi, and Hirayama seem to spend as little time as possible at home and are most often found at restaurants, bars, and golf courses, without their wives and children. Indeed, the characters in the film rarely seem to be "at home"; instead, they constantly circulate among various "homes away from home."

These public-house settings also carry connotations of impermanence. One meets in a bar or restaurant for a matter of minutes or hours; one stays at an inn for a few days—and then one departs, goes home, or goes on to other meetings and other places. There is always a definite and imminent end point implicit in such locales.

This sense of impermanence extends figuratively to all relationships in the film. Children grow up, people die, parents remarry, friends part, feelings change, time passes. In one of the film's key scenes (also incidental), Aya and her friend Yuriko stand on the roof of their office building and wave at a train as it goes by in the distance. On it is a friend of theirs who has just been married. She had promised to wave her bouquet at them, but she does not. Aya and Yuriko are bitterly disappointed. "She probably forgot us," Aya reflects. "Time passes—and friends part."

Later in the film, Aya, refusing to marry, estranged by her mother's apparent betrayal, stands on the roof again, this time alone, and sadly watches another train pass by in the distance. Aya is unable to accept the inevitability of change, although she herself had earlier acknowledged this law of life. She wants to remain forever with her mother, outside change, outside age, outside sexuality. Given the quality of sexual and marital relations seen in the film, there is much to be said for Aya's ideal, but it cannot be sustained. All things must pass—childhoods and ideals as well as trains.

The opening and closing scenes of *Late Autumn* are marked by reflections of sunlight off water flickering over the walls and ceilings of the settings. Associated with scenes of death (the funeral) and parting (Aya and Akiko's last trip together and Aya's wedding), this shimmering, unstable light evokes the idea of transitoriness. This association is then contrasted with a large mountain by the lake where the inn is located. Massive, inert, always positioned in the center of the frame, the mountain evokes a timelessness and stability seemingly denied to the human relationships in the film.

With the mountain in the background, a tiny speedboat whizzes by, a paper lantern dangles, a group of schoolgirls pose for a photograph. Speed, fragility, youth: These images of fleetingness are set against a backdrop of fixity and eternity. The image of the photograph (carried over into the next scene, where one sees Aya and Goto posing stiffly for their wedding photograph) represents an attempt to freeze time, to wrest an instant of stability in the midst of flux. Stasis and change are the ultimate parameters of Ozu's world, in which the eternal and the ephemeral are always intertwined, and the one enduring permanence is change.

Martin Rubin

LATE SPRING
(BANSHUN)

Origin: Japan
Released: 1949
Released in U.S.: 1972
Production: Shochiku
Direction: Yasujiro Ozu
Screenplay: Kogo Noda and Yasujiro Ozu; based on the novel by Kazuo
   Hirotsu
Cinematography: Yuharu Atsuta
Editing: no listing
Art direction: Tatsuo Hamada
Music: Senji Ito
MPAA rating: no listing
Running time: 107 minutes

> *Principal characters:*
> Noriko . . . . Setsuko Hara
> Professor Somiya. . . . . Chishu Ryu
> Aunt . . . . Haruko Sugimura
> Hattori . . . . Jun Usami
> Ayako . . . . Yumeji Tsukioka
> Mrs. Miwa . . . . Kuniko Miyake

To the casual viewer of the films of Yasujiro Ozu, there is a great similarity apparent among them. A certain similarity of titles, more evocative of mood than of plot, the use of the same cast over and over again, in the same kinds of roles (Chishu Ryu as a father, Setsuko Hara, a daughter, Haruko Sugimura, an aunt or a neighbor), and the use of similar slight plot structures (most typically, a widower trying to marry off his daughter) do indeed lend Ozu's cinema a great air of similarity among its parts. Yet similarity should not be confused with sameness, for in choosing to work with the same people time and again, and with similar plots, Ozu made the differences between his films stand out all the more. Often these differences may be subtle, but subtlety makes all the difference in the world.

There are many things about Ozu's masterpiece, *Late Spring*, that distinguish it from his earlier films and from the later works that comprise the "season cycle" (his films with spring, summer, or fall in their titles). Perhaps the most outstanding difference rests with the character of Noriko as portrayed by Setsuko Hara. While Hara usually plays a daughter in Ozu's films (often named Noriko), this particular Noriko is not quite as lovable and docile as the other Norikos she has played. This Noriko is strong willed, stubborn, petulant, moody, sometimes childish and uncooperative. She has an irrational hatred of the idea of remarriage; she refuses to wed because she does not want to leave her father, and she is quite explicit about these dislikes and likes. It would be wrong, however, to read into Noriko's devotion to her father any "Oedipal" or "Electra" complexes. Such psychological probing, to which Western critics often wish to subject screen characters, would be most inappropriate in this film. Rather, Noriko should be treasured as a unique Ozu character, one who is a dutiful daughter but who perhaps takes the idea of filial piety too far and neglects her own place in the scheme of things.

Late Spring also diverges slightly from the later works in the relative straightforwardness of its unfolding. This is not to say that the film comfortably fits into the Western style and sensibility, but rather that Ozu was only beginning to find his mature film sense. *Late Spring* still presents certain kinds of narrative ellipses that no American filmmaker would dare try; Ozu still directs scenes whose dramatic impact rests not on their narrative function but on their emotional content. *Late Spring* does, however (and almost shocking to an Ozu aficionado who has not seen this film) possess a number of scenes that seem to be out of a Hollywood film, in which the principles of montage and camera movement are used to build a sequence.

Late Spring begins in typical Ozu fashion with a series of still lifes that set a mood of tranquillity and timelessness while also delivering the spatial proximity of the scene. Here, Ozu shows three shots of the deserted train station at Kita Kamakura. This scene cuts to a shot down a hallway of a typical Japanese house. (A long-shot of a deserted hallway inside a house is the single most common shot in Ozu's cinema.) Ozu finally reveals a group of women participating in the traditional tea ceremony. Ozu singles out Noriko (Setsuko Hara) and her aunt (Haruko Sugimura) through one short conversation. Before setting up the plot of the film, however, Ozu shows another series of still lifes, cuts back to the tea ceremony as it ritually progresses, and cuts away to two more still lifes before finally introducing Professor Somiya (Chishu Ryu), Noriko's father.

Somiya works closely with his assistant, Hattori (Jun Usami), in his house. Noriko comes home and talks to the men. Ozu breezily establishes the playful, close relationship between Noriko and her father. Somiya wants to go play mah-jongg, but Noriko forbids it until he has written more pages of his scholarly paper.

The next day, Noriko and her father travel to Tokyo by train. Ozu shows the train ride through a montage sequence of some seventeen shots, consisting of interiors of the train and exterior, moving camera shots. The narrative information, that Somiya relies on his daughter to pack his papers for him, seems less important than the style of the sequence, rare for Ozu.

Upon arriving in Tokyo, Noriko meets her father's old friend, Professor

Onodera. They take in an art show and a walk in the park before going to a restaurant. Onodera tells Noriko that he has remarried. Noriko finds the idea repellent and says (in a nice way) that Onodera is "unclean" for having done so. Onodera returns with Noriko to her home to visit with her father. Through the men's conversation, the viewer learns that Noriko is recovering from the ill effects of her forced labor during World War II. Their conversation about it is quite casual, and, except in a passing, offhand fashion, her "sickness" never appears again. Such a discussion would be a clue in a Hollywood melodrama, but it is to be taken as a mere fact of life, along with everything else, in an Ozu film. In addition to Noriko's sickness, the subject of Noriko's marriage is broached for the first time.

The scene between Onodera and Somiya ends with a bizarre exchange which, in typical Ozu fashion, has absolutely no narrative value but is quite amusing (if strange) in its own right. Onodera inquires in which direction, vis-à-vis the house, the ocean lies and points forward: He is wrong about the direction. He then asks about other compass points; in each case Somiya corrects him by pointing in the opposite direction. Onodera, totally baffled, concludes that directions and space in this neighborhood are baffling indeed. One wonders if this scene is Ozu's sly way of indicating that he knows how confusing the space can be in his own films. A still-life shot of the ocean ends the scene.

The next sequence involves Noriko and Hattori and is again atypical of Ozu. The scene begins as the camera dollies across a deserted country road. A bouncy musical score can be heard, a kind of traveling tune. Noriko and Hattori are riding bicycles. Ozu uses some fifteen shots from the time they are first seen riding their bicycles until the bikes are seen parked in a clearing. This montage, along with the earlier train sequence, would be ordinary in an American film, yet it is extraordinary in Ozu. The only Ozu-like aspect in the sequence is the mismatched screen direction of Noriko and Hattori—at first riding parallel; at two points Ozu has Noriko moving left to right and Hattori moving right to left. Dramatically, the purpose of this bicycle-riding sequence and the conversation between Noriko and Hattori which follows, is to show Noriko and Hattori's compatibility. Their compatibility inspires Noriko's aunt and her father to discuss the possibility of Noriko marrying Hattori. They both believe that he would make a fine husband. Somiya promises to broach the subject with Noriko, which he does, later at home; Noriko laughs as she tells her father that Hattori is already engaged.

Noriko goes to Tokyo and meets Hattori to talk about his upcoming wedding. Hattori invites her to a concert, but she refuses his invitation. When Noriko comes home, she sees her friend Ayako (Yumeji Tsukioka) waiting for her. The two go up to her room and talk about the class reunion that Noriko was unable to attend. Ayako, who is divorced and working as a stenographer, tells Noriko that most of the girls from their class are married. One girl is pregnant but unmarried, which shocks Noriko. Somiya brings up a tray of tea and bread for the girls but forgets to bring spoons and sugar. Ayako brings up the subject of Noriko getting married; Noriko counters with Ayako's divorce. The two girls speak in baseball metaphors about getting their turn at bat (marriage) and hitting the right pitch (finding the right husband). From here, Ozu, perhaps perversely but certainly humorously, cuts to a Little League baseball game and then to Noriko playfully fighting with her little nephew at her aunt's house. Her aunt introduces her to Mrs. Miwa (Kuniko Miyake) and then brings up the subject of marriage.

Noriko's aunt has found a likely prospect, a Mr. Satake: a graduate of Tokyo University, from a good family, who works for a chemical company, is thirty-four years old, and looks like Gary Cooper. Noriko does not want to marry. She claims that only she can look after her father, who is very eccentric. Her aunt then states that Noriko, with that attitude, will never marry. Noriko does not mind. Her aunt then brings up the possibility of her father marrying Mrs. Miwa; this possibility upsets Noriko. When she gets home, she can not face her father and runs outside.

At a Nō theater performance, Noriko sees her father smile at Mrs. Miwa, and she gets upset. On the way home, Noriko runs away from her father and goes to Ayako's house. Noriko, still upset, tells Ayako that she wants to learn stenography. Ayako suggests that she get married, and Noriko storms out of her house.

Back home, Somiya tells his daughter that her aunt has arranged for her to meet Mr. Satake. Somiya gently suggests that she comply, claiming it is time that she married. Noriko insists that she wants to remain at home, but her father says that he was wrong to take advantage of her and that now he wants her to marry. When Noriko shifts the conversation to the question of who would take care of him, Somiya brings up the possibility of his marrying Mrs. Miwa. Noriko expresses her abject horror at the idea and runs upstairs. Somiya follows and again asks her to meet Satake. She agrees.

At the park, Somiya and Noriko's aunt talk about Noriko. A week has passed since the meeting of Noriko and Satake, and the aunt suggests that the time has arrived for Noriko to make up her mind. At home, Noriko's aunt confronts Noriko on the question of marriage. At first, Noriko refuses to answer; finally, she gives out a weak "yes."

Noriko and her father take a trip to Kyoto to spend some time with Onodera and his family. Noriko realizes that she was wrong to make those comments about his marriage and she apologizes for them. At the inn where they are staying, Noriko once again wonders why she must marry. She is happy enough with her father and with things as they are. Her father, in what amounts to a recitation of the Ozu credo, tells her that she must marry, that a husband and wife build a life together away from parents: It is in this way that human life and history have been carried on. Marriage may not mean happiness from the start and one should not expect that. One does not wait for happiness; one works for it.

The next scene shows a car outside the Somiya home waiting to take Noriko to the wedding. Noriko is dressed in the traditional bridal costume, and there follows another shot of the car. Again, in typical Ozu fashion, the viewer never sees the husband who takes the daughter away from her father.

Somiya meets Ayako in a restaurant and tells her that he never intended to remarry. He told Noriko he was planning to remarry only because he knew that was the only way she would marry. At home alone, Somiya carefully peels an apple. He stops, looks up and away. A still life of the seashore ends the film.

If *Late Spring* contains a number of sequences, such as the train ride or the bicycle ride, which diverge from Ozu's usual manner, it also contains a number of bits which are pure Ozu. The most special of these include the scene at the Nō theater and two scenes in Kyoto. In the Nō sequence, Noriko and her father sit in the theater, watching a performance for five full minutes before the narrative point of the scene becomes clear: that Mrs. Miwa is there. Another five minutes go by devoted to Noriko's reaction to this. Surely, however, Ozu need not have devoted ten minutes for that one piece of information (which was clear already). Ozu is after the juxtaposition of the quality of the Nō performance, its ancient rituals, to the daily problems of these two people. It is significant that Somiya can be genuinely transported out of his daily existence while watching the performance, something Noriko cannot yet do.

Ozu shows a conversation late at night between Noriko and her father in Kyoto, in which she regrets her remarks to Onodera. She wants to talk more but her father has fallen asleep. Ozu then cuts between Noriko lying in bed awake and a single vase she sees. The image of the vase is complex, for it comes to stand as a narrative ellipsis as Noriko's mood changes across the cuts, and for a kind of still life in which the audience can invest its own emotions. This image becomes even more powerful when Ozu cuts from the vase to two shots of a Zen garden, thus bringing home the Zen-like image of the vase. Somiya and Onodera sit on the porch of a temple overlooking the garden and talk about Noriko's marriage. Somiya thinks that a son is better than a daughter. If the daughter is unmarried, one worries; if she does marry, one feels let down. The content of this scene must be juxtaposed to the scene in which Somiya convinces Noriko to marry and to the end, where he does feel let down. Yet what lets him down? What precisely is Somiya feeling? The answer to this is the answer to the whole problem posed by Ozu's entire cinema: the disappointments of life.

It is significant that Somiya makes his speech to Noriko about human history and the life cycle at Kyoto, the heart of traditional Japanese culture. For a Westerner it would be easy to decry the image of Japanese women, with marriage as their only option. Yet to the Japanese, and the Kyoto setting reinforces this, marriage is simply a metaphor for the participation in a cultural process that is greater than any individual. One is first a child, then a spouse, then a parent whose own children follow the same pattern. Along the way, regrets and sadness are inevitable. Yet it is in the realization that one is part of something greater, larger, than oneself that one can transcend the limitations of individualism.

David Desser

THE LEFT-HANDED WOMAN
(DIE LINKSHÄNDIGE FRAU)

Origin: West Germany
Released: 1977
Released in U.S.: 1978
Production: Road Movies Filmproduktion
Direction: Peter Handke
Screenplay: Peter Handke
Cinematography: Robby Müller
Editing: Peter Pryzgodda
Art direction: Christiab Magis and Pim Pjuijerman
Sound: Ulrich Winkler
Music: Johann Sebastian Bach
MPAA rating: no listing
Running time: 119 minutes

Principal characters:
Woman .... Edith Clever
Stefan .... Markus Mühleisen
Bruno............................. Bruno Ganz
Franziska....................... Angela Winkler
Woman with the child.......... Ines de Longchamps
Stefan's friend .... Philippe Caizergues
Publisher .... Bernhard Wicki
Father .... Bernhard Minetti
Actor............................ Rüdiger Vogler

Few films focus the novel-into-film debate as sharply and idiosyncratically as Peter Handke's *The Left-Handed Woman.* Although known primarily as a novelist and playwright, Handke has regularly peopled his literary work with notorious cinephiles and voyeurs, and he has collaborated with Wim Wenders on Wenders' *Falsche Bewegung* (1975; *Wrong Move*) and *Die Angst des Tormanns beim Elfmeter* (1972; *The Anxiety of the Goalie at the Penalty Kick*), a film adaptation of Handke's novel. Slow paced and oblique, *The Left-Handed Woman* was quickly proclaimed a truly poetic film reminiscent of Robert Bresson and Michelangelo Antonioni, and many critics immediately compared Handke to other writer/filmmakers such as Jean Cocteau and André Malraux. The status of *The Left-Handed Woman* as novel and film is complicated, however, by the fact that it was first conceived as a film and only then written as a novel, and this precedence and privileging of images becomes a crucial factor in this story of a woman secluded in an image outside language and social discourse.

The protagonist in the film is an unnamed woman (Edith Clever), who has a sudden "illumination" at the start of the film. She is a German living in the Paris suburb of Clamart with her twelve-year-old son Stefan (Markus Mühleisen) and her husband, Bruno (Bruno Ganz). At the beginning of the film, she picks up her husband at the airport, and, while Bruno talks continually about his business trip and loneliness in a foreign country, the woman remains silent, a silence that continues for the first twenty minutes of the film. After dinner at a hotel, Bruno announces to the waiter that he and his wife wish to sleep together right away. The next morning she tells Bruno of her illumination and decision that they must separate. Significantly, this decision has none (and never acquires any) of the psychological or sociological explanations that usually accompany this kind of marital or sexual separation.

Marked by the printed titles of the months from March through April, the course of the film then follows the woman's various encounters as she attempts to claim and maintain herself as a distinct identity. Hoping to find that her decision was a whim, Bruno returns, at first contrite and then angry. After she applies for a job, a publisher-friend visits her, gives her work translating Gustav Flaubert's "A Simple Heart," and tries clumsily to seduce her. He tells her of a writer who has refused to write another word, and, when the publisher bemoans the writer's desperate isolation, the woman counters by suggesting that the writer may in fact be quite happy. Similarly, when her father visits her, they talk of old age and loneliness as they walk around the city's suburbs, and he warns her that she will become sad and sometimes bitter like he is if she does not learn to compromise. Yet while quietly listening to these complaints, she refuses to budge from her position. Even the society of a feminist group, recommended and urged by her friend Franziska (Angela Winkler) with whom Bruno is now living, does not offer her a viable alternative: She walks to the meeting but turns away at the last minute. Indeed, as this sequence makes very clear, *The Left-Handed Woman* is both more than and less than a feminist film, since the rebellion and alienation of this woman concerns all forms of social discourse, even that offered by women's groups. (If this film belongs to a feminist tradition, it is that of Chantal Akerman and not that of Agnès Varda or, for example Paul Mazursky's *An Unmarried Woman*, 1978.)

As a negation of all that attempts to appropriate her, what this woman aspires to is the presence of a kind of pure image, apart from any social logic. In this, there is the important connection between the vision of Handke and that of Wenders (whose past editor and cameraman provide the technical underpinning for this film); perhaps more important, this sense of an authentic image pinpoints the debt of both filmmakers to the Japanese director Yasujiro Ozu. Several times the film refers directly to Ozu: once when the woman and her son watch an early Ozu silent film, *Tokyo Chorus* (1931), and another time when the woman sits beneath a picture of Ozu in

her home. In addition, Handke frequently employs the disconnected, sometimes long, takes of particular objects and images that are so characteristic
of Ozu's films. *The Left-Handed Woman* opens with a series of these shots:
grass rustling as a train races by, newspapers sweeping across an empty station platform, an urbanscape, and a frontal shot of the woman's home.
Throughout the remainder of the film, the woman is identified carefully and
rigorously with these images and a perspective secluded in its singularity and
authenticity: Regularly framed or seen looking out of sharp frames, this
woman becomes equated with those nonnarrative moments which punctuate
the story, moments focused in the romantic and isolated brilliance of images
such as the tulip dropping a petal on the restaurant table.

Yet the woman's position as an independent image outside the demands
of society and its discourses continually collides with those demands and
other discourses. While, on the one hand, she attempts to separate herself
from the world around her, she finds herself, on the other hand, running up
against unavoidable social forces and other individuals. Dramatized most
obviously in the domestic demands of her home and son, the jolts, collisions, and quiet disruptions that result are the heart of the film's understated plot, and they function on both a thematic and formal level to suggest
the problem of finding a place in modern society which would still preserve
one's individuality. Like the central predicament of a German woman displaced in a French city, many shots and sequences in the film describe
disturbing confrontations between different realities and images, often
compositionally divided within the frame or linked by subtle shock cuts:
There is, for example, the striking shot in which the woman, a horse and
rider, and a train move across the image on parallel but distinctly separated
paths. For Handke, this tense harmony between characters and images indicates and describes, above all else, the difficulty of maintaining what he has
called a separate togetherness. As an explicit illustration of this, moreover,
there is a sequence at a photographic booth where the woman and her
father meet an unemployed actor. Indirectly echoing the woman's desire for
a pure self-image, the father tells the actor to create a more natural image
of himself on the screen and not to mimic conventions, but, as the actor and
the woman prepare to shake hands and part, a static electric shock anticipates their fingertips and they jump away from each other. As throughout
the film, here the demand for an authentic self-image is juxtaposed with the
confrontations and collisions which occur when that image enters society.

One of the dominant and most specific forms this confrontation takes in
The Left-Handed Woman is between language and the singularity of the image, and in this confrontation one witnesses the woman's effort to move
slowly back into the social world from which she has separated herself. Her
overwhelming silence is one of the most effective ways she resists the
conventions and discourses of society, her status as image marking her off

sharply from a world defined by language. The speech and terminology of others constantly seeks to appropriate her, as when her husband calls her a mystic or Franziska attempts to see her actions as part of a feminist discourse ("We need someone like you, at war with the world," she says). Yet her passive silence—so different from the violent silence of Elisabeth in Ingmar Bergman's *Persona* (1966)—rebuffs these attempts and maintains her as a self-contained image, outside linguistic logic. Even the allegorical street signs, such as "rue Terre Nueve" (new ground), serve mainly to mark an ironic distance between the traditional words used to designate this woman's actions and the reality of her independence. Gradually, however, she begins to insinuate herself back into society, and the salient metaphor for this movement is her translation of the Flaubert story through the course of the film. By the end of the film, she has finished the translation and to some extent she has also translated her own image into the social languages with which she has collided. By the conclusion, the woman has made a gesture of friendship toward her husband (buying him a pair of shoes), and the strange party which gathers the principal characters from the film for an awkward, impromptu, and nervous meeting remains, for all of its strangeness, a social gathering. The Ozu-like shots which close the film are now occasionally populated with human beings, and the final quotation from Yugoslav film director Vlado Kristl indicates the ultimately social direction of this film about an intensely private space: "Have you noticed there's only room for those who make room for themselves."

If *The Left-Handed Woman* is both criticized and praised as a feminist film made by a man, it is equally provocative as a film about pure visual images made by a celebrated man of words. If it is a film of aggressive isolation, it is also a film that speaks of society and history through the negative terms and structures that define that isolation. In this intendedly difficult film, the translation of the individual as image into the language of society is accomplished only by being adamantly faithful to the original; the chief irony of the film is that the left-handed eccentric of the title is by nature a right-handed Everywoman.

Timothy Corrigan

LENIN IN OCTOBER
(LENIN V OKTYABRE)

Origin: U.S.S.R.
Released: 1937
Released in U.S.: 1938
Production: Mosfilm Studio
Direction: Mikhail Romm
Assistant direction: Dmitri Vasiliev
Screenplay: Alexi Kapler
Cinematography: Boris Volchek
Editing: no listing
Art direction: Boris Dubrovsky-Eshke
Music: Anatoli Alexandrov
Running time: no listing

Principal characters:
Lenin .... Boris Shchukin
Stalin .... I. Golshtab
Worker .... Nikolai Okhlopkov

He was one of the most gifted politicians of the modern era, and his image, after Karl Marx's, is the physical symbol of Communism: Vladimir Ilich Ulyanov, best known by the name he adopted during the Czarist reign, Lenin. Besides being an astute tactician of the way to achieve power and a major theoretician of modern Marxism, Lenin became a historical figure whose image dominates the film industry that he helped establish in the first years of the Soviet Republic. Some thirty major films have been produced in the Soviet Union that include him as a character either in the wings or at center stage, besides the numerous documentary features and shorts. Not only did his dictum to Communist leader and educator Anatoli Lunacharsky, that "film is for us the most important art," become a well-known epigram, but also his image became a staple in Soviet film production.

The very first appearance by Lenin on-screen occurred in the 1919 film by Dziga Vertov, *Ninety-Six*, which combined enacted scenarios with newsreel footage. Later, Vertov included scenes of Lenin's funeral in his ode to the founder of the Soviet state, *Three Songs of Lenin*. The most famous characterization of Lenin by a performer was, and probably remains, the short episodes in Sergei Eisenstein's *October* (1928) in which a worker with a startling resemblance to Lenin, Nikandrov (oddly, no first name has come down to researchers), played the part. The use of Nikandrov, however, caused a controversy in which the famed poet Vladimir Mayakovsky played a role, and for about a decade no mere actor was given the role again.

The film that made the role popular, Mikhail Romm's *Lenin in October*, appeared more than a decade after Lenin's death. Scripted by Alexi Klaper and completed in record time, *Lenin in October* presents a fully characterized revolutionary leader. Played by Boris Shchukin, Lenin boasts of his simple workman's shoes and thinks nothing of having to rough it in a railway worker's house. The worker (Nikolai Okhlopkov) is more than a minor figure, since he has to represent the Russian proletariat as a fully realized individual who can give Lenin advice and make sure that he has enough blankets at night. In its way, Romm's film is a fleshed-out version of Eisenstein's abstraction. Instead of the revolutionary masses, there is one warm, friendly, and practical worker; perhaps more crucial, in place of the revolutionaries, there is the solitary leader, Lenin. Where Eisenstein shows a pencil on a Petrograd map marking the places where the Bolsheviks must seize control, Romm has a ruminating Lenin sketch in the plans at his host's dining-room table. If Lenin can accept the advice of a simple worker, he can also confer with his comrades, and in this film a very young Joseph Stalin (I. Golshtab) is shown suggesting key ideas about when to seize power.

The major action of Romm's film revolves around a plot to assassinate Lenin, another indication of the new emphasis on the role of the leader. A police spy and a virtual truckload of goverment soldiers are on Lenin's trail on the eve of the Bolshevik Revolution. Several close calls culminate in a fight between the troops and the lone worker, who not only stalls them but also manages to disable their truck. The successful Revolution can be seen as the result of Lenin's brilliance and the worker's self-sacrifice.

The storming of the Winter Palace, too, seems to be a reduced vision of *October*. Rather than the mass charge through the ornate imperial gates, the viewer is shown a carefully choreographed advance up a wide staircase. The film was well received, and following the relatively innovative depiction of Lenin and Stalin on film, "the floodgates were open," to quote Jay Leyda's monumental history of the Russian and Soviet cinema, *Kino*.

Ironically, Shchukin died after the film was completed, and Golshtab was replaced by Mikhail Gelovani in the numerous films that portrayed Stalin. The mantle of Lenin was soon borne by Maxim Straukh. Straukh played Lenin in numerous films throughout the 1930's and 1940's: *Man with the Gun* (1938), *The Vyborg Side* (1939), *Yakov Sverdlov* (1940), *Stories About Lenin* (1958). *Stories About Lenin* has been cited as his best characterization, but a film made nearly ten years later, *Lenin in Poland* (1966), featured a relatively humane figure: Sergei Yutkevich chronicles Lenin's exile in Poland in the years before the outbreak of World War I. Except for a brief meeting of Bolshevik emissaries that has all the earmarks of a picnic, Lenin appears as a friendly countryman—a sort of Red country squire—giving legal advice off the cuff to the local peasants. His most explicitly political speech is his condemnation of the plight of the young Polish workers, who must confront one another as soldiers in either the czar's or the Austrian kaiser's army. This pacifism was well suited to the mid-1960's, when the film was made, and provides the thematic background to Lenin's eventual arrest and expulsion from Austrian Poland. He moved to neutral Switzerland, from which the Soviet audience could be expected to know the eventual story.

Although Straukh did not have a complete monopoly over the Lenin role (Nikolai Plotnikov had the part in a 1956 film, *Prologue*, directed by Yefim Dzigan), his performances did set the standard for the cinematic portrayal of the man. Only near the end of the 1960's has a successor been seen whose performance has been termed the "best and most mature" of the Lenin portrayals. This is Yuri Kayurov in the 1968 film *The Sixth of July*. Directed by Yuli Karaskik and adapted from a screenplay by Mikhail Shatrov, this film examines the opposition raised by the Bolsheviks' allies, the Left Social Revolutionaries, to the peace treaty with Imperial Germany. That treaty, signed at Brest-Litovsk, sacrificed enormous tracts of land and gave the Germans almost total control of the Ukraine in exchange for an end to their remorseless advance. It was a calculated sacrifice, since Lenin believed that either the German proletariat would soon have their own "October" or the Western Allies would soon crush the Imperial Army in France. Lenin emerges as a grand master in this political chess game, although the other Bolshevik leaders and even the Left Social Revolutionaries receive a fair characterization. Kayurov also appeared in *Lenin in Paris*, a 1981 release.

Lenin has not always been the center of films that feature him as a character. Mark Donskoy's *A Mother's Heart* (1966) and *A Mother's Devotion* (1966) focus on Maria Alexandrovna Ulyanova, Lenin's mother. Some films feature Lenin as a secondary character, as in *On the Same Planet*, a 1965 release, and the 1982 film *Red Bells*, the Soviet cinematic biography of John Reed.

Lenny Rubenstein

THE LEOPARD
(IL GATTOPARDO)

Origin: Italy
Released: 1963
Released in U.S.: 1963
Production: Goffredo Lombardo for Titanus/SNPC/SGC
Direction: Luchino Visconti
Assistant direction: Rinaldo Ricci, Albino Cocco, Francesco Massarto, and
  Brad Fuller.
Screenplay: Suso Cecchi D'Amico, Pasquale Festa Campanile, Enrico
  Medioli, Massimo Franciosa, and Luchino Visconti; based on the novel by
  Giuseppe Tomasi di Lampedusa.
Cinematography: Giuseppe Rotunno
Editing: Mario Serandrei
Art direction: Mario Garbuglia and Ferdinando Giovannoni; set decoration,
  Giorgio Pes and Laudomia Hercolani
Makeup: Alberto De Rossi
Costume design: Piero Tosi
Sound: Mario Messina
Music direction: Franco Ferrara
Music: Nino Rota, Georges Bizet, and Giuseppe Verdi
Running time: 205 minutes
Running time in U. S.: 163 minutes

Principal characters:
Don Fabrizio	Burt Lancaster
Tancredi	Alain Delon
Angelica Sedara	Claudia Cardinale
Don Calogero Sedara	Paolo Stoppa
Concetta	Lucilla Morlacchi
Princess Maria Stella	Rina Morelli
Father Pirrone	Romolo Valli
Don Ciccio Tumeo	Serge Reggiani
Chevalley	Leslie French

Luchino Visconti has been called the founder of neorealism in Italy, but
he did not remain a neorealist for long; like Federico Fellini and Michelangelo Antonioni, he defies such labels. Nevertheless, it is possible to trace
certain recurring patterns in his films.

One such pattern is Visconti's fondness for adaptations of literary works,
a taste evident in his first film, *Ossessione* (1942), which was based on
James M. Cain's 1934 novel *The Postman Always Rings Twice. Senso* (1954),

based on the novel of the same title by Camillo Boito, has much in common with *The Leopard*: Both films deal with an aristocrat coming to grips with the new order; both are set in Italy during the years after 1860; both depict the process of *trasformismo*, the changing of rebels into men who become part of the system. Visconti's next adaptation was *Le notti bianche* (1957; *White Nights*), based on the story by Fyodor Dostoevski. After *The Leopard*, Visconti adapted a poem, "Le Ricordanze," by Giacomo Leopardi, into *Vaghe stelle dell'Orsa* (1965; *Sandra*). Albert Camus' novel of the same title was the basis for *Lo straniero* (1967; *The Stranger*). Other Visconti adaptations include *La caduta degli dei* (1969; *The Damned*), *Morte a Venezia* (1971; *Death in Venice*) from a Thomas Mann story, and *Ludwig II* (1972).

Another unifying element in Visconti's work is his idiosyncratic Marxism. At the heart of a Visconti film is the inner conflict of the central character, a conflict which invariably pits that character against the conventions of middle-class society. Visconti was a nobleman by birth and a Marxist by choice. His films reveal a tortured sense of ambivalence concerning the culture and grace of the old families and the crass, materialistic ways of the new. The new men in his films are successful men of action who venture and get things done; the old aristocrats, by contrast, give up everything too soon and without a fight.

It is ironic that Visconti turned to Twentieth Century-Fox in an effort to gain international distribution for *The Leopard*. They severely cut his longer version and dubbed it into English. The resulting short version leaves out much of the plot and continuity. Even in the short version, however, one can sense Visconti's design.

Fortunately, Burt Lancaster did his own dubbing into English, and he manages to convey the aristocratic nihilism of the film's protagonist, Don Fabrizio, Prince of Salina, in a subtle and restrained performance. The film begins in 1860. The conflict between the old and the new is immediately introduced with the opening shot, which shows the prince's family motto: Things will have to change to remain the same. The prince and his family are at prayer in their chapel. Suddenly, a man is heard crying out off camera, and members of the family are seen turning toward the shouting. Then the camera shows the prince (Burt Lancaster) praying. He has a mustache, long sideburns, and busy eyebrows which curl up. He genuflects and moves outside to find that a man has been shot in his garden. Thus, in this opening sequence, Visconti shows how the Garibaldi revolution intrudes on the quiet habits of the aristocracy. The sequence ends as the prince takes out his handkerchief and covers the dead man's face with it.

The prince is shown riding in his carriage that night with Father Pirrone (Romolo Valli). He drops the priest off at the church in Palermo and then proceeds to visit his mistress. The next morning his favorite nephew, a man of action, Tancredi (Alain Delon), is seen reflected in the prince's shaving mirror. Tancredi is leaving to fight for Victor Emmanuel. He repeats the family motto, and his uncle gives him money. He kisses his quiet, aristocratic cousin, Concetta (Lucilla Morlacchi), and leaves. There are mountains in the background—a green, lush vista of the Sicilian countryside. The camera pans among the trees growing in wild profusion.

The character of the prince is further established in a scene in which Father Pirrone asks him to confess his adultery. The prince refuses, telling the priest that he considers his wife the real sinner because he has given her seven children and has never even seen her knee. Here again, as in the opening sequence in the chapel, the rituals of the Church are mocked, depicted as out of touch with real life.

Tancredi is shown fighting the Bourbon soldiers in the streets while the camera cuts to the prince taking a trip in a caravan of four horse-drawn carriages. The purpose of the trip is a picnic the family shares with Tancredi, who spends his time with Concetta. Tancredi returns home, promoted to captain. He wears a black eye patch over his right eye when it is convenient to do so. During a key sequence in which the family journeys to church, Visconti uses music to comment on his characters. As the street orchestra plays the smuggler's song from *Carmen* (1875), Tancredi, the prince, and his family enter the church, where an organ is playing the death theme from *La traviata* (1853). The camera pans the artwork in the church, shows the priest and choirboys, then pans the faces of the prince's family. Coated with white dust from the road which gives them a corpselike look, they are seated alongside the wall—where the dead are typically buried in cathedrals. In contrast, the vigorous congregation is standing in the center of the church.

In the next sequence, the priest bursts in on the prince, who is taking a bath, to tell him that Concetta is in love with Tancredi. The prince suggests to the priest that he, too, should try bathing once in a while. He says that Tancredi needs a wife who can bring him the money he needs and that Angelica (Claudia Cardinale), the daughter of Don Calogero (Paolo Stoppa), would be a better match. What remains unspoken is the casual way the prince betrays the feelings of his own daughter for material gain.

At a dinner party, the prince's son laughs at Don Calogero for wearing the wrong type of coat, a coat with tails. Don Calogero's beautiful daughter makes a late entrance. Everyone turns to see Angelica, and all are impressed by her poise and beauty. At dinner, Tancredi tells her a risqué story, and she laughs uncontrollably. The laughter of the prince's son ridiculed a middle-class social climber; her laughter comes partly from her fear of not being accepted, partly to link her to Tancredi as a fellow spirit. He joins her in laughing, and the moment cements their relationship. Concetta, seated uncomfortably between them, takes offense, gets up, and leaves. The next day, the prince observes Tancredi bringing gifts to Angelica.

The prince walks down a dusty street to vote for Victor Emmanuel. Don

Calogero is in charge of the election. He sees to it that the king of Sardinia becomes unanimously elected first king of Italy, at least as far as Sicily is concerned. While the prince is hunting, he learns that his companion, Don Ciccio (Serge Reggiani), voted against Victor Emmanuel. In this way the viewer learns that the election was rigged. Don Ciccio tells the prince that Angelica is a beauty but that she is unfit to marry Tancredi. The prince fears that Don Ciccio will talk and spoil the match; thus, he asks him to wait with his hunting dogs until the match is made. The prince hears Don Calogero assign two thousand acres of farmland, one thousand acres of vineyards, and twenty sacks of gold. He and the priest leave before the proud father can explain that his daughter is a baroness. The prince releases Don Ciccio, who has been patiently waiting with the hounds.

The prince is reading aloud to the family when Tancredi arrives during a rainstorm. He brings Angelica a ring. As he explores the palace with Angelica, dust covers everything.

A visitor, Chevalley (Leslie French), asks the prince to become a senator in the new government, but the prince refuses to accept: He is completely without illusions. He recommends Don Calogero for the senate. Chevalley says that if honest men refuse to serve, the senate will be forced to accept lesser men. "We are the leopards, the lions," the prince tells Chevalley. "Those who take our place will be jackals and sheep." The camera pans the hillside with men working in the foreground with pickaxes. The beautiful scene is destined for destruction for the sake of something practical. The sound of an orchestra playing a waltz already fills the background while the men are working. The music provides a transition to the next sequence, the extended ballroom sequence, the longest in the film.

The ballroom sequence pulls together all the strands of the plot, all the characters, in a trenchant social commentary on the era. It is one of the best-sustained sequences in all of modern film, and by itself ensures the film's importance. In the midst of the dancing, a group of soldiers arrive, among them a noisy, pushy colonel who seems to embody all the faults of the new government. Tancredi, unquestioningly in league with the new order, is dancing with Angelica. The prince, weary and tired, looks at some noisy young women, looks sorrowfully into a mirror, sinks into a chair, and wipes his brow. He murmurs that he is sorry he came.

The prince goes to the library, where he sits, staring at a painting of a dying man whose children strike frantic poses around his bedside. The pale man in his dusty bedclothes is in the center of the painting. The prince wonders if his own death will resemble that of the man in the painting. Angelica enters and asks him to dance. At first he refuses, but finally he is persuaded to leave the library. As the orchestra plays a waltz, he leads her to the dance floor, where they waltz flawlessly in the grand old manner. Suddenly, the prince is a man of action again. All eyes are watching the beautiful couple.

Angelica thanks him for helping her win Tancredi, but he tells her a gallant lie: It is her own beauty that has won Tancredi for her. Tancredi asks him to dine with them, but the prince refuses. He decides not to eat anything, but the noisy colonel invites him to join his table. The prince drinks some wine and eats something, painfully listening to the boastful colonel. He loses his temper, leaves the colonel's table, and without being seen, watches Tancredi with Angelica and Concetta. Tancredi tells Angelica that the deserters will be shot a dawn. Concetta tells Tancredi that she liked him better the way he used to be and she leaves, crying. Tancredi kisses Angelica; the dancers surround them. The prince sheds a tear and walks away.

The colonel and the soldiers leave the ball to carry out the execution. Tancredi says goodbye to the prince, who decides to walk home alone. The prince kneels in the street before the church just as the shots ring out. He stands up and slowly walks home.

The prince is very much like Ashley Wilkes in *Gone with the Wind* (1936), while Tancredi and Angelica are like Rhett Butler and Scarlett O'Hara. Yet Visconti's producer lacked the power to control his film to develop an Italian *Gone with the Wind*, instead developing a poorly edited attempt at an Italian counterpart to an American masterpiece. Too much has been cut from Visconti's film. The points he is making about the aristocracy and the middle class are there, but only a glimpse of the working class remains. It is clear that this film ranks with *Intolerance* (1916) and *Greed* (1924) as spectacle with strong content. Like those films and *Cleopatra* (1963), however, another spectacle botched by Twentieth Century-Fox in the same year, *The Leopard* was badly cut on the mistaken assumption that audiences would be unwilling to sit through a long film.

Michael Porte

A LESSON IN LOVE
(EN LEKTION I KÄRLEK)

Origin: Sweden
Released: 1954
Released in U.S.: 1960
Production: Svensk Filmindustri
Direction: Ingmar Bergman
Screenplay: Ingmar Bergman
Cinematography: Martin Bodin
Editing: Oscar Rosander
Narration: Gunnar Björnstrand
Art direction: P. A. Lundgren
Music: Dag Wirén
Running time: 95 minutes

Principal characters:
Dr. David Erneman............Gunnar Björnstrand
Marianne Erneman.................Eva Dahlbeck
Nix Erneman..................Harriet Andersson
Carl Adam ....Åke Grönberg
Suzanne ....Yvonne Lombard
Professor Henrik Erneman.......Olof Winnerstrand
Svea Erneman....................Renée Björling
Sam.............................John Elfström
Salesman.......................Helge Hagerman
Lise............................Birgitte Reimar
Nurse..........................Dagmar Ebbesen
Uncle Axel ....Carl Ström
Pastor.............................Sigge Fürst
Hotel manager ....Arne Lindblad
Passenger in beret ....Ingmar Bergman

Of Ingmar Bergman's handful of comedies, only the sequence from *Kvinnors väntan* (1952; *Secrets of Women*) and *A Lesson in Love* and his masterful *Sommarnattens leende* (1955; *Smiles of a Summer Night*) succeed in delighting. Their success results largely from the witty, stylish performances of Eva Dahlbeck and Gunnar Björnstrand, a team comparable to Hollywood's famous pairings of William Powell and Myrna Loy, Katharine Hepburn and Spencer Tracy, Rosalind Russell and Cary Grant.

Bergman's film prior to *A Lesson in Love*, *Gycklarnas afton* (1953; *Sawdust and Tinsel*), had been a box-office and critical catastrophe, so he was worried that his filmmaking career might be in jeopardy. He needed a commercial success. Recalling the laughter that the comic sequence in his *Secrets of Women* had received, he wrote a script that revived its theme— that marriage can be the death of love—and reunited the pair that had made its humor work. To be sure, themes from his serious films—fear of death, sexual ambivalence, the inability to feel deeply for others, and the inevitable violence (verbal and physical) that emerges in male-female relationships—do appear in *A Lesson in Love* to cloud the levity, but these touches of anguish, which distinguish the work as Bergman's, ultimately enrich the film's fabric.

The story concerns a Stockholm gynecologist, Dr. David Erneman (Gunnar Björnstrand), who has discovered that his philandering is driving his wife, Marianne (Eva Dahlbeck), into an affair with their old friend, sculptor Carl Adam (Åke Grönberg). David sets out to win her back. He also wants to save his marriage because, being middle-aged, he has not the energy for complicated emotional entanglements, and he has come to regret having to neglect the pleasures of study and work for those of the flesh. He realizes now that his favorite witticism—"Marriage needs a shock to wake it up. The marital bed is the death of love"—though it contains a measure of truth, has served to rationalize his lust and vanity. Besides, he is afraid of loneliness.

The action begins in David's office the morning he breaks off with his young mistress, Suzanne (Yvonne Lombard). The history of their affair is conveyed subsequently in two flashbacks as David is being driven by his chauffeur, Sam (John Elfström), to catch the train to Malmö. As Sam drops him off at the depot, David reminds him that they are to meet that evening outside a harbor bar in Copenhagen.

Once on the train, David—after passing Bergman, who here makes a Hitchcock-like appearance—settles down in a compartment occupied by a woman and a man. When the woman leaves the compartment for a moment, the man, a salesman (Helge Hagerman), brags that he is certain that the beautiful lady is attracted to him and, after provocation from David, wages a small sum that he will get her to kiss him before they arrive at the next station. When the man leaves to try to win the bet, David relaxes and turns to his medical book. Photographs of his young son and fifteen-year- old, tomboyish daughter, Nix, fall out. He smiles, leans back, and allows memory to take over. (Throughout the first half of the film, rain and thunder reflect emotional states, and rain-blurred car and train windows facilitate entry into the frequent flashbacks.)

The flashbacks show David—his voice introduces the scene—coming upon Nix (Harriet Andersson), who is running away from home. He invites her for ice cream, and at the parlor she expresses her anger at his neglect. Her parents' separation and sexual behavior also upset her. Her distaste for their sexual indiscretions is fueled by her own sexual ambivalence. Displaying her hands, she proclaims that she wants to make things with them like men do. Can he operate to change her into a man? She voices her detestation of women's passivity, their obsession with pleasure and love, and their dependence on men.

David takes her next to the home of Uncle Axel (Carl Ström), the potter, where father and daughter sit, facing the audience behind potter's wheels, each shaping a spinning lump of clay into an elementary pot. Nix's unhappiness over her parents' possible divorce flows into her voice and hands. As the security of childhood collapses, she crushes her pot and pounds its deformed shape with her fist, crying, before running out, that she never wants to love anybody. After David follows her, the camera moves in on the slightly lopsided but still upright pot he has thrown.

Outside, as she sits with David on the grass, Nix surprises him with the news that her mother is seeing Carl Adam, and she elaborates on her own disgust with sexuality—"behaving like cows or hens." Smiling, David admits that wallowing in physical love is baboonlike but assures her that real love is something more. Referring to his affair with Suzanne, Nix asks if he despises himself. He answers, with frightening poignance, that "everything leaves [him] cold." Does this include, she naturally asks, her, her brother, and her mother? No, he reassures her, they are *all* that he cares for. David arranges for Nix to be apprenticed to Uncle Axel, and that evening a more secure Nix falls asleep in her father's arms.

David is startled out of his memory by the lady, much agitated, reentering the train compartment. A moment later the salesman, rubbing his cheek, returns, hands David the wager, silently gathers his belongings, and moves to another compartment. When something seems to have blown in the woman's eye, David, who has struck up a conversation with her, deftly extracts it, pressing his body against hers as discreetly as possible. Learning that he is a gynecologist, she comments that she has often wondered how men in that specialty avoid temptation. David admits that he *has* lost his head, but, he adds, so too has his wife. Furthermore, "marriage needs a shock to wake it up. The marriage bed is the death of love." Controlling her exasperation at this and his statement that women "adore" being married, the lady insists that "a woman wants to feel she is a woman, not a wife." David replies, "You're beautiful, witty—a perfect example of your sex—I love you, I've always loved you, and always will." The viewer is delighted to discover the lady is Marianne, his wife.

Shortly afterward, when David goes to get Marianne a package of cigarettes, he makes another wager with the salesman whom Marianne slapped—that he will succeed where the man failed. Marianne, meanwhile, in flashback, recalls having confronted David, alone in his lab, with his infidelity. He denied it, but she spied a note he had written to himself about hotel reservations for the weekend. Showing up at the hotel, Marianne, cheerily announcing "Tea for two," delivers David's and Suzanne's breakfast tray.

She is jolted back to the present by David, who is lighting her cigarette. The witty repartee that follows—as David tries to get her to forget Adam and return to him—convinces the viewer that these two are a perfect match. He begs her for a kiss; Marianne winks and leads him out of their compartment to stand outside the gentleman's compartment. She had overheard the bet: "kiss me . . . and win the money," she says, "but I want half." She responds, however, more passionately to David than she intends. (The salesman watches, stunned.) Flustered by her loss of self-control, she hurries angrily back to the compartment. David tells the man to keep the money and buy his own wife flowers and then rushes after Marianne. In their compartment, Marianne angrily cries out, "Never again!" "Never again what?" he inquires. "I don't know, but never again!" she replies in frustration.

In a moment, the two are laughing heartily at the memory (another flash-back) of the day they married. Marianne, engaged to Carl Adam, had not shown up for the wedding ceremony at Adam's studio, so Adam had sent his friend David to fetch her. Alone together, however, Marianne and David confessed their love for each other. On their return to Adam's studio, the jealous fiancé had knocked David down and Marianne had retaliated by pummeling Adam's life-size, nude sculptures—many for which she had modeled—with a jug. Impressed with her spunk, the moody sculptor had apologized and toasted the lovers, who were then wed.

Marianne's resistance seems to be weakening. "Sometimes you might have praised my beauty, pretended I was the best lover in the world . . . although we both know I'm not." The viewer gradually recognizes that this extraordinary, self-deceptively liberated, bourgeois couple is at last accepting not only their own limitations but also the limitations of their fantasies. Their goal: to reestablish a revitalized status quo.

Both worry about how a divorce would affect David's parents and recall celebrating his father's seventy-third birthday. The viewer watches David's mother, Svea (Renée Björling), Marianne, David, their two children, and Sam perform the yearly ritual of ascending the stairs to deliver breakfast in bed to the delighted father, Professor Henrik Erneman (Olof Winner-strand). Another part of the ritual is a picnic, which Henrik hates. As they set out, Svea sends Henrik back to put on his long underwear. Nix accompanies him, and, as he changes, asks him if he is afraid of dying. The old man says no, that he believes in life—"in this life and the next and all kinds of life," adding, "How dull if everything were always the same. . . . Suppose I had to wear long underwear all eternity!" Though this does not completely dispel her apprehensions, it quiets them, and she shows her love for her grandfather with a gift which she herself made. Another heartwarming and amusing scene follows as Henrik, David, and Sam "operate" on the sabotaged car, only to be defeated by the resourceful Svea, who produces a horse and buggy. A brief, lyric montage transports the viewer to the countryside and re-creates the picnic, ending with a contented David and Marianne in an idyllic, wooded setting, lying head to head, the camera hovering just above their faces. Marianne confesses that even though she is totally satisfied with her life, she would like another child—a small one: "Sometimes my body aches for a baby." "I'd have no mistress then," David replies. (Earlier Marianne had shocked David by telling him that he was jealous of the attention she paid their children.) The viewer also learns David's supreme fantasy: Alone in a diving suit (thus combining escape and womblike security), he wants to hunt deep-sea treasure and sharks. Dancing with Marianne that evening, David kisses her bare shoulder and whispers the promise that he had uttered earlier: He always will love her.

As this flashback ends, the viewer expects Marianne to allow David to carry the day, but she wants him to pursue her further. She, however, has not reckoned on Carl Adam showing up as they detrain at Malmö. (David has conspired to get Adam, whose excessive drinking and behavior he counts on to drive Marianne back into his arms, to meet Marianne.) The bull-like man—in every way David's opposite—shouts "Hello my girlie!" over the heads of the crowd, rushing up to hoist and swing her around. In Copenhagen, David insists that they have one last drink together before he turns his wife over to his best friend. (They will not marry, says Adam; that is too bourgeois.) At a seashore dive, while David is dancing with Marianne, Adam does a little conniving himself. He has the bartender mix David a "Volcano" and sets a spicy looking prostitute named Lise (Birgitte Reimar) to pretend that she and David are familiar with each other. David has just downed his Volcano and ordered a second when Lise accosts him, throws her arms around his neck, and screams for a kiss. Björnstrand superbly conveys the nonplussed, embarrassed David's attempt to remain poised and gracious. "Are you one of my patients?" he asks. The Volcano erupting within him, David takes Lise in his arms and kisses her. Marianne attacks, screaming and scratching. The cry, "police," ends this (indifferently staged) brawl and sends people for the exits.

Outside, in the one memorably shot scene of this conventionally photographed film, the camera dollies along one side of the canal while on the other side, Marianne, almost in tears and looking small and overwhelmed by the dockside bars in the background, hurries along berating (in close-up sound) David, who backpedals in front of her, trying wittily, if none too diplomatically, to soften her hurt and outrage over his kissing Lise. When she cries that she would like to drown herself, he calls her attention to the canal a few feet away. Then, raising his hand as if to slap her, he throws both of his arms around her. She capitulates utterly as Sam drives up. They get in the car and Sam delivers them to the hotel, where David has reservations. To a buoyant waltz, the hotel staff, bearing luggage and champagne—in a procession that reminds one of the Erneman family's trip upstairs to celebrate the old professor's birthday—escort the couple to the bridal suite. "You wretch! Were you so sure?" asks the obviously pleased yet outwitted Marianne. "A strategist must foresee all eventualities," replies David in his cockiest, most charming manner. Sam, the staff, the hotel manager, and the camera retreat from the room, leaving David and Marianne sitting on the edge of their bed. As the manager closes the door he hangs a "Do Not Disturb" sign on the doorknob. There is a moment of silence after he departs, and then from around the corner of the empty hallway a little, diapered boy, wings on his back and carrying a bow and arrow, approaches the door, smiles toward the viewer and enters. When Cupid closes the door, the sign reads, "Silence: A Lesson in Love."

A Lesson in Love fitfully succeeds—but it does succeed—in balancing the comic with the potentially tragic. (A voice-over at the film's start instructs the viewer, "This comedy might have been a tragedy, but the gods were kind.") Nor has time dimmed its charm; it still beguiles one with its wit and honesty.

Hubert I. Cohen

LET JOY REIGN SUPREME
(QUE LA FÊTE COMMENCE)

Origin: France
Released: 1975
Released in U.S.: 1977
Production: Michelle de Broca for Fildebroc/UPF/La Gueville
Direction: Bertrand Tavernier
Screenplay: Jean Aurenche and Bertrand Tavernier
Cinematography: Pierre William Glenn
Editing: Armand Psenny
Art direction: Pierre Guffroy
Music: Philippe d'Orléans; based on writings by Antoine Duhamel
MPAA rating: no listing
Running time: 119 minutes

Principal characters:
Philippe d'Orléans .... Philippe Noiret
Abbé Dubois .... Jean Rochefort
Marquis de Pontcallec .... Jean-Pierre Marielle
Émilie .... Christine Pascal
Villeroi .... Alfred Adam
Cardinal .... Jean Roger Caussimon
Duc de Bourbon .... Gérard Desarthe
Mme de Parabère .... Marina Vlady

Let Joy Reign Supreme was the second feature film that Bertrand Tavernier directed. Moving from a respected French film critic to a vibrant and challenging filmmaker, Tavernier based his first film, *L'Horloger de Saint-Paul* (1974; *The Clockmaker*), on a Georges Simenon novel, transferring the action to modern-day Lyons (where Tavernier was born). Using a crime-thriller format, Tavernier managed to raise a host of relevant political issues as the watchmaker comes to terms with his son's murder of a policeman and learns to respect his life-style in the process. By contrast, *Let Joy Reign Supreme* moves back some 350 years in time to look at the brief period between 1715 and 1723, when France was ruled by the Regent, Philippe d'Orléans. Philippe's outlook was a humane one, and he tried to rule fairly, but in the eight years of his reign, the winds of change which resulted in the French Revolution can clearly be seen.

At first sight, a historical costume drama may seem an unusual choice for a politically committed director, but Tavernier, in an interview in *Cinéaste*, explained his reasons for locating his film in early eighteenth century France:

> I chose the Regent because I could easily approach some modern
> feelings and facts, some political ideas which fascinate me. I was
> interested in the Regent's character because he seemed unusual and
> dramatic and very modern. The Regent's story was one of a man
> who saw very clearly what he had to do, and because of the pres-
> sures on him and the nature of his character, was too weak to do it.
> It was a situation representative of the political conflicts in any
> transition period.

Like his earlier film, *Let Joy Reign Supreme* was made within a specific
genre but was intended to break the established stylistic conventions of that
genre. Coscripted by Tavernier and veteran writer Jean Aurenche, the film
attempts to portray history in the present tense, as if it were actually happening at the time it was being filmed. In both film and literature, history is
traditionally represented either by concentrating on particular central characters, elevating their lives to coincide with the key moments of the period,
or with hindsight, bringing contemporary trends and forces deliberately to
the foreground. On the other hand, history can be conjured up by relating
anecdotes (in cinema, this often occurs in the form of comedy). Tavernier
takes elements from all three styles, combining them in various ways to give
a picture of the past that does not assume a privileged viewpoint but rather
presents the narrative as contemporary to its filming. The result, although
an interesting challenge to genre conventions, can often be confusing, making it difficult for the viewer to abstract the main thread of the narrative
from the surrounding wealth of detail.

This deliberate antigenre stance is reflected in the choice of leading characters. The Marquis de Pontcallec (Jean-Pierre Marielle), the leader of the
Breton rebellion, is no romantic hero of historical fiction, but rather an
eccentric, well-meaning buffoon. He is a man who designs his own rather
strange weaponry, but who has no knowledge of battle techniques; a noble
in his own region, he has no sense of court etiquette and no standing among
the Parisian-based aristocracy. The predicaments in which he finds himself
have comic undertones: He escapes from his pursuers by hiding beneath a
girl's petticoats in a bathtub; he is arrested while indulging in the pleasures
of prostitution; and he finds himself married to a woman who never opens
her mouth.

Similarly, the Abbé Dubois (Jean Rochefort), a pimp who wants to be an
archbishop, rarely resembles the black-hearted villain familiar to devotees of
costume drama. Instead, Tavernier depicts an almost pathetic, slightly sinister climber. Having reached the position of abbé without the faintest trace
of religious consciousness, Dubois is afraid to let pleasure stand in the way
of ambition and continually schemes to drag the last bit of advantage out of
any situation, until he induces sympathy in his audience instead of revulsion.
Tavernier draws on Duc de Saint-Simon's *Memoires* (1788-1789) for ac-

counts of how the abbé would climb over furniture in times of distress to supply disconcertingly comic moments. At the center, Philippe Noiret (Tavernier's stock actor, who has starred in many of his films) as Philippe d'Orléans is a recognizably human Regent. A liberal who realizes that the world ought to be a better place, he, like most liberals, is ineffectual, trapped between historical trends. His impotence is his weakness, and he consoles himself with wild, crude parties and masquerades, even hiring men to gratify his whores if he is unable to perform satisfactorily.

Tavernier surrounds the main narrative with a wealth of detail, incidental episodes, and bizarre images, making the story occasionally difficult to follow. In Brittany, the Marquis de Pontcallec calls a meeting of his fellow nobles to raise money to talk to the Regent in Paris before resorting to rebellion in order to achieve an autonomous republic. At the court, Philippe d'Orléans has just buried his daughter, a beautiful girl rumored to be more than a passive participant in her father's lewd activities (she is also thought to have died of drink). The Abbé Dubois, utilizing Philippe's sadness, seizes the growing Breton rebellion as a chance to further his own ends.

Pontcallec uses his time in Paris to indulge in the renowned pleasures of the capital, but while consorting with a prostitute, he is arrested and taken with the other vagrants to be transported to the new colony of Louisiana. He buys his way out and makes his way to court only to be arrested by Dubois and once again returned to prison for deportation. Pontcallec escapes and returns to Brittany to raise an army with Spanish aid.

In order to impress the English, Dubois exaggerates the Breton revolt and sends a large contingent of troops to conquer the rebels. Pontcallec's men are few and hungry, and their revolt consists of an abortive, and slightly comic, kidnaping attempt (the victim stays at home and the peasants, in any event, refuse to fight a nobleman's war). On the run, Pontcallec hides in a nunnery, in a bathtub, ironically beneath the skirts of the Regent's godchild, an innocent young girl whom the Regent is trying to tempt to Paris to participate in his charades. Finally, on the beach, Pontcallec and his two allies are arrested. The quiet humor of this section of the film is underlined by the moment when, as the army surrounds the rebels, a postman walks into the battle to deliver a letter to Pontcallec, which is from his wife, asking him if he will be dining at home this evening.

At the court, the plotting continues. Dubois forces Philippe to sign a death warrant for the Bretons. Meanwhile, in Paris, all is confusion. Nobles, trying to undermine the establishment, exchange their paper money for cartloads of gold. In the middle of the fever, an aristocrat is arrested for murdering a moneylender. Still annoyed at having been bullied into condemning the Bretons to death, Philippe decides the murderer will die on the wheel, placing him and his family in deep disgrace while the rebels go to a more noble end on the scaffold.

At one of Philippe's masquerades—where, symbolically, Misery, Crime, and Despair are joined by the Bank—Philippe imagines that his arm smells of rotting. He tries to force Dubois to amputate it, but on the way to the hospital, his coach tips over and kills a young peasant boy. Philippe's offer of money is spurned by the dead lad's sister, who, when the royals have departed, sets fire to their broken coach. She refuses to let anyone close her brother's eyes, saying, "See how well it burns and we'll burn others." The moral is clear: Even Philippe's enlightened rule cannot prevent the coming revolution. It is not the main characters of history that institute change but the people themselves.

Tavernier mixes styles and ideas with often bewildering speed, moving from intimate details to surreal commentary almost within a single scene. From the pomp of the Church, as field mice are excommunicated for destroying crops, to the whims of the young king, who prefers his education in cannonry to be taught with live targets, the bizarre is incorporated into the plot. Other moments seem gratuitous: The surgeons performing the autopsy on Philippe's daughter wear long-beaked masks, underlining their lack of skill at surgery; the enforced marriages for prisoners about to be shipped to Louisiana take place with dozens of couples standing in line for a two-second ceremony; the red-clothed guards, in their frenzied search for Pontcallec, knock over black-clothed nuns at prayer. All of these scenes seem more appropriate to British comedy troupe Monty Python's idiosyncratic view of the world. Although incidental to the plot, these touches give the film its distinctive appeal, showing decadence and hypocrisy without indulging in banality.

Royalty is, at the same time, brought down from its traditional pedestal in the film. Life at court is demythologized in simple ways: Nursemaids and servants discuss the young king's bed-wetting habits; nobles publicly relieve their bladders into metal buckets. These events bring royalty into the realm of the ordinary. Tavernier uses the comments of the below-stairs staff to build atmosphere and to comment on the unfolding action, once again providing a new and refreshing kind of historical fiction.

Whatever Tavernier's attempts to undermine genre convention, in the last analysis, *Let Joy Reign Supreme*, like most serious historical fiction, is about power—or, to be more accurate, powerlessness. It is no accident that all of Tavernier's characters consort with prostitutes; it is common to compare the selling of flesh to the selling of loyalty and commitment, and considering that, within the film's time frame, paper money and foreign investment had been introduced recently, the depicted prostitution has an economic ring to it as well.

Philippe spends his entire social life with prostitutes, turning even his daughter and his cherished godchild into ladies of the night; this behavior is symbolic of his inability to implement his convictions. One wealthy lady brings her priest to a sexy masquerade, explaining that if he sees it with his own eyes it will save time in confession. Even the Church is not above lowering its morals. The Abbé Dubois goes further: His rule is that of a pimp. Rarely partaking of pleasure himself, he treats women as pawns for his own advancement. Only Pontcallec, whose competence rather than honesty is in doubt, has the decency to marry his bed partner.

By the final scene, the peasant girl whose brother has been killed by the royal coach is the only woman who remains fresh and uncompromised. In the historical context of the film, it is in her hands that the future lies. Tavernier has played a last trick on the audience, showing that the characters whom they have been so avidly following are, in reality, irrelevant to the course of history.

Sally Hibbin

LETTER FROM SIBERIA
(LETTRE DE SIBÉRIE)

Origin: France
Released: 1958
Released in U.S.: 1982
Production: Argos/Procinex
Direction: Chris Marker
Screenplay: Chris Marker
Cinematography: Sacha Vierny
Editing: Anna Saurraute
Art direction: no listing
Music: Pierre Barbaud
MPAA rating: no listing
Running time: 60 minutes

> *Principal character:*
> Voice of commentator .... Georges Ruquier

For contemporary French critics, *Letter from Siberia* marked a turning point in film language. Ostensibly a travelogue (the documentary subgenre of personal journeys), the intricacy of its discourse almost defies synopsis. The following gives some idea of its major forms, its themes, its sections, and its essentially poetic continuity.

The typewritten credits and clicking of keys suggest a tourist's personal letter, but the first sentence has a poetic ring: "I write to you from a far-off land." Spectacular geographical contrasts are eschewed as the camera eye moves sideways from a birch forest to a lone telegraph pole; one of the thin, long lifelines that challenge the cold chaos of what is called a "devil's forest." A lighthearted cartoon sequence evokes the rediscovery of mammoths, which had been encrusted with superstitious legends by Chinese and Europeans alike.

Siberia's highways are the Trans-Siberian Express and the River Lena; their freight has ranged from bulldozers and caged sables to French travel writers such as Blaise Cendrars and Armand Gatti. Others, such as Jules Verne, traveled to Siberia via their imagination. The theme of "Romanticisme plus electrification" (parodying a phrase of Vladimir Ilich Lenin) takes on new significance as huge cranes build a dam. The size of King Kong, they obey the gestures of a woman construction worker.

Traditionally, Siberian transportation, and Siberia's entire economy, depended on the reindeer, and this inspires the film to break into an extended television commercial for the entire range of reindeer products. The filmmakers are offered police protection to film a half-tamed bear, but "we declined politely, as we are more frightened of policemen than of bears."

The film crew provokes only friendly curiosity from Iakoutsk pedestrians. A Russian song about the songs of Yves Montand (who was one of the few Communist film stars) provokes the film to demonstrate how political preconceptions can alter one's perception of the simplest scene. A sequence of roadworkers and traffic appears three times, and each time the images seem transformed by the differing commentary: one pro-Soviet, one anti-Soviet, the third more human in its sense of need and effort.

To cope with the diversity of Siberia's economies and life-styles, the film speculates about an "imaginary newsreel," which the viewer simultaneously sees in black-and-white footage. Color returns with spring, along with poetic reflections on the "fraternal opposition" of bear and shaman, wilderness and order, the political past and the technological future. A hobbled horse limps through a dreary Culture Park.

Nineteenth century Siberia is compared to Alaska with its gold rush, its "Indians," its saloon brawls, and its civilizing schoolmarms (Bolshevik teachers). The last independent gold-seekers are sometimes tolerated, sometimes harassed. Is it really freedom they seek, or are they merely pursuing obsessive dreams of wealth? Meanwhile, the Lena flows in a sunset light, gleaming like an African woman bedecked with costume jewelry. She nurtures the legendary spirits of Yakut folk myths. Even now, a larch tree is regularly hung with votive offerings, including engineering objects such as screwbolts.

The folk hero in a Chinese-style opera bends a bow whose arrow becomes the rocket bearing the first Sputnik, with its little Siberian dog. Upward it speeds, toward constellations with animal names such as The Great Bear. Siberia is a thin crust of soil and forest, delicately suspended between the Permafrost and the sky, "between the Earth and the Moon, between the Middle Ages and the twenty first century, between humiliation and happiness," according to the narration.

Critics recognized that these documentary descriptions were also meditations on film and thought. The suite of variations on the road menders' scene immediately became famous. The same theme inspires the critical/affectionate use of cartoon, commercial, and newsreel forms. Finally, this low-budget travelogue matches in the sophistication, finesse, and critical self-consciousness of its discourse some still ill-defined genres of literary *belles lettres*: the essay, the prose poem, the pastiche.

Cultural history has few absolute firsts. Earlier travelogues occasionally became poetic, personal, subversive, or all three together. They include Jean Vigo's *À propos de Nice* (1930) and Luis Buñuel's *Las hurdes* (1932; *Land Without Bread*). There are earlier films by Chris Marker himself, as well as by Georges Franju, Alain Resnais, Rolando Klein, and Agnès Varda, who are traditionally grouped with Marker within the New Wave's

"Left Bank." (These are the left-leaning directors associated with the subversive, cosmopolitan spirit of Saint-Germain-des-Près, on the Left Bank of the Seine, as distinct from the *Cahiers du cinéma* group, whose offices were on the Right Bank and whose preoccupation was with youthful bourgeois anarchism.) Older than the *Cahiers du cinéma* group, the Left Bank came to feature films after working in quality short subjects, which perhaps constitute a genre, and were for a long time France's avant-garde laboratory. *Letter from Siberia*, however, was rather more elaborate, more prosaic and political, than anything before. It resembles Resnais' *Hiroshima mon amour* (1959) in transcending travelogue aspects. A place (Hiroshima, Siberia) becomes a cosmopolitan zone, a locus of self-alienation (in this case, French irony at the expense of Siberian enthusiasm about the basics of survival). In both films, the commentary ceases to *caption* the visuals, but rather soars above them like an aria in opera: "I write to you from a far-off land." "No, you have seen nothing at Hiroshima."

If Marker's is the earlier, more modest, film, it more clearly prefigures two aesthetic modes. First, it is a "free form" stream of poetic, personal associations, evoking the American underground cinema. Second, it heralds the mainly European genre of ideological-intellectual films, notably Jean-Luc Godard and Jean-Pierre Gorin's *Pravda* (1969).

Using a sixteen-millimeter camera, Marker and Vierny shot "in complete freedom" and "unpremeditatedly," which presumably means with no preconceived structure, in the spirit shared by Jean Rouch, Louis Malle, Klein, and François Reichenbach, four French filmmakers responsible with Marker for rendering the documentary less preshaped, less convention-bound. One development led toward *cinéma vérité*, another toward more personal, impressionistic style. The monochrome footage is presumably preexisting material.

English critic Nöel Burch believed that Marker had striven to enliven banal material by a high-flying commentary and editing-table high jinks. On close inspection, however, the shots are inconspicuously sophisticated (like the quiet contrast of birch forest and solitary telegraph pole). Marker is also interested in off-screen space (Siberia's), but he uses very precise, very local, scenes: In the midst of what seems virgin forest, for example, there is shown a traffic policeman at work. The space around the details is "woven" by cutting and commentary. Although critic André Bazin is often supposed to have disapproved of montage, he admired Marker's use of it here.

Clearly there are constraints on the material. Some are practical (and financial), others political. The former, which need little explanation, include that politeness toward one's hosts which is normal in international film production, as in diplomatic and cultural exchanges. The political issues are more complex. Even here, Marker can fairly ask his spectators to put aside, at least for the space of this film, any preoccupation with Siberian labor camps, Soviet cultural imperialism toward these vast ethnic minorities, and other negative aspects, and to interest themselves in the positive side of Siberia's progress.

Nevertheless, the film's position seems to be a pro-Soviet one, of a type that was common in French left-wing culture at the time (like Montand's). First there was a refusal to believe, or openly to discuss, anti-Soviet evidence, which was thought to be discredited by its right-wing sources or effects. This was then complicated by excessive optimism about the de-Stalinization campaign initiated by Nikita Khrushchev in 1956 and by Charles de Gaulle's "anti-Americanism" from December, 1958.

In this respect, Marker's "poetic" mode solves two problems generated by the practical and political limitations on his material. They are the need to go around unmanageable political issues and the wish to replace the predictably dreary monolithism (both political and geographical) of most accounts of Siberia by a revelation of its myths and metaphors, paradox and color, ingenuity and sparkle. This Siberia is a kaleidoscope (and therefore a montage)—as all human thinking is.

First, a simple example: The Stalin-era imagery of heavy cranes is both poeticized, by comparing the cranes to prehistoric monsters, and humanized (in favor of mass affluence, anathema to Stalinism), by comparing their loads to house-sized chocolate boxes offered to a woman. Second, a more esoteric example: When the River Lena is compared to an African woman, her displacement to this Arctic climate is a kind of poetic Surrealism, but many French spectators will know their Charles Baudelaire and their Jean-Paul Sartre well enough to catch another undertone: Unlike the indolent African in her fake jewels, this part of the Third World is not in thrall to sterile bourgeois decadence. She works, nurtures, braces—and is as breathtakingly lovely.

Marker's very French, and densely packed, puns, allusions, and verbal metaphors will escape, or confuse, most Anglophone spectators, and this probably explains the less enthusiastic response. Siberia can be known in an oblique way by the mind's constructions, and in itself it is as ungraspable as the external world always is. There is also, however, an objective side. A widespread expectation of the 1950's was that technology and affluence would render the United States and the Soviet Union rather more alike. As a model for Siberia's future, the United States is a promise and a threat. Marker especially likes its crazy, anarchistic side.

The film's solipsistic side is balanced by a traditional Marxist emphasis on brute material realities: the cold, the forest, the dams. Even the myths and legends are hard realities, just as ethnic cultures are hard social facts. Siberia faces, in its own way, the problem of all modern cultures: how to reconcile diverse roots in the past with a shiny future?

Siberia was the devil's forest: cold, wild, hard. As in Jack London's

Alaska stories, injustice has been the price of survival. Man has lived in these climes by a "fraternal exploitation" of animals—which may stand for something basic in human nature. The bears, from whom the Russian police offer protection, are all solitary individuals. Yet Nature also knows the social, collective spirit—of flocks, herds, tribes, collective farms, and Communism. Marker admires a reindeer race "where everyone wins and everyone shares the prize, which is the return of Spring, and, with it, color." For him, the positive side of socialism is its emphasis on cooperation over cutthroat competition. Nevertheless, that hobbled, abandoned horse, forlornly wandering from the dreary Culture Park, could be a metaphor for a failure within Communism, for its *wrong* counterpart to the Hollywood style cartoon about reappearing mammoths.

It has already been suggested that *Letter from Siberia* challenges most audience expectations of narrative and form. Its self-reflexivity, however, aims not at the solemnly Brechtian kinds of alienation but rather at simple awareness and humor about the craziness of everything. It could be the only documentary to apply, seriously, the aesthetic strategy of *Hellzapoppin'* (1941)—including jokes about the film itself. In a very real sense, it anticipates the subsequent combination of travelogue and crazy comedy in Werner Herzog's *Fata Morgana* (1971), but where Marker is radical, optimistic, and collectivist, Herzog is conservative, tragic, and obsessed with isolation.

The emphasis on the difficulty and delicacy of learning to see Siberia (and, by implication, the external world in general) resembles, apparently at least, the conjunction of Marxist and structuralist ideas, which were very shortly to revolutionize French Marxism and to affect even non-Marxist film culture worldwide. This new, structuralist Marxism tended to reduce knowledge, and thought itself, to ideology. It wildly exaggerated the difficulty of observation departing from assumption. In contrast, Marker's subtle, poetic, apparently wayward "stream of consciousness" follows the rich unpredictability and autonomy of human thought processes. Although the roadsweeper sequence emphasizes the *influence* of ideology, the film's semantic ingenuity and originality suggest how ideology, in its turn, is the product of thoughts and observations which are still unorganized by any one structure of ideas. Against the new (and unproven) dogmas of one-way causation, it postulates a *dialectic* of assumption and learning.

Very probably Marker's emphasis on the autonomy of thinking was encouraged by his exposure to a diverse plurality of cultures—political and literary, verbal and filmic, French and American (and the various nations and classes inspiring his other films). Godard had shared something of this experience, and the tangle of French and American ideologies is a major theme of his first feature, *À bout de souffle* (1960; *Breathless*). Yet where Godard chose to follow the newer tendency of *reducing* thought to ideological assumptions, Marker juggles the various styles, strategies, and purposes which constitute his oeuvre and whose lessons remain unassimilated by film culture's academic Left. Tentative in some respects, *Letter from Siberia* is a rich microcosm of his whole work, and of a generation's minds working.

The commentary was spoken by Georges Ruquier, the director of the celebrated documentary *Farrebique* (1946). The film won the 1958 Prix Lumière.

Raymond Durgnat

LIEBELEI

Origin: Germany
Released: 1932
Released in U.S.: 1936
Production: Fred Lissa for Elite Tonfilm
Direction: Max Ophüls
Screenplay: Curt Alexander, Hans Wilhelm, and Max Ophüls; based on the
  play by Arthur Schnitzler
Cinematography: Franz Planer
Editing: Friedel Buchott
Art direction: G. Pellon
Music: Theo Mackeben
Running time: 88 minutes

Principal characters:
Christine Weiring	Magda Schneider
Lieutenant Fritz Lobheimer	Wolfgang Liebeneiner
Mitzi Schlager	Luise Ullrich
Theo Kaiser	Willy Eichberger
Baron Eggerdorff	Gustaf Gründgens
Baroness Eggerdorff	Olga Tschechowa
Hans Weiring	Paul Hörbiger

Liebelei was Max Ophüls' fifth film and the last he made in his native
Germany before the rise of Nazism forced him to move on to France, Italy,
the Netherlands, the United States, and, finally, back to France. More
significantly, *Liebelei* was the first great success both critically and commercially for this master of *fin de siècle* romance. Although his style had not yet
evolved into the dazzling display of perpetual motion associated with his
later films, the fundamentals of Ophüls' approach are clearly present and
the material is ideal. Like his American-made *Letter from an Unknown
Woman* (1948) and *La Ronde* (1950), *Liebelei* is set in Vienna at the turn of
the century, and like *Letter from an Unknown Woman* and *Madame de...*
(1953; *The Earrings of Madame de...*), set in early twentieth century Paris,
it is a tragic love story climaxed by a duel in which the conclusion is cruelly
inevitable. Although romantic love is at the heart of all Ophüls' films, the
director's Old-World romanticism is discernible even in his work in other
genres. For example, in another American film, *The Reckless Moment*
(1949), which has a contemporary setting in the United States, a low-class
blackmailer is transformed by the unusual casting of suave British actor
James Mason as a gallant figure ultimately destroyed by his tender romantic
feelings. Ophüls was as versatile as he needed to be and was able to treat

any subject in a personal manner, but the world evoked in *Liebelei* was understandably closest to his heart. This world moved at a more deliberate and graceful pace, and the most innocent and simple emotions could lead to irreversible tragedy.

Liebelei begins at the opera, where two young Austrian soldiers, Fritz (Wolfgang Liebeneiner) and Theo (Willy Eichberger) and two lovely young women, Christine (Magda Schneider) and Mitzi (Luise Ullrich), are in attendance. During the playing of the national anthem, Mitzi accidentally drops a pair of binoculars, which fall on Theo's arm. Unhurt, Theo keeps the binoculars to return to Mitzi later. In the meantime, it develops that Fritz is using attendance at the opera to cover up a love affair. He leaves after the opera has begun, planning to return just before the end. He is involved with a baroness (Olga Tschechowa) whose husband, Baron Eggerdorff (Gustaf Gründgens), is a cold and forbidding man not disposed to look lightly on any transgression. Fritz is becoming weary of the affair but does not know how to end it. By contrast, his friend Theo is a more carefree type who chooses women with whom romance can remain light and simple. With Mitzi, he achieves an immediate rapport. During their first meeting later in the evening, they are briefly joined at a café by Fritz and Christine. Fritz is preoccupied with his own problems and Christine is shy, thus preventing them from recognizing their attraction to each other.

The turning point occurs when Fritz walks Christine home. Initially, he is aloof and withdrawn, but Christine's wholesome sincerity ultimately has an effect on him and he warms to her. Within a short time, the two have fallen deeply in love. They go on a sleigh ride together and pledge to each other eternal love. Fritz has broken off with the baroness, but his identity as her former lover finally comes to the attention of Baron Eggerdorff, who demands satisfaction. Fritz fails to inform Christine of his impending duel. In the meantime, Theo makes an impassioned plea to the commanding officer not to allow the duel to be held. The baron is a crack shot and sure to kill the inexperienced Fritz. Arguing against the conventions of his time and place, Theo insists that dueling is murder. He is rebuffed, and the commanding officer informs him that his attitude will cost him his commission, a commission which has long been in the tradition of Theo's family. On the day of the duel, Theo and Mitzi wait anxiously for the outcome. They hear only one shot, which means that the baron has won. Along with Christine's father, Hans Weiring (Paul Hörbiger), a musician at the opera, they go to inform Christine. Learning of Fritz's death and the history behind it all at once is a horrible shock to her. Left alone for a moment, she jumps from a window to her death.

In some treatments of romantic love, the submission to love is itself a justification for the lovers to be destroyed. That is not the case with *Liebelei*. The deaths of Fritz and Christine are attributable entirely to factors outside their relationship. Their love is not treated as a forbidden or sinful love. As if to underscore this, Ophüls gives great weight to the romance of the secondary couple, Mitzi and Theo. Although initially lighter, it, too, remains constant throughout the film. It appears that Theo and Mitzi are in the story to provide comic relief, but they are ultimately no less moving than the two leading characters. When the occasion requires seriousness, they both show themselves to be very sensitive. Theo's attempt to stop the duel is one of the most dramatic scenes in the film, especially in the light of the revelation that he is destroying his career.

The poignant sleigh ride sequence foreshadows the tragic fate of Fritz and Christine and establishes the feeling, the sense of movement and symbolic purity, in which their love is immortalized. The film's final sequence is an exact re-creation of the sleigh ride—the identical shots of the same snowy landscape with the camera moving precisely as before—but without the sleigh and without the two characters. The texture of the film reveals Ophüls' unreserved endorsement of the relationships of his two young couples, his celebration of love's joyful abandon as well as its quieter communion. The causes of the story's tragedy lie completely outside the values of the two couples. That Fritz must be responsible for an earlier mistake seems not only unfair but also unaccommodating of his own transformation. The affair with the baroness is over, and Fritz has become more completely himself in his relationship with Christine. It is clearly social values which cause the tragedy. It is not the baron who is a villain, but rather the military and cultural hierarchy that demands Fritz's fidelity to a code of honor which virtually guarantees his death in the duel.

In later films such as *Letter from an Unknown Woman* and *The Earrings of Madame de...*, Ophüls persists in his sympathetic treatment of love as life's most positive force. Yet the duels which bring a tragic resolution to those stories are not treated as critically, even though the challenger is again certain to kill his opponent in both cases. The lack of suspense is deliberate and serves as a proof of the injustice of these strict conventions in a stratified culture such as that of Austria toward the end of the Austro-Hungarian Empire. The vigor of the social criticism in *Liebelei* can be directly related to its place in Ophüls' career. This passionate attack on values which presumably had died years before is interesting for several reasons. First, it does not inhibit Ophüls from exhibiting the same affection for the place and the period which is evident in the later films. Moreover, it indicates a clear perception that those earlier values were not moribund: The rigid moral and social attitudes underlying that way of life seem to have remained a part of the collective consciousness. Indeed, *Liebelei* still retains a validity in its social observations, even decades after its release.

A socially purposeful work such as *Liebelei* reveals aspects of Ophüls' artistry which are often neglected, but this should not obscure its more essential qualities. Ophüls' style imparts a tangible reality to a narrative mode and a stylized re-creation of the past which are often thought of only in terms of storybook romance. The players in *Liebelei* go beyond striking poses in artificial sets. The acting is distinguished by an understated naturalness, and the decor is richly suggestive of lives actually being lived: Ophüls possesses a gift for inspiring *belief* in the story as a credible series of events which seem very immediate.

Although Ophüls' predilection for almost continuous camera movement is not yet on display in *Liebelei*, his tendency to define key moments in terms of the camera's relationship to the action is impressively evident. The sequence in which Fritz walks Christine home, for example, begins with a series of fixed shots, each one showing the couple walking from one point to another. It is natural to wonder why Ophüls, of all directors, would not utilize a long tracking shot for this sequence, but his strategy quickly becomes evident. When the melancholy silence of Fritz and Christine is finally overcome and they begin to interact, a fully characteristic Ophülsian tracking shot accompanies them for the remainder of the walk.

In another instance, the sleigh ride is conveyed in a very deliberate series of shots. Initially only the background moves and the camera rests in the sleigh with Fritz and Christine, but as the sequence progresses and comes to an end, the camera's vantage point changes. The final beautiful image in the sequence is a panning shot from behind a snow-covered graveyard as the sleigh disappears from the frame. The emotional and aesthetic effect of this final image within the sequence is so precise that when it reappears in the altered context of the ending, the response it evokes is ineffably heartbreaking. The image, accompanied by the same beautiful music and the sound of sleigh bells, becomes a ghostly echo, forcefully reminding the audience of the fragile love of the now absent couple.

Compositional elegance came easily to Ophüls, as is evident in shots such as the one from the graveyard and others in which several characters interact within expressively decorated settings. There is, however, a quiet reflectiveness in his treatment of other moments which also deserves attention. When Theo, Mitzi, and Christine's father come to inform Christine of Fritz's death, the camera holds in a close-up on Christine's face as a series of halting explanations are offered offscreen. No one moves into the frame to offer solace. The intimacy of Christine's grief is respected by the other characters and compassionately observed by Ophüls' camera. When the shot finally ends, the camera describes the ensuing suicide with a series of harsh and abrupt camera moves uninflected by sentiment, in contrast to the loving resurrection of the sleigh ride which follows.

Liebelei is apealing on every level. Its four young leading players are exceptionally attractive and genuine, the music is beautiful, the decor eloquent, and the black-and-white cinematography of Franz Planer lustrous.

Ophüls responded thoughtfully to the source material by Arthur Schnitzler, an author to whom he later returned for *La Ronde*. In *Liebelei*, Ophüls achieved a mature harmony of form and substance no less masterly than that of his finest works of the 1940's and 1950's.

Blake Lucas

THE LIFE OF OHARU
(SAIKAKU ICHIDAI ONNA)

Origin: Japan
Released: 1952
Released in U.S.: 1964
Production: Hideo Koi and Isamu Yoshii for Shin Toho
Direction: Kenji Mizoguchi
Screenplay: Yoshikata Yoda; based on the novel *Koshoku ichidai onna*, by
  Saikaku
Cinematography: Yoshimi Hirano
Editing: Toshio Goto
Art direction: Hiroshi Mizutani
Music: Ichiro Saito
Running time: 146 minutes

> *Principal characters:*
> Oharu .... Kinuyo Tanaka
> Katsunosuke .... Toshiro Mifune
> Kikuoji .... Masao Shimizu
> Shinzaemon .... Ichiro Sugai
> Tomo .... Tsukue Matsuura
> Harutaka Matsudaira.............. Toshiaki Konoe
> Matsudaira's wife .... Hisako Yamane
> Otsubone Yoshioka .... Yuriko Hamada
> Kabee Sasaya..................... Eitaro Shindo
> Owasa .... Sadako Sawamura
> Bunkichi......................... Hiroshi Oizumi
> Taisaburo Hishiya .... Masao Mishima
> Counterfeiter.................... Eijiro Yanagi
> Yakichi Ogiya .... Jukichi Uno
> Old nun Myokai .... Chieko Higashiyama
> Clothing store owner .... Tozen Hidari
> Jihei .... Benkei Shiganoya
> Old man...................... Takashi Shimura

The Life of Oharu is surely one of Kenji Mizoguchi's most important films. Artistically, it ended a series of critical failures and initiated the half-dozen masterpieces that close his career. Financially, it ultimately made enough money to win for Mizoguchi a carte blanche contract with Daiei Films, resulting in the artistic freedom that he enjoyed toward the end of his career. Critically, *The Life of Oharu* marks the recognition of Mizoguchi by the West, for the film captured the Golden Lion at the Venice International Film Festival and made him the cult hero of the cinema magazine *Cahiers du cinéma*. Mizoguchi may have made better films—Westerners prefer *Ugetsu monogatari* (1953; *Ugetsu*) and the Japanese prefer *Chikamatsu monogatari* (1954; *A Story from Chikamatsu*)—but seldom has a film meant so much to a director and his future.

Beyond these practical considerations, *The Life of Oharu* was, of all Mizoguchi's films, the one he struggled longest to get on the screen. The idea of adapting Saikaku's classic seventeenth century picaresque novel came to Mizoguchi at the beginning of the World War II, and he actively sought to produce the film once the war had ended. Yet American restrictions against historical subjects and the evident expense this film would entail frightened all the studios he approached. When the Americans pulled out of Japan in 1950, Mizoguchi could count eight films made during their stay, not one of which satisfied him or pleased the critics. He needed a big success. While shooting the last of these films, he was galled to learn that Akira Kurosawa had received the top prize at Venice for *Rashomon* (1950). How could a comparative youngster with only a handful of films and little personal experience win such a prize? In a rare interview, Mizoguchi claimed that no artist really achieved anything truly great until after he was fifty. Mizoguchi was fifty-two when he said this, and it was clear that he intended to waste no more time. He wanted greatness. His ambition was matched by that of his longtime leading actress, Kinuyo Tanaka, whose trip to the United States had halted a decline in her artistic reputation. Mizoguchi had been appalled at the gaudy welcome she received at the airport on her return. He shamed her into working with him, and together they agreed to risk their careers on *The Life of Oharu*.

Mizoguchi was able to subcontract the film from a recently established company through Shin Toho, assuring it some distribution, though he would have no studio at his disposal for its production. Filming took place in a bombed-out park midway between Kyoto and Osaka. Every fifteen minutes a train between these cities passed nearby, the noise allowing no more than one of Mizoguchi's invariably long takes at a time: to Mizoguchi, the idea of dubbing was unacceptable. Planning went on for days, since he refused to begin until his valued crane arrived from Kyoto and until his assistants returned from museums, where they were trying to secure authentic props to replace the copies which had already been prepared. The concentration on the set was legendary. When his chief assistant argued with him over a problem, Mizoguchi fired the assistant. After an unexpected snowfall, he had thirty men spend an exhausting three hours clearing away the snow, only to scrap the proposed site when he noticed a snowcapped peak in the background.

The film took months to complete and cost forty-six million yen. Japan had never seen a film to match its scope and rigor; it was perhaps too taxing a film for Japanese audiences. Intellectuals complained that Mizoguchi had lost Saikaku's irony and humor in his realistic and sympathetic treatment of Oharu. The populace was no doubt frustrated by the film's length, tempo, and the inevitability of the events it portrayed. The film virtually destroyed Shin Toho, but the critics continued to discuss it. While it placed only ninth on the annual list of Japan's ten best films, it was selected to represent the country at the Venice International Film Festival, where it stunned the jury, which gave it the festival's grand prize, the Golden Lion.

The film opens in seventeenth century Japan with an old prostitute wandering the dark streets in search of clients. Refused, she joins some companions, who are warming themselves by a fire under a bridge. After they are warned about making fires there, she seeks shelter in a nearby temple and is mesmerized by a wall of statues representing samurai warriors. One face particularly affects her, so much so that she superimposes on it the living representation of a man who will soon prove to have been her first and only true lover. A shawl falls wistfully from her head, as she begins to recall the course of life that brought her to her lamentable state.

Her life seemed destined to be one of ease and serenity, as Mizoguchi shows by returning the viewer to the woman's youth. A young woman of modestly noble extraction, Oharu (Kinuyo Tanaka) is welcome at the local manor, where her grace and beauty are highly appreciated, especially by a certain young lord. Her routine at court is upset, however, when Katsunosuke (Toshiro Mifune), a minor samurai in the employ of the lord, stops her on her daily visit to a shrine to insist that she see his lord at a nearby house. When Oharu arrives there, she finds herself alone not with the lord, but with Katsunosuke, who has used this ruse to declare his love for her. Flustered, Oharu at first scolds him for the impropriety, even illegality, of this declaration, but soon, in the garden of the house, she swoons under his impassioned pleas, for she has secretly admired him for some time. Katsunosuke's success is momentary, however, for no sooner has he carried her inside than the police arrive, exposing the tryst.

In the formal hall of the manor, Oharu and her parents kneel before the lord to receive the sentence for her misconduct: perpetual banishment from the State. They are led to the frontier and disappear beyond a bridge. In their new home in exile, Oharu's parents berate her for ruining her chances and their comfort. Katsunosuke, meanwhile, is beheaded for initiating the affair, but before the sword falls, he leaves a message for Oharu and cries out in prophecy for a time when true love will not be repressed. News of Katsunosuke's execution and of his last words completely unnerves Oharu. Grabbing a knife, she races through the woods, prepared to kill herself. Her mother, Tomo (Tsukue Matsuura), pursues and finally catches her.

Much later, Oharu's village receives a royal messenger. The head of the great Matsudaira clan is without an heir and has sent his servant to seek a mistress who might bear him a son. His specifications are absurdly exacting, as both the servant and the town's leading merchant agree. Nevertheless, various eligible girls are brought together. When none proves acceptable, the servant is in despair, but he grasps at one final hope in going to visit a nearby dancing entertainment whose music has caught his ear. There, beyond the draperies, he sees in one of the dancers the woman with the looks he has been seeking. Oharu fits each requirement perfectly. A bargain with her parents is soon concluded, and despite her protests, Oharu's avaricious father, Shinzaemon (Ichiro Sugai), sends her off to the faraway Matsudaira palace.

In her new home, Oharu finds herself well treated but by no means well accepted. The barren wife of Lord Matsudaira is particularly chagrined by her presence and, in humiliation, walks out of a puppet-theater performance. In time, Oharu delivers the heir expected from her. Although the infant makes her feel a measure of benevolence and loyalty to the house, the converse is far from true. She finds that the lord's administrators will not permit her to nurse or in any way rear the baby.

Meanwhile, her parents, filled with pride and the certain hope of reward descending on their daughter, indulge themselves in extravagant boasts and purchases. All hopes come to an end, however, as Oharu is dismissed from the palace, her job completed. To avert any claims she might have on the Matsudaira clan, the administrators of the palace release her from service with very little financial compensation. This disappointment arouses the anger of her father, who has imprudently steeped himself in debt. He beats his daughter and sells her to a house of pleasure. Known there for her haughty ways, Oharu interests one free-spending client after another. An exceptionally liberal and uncouth merchant causes her downfall when she refuses to entertain him. He clamors for her dismissal. The commotion is doubled when he is discovered to be a counterfeiter.

Returning once more to her parents, Oharu is placed in service to Owasa (Sadako Sawamura), the wife of the local dry-goods merchant, Kabee Sasaya (Eitaro Shindo). A disfiguring disease has robbed her of nearly all of her hair, and she employs Oharu's skills in coiffure to disguise this fact from her husband. One day the counterfeiter from the house of pleasure happens to stop in, and in his boisterousness, he quickly reveals that Oharu is a famous ex-courtesan. Later, the merchant cannot resist trying to seduce her. Owasa now suspects Oharu of stealing the affections of her husband and violently fires her. That night, Oharu vindictively exposes her lady's baldness with the help of the family cat. She leaves quickly and returns to her aging parents.

Oharu then marries Yakichi Ogiya (Jukichi Uno), a poor merchant of fans whom she met at the dry-goods store. Just as she is growing used to the routine of an unambitious, quiet domestic life, her new husband is killed by thugs on the highway. Completely disillusioned, Oharu puts herself under the tutelage of a Buddhist nun. She is outfitted without charge by Bunkichi (Hiroshi Oizumi), a servant of the dry-goods merchant who has always been struck by her beauty. When Jihei (Benkei Shiganoya), the chief clerk, learns of this "gift," he rushes to the convent to reclaim his master's wares. At the sight of Oharu, he loses control of himself and forces her to make love with him. The nun discovers them and sends Oharu away in disgrace. For a short time, Oharu and Bunkichi live on the run, with money taken from the dry-goods merchant, but inevitably they are tracked down.

There is nothing left for Oharu now but to beg for a living. One day, as she strums her samisen by the wayside, the prince's entourage passes by. She struggles forward to catch no more than a glimpse of her son, now an adolescent. Oharu has now taken on the life of a common prostitute. The nadir of her humiliation comes when an old man (Takashi Shimura), leading a pilgrimage, gives her money—not for sex, as she supposes, but to serve as a living example of the rot of the body and the destitution of the soul. She makes her way proudly to the doorway but then quickly returns to scoff at the pilgrims' self-righteousness. The film comes full circle now, returning to the present with which it began, as she wanders the streets forlorn and wakes up in the temple under the statue resembling Katsunosuke. She is terribly ill. Her mother, who has been looking for her, arrives at her bedside and nurses her. She tells Oharu that Lord Matsudaira has died and that Oharu has been summoned to return to the palace.

Oharu goes to the palace, breathless with expectation. The court ministers, however, have their way and command her exile to a distant district where she may never bring pressure to bear on her son. Before binding her away, they grant her request to catch a glimpse of her son as he walks by with his retinue. Unable to restrain her emotion after seeing him, she breaks loose and rushes toward the royal suite. Blocked, she nevertheless manages to escape the bonds of the guards chasing her.

As a mendicant nun, Oharu chants prayers from home to home. One person slams the door in her face; another tosses her a coin. She bows respectfully to a distant temple, turns, and slowly makes her way offscreen.

What makes the film so exceptional is the camera perspective, which is omniscient yet sympathetic. As Oharu descends from a privileged life at court to that of the untouchable, nameless mendicant nun at the end, she achieves nobility and wisdom. Where Saikaku had parodied her erotic exploits and used her to satirize all levels of Tokugawa culture, Mizoguchi finds her odyssey painful and sacred. She is the purest of all his sacrificing women, who suffer at the hands of a male world not worthy of them.

This hagiographic tone is felt in the extraordinary camera flourishes that terminate so many sequences. The falling of the camera away from the beheading of Katsunosuke is not a hysterical fall; indeed, its point of rest is a perfect composition, which includes the sword still glistening from its bloody work. When the family flees in exile from the court, the camera coolly watches them cross the bridge, only to dip under the bridge at the last moment and catch a final glimpse of them passing a single tree far away. The graceful movement here serves to keep the subject in view, but, more important, it is the melancholy reaction of an observer to a woeful tale. In the final shot, Oharu, bowing to the temple, passes out of frame, allowing the camera to hold on that temple in a sacramental finale that comprehends a life gone so low that it is now forever out of view. Long and solemn, *The Life of Oharu* is an immensely mature work of art.

Dudley Andrew

LIFE UPSIDE DOWN
(LA VIE À L'ENVERS)

Origin: France
Released: 1964
Released in U.S.: 1964
Production: Alain Jessua for A J Films Production
Direction: Alain Jessua
Screenplay: Alain Jessua
Cinematography: Jacques Robin
Editing: Nicole Marko
Art direction: Olivier Gérard
Music: Jacques Loussier
Running time: 92 minutes
Also known as: Inside Out

Principal characters:
Jacques.........................Charles Denner
Viviane...........................Anna Gaylor
Fernand ....Guy Saint-Jean
Nicole ....Nicole Gueden
M. Kerbel...........................Jean Yanne
Mme Kerbel.......................Yvonne Clech
Paul ....Robert Bousquet
Ina ....Françoise Moncey
Mayor...........................Jean Dewewer
Doctor...........................André Thornent
Inspector ....Bernard Sury
Concierge.........................Jenny Orleans
Mother ....Nane Germon

During the turbulent and iconoclastic years of the 1960's, many major artists saw modern society in one of two ways: It was either alienating or
absurd. The alienated vision tended to tragedy, since the artist felt no contact with a society characterized by featureless architecture, heartless technology, and materialist values. The Absurdist vision tended to grim comedy,
since the artist could view certain unpleasant features of modern life—its
conformity, authoritarianism, absence of spiritual feeling—with a wry and
ironic detachment.

In the cinema of that decade, some of the masters of artistic alienation
were Michelangelo Antonioni, Jean-Luc Godard, and Robert Bresson, and
they responded to what they saw as the devitalized values of conventional
society with, respectively, anguish, anarchic anger, and a ruminative resent-

ment. In the theater, where the vision of the Absurd began in the 1950's, dramatists such as Samuel Beckett, Edward Albee, Eugène Ionesco, and Harold Pinter offered varied responses to what they saw as a universe that had lost its sense of purpose, ranging from the music-hall melancholy of *En attendant Godot* (1952; *Waiting for Godot*) to the whimsical moralizing of *Le Rhinocéros* (1959; *Rhinoceros*). There was room for a film which could straddle the two traditions and make a statement which would somehow combine the social polemic of the alienated with an Absurdist recognition of the comic incongruities of life. This work was to come from a wholly unexpected source: a modest black-and-white French film, from an unknown director, which rapidly became one of the art-house successes of 1964.

Life Upside Down was the feature-film debut of Alain Jessua, who was born in Paris in 1932, and who had served his film apprenticeship as an assistant to directors such as Jacques Becker, Max Ophüls, and Marcel Carné. His short film *Léon la Lune* (1957) had won high praise for him, but nothing had quite prepared the press or public for the insolent assurance and originality of his first feature. In a competitive field that included such modern classics as Grigori Kozintsev's *Gamlet* (1964; *Hamlet*), Pier Paolo Pasolini's *Il vangelo secondo Matteo* (1964; *The Gospel According to St. Matthew*), Ingmar Bergman's *För att i nte tala om alla dessa Kvinnor* (1964; *All These Women*), Joseph Losey's *King and Country*, Antonioni's *Deserto rosso* (1964; *The Red Desert*), and Godard's *La Femme mariée* (1964; *The Married Woman*), Jessua's film still managed to pick up a major prize at the 1964 Venice International Film Festival.

The action of *Life Upside Down* takes place over a period of two months. The hero, Jacques (Charles Denner), works as an estate agent in a big city. He is shortly to be married to a pretty model, Viviane (Anna Gaylor), although his only friend, an acrobat, is trying to dissuade him from taking such a perilous step. The wedding goes ahead, but already Jacques is showing signs of dissatisfaction with the external world and is retreating into his private shell—so much so that he feels relieved when he loses his job. His serene detachment cannot be shaken even by the attempted suicide of his loving but talkative wife, who is being driven to distraction by his strange behavior. Jacques does not rebel against society: He simply retreats. By an act of will, he trains himself to eliminate extraneous objects and human beings, finally reducing his world to a bare room in a mental clinic. At the end, this thin, vaguely identifiable figure, his back to the camera, stares intently at the blank wall and congratulates himself for having, as he puts it, outwitted them all. He has certainly escaped the crippling conventions of society, but has he lost his wits in so doing?

Such an internalized, private, and esoteric subject might seem more suitable to the novel than to the cinema. Yet what is immediately remarkable about the film is its technical assurance, its blithe refusal to recognize the filmic problems of this intensely difficult subject. Jessua's technique rejects superfluities, becoming as refined and as clear-cut as Jessua's own mind. The camera at key moments becomes the mind's eye of the film's hero. Shots of a tree, a slice of bread, a table leg, a broken egg are composed so that familiar objects suddenly seem strange, and one is drawn into Jacques's intent, fresh vision of them. When the camera tracks away from a conversation at the table, the movement corresponds to Jacques's mental withdrawal from the scene and the diminishing impact on him of the trivia of domestic and social chitchat. Paradoxically, in moving away from the hero physically at this juncture, the camera is leading the viewer further and further into the private silence of the hero's consciousness.

At times, Jessua reveals a nice flair for social comedy. The wedding ceremony of Jacques and Viviane is sharply observed, as if all the pomp that goes with society's institutionalizing of love were suddenly seen as absurd for the first time. Yet Jessua's main achievement is in finding the appropriate imagery and tempo to convey the inner intensity and logic of his hero's outlook (or, more properly, his inward look). A subtle employment of silence and space, of misty pauses and lyric calmness, forms an effective visual and aural correlative to Jacques's languid inner tranquillity. Individual scenes and shots effectively convey the progression and peculiarity of Jacques's mental processes. He strolls obliviously through crowded bars and stations. A letter to his mother slowly disintegrates into a meaningless jumble of straight lines. He turns to look at his wife in a mirror and no reflection comes back to him.

Two other features intensify the viewer's identification with Jacques's condition. Jacques Loussier's music seems to simplify itself into a crystalline five-finger exercise. Loussier was undoubtedly influenced in his score by the spare, pellucid piano works of Erik Satie—who, incidentally, was also a haunted recluse spending his final days in an almost totally denuded room. As the film develops, Jacques Robin's cinematography moves subtly and gradually into a higher key. The film frame is progressively emptied of objects, of time, of desire, becoming as pristine, blank, and beautifully simple as the life of its hero, who has transformed a sense of loneliness into a transcendent solitude. The philosopher Blaise Pascal said that man's happiness was assured if he could only stay quietly in one room. At the end, Jacques seems to have attained a state of Zen-like philosophic grace.

The film is beautifully done, but what about the implications of its theme? Much of the discussion engendered by the film was undoubtedly caused by its ambiguity. Is one meant to see Jacques as quite mad, or as the last sane man on earth? Some observers saw it as a film about a kind of inner death, the relentless superficiality and trivia of modern life driving a sensitive human being to madness. In these terms, a comparison which suggested itself was Roman Polanski's film made at roughly the same time,

Repulsion (1965), an unnerving study of solitude in which the leading character's ostensibly stoical exterior conceals a profoundly sick and twisted psychological state that ends in insanity. On the other hand, it was equally common to see the film as a comedy of protest, on the theme (very topical in the 1960's) of how to live in society and escape it at the same time. The tone was interpreted as serenely euphoric, appropriate to a hero who had achieved total victory without a semblance of conflict. From this perspective, Jacques's rejection of and freedom from the urban round of homework-wages was seen as heroic more than tragic, a triumph for the contemplative over the competitive outlook. The film's upside-down look at life in these terms suggested a comparison with Jacques Tati—a master at revealing the ridiculous through a detached watchfulness and a slight tilt of his alert camera, like the raising of an eyebrow.

It would be fairest to say that *Life Upside Down* is poised between these two extremes. It leaves an audience free to make up its own mind about the hero's predicament—whether he is a tragic outsider in the manner of Meursault in Albert Camus' great Existential novel, *L'Étranger* (1942; *The Stranger*) or a poker-faced clown such as director Pierre Étaix, who retains a grave serenity in the midst of the endless provocations of modern life. The performances are very appealing. As Viviane, Anna Gaylor (Jessua's wife) contributes an attractive and judicious performance that manages convincingly to irritate Jacques without irritating an audience. Charles Denner seems particularly well cast as Jacques. Immediately prior to this film, he had appeared as the charming murderer of Claude Chabrol's *Landru* (1963; *Bluebeard*)—another man who could make people disappear—and he was to make a particularly telling appearance in the following decade in François Truffaut's *L'Homme qui aimait les femmes* (1977; *The Man Who Loved Women*). The ingredients of a disquieting, amusing, eccentric obsessive that constitute Denner's screen *persona* found a most congenial home in *Life Upside Down*.

Curiously, Alain Jessua has broadly failed to live up to the promise of this early film. His following work, *Jeu de massacre* (1967; *The Killing Game*) concerned a comic-strip cartoonist who notices that his best friend seems to be imitating the antics of his cartoon hero; or is it that he is relying on the quirkiness of his friend for the inspiration of his cartoon hero? Like *Life Upside Down*, the film is about liberating dream worlds and the thin line between fantasy and reality, but it is done with much less flair and conviction. Later melodramas such as *Traitement de choc* (1973; *Shock Treatment*), with Alain Delon, and *Les Chiens* (1979; *The Dogs*), with Gerard Depardieu, have something of the quirky observation of the earlier film and a similar interest in varieties of personal and social madness. Yet they are more commercial and have less depth and richness. For the most interesting examples of the influence and legacy of *Life Upside Down*, one has to look away from Jessua's own subsequent work. One looks instead, for example, to a beautiful film such as Claude Goretta's *La Dentellière* (1977; *The Lacemaker*), which ends in a manner similar to Jessua's film, with its heroine in a mental clinic staring vacantly into a world of private imagination that affords some relief from the devastations of romantic and social disillusionment. One is also reminded of Jessua in the atmosphere and irony of Paul Cox's Australian art film *Man of Flowers* (1983), a tragicomic study of a man's phased withdrawal from so-called normal life.

Both *The Lacemaker* and *Man of Flowers* were highly acclaimed, but strangely, no critic alluded to *Life Upside Down* in a discussion of them. Perhaps because Jessua has never become a cult director or rediscovered the eminence he enjoyed for a brief time with *Life Upside Down*, the film itself has followed the fate of its hero, becoming rather forgotten and neglected. It is now buried under the weight of the more publicized products of the New Wave and of the earnest exegeses that have been produced about the complete works of Truffaut, Godard, Chabrol, Eric Rohmer, Alain Resnais, and Jacques Rivette. Yet Jessua's film was one of the most intriguing and affecting French films of the decade: wry, thoughtful, unpretentious, and provocative. It not only warrants rediscovery: It deserves a permanent place in the repertory of art cinema.

Neil Sinyard

LILI MARLEEN

Origin: West Germany
Released: 1980
Released in U.S.: 1981
Production: Luggi Waldleitner for Roxy-Rialto-Lex-Film
Direction: Rainer Werner Fassbinder
Screenplay: Manfred Purzer, Joshua Sinclair, and Rainer Werner Fassbinder;
    based on the autobiography *Der Himmel hat viele Farben*, by Lale Andersen
Cinematography: Xaver Schwarzenberger
Editing: Juliane Lorenz and Franz Walsch
Art direction: Rolf Zehetbauer
Music: Peer Raben
MPAA rating: R
Running time: 116 minutes

        Principal characters:
           Robert . . . . Giancarlo Giannini
           Willie . . . . Hanna Schygulla
           David Mendelsson . . . . Mel Ferrer
           Henkel . . . . Karl Heinz von Hassel
           Von Strehlow . . . . Erik Schumann
           Taschner . . . . Hark Bohm
           Aaron . . . . Gottfried John
           Anna Lederer . . . . Karin Baal
           Miriam . . . . Christine Kaufmann

Lili Marleen appeared during the golden period of Rainer Werner
Fassbinder's tragically aborted career. One of the most productive directors
in film history, Fassbinder released *Lili Marleen* during a four-year period,
from 1978 to 1982, in which he completed his celebrated postwar trilogy,
Die Ehe der Maria Braun (1978; *The Marriage of Maria Braun*), *Lola*
(1981), and *Die Sehnsucht der Veronika Voss* (1982; *Veronika Voss*), as well
as three of his most stylistically complex films—*In einem Jahr mit 13
Monden* (1978; *In a Year of 13 Moons*), *Die dritte Generation* (1979; *The
Third Generation*), *Querelle* (1982)—and the extraordinary fifteen-hour
epic *Berlin Alexanderplatz* (1980). That this prodigious effort occurred at a
time when many were proclaiming the old age of the latest European new
wave, the New German Cinema, indicates either that the claim was pre-
mature or Fassbinder's abilities and strengths went well beyond any school
or movement. The New German Cinema was, in many ways, born out of
the ashes of World War II, and, like many of his colleagues in that movement, Fassbinder grew up in an Americanized West Germany, making films

in the 1960's as a protest against the impoverished state of the German film industry and the cultural amnesia that pervaded postwar Germany. By the mid-1970's, the New German Cinema comprised the most acclaimed group of directors on the international scene, and Fassbinder, its leading light, was demonstrating better than anyone that the movement's most complex and most important question was: How did Germany generate World War II, and why did it attempt to misrepresent or repress that horror during the 1950's? By 1980, the New German Cinema may have lost some of its youthful energies, and *Lili Marleen* may represent compromises with the established hierarchy that Fassbinder had once detested and denounced (specifically, producer Luggi Waldleitner and scriptwriter Manfred Purzer). Yet, if this film is the failure that many claim that it is, it is not because Fassbinder changed his methods or his concerns. Rather he was focusing them, as never before, on the spectacle of Fascism that was both Germany's past and, for Fassbinder, its present.

Lili Marleen, however, is history deflected: history as it is made through the popular imagination. Indeed, an easy mistake with this film, as with any Fassbinder film that deals with a specific historical period or figure, would be to look for an accurate depiction of events or political intricacies. Lale Anderson, upon whose personality and career the film is based, was a real Nazi radio star during World War II: Her song "Lili Marleen" was, as the film shows, almost accidentally discovered by a propaganda officer looking for new material. Against Joseph Goebbels' protests, she and her song did rise meteorically in the affections of not only the Nazi troops but also the Allied soldiers. Yet, if Fassbinder takes many liberties with Andersen's story, it is because, for him, the story is important mainly as an index of how private sentiment is the real measure of public events and history. The roots of Nazism, for Fassbinder, are closely connected with sentimental idealism, and to understand the popular fascination with and the support for Fascism, one must look through the facts to the emotions and myths that created those facts. That two years earlier *The Marriage of Maria Braun* was hailed for its historical accuracy, despite its clear detour away from historical figures and specifics of the postwar years, suggests that Fassbinder's depiction of the sentiments and the images of history can, in fact, be more faithful to a period than a more detailed analysis. *Lili Marleen* tells the tale of the futile last days of Nazi Germany by focusing on the song of one of its stars in a similar attempt to show that Fascism lives in the illusions that it can sustain, and that those illusions have little to do with historical geography or with epochs.

Like many of the later Fassbinder films, the narrative is a relatively straightforward story line, perhaps misleading audiences into thinking that they are getting straightforward history. *Lili Marleen* opens in Zurich, in 1938. A young German woman named Willie (Hanna Schygulla) is entertaining tourists and soldiers with her American burlesque routine. Outside this frivolous setting, German troops have invaded neighboring countries; secluded in Switzerland, Willie falls in love with Robert Mendelsson (Giancarlo Giannini), the son of wealthy, aristocratic parents and an aspiring musician. Robert and his family lead an underground movement that helps Jews escape from Germany, and, although his father sternly objects, Robert brings Willie with him to Germany when he goes there for a secret rendezvous. When they try to return to Switzerland after this meeting, Willie is refused entry because she has so many debts. Robert, though, carries important and sensitive documents, and to remain undetected, he must desert Willie.

Abandoned in Germany, Willie seeks out a Nazi official whom she had met while performing in Switzerland and who had meanwhile become a cultural affairs officer. She performs in a local beer hall and is urged by him to record a sailor's song called "Lili Marleen." During a break in this recording, Robert and Willie secretly meet outside, and the emotional impact of this reunion inspires Willie to sing her song as never before. Later, "Lili Marleen" is accidentally played at a radio station. The response from the troops is so immediate and so strong that Willie and her accompanist Taschner (Hark Bohm) become instant celebrities. They are catapulted into a life of opulence and ease, dramatically at odds with the hardships suffered by the rest of Germany. Adolf Hitler himself becomes one of Willie's fans, and at one climactic point, she is brought to meet him.

As she travels around war-torn Germany, attempting to rally the troops, Willie is approached by a leader of the underground—played, as is the scruffy black marketeer in *The Marriage of Maria Braun*, by Fassbinder himself. Because she is able to move freely and is privileged because she is a star, Willie is asked to help smuggle out secret films, which reveal the atrocities of the concentration camps. Showing these horrors to the Allies, she is told, will fire their anger and hatred of the Nazis. The Nazis soon suspect Willie of treachery, but since she is favored by Hitler, little can be done until she is finally caught in a meeting with Robert. Although they are not sure who he is, the Nazis arrest Robert and torture him by forcing him to listen to one phrase from "Lili Marleen" played again and again. Put together in a room, Willie and Robert are watched from a one-way window to see if they reveal their true relationship.

Robert is later returned to Switzerland in an exchange of prisoners at the border. Willie, on the other hand, is forced to visit hospitalized soldiers in an effort to quiet rumors that she has been mistreated by the Nazi leaders. At one key point, Willie becomes part of a mammoth Nazi propaganda spectacle, replete with huge swastikas, fireworks, and flowers. Visibly broken, she stumbles onstage for one last radio broadcast of her song.

When the war ends, she escapes Germany, escorted by a sympathetic

Nazi officer. When she arrives at the Zurich opera house where she hopes to find Robert, however, she is first met by Robert's new, fittingly aristocratic wife. Robert has just finished conducting the orchestra, and, as he comes backstage, leaving wild ovations, he meets the two women. Torn and confused, he leaves Willie as he did years earlier, this time returning to the stage and the applause of the audience. Willie walks slowly from the theater.

This closing sequence is the typically precise ending of a Fassbinder film: In a film that is so much about spectacles and performances, the ending deflects the film's focus from the longed-for reunion of the lovers to the glare of the stage and the clamor of audience approval. Like the Nazi propaganda spectacles, Willie's various radio performances, the underground's plan to distribute the concentration-camp film, and the obsession with class appearances in Robert's family, this final retreat to the stage makes clear that the center of this society is illusory spectacle. From the opening shots, illusions define the terms by which individuals relate and through which public politics are put into play; according to these terms, the person who directs the show usually uses that power to victimize and manipulate those who merely watch or who blindly participate. These dynamics of spectacle form the crucial interface where the tragedy of Willie as Lili Marleen becomes the tragedy of "Lili Marleen" and Nazi Germany. Just as Willie is exploited and ultimately left destitute by the song which becomes her alter ego, Germany, in this film, becomes the naïve dupe of a fantastic and impossible image of itself that is put in place by those overwhelming propaganda spectacles, which are ultimately, in this film, summarized in a song. Therefore, when Willie is abandoned at the end, her resignation suggests at least an implicit recognition that she is again being victimized by the stage that has destroyed her life and love from the outset.

Seen in this light, the indignation that this film often elicits follows in part from its argument that the abuses and violence of Fascism are not the exclusive property of the Nazis but are equally present in other, more accepted social forms. The snobbish proprieties of Robert's family and Robert's inability to denounce them are both, on a private level, as cruel and oppressive as any political party. This despairing structure is, moreover, a common one in Fassbinder's work: This is a world of individuals—usually women—who are victimized and destroyed by their emotions and by their love, who are made to surrender and so to sacrifice themselves to the spectacle of another. Sometimes this theater of suffering occurs between individuals, such as Willie and Robert; sometimes it occurs between an individual and his or her art (for example, when Willie sacrifices herself to her song or when Robert sacrifices himself to his music); sometimes the violence of the spectacle erupts when a people give themselves up desperately to the emotional image of a national identity, such as Nazi Germany.

The historical backdrop that informs this film about spectacles is clearly the *Revuefilm* of Nazi Germany. Fassbinder does not, however, simply imitate these theatrical parades of mass enthusiasm but rather exaggerates their style so that their excesses become part of his critical commentary. *Lili Marleen* certainly demonstrates Fassbinder's standard techniques. The redundancy of internal frames and scenes shot within mirrors or through glass panes suggests how, in this reality, all is mediated by or is the product of a framed perspective (dramatized when the Nazi officials attempt to "frame" the lovers by spying on them through a one-way window). The dense overlapping of visual and auditory tracks is likewise a technical strategy with which Fassbinder frequently experimented as a way of emphasizing the materials of representation and of showing how the illusory unity of any image hides, in fact, a more cluttered and dissonant reality. Yet, of these many sophisticated technical motifs, it is the visual excess of *Lili Marleen* which is most prominent. The sets and lighting, in particular, are frequently exaggerated in their art-deco design, plush colors, and increasingly dazzling tones: These are the visual corollaries of a truly spectacular society, and the excessive qualities of these images mark, through the course of the film, their growing distance from the dark and bitter world they are supposed to reflect.

If viewers are upset or confused by *Lili Marleen* (as many are), it may be because of this irony of excess. War depicted as a series of static tableaux seems, at first, a perverse stylization. When Willie walks up majestic steps to meet Hitler and the doors open to greet her with a flood of white, celestial light, the effect would be shocking, if it were not so outrageous. Mistaking sequences like these for legitimate representations of events can, however, only degrade the film, since *Lili Marleen* is describing not so much the war (or even one part of it) but rather the way the popular imagination can create images—including images of songs—as surrogates for that war. By making his audience participate in the luxury and visual pleasure of those images, Fassbinder does more than describe that popular imagination: He enlists the viewer in its action and so makes it very difficult to maintain a safe historical distance from the most catastrophic of twentieth century events. *Lili Marleen* may simplify a complex national disaster, but the sensational irony implicit in that simplification is meant to suggest that this kind of reduction is precisely the way a public deals with those events—how it turns politics into a slogan or a song.

Timothy Corrigan

LOLA

Origin: France and Italy
Released: 1961
Released in U.S.: 1962
Production: Carlo Ponti and Georges de Beauregard for Rome-Paris Films
   and Euro International Films
Direction: Jacques Demy
Screenplay: Jacques Demy
Cinematography: Raoul Coutard
Editing: Anne-Marie Cotret and Monique Teisseire
Art direction: Bernard Evein
Music: Michel Legrand, Ludwig van Beethoven, Johann Sebastian Bach,
   Wolfgang Amadeus Mozart, and Carl Maria von Weber
Running time: 90 minutes

> *Principal characters:*
> Cécile (Lola) . . . . Anouk Aimée
> Roland . . . . Marc Michel
> Mme Desnoyers . . . . Elina Labourdette
> Cécile . . . . Annie Duperoux
> Frankie . . . . Alan Scott
> Michel . . . . Jacques Harden
> Jeanne . . . . Margo Lion
> Claire . . . . Catherine Lutz

   Like their creator, the characters of Jacques Demy are incurable romantics who persist in the belief that perfect happiness and fulfillment may be only a heartbeat away. Such faith is extremely touching in Demy's world because invariably the capriciousness and remorselessness which have a telling effect on every human life have given these characters reason to be bitter and disenchanted. In a key scene of *Lola*, Anouk Aimée as Cécile and Marc Michel as Roland find themselves at cross-purposes, and an exchange occurs in which resentments, frustrations, disappointments, and insecurities abruptly surface. The two characters ultimately reconcile, but it is important to remember that Demy's apparently rosy vision is not all sweet music and lyric encounters. His romanticism derives from a view of the world as despairing as the cinema can offer. For such a sensibility, the creation of a single work which offers escape from the pervasive melancholy of life would not suffice.
   Lola marked the beginning of the director's attempt (continuous in his first five films) to create his own self-contained world, a world necessarily limited to his films but not doomed to perish at the fadeout. Characters

would recur or be alluded to in subsequent films, endlessly meeting and parting in new configurations. The practical realities of making films, however, made it ultimately impossible for Demy to carry out this intention (something which a novelist might accomplish more easily), but the grace and beauty which distinguish his cinematic world have maintained an undiminished hold on those who respond to his films.

Lola was Demy's first feature film. Like its four successors, it is set in a coastal town, in this instance Nantes, where Demy himself grew up. His second film, *La Baie des anges* (1963; *Bay of the Angels*), is set on the French Riviera, while *Les Parapluies de Cherbourg* (1964; *The Umbrellas of Cherbourg*) and *Les Demoiselles de Rochefort* (1967; *The Young Girls of Rochefort*) are set in the towns named in the titles and *The Model Shop* (1969), an extremely underrated American effort, is set in Los Angeles (where the hero lives in Venice Beach). The coastal setting of *Lola*, more than those of the subsequent films, alerts the audience to the presence of one of Demy's themes. The human spirit thrives on a yearning for change, and the sea manifests the possibility of change. It offers a sense of unknown adventure and new worlds. Whether the odyssey which the sea symbolizes will actually offer people the rewards they truly desire is a moot point, but in the vision of life which a film makes possible, romantic belief may be confirmed. Demy recognizes this by having a scene in which Roland goes to a film (the 1953 *Return to Paradise*, a Technicolor adventure directed by Mark Robson). Speaking with his friend and confidante, the waitress Claire (Catherine Lutz), Roland describes the film, in which Gary Cooper plays a rugged wanderer who creates his own paradise on the island of Marateva. Later, Lola's long-absent husband, Michel (Jacques Harden), relates his own experiences, and it develops that the turning point in his fortunes occurred when *he* was on the island of Marateva. Since the audience already knows that Marateva does not really exist and was created for an American film, they are reminded that *Lola* is also a film and one no less fanciful than its predecessor.

Lola is not so much one story as a passage of a longer narrative in which the earlier existence of the characters is as significant as the present action and in which the future beyond the fadeout promises resolution for some lives and redirection for others. At the center of this flowing fragment of a more elaborate world are Cécile (Anouk Aimée), who works as a cabaret dancer under the name "Lola," and Roland Cassard (Marc Michel), a young dreamer who is drifting through life without any clear motivation or ambition. In the period of a few days in which the film is set, Cécile and Roland, childhood friends, meet once again. Each is at a turning point in life, and the lives of other characters in the film intersect with those of Cécile and Roland in coincidences that seem extremely contrived yet unfailingly meaningful. The most significant of these characters are Mme Desnoyers (Elina

Labourdette), her daughter Cécile (Annie Duperoux), and an American sailor, Frankie (Alan Scott).

As the film opens, Michel (whose identity remains ambiguous for most of the film) is staring out to sea during the early morning hours. Dressed in a white suit, he gets into a white Cadillac convertible and begins to drive along by the ocean as the credits roll. A sense of fatality is immediately imparted to the viewer by the dedication to German-born director Max Ophüls (the comparison Demy dares to invite by this dedication turns out to be well-earned) and the effective use of the second movement of Ludwig van Beethoven's Seventh Symphony. After the credits, the viewer is introduced to Roland speaking with the sympathetic Claire and with Jeanne (Margo Lion), the café owner and an amateur painter who also happens to be Michel's mother. The hapless Roland has stayed up late reading *La Chartreuse de Parme* (1839; *The Charterhouse of Parma*), by Stendhal. As a result, he has overslept and is late to work. His honest explanations of his apathy toward his job elicit from his employer both sympathy and a dismissal. His immediate solution to his problems is to spend the next few hours watching *Return to Paradise*, an act which Demy knows is bound to endear him to any cinema devotee. Of greater significance is the fact that his unexpected freedom leads to his chance meetings with the young girl Cécile and her mother Mme Desnoyers in a bookshop, and later with his childhood friend Cécile (hereafter called Lola). Roland falls in love with Lola almost immediately. For her part, Lola has been waiting patiently for seven years for her lover Michel to return, raising their son and working as an entertainer in a dance hall. Lola is not a vulgar woman with a lot of male friends. She does, however, have a weakness for Frankie, because his blond hair and sailor suit remind her of Michel as he was when they first met.

As the film progresses, Roland makes a deal to smuggle diamonds, which he is prepared to abandon for love of Lola. When she disappoints him, he resolves to go through with the plan in spite of the arrest of his employer. Frankie, who is in Nantes on leave, sleeps with Lola and also meets the younger Cécile during his wanderings around town. Meanwhile, Cécile and her mother are visited several times by Roland. Michel cruises around town learning about Lola and finally reveals himself to his mother, who is overjoyed to see him. He then reconciles with Lola, and the now reunited family—man, woman, and son—drives off in the white Cadillac. At the same time, Mme Desnoyers has left with Cécile for Cherbourg in order to reunite with the love of *her* life, her daughter's father.

Demy loves all of his characters, and, in a sense, they are reflections of one another. The resemblance between Frankie and Michel is obvious. The carefree young sailor is the image of what the now rich Michel had once been. In the same way, the young Cécile is the image of the younger Lola whom Roland has always remembered. No less important is Mme Desnoyers' kinship with Lola. She, too, is rearing an illegitimate child and dreaming of a love that she believes has been lost to her, and her imminent reconciliation with that unseen lover is as grandly melodramatic as Lola's abrupt reunion with Michel. At the same time, Roland's departure for an adventurous future at the film's conclusion is a reminder of Michel's journey to seek his fortune seven years earlier. The fateful meeting of Lola and Roland crystallizes the dreams of a romantic past which are Lola's *raison d'être* and the dreams of a romantic future which sustain Roland during an uncertain period of his life. Although Roland's romantic expectations of Lola are disappointed and she regrets her inability to fall in love with him prior to Michel's return, the two part as friends. The film implies that their encounters have sharpened the focus of their hearts' desires.

The most beautiful sequence of *Lola* is reserved for Frankie and the young Cécile. Far from being incidental, their second meeting is the heart of the film–a hallucinatory memory image occurring in a vivid present. Frankie takes the little girl to a carnival, just as Michel had done with Lola many years earlier. The two go on several rides, the second a fast "thrill" ride, and Cécile leans her head on Frankie's shoulder as he puts his arm around her. When the ride ends, the two jump off in lyric slow motion, accompanied by the second of two Johann Sebastian Bach preludes from *The Well-Tempered Clavier* utilized for the sequence. The innocent eroticism of the sequence has a special magic which derives from Demy's ability to perceive the joy of the brief experience with a lack of self-consciousness which he shares with the two characters. The slow-motion descent from the ride, as the man and girl skip hand in hand in breathless happiness, is completely free of affectation or miscalculaton. Countless directors have attempted to impart lyricism to sequences of their films by using slow motion, but what seems mannered and disingenuous in their films remains fresh and spontaneous in *Lola*. The immediate aesthetic effect is rivaled by the formal accomplishment of evoking the past relationship of Lola and Michel without a flashback. All of *Lola* takes place in the present, but the audience is acutely aware of the characters' present experiences as events in an endlessly recurring cycle of romantic moments and of hopes and dreams which refuse to fade.

Demy was intent on filming *Lola* in color, but for economic reasons it was made in black-and-white. While Demy himself might have regretted this, the resulting visual tone—a subtle artificiality of design and lighting in which white naïvely dominates shades of gray and black—has a mesmerizing effect. Location shooting tends to emphasize the naturalistic aspects of a work, but in *Lola* this does not occur. Demy's use of color in *The Umbrellas of Cherbourg* and *The Young Girls of Rochefort* emphasizes the relationship of those films to the soundstage musicals of Hollywood's past, films for which the director has a deep admiration. By contrast, the extent to which

Demy's romantic visualizations derive from his most profound feelings is more poignantly experienced in the CinemaScope imagery of *Lola*, a film even more lilting and lovely than the others, precisely because it achieves its effects without recourse to storybook color schemes and overtly stylized decor. This impression is confirmed by *Bay of the Angels*, for which black and white was again imposed, in a gambling fantasy which charmingly extends the "white" motif by presenting Jeanne Moreau in a blonde wig. As Demy's style has developed, he has restrained the mobility of the camera and has tended to deliberate more over the effect of each shot. *Lola* presents his style at its purest and most spontaneous. In this first film, he seems more willing to trust to impulse (as in the carnival sequence with Frankie and the young Cécile); his instinct for seizing the dramatic meaning of a moment appears to be infallible.

The freshness of *Lola* is very typical of early films of the French New Wave. For this reason, it should be emphasized that it has stood the test of time much better than other celebrated films of the period. Among the first films of directors of Demy's generation, only Jean-Luc Godard's *À bout de souffle* (1959; *Breathless*) also stands up to reappraisal as an unqualified masterpiece. (Interestingly, Demy refers to *Breathless* in *Lola* by having Roland claim that his one friend, Michel Poiccard—the "hero" of *Breathless*—was shot by the police.)

Also characteristic of the New Wave is Demy's assured eclecticism, particularly his taste for American genre films. The joie de vivre of Gene Kelly in Stanley Donen's musicals (such as *On the Town*, 1949, with its carefreee dancing sailors) and the melancholy of Vincente Minnelli's musicals and comedies are joined in Demy's vision. The dedication to Max Ophüls acknowledges another debt: Demy's Lola is named after the heroine of Ophüls' *Lola Montès* (1955); like Lola Montès, she is both a character and a focus of artistic intention. She is the embodiment of the dreams and desires of both the women and the men in Demy's world.

On the strength of *Lola*, Jacques Demy would have seemed as likely as any director to become one of the greatest masters of the cinema. Sadly, his career has been plagued by setbacks, and he has never quite equaled this captivating first film, although *The Umbrellas of Cherbourg*, a love story performed completely in song, is also a masterpiece and has enjoyed continued popularity. His first five films are admirable, and each has a distinctive quality. The recurring characters contribute an additional element to the aesthetic and emotional unity of the films. Lola turns up in Los Angeles in *The Model Shop*, and she explains to the young American hero of that film that Michel ran off with Jackie (the gambler played by Jeanne Moreau in *Bay of the Angels*). Meanwhile, Roland reappears in *The Umbrellas of Cherbourg*, singing of Lola (to the same Michel Legrand melody which served as the main theme of *Lola*) but falling in love with the pregnant heroine of that film and now possessing both the wealth and wisdom to win her for his wife. The many charming characters of *The Young Girls of Rochefort* were obviously also intended to be resurrected, but after *The Model Shop*, Demy seemed to lose his way.

The fairy-tale aspect of his first five films had transformed the real world in which all of these films were set. The rawness of modern reality had been softened by Demy's gentle reimagining of life as fairy tale. By contrast, his attempt to treat an actual fairy tale in *Peau d'âne* (1971; *Donkey Skin*) had the paradoxical effect of laying bare his coldly pessimistic vision of life. Its sweet and pretty surfaces could not conceal the sourness and gloom within. Other projects not wholly suitable to his sensibility followed, but he belatedly made a heartening return to form with the beautiful *Une Chambre en ville* (1982), another completely sung musical drama, set in Nantes in 1955. Even without this reassertion of his special gifts, the films of his first decade would assure his high critical standing. *Lola* alone warrants eternal regard for this most wistful of cinematic artists.

Blake Lucas

LOLA

Origin: West Germany
Released: 1981
Released in U.S.: 1982
Production: Horst Wendlandt for Rialto-Film/Trio-Film
Direction: Rainer Werner Fassbinder
Assistant direction: Harry Baer
Screenplay: Rainer Werner Fassbinder, Pea Fröhlich, and Peter
  Märthesheimer
Cinematography: Xaver Schwarzenberger
Editing: Juliane Lorenz
Art direction: Rolf Zehetbauer; set decoration by Raul Gimenez
Costume design: Barbara Baum
Music: Peer Raben
MPAA rating: R
Running time: 114 minutes

Principal characters:
Lola	Barbara Sukowa
Von Bohm	Armin Mueller-Stahl
Schuckert	Mario Adorf
Esslin	Matthias Fuchs
Hettich	Helga Feddersen
Lola's mother	Karin Baal
Wittich	Ivan Desny
Timmerding	Karl-Heinz von Hassel
Mayor Volker	Hark Bohm
Frau Schuckert	Rosel Zech
Marie	Ulrike Vigo

Lola is the third in Rainer Werner Fassbinder's trilogy of films dramatizing the history of postwar Germany. Like *The Marriage of Maria Braun* (1978) and *Veronika Voss* (1982), *Lola* treats the decade of the 1950's, the period of German rearmament and of the *Wirtschaftswunder* (Economic Miracle) that accompanied it. In each of these harsh exposés of the corruption and dehumanization of a capitalist society, a female protagonist occupies the center. She acts as a vessel charting the political, social, and economic currents of this particularly materialistic and smug period of German history. Lola, a composite of Maria and Veronika, is a talented performer, a prostitute, and ultimately a successful businesswoman. Maria is a war widow who briefly becomes a prostitute before attaining success as an industrial magnate. Veronika, a faded film star from the Nazi era, becomes a heroin addict after the war and retains her narcissism but not her talent. In *Lola*, the men who control the town (supposedly Coburg in Bavaria, in 1957) use Lola as a bargaining tool for their corrupt business and political deals. Interestingly, however, she occupies so much screen time, with such animated allure, that her cinematic presence tempers her ultimate powerlessness. In spite of this powerlessness and her lack of any real self-awareness, which both Maria and Veronika have, Lola is the only one of the three with any sort of success at the film's conclusion. The irony is that *Lola*, superficially the least cynical and depressing film of the trilogy, is upon reflection the most pessimistic. It refuses conventional resolution, opening itself up to the cyclical, unjust realities of postwar German society. The corrupting effect of capitalism, for which Lola's prostitution is a metaphor, will continue.

Lola begins with a scene presenting Lola (Barbara Sukowa) and one of her lovers, Esslin (Matthias Fuchs), a young leftist who works for the city by day and as a drummer for the nightclub/brothel that employs Lola by night. Her other major lover, Schuckert (Mario Adorf), the town's biggest building contractor, keeps her. Schuckert uses the nightclub to plot his corrupt business alliances with Volker, the town's mayor (Hark Bohm), and bank director Wittich (Ivan Desny). A huge housing development, the Lindenhof project, is in the works. The arrival of the town's new building superintendent, the idealistic, intelligent, and naïve Von Bohm (Armin Mueller-Stahl), upsets the men's carefully calculated plans. Von Bohm rents a room in the home of Lola's mother (Karin Baal), who keeps Lola's daughter by Schuckert. Lola, in a fit of anger at Schuckert for belittling her low position in society, presents herself as a cultured, educated, innocent young woman to Von Bohm, who falls in love with her. Esslin, jealous of Schuckert as a competitor, exposes the sham. He takes Von Bohm to the nightclub, where the new superintendent watches her bestially perform a rendition of "The Capri Fishermen" and learns of her affair with Schuckert. Hurt and vindictive, Von Bohm decides to unmask the contractor and prevent the implementation of the development plans. Esslin offers to help Von Bohm, but Schuckert easily buys off the leftist with the promise of a job. Von Bohm is unable to contain his obsession with Lola; he sublimates his sexual longing by playing the violin franticly. Schuckert seizes his opportunity by offering Lola in marriage in exchange for approval of the building project. Lola's reward from Schuckert is the title to the club which employs her; she becomes an entrepreneur. After her marriage to Von Bohm, Lola maintains her affair with Schuckert, who has brilliantly orchestrated the entire business transaction and the obligatory construction of a new nuclear family.

Lola evokes the cultural mood of both Germany and Hollywood in the 1950's. The choice of furnishings and costumes is meticulously appropriate. The garish color schemes, such as the aquas and lavenders of the interiors, and the pink, blue, and gold filters and lights flooding certain shots, are endemic to the period. Often two differently colored filters or lights are used in a single shot, such as the two colors which bathe the faces of Lola and Von Bohm, respectively, in the car during their first, interrupted embrace. The brashness of the decor of the brothel extends to the rest of the film's sets, including Von Bohm's office and the homes of Schuckert and of Lola's mother. Stylistically, Fassbinder clarifies the analogy between prostitution and capitalism.

The style of *Lola* is an homage to the Hollywood color melodramas of the 1950's, especially those of Douglas Sirk at Universal, in which artifice was often deployed for the purpose of social criticism. Yet Fassbinder retains the Brechtian distancing devices and the irony of his earlier works. The exaggerated color contributes to the distancing strategy, but it is the editing structure that prevents the spectator from becoming uncritically absorbed in the narrative. Rapid, out-of-focus zooms mark the transition between scenes. A monotonous, irritating musical chord accompanies these cuts, as in *Fox and His Friends* (1975). The last scene exemplifies the Brechtian irony, which Fassbinder magnifies with outrageous humor. While the passive Von Bohm stands with his new stepdaughter, Marie (Ulrike Vigo), who will eventually inherit the brothel, the bride, Lola, still in her wedding dress, begins to make love savagely to Schuckert.

The sound track strongly reinforces the feeling of German culture in the 1950's. "The Capri Fishermen" was one of the popular but banal songs of the period. During the credit sequence, a male voice accompanies the image of then Chancellor Adenauer with an incredibly romantic and nostalgic popular song. The legacy of German Romanticism is the song's inspiration. A German sailor abroad speaks to the wind and clouds of his longing for the homeland. As well as presenting German history as cyclical, Fassbinder proffers a continuity of the German cultural heritage: The National Socialist ideologues perverted the nationalistic nostalgia lingering from the eighteenth century Romantics; *Blut und Boden* (blood and soil) was a watchword for the Nazi cause.

The artifice and metaphor of *Lola* refer to concrete social, political, and economic events in West Germany in the 1950's. Fassbinder refuses to isolate these specific events; rather, he maintains a sense of historical continuity. Still photographs of Adenauer, flanked by vertical bands with the colors of the German flag, bracket the film and sustain the film's references to actual events. The choice of Schuckert's profession as a developer is not accidental. A priority of the postwar German economy was building reconstruction, especially housing. The government in fact provided half of all housing costs; by 1967, more than half of German housing units had been built since the war. By exposing the corruption associated with the Lindenhof project at all levels of political and economic power, Fassbinder hits a sensitive nerve in the psyche of postwar German society.

The rather brief scenes of protesters demonstrating against nuclear armament refer to actual opposition to Adenauer's policies of rearmament, especially to the deployment of nuclear arms. Adenauer had in fact succeeded in ridiculing and dismissing the antinuclear protesters. In actuality, the occupying Allied countries rearmed Germany in the early 1950's, during the Cold War and the Korean War. By 1958, the *Bundestag*, the German parliament, had approved the implementation of nuclear weapons on German soil. Fassbinder forges the link between the rapid industrialization of Germany during the Economic Miracle and the nation's rearmament, much like what happened during the Third Reich.

Lola alludes to other social issues involved in the rapid economic growth of a stratified, capitalist society in Germany. The rigidity of class distinctions, for example, ties in with the resentment of the newly displaced immigrants, especially those from Eastern Europe. Lola, out of necessity a prostitute, supports her family, including her immigrant mother. The arrogant Frau Schuckert (Rosel Zech), a member of the old, wealthy German aristocracy whose credentials rest tenuously on anachronistic notions of power, belittles Lola's mother at the latter's dinner party: She projects her class-consciousness onto the cuisine. Von Bohm is also from the aristocracy but from the less wealthy strata that traditionally bred civil servants. Both types of aristocrats have been superseded by men such as Schuckert, members of the new commercial class of businessmen, whose power and prestige have grown with Germany's reindustrialization. Schuckert has few traditions and few rituals of class behavior to limit and regulate his dealings with others. Refreshingly spontaneous and charming, he is able to manipulate people across class lines.

The sense of cultural continuity extends to the overall plot and to the delineation of character. *Lola* is consciously derivative of the classic German film *The Blue Angel* (1930), directed by Josef von Sternberg, and the novel by Heinrich Mann, *Professor Unrat* (1905), on which it is based. In both films, the central character is a woman surviving as a singer-prostitute in a nightclub/brothel. Each meets a respectable, idealistic, and thoroughly anachronistic man who succumbs to her charms, and whom she manipulates mercilessly, eventually into marriage. In *The Blue Angel*, the male victim is an elitist teacher at the town's advanced high school. The conflict is essentially the intellectual versus the libidinal, the splitting of the German psyche into two mutually incompatible camps. In *Lola*, the male victim is also an intelligent and cultured civil servant, but his profession as building superintendent links him to the vested commercial interests of his society. Whereas Professor Rath in *The Blue Angel* remained aloof from the world of the everyday, Von Bohm not only analyzes that world but also must judge its functioning. His fall from grace occurs when his desire for Lola obscures his professional judgment and moral principles. Whereas *The Blue Angel* mourns a dying tradition of erudition and rational analysis, *Lola* is essentially a Marxist critique, exposing the economic base which perverts the entire social and moral fabric of society.

By borrowing freely from the condition of German culture in the period immediately preceding the ascendancy of the National Socialists to power, Fassbinder comments cynically on the future of the German society represented in the film. Lola-Lola of *The Blue Angel* and Lola of *Lola* both triumph at the climax of the film. Each has used beauty and sexual allure, tools of powerless women, to succeed within her circumscribed world. The degraded Professor Rath dies in *The Blue Angel*, providing some resolution to the conflict in a society with rapidly changing mores. In *Lola*, however, the woman's victory is less convincing. She achieves her dream, and Marie will inherit the brothel; historical progression is assured. Fassbinder formalizes this sense of continuity by placing Marie in a hayloft at the end of the film in the same reclining position in which her mother had appeared earlier. Lola's success is inconsequential, for her achievement is the result of appeasement among men in power. Whereas Professor Rath died, Von Bohm lives and will rear Marie.

Fassbinder, by leaving the narrative open-ended, implies the repetition of the vicious cycles of capitalism and its undermining of fair and just standards of behavior. The political model is anarchism, the stepchild of Marxism: Anarchist theorists rebelled against Marxism's definite blueprints for a new society of the future; they believed that such a strategy would lead only to the repetition of the conflicts and injustices of the old order. Fassbinder offers no solutions; he merely lays out contradictions. He forces the spectator to contemplate the social issues embedded in the narrative.

Howard Feinstein

LOLA MONTÈS

Origin: West Germany and France
Released: 1955
Released in U.S.: 1969
Production: Ralph Baum for Gamma Films, Florida Films, and Union Films
Direction: Max Ophüls
Screenplay: Max Ophüls, Annette Wademant, Jacques Natanson, and (for the German version) Franz Geiger; based on the novel *La Vie extraordinaire de Lola Montès,* by Cecil Saint-Laurent
Cinematography: Christian Matras
Editing: Madeleine Gug
Art direction: Jean d'Eaubonne
Costume design: Georges Annenkov and Marcel Escoffier
Music: Georges Auric
MPAA rating: no listing
Running time: 110 minutes
Also known as: The Sins of Lola Montes and *The Fall of Lola Montes*

Principal characters:
Maria Dolores Porriz y
Montez, Countess of
Lansfeld (Lola Montès) . . . . Martine Carol
Ringmaster . . . . Peter Ustinov
King Louis I (Ludwig I) . . . . Anton Walbrook
Lieutenant James . . . . Ivan Desny
Franz Liszt . . . . Will Quadflieg
Student . . . . Oskar Werner
Maurice the Coachman . . . . Henri Guisol
Joséphine the Chambermaid . . . . Paulette Dubost
Mrs. Craigie . . . . Lise Delamare

Lola Montès was a resounding commercial failure that ran the gamut of critical opinion. At one extreme, Andrew Sarris called it the greatest film ever made, while Claude Beylie compared it to the Sistine Chapel; on the other hand, Manny Farber thought all its virtuosity was like hauling a corpse around a circus ring. The compromise category of "flawed masterpiece" could be useful. In art-house repertory, the film generates, at the very least, an amazed respect for its extravagant poetry.

It belongs to a genre with many names, all unsatisfactory: romantic drama, women's film, soap-opera, melodrama. It involves two themes conspicuous in its time. First, it considers woman in relation to shows, truth, scandal, and her freedom—like Jean Renoir's three costume Technicolor spectaculars, French actress Martine Carol's other films, and, in Hollywood, *A Star Is Born* (1937; 1954; 1976). Second, its circus setting takes on a spiritual sadness, as in Federico Fellini's *La strada* (1954) and Ingmar Bergman's *Gycklarnas afton* (1953; *The Naked Night*).

Martine Carol was an absolute condition of the production, and although director Max Ophüls feared miscasting, he came to hope that the not uncommon procedure of "casting against type" might generate a poignant discomfort. CinemaScope was another awkward stipulation, but by affixing black velvet maskings to the camera, Ophüls successfully varied its crushingly flat proportions. Ralph Baum, the producer, suggests that Ophüls' initial fears, lest spectacle swamp intimacy, gave way to the strategy of elaborating on the spectacle itself. Ophüls became steadily more possessed and demanding, massively increasing the already lavish budget.

Possibly the most expensive European production up to its time, *Lola Montès* was filmed simultaneously in French, English, and German versions. The sets are visibly vast. Twelve hundred extras wore seven hundred different costume designs. Eighty-five kilometers of film were exposed. Miles of road were color-sprayed by water-carts daily; an entire mill was swathed in tulle and airlifted from Brussels to achieve a particular autumnal tint.

After his first 140-minute edit, Ophüls agreed to the 110-minute release version. After its hostile reception, the producers reissued it, despite all protests, in a ninety-two-minute version. This replaced the flashback structure by a more chronological narrative and hinted at a happier end. It became *The Fall of Lola Montes* in Great Britain, while in the United States the title *The Sins of Lola Montes* was used on three edited versions (ninety-three, ninety, and even seventy-two minutes). The 110-minute version was rereleased in 1968 and is the standard.

In New Orleans, the Ringmaster of the Mammoth Circus (Peter Ustinov) proudly presents Lola Montès (Martine Carol): dancer, courtesan, and consort of bankers and kings. She will answer the public's most indiscreet questions and reenact her life as a series of circus acts and tableaux. The show must proceed despite Lola's fainting-fit and the doctor's warning of a worsening heart condition.

This gaudy production is interrupted by the flashbacks' quieter versions. Lola's affair with Liszt (Will Quadflieg) ends as their coaches rumble their separate ways, suggesting two rootless bohemians of romantic passion. The next flashback plunges further back, to Lola's girlhood. Her shallow-spirited mother banishes the too-pretty child from a ship's salons to its lonely deck, but she returns to steal her mother's admirer, Lieutenant James (Ivan Desny). Next, she escapes from her stultifying domesticity with him to blaze a trail of scandals and diplomatic incidents across Europe, which are developed less in flashback than in ingenious circus tableaux.

Flashbacks resume with the Ringmaster's first attempt to hire her, to create an attraction for scandal-mongering. As her coach approaches Munich (presumably, but not certainly, continuing the departure from Liszt), she picks up an idealistic student revolutionary (Oskar Werner)—and after enjoying him, deposits him. Arriving in Bavaria in poverty, she soon compels the attention of King Louis I (Anton Walbrook). Elderly as he is, they enjoy domesticity and love of a kind, until the scandal provokes the 1848 Revolution. The student helps her flee, but she again leaves him, this time because something has been broken in her.

Back in the circus, the Ringmaster goads her to risk a leap without the safety net. She survives but is last seen enclosed in a cage, like an idol, with her hands protruding through the bars, for the public to file past and kiss at a dollar a time.

The novel on which the film is based was not published, and presumably the author of sexy romances was hired for his name and to provide a treatment to which Ophüls would not have been very faithful. Ophüls clearly knows the history, for he plays little games with it, right down to the colors and slogans of the student political leagues.

The real Lola Montès also inspired the Joan Crawford character Vienna, in Nicholas Ray's *Johnny Guitar* (1954). She was hardly Ophüls' quiet, inarticulate, indecisive figure. An Irish girl posing as a Spanish aristocrat turned dancer, she was intellectual enough to hold her own in the Liszt-Georges Sand circle (Ophüls even endows her with a resemblance to Sand in that sequence). Her domination of Louis I was indeed a major catalyst of that revolution, but she had been politically active as a Lammenais republican and Socialist. Combined with all these characteristics were her wild temperament and extravagant tastes. Thus, her biography accommodates innumerable themes, some resurgent since Ophüls' death: revolution, feminism, German Romanticism, alienated individualism. Ophüls neither suppresses nor highlights them, but his Lola belongs to his personal mythology, not to the 1840's.

One might diagnose Ophüls' interest in old-fashioned women or the feminine mystique of the film's time (or both). He had stated that he had in mind Judy Garland's nervous breakdown, Zsa Zsa Gabor's brief rise to stardom on the strength of several wealthy marriages, and certain starlets exposed beyond their talents. Television and radio programs inspired the idea of cruel questioning by the public.

Lola's men are no less complex and weak. The "inspired," idealistic Liszt deals in politely dishonest courtesies. The revolutionary student is confident of always finding employment—for all countries must need Latin tutors. Louis I so immerses himself in domesticity as to provoke revolution. Such ripples of contradiction and paradox flow through all the characters and situations.

Not that such quiet ironies are as conspicuous as the visual spectacle, but

Ophüls was infamously obsessed with details. The cut of a mustache or the gesture of a hand, according to him, could say more than a page of the script. This film builds as a ballet of details, colors, movements, and virtuoso camera movements, which set landscapes and architecture moving in their turn. Thus, Ophüls develops, through "pure film" form, the "pictorialist" tradition of stage *mise en scène*, in particular the idioms developed by Max Reinhardt in Berlin and Austria between 1905 and 1933. Ophüls' own theater productions had all but established him as Reinhardt's heir apparent before he turned to film. (In film, expressionist decor represents a distinct, but simultaneous, influence of theater on film; the two can be crossbred, as was briefly done here.)

Theatrical pictorialism accepts realism and artifice together. Here the circus spectacle affords a pretext for strident antirealism, like the male figures with coins for heads. Ophüls, however, sweeps on to unabashed artifice without pretext. Among the circus spectators are dummies and life-size photographs (black-and-white stills) pasted onto flat plywood. Their fixed, convergent stares are subtly eerie.

Ophüls is rightly associated with the baroque, especially with the Austrians, even though he was a Berliner. In the circus, Lola, queen and martyr, sits enthroned—a silent hub of concentric and contrarotating circles and ellipses. The visual counterpoint includes her turntable, the ringmaster's 360-degree stalkings back and forth, the tiers of spectators whose voices stab inward, and the big top curving over everything, even over the camera, on which it seems to ride, fly, and fall. Intermittently, files or squadrons of clowns, freaks, or glittering props surge or scatter in spokes, chords, or tangents. These torsions and distensions are diversified by vertical movements or screens of ropes from which chandeliers and people hang like monstrous jewelry. Eventually, Lola's own "rise" begins, an odyssey on platforms, rope ladders, and trapezes, which sketch the most terrifying—and paradoxically tenuous—of baroque staircases.

Many other scenes are also structured on visual motifs associated with ascending/descending spirals, counterturns, domes, drums, and canopies, corridors arranged like the chords around a circumference, or ascents beyond tiers of balconies, or spoke movements around rooms. Scenes are conceived and written to constitute dynamic walk-throughs, as the characters, and the camera with them, stalk reverse, prowl, diverge, and converge. Here is a choreography of momentum and inertia, of orbits through architecture. One need only cite Lola's trajectory from a wallowing rowboat through the variously gloomy spaces, rhythms, and moods above and below a ship's deck. She ends, alone, beside a heaving prow which becomes her partner in a waltz under the stars. Promptly, the camera tilts up toward them—only to encounter, through a lap-dissolve, a descending theater curtain.

Very different is Lola's arrival at an inn. Her sweeping ascent, with her entourage, up through three stories, is irresistible, despite the landlord's obsequiously persistent attempts to divert her into various rooms all the way up. When Lola rips her bodice to conquer the king, the movement of her arms sets off a volley of cuts to ever-further parts of the palace, as servants relay orders and scurry for needle and thread. Palatial space for stitch space. In contrast, the next scene is a loitering ritardando: Louis and Lola while backstage make little, listless movements, while bored courtiers make space: dead, vacant. Amid imposing decor, the characters may relate via the miniscule. Needle and thread, specks of dust, or even a chart of the ear.

There is much truth in the critical association of Ophüls with F. W. Murnau and Kenji Mizoguchi in a cinematic style of camera movement and continuous flow, as opposed to the collisions between shots practiced by Sergei Eisenstein and the cinema of montage. Nevertheless, Ophüls' continuity often works from thrust, deviation, violent turn, and penetration. The needle-and-thread sequence is a montage explosion. Likewise, in Lola's flashback with the Ringmaster, the continuous space of her room is arbitrarily segmented into shots angled at different tilts.

Before costume designing began, Ophüls explained to Georges Annenkov his color-plan for the film's series of dramatic atmospheres. The Liszt sequence is dominated by autumnal tints (gold, red, violet) and, with them, sunset light. Lola's sad childhood is black, blue, and gray. Bavaria is white (hence snow, but a soft, pastel snow) with blue, silver, and gold. The circus is a kaleidoscope of colors, lurid against black. These motifs, however, only dominate: other colors diversify, contrast, vary the mood, or trace other patterns (Lola's dresses).

A similar tactic is used with every kind of physical-visual patterning. For example, a general theme of spatial design ranges from motifs of enclosure (notably coaches, cages, boxes, foreground screens) to open-plan mazes (a dormitory, theater wings). These varied motifs, however, are not simple repetitions of one meaning, such as, perhaps: "false freedom." On the contrary, the theme is worked through a diversity of variations so as to provide differences, changes, surprises, complementary or countervailing experiences. Interpretation must never crush variation under "theme." The dramatic components are equally complex. The references to Louis' deafness are equivocations rather than repetitions; each time they draw in something different from the local issues, setting, or ideas. Thus, all structures are open-ended and, through that, dependent on each other, urging multiple viewings to appreciate its many levels. Such riches by no means rule out major fractures and failures. Apart from the central miscasting (some Ophüls admirers feel that his first fears were justified), the film's intimate side (acting, lighting, atmospherics) lacks his usual precision and intensity.

Raymond Durgnat

LONE WHITE SAIL
(BYELEYET PARUS ODINOKY)

Origin: U.S.S.R.
Released: 1936
Released in U.S.: no listing
Production: Soyuzdetfilm
Direction: Vladimir Legoshin
Screenplay: Valentin Katayev; based on his novel
Cinematography: Bentsion Monastirsky and G. Garibian
Editing: no listing
Art direction: Vladimir Kaplunovsky and S. Kuznetsov
Sound: N. Ozornov
Music: N. Rauchberger
Running time: 92 minutes
Also known as: A White Sail Gleams

Principal characters:
Gavrik................................Igor But
Petya ....Boris Runge
Rodion Zhukov ....A. Melnikov
Grandfather........................Ivan Peltser
Terenty ....A. Chekayevsky
Gavrik's father ....Fedor Nikitin
Government agent ....Nikolai Plotnikov

Films about and for children have been an important part of Soviet cinema since its inception. The very first Soviet children's production, *Signal* (1918), directed by Aleksandr Artatov for the Moscow Film Committee and photographed by the great Eduard Tisse, is based on a popular children's story by Vsevolod Garshin.

One of the best-loved Soviet films of all time is *Krasnye diavolyata* (1923; *Red Imps*), an exciting adventure story about three youngsters—two white and one black—who call themselves "The Elusive Avengers" and who win the Order of the Red Flag after acting as volunteer scouts for the Red Army during the Civil War. Made by Ivan Perestiani in the Georgian studios, it was the first Soviet film to beat foreign productions on the home screens and the first to be reviewed in *The New York Times*. The *Times* correspondent of the period, Walter Duranty, described the film as a Russian-revolution version of the tales of Huckleberry Finn or Tom Sawyer produced in a Tarzan manner and tempo. Several sequels have been made over the years.

One of the first films scripted and made for sound, *Putyovka v shiza*

(1931; *Road to Life*), was also about children. It was based on a true account of a scheme to rehabilitate orphaned youngsters running wild in the street by involving them in a residential educational farm.

In 1934, as part of a training program initiated by Sergei Yutkevich, a highly experienced filmmaker and a brilliant teacher, two young men, Vladimir Legoshin and Mark Donskoy, collaborated on their first feature film, *Pesnya o schastye* (*Song of Happiness*), a lighthearted tale about young people from the Mari community in the Volga region who are learning musical skills. When Soyuzdetfilm (Children's Film Studio) was established in 1936, both of these gifted young directors joined it and made films that became classics of world cinema. Donskoy made *The Childhood of Maxim Gorky* (1938; *Detstvo Gorkovo*), the first part of the celebrated Gorky trilogy. Legoshin's film, *Lone White Sail*, made in the tradition of *Red Imps*, was immensely popular at home and abroad and had a far wider distribution in the West than was usual for Russian-language films.

The action of *Lone White Sail* takes place in 1905, the year of the first Russian revolution, which was sparked by the mutiny on the battleship *Potemkin*. The *Potemkin*, a title informs the audience, has been captured by the Romanians and taken to Constanza; its sailors are making their way back in secret to their home port of Odessa to rejoin the revolutionary struggle.

The passenger steamer *Turgenev* is about to sail for Odessa when it is boarded by military police. They are looking for a sailor from the *Potemkin*. Gavrik (Igor But), a wide-eyed, solemn little boy, his younger sister, and his father (Fedor Nikitin), have retired, as ordered, to their first-class cabin. A sailor (A. Melnikov) rushes into the cabin and hides under one of the bunks. When the military police burst in to search the cabin, Gavrik's father, who is a senior academic, reprimands them for their impertinence and they leave apologetically. The sailor slips out, but just as the ship is reaching Odessa he is spotted by a government agent (Nikolai Plotnikov), who tries to arrest him. The sailor plunges overboard and is picked up by a fishing boat, crewed by a cheerful little boy, Petya (Boris Runge), and his grandfather (Ivan Peltser). They take him to their tiny, cliffside dwelling.

The two little boys meet at a quayside market and swap stories about the sailor. They play a gambling game on the ground, using brass buttons as tokens. Petya is an expert; Gavrik loses and goes home to get some more buttons and some money to pay his debts. When his father proves difficult, he rifles his sister's money box and rips the buttons off his father's uniform.

While Gavrik is at home, the government agent tries to bribe Petya into giving him information about the sailor. Petya puts him off the scent and goes to see his grown-up brother, Terenty (A. Chekayevsky), who is in the revolutionary movement. Terenty and another revolutionary go to the hut, recognize the sailor as Rodion Zhukov, a leading figure in the *Potemkin* mutiny, and arrange to take him to the Workers' Council. As they are leaving, the agent and the military police burst in. The men escape, but the police manhandle Petya and beat up and arrest the grandfather.

On October 18, 1905, in the center of Odessa, a man is pasting up the czar's manifesto promising freedom of thought, speech, and assembly. The wealthier citizens welcome it, but the workers treat it with great scorn and anger. At a huge workers' rally, a speaker denounces the manifesto as sheer hypocrisy.

Unaware of all this, Gavrik, in school uniform with a satchel strapped to his back, finds Petya and plays the button game with him. When he loses, he tears off the buttons of his uniform as payment.

The atmosphere in the town is becoming increasingly tense, with crowds scattered by the military, gun-carriages racing through the streets, and the sound of gunfire growing louder. The militia sets up barricades which encircle the Workers' Council's hideout in a tenement block.

The workers inside the encirclement are short of ammunition. Terenty gives Petya the task of smuggling the ammunition past the guards. Petya loads the bullets into Gavrik's satchel from behind him, pretending that they are brass buttons. The two boys manage to get past the guards and deliver the ammunition to the workers. Some of the bullets fall to the ground, and Gavrik at last realizes what is happening. The two boys are urged to go back for more ammunition.

They are about to make a second attempt to cross the barricade when Petya spots the government agent and tells Gavrik that he must go ahead alone. Gavrik passes the guard without difficulty, but the bombardment is getting heavier and the soldiers are closing in. Gavrik, Zhukov, and others are forced to flee across the rooftops. Zhukov is captured, but Gavrik escapes.

At Gavrik's home, his little sister is celebrating her birthday with a party. Gavrik has been out all day, and the parents are very worried, especially when the little girl announces that her money box is empty.

When Gavrik returns, tired, dirty, and with no buttons on his uniform, his father berates him for supposedly keeping bad company and getting involved in gambling. He grabs hold of Gavrik's satchel, finds a package in it and, assuming it to be gambling tokens, thrusts it into the kitchen range. Gavrik tries in vain to stop him. There is a violent explosion.

A year has passed. Gavrik, recovering from a long illness brought on by his experiences, seeks out Petya and finds him on the shore below his hut. The grandfather has died. Petya is getting the boat ready for Zhukov, who has been sprung from prison by his comrades. Gavrik and Petya's sister mount the cliff to act as lookouts. Zhukov arrives and sets sail. The three children stand on the cliff and watch the little boat as it sails into the distance.

The film runs at a tremendous pace, with swift, sure cutting that deftly ushers in the surprising twists and turns of the plot and maintains the suspense throughout. There are many humorous touches and even a hint of romance between Gavrik and Petya's sister.

The young boys are delightfully portrayed and well contrasted. Their carefully delineated relationship is of central significance to the film. Petya, with his broad, Slavic face, fair, tousled curls, and ragged clothing, is a natural revolutionary. Gavrik, dark-eyed and sensitive, is overeager to gain Petya's confidence. Like his father, who is depicted as a well-intentioned liberal, he cannot be wholly trusted; his loyalty has to be constantly put to the test.

There is a very engaging scene in which Petya promises to tell Gavrik about the real situation if he will first swear secrecy by eating a mouthful of soil. Gavrik obeys, with evident distaste. At that moment, Petya spots a column of striking workers who are being marched off to prison. He looks at them, and then at Gavrik's polished shoes, and refuses to tell. Gavrik's face is a picture of hurt and frustration. It is not until Gavrik delivers the ammunition alone that he gains Petya's wholehearted trust. In the final cliffside sequence, he is at last accepted on equal terms.

The class difference between the two boys is also emphasized by the attitude taken toward them by the guards at the barricade. Petya is roughly treated by the militia; Gavrik, with his neat appearance and middle-class voice, is let through with only a mild reproach. A further class contrast is made by a swift cut from the poor district in which the battle takes place to the elegant home of Gavrik's family, with the children in party clothes dancing to a tinkly polka tune.

It is Gavrik, however—and by implication the intelligentsia—who provide the film's cultural framework. At the beginning, before the military police enter the cabin, he recites a Mikhail Lermontov poem for his father. He repeats the poem at the end, as the three children watch Zhukov sail into the distance. The opening words, "A white sail gleams in the blue sea mist . . ." supply the film's title.

Although the children's characters are fully rounded, the other characters are stereotyped. The revolutionaries are kindly and stalwart. The militia are fierce and brutal; they all wear handlebar moustaches, as does the government agent, who is a very sinister character indeed.

Soviet audiences of the period would have been familiar with the legendary *Potemkin* incident, which was in any case immortalized on the screen by Sergei Eisenstein in his silent masterpiece *Bronenosets Potyomkin* (1925; *Potemkin*). In the English-subtitled version of *Lone White Sail*, a long opening caption sets the scene.

Titles are also used to explain some of the more complex situations and to indicate the passage of time, but most of the historical background emerges through the characters and situations. The announcement of the czar's proclamation is particularly well handled by showing a variety of ironic reactions to it. A pompous man in a horse and carriage welcomes the news as a great step forward for democracy and in the same breath berates and curses his driver. While the words "freedom of assembly" are ringing out, the police are brutally dispersing the crowds.

Bentsion Monastirsky's camera work achieves some striking visual effects. In the scenes in the tenement courtyard leading to the workers' hideout, the camera lingers on the intricate structure of the exterior wrought-iron staircases—imagery which harks back to the famous tenement-staircase scene in Eisenstein's *Stachka* (1925; *Strike*). In the final clifftop scene, the children's figures are silhouetted dramatically against the sky as the white sail of the boat, gleaming against the dark sea, gets smaller and smaller.

The most impressive visual qualities of the film come from Legoshin's handling of the crowd scenes—the packed decks of the *Turgenev*; the quayside scene with a brass band welcoming the disembarking passengers; the police charging the demonstrators in the center of Odessa; the house, street, and rooftop fighting. The waterside scenes, in particular, are comparable to the much-praised period reconstructions in Donskoy's Gorky trilogy.

After completing the trilogy, Donskoy continued to make films of great distinction throughout his life. Legoshin's career was less successful. During the 1940's and the early 1950's, he worked on a number of war films and educational films. None of his later films, however, could compare with the excitement, high spirits, charm, humor, and warmth of *Lone White Sail*.

Nina Hibbin

THE LOST HONOR OF KATHARINA BLUM (DIE VERLORENE EHRE DER KATHARINA BLUM)

Origin: West Germany
Released: 1975
Released in U.S.: 1975
Production: Eberhard Junkersdorf for Paramount-Orion/Westdeutscher Rundfunk (WDR)/Bioskop Film
Direction: Volker Schlöndorff and Margarethe von Trotta
Screenplay: Volker Schlöndorff and Margarethe von Trotta; based on the novel by Heinrich Böll
Cinematography: Jost Vacano and Peter Arnold
Editing: Peter Przygodda, Heidi Handorf, and Ursula Götz
Art direction: Günther Naumann and Ute Burgmann
Sound: Klaus Eckett, Willi Schwadorf, and Wolfgang Loper
Music: Hans Werner Henze
MPAA rating: R
Running time: 106 minutes

Principal characters:
Katharina Blum . . . . Angela Winkler
Inspector Beizmenne . . . . Mario Adorf
Werner Tötges . . . . Dieter Laser
Hubert Blorna . . . . Heinz Bennent
Trude Blorna . . . . Hannelore Hoger
Walter Moeding . . . . Harald Kuhlmann
Ludwig Götten . . . . Jürgen Prochnow
Sträubleder . . . . Karl-Heinz Vosgerau

Filmmaker Volker Schlöndorff (born March 31, 1939, and trained at the Institut des Hautes Études Cinématographiques in Paris) codirected the film version of Heinrich Böll's novel *The Lost Honor of Katharina Blum* (1975) with his wife, Margarethe von Trotta (born February 21, 1942), who was later to become a respected filmmaker in her own right. This proved to be an effective collaboration, the husband concentrating on action sequences, the wife exploring internal character motivation and psychology. Von Trotta's contribution gives the film a distinctive personal impact and authenticity as a woman's film. In this respect, the film may seem more substantial than the novel, which is an exquisitely structured polemic against right-wing paranoia and the violation by the State apparatus of privacy and personal freedom.

Volker Schlöndorff served an apprenticeship as assistant director to French New Wave filmmakers Alain Resnais and Louis Malle, then carried the liberating influence of that movement back into his native Germany, where he specialized in cinematic adaptations of literary works: *Der junge Törless* (1966; *Young Törless*, adapted from the novel by Robert Musil), *Michael Kohlhass—Der Rebell* (1969, from the novella by Heinrich von Kleist), *Baal* (1970, a television production adapted from the work of Bertolt Brecht), *Der Fangschuss* (1976; *Coup de grâce*, adapted from the novel by Marguerite Yourcenar), and *Die Blechtrommel* (1979; *The Tin Drum*, adapted from the novel by Günter Grass). Schlöndorff also wrote or collaborated on the writing of nearly all of these projects. Though particularly respected for his skill at adapting literary texts to cinema, the artist has also been drawn toward films that raise political issues and offer an opportunity for social criticism.

In this respect, then, Heinrich Böll's novel is a typical project for Schlöndorff as well as a remarkable achievement in cinematic transformation. Böll's novel resembles a polemical tract, elevated to the level of art by the novelist's command of metaphor, which is combined with a seemingly detached journalistic style and is given additional impact by the brittle irony that pervades the work. The point of the narrative is made clear by the novel's subtitle: *How Violence Can Develop and Where It Can Lead*. The political and psychological discourse of the novel is conveyed by a narrator who emphasizes the importance of the process that impels the central character toward the desperate act, an innocent woman driven to the act of murder. The narrator is no longer present in the film, which dramatizes that process in its own way while simplifying and clarifying the issue. As a consequence, the novel's tonal nuances are sacrificed in the interest of sheer emotional power.

Heinrich Böll has been recognized in his own country as a popular, master storyteller. His international reputation was established in 1972, when he won the Nobel Prize for Literature. Böll, who has described himself as "a Communist *manque*, prevented from becoming a Communist on the one hand by Hitler and on the other by Stalin," has generally focused his fiction on World War II and its aftermath in Germany. *The Lost Honor of Katharina Blum*, however, is linked to the political atmosphere of Germany some thirty years after the war and was inspired by the governmental antagonism that the novelist experienced in 1972, the year that he won the Nobel Prize. First, Böll was attacked by the press as a consequence of his writing an article for *Der Spiegel*, criticizing the hysterical coverage of the Baader-Meinhof gang and arguing that the terrorist Ulrike Meinhof should be given a fair trial. This was an unpopular position to take and was interpreted as a mark of sympathy for the terrorism that Meinhof had come to symbolize. The novelist's house was searched and he was antagonized by the police as well as by Axel Springer's widely read paper, *Bild-Zeitung*.

The story of Katharina Blum (Angela Winkler) presents an innocent, hardworking, and well-structured young woman who meets and falls in love with Ludwig Götten (Jürgen Prochnow), who is being tailed by the police as a suspected terrorist. The two are introduced at a party during the carnival season and immediately fall in love. Götten escorts Katharina home and spends the night. The police mount an early morning raid on her apartment the next day, but Götten escapes. Katharina is jailed as a possible accomplice, and, though later released, she is constantly harassed by the police thereafter. The most psychologically damaging consequence, however, is the way that her reputation is defiled by the press, particularly the way that she is treated by an unscrupulous reporter named Werner Tötges (Dieter Laser), who invents details to make his reporting more spectacular and turns her into a notorious celebrity by making her appear to be a terrorist sympathizer and a whore.

Finally, the reporter attempts to capitalize on her notoriety, which he has himself created, and to exploit her sexually as well. At this point, she snaps, arms herself, and shoots the man when he comes to visit her in her apartment. After having been victimized and brutalized by the State and the press, she is desperately driven to criminal behavior by the way that Tötges and his newspaper, the popular *Zeitung* (read by all of her friends), have scandalized her reputation. The film makes clear that the shock of his methods brings about the death of Katharina's mother, who is recuperating in the hospital. The scandal also damages the careers of her employers, Hubert Blorna (Heinz Bennent) and Trude Blorna (Hannelore Hoger). Götten, the presumed terrorist, is later apprehended at the holiday estate of a man named Sträubleder (Karl-Heinz Vosgerau), who had earlier tried unsuccessfully to take sexual advantage of Katharina. The suspect's crimes, however, seem only to involve his having deserted from the army and stolen money from the regimental safe. As Blorna says of Götten in the film, "We know only that he was a deserter from the Bundeswehr and that he helped himself to the pay shipments."

Heinrich Böll's novel represents a much more complicated version of the story, moving back and forth in time in a calculated attempt to demonstrate the process of "how violence can arise and where it can lead." Böll sent proofs of his novel to Schlöndorff and von Trotta while the book was in production and later collaborated with them in reshaping the narrative for the film version, which took a more straightforward, chronological approach and was intended to reach a wider, more popular audience than the novel. The film makes the plot linear and begins with black-and-white, documentary images of the terrorist suspect, Götten, on a ferry, demonstrating the process of police surveillance. These shots parallel later black-and-white photographs taken by the newspaper photographer for the *Zeitung*. The documentary police camera captures the suspect in the cross hairs of a viewfinder that resemble the cross hairs of a rifle scope and suggest that the camera can also function as a weapon.

The police follow their suspect to a bar, where he joins a group of young women on their way to the party where Götten will first meet and fall in love with Katharina. The film emphasizes the Carnival atmosphere of the setting and shows a pervasive process of undercover police work, with police agents disguised as Arabs. The film serves to clarify the issues (such as police spying and the invasion of privacy) by placing them in bold relief. After Katharina is taken to police headquarters, the film makes perfectly obvious the idea of police collusion with the press. One sees Inspector Beizmenne (Mario Adorf) giving police records to the reporter Törges, who has not yet been identified in the film but who is later to become Katharina's nemesis.

The film tends to emphasize the major characters more clearly. The Blornas do not enter the picture until they return home from an Alpine vacation later on in the film narrative, in keeping with the chronological restructuring of the story. As a consequence of their later introduction, their significance is reduced in the film. On the other hand, the unscrupulous reporter Tötges has a much larger role in the film, which turns him into an absolute, unfeeling villain. In the novel, Böll attacks yellow journalism in general, as a destructive process, but Schlöndorff and von Trotta narrow the attack to a specific character, who is presented in an overstated and despicable way. Early in the picture, the emphasis is on the sinister Inspector Beizmenne, who is later replaced as the primary villain by Tötges. In the novel there is more balance between these two characters.

The detached, objective reporting technique of the novel gives way in the film to a more sentimental presentation of character. Katharina herself is humanized to a larger extent by Schlöndorff and von Trotta and made less enigmatic and more sympathetic. The police invasion of her apartment in the film is brutal and humiliating. She is ordered to change clothes, and the prying eye of the camera follows her into her bathroom, revealing her nudity and affording her no privacy in her own home. Her infatuation with Götten, moreover, is presented as a conventional film romance. Romantic flashbacks are later inserted to demonstrate Katharina's "tenderness" toward Götten. In the novel, Böll does not take the reader into this dimension of her character.

In the film, Katharina's feelings toward her ailing mother, who is visited by the reporter—who breaks into her hospital room and contributes to her death by telling the mother about Katharina's alleged scandalous behavior—are dramatized when Katharina sits, sobbing, on a bench, after a doctor at the hospital has told her that her mother was well on the way to recovery and that there is no apparent reason for her death. There is no similar loss of self-control on Katharina's part at this point in the novel.

The most striking visualization of theme, however, comes toward the end of the story, when Katharina wrecks her tidy apartment in a fit of passionate anger and resentment, then sits in the shambles of her once well-organized life, contemplating the murder of the man who has spoiled her happiness.

The film begins by stating that "Although the names of the characters are fictitious, the story you are about to see is based on an actual occurrence," before going on to the documentary, day-by-day chronology that starts on "Wednesday, 5 February 1975." The film ends with the same statement that Böll uses to begin his novel: "The characters and action in this story are purely fictitious. Should the description of certain journalistic practices result in a resemblance to the practices of the *Bild-Zeitung*, such resemblance is neither intentional nor fortuitous, but unavoidable."

In general, the film places its emphasis on character rather than on theme. This tendency is reversed at the end of the film, when Schlöndorff and von Trotta provide an epilogue to correct the balance and to emphasize the discourse rather than the story and its characters, after sympathy has been fully established and after Katharina and Götten have been captured and imprisoned. The epilogue is set at the cemetery, where Werner Tötges is being buried. The Sträubleders are in the foreground, the disgraced Blornas in the background, as the owner of the *Zeitung* delivers the funeral elegy and a political message that is ironically overturned by the story witnessed: "The shots that killed Werner Tötges did not hit him alone. They were aimed at the freedom of the press, one of the most precious values of our young democracy. And these shots for us who stand here in grief and horror, they hit us just as they struck him. We all feel the wound, we all feel the sorrow far beyond personal considerations. We all feel the breath of terror, the savagery of anarchy, the violence which is undermining the foundations of our liberal-democratic order which is so dear to us. Here allegedly private motives have led to a political assassination, and we can say once more: Watch how it is starting! Look out, for freedom of the press is the core of everything: well-being, social progress, democracy, pluralism, diversity of opinions. And whoever attacks the *News* attacks all of us."

It was clearly Heinrich Böll's original intention to attack the *Bild-Zeitung*. In his book *The New German Cinema* (1980), John Sandford notes that as a consequence of the film, Schlöndorff, like Böll, was labeled in the *Bild-Zeitung* as a "Baader-Meinhof *Sympathisant*," indicating that the journalistic abuses dramatized by the film were not necessarily corrected by either the novel or the film and that an intelligent concern for individual rights crushed by the power of the State and the press could still be distorted and interpreted as terrorist sympathy.

Interviewed by the French film journal *Ecran*, Schlöndorff contended that Böll's political discourse was his primary concern: "*Katharina Blum* is not a film version of a novel in the same way that *Törless* was," the director stated, "What is of importance is the subject matter which Böll treated in his book. What interested us was not the literary quality, but the issues raised." Schlöndorff concluded that the project was regarded "more as an engagement with matters of topical concern rather than the film version of a novel." This, then, accounts for the absence of Böll's original structure and technique and the loss of the narrator who commented so effectively on the action as he reported it. What is lost in irony and perspective is compensated by the emotional intensity of the film and the integrity of Böll's social and political criticisms, generally maintained, though the scope is reduced to a more limited and personal level.

James M. Welsh

THE LOST SON
(DER VERLORENE SOHN)

Origin: Germany
Released: 1934
Released in U.S.: 1983
Production: Deutsche Universal-Film
Direction: Luis Trenker
Assistant direction: Werner Klinger
Screenplay: Luis Trenker, Reinhardt Steinbicker, and Arnold Ulitz; based on
  the novel by Luis Trenker
Cinematography: Albert Benitz and Reimar Kuntze
Editing: no listing
Art direction: Fritz Maurischat
Music: Giuseppe Becce
MPAA rating: no listing
Running time: 102 minutes

>*Principal characters:*
>Tonio Feuersinger . . . . Luis Trenker
>Barbl . . . . Maria Andergast
>Miss Lilian Williams . . . . Marian Marsh
>Teacher . . . . Paul Henckels
>Hobby . . . . Jimmie Fox
>Mr. Williams . . . . Franz W. Schröder-Schromm
>Tonio's father . . . . Eduard Köck
>Barbl's father . . . . Bertl Schultes

Until the 1983 Telluride Film Festival, at which Luis Trenker's *The Lost Son* and *Der Kaiser von Kalifornien* (1931; *The Emperor of California*) were shown as part of a retrospective of his films with the then almost ninety-year-old director present, it had almost appeared as if the name of Luis Trenker were destined to fade into oblivion in the United States, or at best to be relegated to a few short paragraphs in historical surveys of films made during the Third Reich. This would have been ironic and unfortunate, because *The Lost Son* and *The Emperor of California* both reveal Trenker's obvious fascination with the United States: its myths, its people, its ideals, its potential, its social structures, and its vast panoramas of landscapes and cityscapes. The two films form what may be called Trenker's American diptych: *The Lost Son* tells the story of an immigrant who flounders in New York during the Depression, and its sequel, *The Emperor of California*, presents the history of Johann August Suter, later John Augustus Sutter, a nineteenth century immigrant whose success in America is brought to an end by the California gold rush. These two films were appropriately chosen to be part of the "Focus America: America in German Film" series which Goethe House organized in commemoration of the 1983 tricentennial of German immigration to America. After the Telluride festival, the two films were shown at Goethe House New York, at Chicago's Art Institute, and in other cities, where they impressed American audiences. *The Lost Son* had not previously been released in the United States, and *The Emperor of California* had been out of American distribution for several decades. New thirty-five-millimeter prints (Trenker refused to have the prints reduced to sixteen millimeters because the quality of the images would have suffered) became available for viewing by a new generation of cineasts.

The multitalented Trenker is a household name in Alpine countries, where he is known as a skier, a mountain climber (with eleven first ascents of various peaks to his credit), an active conservationist, an author (of film scripts, memoirs, fifteen novels, and numerous books on mountaineering), an actor, a director, and a producer. Trenker began his acting career in Arnold Fanck's mountain film *Der Berg des Schicksals* (1924; *Peak of Fate*). The *Bergfilm*, or "mountain film," is a genre which typically depicts the perilous adventures of skilled mountain climbers as they conquer dangerous Alpine peaks. The stunning scenery, with its clouds, snow-covered peaks, and shots of skiers and climbers, is often breathtaking, and these sequences often take precedence over the dramatic narrative. Under Fanck's direction, Trenker starred together with Leni Riefenstahl in *Der heilige Berg* (1926; *Peaks of Destiny*) and *Der grosse Sprung* (1927; *The Big Jump*). After appearing in nine films (three being mountain films directed by Mario Bonnard) between 1923 and 1930, he went on to direct fourteen feature films between 1930 and 1962, usually writing the scripts, playing the leading roles, and occasionally producing the films himself. He has also made thirty-five short documentary films, mostly about the South Tyrolean Alps and their mountaineers.

It was thus fitting that the festival in the Rocky Mountains should pay tribute to a filmmaker whom William K. Everson has described as John Wayne and John Ford rolled into one. The suspense-filled mountain films were to Germany and Austria what the Western was to the United States. Like the heroic characters portrayed by Wayne, Trenker's characters are rugged and athletic individuals who risk life and limb for their ideals and their community. As a director, Trenker knew how to film a landscape to its best advantage. Like Ford, he used it as a concrete spatial setting and also made it an agent in the film's conflict, letting it determine the decisions and actions of the characters. On a thematic level, Trenker can also be compared to Ford in his affirmation of the eternal values of home, family, and community.

The Lost Son was the third film Trenker directed. He was inspired to make it while waiting to leave from New York for Europe after completion of the Hollywood version of his film *The Rebel* (1933). *The Lost Son* is a variation on the theme of the prodigal son. The film begins in the tradition of the *Heimatfilm* (a sentimental film genre usually set in Southern Germany or Austria) with idyllic images of the Alpine countryside and its inhabitants: Tonio Feuersinger (Luis Trenker) and Barbl (Maria Andergast) sit in a meadow, lumberjacks wrestle merrily, trees are chopped down, and huge logs slide down flumes into the water. Tonio, however, suffers from wanderlust; he is tired of the mountains and longs for a big city. After work, he visits the teacher (Paul Henckels), who tells him about distant lands.

In a ski race, Tonio's team wins the first prize, which has been donated by the rich American Mr. Williams (Franz W. Schröder-Schromm). In a woodcarver's shop, Mr. Williams sees a large sun mask and orders a copy made for his daughter Lilian (Marian Marsh). The sun mask is used by the peasants during the *Rauhnacht* festival (an Alpine version of Twelfth Night festival which celebrates the elemental forces in nature). Tonio has been chosen to be the next *Rauhnacht* sun king, and from twelve maidens he is to choose his bride during the festival.

Tonio and Jörg, another mountain guide, take Lilian on a mountain tour. The mountain has never before been climbed in the winter, and the pleasant trip turns to tragedy when an unexpected snowstorm comes. Jörg slips, falls, and dies on the mountain. With great effort, Tonio manages to save Lilian. Tonio now hates the mountains and decides to leave for New York. The teacher tries to console Barbl by telling her that someone who never goes away can never return home.

Tonio's trip is never shown but rather is implied through the images. Shots of moving clouds cut to a shot of the Dolomite peaks, which, through a beautiful montage, blend into the New York skyline. Tonio is then seen walking the streets of the city and, through a series of long-shots, the camera, looking up at him and down at him, shows him on various levels of the Empire State Building. In New York, Tonio meets with one disappointment after another: Mr. Williams and Lilian are out of town; he runs out of money and is thrown out of his apartment. After sleeping on a park bench, he meets Hobby (Jimmie Fox), who has been sleeping on the bench next to him. In a laconic conversation, Tonio says that he is from Bavaria, Hobby says that he fought in the war, Tonio says that he did also, and Hobby offers Tonio half of his last cigarette—the two former enemies become united in comradeship through poverty. For a brief period, they find work building skyscrapers. Tonio's mountains are now replaced by high girders above the city's streets, which he climbs. Soon, however, a policeman comes to take Hobby away, and Tonio loses his job.

Homesick, Tonio walks through New York and looks longingly at ships going out to sea. Here Trenker presents a series of realistic shots of derelicts and unemployed men during the Depression. These images foreshadow the Italian neorealism of the late 1940's and 1950's. Tonio is seen staring into grocery store windows and restaurants—these and other sequences were filmed mostly with concealed hand cameras. Tonio steals a loaf of bread and a policeman runs after him. When the policeman catches up with him and sees Tonio eating the bread, he simply turns his back. While standing in line at a Salvation Army soup kitchen and hearing the hymns, Tonio is reminded of a procession in honor of the Blessed Virgin back home. The two sequences dramatically contrast with each other: the dark and lonely night in New York is juxtaposed to the bright daylight and brilliant white light of the village's religious procession.

Tonio and Hobby find work as water boys for a boxer. During a fight actually filmed in Madison Square Garden, one boxer beats his opponent while he is down, whereupon Tonio jumps into the ring and knocks out the boxer with a punch, creating a great sensation. By chance, Mr. Williams and Lilian are in the audience, and they take Tonio to their luxurious townhouse. Tonio falls in love with Lilian, but when he sees the copy of the sun mask, he remembers that he was chosen to be the next sun king and returns home.

He arrives on the eve of Epiphany as the *Rauhnacht* festival is being celebrated. For this festival, Trenker combined elements from the Twelfth Night celebrations of several villages. These sequences consist of beautiful night scenes of skiers wearing masks and carrying torches as they ski downhill, peasants in costume representing the different aspects of nature, and shots of masks and faces superimposed on fires. Tonio and Barbl are reunited, and in the final scene they follow the other villagers and the youths who are dressed as the Magi into church, where they pray to the Blessed Virgin.

Although some of the film's sentimentality appears dated to a modern audience, most critics agree that *The Lost Son* is Trenker's best film, and many have called it a masterpiece. According to Trenker, American distributors refused to release the film in the United States because it presented the story of a German immigrant who suffered and hungered in New York during the 1930's. The shots of New York during the Depression were innovative for the time and document in a *cinéma vérité* manner a stark reality almost never seen in American films of the period. Eric Rentschler has pointed out, however, that the realism at times gives way to stylization: Some of the characters in New York, such as the butler and the white actor in blackface, have German accents when they speak English. This probably went unnoticed by European audiences at the time. The portrayal of poverty and hopelessness in New York is in no way anti-American, partly because there was little anti-American sentiment in Germany in 1934 and partly because Trenker's cosmopolitan and unprejudiced curiosity permitted him to seek and marvel at the new and foreign. Tonio's displacement in

Manhattan serves as a contrast to Trenker's beloved mountains, where the poor peasants have a sense of belonging and are freer than Manhattan's millionaires.

At the 1935 Venice International Film Festival, *The Lost Son* was awarded the Prize of the Italian Minister for Popular Culture, an award reserved for the foreign film with the "most important moral message." Because of the Venice award, Joseph Goebbels did not pursue his plans to suppress the film in Germany, and the film was given the Prädikat (merit award) "Artistically Especially Valuable." Initial criticism of *The Lost Son* came from the leaders of the Hitler Youth, who viewed it as a work filled with concealed Catholic propaganda financed by the Catholic Church, and the Communist papers in Vienna also attacked the film. Nevertheless, critical and audience responses to the film were most favorable. It is ironic, however, that although the film received the Italian Minister's Prize and was released in Italy, the anti-German Fascist prefect Mastromattei banned the film in the Southern Tyrol, making it impossible for Trenker's fellow South Tyroleans to see the film in their homeland.

Franz A. Birgel

LOVE AFFAIR
Or, The Case of the Missing Switchboard Operator
(LJUBAVNI SLUČAJ, TRAGEDIJA SLUŽBENICE PTT)

Origin: Yugoslavia
Released: 1967
Released in U.S.: 1968
Production: Avala Film
Direction: Dušan Makavejev
Screenplay: Dušan Makavejev
Cinematography: Aleksandar Petković
Editing: Katarina Stojanović
Art direction: Vladislav Lazić
Sound: Dušan Aleksić
Music: Hanns Eisler
MPAA rating: no listing
Running time: 69 minutes
Also known as: An Affair of the Heart, Love Dossier, The Switchboard Operator, Tragedy of a Switchboard Operator

Principal characters:
Isabela...............................Eva Ras
Ahmed......................Slobodan Aligrudić
Ruza ....Rušica Sokić
Mica..........................Miodrag Andrić
Sexologist..................Dr. Aleksandar Kostić
Criminologist ....Dr. Živogin Aleksić

The cinema of Dušan Makavejev, with its strongly sexual content and acerbic criticism of social and political structures, has raised controversy from its beginnings. His short film *Spomenicima ne treba verovati* (1958; *Don't Believe in Monuments*) was judged too erotic by the censors, his landmark *WR—Misterije organizma* (1971; *WR—Mysteries of the Organism*) was banned in his native Yugoslavia, and the French-Canadian production *Sweet Movie* (1971) proved too scatalogical and sexually provocative to find its audience. Makavejev's style expands upon the revolution in film rhetoric begun by the French New Wave filmmakers (most notably Jean-Luc Godard): He uses startling juxtapositions of contrasting images and a mixture of Surrealism and *cinéma vérité* for outrageous comic effect. Makavejev is, in the words of critic John Simon, a curious blend of artist and prankster.

Love Affair: Or, The Case of the Missing Switchboard Operator, Makavejev's second feature-length film, brought its director to international attention. The collage approach to the narrative, in which certain elements in the history of the love affair are presented out of sequence and interspersed with illuminating commentary by scientific experts, prefigured Makavejev's most widely known and respected film, *WR—Mysteries of the Organism*. The "WR" of the title is Wilhelm Reich, former Freudian psychologist and discoveror of the orgone, the life force of sexual energy. Part documentary on Reich and his work, part exploration of sexual liberation that appears superficially Reichian, and part fictional narrative of the sexuality of two women, *WR—Mysteries of the Organism* is the clearest statement of Makavejev's recurring theme of the correlation between repressed sexuality and totalitarianism. This theme is central to *Love Affair*, in which the conflicting forces of technology and nature are added to the sexual tensions, which themselves are related to the lovers' attitudes toward political ideology. Both characters are outsiders in Yugoslavia who experience conflicts with ideology and varying forms of sexual repression.

Makavejev has his roots in disparate cultural traditions. His fascination with the cinema dates to his childhood, when Western films and cartoons were his favorites. From a synthesis of Western popular culture and Eastern culture, of an anti-Stalinist upbringing and Serbian folklore, Makavejev developed an eccentric sensibility. The title *Love Affair: Or, The Case of the Missing Switchboard Operator* evokes a romantic melodrama (indeed, it calls to mind Leo McCarey's 1939 film of the same name) crossbred with a pulp thriller, and stylistically the film is very much a hybridization.

Although his exposure to Western popular culture is significant, Makavejev's cinematic roots can be found in Soviet cinema. Sergei Eisenstein and Dziga Vertov seem to be Makavejev's antecedents with the creation of heightened forms of realism in film. From Vertov, Makavejev may have learned the technique of startling juxtapositions; in homage, a sequence from Vertov's *Enthusiasm* (1931) is shown in *Love Affair*.

Makavejev's literary antecedents are Bertolt Brecht and John Dos Passos. The mixing of documentary and fictional elements in *Love Affair* into a flowing, self-illuminating montage is reminiscent of Dos Passos' fiction. Makavejev's use of distancing techniques and his detailed examination of the minutiae of everyday life are similar to Brecht's drama. As Brecht did in drama, Makavejev uses documentary realism and distancing techniques as a means of rejuvenating the film audience. *Love Affair* is like a mystery whose solution only raises a new set of questions.

The film opens with a display of Brechtian titles that ask "Will man be remodeled?" "Will future man preserve certain old organs?" The sexologist (Dr. Aleksandar Kostić) delivers an anthropological overview of sexuality in society and how contemporary society, although interested in sex, has paradoxically repressed its sexuality under the guise of frankness. After the credits (a montage of sexual paintings and drawings), the narrative begins. Isabela (Eva Ras) and her friend Ruza (Ruŝica Sokić) are working at the switchboard when Mica, the telegram deliverer (Miodrag Andrić), a predatory and shallow rakehell, appears and flirts with them. The women leave the office discussing their sexuality. Ruza is more open and promiscuous; Isabela is more demure.

Makavejev at this point introduces political icons and advertising displays, both of which seem to incorporate sexual elements: An idealized toothpaste tube, for example, recalls a giant phallus from the sexologist's lecture that was the center of an ancient ritual of fertility. These images, partially intended for humorous effect, when placed in such proximity to the sexual discussion that preceded them, become ambiguous. Whether the implied sexuality is actually present in these images or merely seems to be there is the question Makavejev wants his audience to ask. Society, the film implies, has substituted sexual imagery for human sexual emotions.

Isabela and Ruza meet Ahmed (Slobodan Aligrudić), who takes them for drinks at a nearby café. A quick leap in time shows a woman's corpse being discovered in a well. Although no identification of the body is made, the audience assumes that it is Isabela. The criminologist (Dr. Živogin Aleksić), surrounded by implements of crime and other trappings that suggest scientific research, delivers his lecture on detection. In a dispassionate and rational tone, the criminologist points out that the police have perfected their science, and the criminal is almost always apprehended.

The next scene shows a nervous Ahmed at Isabela's apartment. He tells her that he is a sanitary inspector (he is, in fact, an exterminator) and describes himself as clean and orderly. Since the audience has made a connection with the dead body and Isabela, and since the criminologist's lecture precedes the appearance of the agitated Ahmed, this sequence develops a menacing irony. As they watch a documentary on television about the demolition of churches in the Soviet Union, Isabella and Ahmed make love. As the lovers are in bed, they discuss their lives. Isabela is Hungarian, which reminds Ahmed of the stories he has heard of the wild sexuality of Hungarian women. It also serves as a political contrast—the Hungarians are more formal Communists than are the Yugoslavians, but Isabela is totally uncommitted; Ahmed is Middle Eastern and completely outside the Eastern European Marxist experience, yet he is a dedicated Party member. This scene introduces the two forms of repression that Ahmed has experienced: his Muhammadan upbringing and the strict demands of his Party affiliation.

Another leap forward shows the morgue, where an autopsy is to be performed on the corpse of the woman found in the well. The woman, it seems, was pregnant at the time of her death. An inventory of the woman's belongings ends with a close-up of a pendant. In the next scene, Isabela is searching for her pendant, which is lost among the bedclothes. At this point, the film beautifully catalogs Isabela's sensuousness: her casual and earthy beauty as she walks about the apartment or as she lies naked on her bed with a black cat upon her buttocks. These images form a morbid contrast with the scene of the corpse, which the viewer now knows is Isabela's, on the autopsy table; the contrast is particularly morbid in view of her deathlike gaze as she lies absently upon her bed.

The next juxtaposition begins with a documentary on the rodent problem in Belgrade, a documentary in which Ahmed is shown exterminating rats. The exterminators are called by the narrator "the avant-garde of humanity." This scene is followed by the text of a poem on the death of a rat. An uneasy connection is made between Isabela and the rats, the symbol of nature that gnaws voraciously on the infrastructure of technological society. Ahmed controls the rodents for a living, and he controls Isabela in a slightly repressive way; he confines her to a life of modulated domesticity held in place by his male supremacy. At this point in the film, the audience must question whether, if Isabela could not be controlled, Ahmed would exterminate her as he exterminates the rats.

Isabela makes a strudel for Ahmed (the musical score playing the grand march from *Aida*). This sequence, made in a painstakingly realistic, almost documentary style, is an intricate cross-referencing of sexual images: Isabela's buttocks, an egg, the egg being cracked into a mound of dough. This is followed by a second lecture by the sexologist on the perfection of the egg as a reproductive element and symbol.

Cutting back to the apartment where Ahmed and Isabela are now staying, Ahmed plays a Communist song sent to him by friends ("Crush to Dust the Rotten Vermin"). As he tries to work, Isabela sings a Hungarian folk song ("A Man Isn't Made of Wood"). The growing gap between the two of them appears not so much personal as philosophical—his orderly formalism, her emotional earthiness.

Although Ahmed is not inattentive (in another sequence of documentary realism, Ahmed and a friend install a shower for Isabela), and although she loves him, Isabela one night succumbs to the attempts of the telegram deliverer to seduce her. The seduction is followed by another series of crude representations of sexual scenes.

Isabela goes to a doctor and discovers that she is pregnant. She tells Ahmed, who is pleased, but it is obvious that she does not want the child. She feels trapped in her role as housewife, concubine, and now mother.

Ahmed goes out and gets drunk (he has previously told Isabela that, as a Party member, he does not drink). Isabela tries to find him, but another leap forward shows the police identifying Ahmed's photograph as the main suspect in Isabela's murder.

Isabela pursues the now intoxicated Ahmed, who in despair wants to commit suicide by jumping into the well. Isabela tries to stop him, but he accidentally pushes her too hard; she falls to her death. Eventually, the police find Ahmed sleeping in the garden and they lead him away.

That Makavejev can fit a narrative of such complexity into a film with a running time of only a little more than an hour demonstrates the efficacy of his style. Other films have attempted this blend of mock-documentary and fictional narrative—most notably Anthony Simmons' *Four in the Morning* (1965; much admired by Makavejev and which may have served as a model) and Alain Resnais' *Mon Oncle d'Amerique* (1980; clearly inspired by Makavejev's work)—but none has so successfully mixed the blackly comic with the tragic, and none has developed such a unified theme of the conflict between life or nature and repressive rationalism and technology.

Love Affair, with its intricate cross-cutting and detailing of the inconsequential aspects of life, deals with archetypes. Each character is defined in terms of his or her technological role and emotional liberation. Isabela, the switchboard operator, is linked to office technology, but through imagery she becomes the manifestation of natural beauty, sexuality, and unbridled emotions. Her job is to make connections, but her function in life seems more closely defined by the egg in the sexologist's lecture. Ahmed, the Party member, one of the avant-garde of humanity, has repressed his emotions and for a living destroys the natural force (the rats) that threatens technological society. Although it is she who is killed in the struggle, it is his life that seems the most tragic, as he has been deprived of emotional connections.

The film reaches a sort of dialectic by pitting diverse elements against one another: the sexual artwork, the lectures, the incongruous imagery, the partially melodramatic plot. Its unusual structure is a deliberate attempt to create a new realism that challenges its audience. Some of the images are purely comic, some have a lyric beauty, and some are horrific (a mutilated corpse shown during the criminologist's lecture). One element of the plot refers to another in what Makavejev is said to call mutual irradiation. Although not fatalistic, Makavejev's universe is ruled by determinants—social, political, and, primarily, sexual—and this structural associative technique allows for the visual representation of life determined by those forces. It shows all aspects in one multifaceted montage.

Love Affair, like most of Makavejev's films, is paradoxically a celebration of humanity, of human folly, innocence, emotionalism, sexuality, and freedom. The cross-referenced scientists can analyze human behavior (relegating sexuality to clinical behaviorism and murder to dispassionate extermination), and the two protagonists are destroyed by forces completely beyond their understanding, but the images that dominate Makavejev's film are those of Isabela and Ahmed in the formative stages of their love affair.

Dušan Makavejev has been quoted as saying: "Men live their beautiful, wild lives quite close to magnificent ideas and progressive truths. Only seemingly they have no connection. This film is dedicated to those interesting undefined in-between spaces . . . [giving] the greatest value to marvelous trivialities, to senseless moments, to people who do not think." The film, in other words, is about the failure of scientific theory, political forms, and sociological forces to have an impact on the triviality of everyday human life.

The film's complex plot and interpolated images, with its Brechtian, perhaps one should say post-Godardian, estrangement techniques, deals with the problems of realistically drawn characters in an absurd universe. The versimilitude only exaggerates this sense of absurdity, yet the film remains involving on a human level. Isabela's strudel baking and her singing of the Hungarian folk song give the character a cultural background and historical tradition, but in the film she seems only an archetype. Makavejev's strength lies in his ability to create both a real sense of the humanity of his characters and the controlled posturing of the characters as symbolic representations. *Love Affair: Or, The Case of the Missing Switchboard Operator* is an audacious and personal work whose theme contradicts the impersonality of its tone, but it may be Dušan Makavejev's most passionate statement of the liberating qualities of love, human sexuality, and emotions.

Ronald Koltnow

LOVE AND ANARCHY
(FILM D'AMORE E D'ANARCHIA)

Origin: Italy
Released: 1973
Released in U.S.: 1974
Production: Romano Cardarelli for Euro International Films Productions and Steinmann-Baxter Company
Direction: Lina Wertmüller
Screenplay: Lina Wertmüller
Cinematography: Giuseppe Rotunno
Editing: Franco Fraticelli
Art direction: Enrico Job
Music: Nino Rota
MPAA rating: R
Running time: 108 minutes

> *Principal characters:*
> Tunin . . . . Giancarlo Giannini
> Salome . . . . Mariangela Melato
> Tripolina. . . . . Lina Polito
> Spatoletti . . . . Eros Pagni
> Madame Aida . . . . Pina Cei
> Donna Carmela . . . . Elena Fiore

Love and Anarchy, released in Italy in 1973, was one of director Lina Wertmüller's first major film successes. Before this film and *Mimi metallurgio ferito nell'ornore* (1972; *The Seduction of Mimi*), the Socialist filmmaker was primarily recognized for her work in radio, television, and theater; her early film *I basilischi* (1963; *The Lizards*) was critically lauded but commercially unsuccessful. Especially significant to her development as a filmmaker was her experience as Federico Fellini's assistant director on his acclaimed film *Otto e mezzo* (1963; *8½*). This apprenticeship undoubtedly left an imprint on Wertmüller films, particularly the earlier ones.

As is characteristic of Wertmüller films, *Love and Anarchy* is a bawdy satire on sex and politics, two themes dominant in contemporary Italian cinema. In this film, as in most of her work, moments of stark cruelty are juxtaposed with scenes of outrageous slapstick. Wertmüller's comedy is alternately grotesque and sensitive; she offers both thoughtful close-ups of ordinary people and monstrous, Fellini-esque caricatures.

This last emphasis in Wertmüller on vulgar distortion, particularly of female anatomy and of women's role in society, has provoked much controversy among feminist film critics, who have frequently labeled Wertmüller a misogynist and a traitor to her own sex. In her own defense, Wertmüller, a professed feminist, states simply that the conservative bourgeois female audience (itself chauvinistic) has misjudged her. Furthermore, she contends that as a filmmaker, despite her radical political leanings, it is not her role to preach feminism or revolution so much as to provoke independent thought and to raise pertinent social questions. Controversy underscores every Wertmüller film, each of them, like *Love and Anarchy*, a dialectic on man and his mores.

Love and Anarchy opens with a brilliant montage of aging photographs of Benito Mussolini, which collectively form a visual overture to the body of the film. As the photographs snap by, they are accompanied by incessant drumming and by old recordings of Mussolini haranguing crowds. Together, the photos, drums, speeches, and the crowds' cheers serve to evoke the bombastic posturing of the Italian dictator as well as to jibe at the glittering façade of Fascism. After a final menacing crescendo of close-ups, which include Mussolini's helmet, his clenched fist, and his curled lip, the photo collage and the drums abruptly cease. For a brief moment there is dead silence as the screen goes dark and the scene changes dramatically.

The next scene opens on an idyllic, 1930's Italian countryside, a pastoral setting in which birds twitter as a delicate morning mist rises above the river. The contrast between this moment and the previous one is stunning, highlighting the difference between sanity and madness, between man's unnatural and natural states. Here, in man's honest element, the audience is introduced to the film's protagonist, a naïve bumpkin named Tunin (Giancarlo Giannini). The next sequence of events is brief and reveals Wertmüller's fine sense of dramatic economy. Tunin is feeding the chickens when he is approached by a dear old friend, an ardent anarchist on a mission to assassinate Mussolini. Almost wordlessly the anarchist entrusts his suitcase to Tunin and departs. A few moments later, gunshots shatter the stillness of the peaceful scene and the camera reveals the dead anarchist, who has been martyred by the Fascist police and left spread-eagle, Christ-like, in the branches of a tree on the riverbank. The camera's attention next shifts to a crowd of onlookers and then to a close-up of Tunin that becomes a fond tribute to actor Giannini and is repeated in subsequent Wertmüller films starring this same actor. Immense surprise, then pain, and, finally, anger register on Tunin's face. At last he turns and shuffles off in a long-shot too reminiscent of Charles Chaplin's "little fellow" to be mere coincidence.

The next scene establishes Tunin in Rome. By way of information gleaned from the dead anarchist's suitcase, he has himself become involved in the plot to kill Mussolini and has volunteered to substitute for his friend as the assassin. His Roman contact is Salome (Mariangela Melato), a prostitute in a high-class bordello and one of Wertmüller's better developed female characters. Actress Melato, in this film a delicate blonde often filmed in soft focus, adds a splendid note of irony to the role, her gutter-mouthed brawling contrasting nicely to the virginal aura of a Renaissance Madonna that she creates. Ethereal beauty, intelligence, and wit thus often lift the character above the cliché-ridden image of the prostitute and transform her into a sensitive, fragile human being.

Also appealing in the film is the sharp contrast drawn between Salome and Tunin: she willowy, elegantly groomed, savvy, and patrician; he stubby, dirty, simpleminded, and plebeian—his face covered by enormous freckles and his head topped by a haircut apparently achieved with a dull paring knife. That Wertmüller herself delights in the natural incongruity of this Giannini-Melato pairing is testified by the number of her films in which the two actors have appeared together.

In their initial encounter, Salome tells Tunin the tragic events which have made her an anarchist, and then she introduces him to life in the bordello. The scenes in the brothel are generally considered to be those which are the most Felliniesque. In one scene reminiscent of Fellini's *Roma* (1972), a troop of scantily clad prostitutes descends on prospective clients; they roll their breasts at the camera and bawl and caper suggestively. In another, more moving scene, a bug-eyed Tunin, sexually inexperienced and over-whelmed by the exhibitionism around him, uneasily dines at a long table of bickering ladies of the night while desperately trying to appear unaffected.

In this poignant scene, similarities between Wertmüller and Fellini fade to superficialities. Sex and nudity in Wertmüller, though perhaps as explicit as in Fellini, are never as voyeuristic. Unlike Fellini, Wertmüller never uses the camera as voyeur, is never sly or insinuating. Instead, in her films an element of pathos often underscores even the bawdiest scene. For example, the dinner scene described above concludes when a still-young yet world-weary prostitute plays her guitar and sings a tender, mournful love ballad for the melancholy assemblage of those living in the brothel. This melody becomes part of the film's leitmotif and has been chosen with sensitivity, as are the scores of all of Wertmüller's films.

As the film continues, it is learned that Tunin must shoot Mussolini at an upcoming public rally. Useful details of the rally are to be gathered for him by Salome from one of her customers, Spatoletti (Eros Pagni), an important Mussolini henchman. In a comical sequence, Salome, Tunin, and another prostitute, Tripolina (Lina Polito), accompany the loud and loquacious Spatoletti on a wild motorcycle ride to a rustic country inn. Once there, Salome seduces Spatoletti in order to gain information, leaving Tripolina and Tunin together.

In a swift series of tender vignettes, a love bond is established between Tunin and Tripolina. The two characters have much in common, for they belong to life's downtrodden masses. Both are naïve, separate from society, and even physically small and disadvantaged. Wertmüller loves to emphasize the smallness of her heroes, if only to underscore their alienation and in-significance. In several Chaplinesque scenes, she shoots Tunin from an incredibly long, low angle posed against an enormous, white monolithic, Fascist monument in order to emphasize his slight stature and anonymity. The political message seems clear enough: The proletariat is small, helpless, and nameless; the mechanism of government is enormous, overwhelming, and indifferent.

The image of Spatoletti also serves to reinforce the discrepancy between the little man and big government. Furthermore, the character is a fine example of Wertmüller's gift for the grotesque: a larger-than-life caricature of Italy's most infamous dictator. His macho posturing, bullish insensitivity, and obscene vulgarity furnish a darkly humorous commentary on the falsity and injustice that was Fascism.

With the Fascist rally approaching, Tunin reaches a surprising decision. He will devote what might be his last days of life to love. Striking a bargain with the bordello's madam, he acquires Tripolina's exclusive services, and together the couple spends two idyllic days together. On the last night Tunin extracts a promise from Tripolina and Salome to wake him early the next morning for the attempted assassination. Instead of waking him, however, the two women agree to let him oversleep, miss the rally, and thus be spared from danger. When Tunin awakes late, he goes berserk and attacks the two women. When the police arrive for a routine inspection of the brothel, he mistakes them for officers coming to arrest him and starts shooting. After a slapstick chase, comic in structure but grim in outcome, Tunin is arrested and jailed. In a brisk sequence he is interrogated and tortured and then bru-tally murdered, as the sound track cynically blares the film's mournful love theme.

The film's rapid-fire conclusion, its combination of low-comedy high jinks and tragic expediency summarize the essence of Wertmüller's best works. Like Fellini and like many Italian directors of her time, Wertmüller sees cinema as a means to satirize modern man and his faulty mores. Like other political filmmakers, she perceives life and love as inextricably caught up in politics. She delights in leveling the pompous authority figures of high gov-ernment at the same time that she exults the little man, if not for his ade-quacy, then at least for his humanity. Her humor plays with life's incongru-ities, pitting man against government and man against woman.

Although Lina Wertmüller insists that she is a feminist, her films do not support her claim. Women in her films, with rare exception, are depicted as unlovable, petty, and bovine. Whether they are ineffectual by natural proclivity or because society has rendered them so is never made plain, since the female characters remain underdeveloped. *Love and Anarchy*, like other Wertmüller films, reveals the director's marked preference for male protagonists, closely modeled after Tunin. Only the male character in

Wertmüller is carefully portrayed, only his thoughts are explored. Only the male confronts grave dilemmas, feels deep emotions, and therefore achieves true humanity.

Love and Anarchy opened in the United States in 1974, and it achieved considerable success for its abrasive wit and exuberant vitality. Although it is not considered to be a film of the same stature as Wertmüller's later masterpiece *Pasqualino settebellezze* (1976; *Seven Beauties*), *Love and Anarchy* established the director as a major film talent and opened the area of commercial world cinema to an Italian woman.

Constance Markey

THE LOVERS
(LES AMANTS)

Origin: France
Released: 1958
Released in U.S.: 1959
Production: Nouvelles Éditions de Films
Direction: Louis Malle
Assistant direction: Louis Cavalier and François Leterrier
Screenplay: Louis Malle and Louise de Vilmorin; based on *Point de lendemain*, by Dominique Vivant
Cinematography: Henri Decaë
Editing: Léonide Azar
Production design: Irenée Leriche
Art direction: Bernard Evein and Jacques Saulnier; set decoration, George Houssaye
Makeup: Giselle Jacquin
Costume design: Renée Pellemoine
Sound: Pierre Bertrand
Music: Johannes Brahms
Running time: 90 minutes

> *Principal characters:*
> Jeanne Tournier . . . . Jeanne Moreau
> Henri Tournier. . . . . Alain Cuny
> Bernard Dubois-Lambert. . . . . Jean-Marc Bory
> Maggy Thiébaut-Leroy . . . . Judith Magre
> Raoul Florès . . . . José-Luis Villalonga

Louis Malle's career is primarily noteworthy for its eclecticism; the difficulty of including his diverse projects under a glib thematic umbrella has, ironically, led to a certain critical neglect of his far-ranging oeuvre. Malle's films, whether emulating the hard-boiled veneer of American *film noir* in *Ascenseur pour l'echafaud* (1958; *Frantic*) or examining incest with peculiarly Gallic whimsy in *Le Souffle au cœur* (1971; *Murmur of the Heart*), combine a pervasive lyricism with a gentle irony. It often seems that the attempt to assume a pose of ironic detachment in films such as *Lacombe, Lucien* (1974) or *Atlantic City* (1981) is actually an elaborate ruse meant to offset a surge of overweening sentimentality. Malle's worst films, in fact, tend toward undiluted treacle.

The Lovers, Malle's first popular and critical success, is remembered for reasons that are as much sociological as aesthetic. Banned in many towns in rural France, the film became the focus of a landmark censorship battle that culminated in a historic Supreme Court decision. The manager of the Ohio cinema that was featuring *The Lovers* was eventually cleared of obscenity charges after Justice William Brennan ruled that material dealing with sexual matters could not be deemed obscene if it possessed "literary . . . social or scientific importance." Although the erotic sequences in *The Lovers* seem tame, even laughable, by contemporary standards, the unprecedented explicitness of its final reel made it a *cause célèbre* in 1958.

Despite its salacious reputation, *The Lovers* is primarily devoted to the concerns of the characteristically French comedy of manners. The film opens with an exchange of bons mots at a Parisian polo match, as Jeanne Tournier (Jeanne Moreau) and her childhood friend Maggy Thiébaut-Leroy (Judith Magre) assess the charms of Raoul Florès (José-Luis Villalonga), a particularly gifted and handsome polo player. Jeanne is bored with her marriage to the lackluster provincial newspaper editor, Henri Tournier (Alain Cuny), and, with the encouragement of her constant confidante, Maggy, she initiates a rather frivolous offscreen liaison with Raoul.

The scene shifts to the more prosaic surroundings of Henri Tournier's bourgeois manor. Jeanne and Henri's indifference to each other is conveyed in a series of blasé reaction shots, and Henri's gruff, indifferent manner betrays little interest in his wife's obsession with the Parisian social whirl. In the following sequence, Henri chances upon a newspaper photograph of Maggy and Raoul taken at the polo match, and Jeanne cannot resist an audacious expression of admiration for Raoul's gallantry and good looks. Nevertheless, she remains convinced that her husband does not have the slightest suspicion of her infidelity. She even makes a perfunctory visit to her husband's office, slyly checking to see if any change in his placid demeanor can be ascertained. When this proves impossible, she experiences a feeling of tremendous liberation and is determined to visit Paris often in order to escape the humdrum existence endemic to the provinces.

Freed from the yoke of country life and Henri's rather malevolent indifference, Jeanne visits Maggy in Paris. Maggy encourages Jeanne to continue her amorous interludes with Raoul, since she claims that he is madly infatuated with her. When Jeanne finally has a rendezvous with Raoul, he passionately confesses his love for her. Jeanne sheepishly admits her own emotions, although her avowal seems to lack commitment. These heartfelt exchanges are slightly ludicrous. Although Jeanne yearns for a grand passion, she seems merely pleased by Raoul's playboy aura and affluence. Above all, the allure of a marital "double life" entrances Jeanne and remains the constant inspiration for her frequent sojourns to Paris.

Yet when Jeanne returns home after this rapturous encounter with Raoul, the previously nonchalant Henri has become more irritable. Henri believes that Jeanne is mocking him with her incessant forays to Paris and demands an explanation for her weekly departures. When Jeanne insists that she must leave again for a dinner party that Maggy has arranged for Raoul in Paris, Henri insists that a similar dinner party be held at their country estate. Jeanne agrees to this suggestion with reluctance, since it is clear that her husband has become increasingly aware of the extent of her relationship with Raoul. A trip to Paris is, however, necessitated by the need to inform Raoul of this impromptu social event.

On her way back to the country and to the burden of this imminent, profoundly embarrassing social event, Jeanne's car breaks down: A recalcitrant motor is the culprit. She enlists help from Bernard Dubois-Lambert (Jean-Marc Bory), a passing motorist. After it becomes evident that her engine cannot be resuscitated, Jeanne accepts a ride with Bernard. Jeanne regales him with impertinent stories concerning her oafish husband, and a meticulously edited series of close-ups establish the fact that their congenial exchange of glances are leading to a special rapport.

As Jeanne and Bernard arrive at her estate, the camera pans slowly to a frontal view of the palatial manor, gradually revealing the clearly nervous visages of Maggy, Raoul, and Henri.

After an awkward series of introductions, the guests finally settle down to one of the most strained dinner parties in film history. All the guests try their best to encourage civilized banter: The architecture of the Avenue Foch, Raoul's adventures, and the national characteristics of Germans, Russians, and Spaniards are all part of a hilarious subterfuge in which the guests vainly attempt to avoid any scandalous or controversial subject matter. This sequence is an excellent example of Malle's cinematic adroitness; a succession of close-ups and two-shots reveal the constricted body language of all the participants. At one point, Maggy's discomfort with the proceedings leads her to cover her head with her napkin, while a subsequent shot reveals one of Henri's most unrestrained grimaces. The tone of good-natured social hypocrisy that prevails in this sequence is worthy of Molière or Beaumarchais. Toward the end of this exquisitely choreographed verbal Ping-Pong match, Maggy compares love to a sporting event, and the carefully modulated dinner-table chitchat of this sequence establishes the truth of this aphorism with finesse.

After another series of fatuous pleasantries are exchanged in Henri's library, the guests finally prepare for bed. Raoul implores Jeanne to stay with him, once more playing the role of the earnest suitor.

Ensconced within her bedroom, Jeanne is unable to sleep. Riled by thoughts about her desolate marriage and her unfulfilling affair with Raoul, she descends the stairs to the forbidding environs of Henri's library. She is astonished to discover Bernard lurking outside the doorway but proceeds to pour herself a whiskey.

At this juncture, *The Lovers* abruptly changes tone and moves from a detached examination of social mores to a frenzied lyricism that unabashedly exalts the growing passion uniting Jeanne and Bernard. The restrained, analytical editing that has dominated most of the film gives way to sweeping, lush camera movements that capture the mounting ecstasy of this unexpected amorous eruption. This climactic celebration of sensual pleasure evolves gradually. After Jeanne and Bernard intuitively begin to realize the extent of their amorous bond, the claustrophobic cinematic space of the manor house (a metaphorical allusion to Henri's bourgeois smugness) is replaced by the glistening, even resplendent surface (enhanced by Henri Decaë's superb cinematography) of the lake adjacent to the manor. Perhaps since Malle served his apprenticeship with Jacques-Yves Cousteau on *Le Monde du silence* (1956; *The Silent World*), he proved extremely adept with aquatic settings. It is this pristine locale that serves as the site for Jeanne and Bernard's first protracted session of lovemaking. After their first halting union on a rowboat, they return to the house with some trepidation. As a Johannes Brahms sextet swells mellifluously on the sound track, their lovemaking continues in Jeanne's bathtub and finally reaches its apex within the confines of her boudoir.

Jeanne's belated rediscovery of sexual passion with Bernard leads her to reassess her prospects for future happiness amid the debris of her failed marriage. Should she renounce her newfound love for Bernard for the sake of her husband and child, or should she follow her daring instincts and abandon her life of ennui for a more adventurous future? Ultimately, she chooses the latter course and drives off with Bernard, facing an ambiguous, but hopefully not a dull, future.

In retrospect, *The Lovers* can be viewed as a witty rendering of the traditionally French tension between city and country. Jeanne Moreau's brilliant performance as a more buoyant incarnation of Emma Bovary, and Louis Malle and Louise de Vilmorin's graceful and incisive dialogue transform a hackneyed premise into a memorable, albeit a slight, film. Moreau's sporadic voice-over commentary, in the form of concise internal monologues that reveal the progress of her sentimental journey, help the audience to identify with a protagonist who would have been condemned by earlier generations. Despite its weaknesses, *The Lovers* represents the great strides filmmakers have made as they attempt to find a cinematic language supple and versatile enough to depict the nuances of sexual experience.

Richard Porton

LOVES OF A BLONDE
(LÁSKY JEDNÉ PLAVOVLÁSKY)

Origin: Czechoslovakia
Released: 1965
Released in U.S.: 1966
Production: Barrandov Film Studios
Direction: Miloš Forman
Assistant direction: Ivan Passer
Screenplay: Miloš Forman, Jaroslav Papoušek, Ivan Passer, and Václav Šašek
Cinematography: Miroslav Ondříček
Assistant cinematography: Ladislav Chroust
Editing: Miroslav Hájek
Art direction: Karel Černý
Sound: Adolph Böhm
Music: Evžen Illín
Running time: 88 minutes
Also known as: A Blonde's Love

Principal characters:

Andula	Hana Brcjova
Milda	Vladimír Pucholt
Vacovský	Vladimír Menšík
Maňas	Ivan Kheil
Burda	Jiří Hrubý
Milda's mother	Milada Ježková
Milda's father	Josef Šebánek
Marie	Marie Salačová
Jana	Jana Nováková
Jaruška	Jana Crkalová
Zdena	Zdeňka Lorencová
Girl with guitar	Táňa Zelinková
Colonel	Jan Vostrčil
Pokorný	Josef Kolb
Tonda	Antonín Blažejovský
Educator	M. Zedníčková

As one of the many films which called the attention of the world to the film renaissance in Czechoslovakia during the 1960's, *Loves of a Blonde* opened the New York Film Festival in Philharmonic Hall on September 12, 1966. The event, celebrated by a reception that followed at the Promenade of the New York State Theatre, augured well for the series of films to follow and for the reputation that Czechoslovakian films were to earn during that eventful decade. Chosen by *The New York Times* as one of the ten best films of that year, *Loves of a Blonde* appeared at a time when its studios, Barrandov Films, would win the New York Film Critics Circle Award for Best Foreign-Language Film for *Obchod na korze* (1965; *The Shop on Main Street*, honored with an Academy Award the previous year). Still a third Czechoslovakian film from the same studios, *Ostře sledované vlaky* (1966; *Closely Watched Trains*), won the Academy Award in 1967, completing a trio of acclaimed films from an Eastern bloc country. All three films catapulted their directors—Miloš Forman, the team of Ján Kadár and Elmar Klos, and Jiří Menzel, respectively—into the spotlight of the film world.

In addition to its place in the Czechoslovakian film renaissance, *Loves of a Blonde* is important in the early career of Forman, who later emigrated to the West, where his directorial reputation was enhanced with such films as *One Flew over the Cuckoo's Nest* (1975) and *Hair* (1979). In an article in *Saturday Review* (December 23, 1967), Forman described himself as one of fifteen eager, self-confident new graduates at the Film Faculty of the Academy of Music Art (FAMU) in Prague, graduates who made their first full-length films between 1962 and 1965, when ideological barriers were lifted and a new wave of filmmaking was underway. The new wave soon came under pressure, this time commercial rather than ideological, and some of its members, including himself, dispersed to American and other western locations. In Paris in the summer of 1968, when the Russians invaded his country, Forman found his way eventually to New York. His native film career was a brief one, consisting of only two other full-length films (*Black Peter*, 1964, and *The Fireman's Ball*, 1967) and two shorter films (*Audition/Talent Competition/Competition*, 1963, and *If There Were No Music*, 1963).

Loves of a Blonde achieves its importance from the unforgettability of its treatment of adolescent sexuality, an experience laced with painfully romantic feeling that holds firm even when its victim, a female shoe factory worker, faces the disillusioning reality of having been deceived by a working-class Don Juan of sorts. If the passion for romance is at its grandest in Emma Bovary and Anna Karenina, it could hardly be smaller and duller than in the heroine of this film, Andula (Hana Brcjova). Yet the director's shrewd eye for detail and his genius for transmuting banalities into poignantly humorous, sometimes bittersweet, moments which illuminate trivial details, remind the viewer of Anton Chekhov's definition of art (spoken by Trigorin in *The Seagull*, 1896) as moonlight shining on bits of broken glass.

The story of the film is simple, in itself banal. To alleviate the boredom of his female employees and thereby increase productivity, the foreman of a shoe factory arranges a dance to which nearby military reservists have been invited. The girls for the most part are plain, and the soldiers, much to the disappointment of the younger girls, are middle-aged and unromantic. The party scene gradually focuses on three girls and their partners for the evening. This focus in turn narrows to Andula and Milda (Vladimír Pucholt). Andula's local admirer, Tonda (Antonín Blažejovský), like the visiting soldiers, does not hold Andula's attention. She is attracted, instead, to the young piano player, Milda, with whom she enjoys a liaison later that evening. Milda returns to his home in Prague. The next weekend, Andula surprises his parents by arriving at their home while he is off on another engagement. When he returns, a long scene follows in which the parents attempt to keep him from Andula by forcing him to sleep with them, while Andula overhears the goings-on through a door in the adjoining room. She leaves the following day for her small factory town and for the resumption of life among the women at the factory, hiding her disillusionment by recounting her "romantic adventure" to a friend. Like the Chekhovian plot in which events that appear to change the lives of the characters in the end do not, Forman's plot ends with the resumption of the normal pattern of life.

What transforms this story into something beyond the banalities are those poignant insights that catch the viewer off guard, as in the scene in which Milda lures Andula by pretending to read her palm and the scar on her hand becomes visible, the result of a suicide attempt when her parents were divorced. A routine seduction scene is suddenly pierced by a momentary flash of pain. A similar transformation of the ordinary occurs when, during the dance, a wedding ring slips from the hand of one of the soldiers and the camera follows the journey of the ring, humorously and embarrassingly spotlighting its middle-aged wearer. Earlier, this same irony is experienced at the station as the girls' prospects for romance are dimmed when the military guests turn out to be most unromantic.

The big scene of the film is the long evening in the Prague home of Milda's parents, who become an extension of the adult world represented by the soldiers. They have their boredom and frustrations from which they escape temporarily by watching television and engaging in domestic wrangling. Andula's arrival provides them with more opportunity for venting their frustration with their son. She listens to their rationalized explanations of their son's behavior. When he finally arrives home from another evening of piano playing, he becomes the target of his parents' tirades. He is forced to sleep between them in bed and is lectured continuously. He responds by jumping up and down, shouting about his innocence and his lack of interest in Andula. The three-way shouting match goes on into the night, in a scene whose hilarity is broken only by the picture of Andula on the other side of the door, listening. As in the earlier seduction scene with Andula in which Milda kept running to the window to shut out the light, so in this scene of the same kind of bumbling activity, he attempts to justify himself. The hilarity of the wrangling, physical and verbal, never quite reaches farcical proportions, since it is too close to actuality and too strongly tinged with misunderstandings that are never clarified. Beyond the conflict caused by the generation gap and by the sexual rites of passage of Andula is the ever deepening sense of the sad and lonely Andula, the callow and opportunistic Milda, and the bored and frustrated parents. It is on this note that Andula returns to her factory milieu to fabricate a story of a romantic weekend that never was. Her dream is still a dream.

As a shrewd observer of the human comedy, Forman does not exploit individual or social foibles cheaply nor does he draw caricatures from those foibles. In a conventional comedy it is the humor that undercuts the potential seriousness of tragedy. In this film, however, it is the pain or the embarrassment that undercuts the humor. There is nothing here like the farcical stationmaster of *Closely Watched Trains*, who literally stamps the derriere of his latest sexual conquest, or like the farcical maneuvers of the young man in that film during his first sexual experience.

Much of the humor and poignancy of the film stems from the director's choice of nonprofessionals for all but the leading roles. Even the mother and father had never played in a film before, and the factory girls and soldiers were recruited from factories and military posts. In fact, the basic premise of the story—a foreman's arranging of a dance for his bored female employees—derives from an actual event. The plot does not depend on the conventional contrivances of comedy, nor are the characters puppets for their director to manipulate. All is as unself-conscious as life itself and, indeed, as inconclusive.

There is something in the Eastern European experience caught by writers such as Chekhov, Jaroslav Hašek, and Karel Čapek, to mention only a few, that has evaded Western writers: It is that illumination of a moment in which a deep-seated and universal truth is captured in the trivial object or in a brief moment; it is that truth felt but not articulated verbally by either the character or the viewer. Andula, Milda, and Milda's parents become everymen and everywomen of a sort.

There is in Forman's art the art of Nikolai Gogol, in one of whose stories a nose departs from its owner and takes on a life of its own. In *Loves of a Blonde*, the scar on Andula's wrist and the rolling wedding ring of the soldier are stories that need not be told but are there. The catalyst for these epiphanies or revelations is usually a celebration: a birthday party or a wedding. In this film, it is a dance; in *The Fireman's Ball*, it is a raffle, a beauty contest, and the honoring of an old fireman, all wrapped into one. These situations provide the opportunity for everything that can go wrong to do so. The dream gone wrong or the disparity between the dream and waking states is the stuff of life, and the clinging to the dream in the face of reality is the stuff of Forman's art.

Reviewing the film in *The Film Quarterly* (Fall, 1967), Claire Clouzot calls attention to an incident omitted in the European release of the film but added in American showings. It involves Milda's having been tricked by one of his female friends into visiting her, only to discover that he has intruded on a couple in bed. Too much like the bed-hopping games that are such an integral part of the highly artificial comedy of manners, the scene disrupts the natural rhythm of the remainder of the film and violates the realism so successfully realized by Forman in his use of characters, actors, and situations from actual life.

Not to be overlooked in this discussion is the use of black and white rather than color. The black and white complements the drabness of the lives of the factory girls, soldiers, Milda, and his parents. In addition, the inconclusiveness of the story of the film is handled ingeniously by both director and photographer as they studiously avoid any glance, expression, or movement of a decisive nature. The momentary hesitation of a character, the obliqueness realized by a shot of a wedding ring or a scar, and the final indefiniteness of Andula's unresolved romantic pain constitute the texture of the film. There is no moralizing or sociopolitical posturing, much as some reviewers might see it as a film about the drabness of life in a Socialist society. Except in superficial ways, the drabness is no different from that experienced by Chekhov's nineteenth century Russian gentry or John Cheever's twentieth century middle-class suburbanites. Adolescents and adults, males and females, romantics and cynics, actors and audiences—all partake of Forman's human comedy of life.

Susan Rusinko

THE LOWER DEPTHS
(LES BAS-FONDS)

Origin: France
Released: 1936
Released in U.S.: 1937
Production: Alexandre Kamenka for Albatros Films
Direction: Jean Renoir
Screenplay: Eugène Zamyatin, Jacques Companeez, Charles Spaak (adaptation), and Jean Renoir (adaptation); based on the play by Maxim Gorky
Cinematography: Jean Bachelet
Editing: Marguerite Renoir
Art direction: Alexandre Kamenka
Music: Jean Wiener and Roger Désormièrs
Running time: 90 minutes
Also known as: The Underworld

Principal characters:
Baron	Louis Jouvet
Pepel	Jean Gabin
Vasilissa	Suzy Prim
Kostylev	Vladimir Sokoloff
Natacha	Junie Astor
Felix	Léon Larive
Police inspector	André Gabriello
Luka	René Génin
Nastia	Jany Holt
Actor	Robert Le Vigan
Aliosha	Maurice Baquet

Producer Alexandre Kamenka suggested that Jean Renoir make *The Lower Depths*, from the 1902 play by Russian author Maxim Gorky because the Utopian yearnings of prerevolutionary Russia were very much in tune with the social climate of France in 1936. Jacques Companeez and Eugène Zamyatin adapted the play and sent the script to Gorky, who approved it but died before seeing the final version, which was a reworking by Charles Spaak and Renoir. According to the prologue of the print owned by the Museum of Modern Art in New York City, Gorky felt that the screenplay "retained the essential spirit of the play." At the film's premiere, in December, 1936, Renoir said, "I have not tried to make a Russian film; I have tried to make a human drama, a drama of the degradation of a class, a drama of the loss of human dignity." Renoir did, however, use theatrical conventions in his film, raising and lowering a filmic curtain upon many of the scenes. The characters speak French, use rubles and kopecks, have Russian names, wear modern dress, and live within or outside some great European city, but their attitudes and attributes are ageless and universal rather than local.

Although *The Lower Depths* is not ranked among the greatest of Renoir's films—perhaps because of the theatricality of some of the acting rather than because a French director worked on a Russian play—it is nevertheless a strong, affecting and effective motion picture. The story, by itself, is not worth recounting, except as it introduces the crucial *dramatis personae*: The Baron (Louis Jouvet), who is a discredited, bankrupt officer, meets Pepel (Jean Gabin), a thief, the night before the Baron's furniture is to be impounded by the marshals. The Baron and Pepel form a strong bond, and Pepel invites the Baron to the doss house where he lives, on the outskirts of town. The lodging is run by Kostylev (Vladimir Sokoloff), a hypocritical old fence, and his mistress, Vasilissa (Suzy Prim), who is having an affair with Pepel. Pepel is in love with Vasilissa's younger sister Natacha (Junie Astor), who is attracted to him but loathes his profession. Kostylev and Vasilissa try to marry Natacha off to a venal, fat police inspector (André Gabriello) so that he will not interfere with their business, but Pepel intervenes and kills Kostylev. The other residents protect Pepel, telling the police that they helped murder Kostylev. Pepel goes to prison for a short time, says goodbye to the Baron, and then, taking Natacha by the hand, he departs.

The other *habitués* of the house include an alcoholic actor (Robert Le Vigan) who dreams of recuperating in a luxurious hospital and who recites Hamlet's soliloquy before hanging himself at the end of the film; Nastia (Jany Holt), a prostitute who reads romances and incorporates the stories into her own history; Aliosha (Maurice Baquet), an acrobatic accordion player; Luka (René Génin), the old philosopher who tries to comfort the homeless wretches; and a nameless group who play cards and welcome the Baron to their game.

The Lower Depths works on two levels: as a dissection of social classes and as a series of character studies. With the exception of Pepel and the Baron, and to a lesser degree, Vasilissa, these individuals are not particularly interesting. They are caricatures, simply drawn and broadly acted—philosophical drunk, wistful waif, and the like. They often utter the clichés of their class or character-types. Pepel and the Baron are played by the famous French film actors, Jean Gabin and Louis Jouvet, respectively, who lend more depth to these leads than is accorded the other figures. Suzy Prim plays Vasilissa and is granted a few moments of pathos when talking to Pepel, who is disgusted with her and with all that she represents and tired of her clinging to him. She manages to create a pitiable and comprehensible woman who is also an object of revulsion.

Renoir's great accomplishment in *The Lower Depths* is not to be found in the repetitive sociopolitical mumbo jumbo of the lodgers, nor should the film be seen as an attempt to elicit pity for the miserable dispossessed. Rather, the strength of the film lies in its depiction of the friendship between the dishonored Baron and the disaffected Pepel. Full of the familiar Jean Gabin charm, ennui, and stoicism, Pepel meets the equally charming, bored, and resigned Baron the night that he attempts to rob the Baron's house. They are almost peers, but when the Baron suggests that Pepel join him for a late dinner, Pepel demurs because he knows his place. "We'll pretend you stole the food," the Baron tells him, and Pepel responds, "That's how I like it." "Call me partner," the Baron replies with evident sincerity. They are friends as they play cards till dawn, with the Baron in his shirt-sleeves and Pepel in the Baron's robe. The stakes are "Your share of paradise," as Pepel says when he has won the final game. They divide the last cigarette, and Pepel accepts the Baron's cigarette case but refuses the robe on the grounds that he would be laughed at back at the doss house. Now that his possessions are no longer his, the Baron is very generous. He offers the robber anything in the place, and Pepel chooses a bronze equestrian statue.

The Baron likes Pepel's style; Pepel is a thief, but he has pride. He takes what comes his way, whether it is the life of a housebreaker existing on the fringes of society or the Baron's dinner and presents. Pepel desires nothing from the Baron but what he can steal and a friendship based not on class similarity but on an affinity of outlook and mutual acceptance. Pepel has nothing the Baron wants but his rooming quarters, the last outpost of the spiritually disenfranchised.

The statue that Pepel takes, however, is a two-edged sword. As soon as he leaves the Baron, Pepel is arrested. Natacha visits him, bringing gifts which Pepel accepts, protesting that he would rather have a kind word from her. She believes that he stole the cigarette case and the bronze; he is condemned in her eyes by his history and his environment. The Baron testifies to the captain of the jail that he gave Pepel the items and, in an ironic ceremony, Pepel is released. The Baron's house is empty, but the captain treats him with the old deference, clicking his heels and bowing.

Another scene delineating the relationship between Pepel and the Baron shows them lounging on the grass on a hot summer day. The Baron chews a blade of grass and contemplates a snail crawling on his hand. In one of the finest speeches designed to reveal character ever written for a film, he describes the outward appearance of his former life, although he says that he cannot comprehend its inner significance: "When I think of my life, it seems to me I have never done anything but change costume." He describes the various outfits associated with his identify as a student or bridegroom or a government official and how the uniforms, and implicitly those identities, have become increasingly threadbare. He concludes that what he is wearing seems to be part of a dream. This "dream" (that is, the life of social roles) is not as important or as substantial as the Baron's dignity and human worth.

Louis Jouvet employs a unique walk to characterize the Baron: He tilts and lurches, throwing his torso out and bowing his knees, looking rather like a pregnant ostrich. As an actor, Jouvet always had a rueful quality. From *La Kermesse héroique* (1935; *Carnival in Flanders*) to *Quai des Orfèvres* (1947; *Jenny Lamour*), he developed a character that led him to be typecast as a cynical, worldly, and for the most part, humane gentleman. *The Lower Depths* uses Jouvet's attributes to their best effect and allows the Baron to be a delightful skeptic—bemused, civil, and considerate.

Pepel is a recognizable figure, drawn from the characters that Gabin played in *Pépé le Moko* (1937), *Quai des brumes* (1938; *Port of Shadows*), and *Le Jour se lève* (1939; *Daybreak*). Cursed from birth as the son of a jailbird/thief, Pepel has lived out his destiny but longs to reform. "Stop dreaming . . . what does it get you?" he tells Vasilissa, but he dreams of a "kind word" and a new start with Natacha. Pepel grabs Kostylev by the throat and rants at him in a manner precursive of his attack on Jules Berry in *Le Jour se lève*, but this is a gentler Gabin, one who prefigures his Maréchal in Renoir's next film, *La Grande Illusion* (1937). There has been considerable speculation that once Gabin became popular enough to force the issue, he insisted that his scripts include a scene in which he gives vent to enormous anger, kills someone, or commits suicide. He is refused only the latter option in *The Lower Depths*. His screen *persona* changed after the war and softened to the point that in *Un Singe en hiver* (1962; *A Monkey in Winter*), a grizzled, white-haired Gabin played a kindly ex-drunk opposite Jean-Paul Belmondo, whom he called his logical successor.

There is one scene in *The Lower Depths* which exists as a kind of show piece for Gabin's talent. Speaking to his jailer—and into the camera to the viewer in a form that prefigured the *cinéma vérité* of the latter New Wave French films—Pepel explains why he should be released. He would prefer to stay in jail in order to avoid bad company, he says, but if he is let out, it will prove to Natacha that he is not a bad person. Gabin's mobile face and ingratiating smile, his proud attitude of asking without begging, and his gestures are subtly yet forcefully illustrated. The economy of his style and the charm he evinced while playing an outcast are examples of an ability that subsequent screen performers have seldom demonstrated.

Other roles suffer by the comparison. Junie Astor's makeup gives her face too sharp an appearance, making Natacha look peevish. Very rarely does she hint at the soft, loving girl beneath the misused, perplexed drudge. Vladimir Sokoloff's hammy portrayal of Kostylev is all smiles and self-pity. He is Fagin and Uriah Heep combined in one ratty, dirty little hypocrite. Similarly, Robert Le Vigan as the Actor and René Génin as Luka have an annoying tendency to overact in parts that are too obviously written. André

Gabriello as the inspector provides a neatly done portrayal of an anxious romantic, too fat and sweaty to court Natacha without a go-between, too overbearing to succeed. Jany Holt, as Nastia, conveys the character's loneliness and her longing for a romance that goes beyond commerce. Léon Larive as Felix, the Baron's almost obsequious servant, is cast from the same mold as the Hollywood butler of the same period, usually portrayed by Robert Grieg, rotund, proud, and sure of himself in a world that threatens to shift from under his feet.

Renoir's restlessly tracking and panning camera achieves its task of creating a credible milieu for the cast. In showing the shelter, the camera tracks through the large room, past the men's pallets, the broken furniture, introducing the viewer, not to the guests, but to the ambience of despair and decay which remind those inhabitants constantly of exactly how low the lower depths are.

The doss house is a social arena as rigidly stratified as the arena that the Baron leaves. Upstairs are the bosses, Kostylev and Vasilissa; halfway down the stairs in a room by himself is Pepel, who has an occupation, albeit a dubious one; below him are the dormitory residents who live on air, liquor, talk, and cards. In accepting his lot with the regulars, the Baron has made what he thinks is his last compromise with life. He stops there and vegetates. He retains the niceties of his class—a suit and tie, exchanging chitchat with Nastia and philosphizing with Pepel—but he is like Boieldieu in *La Grande Illusion* seen from another angle. He knows that his class is doomed; he is still gallant and suave, but dispirited.

The Lower Depths is a curious film, beautifully shot in rich chiaroscuro, and poignantly observant. It delineates characters who seem to draw more life from the actors than from Gorky's words. Their theatrical origins are evident. The interpretation of their theatricality within the drama is a notable achievement of Renoir's actors.

Judith M. Kass

LUCÍA

Origin: Cuba
Released: 1968
Released in U.S.: 1974
Production: Raúl Canosa for Instituto Cubano del Arte e Industria
  Cinematográficos
Direction: Humberto Solás
Screenplay: Humberto Solás, Julio García Espinosa, and Nelson Rodríguez
Cinematography: Jorge Herrera
Editing: Nelson Rodríguez
Art direction: Pedro García Espinosa and Roberto Miqueli
Costume design: María Elena Molinet
Sound: Ricardo Istueta and Carlos Fernández
Music: Leo Brower
MPAA rating: no listing
Running time: 160 minutes

> *Principal characters:*
> **1895**
> Lucía..........................Raquel Revuelta
> Rafael..........................Eduardo Moure
> **1932**
> Lucía............................Eslinda Núñez
> Aldo..............................Ramón Brito
> **196..**
> Lucía..............................Adela Legrá
> Tomás..........................Adolfo Llauradó

Within weeks of the triumph of the Cuban Revolution, Fidel Castro summoned one of the very few native filmmakers, Alfredo Guevara to formulate a law founding the Cuban Film Institute, Instituto Cubano del Arte
e Industria Cinematográficos (ICAIC). On March 24, 1959, less than three
months after Juan Batista's overthrow, the act was passed, the first of many
on cultural matters under the revolutionary regime. ICAIC, in essence a
ministry of film, was set up to oversee the development of an indigenous
Cuban film industry and exhibition network and training for filmmakers and
audiences alike. By the time of the first projected United States festival of
ICAIC products in March, 1972, approximately fifty medium- to full-length
films, almost three hundred documentary shorts, and even more *noticieros*
(newsreels) had been made. The United States government intervened, and
in the middle of the first screening of Humberto Solás' *Lucía*, the festival
was closed. Another two years would elapse before an American audience

could view Solás' 160-minute epic complete, some six years after it was made in Cuba, and too late for it to garner the attention it deserved for, at the very least, foregrounding women's issues.

Lucía is a three-part narrative film. Each part concerns the life of a Cuban woman named Lucía (portrayed by a different actress in each part), and each takes its subtitle from the year in her life on which it focuses. In *Lucía*, "1895," the central character of the title (Raquel Ravuelta) is a member of the landowning plantocracy. She spends her time almost exclusively with other women and appears to be destined for the unfavored status of "old maid." Though of the upper class, Lucía's family consider themselves to be Cuban rather than Spanish, and during a peasant uprising against the colonials, her brother fights with the rebel patriots against the Spanish. Lucía meets a Spaniard, Rafael (Eduardo Moure), who claims to be an apolitical businessman, and falls madly in love with him. He functions as a spy for the colonial regime, however, and by seducing her he finds the rebels' hiding place at her family's coffee plantation in the mountains. In the ensuing struggle, her brother is killed. When Lucía learns of her betrayal by Rafael, she stabs him to death. At the end of the story she is dragged away from the scene of her crime. She is alone and probably insane.

In the second episode, "1932," Lucía (Eslinda Núñez) is a member of the middle class, but, like her nineteenth century namesake, she is introduced as a single woman, though of a somewhat younger age. She has fewer social restrictions and is able to take a job in a tobacco factory. She meets a man, Aldo (Ramón Brito), and she falls in love, but in contrast to her predecessor's fate, this love is requited. Again, the background action is historical and specific—a political uprising against the dictator Gerardo Machado and his overthrow. Aldo is actively engaged in the revolution and together with his friend and political ally and his friend's wife, he and Lucía celebrate. Celebration leads to decadence for the other couple, however, and Aldo and Lucía become estranged from them. The decline in personal standards is matched by the political as the Left is shown to be unable to consolidate its victory. Aldo leaves his party job, and in the counterrevolutionary purge, he is killed. Again the Lucía of the title is alone, but this time some hope remains since she is pregnant.

The final segment is titled "196.." and examines the immediate present and the future. Following the pattern of the previous stories, the central character is of a lower class and younger than the "1932" Lucía. This modern Lucía (Adela Legrá) is a peasant worker, living in the country rather than the city, and is mulatto rather than white. The historical background, though less specific than before, is very pointed and linked closely to the main action. It is the time of Cuba's great literacy campaign, and Lucía wishes to read and write. She marries macho Tomás (Adolfo Llauradó), a cigar-chomping truck driver, and he decides that she must now work for him, not in the fields. He boards up the house in order to keep her at home, and when a teacher arrives he tries to stop Lucía from gaining an education. Tomás is overruled by the village officials on this matter, but his jealousy rules. Lucía is determined to work on both fronts, however, and the film ends with the couple still engaged in struggle while a much younger girl (the next Lucía, one assumes), observes the modern political struggle with amusement.

In interviews, Humberto Solás has argued that *Lucía* is not specifically a film about women, but one about society. He chose a woman as the central character because women have always been the most "vulnerable" to changes and contradictions in society. Thus, while the narrative focus of *Lucía* is on the plight of women, thematically the intention was to expose repression, generally, under colonialism ("1895"), neocolonialism ("1932"), and, even in revolutionary Cuba ("196 . ."). In the first two segments, the title characters are conspicuously outside the depicted struggle. (As mentioned, the first Lucía kills her lover, a Spaniard, but, on the surface, this is an act of passion caused by betrayal, not "anticolonialism.") If the emancipation of Cuba was far distant in 1895 and 1932, then that of Cuban women was even more so. Significantly, it is only in the modern story that Lucía has any possibility of acting positively to change and improve her own situation, and, by implication, that of all underprivileged Cubans. Nevertheless, far from glorifying the "new Cuba" and patting itself on the back for bringing emancipation to everyone, the third segment presents a woman in the midst of battle (albeit a humorous one) with her man and his archaic values. In this way, through the struggle of women (rather than a "women's struggle") Solás' film fits the prescription of Cuba's leading film theorist, Julio García Espinosa, who has called for an "Imperfect Cinema": aimed at audiences engaged in struggle, and at people who believe that the world can be changed.

Though Cuba is situated geographically in the Caribbean area (and is building closer associations with other islands), it also has profound connections with the mainland of South America. Its historical, cultural, and linguistic ties with Latin America are so pronounced that ICAIC's policy is to make films as much for liberation movements on the mainland as for its own people (and potentially for all Spanish-speaking Americans). In "1895," the war of liberation with Spain that is depicted could conceivably be located anywhere else in Latin America. The ill-fated Socialist movement depicted in "1932" must also have strong resonances in other Latin American countries where dictatorial regimes such as that of Machado in the film still prevail. Solás has stated that this part of *Lucía* means the most to him—is the most "autobiographical"—since his own father was a part of that insurrection.

Julianne Burton, who has written extensively on Cuban cinema, believes that history and underdevelopment are its two major concerns. This assessment can be readily applied to *Lucía*, in which three stages of underdevelopment are depicted in the three phases of Cuban history. What is important is not simply the successive improvement of conditions that exist through time shown between the three parts, but the changes that take place within them, particularly the raising of each Lucía's consciousness. In "1895," Lucía, in abject passivity and naïveté—she has waited years for a suitable man to come into her life—learns of her double betrayal: Rafael's fighting against Cuba and killing her revolutionary brother. The second Lucía, though essentially more in control of her own life (since she works in a factory), is a passive witness to Aldo's destruction. Despite an aura of hopeless alienation at the end, it is inferred that she has come to understand well the evils of neocolonial oppression. In "196. . ," learning itself is a theme. The third Lucía is dynamic, as opposed to passive, and she struggles with her husband in order to admit a teacher into their house. She takes on the role of being an agent for change and tries to educate her "ignorant" husband. In this segment, the display of, and confrontation with machismo can be understood as being a remnant of colonialism. In "1895," women exist only to serve men. A sequence involving a Lucía-look-alike prostitute presents woman's place in a colonial society. Man's dominance is exercised aggressively. Though given more dignity in "1932," Lucía, if not servile, is singularly supportive of her man, Aldo. In neither of the first two parts can machismo be realistically criticized directly in the narrative, since it was too firmly entrenched as a condition of life.

Argentinians Fernando Solanas and Octavio Getino clandestinely codirected the extremely important Third World Film *La hora de los hornos* (1968) and also cowrote the seminal revolutionary film text *Cine, cultura, y descolonizacion* (1973). They also cowrote an article, "Toward a Third Cinema," in which they argued that documentary film forms the basis of the struggle against colonialism and neocolonialism. ICAIC's director, Alfredo Guevara, has often stated that Cuba's primary mode of filmmaking is the documentary and that the documentary's principles are carried over into fiction films. *Lucía* is a film that incorporates documentary style. While there are features of documentary throughout *Lucía*, it is only in the third part that Solás chose to make it the dominant "style" of the segment. The only striking "documentary" aspect of "1895" is the use of extremely high-contrast stock for the sequence involving the prostitute. The graininess is characteristic of *cinéma vérité*. In "1932," the film takes on a definite documentary tone when the Socialist insurgents begin their revolution. On the streets during the strike, people continually pass in front of the lens as the frenetically hand-held camera gets involved in the action. Flash pans and a high noise level on the sound track accentuate the visceral quality and immediacy of the sequence. At this point, the film looks very much like Gillo Pontecorvo's *La battaglia di Algeri* (1966; *The Battle of Algiers*), another key Third World film which, though fictional, is styled to encourage the audience to believe that the events were filmed as they actually happened. "Documentary" is here associated with the oppressed and their struggle (and this could retrospectively be the interpretation of the style usage in "1895," also). After the fall of Machado, the film reverts to another tone in following the misfiring of the revolution. In "196. . ," a documentary flavor pervades. After the introduction, and until the last sequence, the episode consists mostly of intimate, engaged close-ups and medium-close-ups, not of the soft-focus Hollywood variety, but with the hard-edged realism of *cinéma vérité*. In fact, the entire segment may have been filmed in the same high-contrast stock that was used for the allegory in "1895." It is clear that Solás, in the new Cuban tradition, equates a documentary style with anticolonialism.

Interestingly, on a cinematic level, *Lucía* also criticizes Western European, "bourgeois" forms of filmmaking. Solás admires Luchino Visconti's earliest work but criticizes his later films along with those of Michelangelo Antonioni. In "1932," often the composition of the frame is unbalanced with a character placed at one extreme edge. The segment also contains many relatively silent, extended takes in long-shot and extreme-long-shot (particularly on Lucía after Aldo's death), and both of these techniques recall much of Antonioni's work and convey the same alienation from the landscape. Also, in the beginning of "1932," extended panning shots are employed to follow Lucía walking, again in the distance. These recall the Visconti of *Morte a Venezia* (1971; *Death in Venice*) and, with music in the style of Francis Lai, evoke the phenomenally extraneous, wasted footage in some of the features of Claude Lelouch, which resemble slick television commercials. Whereas the overall tone of "Lucía, 196. ." is involved, "1932" is alienated. Thus, it is suggested that Solás did not simply employ elements of the European art-film style to match the characters' state of alienation in the counterrevolutionary Havana of 1932, but that he also, implicitly, criticized such a style.

The first part, "1895," is stylistically complex. It has been compared favorably to *Senso* (1954), from Visconti's politically engaged period, a film which it resembles in its plot as well as in its decidedly operatic tone. Cinematic hyperbole can even be found in the use of a hand-held camera, which is frequent, but seems to be used more in the style of Glauber Rocha than in the style of documentary. Solás has praised Rocha's work, and it is unlikely that a borrowing from the most flamboyant director of the Brazilian *Cinema Novo* would carry implicit criticism of his style. In fact, on the evidence of Solás' other films—for example, *Simparele* (1974), *Cantata de Chile* (1975), and *Cecilia* (1982)—of the three parts of *Lucía*, "1895" most closely represents the director's own style. In its hyperbole, even outrageousness (the phallic imagery is at times crude to the point of comedy), the segment criticizes the histrionics and operatic melodrama of traditional, personalized portrayals of history in film (for example, *The Birth of a Nation*, 1915), while simultaneously allowing the director to display his vibrant mastery of the medium.

In its allusions to documentary film, in the appropriateness of its stylistic choices, and its seriousness in dealing with Cuban history and society, *Lucía* is quintessentially Cuban. More important, the average Cuban film spectator would even be able to understand to some degree the subtleties of these strategies because the literacy campaign was carried over into film. Both Solás and Guevara have emphasized the importance of the Cuban television shows *Twenty-four Times a Second* and *History of Film* in explaining film techniques and demystifying the workings of cinema, particularly the "tricks" of the commercial variety, for the Cuban spectator. Though it may not have found its audience in the United States, *Lucía* can at least be appreciated in its own country as a brilliant work of anticolonialist filmmaking.

Peter Rist

LUCKY LUCIANO

Origin: Italy and France
Released: 1973
Released in U.S.: 1973
Production: Franco Cristaldi for Vides/Films La Boétie
Direction: Francesco Rosi
Screenplay: Francesco Rosi, Lino Jannuzzi, and Tonino Guerra
Cinematography: Pasqualino De Santis
Editing: Ruggero Mastroianni
Art direction: Andrea Crisanti
Music: Piero Piccioni
MPAA rating: R
Running time: 115 minutes
Running time in U.S.: 94 minutes

Principal characters:
Lucky Luciano	Gian Maria Volonté
Gene Giannini	Rod Steiger
Harry J. Anslinger	Edmond O'Brien
Charles Siragusa	Himself
American colonel	Vincent Gardenia
Vito Genovese	Charles Cioffi
Italian captain of police	Silverio Blasi
French commissioner	Jacques Monod
Igea	Karin Peterson
Countess	Magda Konopka
Herlands	Larry Gates
Don Ciccio	Dino Curcio

Although respected throughout Europe as one of the most accomplished heirs of the Italian neorealistic tradition, Francesco Rosi has not enjoyed similar success in the United States, partly because his explorations of the theme of power have been rooted in Italian settings and feature, for the most part, historical figures and events unfamiliar to American audiences. Moreover, in his quest for truth Rosi presents facts—he relies heavily on primary "documents"—but he offers his audience neither an interpretation of these facts nor an ending which resolves the issues that he has explored. As he has often stated in interviews, he wants his audiences to participate, to arrive at their own truth. In many ways his films seem like documentaries, but they are more appropriately described as documented and dramatized explorations of what lies behind the ostensible subject or character. The historical figures are important not only in themselves, as is the case with biography, but also as a means of exploring the complex relationships between powerful institutions—legal and illegal—in Italy after World War II.

As a study of power, *Lucky Luciano* resembles Rosi's *Le mani sulla città* (1963; *Hands over the City*) and *Uomini contro* (1970), but it has more in common stylistically with his *Salvatore Giuliano* (1962) and *Il caso Mattei* (1972; *The Mattei Affair*). All three films use historical figures to probe the ties between legal and illegal power and to suggest their interdependence. *Lucky Luciano* is not a gangster film, though it has obligatory scenes of violence, nor is it a biography which details a man's life. Instead, it focuses on one phase in the career of Luciano (Gian Maria Volonté), his decline, and on the ambiguous alliances among the Mafia, American politicians, and the American military establishment. Against this political backdrop the characters are presented as committed but powerless pawns who can, like the audience, only speculate about the motives and machinations of the institutions. The audience cannot "know" the characters or the truth because Rosi insists on maintaining a distance between his audience and the film characters: Rosi largely ignores the private lives of his characters, and he films his characters mostly in long-shots. The audience sees characters speak, but Rosi's sound track often deletes dialogue—especially when it would resolve ambiguity—and stresses background sound or the narrator's voice. For the most part, the only dialogue that the audience hears pertaining to Luciano's criminal activities in Italy is based on primary documents, such as Luciano's last interrogation by the Italian police, a narcotics agent's official report, and a commission's report on drug traffic. The question of Luciano's criminal activities in Italy is not ultimately resolved by the film.

The basic plot of *Lucky Luciano* concerns the events following Luciano's deportation to Italy in 1946. In fact, opening credits are shown over a newspaper account explaining Luciano's release: After serving only nine years of a thirty-to-fifty-year sentence on charges brought against him by District Attorney Thomas A. Dewey, Luciano is freed—because of special services provided to the Navy in World War II—by the governor of New York, the same Thomas A. Dewey. The United States Narcotics Bureau, headed by Harry J. Anslinger (Edmond O'Brien), suspects Luciano of controlling the flow of drugs from legal Italian pharmaceutical firms to the United States, and Charles Siragusa (Himself) is the agent who attempts to return Luciano to jail. At a 1952 United Nations Drug Conference, Anslinger accuses the Italian police of indifference and urges that the legal drugs be made illegal. The Italian response is that the United States Armed Forces must bear some responsibility for the Mafia's criminal activities, since army officers installed known mafiosi in political positions and allowed them to control the black market. In fact, one lengthy flashback details the collaboration between an army colonel (Vincent Gardenia) and Vito Genovese (Charles Cioffi), a Mafia chieftain. When the conference fails to resolve the problem,

Siragusa tries to get Gene Giannini (Rod Steiger) to implicate Luciano and
finally forces Giannini to return to the United States to testify. Giannini,
however, is killed, and Siragusa, who lacks the evidence to convince a
Dewey crime commission of Luciano's guilt, is transferred off the case. The
Italian police, however, persevere and bring Luciano in for questioning.
During the interrogation, Luciano is sick and reveals that he has had two
heart attacks. When he later goes to the airport to meet a writer who has
scripted his life story for film, Luciano suffers a fatal heart attack. The final
credits are run over an image of the sprawled, lifeless body of Luciano.

Rosi's film raises many unresolved questions about the connection
between Luciano's release and an alleged political donation to Dewey's campaign fund, the nature of Luciano's special service to the United States
Navy; the reason for the Army's installing Mafia chieftains in positions of
power; the nature of Luciano's Washington connections; and the need of the
American Mafia, the American and Italian politicians, and the police to insist upon or to deny Luciano as the "boss of bosses." Near the end of the
film, Luciano, in a rare revelatory speech, declares cynically that everyone—Mafia and police alike—is used by the politicians, who want to keep
the people in the dark. Certainly, one has the sense that in this film the Mafia is so intertwined with politics that, from a pessimistic view, the system as
a whole is a "Mafia," one complete with payoffs and favors.

Rosi's opening credits suggest that he is conducting an inquiry, that he is
attempting to go beyond the printed story to find the truth about Luciano
and about power. Though there is no "Rosebud," the search for Luciano is
much like the search for Charles Foster Kane in *Citizen Kane* (1941). That
the search will be difficult is obvious from the New York City waterfront
sequence, in which Rosi demonstrates the problem of seeing the truth. The
establishing shots of the ship and the arriving car seem typical enough, but
then Rosi uses the hand-held camera to force his audience abruptly into the
crowd gathering about the car. Subsequently, Rosi moves his camera behind
a fence so that the audience is slightly removed from the conflict between
the longshoremen who support Luciano and the press who have had "Immigration" arrange their presence. Then the audience looks through a window at an even greater distance from the action and realizes that the first
shots were also taken from the same window, behind which the police film
Luciano's farewell party. This would seem to suggest that the audience's
view is consonant with the police view, but since the camera includes the police, the audience senses—and soon learns—that the police "view" is
incomplete, inadequate because of the barriers, visual and aural.

In this scene, Rosi also establishes a tie between Luciano and Siragusa:
Both are Sicilians, though they represent, according to Rosi, the two opposing faces of Sicily. At one point, Siragusa discusses Luciano with Anslinger
and then turns abruptly to the camera and tells the audience that he hates

Luciano because he is a black mark on all Sicilians. This apparent opposition and conflict is, however, overshadowed by Rosi's insistence on the interdependence of the Mafia and the police, nowhere better illustrated than in the methods that both employ to achieve their ends. Giannini suspects Siragusa of having been responsible for his year in prison on a counterfeiting charge, and Siragusa is ultimately responsible—despite his legalistic denials—for Giannini's death, because the prison term has placed Giannini in an untenable position, one in which he must return to New York. When he understands his plight, Giannini declares that he does not know who is worse, Luciano or Siragusa. This blending of Mafia and police is compounded when the Dewey Crime Commission accuses Siragusa of causing Giannini's death, prompting him to ask who is on trial. He is told that it is not a bad idea for police to be placed on the other side of the law, to which Siragusa responds that it would be appropriate for judges (who apparently serve on the Commission) to experience the same fate.

Rosi suggests that if well-intentioned people such as Siragusa employ questionable means, then the Mafia atmosphere is indeed pervasive. At the deportation party, a New York City policeman, who is Italian, talks with Luciano about a promotion, and Luciano mentions Washington connections. When Luciano returns to his hometown in southern Italy, Rosi visually suggests that violence has been and is an ongoing part of life: His tour includes a cemetary, and the camera pans from one memorial to another as the narrator reads about the assassinations of the victims. Shortly thereafter, as Luciano and Don Ciccio (Dino Curcio), the parish priest, drive away from the church, the two men and the expensive American car are visually contrasted with an old peasant astride a donkey. As the car passes out of the frame, Rosi's camera remains on the peasant, who carries his rifle. The past and present are fused.

Similarly, when Rosi reconstructs the alliance between the American military and the Mafia in Italy during World War II, he not only blurs the distinction between the two but he also demonstrates that selling goods was not the sole province of the Mafia. As the American colonel struts, spouts chauvinistic psychology, and asks his entourage for perfunctory agreement, Genovese is constantly at his side, and, as he gains the colonel's trust, he actually assumes command, even to the point of assuming the colonel's verbal mannerisms. When they drive away from the base together, a two-shot effectively shows their alliance. The colonel sells official positions, the Mafia sell black-market goods, and women outside the base sell trinkets. Everyone has a hand stretched out, and in a long-take Rosi foregrounds the "sales" against the background of a train moving military equipment to the front, thereby commenting ironically on the values of the military.

The Mafia maintain the power that they gain because they understand the nature of power and because they adapt to the times. According to one of

Luciano's cohorts, a "boss" puts things "in order" (here Rosi alludes to Benito Mussolini, the "boss" of Fascist Italy), thereby producing peace and prosperity. Following this definition, Rosi illustrates "order": The audience sees a montage of stylized, choreographed, slow-motion executions that resemble, because of the lighting, dreams, or nightmares. Aside from Giannini's murder, also a stylized execution, and the murder of an ambitious young hoodlum, these are the only violent shots in the film. Rosi clearly does not sensationalize violence but instead uses it to show how Luciano came to power in 1931 by eliminating the old-guard Mafia bosses and establishing order and peace in a new "corporate" Mafia. Rosi's emphasis is not on the violence but on the forces behind the violence.

Rosi contrasts the Mafia power with the well-intentioned but futile efforts of Anslinger and Siragusa, who are apparently powerless. The Mafia gatherings and festive occasions are crowded with people and food (much like the American Officers' Club), while Anslinger and Siragusa are photographed by themselves in enormous rooms which serve to stress their insignificance. On one occasion they are shown in the foreground at one table; behind them are countless empty tables. Rosi then reverses the shot and shows the empty tables in the foreground with Anslinger and Siragusa in extreme longshot.

It is in this scene that Siragusa discovers that he and his boss are "in the middle"; Anslinger says that while they chase Luciano, Dewey chases them and Kefauver chases Dewey—with the result that everyone will in the end be back where he started. Luciano himself comments that the police are chasing in circles, and Rosi ends his film with a repetition—over the shot of Luciano's dead body—of Anslinger's words.

By the end of the film Rosi has provided his audience with scenes reconstructed from primary sources, television coverage of Senate hearings, voice-over testimony of Mafia hit men, teletype headlines, newspaper stories, and press conferences with Luciano—and the audience is left with only the frozen image of the dead Luciano. Rosi has kept his audience at a distance from Luciano, who often is absent from the film (as in the Genovese and Giannini sequences) and who has comparatively few lines of dialogue. (He is in marked contrast to the voluble and superficial Giannini). The audience is almost where they were at the beginning of this pessimistic film. Yet if they have participated with Rosi in the search for truth, Rosi's social and political effort at reform has partially succeeded.

Thomas L. Erskine

LUMIÈRE D'ÉTÉ

Origin: France
Released: 1943
Released in U.S.: no listing
Production: André Paulvé
Direction: Jean Grémillon
Assistant direction: Serge Vallin
Screenplay: Jacques Prévert and Pierre Laroche
Cinematography: Louis Page
Editing: Louisette Hautecœur
Art direction: Alexandre Trauner; set decoration, Max Douy and André Barsacq
Costume design: Robert Clavel
Sound: Jean Monchablon
Music: Roland-Manuel
Running time: 108 minutes
Also known as: Summer Light

> *Principal characters:*
> Cri-Cri .... Madeleine Renaud
> Patrice .... Paul Bernard
> Michèle .... Madeleine Robinson
> Roland .... Pierre Brasseur
> Julien .... Georges Marchal

Looking at Jean Grémillon's films, one can easily be astonished that it took so long for his name to become known and respected outside France. Yet there were two strong reasons for this. After several promising silent films, Grémillon directed *La Petite Lise* (1930), an early sound film which can now be seen as an outstanding achievement, but its restraint and somber atmosphere made it a commercial failure. As a result, while directors such as Jean Renoir and Marcel Carné were attaining success and independence with an almost continuous succession of films, Grémillon had difficulty finding work: He went to Spain to make the screen version of a popular sentimental operetta, and two of his subsequent films, including the excellent *Gueule d'amour* (1937), starring Jean Gabin, were made for a German company with studio scenes shot in Germany. When Grémillon finally began to hit his stride again with congenial films made in France, the completion of *Remorques* (1941; *Stormy Waters*), which also starred Gabin, was delayed for two years by the outbreak of World War II. The two films that are generally considered to be Grémillon's masterpieces—*Lumière d'été* and *Le Ciel est à vous* (1944)—were made during the Occupation, at a time when they could have little or no international impact.

Yet even if Grémillon had had better luck in his career, it might still have taken time for his films to be appreciated. Unlike other leading French directors of the 1930's and 1940's, Grémillon did not have an obvious or easily labeled source of appeal. The films of Renoir (whatever else they might offer) could always be counted on for social comment, those of Julien Duvivier, for romantic melancholy, and those of Carné for fatalism tinged with fantasy. Yet the films of Grémillon are full of equally matched opposites: social concern plus a strong focus on individuals; melancholy infused with confidence and hope; fantasy emerging from a sharp sense of realism. The differences between Grémillon and his contemporaries emerge with particular clarity in *Lumière d'été* because the script was coauthored by Jacques Prévert, the dominant French screenwriter of the 1930's. Prévert had written the scripts for important films by both Renoir—*Le Crime de Monsieur Lange* (1936)—and Carné—*Quai des brumes* (1938; *Port of Shadows*) and *Le Jour se lève* (1939). He had also worked on Grémillon's *Remorques*, but there the settings—busy port, bustling tugboat, open sea—provided an easy counterbalance to the enclosed worlds that Prévert favored—a handful of varied characters generating romance, gloom, and fantasy in near isolation. With *Lumière d'été*, however, Prévert was on much more familiar ground.

The action takes place in an arid region of southern France. The meeting place for the film's assorted characters is a hotel that clings to a bare mountainside. The owner of the hotel is Cri-Cri (Madeleine Renaud), the former lover of—and still in love with—Patrice (Paul Bernard), an aristocrat who lives in a nearby château. A young woman, Michèle (Madeleine Robinson), arrives at the hotel to await her lover Roland (Pierre Brasseur), who has created a ballet in Paris. When he arrives, he turns out to be a drunkard and his ballet, a failure. Meanwhile, a young construction worker from a nearby dam site, Julien (Georges Marchal), has also arrived. Both Patrice and Julien fall in love with Michèle, and Patrice engages Roland to design an interior at the château in the hope that Michèle will accompany Roland.

The climax begins at a fancy dress ball given by Patrice. He tells Cri-Cri that he plans to marry Michèle; Cri-Cri confronts Michèle, who says that she is independent; Cri-Cri then confronts Patrice, and it is revealed that his wife died in an "accidental" shooting that was probably murder. At the end of the ball, Patrice, Cri-Cri, and Michèle pile into a car that is driven off by Roland, who has spent the evening getting drunk. The car crashes, injuring Roland, whom the others carry to the nearby dam site. A doctor is summoned, but the cable hoist bringing him across the ravine breaks down. When Julien climbs along the cable to repair the hoist, Patrice seizes a rifle and tries to shoot him, but other workers confront him and he falls over the edge of the ravine to his death. Julien and Michèle leave together.

In its broad outline, the plot is predictable: There is little doubt that Michèle will reject both the drunken dilettante and the decadent aristocrat and end up with the young, brave, and honest worker. For a film made under the Occupation, however, it is surprising to find the working class and the young generation presented so unambiguously as the hope of the future. At the same time, the script has other problems that are not diminished by historical perspective. The characters are flimsy, tending to repeat the same attitudes to the point of monotony. This is particularly obvious with Cri-Cri, who is allowed hardly any speech or action that does not spring from her jealous love of Patrice. It is less obvious with Patrice, only because his nastiness is revealed little by little, but compared to the complex figure of aristocratic decadence that Paul Bernard would later play in Grémillon's *Pattes blanches* (1949), Patrice is a stereotype. In addition, the climax and ending of the film are overly filled with melodramatic and sometimes implausible action. It is in this situation in which Grémillon's abilities come into play: He does not try to conceal the flaws; instead, he infuses them as far as possible with fascination and meaning.

The term "poetic realism" could be applied to almost all of the leading French directors of the 1930's and early 1940's, but none relied more than Grémillon on the power of simple realism to create poetic effects. In *Lumière d'été*, true to the film's title, Grémillon rejects the easy mystery of darkness or fog and insists on clarity even in the night scenes. After establishing the barren, sunburned setting of the hotel, he does not exaggerate the contrast with deep shadows when the film moves inside: The sheer normality of the bright and airy interiors is contrast enough. The one shadowy scene inside the hotel is indeed romantic, but not because visual detail is obscured. When Julien arrives, he is directed by mistake to Michèle's room: Unable to find the light switch, he feels his way—past a vase of sunflowers—across to the bed, where Michèle, taking him for Roland, kisses him. "It was like a dream," Julien later tells a friend; the power of this oneiric interlude is in no way weakened by what turns out to be the sketchy characterization of Julien and Michèle.

Roland's eventual arrival begins with the distant roar and headlight of a motorbike amid near darkness and quickly culminates in a skid and drunken collapse in front of the hotel. In retrospect the viewer may find further meaning in this vivid sequence, which foreshadows Roland's car crash near the end, and both incidents symbolize the dash and failure of his artistic ventures. Thus, Grémillon adds interest to another perfunctory character.

The script contains some fairly heavy symbolism that Grémillon does his best to lighten. At the hotel, Julien's friend has a pet cricket in a cage, and Michèle asks him to set it free because "No one belongs to anyone else." Before this, however, Grémillon has used the sound of the cricket without revealing its origin. This mysterious ticking, about which Julien shows no unease, suggests both the disturbing undercurrents beneath the normality of the hotel and Julien's detachment from them.

The fancy dress ball also offers opportunities for lavish symbolism. Patrice, for example, wears the costume of an eighteenth century dandy, which led Georges Sadoul to compare him to a "frenetic De Sade hero." Roland and Michèle are dressed as Hamlet and Ophelia, as if to demonstrate the former's self-disgust and the latter's naïveté. Yet the mere presentation of such symbolism adds no depth to the characters and their interactions. The costumes gain interest only when they are involved in the action. Thus, when Cri-Cri confronts Michèle with Patrice's plan to marry her, Michèle removes her long Ophelia wig. The emergence of the real simplicity behind its make-believe counterpart brings the symbolism to life and fleshes out the stereotype of Michèle's character. After the car crash, when the film's main characters arrive at the dam site, the visual incongruity between their costumes and the setting underscores the distance between the worlds of the leisured and working classes. This contrast originated in the script, but the fact that it emerges casually amid flurries of action, without the overemphasis of carefully composed tableaux, is to Grémillon's credit.

This listing of Grémillon's improvements on the script is not intended to deny the importance of Prévert's and Pierre Laroche's contribution: The film could not exist without it. The point is that Grémillon's approach was well suited to neutralizing the script's flaws or even turning them into advantages. In other scripts filmed during the Occupation, Prévert and Laroche usually placed their characters in an entirely make-believe world, either of outright fantasy, as in *Les Visiteurs du soir* (1942; *The Devil's Envoys*) or of the past, as in *Les Enfants du paradis* (1945; *Children of Paradise*). The studied, carefully composed approach of Marcel Carné was ideal for such scripts, but it would undoubtedly have magnified the discrepancies between the make-believe and contemporary worlds of *Lumière d'été*. Grémillon, at home in both worlds, knew how to fuse them together.

Despite the fact that *Lumière d'été* was highly praised by such contemporary French critics as Sadoul and André Bazin, it had no foreign release after World War II. In 1949, it was selected for showing at a Festival du Film Maudit (maligned or rejected films) in Biarritz, France. Seen today, *Lumière d'été* presents an extraordinary summary of the major themes and styles that emerged in French filmmaking during the 1930's. Though overly rich and flawed, the film nevertheless holds together under Grémillon's broad directorial reach and still offers both pleasure and excitement.

William Johnson

M

Origin: Germany
Released: 1931
Released in U.S.: 1933
Production: Seymour Nebenzal for Nero Film
Direction: Fritz Lang
Screenplay: Fritz Lang and Thea von Harbou
Cinematography: Fritz Arno Wagner and Gustav Rathje
Editing: no listing
Art direction: Karl Vollbrecht and Emil Hasler
Music: Edvard Grieg
Running time: 99 minutes

Principal characters:

Franz Becker	Peter Lorre
Inspector Karl Lohmann	Otto Wernicke
Schränker	Gustav Gründgens
Inspector Groeber	Theodor Loos
Mrs. Beckmann	Ellen Widmann
Elsie Beckmann	Inge Landgut
Blind man	Georg John
Lawyer	Rudolf Blümner
Franz	Fritz Gnass

Late in life, after his career as a director had ended, Fritz Lang was asked to play the role of a director in Jean-Luc Godard's *Le Mépris* (1963; *Contempt*). The invitation to play himself was in part a tribute to a deeply influential filmmaker, whose work in silent and sound films in Germany and then in the United States spanned more than five decades. Yet Lang's appearance in *Contempt* was a meaningful critical gesture as well as a tribute: In Godard's film and indeed in the history of modern film, Lang is an imposing figure, representing both constant experimentation with the film form and an attempt to use films to inquire into basic moral, social, and political dilemmas. Contrasted with the wishy-washy screenwriters and thrill-seeking producers envisioned by Godard, Lang is an uncompromising Olympian—it is no coincidence that in *Contempt* he is asked to direct Homer's *Odyssey*—and though he is not contemptuous of the world, he does view it according to morals and ideals that are at once necessary and impossible.

Lang worked successfully in an impressive variety of genres: *Dr. Mabuse der Spieler* (1922; *Dr. Mabuse the Gambler*) and *Das Testament des Dr. Mabuse* (1933) are metaphysical crime thrillers; *Die Nibelungen* (1924) is a mythological epic; *Metropolis* (1927) is an allegorical-fantastic epic; *Fury* (1936) is a realistic social drama; *The Return of Frank James* (1940) is a Western; and *The Big Heat* (1953) is an example of *film noir*. His greatest films, in these and in other modes, share what some critics have described as a cynical view of human nature and social institutions: Mankind is portrayed as frail at best, and relentlessly psychopathic at worst, which occurs more frequently than one would like to admit, and the forces designed for human comfort and protection—the community, laws, government officials, even the family—seem impotent or irrational. Whether this view is truly cynical—Lang protested that he was not cynical but merely honest—it is absolutely central to *M*, perhaps Lang's most typical and fully realized work, and in any event one of the few indispensable films of the modern period.

Based in part on a series of murders that had occurred only a few years earlier in Düsseldorf, *M* focuses not only on the tormented child murderer Franz Becker (Peter Lorre, in his first film role) but also on the minds and methods of his various pursuers, including both lawmakers and lawbreakers. The film opens with a scene that is grimly ironic: A group of children stand in a courtyard playing a game about an evil man in black coming to kill them with a chopper, much to the horror of a mother high above them on a porch, clearly too far away to protect them from the real murderer that she knows is terrorizing the city. (This simple scene is not only ironic but also reflexive: Like the children's game, Lang's film itself is an example of the inescapable fascination of violence and terror.) Young Elsie Beckmann (Inge Landgut) is barely able to stay clear of the normal dangers of everyday life—she is almost struck by a speeding car in the street—but she is not so fortunate when approached by Becker. He appears first only as a shadow across a poster offering a reward for the child-murderer; then, as he entices Elsie with a balloon, he nervously whistles an eerie tune from Edvard Grieg's *Peer Gynt*. Later, as the police plod along, trying to trace his handwriting on a note bragging of his murders, this musical signature gives him away to his underworld pursuers.

Elsie's murder not only outrages the citizens but also provokes a growing irrationality and hysteria, with ominous results. The social order seems especially precarious, perhaps mirroring the chaotic last days of the unstable Weimar Republic and in some ways prophesying the ascendancy of Nazism in German during the early 1930's: A convivial round-table meeting of well-dressed gentlemen turns into a nasty shouting match as one accuses another of being the murderer, and the kindness of an old man to a young girl is seen as suspicious by a quickly formed, uncontrollable mob that administers its "justice" to him—a frightening spectacle that appears repeatedly in Lang's films. The police carry on an extensive investigation to find the murderer who has disrupted the entire city. Lang inserts documentary-style footage to show how all the latest scientific methods are being used, and

Inspectors Groeber (Theodor Loos) and Lohmann (Otto Wernicke) are presented sympathetically, though occasionally humorously. They are, however, simply inefficient and overmatched, as is dramatized neatly in one scene composed of rapid-fire shots of two investigators arguing inconclusively about even so simple a matter as whether a minute piece of evidence is red or green.

Ironically, the greatest success of the police comes as they inadvertently rouse the underworld to action. The activities of the gangsters are interrupted by the police search, so it is much to their advantage to catch the murderer and return to business as usual. In a masterful set piece of parallel editing, Lang compares the simultaneous conferences of the police and the gangsters and shows that the gangsters have nearly all the advantages: They are unhampered by laws and fanciful speculations about the criminal mind; they have an enormous network of beggars for surveillance and communication; and they are led by a mysterious master criminal, Schränker (Gustav Gründgens), wanted for murder himself. Although the viewers' great respect for Schränker and the gang is undercut at the conclusion, when Lang shows that the price of their efficiency is inhumanity and insensitivity, throughout most of the film they seem to be the only ones able to catch a murderer who is farther outside the law than they are.

The police would eventually have caught up with Becker—they miss him by only a few moments when they go to stake out his apartment, where they find more evidence of his guilt—but the criminals catch him first. When Becker buys a balloon for a new victim, as he had for Elsie, the balloonman (Georg John), who is blind, recognizes his nervous whistling and alerts the network of beggars to follow him. One beggar chalks an "M" on his hand and bumps into Becker to mark him as the murderer. Even apart from the allegorical meaning of this sign of Cain, the image of the meek, shadowy murderer walking down dark streets with an almost glaringly luminescent white "M" on his black overcoat is visually stunning. The moment of discovery is equally effective as Lang exploits a common symbol from German Expressionist films of the time, a mirror, to portray a split or disordered personality: The shock on Becker's face as he sees the mark on his back in a store mirror comes as much from his awareness of himself as a brutal murderer as from his knowledge that he is being followed. He attempts to hide in an office building, but the criminals break in, seize him, and drag him, screaming, to their hideout for a trial.

The pursuit of Becker in the streets and the search for him in the menacingly barred and enclosing attic of the office building are suspenseful and edited to create a dramatically increasing tempo, but the real climax of the film comes in the trial scene. What were intriguing ironies earlier in the film now suddenly become serious moral quandaries: The legitimacy of the lawbreakers as agents of the law is challenged as they mistreat their prisoner; Schränker seems more a snarling, inhuman tyrant, totally devoid of compassion, than a figure of justice; and Becker, because of Peter Lorre's tour de force acting, becomes pitiable, a victim of a demon inside and a brutal mob outside. Even though the police rescue Becker from the criminals and deliver him to the court, this brings no final resolution. Interestingly, two different versions exist of the ending of *M*. In many prints, the film ends with the recapture of Becker by the police, followed by a voice-over by Mrs. Beckmann (Ellen Widmann) urging mothers to watch over their children more carefully. The original ending, though, was much more problematic and troubling: The final scenes in the original version show a judge about to pronounce a verdict on Becker, but this is never heard because of the voices of three mourning women, including Mrs. Beckmann, who cries that whatever the verdict, it cannot restore the dead children. Even though throughout the film justice has been debated and strenuously sought, from a certain perspective, it is finally inconsequential. One can well understand why Lang's films have often been described as bleak, if not cynical.

One reason that Lang is so influential and admired is because of his meticulous attention to the technical details of filmmaking. *M* was his first sound film, and he used the new medium cautiously but innovatively. Lang succeeded where many failed during this difficult transitional period because he used sound to enhance rather than replace a cinematographic and editing style rooted in the silent era. He does not rely on dialogue to provide a great deal of narrative information, thus avoiding the tendency of many early talkies to become static and visually uninteresting. On the contrary, in *M* Lang often uses dialogue musically to convey certain tones and moods rather than bits of information. For example, the anxious questions and then mournful cries of Elsie's mother express her deep sorrow; the droning voice-over of the police inspector describing the latest investigative techniques suggests his inefficient officiousness; and the biting, violently animated delivery of Schränker's speeches, even apart from the content of what he is saying, confirms his callous arrogance. Lang is equally careful in his use of other sound effects, often cutting his scenes on a noise, such as the chiming of a clock, continued or echoed in the next scene. Finally, it is sound that gives the murderer away: Whistling betrays his identity to the blind balloon-man, and the banging and scratching as he tries to escape leads the gang directly to his hideout.

The most interesting technical details of *M*, however, are visual. Many of the images that Lang presents are strikingly unusual or grotesque, necessarily so to portray a troubled and disordered world. Early in the film, for example, as Mrs. Beckmann waits anxiously for news of her daughter, she twice looks down the long staircase in her building. These shots from high above picture a disturbing vortex that introduces and represents the disorienting journey that lies ahead in the film. Alfred Hitchcock may well have had these shots in mind when he filmed the staircase scenes in *Vertigo* (1958). Later in *M*, when ordinary people walk by in the street, the store windows contain the usual assortment of everyday merchandise, games, and advertisements, but when Becker stalks a new victim (only to be disappointed when she escapes safely with her mother), he stares into a window containing a huge phallic arrow moving up and down, casting a shadow onto a large wheel spinning hypnotically. These images are both realistic— store advertisers actually used such spinning wheels, as captured in Walter Ruttmann's documentary *Berlin—die Symphonie einer Grossstadt* (1927; *Berlin—Symphony of a Big City*)—and surrealistic, suggesting that Becker is a prisoner of unconscious drives.

Lang also uses familiar images to set up highly articulated repeated patterns. From beginning to end, *M* is filled with railings, wooden slats, and bars (and the shadows cast by these objects, often directly onto the murderer), creating a vivid sense of entrapment. (In this respect as well, Hitchcock may be indebted to Lang.) Another insistent image system used throughout the film is somewhat more complicated: Lang seems absolutely fascinated by smoke. Smoking is a nervous habit indulged in by a number of the main characters—a cigarette left by Becker near the site of a murder is the clue used by the police to track him down—and many scenes are literally filled with a smoke screen, suggesting the inaccessibility of truth. Smoke also provides one of the few comic moments in the film: When Franz (Fritz Gnass), a burglar, casually announces that they have kidnaped the murderer, Lohmann first drops his cigar, then puts it back into his mouth and blows a tremendous cloud of smoke that nearly covers him completely. More important, though, because smoke wanders freely in a room and, though insubstantial, reflects light, it very subtly helps to animate and brighten some scenes that might otherwise be somewhat static and dark. Though Lang does not exploit this technique as fully as D. W. Griffith, smoke allows Lang to paint with light.

Influenced in may ways by his early studies as a painter and experiments with light and shadow by German Expressionist artists, stage designers, and filmmakers, Lang also uses *chiaroscuro* lighting effects throughout *M*. As in *The Cabinet of Dr. Caligari* (1920), which Lang was offered but was unable to direct because of other commitments, darkness and light are obvious but effective symbols, and the world that the murderer inhabits is, like his mind, shadowy, unfathomable, and alien. Besides creating a moody, mournful atmosphere, Lang skillfully directs the viewers' sympathy by lighting techniques. When the police invade the Crocodile Club to harass the gangsters, they are pictured as a shadowy, impersonal, unsympathetic force. Later, when the criminals capture Becker, they take on the form of a dark, faceless mob. Finally, the humanizing of the pathetic murderer, a major theme in the film, is brought about in part by raising him from darkness to light. He delivers his confessional monologue in bright, clear light, and while this by no means completely redeems him from his dark unconscious compulsions, it helps transform him from an object of hatred to a subject of compassion.

Lang's camera techniques are also consistently effective. While for the most part the camera is rather immobile, several scenes benefit greatly from simple camera movement: For example, purposely unsteady dolly and tracking shots communicate Becker's terror as he is literally tracked down the streets by the criminals, and the long, slow pan across an almost endless sea of faces as Becker confronts his accusers in the trial scene underscores the enormity of his crimes and the impassive force of the threatened judgment. A few of the camera angles are obtrusively predictable, such as when the kindly old man helping the young girl is shot from above to make him seem ridiculously small while the suspicious bully is shot from below to make him appear more intimidating. In general, however, Lang's camera angles are carefully planned and evocative. One characteristic angle is from high above the action, establishing, at least for the moment, a sense of distance between the viewer and the protagonists (whether schoolgirls in the courtyard or the frantic murderer in the streets below), who seem locked within an uncontrollable and inscrutable destiny. Lang also perhaps borrowed from the famous Odessa Steps sequence in Sergei Eisenstein's *Potemkin* (1925) when he filmed the entrance of the police down the steps of the gang's Crocodile Club: Shooting from a low angle makes the police appear not only threatening but also inhuman, since, like Eisenstein's attacking Cossacks, their heads are often cut off by the frame. In addition to using a variety of camera techniques that call attention to them, Lang also works subtly. Most memorably, Becker's long concluding monologue is shot naturalistically rather than expressionistically, emphasizing his painful and moving honesty, but through nearly all of it, the camera is tilted somewhat to the side, presenting a cinematic emblem of his continuing instability. Without this simple maneuver, this climactic scene would lose much of its magnificent tension and drama.

Lang's obvious care for the construction of individual scenes and the composition of particular shots is complemented by his skillful montage effects. Perhaps the most famous of these is the sequence telling of Elsie's murder: Quick shots of her empty chair at the dinner table, her ball rolling away on the ground, and her balloon floating aimlessly upward, only to be tangled in wires overhead, convey Elsie's pathetic fate and also allow the viewers to imagine much more gruesome details of the murder than Lang could ever have shown on-screen. Later, in one of his more extended sequences of parallel editing, Lang shifts back and forth between the criminals and the police, emphasizing by technical devices the ironic similarities between their respective conferences: The settings and the scene arrangements are nearly identical, and Lang frequently cuts on a word, sound, or gesture in one place that is then continued in the other.

It is a sure sign of Lang's technical virtuosity that such self-conscious montage effects do not clash with but rather highlight the few key scenes presented with a bare minimum of editing. When Becker is hiding in the attic, for example, the rapid pace of the editing, alternating between his attempt to get out and the gang's attempt to get in, creates increasing excitement, but at the climax of this buildup, Lang suddenly focuses the camera on Becker for a long take, trusting Peter Lorre's extraordinary acting ability to continue the accelerating tension. Lang also shows his remarkable editorial restraint in presenting Becker's final monologue in long, uninterrupted takes: The superb acting and writing here require no further embellishment, a fact that might not have been recognized by a lesser director.

Like many other great works of art, *M* is unpleasant, not only because it focuses on the dreadful subject of child murder but also because Lang relentlessly subverts or criticizes many of the audience's traditional sympathies and views. By the end of the film, it is difficult to know what to believe in, and the viewer may well feel exactly like the exhausted and forlorn women mourning in the concluding scene: Trust in the normal channels of justice is, for obvious reasons, impossible; criminals cannot be glorified as redemptive heroes after it is seen how easily they degenerate from a finely organized group to a mob; and one cannot even indulge in a feeling of rage against an abhorrent outsider because the murderer is an all-too-human figure, apart from but undeniably a part of mankind.

Although *M* is challenging, even disorienting, it is not a counsel for despair. Behind its convincing attacks on an unrealistic belief in the innate goodness of mankind and the beneficence of its social institutions lie powerful pleas against poverty, capital punishment, and violence, evils that can be combated only if mankind is prepared to step toward a deeper, more compassionate understanding of the complicated workings of the human mind. It is such an understanding, conveyed by brilliantly conceived and executed cinematic means, that is the legacy of *M*.

Sidney Gottlieb

MADAME BOVARY

Origin: France
Released: 1934
Released in U.S.: 1934
Production: Gaston Gallimard for Nouvelle Société de Films
Direction: Jean Renoir
Assistant direction: Jacques Becker and Pierre Lesouches
Screenplay: Jean Renoir; based on the novel by Gustave Flaubert
Cinematography: Jean Bachelet and Gibory
Editing: Marguerite Renoir
Art direction: Eugène Lourié and Robert Gys
Costume design: Lazare Medgyes
Sound: Marcel Courme and Joseph de Bretagne
Music: Darius Milhaud and Donizetti
Running time: 120 minutes
Running time in U.S.: 102 minutes

Principal characters:

Madame Bovary	Valentine Tessier
Charles Bovary	Pierre Renoir
Homais	Max Dearly
Léon	Daniel Lescourtois
Rodolphe	Fernand Fabre
Charles Bovary's mother	Alice Tissot
Hippolyte	Pierre Larquey
Lheureux	Robert Le Vigan
Mme Homais	Maryanne
Prefect	Léon Larive
Abbé Bournisien	Florencie
Notary	Romain Bouquet
Rouault	Georges Cahuzac
Surgeon	Alain Dhurtal
Canivet	Henry Vilbert
Bailiff	Robert Moor
Marquis	Georges Deneubourg
Binet	Edmond Beauchamp
Justin	André Fouché
Prefect	Jean Gehret
Old Nicaise	Marthe Mellot
Mme Lefrançois	Christiane d'Or
Mlle Musette	Odette Dynès

Legend has it that Jean Renoir agreed to direct *Madame Bovary* over the telephone one night while talking with his producer. Renoir wrote the screenplay, closely following Gustave Flaubert's 1857 novel and shot the film during September and October, 1933, in and around Lyons-la-Forêt and at the Billancourt Studios. The final cut ran some three and a half hours. In spite of Renoir's objections and over the protests of his producer, the distributors insisted that the film be shortened before they would show it, and it was edited down to 120 minutes and released. A slightly shorter version was exported to the United States. The final editions of the film pleased no one, neither the critics nor the public and certainly not Renoir, and *Madame Bovary* slipped quietly into obscurity.

Although the film has received somewhat better treatment in later years, especially with Renoir's reputation gaining in strength, it still poses obstacles to analysis. First, there is only a little more than half of the film to examine since the balance of the original footage plus all the outtakes apparently were destroyed after the editing in 1934. Second, Renoir's adaptation of such an icon of French literature, of international literary fame, presents its own set of problems, among which are included the invidious comparison between Flaubert's novel and the film. Such a comparison is unfair, since neither a close adaptation, which for the critic is somehow never close enough, nor the impressionistic approach, which calls forth howls from another direction, ever seems to satisfy those who would make such comparisons in the first place. Third, the scant treatment given to the film by Renoir himself both in his autobiography, *Ma Vie et mes films* (1974; *My Life and My Films*), where the film is mentioned only in passing, and in the interviews he granted over the years, in which he only talked about the film to describe it as "boring" in its present form, has given Renoir's critics the impression that the director himself did not care for the film, so it must be inferior and therefore not worthy of attention.

None of these objections, however, provides sufficient reason for ignoring the film. Indeed, on closer inspection, Renoir's *Madame Bovary*, both stylistically and thematically, forms an integral part of the director's most exciting period during the 1930's between *La Chienne* (1931) and *La Règle du jeu* (1939; *The Rules of the Game*). In spite of the obvious problems of discussing a film which is literally only half there, what remains is sufficiently interesting enough to warrant close examination, especially since in the film Renoir explored his interest in the theater and in the cinematic use of theatrical elements which form one of the central motives of Renoir's most important films of his French period.

Renoir's film follows the general outline of Flaubert's narrative rather faithfully, with a few minor exceptions, when events are either telescoped or combined for the sake of economy and when one was added, the meeting between the Bovarys (Pierre Renoir and Valentine Tessier) and the Marquis de Vaubyessard (Georges Deneubourg) which is counterpointed with an earlier carriage ride of Charles and Emma. The story is a familiar one. Emma Bovary, née Rouault, lives in rural isolation with her widowed father following her education at a convent. In spite of, or perhaps because of her confining education, Emma succumbs to various and unrealistic notions of romanticism, including the idea that a salvation for her boredom can be found through romantic love. When the local doctor's wife dies, freeing Charles Bovary to marry again, Emma perceives him as providing her with an escape from her provincial ennui. After their marriage, Emma moves to a small town, where Charles has comfortably established himself in his practice. At first happy both domestically and sexually, Emma quickly tires of small-town life as well. Unable to change either financially or emotionally, Charles resists all of Emma's attempts to elevate their lives socially. A brief flirtation with Léon (Daniel Lescourtois), a local young man, comes to naught when he departs for schooling in Paris. Emma's second flirtation is with the more experienced and manipulative Rodolphe (Fernand Fabre), who quickly seduces her and employs her romantic notions for his own ends. An escape with Rodolphe, planned after an operation which was supposed to make Charles a fortune goes awry, is also aborted when her lover bolts. After her period of repentance and illness, Charles is encouraged to take Emma to the theater in Rouen, a nearby city. There she once again meets Léon, who has returned from Paris to take up the study of law. The two begin a love affair in earnest.

Meanwhile, Emma, ever driven by her romantic excesses, has ruined the Bovary household financially, driving her husband deeper and deeper into debt, a fact kept from him until the bailiffs arrive to confiscate the furniture. Emma, now frantic to save herself and her husband from ruin, tries in vain to secure enough money to hold the creditors at bay. Failing to raise the eight thousand francs that she needs, driven by despair of having been betrayed by Léon also, Emma takes poison and dies while Charles looks on, helpless and bewildered.

The version of Renoir's film which survives has divided this narrative into three parts. "Les Bertaux—1839" forms the first part and takes Emma from the farm, Les Bertaux, through her marriage, settling in, and her first dalliance with Léon. In this section, Emma is shown as being quite at odds with her rural environment and yet strangely at home in the farmyard, as if on some level below which Emma is even aware, she is perfectly at ease with nature. Her sexual behavior later and her obvious sensuality even in these early scenes, would also suggest that she responds to life on a very natural and elemental level much at odds with the social and artistic pretensions of her romantic posing. Unlike the first Madame Bovary, who dies of a heart attack in the rain, Emma blooms in the out-of-doors, among the rooting pigs. Only when she is divorced from nature does she languish.

Besides introducing the theme of nature and artifice, this section also initiates a pattern of stylistic metaphors. Much is done with both framing and with deep-focus shooting, a visual trope which both separates nature outside from society inside and makes the obvious connection between the two by visually linking them through windows and doorways. The framing also serves to suggest the theatricality of much of Emma's response to life and works to suggest the sense of confinement that Emma feels in her provincial life. The expansiveness which nature provides is greatly restrained by the interiors and their clutter of pseudoart and knickknacks which are so defining of bourgeoisie life and emblematic of its restrictions both emotionally and intellectually.

These conflicts are introduced in the initial section of the film. The viewer also sees the beginnings of Emma's financial ruin as old Lheureux (Robert Le Vigan) insinuates himself into her life by playing on her need for things to authenticate her rise in class or her pretended, at least intended, climb up the social ladder. The beginnings of her sexual fall are introduced with the unfulfilled flirtation that Emma has with Léon. Perhaps necessary to Emma's sense of herself as a romantic heroine, this flirtation lacks only Rodolphe's insistence to be turned into the real thing, with consequences far beyond Emma's ability to control. Like the financial theme—and what could be more middle-class than money?—the sexual theme also progresses quickly to destructive levels.

The second section of the film, "Agricultural Fair—July 1841," covers Emma's affair with Rodolphe, the worsening financial condition of the Bovarys, and the increasingly ineffectual efforts of Charles, which merely widen the rift between him and Emma. The distance between Emma's romantic dreams and the provincial reality of her life is nowhere more evident than at the agricultural fair where she first meets Rodolphe. Later, Rodolphe and Emma ride together in the woods, and in him she finds the embodiment of her notions of a romantic hero; he plays the part for his own purposes. The artificiality of the relationship between the two is suggested on a number of occasions by the use of draped windows, which hint at the theatrical conditions of their affair. Even the exterior scenes are played for their dramatic effect, an effect which is most seductive to Emma and finally is responsible for her downfall.

Running parallel with the love plot is the financial one. Growing deeper in debt to Lheureux, on his suggestion, Madame Bovary, in a scene dripping with duplicity, obtains power of attorney from her husband. The sexual and financial themes merge in the escape that Emma plans with Rodolphe after she is humiliated over Charles's failure to cure a clubfooted man and thereby secure their fortune. Emma orders expensive traveling clothes for the trip, but Rodolphe leaves without her. Her life shattered by Rodolphe's betrayal, she becomes ill and later seems to have changed. Yet when Léon reenters her life—she meets him at an opera in Rouen—she begins an affair with him. This section concludes with a ride in the country in a closed carriage in which Emma acquiesces to Léon's advances: Once again, Emma responds to a romantic setting and to her sense of theater.

The third part of the film, "Rouen—November 1842," opens with a scene in the hotel room where Emma and Léon have been carrying on their affair. Emma announces that nothing but death could replace her happiness of the moment, and the camera pans down to a blind beggar singing in the streets; both the drapery of the bed on which Emma reclines and the blind beggar will appear again during Emma's death scene at the film's conclusion. From the opening of this third part, Emma progresses from happiness to disillusionment to despair to death in a never-ending cascade of emotions.

Upon her return home, she is accosted by Lheureux, who informs her that the bailiffs will confiscate her goods if she cannot raise the necessary funds to repay her debts. Both Léon and Rodolphe fail to supply her with the money she needs, again reinforcing the love/finance connection established early in the film. Emma is abandoned by her lovers, manipulated by Lheureux, misunderstood by her father, and mismatched to Charles Bovary. The conclusion of the film shows not simply a woman who foolishly has succumbed to the romantic nonsense of popular writing, but also a woman manipulated and misused by the men around her.

Driven to despair by her attempts to raise money, Emma takes poison and prepares to die. Ever the romantic heroine, she stages her deathbed scene as a piece of drama. The scene is shot in soft focus; Emma, swaddled in white, dies in an ecstasy of suffering, clutching the cross from the priest, embracing and forgiving Charles. This scene, like many others in the film, because it is so overdone, could have bordered on the laughable, but it does not, primarily because the viewer has seen genuine suffering on Emma's part. She has been exploited by those around her, and her culpability becomes softened by such recognition.

In spite of the critical objections to the film, Renoir's *Madame Bovary* is both solidly within the tradition of his films of the 1930's and a considerable film in its own right. Some of the concerns, such as whether or not Valentine Tessier was too old to play Emma, have faded, as they should. Even the controversy over the length of the film, once a *cause célèbre* for enthusiasts, has disappeared as well, allowing critics to worry less about what was cut and to concentrate more on the properties of the footage that remains. What remains is far better—actually quite good, in fact—than might be suggested by the history of the film. Dealing with one final objection may help to clarify this point.

Much has been made of the artificiality and theatricality of Renoir's adaptation. For those writing about the film in 1934, Renoir's interest in the theater may have not been as clear as to those writing about his films after the 1930's. The theater and the uses of both the topic of theater and of theatricality within his films became a thematic preoccupation of Renoir's middle period, especially in those films from *Madame Bovary* through *The Rules of the Game*. Thus, most critics would now see the theatricality of *Madame Bovary* not as a drawback but as one of the important reasons for examining the film. Emma's romanticism and posing dovetails nicely with the importance of this theme. The use of windows and doorways and of draped alcoves, especially beds, which form little theaters, provides a background against which to act out the events of the unfolding drama. The world of the cinema is as artificial as the theatrical world depicted within it.

Renoir's adaptation of Flaubert's masterpiece was not his first. In *Nana* (1926), he adapted Émile Zola's novel to the screen with little protest, as later in his career Renoir would transfer literary works from Honoré de Balzac to Georges Simenon to the screen. One consistent theme which ties many of these films together is the softening of the criticism of the middle class inherent in the literary originals, and in this respect *Madame Bovary* is no exception. Flaubert's novel is quite harsh in its treatment of Emma's world, and while Renoir's film pokes fun at the foibles and excesses of the bourgeois life, he does so with both understanding and compassion. Emma may be foolish and misguided, Charles may be bumbling and insensitive, but they are not condemned for these human failings. In the world of Renoir, the focus is always on understanding people, not on judging them. It is for such insights into human nature that one returns again and again to his films. *Madame Bovary* is a triumph of such compassion.

Charles L. P. Silet

MADAME ROSA
(LA VIE DEVANT SOI)

Origin: France
Released: 1977
Released in U.S.: 1978
Production: Lira Films (AA)
Direction: Moshe Mizrahi
Screenplay: Moshe Mizrahi; based on the novel *La Vie devant Soi*, by Émile
  Ajar
Cinematography: Nestor Almendros
Editing: Sophie Coussein
Art direction: no listing
Music: Philippe Sarde and Dabket Loubna
MPAA rating: PG
Running time: 105 minutes

> *Principal characters:*
> Madame Rosa . . . . Simone Signoret
> Momo . . . . Samy Ben Youb
> Dr. Katz . . . . Claude Dauphin
> Nadine . . . . Michal Bat-Adam
> Hamil . . . . Gabriel Jabbour
> Ramon . . . . Constantin Costa-Gavras
> Madame Lola . . . . Stella Anicette
> Momo's father . . . . Mohammed Zineth

When Simone Signoret was offered the title role in Moshe Mizrahi's
Madame Rosa, she was understandably reluctant to take it. The German-
born French actress had long since established the screen *persona* of a ra-
diant, sensual, desirable woman in such films as *La Ronde* (1950), *Thérèse
Raquin* (1953; *The Adultress*), *Les Diaboliques* (1955; *Diabolique*), *Room at
the Top* (1959), and *Ship of Fools* (1965).

Yet here was a role that required the fifty-seven-year-old Signoret to play a
fat, swollen, squint-eyed character ten years her senior; to wear the least flat-
tering costumes and makeup; to be subjected exclusively to camera angles
designed to make her look far heftier and puffier than she was in actuality—in short, to demonstrate and chart her ongoing physical deterioration.

Nevertheless, Signoret was persuaded to take the role by director
Mizrahi, whose previous work—especially *I Love You Rosa* (1972)—had
impressed her. Her decision pays a substantial dividend in the finished film,
as the bravery of the actress reverberates within her characterization, reinforcing the essential courage of the character Rosa.

In winning the 1977 Academy Award for Best Foreign-Language Film (as France's entry), *Madame Rosa* was the third film directed by Moshe Mizrahi to have been nominated in the Foreign-Language Film category, having been preceded by two entries from Israel—*I Love You Rosa* in 1972 and *The House on Chelouche Street* in 1973.

The film's commercial appeal in the United States was further enhanced in 1978 by its selection by the Los Angeles Film Critics Association as Best Foreign-Language Film and by its selection by the National Board of Review as one of the Best Foreign-Language Films.

An Egyptian-born Jew, Moshe Mizrahi moved from Alexandria to Israel when he was fourteen, having been brought up speaking not only Hebrew but also Arabic and Castilian Spanish. As an adult, he maintained residences in Tel Aviv and in Paris. His immersion in both Israeli and Arab culture served him well in gaining the necessary perspective to tackle *Madame Rosa*, the central relationship of which involves an aging Jewish woman and a fourteen-year-old Arab boy.

Madame Rosa is set in Paris, in 1974, in the Belleville quarter, a multi-ethnic, working-class slum with a large population of pimps and prostitutes. When the film opens, Madame Rosa—a bloated, broken-down woman in her late sixties with a thick elastic bandage wrapped around one of her failing legs—is making her weary way home in the tortuous, torturous climb that she must make to get to her cramped, sixth-floor flat.

The opening sequence not only establishes character and setting but also serves—perhaps intentionally—to allow startled audiences to overcome their disbelief and discomfort gradually and accept the fact that this is indeed the same Simone Signoret—no longer youthful or sturdy, no longer glamorous or voluptuous or sultry—whom they have come to know in dozens of films spanning more than thirty years.

Waiting for Rosa in the crowded sixth-floor apartment of the run-down building is a gaggle of multiracial and multicultural children, ranging in age from two to fourteen. They are all the children of working prostitutes, from whom Rosa—an ex-hooker who gave up prostitution at the age of fifty "for aesthetic reasons"—gets money to make ends meet. In return for boarding the fatherless children of her friends and former colleagues—a service which allows the prostitutes to avoid being turned in to the welfare department by neighbors and prevents their pimps from using their children for any kind of coercion—Rosa gets money to pay the rent and children to love.

The older children watch over the younger ones, and Rosa makes them all promise not to live off the streets, not to steal, not to sell themselves. She also takes great pains to assure their various cultural identities. A Vietnamese child is sent out regularly for meals with a Vietnamese family; black children are sent to mix with the Senegalese populace; an Arab boy receives regular lessons in Arabic as well as Muslim religious instruction.

The Arab lad, named Momo (Samy Ben Youb), is fourteen and gets the most attention, either because he needs it or because he is Rosa's favorite—or both. "Momo," short for Mohammed, is a fretful youngster who has been with Rosa the longest, apparently abandoned by parents about whom he can get no information. Rosa has cared for Momo since infancy, rearing him as a Muslim, but she will not reveal to him the truth about his origins—that his mother was murdered by her pimp in a jealous rage. She even lies to him about his age, telling him that he is eleven—perhaps to delay his growing up and abandoning her. At Momo's school, his teacher confronts Rosa about Momo's actual age.

Like Rosa, Momo is a born survivor. Rosa ekes out a living, and Momo follows suit, doing illegal street performances with a homemade puppet and lifting food from outdoor food stands. One day, he steals a dog from a pet shop, forms an attachment to it, sells it to someone on the street, and then, curiously, drops the five hundred francs that he has been paid into a sewer.

Momo is angry that Rosa has kept his parentage a secret, but he also fears that Rosa—his surrogate mother and only emotional link—will soon be abandoning him one way or another.

The tattooed number on Rosa's arm remains from her victimization at a concentration camp after her lover betrayed her to the Nazis; Auschwitz still haunts her in nightmares, and she still worries about the French authorities: Will they collaborate with the Germans again?

Meanwhile, she grows old, sick, and ugly; continues trudging up those awesome stairs; challenges her own agnosticism by creating a hidden religious shrine in the basement; and approaches senility with reminiscences: of her unhappy love affair, of her thirty-five years as a much-in-demand hooker, of how she became a foster grandmother and wet nurse for the children of the whores.

The love and interdependence that Rosa and Momo share is intensified in the distress each feels: Rosa worries about Momo's friendships on the street, as pimps and prostitutes attempt to bring him into "the life." Momo is concerned about Rosa's rapidly deteriorating health—she has emphysema and hypertension and suffers blackouts. When elderly Dr. Katz (Claude Dauphin), Rosa's sympathetic doctor, suggests that she go into a hospital, it triggers yet another paranoid hallucination about being taken away by the police to a concentration camp. At one point, Momo, with the best of intentions, suggests tactfully to the abashed doctor that he put Rosa out of her misery.

Knowing that she is dying, Rosa gradually releases the children to their mothers so that other arrangements can be made for them. Momo, who has no mother and no place to go, stays on.

An Arab man (Mohammed Zineth) turns up at Rosa's door one day, claiming to be Momo's father. An ex-convict who has spent years in a psychiatric hospital without having borne any of the financial burden of rearing the boy for more than a decade, he now wants his son back. Rosa keeps the truth from the man, diverting his attention to the other child still in her care, but in the process, she reveals the truth to Momo about the specifics of his birth. Rosa and Momo remain together.

As Rosa edges closer to the end of her life, Momo is befriended by an affluent film editor (Michal Bat-Adam) and her husband (played by director Constantin Costa-Gavras), who represent a potential family for Momo after Rosa dies.

To accede to Rosa's wish that she not die in a hospital—which she is now confusing with a concentration camp—Momo attends her till the end. Upon her death, he lights the menorah for her in her Jewish basement hideaway—now a virtual mausoleum—and applies makeup to her already decaying face.

Signoret so dominates *Madame Rosa* in her titular role that it is easy to overlook the qualities of director Mizrahi's film beyond the striking central performance. Unashamedly sentimental and warmly compassionate—tones which spill over into mawkishness and ingenuousness for the film's detractors—*Madame Rosa* paints a calculatedly stacked-deck picture of dignity, nobility, and togetherness in the face of squalor and degradation. The concentration with which Mizrahi and cinematographer Nestor Almendros focus on Signoret's expressive face, however, renders objections regarding verisimilitude academic.

Mizrahi's screenplay is based on Émile Ajar's 1975 Prix Goncourt-winning novel, published in English as *Momo*—the title change speaking volumes about the switch of emphasis from book to film. The latter offers a fluid progression of elliptical set pieces, its potentially lugubrious material leavened with moments of wry humor and a superbly integrated, violin-dominated score by Philippe Sarde.

Nevertheless, it is Signoret's commanding performance—for which she was awarded France's César Award—which makes *Madame Rosa* such an indelible cinematic work. Mizrahi's ultimate achievement was the result of his choice of and confidence in Signoret, complemented by Almendros' bold photographing of the consummate actress' ravaged face, itself mocked by actual photographs of the much younger, prettier, and healthier Simone Signoret which stare out at Rosa from her bedroom mirror. It is precisely Signoret's willingness to reveal and use much of her own physical unwinding—embellished by padded hips and grotesque facial makeup—that engages the audience's faculties and feelings so quickly and unyieldingly.

Signoret's is far from the only acting contribution to *Madame Rosa*. Mizrahi's casting—effective from the lead roles down to the walk-ons—and subsequent directing give the film a gritty kind of reality when the scenes call for it. Samy Ben Youb's Momo is a marvelous blend of wide-eyed innocence and emerging adult resourcefulness, and veteran actor Claude Dauphin is convincing as the gallant, ailing doctor who has to be carried up the steps to make house calls.

Madame Rosa can be viewed as a fable of sorts—old Jew and young Arab united in their misery and love—but it works best when not burdened with too much Middle Eastern political significance. Rather, it is a story about love and need, with strong undercurrents of loss—loss of one's loved ones, loss of one's faculties, loss of one's physical beauty. Accepted on its own terms, it is a moving and eloquent film that serves as a tribute to the human spirit.

Bill Wine

MÄDCHEN IN UNIFORM

Origin: Germany
Released: 1931
Released in U.S.: 1932
Production: Deutsche Film Gemeinschaft
Direction: Leontine Sagan
Screenplay: F. D. Andam and Christa Winsloe; based on the play *Gestern und Heute*, by Winsloe
Cinematography: Reimar Kuntze and Franz Weihmayr
Editing: no listing
Art direction: F. Maurischat and F. Winkler-Tannenberg
Music: Hanson Milde-Meissner
Running time: 98 minutes
Also known as: Girls in Uniform

> *Principal characters:*
> Fraulein von Bernburg.............Dorothea Wieck
> Manuela von Meinhardis..............Herta Thiele
> Frau Principal ....Emilia Unda
> Ilse von Westhagen ....Ellen Schwannecke
> Fraulein von Kosten ....Hedwig Schlichter

In 1931, John Krimsky, president of *Playchoice*, and Gifford Cochran, an artist with a studio in Munich, saw *Mädchen in Uniform* in Paris, flew to Berlin, and arranged for the American rights to the film. The following autumn, the original German-language version opened in New York City, where it received consistently good reviews. The first foreign-language talking picture to be shown in a Broadway theater, it ran seventeen weeks. Herman Schumlin, the theatrical producer, tried to prevent Krimsky and Cochran from showing *Mädchen in Uniform*. Schumlin claimed that the use of English subtitles was an arrogation of his rights, acquired from Christa Winsloe, the author of the play on which the film was based, to produce the film in English. Thereupon, the film was lip-synced in English and reopened in January, 1934. Krimsky ran into trouble again when Joseph Breen, administrator of the Production Code, refused to grant the film a "purity seal," deeming it unfit for showing to mixed audiences. The film was remade in 1958 in color with Romy Schneider and Lilli Palmer.

The controversy which surrounded *Mädchen in Uniform* when it opened has subsided with the passage of time. The reputed lesbian theme is, in fact, restrained to a few harmless jokes and one unerotic, although heartfelt, kiss on the lips. The men in the film are limited to a few statues, a line of soldiers marching near the boarding school and a collage of photographs stuck to the locker of the school cutup, Ilse von Westhagen (Ellen Schwannecke). The lesbian notion is introduced through such devices as sprinkling some women's photographs among those pictures, the students linking arms occasionally, and two girls wistfully pressing their heads together at a window drenched in moonlight. One scene shows the girls teasing a well-endowed pupil into demonstrating her specialty—popping the buttons off her blouse by expanding her chest.

The film's real subject is repression and its harmful effects. The institute is so oppressive that naturally, when the girls do have a chance to behave freely, they go overboard, at least within the rules director Leontine Sagan intends her audience to understand were prevalent at the time. Any respectable boarding school today would be delighted if its students' antics were restricted to spiked punch, cow-eyed crushes, and an innocent snuggle or two.

Manuela von Meinhardis (Herta Thiele), a motherless fourteen-year-old, arrives at a Potsdamm school for the daughters of army officers. She is already in uniform—the ubiquitous sailor outfit worn by boys and girls alike in the early twentieth century. Manuela is readily accepted by the other girls, who exhibit various degrees of resentment at the authoritarian methods of the teachers and the Teutonic headmistress, the Frau Principal (Emilia Unda). As a disciplinarian, the Frau Principal is seconded by a cringing assistant, Fraulein von Kosten (Hedwig Schlichter), who pads through the halls spying on the girls, reporting disobedience and making herself unpopular in the service of her employer. The chief insurgent among the pupils is Ilse, whose letter home asks, "Why is one hungrier on Sunday than weekdays?" The answer is not only that the food is inadequate—a half-pound of butter divided among fifty girls demonstrates both stinginess and the size of the school—but also that without lessons to distract them from their boredom and confinement, they feel their emotional starvation more acutely.

The students' lack of spiritual nourishment is alleviated by one teacher, Fraulein von Bernburg (Dorothea Wieck), who is too paradigmatically virtuous to be a realistic figure. In a film in which every character is a symbol, however, she is more than acceptable as a saint in a gray uniform. All the girls focus on Bernburg, who kisses them goodnight, listens to their pleas, and tries to be both a mother and a teacher to schoolgirls who have no positive role models for either. For example, when Ilse packs to run away after being disciplined severely, she is interrupted by Bernburg, who halts her impetuous rush with one kindly sentence. Although the viewer understands the instructress' influence on the pupils, she is not omnipotent, and Sagan and Winsloe undermine their thesis by oversimplifying the struggle between authoritarianism and a more temperate attitude.

Manuela becomes fixated on Fraulein von Bernburg. Praised for her performance in the leading role of Friedrich Schiller's *Don Carlos* before the school and its visitors, she becomes drunk on spiked punch and, still costumed as the "Don," declaims her love for her teacher. Then, distraught and embarrassed, Manuela rushes to the top of the school's central staircase; the girls, united in their love for their fellow sufferer and their hatred of the regime, scour the school for her. Manuela slumps into a faint before she can commit suicide, and the girls catch her. Fraulein von Bernburg tells the Frau Principal that the "children prevented a tragedy," as the headmistress, temporarily defeated and ashamed, stalks down the hall alone.

The astonishing achievement of *Mädchen in Uniform* has little to do with the trite and reductive plot, but rather with the way it is interpreted visually. An opening montage of military statues, soldiers at drill, and barred gates gives way to the girls walking through an arcade in their striped uniforms, the stripes correlating with the heavy verticals of the previous images. Clothing is of particular importance, since the last link the girls have with their homes and their individuality is the dresses in which they arrive at the school. Manuela's chemise is torn and Bernburg gives her a new one, forging yet another link between them. The institute's hierarchy is enforced by its uniforms: dark gray for the Frau Principal, who supports herself on a cane; light gray for the teachers; and stripes and aprons for the students. Members of the administration wear medals; the students, rosettes, stressing the parallels with militarism. Since the school is attended by the daughters of officers at a nearby army garrison, recurring bugle blasts govern the girls' lives as emphatically as they do those of the soldiers.

Yet the film focuses on the girls themselves, their feelings of abandonment—their yearning for affection, and their reliance on one another for support—as much as it does on Prussian tyranny. Photographed in soft focus against light backgrounds, blonde Manuela is a luminous, sensitive mouthpiece for Sagan's and Winsloe's opposition to repression.

Sagan foreshadows Manuela's suicide attempt by staging her first meeting with Bernburg on the stairs. Next, the steps are used for an impromptu physics exercise to relieve the girls' boredom on their day off. Repeated references to the height of the staircase increase the viewers' awareness of Manuela's danger when she climbs over the top railing.

Sagan relieves the constant Germanic chiaroscuro with brightly lit scenes showing the pupils dressed in white, at play in their dressing room. Here the viewer sees how fear has already undermined their girlish hearts and what they do to counteract that oppressiveness. The nonconformist Ilse plays pranks, mugs, laughs, and generally tries to relieve the tension.

It was not the intention of Winsloe or Sagan to rebel openly against Teutonic despotism through their spokeswoman, Fraulein von Bernburg. Fraulein von Bernburg wants to incorporate kindliness within the autocracy. As Siegfried Kracauer points out in *From Caligari to Hitler*, "One is tempted to suspect that [Bernburg's] understanding, if not motherly, attitude toward the girls originates in patriarchal notions inseparable from the authoritarian regime. Fraulein von Bernburg is a heretic who never dreams of exchanging the traditions she shares with the headmistress for a 'new order.'"

Director Leontine Sagan was a woman of the theater; first an actress, she was trained by Max Reinhardt. She directed *Mädchen in Uniform* for the stage, then made this, her film directing debut with the guidance of the more experienced German director, Carl Froelich. Her second, and seemingly last, job as a film director was for *Men of Tomorrow* (1932) for Alexander Korda in England. It is distinguished only as a vehicle for Robert Donat's film debut. The rise of Nazism (*Mädchen in Uniform* was banned in Germany) forced Sagan and the principal actors to leave Germany. She returned to stage work in England and South Africa, where she was a cofounder of the National Theatre of Johannesburg. She died in Vienna in 1974, at the age of eighty-five.

Judith M. Kass

THE MAGIC FLUTE
(TROLLFLÖJTEN)

Origin: Sweden
Released: 1975
Released in U.S.: 1975
Production: Ingmar Bergman for Sveriges Radio A.B. Production
Direction: Ingmar Bergman
Screenplay: Ingmar Bergman; based on the opera by Wolfgang Amadeus Mozart, libretto by Emanuel Schikaneder
Cinematography: Sven Nykvist
Editing: Siv Lundgren
Art direction: Henny Noremark
Music: Wolfgang Amadeus Mozart
MPAA Rating: G
Running time: 134 minutes

Principal characters:

Tamino	Josef Köstlinger
Pamina	Irma Urrila
Papageno	Håken Hagegård
Papagena	Elisabeth Eriksson
Sarastro	Ulrik Cold
Queen of the Night	Birgit Nordin
Three ladies	Britt-Marie Aruhn
	Kirsten Vaupel
	Birgitta Smiding
Monostatos	Ragnar Ulfung
Speaker	Erik Saedén

Despite a long history of attempts which date back to the earliest days of silent films, successful film adaptations of opera have been relatively few. Most opera stars either have never ventured before a motion-picture camera or have found themselves ill-suited to scrutinizing close-ups. More important, most film directors have shown little or no familiarity with opera. Notable exceptions have been the Italian directors Luchino Visconti and Franco Zeffirelli and the Swedish director Ingmar Bergman. In the opinion of most critics, it is Bergman's production of *The Magic Flute* which finally put to rest the belief that opera could not be successfully translated to the screen.

Bergman himself once said that he believed opera was better suited to television than to film, and, indeed, his adaptation of *The Magic Flute* began as a television show to commemorate the fiftieth anniversary of the birth of Swedish radio. This effort required a year to complete at a reported cost of more than two and a half million Swedish krøners, or $650,000. Following its Swedish television premiere on New Year's Day, 1975, *The Magic Flute* was released to theaters.

Ingmar Bergman is an ideal choice to stage Wolfgang Amadeus Mozart's opera. His reputation as one of the world's foremost film directors has kept many people, especially American audiences, from realizing that he also enjoys a considerable reputation as a stage director. He has worked with all forms of theater and has been acquainted with opera since childhood. As a young man, Bergman served as an assistant director of the Royal Swedish Opera. Later, in the 1960's, his production of Igor Stravinsky's *The Rake's Progress* won for him wide acclaim, including a rave review from Stravinsky himself.

Since then, Bergman has continued to mix stage and film work in an illustrious career. To those who know him only through his somber, often existential and unrelentingly solemn films of the 1950's and 1960's which secured his reputation as a director of serious cinema, the lighthearted, often comic touch of *The Magic Flute* must seem a shocking departure. Yet the search for love in the face of danger or hopelessness is a theme common to many of Bergman's films; that his characters have often failed in this quest has led to the bleakness which one sometimes associates with his work.

Yet Bergman has on occasion shown a gift for comedy or romance; critics cite such films as *Sommarnattens leende* (1955; *Smiles of a Summer Night*), which Bergman himself called "a bit of Mozart," and *Det sjunde inseglet* (1956; *The Seventh Seal*) as precursors of the romantic fairy tale, *The Magic Flute*.

Bergman for a long time had dreamed of staging Mozart's final opera, which he had first seen as a child of twelve. In a 1962 *Opera News* interview, he said, "To me the most alluring and difficult opera ever written is Mozart's *Magic Flute*. Nothing interests me more than this work; it offers a director more hurdles than any other opera."

The first hurdle that Bergman had to clear was the confusion surrounding the libretto written by Emanuel Schikaneder. For nearly two centuries, scholars have been arguing about abrupt shifts and puzzling references in *The Magic Flute*. Critics now agree that the opera may be interpreted as an allegory on Freemasonry (both Schikaneder and Mozart were Masons) but remain divided on the reason for the unexplained character shifts of two important roles, the Queen of the Night and Sarastro.

Bergman's aim was to re-create the look and spirit of the original production. To approximate the Theater-auf-der-Wieden in Vienna, where *The Magic Flute* premiered on September 30, 1791, Bergman chose Stockholm's eighteenth century Drottningholm Court Theater, built by Gustavus III,

Sweden's playwright-king. The interior of this historic theater (which proved too fragile to accommodate television equipment) was reconstructed in the studios of the Swedish Film Institute under the supervision of Henny Noremark.

Bergman chose a cast trained primarily for opera rather than film, and for the sound track, sung in Swedish, used a playback system whereby the actors meticulously synchronized their performances to their own prerecorded voices and music.

To establish the rapid pace which he deems essential to the opera, Bergman used during the eight-minute overture nearly two hundred shots of a theater audience, mostly close-ups (including one eight-frame shot of himself), and focuses repeatedly on the beatific face of his own young daughter, Linn Ullman. In this sequence, he presents a wide range of ages, races, and nationalities, as if to demonstrate the broad appeal of Mozart's work. Curiously, at no time during this overture does he show the viewer the orchestra or conductor Eric Ericson. Later in the film, he returns to the close-ups of his daughter, often using her facial expressions to signal a change in scene or mood.

The first act of *The Magic Flute* opens with Tamino (Josef Köstlinger), a prince, being pursued by a dragon. When he swoons, he is saved by three ladies (Britt-Marie Aruhn, Kirsten Vaupel, and Birgitta Smiding) who slay the beast, then examine the handsome youth carefully and compete for the task of guarding him. The awakening prince first believes that the dragon has been slain by Papageno (Håken Hagegård), a rustic birdcatcher who appears as the women momentarily depart and who does nothing to correct Tamino's mistaken assumption. For this fib, Papageno's lips are padlocked by the three ladies, who return to present to Tamino a locket containing a picture of Pamina (Irma Urrila), the daughter of the Queen of the Night (Birgit Nordin). Pamina has been abducted by Sarastro (Ulrik Cold), a mighty sorcerer.

The queen arrives and laments her loss, promising her daughter to the prince if he will rescue her, a quest which Tamino, already enchanted by Pamina's portrait, readily undertakes. The queen's three attendants unlock the lips of the birdcatcher, who reluctantly agrees to accompany the prince. They then present gifts to the two travelers: for Papageno, a box of magic bells; for Tamino, a magic flute. The ladies disappear, and three spirits descend in a balloon to direct them to Sarastro's realm.

Tamino, separated momentarily from his companion, finds himself before three entrances to Sarastro's temple. Rebuffed at the first two doors, Tamino encounters a speaker (Erik Saedén) at the third door, who assures him that Sarastro is not an evil man. Confused, the prince plays the flute which magically transports him from the darkness and uncertainty of Sarastro's temple to a sunlit meadow where animals appear and are charmed by the flute's song.

Monostatos (Ragnar Ulfung), a lustful Moor in the service of Sarastro, guards Pamina. Papageno, discovering her and eluding the Moor, acquaints the girl with the prince's quest and his love for her, and the two plan her escape. Tamino, hearing the call of Papageno's pipes, grows confident that he will soon find Pamina. Sarastro arrives, and Pamina confesses her attempt to escape. As act 1 ends, the prince is brought before Sarastro, who declares that Tamino must undergo trials to determine if he is worthy of Pamina.

During a brief intermission, Bergman's camera ventures backstage to glimpse the actors as they relax. Each displays characteristics appropriate to the character he or she is playing. Thus, the wise Sarastro uses the break to study a part from Richard Wagner's opera *Parsifal* (1882), the evil queen puffs on a cigarette directly beneath a no-smoking sign, and the two lovers Tamino and Pamina pass the time together playing chess.

As the second and final act begins, Sarastro addresses his priests and praises Tamino, telling the brotherhood that, should the prince prove worthy, he will be permitted to marry Pamina, who is revealed to be Sarastro's daughter. Tamino and Papageno are led to the House of Trials where they are visited by the three ladies, who urge them to remain faithful to the queen.

Meanwhile, Pamina sleeps fitfully. Monostatos attempts to ravish her but is interrupted by the arrival of the Queen of the Night who, cold with fury, demands that her daughter kill Sarastro.

Tamino and Papageno undergo a second trial of silence, but the birdcatcher is unable to resist the urge to sing a song. Papagena (Elisabeth Eriksson), a beautiful girl, disguises herself as a crone and flirts with Papageno, but when he attempts to kiss her, she vanishes. Pamina arrives and mistakenly interprets Tamino's steadfast silence as rejection. In despair, she contemplates suicide but is dissuaded by the three spirits. Papageno, disconsolate at the loss of Papagena, attempts to hang himself but is also saved by the three spirits, who return to him his magic bells which enable him to call Papagena.

Tamino faces a third trial of fire and water and is joined by Pamina, who brings him his magic flute. Released from his vow of silence, Tamino declares his intentions, and the two lovers successfully withstand the frightful trial.

The Queen of the Night and Monostatos join forces and attempt to destroy the brotherhood but are routed by Sarastro and his priests. After this defeat of the evil forces, Sarastro gives his blessing to the young lovers and abdicates his throne in favor of Tamino.

Although Bergman has shortened the opera by about forty minutes, he has remained faithful to the spirit of Mozart's work but has not hesitated to make some adjustments to the libretto. The most obvious allusions to Free-masonry and all references to Isis and Osiris have been eliminated, and Papageno's traditional costume of feathers has been altered to the simple clothes of a woodland rustic. The most notable change, however, is the identification of Sarastro as Pamina's father, an addition which reportedly stems from Bergman's childhood misunderstanding of the story. Though some critics were disturbed by this interpretation, most agreed that it simply clarified what had been an ambiguous point in the opera.

Bergman has changed the order of some scenes, especially near the end where he juxtaposes Papageno's and Pamina's suicide attempts and lets the attack by Monostatos and the queen fall immediately after Tamino's final trial. This change makes for a more dramatic finale, for the comic relief of Papageno and Papagena's love duet no longer interrupts the flow of the more serious plot elements which now progress from the final trial to the attack and defeat of the evil forces and the alliance of the lovers. The original libretto makes no mention of Sarastro's abdication, but by having him step down, Bergman shifts the final emphasis from a Masonic triumph to a romantic one.

Structurally, the film has much in common with a long-established formula for film musicals: By showing an audience within the film, Bergman provides someone with whom the audience can identify; subsequent shots of the performers speaking directly to the camera no longer seem unnatural or jarring. Close-ups and point-of-view shots establish a second level of identification which allows the viewer to feel like both a spectator and a performer. Backstage shots, which Bergman uses effectively for Papageno's entrance and during the intermission, are a frequent convention of film musicals which sustain the actors' point of view and provide, as Pauline Kael has noted, in her review in *The New Yorker*, the story of the performance as well as the story of the opera.

The film abounds with delightful comic touches: the dragon which prances in comic pursuit of Tamino and dies with smoke and sparkling flames coming from its nostrils, Pamina's picture in the locket which comes to life as the prince looks at it, the three boys who descend in a marvelously creaky eighteenth century balloon, the snowfall that marks the two suicide attempts, and the frequent use of title cards during songs, which Bergman uses as the filmic equivalent of the theatrical aside.

Though some critics regretted that Bergman had not chosen more notable singers, most praised both the singing and acting of the entire cast, with Håken Hagegård deserving special mention for his comic portrayal of the roisterous Papageno.

Bergman's affection for theatrical devices is everywhere apparent in *The Magic Flute,* and the patent artificiality of the sets adds to the film's charm. The stage setting works because the director does not allow himself to be limited by it; he retains the theatrical context, but through shot selection (predominantly closeups, especially for the arias), brisk editing, and occasional camera movement, he avoids the clichés of most filmed operas.

The result is a romantic and comic masterpiece full of naïve charm and theatrical nostalgia, a film entertaining to both Mozart purists and filmgoers unfamiliar with opera. At the time of its release in 1975, critics generally regarded it as the most successful adaptation of opera yet filmed.

Rick Shale

THE MAGICIAN
(ANSIKTET)

Origin: Sweden
Released: 1958
Released in U.S.: 1959
Production: Allan Ekelund for Svensk Filmindustri
Direction: Ingmar Bergman
Screenplay: Ingmar Bergman
Cinematography: Gunnar Fischer
Editing: Oscar Rosander
Art direction: P. A. Lundgren
Music: Erik Nordgren
Running time: 101 minutes

Principal characters:
Albert Emanuel Vogler . . . . Max von Sydow
Manda/Aman . . . . Ingrid Thulin
Doctor Vergérus . . . . Gunnar Björnstrand
Grandmother . . . . Naima Wifstrand
Spegel . . . . Bengt Ekerot
Sara . . . . Bibi Andersson
Ottilia . . . . Gertrud Fridh
Simson . . . . Lars Ekborg
Police Chief Starbeck . . . . Toivo Pawlo
Consul Abraham Egerman . . . . Erland Josephson
Tubal . . . . Åke Fridell
Sofia Garp . . . . Sif Ruud
Antonsson . . . . Oscar Ljung
Mrs. Henrietta Starbeck . . . . Ulla Sjöblom

In *The Magician*, Swedish director Ingmar Bergman explores the general subject of the work of an artist, as well as—to some degree—the more specific subjects of filmmaking and his own life. These topics are by no means the entire substance of the film, however, and none of the many themes of *The Magician* are developed in a clear-cut manner. Such themes as the conflict or differences between rationalism and faith, truth and illusion, and science and religion are intermixed with comedy, drama, and melodrama in a manner that may be seen as artfully ambiguous or as unnecessarily confusing. Bergman himself has mentioned the elements of game playing and of chance that went into the film and remarked that it should not be taken too seriously. *The Magician* is, then, a sincere but not overly serious film that treats many complex matters.

The actors and actresses in *The Magician* have become familiar to those who have seen most of Bergman's previous films. Of the seven most important roles, all are played by actors or actresses who have played major roles in at least one of his five previous films (from *Smiles of a Summer Night*, 1955, to *The Brink of Life*, 1957). As he has done throughout most of his professional career, Bergman was working in both the theater and films at the time, and he says that he was able to keep his theater company together by promising the members parts in his next film. Indeed, Bergman claims that he had tremendous problems devising a film that would accommodate all the people to whom he had promised parts. This difficulty, however, is not evident to the viewer of the film. What is evident is that the director is working with accomplished performers who work well with him. This is undoubtedly part of the reason that most viewers and critics simply take for granted that the acting in an Ingmar Bergman film will be superlative.

Bergman begins *The Magician* by showing the audience a coach carrying a strange troupe through the forest in mid-nineteenth century Sweden. The troupe consists of five people. Vogler (Max von Sydow) is an intense man with dark hair and beard; Manda (Ingrid Thulin) is Vogler's wife but spends most of the film—including this opening scene—disguised as a young man called Aman; the appearance of Vogler's grandmother (Naima Wifstrand) and the fact that she makes the medicine that the group sells suggest that she is something of a witch. Unlike the others are Tubal (Åke Fridell) and Simson (Lars Ekborg). Tubal is a large, lively man who functions as the troupe's manager. He describes his function as getting them out of the scrapes caused by Grandmother and Vogler. Simson is the party's young coachman.

Throughout the film, the audience is made to wonder whether Vogler or anyone in this troupe actually possesses any supernatural powers. A definitive answer to the question is never given, and the members of the group sometimes argue on one side of the question and sometimes on the other.

Soon after the opening of the film, the coach is stopped and the troupe is taken to the house of Consul Abraham Egerman (Erland Josephson), who explains that he and his wife, Ottilia (Gertrud Fridh), are interested in the spiritual world and have arranged for the troupe to meet in his house with the Chief of Police, Frans Starbeck (Toivo Pawlo), and the Royal Medical Counselor, Doctor Vergérus (Gunnar Björnstrand).

The "meeting" is obviously a test, but it is never entirely certain what the officials want the group to prove. Egerman seems genuinely interested in spiritual phenomena, but Starbeck and Vergérus apparently want to prove that the group is fraudulent. Vergérus is the most severe examiner, attacking Vogler's use of Franz Mesmer's principles of animal magnetism to treat sick people. He is also suspicious of the claim that Vogler is mute. Vogler and his troupe, on the other hand, carefully do not claim supernatural or healing powers and tell the medical counselor that their performance is merely a game, that the effects are accomplished with mirrors and other apparatus and are entirely harmless. They are thus put in the position of proving that all their effects are merely tricks. At least three times, in fact, someone in the film claims to be lying.

The first test comes the first evening when Vergérus dares Vogler to hypnotize him. After he tries to do so, Vergérus claims that he has failed, but the Egermans both think that the medical counselor was deeply affected and refuses to admit it. Then the group is told that it can have a permit if it gives a private performance the next morning in the large hall of the Egerman house.

The evening following the first test is filled with incident. Eating with the servants, both Tubal and Simson affect the manners of cosmopolitan men of experience, but each is seduced. Simson gives the serving girl Sara (Bibi Andersson) a love potion and talks of his experiences with women at other places where they have performed, but it is Sara who takes the initiative; she tells him that he talks too much. The cook, Sofia Garp (Sif Ruud), not only invites Tubal to her bedroom but also persuades him to quit the troupe and stay with her.

Meanwhile, Vergérus has seen Manda without her disguise and has offered to help her if she wants to leave the group, and Mrs. Egerman has invited Vogler to come to her bedroom after everyone is asleep. Although the two do not know it, Mr. Egerman hears this invitation as he stands behind a drapery. At the appointed hour, it is Egerman who appears at his wife's bedroom. In the bedroom of Vogler and Manda, Vogler removes his black beard, eyebrows, and wig. The effect is astonishing. Without his disguise he looks defenseless.

The demonstration the next day begins with Starbeck exposing the mechanism that makes it appear that Vogler is causing Manda (now again disguised as a young man) to float in the air. This is not, however, a devastating revelation, since Manda has told them that their performances are merely trickery. The demonstration takes a different direction when Mrs. Starbeck (Ulla Sjöblom) is put under a spell and reveals many embarrassing details about Starbeck, including her opinion of him. Then the Egerman's huge coachman, Antonsson (Oscar Ljung), is tied up with invisible chains by Manda. When she tells him that he is chained, he tries to move, but he cannot. When Vogler moves close to Antonsson, he grabs the throat of the magician and chokes him. This causes much confusion, but when it is over Vergérus looks at the magician lying on the floor and says that he is indeed dead. Later, the audience discovers that Antonsson has hanged himself.

That night Vergérus performs an autopsy on the body, but later, as he is writing the report, he suddenly sees a human eye in his inkwell. Then more and more strange things happen to him in that dark attic, until finally he finds that Vogler is in the room with him.

Later Vogler tells him that it was all only a cheap trick, that the body of an actor called Spegel (Bengt Ekerot—who played Death in *The Seventh Seal*) was substituted for Vogler's supposedly lifeless one. In this last sequence, Vogler for the first time appears without his disguise before everyone. He has no money, and his prospects look bleak. He and Manda prepare to leave, but Tubal is staying with Sofia, and Grandmother reveals that she has saved quite a bit of money and that she, too, is not going on with them. Sara, however, cannot be separated from Simson; so she joins the bedraggled group. Then, at the last moment, word arrives that the king has requested that Vogler give a performance for him at court. Vogler and his group drive away in triumph.

The parallels between the magician and the filmmaker both using apparatus to produce effects upon an audience are obvious, but as Bergman has pointed out, other elements of *The Magician* are also relevant in the director's life. He says that as an artist he has felt the same humiliation that Vogler had to endure and that the happy ending parallels the time Bergman felt despised and then was given a grant from the King's Fund in Sweden. For this reason, the command to appear before the king in *The Magician* is dated July 14—Bergman's birthday. Bergman has also remarked that as a filmmaker "one is in the privileged position of being allowed to ritualize a lot of tensions and complications within and around oneself."

The Magician, in short, delves into a number of themes in a manner that is always compelling, and it is also rather confusing. The film was perhaps best summed up by critic John Simon when he placed it in the category of "striking near-misses of genius."

Timothy W. Johnson

LE MAGNIFIQUE

Origin: France and Italy
Released: 1973
Released in U.S.: 1975
Production: Alexandre Mnouchkine and Georges Dancigers for Films
   Ariane/Mondex Films/Cerito-Oceania-Rizzoli
Direction: Philippe de Broca
Screenplay: Francis Veber and Philippe de Broca
Cinematography: Maurice Chapiron
Editing: Henri Lanoë
Art direction: François de Lamothe
Music: Claude Bolling
MPAA rating: no listing
Running time: 86 minutes
*Also known as: Comment détruire la réputation du plus célèbre agent secret du
   monde* and *The Magnificent One*

   Principal characters:
      Bob St. Clair/François
      Merlin .... Jean-Paul Belmondo
      Tatiana/Christine .... Jacqueline Bisset
      Karpoff/Charron .... Vittorio Capriolo

   In *Le Magnifique*, director Philippe de Broca and actor Jean-Paul Belmondo were reunited after a lapse of ten years. Their first collaboration, *Cartouche*, in 1962, was followed by the enormously successful *L'Homme de Rio*
(1964; *That Man from Rio*), which brought de Broca to international prominence, and then *Les Tribulations d'un chinois en Chine* (1965; *Up to His Ears*).
   All of these earlier outings were comic swashbucklers which involved
Belmondo's considerable athletic abilities as a stuntman. In *Cartouche*, he
played a peasant defector from Napoleon's army who comes to lead a band
of thieves as a sort of French Robin Hood on the eve of the Revolution.
That Man from Rio and *Up to His Ears* were both reminiscent of the classic
silent comedy chases, full of hair-raising thrills and laughter, which hurtled
along at a breakneck pace. In *That Man from Rio*, Belmondo was a plucky,
energetic soldier on leave who pursues his kidnaped girlfriend halfway
around the world to Brazil, survives every manner of danger to rescue her,
and returns to Paris, all in the space of a weekend pass. *Up to His Ears*, on
the other hand—based on a story by Jules Verne—saw Belmondo as the
one who is chased. As a member of the "nouveau poor," he arranges to be
killed so that his heirs can collect on an insurance policy, only to fall in love,
decide that he wants to live, and evade a number of assassination attempts

until the appointed deadline is past.

In *Le Magnifique*, de Broca both celebrates and spoofs these earlier heroic, dashing images portrayed by Belmondo by giving him a dual role. As François Merlin, he appears as a seedy hack writer (with a nagging nicotine cough). Merlin churns out pulpy spy novels featuring Bob St. Clair, a debonair, invincible secret agent of the James Bond school. Belmondo plays both parts to the hilt, giving resonance to the relationship between the author and his fictional creations. St. Clair is everything Merlin would like to be, yet he is so smug and self-assured that he comes off as somewhat obnoxious; Merlin is by far the more human and appealing of the two.

The plot line of *Le Magnifique* is a remarkably simple one, based on the notion that incidents and details from a writer's life are inevitably, if obliquely, reflected in his work. De Broca has said that for him, "a film is less to tell a story than to show a thousand little things, or two or three, but with a cupful of details, an ornamental profusion," and indeed, perhaps the most remarkable aspect of *Le Magnifique* is how rich a film and how much comic invention are derived from such a slender premise. Seldom has so much been made from so little.

The story is actually two stories: that of the rumpled, threadbare writer struggling to finish his latest novel in the Bob St. Clair series on schedule, counterpointed by the glamorous adventures of the superspy, which form a film-within-a-film.

The tone of the comic thriller is established at the outset. While a mariachi band plays in Acapulco, a suspicious-looking man makes a call in a telephone booth. Suddenly, a helicopter descends, captures the phone booth, and skylifts it out to sea. There, it is dumped into the waves in front of a caged shark, which is released to devour the occupant. The mastermind behind the murder is the evil Karpoff (Vittorio Capriolo), head of the Albanian secret police, who is trying to take over the free world. Only the invincible Bob St. Clair, fresh from the fleshpots of Baghdad, can stop him.

Meanwhile, François Merlin pounds at his battered typewriter through a haze of cigarette smoke and aquavit. Surrounded by overflowing ashtrays in his cluttered, decrepit old flat, Merlin is besieged by a multitude of problems: He is battling a head cold in the drab Paris winter; his ex-wife is after him for back alimony, and he is confounded by red tape and diffident repairmen when a plumber whom he has been trying to get to fix a leak for weeks demurs, saying he cannot make the repairs until the electrician has been there, although Merlin points out that the electrician says the same thing about the plumber. The cleaning lady constantly interrupts him and criticizes his work, a policeman threatens him with a parking ticket, the convertible top to Merlin's vintage jalopy refuses to convert and then rips to shreds in a driving rainstorm, and Merlin's stingy editor smoothly refuses him an advance.

By contrast, everything goes easily for Bob St. Clair. Dressed immaculately in tropical whites, constantly flexing his muscles, flashing his grin, and suavely combing his hair, St. Clair is infallible, whether dispatching a score of enemy agents with a twist of his wrist or casually leaping into a hammock to make love to a beautiful woman on a sun-splashed Acapulco beach.

The heart of *Le Magnifique* is the ingenious way that de Broca intercuts between the two characters and stories. People in Merlin's life show up in his novel, with actors playing two parts: The recalcitrant plumber and electrician become dim-witted henchmen who receive their just deserts at the hand of St. Clair, while Merlin's editor, Charron, appears in the role of Karpoff, St. Clair's Albanian archnemesis. When St. Clair finally does catch up with Karpoff, the villain dangles a bribe to join him, entreating St. Clair to consider it as an "advance," which St. Clair coolly refuses. Such is the author's revenge.

The romantic interest in the novel is inspired by an attractive young woman, Christine (Jacqueline Bisset), who is a neighbor in an apartment across the courtyard from Merlin's. He has shyly admired her from afar but does not even know her name. She becomes St. Clair's voluptuous assistant, Tatiana, a perfect companion.

De Broca also uses a wealth of cinematic editing devices to overlap cleverly between the writer and his fictional narrative. In the middle of the Bob St. Clair story, for example, all the characters suddenly develop an odd speech impediment in which they cannot pronounce the letter "r." De Broca cuts to Merlin, furiously attacking his typewriter, whose "r" key has become jammed. In another instance, Merlin's cleaning lady surrealistically appears in the midst of a St. Clair beach sequence, pushing a vacuum cleaner noisily over the dazzling sands of Acapulco. A moment later, the viewer is back in Merlin's apartment, where the cleaning lady's vacuuming has intruded on his concentration. Similarly, the characters may suddenly stop in mid-sentence, question what they are saying, and look quizzically at the camera, waiting while the writer reconsiders the dialogue. A scene from the spy story abruptly wipes violently upward as Merlin, in dissatisfaction, yanks a page out of his typewriter to begin again. Perhaps the most entertaining of these editorial devices occurs when a car plunges off a cliff, and then, the author changing his mind, the film reverses and the parts of the demolished automobile magically fly together again as the car rebounds back up the precipice.

In addition to his imaginative cutting, de Broca displayed his genius for delightful silliness and inspired screenwriting. When a dying Albanian operative, caught in a deadly crossfire, utters a few last words (as in Alfred Hitchcock's *The Man Who Knew Too Much*) in his native tongue, St. Clair has to discover their meaning. He resorts to using a team of translators, who translate Albanian into Serbo-Croatian, then Serbo-Croatian into Romanian, Romanian into Hungarian, Hungarian into Russian, and Russian into French, passing the words along in a ridiculous babble.

Merlin eventually makes the acquaintance of his lovely neighbor and discovers that Christine is a university graduate student in sociology who is interested in Bob St. Clair as a sociological phenomenon. As a result of her fascination, Merlin becomes jealous of his own creation. Back at the typewriter, he proceeds to humiliate his hero, who suddenly is clumsy and buffoonish, becoming entangled in the hammock into which he had leaped so gracefully and making a fool of himself in front of Tatiana. Cackling with devilish glee, Merlin even kills off St. Clair as a result of his own blundering stupidity. Having vented his feelings, Merlin throws the page out and begins again.

The dual stories draw to a parallel conclusion as Merlin's editor meets Christine and attempts to seduce her under the pretense of being interested in her thesis for possible publication. Just as Bob St. Clair arrives in the nick of time to save Tatiana from the clutches of the dastardly Karpoff, Merlin races to rescue Christine from the publishing magnate. In the end, she and Merlin fall in love, and he throws his manuscript out the window, the pages fluttering down into the street. Literature's loss is romance's gain.

The critical response to *Le Magnifique* was mixed. Most reviewers found it mildly pleasant, though not one of de Broca's major works. The satire of action-filled spy capers seems more reminiscent of the 1960's James Bond/Matt Helm/Our Man Flint genre, which did, in fact, turn to satirizing itself in the latter productions. What works even less well is the apparent lampoon of gory Sam Peckinpah-style violence, which serves only to undermine the humor by abruptly turning it pitch-black, despite the point that the director was undoubtedly trying to make.

Le Magnifique lacks the gentle irony and the moments of melancholy, contemplative beauty which gave charm to de Broca's earlier films. Instead, its style is closer to the antic quality of an animated cartoon. Nevertheless, in terms of originality and freshness, comic invention from the slightest of sources, and laughter, *Le Magnifique* is one of de Broca's most rewarding pictures.

Steve Greenberg

MAN ABOUT TOWN
(LE SILENCE EST D'OR)

Origin: France and United States
Released: 1947
Released in U.S.: 1947
Production: René Clair for Pathé-Cinéma/RKO
Direction: René Clair
Screenplay: René Clair
Cinematography: Armand Thirard and A. Douarinou
Editing: Louisette Hautecœur
Art direction: Léon Barsacq and M. de Gastyne
Costume design: Christian Dior
Music: Georges Van Parys
Running time: 100 minutes
Running time in U.S.: 89 minutes

Principal characters:

Émile Clément	Maurice Chevalier
Jacques	François Périer
Madeleine	Marcelle Derrien
Lucette	Dany Robin
Duperrier	Robert Pizani
Joseph	Paul Olivier
Célestin	Roland Armontel
Hairdresser	Raymond Cordy
Camera operator	Gaston Modot
Paulo	Bernard Lajarrige
Sultan	Paul Demange
Marinette	Christiane Sertilange

Man About Town was René Clair's first French film after a hiatus of more than a decade; his last French film prior to *Man About Town* had been *Le Dernier Milliardaire* (1934). In the years between, he produced two films in England, *The Ghost Goes West* (1935) and *Break the News* (1937), and then returned briefly to France, where he was involved in a short documentary and started a feature, *Air pur,* which was interrupted by World War II and was never completed. Clair then went to the United States, where he made four films: *The Flame of New Orleans* (1941), *I Married a Witch* (1942), *It Happened Tomorrow* (1943), and *And Then There Were None* (1945). Then, with some American financing, he returned to France to make *Man About Town.*

Although *Man About Town* is based on a theme often treated in drama and most notably linked with Molière's _L'École des femmes_ (1662; _The School for Wives_)—indeed, Clair himself described the film as Molière's story transplanted to the setting of one of his earlier films, _Sous les toits de Paris_ (1930; _Under the Roofs of Paris_)—it is also an expression of Clair's appreciation for the pioneers of film, such as Georges Méliès, Max Linder, and Louis Feuillade, from whom he had learned so much. The film is set in 1906 in Paris and features characters involved in the making of films in those early days of motion pictures. The charcters do not represent actual persons; rather, they are composites of the filmmakers who gave birth to the cinematic art.

The story concerns a middle-aged filmmaker, Émile (Maurice Chevalier), who expounds upon life and gives practical advice on how to live it to the fullest to his young and timid assistant, Jacques (François Périer). Jacques is particularly shy when it comes to approaching the opposite sex, so Émile— a Don Juan who is always searching for new conquests and avoiding commitments—teaches his protégé how to seduce women.

The film's essential irony derives from the fact that both men, without the other's knowledge, have set their sites on Madeleine (Marcelle Derrien), the daughter of a former love of Émile. Madeleine's father, a traveling comedian and an old friend of Émile, has asked the filmmaker to look out for his daughter, and she has become an actress at the Fortuna studio, where Émile works. By chance, Jacques has met Madeleine on a bus and seeks to win her heart. In encouraging Jacques to pursue the young woman (whose identity is unknown to him), Émile subverts his own aspirations as a lover with his excellence as a teacher of the art of seducing women. The irony is underscored in several scenes: Both men have conversations with Madeleine, on separate occasions, in the same café; both engage in simultaneous inner dialogues about her as they stand on opposite sides of a wall in the studio; and Émile unwittingly directs Madeleine (as a princess) and Jacques (as an explorer) in a film which brings the real-life lovers closer together.

Émile gives Jacques a speech to use on his young lady: He is to tell her not to waste her fleeting youth by marrying without love; to drive the point home, he is to quote to her the admonition of the poet Pierre de Ronsard: "Gather rosebuds while ye may." Jacques delivers this speech to Madeleine, who in turn relays it to Émile: She is not going to waste her fleeting youth, she tells him; she is going to "gather rosebuds" while she may. When Émile asks her the source of this advice, she replies that it is Ronsard, the poet. The full truth is soon disclosed by Jacques himself, who, torn between loyalty to his teacher and attraction to Madeleine, breaks the astounding news to Émile. The irony comes full circle: Now Émile realizes that he has helped Jacques to make a conquest that he hoped would be his own.

Despite the potential of such news to devastate its recipient, Émile musters his sense of humor and philosophical resignation, accepting the situation and giving the young couple his blessing. At the close of *Man About Town*, Émile sits in the audience of a traveling theater, watching *Passion d'Orient*," the film starring Jacques and Madeleine which he, Émile, directed. When the Grand Vizier (clearly Émile's counterpart) aborts the princess' attempted suicide and unites her with the explorer, the two lovers embrace and the film-within-the-film ends. This happy ending, the viewer already knows, is Émile's reworking of an original, tragic one (to which a visiting dignitary had objected) in which the princess committed suicide; the explorer, in despair, followed suit; and the Grand Vizier was left in anguish. Émile asks a young theatergoer if she likes happy endings. When she replies in the affirmative, he adds that he does, too. The viewer of *Man About Town* realizes what the viewer of *Passion d'Orient* does not: Émile's concession to the happy ending mirrors his acceptance of Madeleine and Jacques as lovers; indeed, Émile has used his art to bring the two real-life lovers closer together.

It is not only the ending of *Man About Town* but also the entire film that raises the theme of illusion versus reality, the relationship between art and life. The story provided Clair with an excellent opportunity to deal with this issue by exploring how filmmakers create their own reality—how art can influence life. When Jacques and Madeleine meet in front of the camera that is filming *Passion d'Orient*, Émile initially thinks of them only as characters in his film, not suspecting the corresponding reality of their budding relationship in actual life. Similarly, Jacques, the initially timid protégé, is Émile's "creation" to the extent that the older man has remolded the younger man's approach to women, yet Émile fails to recognize the effect that such a creation will have upon his own life. *Man About Town* reveals Clair's belief that art not only is effected by, but also affects, life.

There were ironies in Clair's own relationship to filmmaking. Friends in the industry got him acting jobs, most notably for Feuillade. Like D. W. Griffith, Clair was somewhat ashamed to be associated with film and therefore took a pseudonym to preserve his real name for a more "respectable" literary career. He was elected to the French Academy on June 17, 1960, ironically as the first person to have been elected solely on the basis of achievements in cinema.

Although Clair did not intend to continue in the cinema, he became fascinated first by film and then by filmmaking. He went to Belgium, where his older brother Henri was assisting on a film, to learn the techniques of filmmaking. Living through the transition from silent to sound film, Clair retained a preference for silent film. Nevertheless, he did express the opinion that it would be possible to develop an art appropriate to sound. *Man About Town* is in many ways Clair's tribute, in a sound film, to the era and makers of silent film.

The technical elements of the production of *Man About Town* presented unique challenges for two reasons: The film was a "period piece," set in the early years of the twentieth century; moreover, the film concerned film-making itself and therefore required that distinctions be made between the "real life" of Clair's film and the artificial world of Émile's film-within-the-film.

Man About Town was therefore doubly dependent on decor, since it is set in a Paris film studio in 1906. Art director Léon Barsacq had to create not only sets depicting Paris in this era but also sets of the film sets in studios of this era. Visual elements were crucial in evoking the atmosphere of the city—with its boulevards, parades, and *café concerts* inhabited by strolling violinists, concierges, flower girls, hackney drivers, and police officers. Visual elements were also crucial in evoking the atmosphere of the Fortuna Studio, where contrived illusions are the business of the day. Barsacq was therefore an essential contributor to the success of the film.

All of this had to be captured on film by cinematographer Armand Thirard. The period setting of *Man About Town*, with its use of gas lamps, opened up opportunities for fascinating patterns of light and shadow, which were well exploited by Thirard.

Perhaps the greatest challenges posed by the demands of the film's dual nature were faced by the actors: In this film, acting is a demanding task because actors often have to say one thing while they express feelings which are quite the contrary. For example, Chevalier, as Émile, reassures a young woman whom he has just met that she need have no fear of his advances by telling her that he is old enough to be her father, but his vocal quality and mannerisms also make it clear to the viewer that this is in fact nothing but a trick designed to lead to seduction. Similarly, Périer and Derrien, actors acting as actors in Émile's film-within-the-film, essentially had to play two parts apiece, often maintaining their "real-life" identities as Jacques and Madeleine while superimposing their fictive identities as explorer and princess being directed by Émile.

Périer, as Jacques, successfully makes the transition from a shy and vulnerable social illiterate to a determined and accomplished suitor. The acting of Chevalier is totally befitting of a character who is as sophisticated, elegant, debonair, and charming as the worldly-wise Émile. He plays the part with exactly the right touch of humor, so that Émile can be taken seriously even as the audience laughs at his antics. Chevalier also helps the audience to accept the resignation of Émile to his fate, even as the viewer feels his hurt when he realizes that all is lost for him. Although the weakest of the three leads, Derrien sufficiently captured her role as a charming, sweet young thing.

Music played an especially important function in *Man About Town*, not only in evoking the atmosphere but also in developing the plot. A sentimental waltz serves as the motif throughout the film. It is used when Émile and

Jacques talk together about their love and when they talk separately with their love. In the scenes in which Jacques and Madeleine, and Émile and Madeleine converse at the same café, the strolling violinist plays this waltz in each instance. It is played by a pianist accompanying a silent film. The musical motif not only ties sequences together but also adds to the ironic quality of the film by its repetition in different contexts.

The literal translation of the French title, *Le Silence est d'or*, is the proverb "Silence is golden." In as richly structured a film as this—as one might expect—more than this one level of meaning is involved: The title also alludes to the irony of an overly talkative older man unwittingly teaching an excessively timid younger man how to beat him in the quest to win the woman whom they both desire. Émile would have served his own interests better if he remained silent. The notion of silence also alludes to the era of silent pictures, in which pioneers such as Méliès, Linder, and Feuillade discovered a technique that was to become both an art and a gold mine for some people. Perhaps the title also bore a hint by the nostalgic Clair that the gold of silent films had become tarnished with the advent of "talkies."

All that glitters is not gold, but in *Man About Town* Clair provided a glittering re-creation of the golden era of films and filmmakers. Ironically, Clair's own determined preference for the traditional method of creating filmic illusions in studios at a time when public taste preferred to have them created on location provoked criticism which tarnished his own reputation as a filmmaker.

Engaging in astute self-criticism, Clair once remarked that the opening of *Man About Town* is too slow and that too much time passes before Madeleine appears. *Man About Town* was not well received in English-speaking countries. Some speculated that the subject matter was of more interest to Latin than to Anglo-Saxon cultures. Clair himself attributed the problem to technique rather than story. In the English-language version, Chevalier comments in English, interspersed between the French dialogue. Clair subsequently decided that the interpolation of an invisible and omniscient commentator prevented the audience from identifying with the characters in the film. The film was, however, very well received in French-speaking countries and won the Grand Prix at both the Brussels and Locarno film festivals.

Harold Hatt

A MAN AND A WOMAN
(UN HOMME ET UNE FEMME)

Origin: France
Released: 1966
Released in U.S.: 1966
Production: Les Films 13 (AA)
Direction: Claude Lelouch
Screenplay: Claude Lelouch and Pierre Uytterhoven (AA)
Cinematography: Claude Lelouch
Editing: Claude Barrois and Claude Lelouch
Art direction: Robert Luchaire
Music: Francis Lai
Running time: 102 minutes

> *Principal characters:*
> Anne Gauthier . . . . Anouk Aimée
> Jean-Louis Duroc . . . . Jean-Louis Trintignant
> Pierre Gauthier . . . . Pierre Barouh
> Valérie Duroc . . . . Valérie Lagrange
> Headmistress . . . . Simone Paris
> Antoine Duroc . . . . Antoine Sire
> Françoise Gauthier . . . . Souad Amidou

A Man and a Woman was the foreign film success of the year in the United States in 1966. Having been named cowinner of the Grand Prize at the Cannes Film Festival, it set foreign-film box-office records when it arrived in the United States. It was nominated for four Academy Awards and won two, for Best Foreign Language-Film and for Best Original Screenplay. Even the recording of its sound track was a best-seller. The film was immensely popular because it combined the romance suggested by the title with interesting and exciting scenes of motor racing and filmmaking, a compelling score, accomplished adult actors and appealing child actors, and imaginative storytelling and camera work.

Since Claude Lelouch was not only the director of the film but also the coscenarist, cameraman, and assistant editor, *A Man and a Woman* is very much his film and demonstrates most of the characteristics that have made him popular with filmgoers but somewhat suspect with most critics. Among critics, he tends to inspire such reactions as Bosley Crowther's remark in *The New York Times* that he "has a rare skill at photographing clichés."

The narrative of *A Man and a Woman* is complex yet accessible, shifting from the present to the past and from real to imaginary scenes from the point of view of both of the principal characters. In addition to alternating between past and present, Lelouch also changes between color and monochrome. Some of the monochrome sequences are in standard black and white, but others are tinted in muted colors such as blue, red, or sepia. Although some critics and viewers have tried to find a logical pattern to these color changes, there is none. In fact, it was reported that parts of the film were not shot in color simply because Lelouch was unable to raise enough money to afford color film for the entire picture. He did, however, use a logically determined mixture of color and black and white in a later film *La Bonne Année* (1973; *Happy New Year*).

The film begins very simply, with a woman, Anne Gauthier (Anouk Aimée), telling a story to her little girl, Françoise (Souad Amidou). This opening scene is paralleled by one with a man, Jean-Louis Duroc (Jean-Louis Trintignant), and his little boy, Antoine (Antoine Sire). The scene is set in Deauville, where both children are attending a boarding school, and the parents are visiting them on a Sunday. At the end of the day, they separately return the children to the school. When Anne misses her train back to Paris and the headmistress of the school (Simone Paris) prevails upon Jean-Louis to give her a ride, the audience knows to a certain extent what will ensue, just as viewers of Hollywood films in the 1930's or 1940's knew what to expect when they saw that Cary Grant and Katharine Hepburn, for example, were the stars of the film.

As Jean-Louis drives Anne toward Paris that first time, both are initially ill at ease, and both say that they are married. As Anne tells Jean-Louis about her husband, Pierre (Pierre Barouh), the audience sees what she is describing. She says that he is a stuntman in films and describes him as a quite romantic and dashing man. When they reach Paris, Jean-Louis offers to drive her to Deauville the next weekend and says he would like to meet her husband. It is then that she tells him—and the audience sees in a flashback—that he was killed in a flaming explosion when he was too reckless during the filming of a battle scene. Jean-Louis can only see that he could not have known her husband was dead from the way she talked about him.

The audience then learns (although Anne does not) that Jean-Louis is a race-car driver. In the original script for the film, Jean-Louis was to be a physician, but Trintignant, who is a racing enthusiast, persuaded Lelouch to change the profession of the character. In the next segment of the film, Lelouch immerses the audience in the motor-racing world as Jean-Louis and other drivers test their cars. This sequence also sets up a bit of humor when Jean-Louis drives Anne to Deauville the next Sunday: He asks her if she rates him as a good driver, and she responds that he is about average.

As they continue the drive to Deauville, Jean-Louis tells Anne that he is a race-car driver, but while he is speaking, images representing Anne's thoughts reveal that she envisions him as a pimp. At Deauville, they spend the day together with the two children; there is a delightful luncheon scene in which the parents (self-consciously) and the children (unself-consciously) all talk to one another. On the way back to Paris, he tries to hold her hand, and she responds by asking about his wife. He tells her—and the audience sees in a flashback—about the twenty-four-hour LeMans race in 1963. When he was seriously injured in a crash, his wife Valérie (Valérie Lagrange) could not stand the shock and the strain of waiting to find out how seriously he was injured and killed herself. This section of the film is presented in the style of a television report, with an announcer's voice telling what is happening in the race and in the hospital where Jean-Louis has been taken.

After this disclosure, Jean-Louis leaves for Monte Carlo to drive in the arduous Monte Carlo Rally. In Paris, Anne follows the race through newspapers, radio, and television, and even buys a racing magazine. When the race is over, she sends Jean-Louis a telegram saying that she loves him. When he receives the message during a postrace banquet, he immediately leaves Monte Carlo and begins an all-night drive in the rain back to Anne. As he drives, the audience hears his thoughts in a voice-over. He speculates on what her reaction will be, on what he should do, on when he will arrive at her flat. The sequence is notable for the background theme music, played loudly as Jean-Louis' car races back to Paris. There is an amusing interruption in the drive back when he has to stop for gas, and the gas-station attendant is oblivious to his impatience.

He arrives at her flat, only to find that she has gone to Deauville, so he continues on. He finds her on the beach with the two children, and they embrace enthusiastically. This embrace is shown in two fairly long hand-held medium close-ups as the two spin around. The second shot of the two is followed by a long-shot of a dog playing on the beach, apparently sharing in their mood. This scene made a strong impression on nearly every viewer, but while some thought it appropriately joyful, others dismissed it as saccharine and contrived.

This is not, however, the happy ending. After they leave the children and go to a hotel room, they go to bed together, but it is obvious that, for Anne, something is wrong. Images show that she is thinking of her husband, and the two dress despondently. Anne decides that she will return to Paris on the train alone, and as she travels on the train and Jean-Louis drives toward Paris, crosscutting reveals that they are both thinking of a scene which the audience had not yet seen. They go to the hotel's restaurant and begin to order a meal, but then Jean-Louis orders a room instead.

Jean-Louis remembers that Anne has to change trains on her journey and meets her train. He walks toward the passengers alighting from the train. He sees Anne before she sees him, but when she does, her face brightens, and the two embrace again, much as they did on the beach. Then the frame freezes, the background turns white, and the film ends.

The use of point of view in *A Man and a Woman* is one of its interesting features. Throughout the film, the audience usually sees things from the point of view of Jean-Louis, both when he is not with Anne and when he is telling Anne about something. In only a few sections of the film is Anne seen when she is not with Jean-Louis: the short scene of her telling the story to Françoise at the beginning; the occasions on which she tells Jean-Louis about a past event; the sequence showing her activities while Jean-Louis is racing at Monte Carlo; and the shots of her alone in the train in the last sequence. If the two are not together, the audience almost always sees Jean-Louis rather than Anne. This pattern gives an added force to the scene near the end that shows Anne's memories of her husband which are interfering with her desire for Jean-Louis. Lelouch employs another imaginative shift in point of view to show that Jean-Louis and Anne are thinking of the same thing even though they are traveling toward Paris separately.

Especially after it became popular, *A Man and a Woman* provoked some scathing criticism for what certain reviewers regarded as its manipulative sentimentality. Lelouch perhaps anticipated that reaction when he had Jean-Louis say to Anne at one point that her story was like that of a television serial. Also, in a later film—*La Bonne Année*—he has a character remark that *A Man and a Woman* was only "windshield wipers and tranquilizers." (A projected sequel to the film, "Twenty Years Later," picks up the now-middle-aged characters who ended their relationship, according to Lelouch, one week after the ending of *A Man and a Woman*—even the writer/director did not completely succumb to the sentimentality of the plot.)

A Man and a Woman, however, does not deserve the occasionally violent dismissals it provoked. It is a successful romantic film with a greater amount of imagination and creative complexity than such films usually contain. In addition, Lelouch—as he has done in many of his other films—was able to cast first-rate actors and actresses and to obtain excellent performances from them.

Timothy W. Johnson

A MAN ESCAPED
(UN CONDAMNÉ À MORT S'EST ÉCHAPPÉ)

Origin: France
Released: 1956
Released in U.S.: 1957
Production: Alain Poiré and Jean Thuillier for Sociéte Nouvelle des
    Établissements Gaumont/Nouvelles Édition de Films
Direction: Robert Bresson
Screenplay: Robert Bresson, with additional dialogue by Bresson; based on
    the true story by André Devigny
Cinematography: Léonce-Henri Burel
Editing: Raymond Lamy
Art direction: Pierre Charbonnier
Music: Wolfgang Amadeus Mozart
Running time: 102 minutes
Also known as: Le Vent souffle où il vent and *The Spirit Breathes Where It Will*

> *Principal characters:*
> Lieutenant Fontaine .... François Leterrier
> Jost......................... Charles LeClainche
> Blanchet...................... Maurice Beerblock
> The Reverend de Leiris .... Roland Monod
> Orsini .... Jacques Ertaud
> Hebrard .... Jean-Paul Delhumeau
> Terry........................... Roger Tréherne
> Prisoner 110 .... Jean-Philippe Delamare
> Chief Warder .... Jacques Oerlemans
> Intelligence officer .... Klaus Detlef Grevenhorst
> Escort .... Leonhard Schmidt

Robert Bresson has made relatively few films, and since 1943 these have been distinguished by an unrelentingly personal vision and style. With the exception of *A Man Escaped*, which was popular in France, his films have not interested general audiences.

The mainstream commercial film tries to work on the viewer's emotions, but Bresson's impersonal, ascetic style, which seems scrupulously impartial, sometimes even indifferent, forces one to contend with issues that transcend emotion. Whereas in most films the plot, acting, cinematography, editing, and music are employed to hide the illusion's seams and the hand of the storyteller, Bresson deliberately calls attention to them. He magnifies mundane sounds, makes few concessions to smooth continuity, and frequently casts nonactors who, unlike professionals, have difficulty narrowing their complex emotional and intellectual responses to those of the scripted character. Furthermore, he will deliberately puncture suspense and create ambiguity about his intentions. The overall effect is to throw the viewer emotionally and intellectually off balance, making him contend with the film's formal patterns and unconventional vision. When Bresson is successful, as he is in *A Man Escaped*, he can understate the dramatic situation, still hold the viewer's attention, and provide a unique spiritual experience.

In this film, for example, the foreign title—literally translated as "a man condemned to death has escaped"—gives away the film's conclusion, shifting the emphasis from the plot's outcome to the process of escape and the human and divine forces influencing it. (The cotitle, taken from Saint John's Gospel, chapter 3—"The Spirit breathes where it will"—even makes explicit part of the film's theme.)

The theme of *A Man Escaped* is broader than the idea contained in the expression that originally was to have been the film's title: "Heaven Helps Him Who Helps Himself." The fierce determination of prisoner Fontaine (François Leterrier) to escape death is responded to not only by God but also by his fellow prisoners.

The story is based upon André Devigny's written account of his own imprisonment by the gestapo at Fort Montluc, Lyon, in 1943, for his activities with the French Resistance. Bresson shot part of the film on location at Fort Montluc. (Fortuitously, the hooks and ropes Devigny used still existed and were used as models.) Devigny was present during the filming to authenticate details, but Bresson, who himself had been a prisoner of war, wrote the script and created the dialogue. These facts, the film's use of nonprofessional actors, and its documentary visual style suggest documentary intent. *A Man Escaped*, however, is far more than a documentary. It is infused with Bresson's existential and religious belief (bursts of religious music cue the viewer at once to this), and, narrated by Fontaine, the visual and auditory point of view is frequently subjective.

During the titles and credits, the camera photographs a commemorative plaque for the prisoners who died at Montluc and then moves to the prison's gray, outer wall. The story immediately underscores Lieutenant Fontaine's will to escape. While being transported to prison with two other prisoners in the back of a car, Fontaine discovers that the door beside him is unlocked. When the car stops for a streetcar, he makes a break for freedom. Through the rear window the viewer sees the accompanying car pull up; men jump out and take off after Fontaine, shouting and shooting. The inevitability of his recapture is foreshadowed by the camera's waiting inside the car, focused on the other two handcuffed prisoners. After a few moments Fontaine is shoved back in through the car's still-open door, handcuffed, and then struck on the head with a pistol.

At the prison, he is taken into a room from which, after an unusual ellipse that deletes showing the beating he has received, he is carried to a cell, his shirt streaked with blood. Accepting his imminent death, he weeps. After he receives a note urging "courage" from the women's quarters and he discovers a way to communicate with his family by means of a fellow prisoner, however, his hope rapidly revives. In turn, Fontaine tries to inspirit his neighbor, a nineteen-year-old boy, by tapping out the words of a Resistance song with his handcuffs on their shared cell wall. Moved to another cell, Fontaine soon learns that the boy has been executed; to drive the thought of this from his mind, he directs his thinking to escape. His new neighbor, Blanchet (Maurice Beerblock), refuses to respond to his tapping and Fontaine becomes concerned with the man's silence. Only after Fontaine comes to Blanchet's aid—when the old man has a dizzy spell and falls as they are emptying their slop buckets in the prison yard—will he speak to Fontaine, but then only to enjoin him not to escape because others will be punished. Blanchet's despair is absolute; he was in the act of committing suicide when, as "chance" would have it, Fontaine's tapping interrupted him. Man's importance to his fellows and God's subtle machinations are already manifest.

Having determined that the soft wood holding the boards in the lower half of his door can be splintered and the boards removed, Fontaine uses his cement floor to hone an iron spoonhandle into a chisel. The film's most engrossing moments are those in which Fontaine is absorbed in fashioning his means of escape and disguising his accomplishments. The process itself embodies Fontaine's passionate will to escape, and Bresson elevates to nearly sacred status the mundane objects—a piece of string, a spoon, a pencil, a blanket, bed springs—that Fontaine almost magically transforms into life-preserving instruments of escape. In addition, Bresson's magnification of the sounds of Fontaine rubbing his spoon on the stone floor, chiseling and splintering the wood in his door, sweeping up the shavings, and slicing and ripping into strips blankets, sheets, and clothes, magnifies their significance and, since the sounds can betray Fontaine, the suspense. Eventually his spoon-chisel breaks.

In the washroom where the men surreptitiously communicate, Reverend de Leiris (Roland Monod), a Protestant minister and also a prisoner, discovers a Bible in his coat pocket. He calls it "luck," but Fontaine, not an intensely religious man (he prays "sometimes," he tells the minister, but believes he must help himself), calls it a miracle. Moments later, Fontaine luckily discovers an extra steel spoon.

At last, Fontaine is able to remove the planks in the lower half of his door and crawl out into the only occasionally patrolled corridor. He talks to the other prisoners through the doors of their cells. His sudden appearance surprises Blanchet who asks him how he will escape. Fontaine admits he does not know.

Events quickly suggest means. Prisoner Orsini (Jacques Ertaud), a man who cannot forgive his wife for betraying him, tries to escape while the men are exercising in the prison yard. He fails, but before Orsini is taken out and executed, Fontaine gains valuable information from him for his own escape. When Orsini is removed from his cell, his fate becomes the topic of conversation. The minister believes that Orsini wanted to be reborn into eternal life, but Blanchet sees his death as sacrificial, as necessary for Fontaine's success. Fontaine recognizes the new hope, if not faith, implicit in Blanchet's observation and points out to him that actually what is extraordinary is that he, Blanchet, noted it.

Soon afterward, Fontaine hears a strange creaking. (Throughout, sounds—streetcars and trains passing in the distance, firing squads, a guard patrolling on a squeaky bicycle—tantalizingly enlarge the dimensions of Fontaine's confined world.) Drawn to his cell door, he sees a German guard cranking open a skylight in the corridor. Fontaine has his means of escape—through the skylight and over the roofs, down into the prison yard, and over the two walls of the patrolled moat. Applying Orsini's experience, he dismantles his cell's steel window frame and bends it to form a hook. With his bedsprings, he reinforces the ropes that he has made by cutting blankets and cloth into strips. (His singleness of purpose is evidenced when he receives a package of clothing from home. He immediately slits into strips his clean, new shirt instead of the bloody one he has been wearing.) Blanchet even contributes one of his blankets and tells Fontaine to believe in his ropes and in himself. He adds that he and Fontaine will meet again in the next world. A measure of the emotional and spiritual progress that he has made through his contact with Fontaine is his final, "Goodbye, my friend."

The prisoners are ordered to turn in all writing instruments or incur a search. Fontaine's pencil is not indispensable, but when the guard arrives at the door to his cell, Fontaine hesitates and, at the last second, stubbornly denies that he possesses any writing materials. So-called luck is once again a factor: The guard only searches Fontaine's package from home.

Time is running out for Fontaine. He has been before the investigator and found guilty. In the washroom, when the minister hangs up his coat, Fontaine slips a note telling of his escape into its pocket. Fontaine and the minister hold their breath when the guard unexpectedly begins searching the coats. They watch him pause and bypass the minister's when he sees the cross in its lapel. The minister whispers, "Mon Dieu!"

Fontaine's efforts are threatened when another prisoner, a youth named Jost (Charles LeClainche), whom Fontaine suspects may be a German plant, is confined in Fontaine's cell. Fontaine studies Jost and weighs his choices: inform Jost of his plans and include him in the escape, or kill him. He informs Jost of his plan. Bresson's refusal to dramatize the details of his characters' mental and emotional states is perfectly illustrated here.

Fontaine's acceptance of Jost forces the viewer—after the fact—to infer his (Fontaine's) inspired faith in his own intuition, his fellowman, and his God. (Remarkably, the more familiar the viewer becomes with Fontaine's plain, sharp-featured, opaque face, which conceals equally his intelligence, his fierce will, and his emotions, the more saintly it becomes.)

Carrying the ropes and hook, the two emerge from their cell, exit through the skylight, and make their torturous journey through the darkness and across the rooftops. During the last, approximately fifteen minutes of the film, it is often too dark to make out Fontaine's and Jost's forms, much less their faces. This lighting plan is not only more realistic because, like the escapees, the viewer must rely more on his ears, but also, by making it difficult to focus on the characters' incidental actions, it permits the viewer to reflect on the human will and divine power behind their achievement. Once on the ground, Fontaine has to kill a German sentry in order to proceed to the next wall. (The camera remains near Jost and the sound of the struggle is covered by a passing locomotive; the viewer must imagine the details from a glimpse of the fallen sentry afterward. Bresson treats this violence just as he did the beating Fontaine received when he arrived at the prison.) On top of the first wall of the patrolled moat, Fontaine realizes that Jost was a godsend because alone he never could have scaled the walls. The final obstacle overcome, the men descend the outside wall into the street and dissolve into the darkness. Wolfgang Amadeus Mozart's triumphant but poignant Mass in C Minor—the startling outbursts of which have punctuated the film during a few, key moments—now cues the release of the viewer's emotions. It also celebrates the rightness and inevitability of Fontaine's success while calling attention to the blend of superhuman will with the "hand that directs all," as Bresson refers to it. One may even think that the Mass conveys human and divine sadness for those left behind and, possibly for all humanity. The reintroduction at this point of the chorus singing for God's mercy also underscores the theme of human solidarity (the chorus is heard only two other times: at the film's commemorative opening and during Orsini's sacrificial attempt to escape).

Though it is unusually elliptical and rigorously eschews the melodramatic, *A Man Escaped* may be—along with Jean Renoir's masterpiece, *La Grande Illusion* (1937), which also ends with two men disappearing into the distance—the most quietly suspenseful and inspiring film ever made about an escape from prison.

Hubert I. Cohen

MAN IS NOT A BIRD
(ČOVEK NIJE TICA)

Origin: Yugoslavia
Released: 1965
Released in U.S.: 1974
Production: Avala Film
Direction: Dušan Makavejev
Screenplay: Dušan Makavejev
Cinematography: Aleksandar Petković
Editing: Ljubica Nešić
Art direction: Dragoljub Ivkov
Music: Petar Bergamo
MPAA rating: no listing
Running time: 80 minutes

> *Principal characters:*
> Raika .... Milena Dravić
> Jan .... Janez Urhoveć
> Barbulović .... Stojan Arandjelović
> Barbulović's wife .... Eva Ras
> Truck driver....................... Boris Dvornik
> Hypnotist................................ Roko

Man Is Not a Bird was thirty-three-year-old Dušan Makavejev's impressive debut feature film, which immediately established him as a leading member of a new generation of Yugoslav filmmakers who emerged in the 1960's. Shot in grainy black and white, this first film points toward themes and jarring juxtapositions for which Makavejev would become well-known. The overall structure and tone of the film, however, remain close to a more traditional form of neorealistic narrative that had developed in Yugoslavia at the time. The title is an ironic reference to a motif used throughout the film, concerning a hypnotist who tries to convince his hypnotized subjects that they are in fact birds. With both humor and sympathy, Makavejev suggests that the hypnotist's volunteers and the main characters of the narrative are, unlike birds, earthbound and fully human in all of the disappointing limitations which that condition involves. Neither wholeheartedly pessimistic nor blithely hopeful, the film, like Yugoslavia itself, emerges as a curious and original "in-between" reality. In this sense, Makavejev's importance stems both from his innovative use of the medium of film itself and the ways in which he reflects moods, themes, and concerns of his native land.

Makavejev, who was born in Beograd in 1932 and received a degree in both psychology and direction from the Academy for Theater, Radio, Film, and Television, has been appreciated internationally since the release of *Man Is Not a Bird* for his fresh presentation of multiple realities through ironic, sudden juxtapositions which create both a humorous and thought-provoking response in audiences. This "cinema of collage" is even more clearly seen in *Ljubavni slucaj: Tragedija službenice PTT* (1968; *Love Affair: Or, The Case of the Missing Switchboard Operator*), *Nevinost bez zaštite* (1968; *Innocence Unprotected*), *WR—Misterije organizma* (1971; *WR—Mysteries of the Organism*) and *Sweet Movie* (1974). In all of these works, plotting is casual and insignificant. What is primary is Makavejev's constant contrasting of individual lives and the desire for sex and freedom against the more generalized forces of politics (Left and Right) which work to repress such expression. His films thus appear as a refreshing blend of celebration of the individual and critique of political power. In his later films, *Montenegro* (1981) and *The Coca-Cola Kid* (1985), in order to reach a larger audience, Makavejev has returned to the stronger narrative line represented in *Man Is Not a Bird*.

Like many important filmmakers, such as Jean-Luc Godard, Makavejev began his career in documentaries and film criticism before turning to feature films. The documentary reality that one senses in *Man Is Not a Bird*, which is filmed against a striking backdrop of a poor factory town in south Serbia, is important to the overall impression of this story of a middle-aged, middle-management engineer, Jan (Janez Urhoveć), and his brief affair with Raika (played by the well-known Yugoslav actress Milena Dravić, who later starred in *WR—Mysteries of the Organism*), a young hairdresser. On the most apparent level, this is a film about another love affair, but in Makavejev's films, nothing is ever that simple. In this early film, the director immediately forces his audience to consider a number of implications and cross-meanings. The engineer is a man of seemingly traditional values and a member of the Communist Party of Yugoslavia. The hairdresser, on the other hand, represents a younger generation, that of Makavejev himself, which is restless, curious, hungry for experience, and uninterested in politics and status in a middle-class socialist state.

Man Is Not a Bird opens at a people's carnival in a bleak, south Serbian town, where a hypnotist-magician (Roko, a real hypnotist) speaks to a crowd about the nature of magic. Next, one sees Jan, the engineer, doing business by phone: By all appearances, he is a respectable man and a member of the local ruling class, since he is a manager at a turbine factory. A third narrative strand appears as the viewer sees Barbulović (Stojan Arandjelović), a drunken worker, in a cheap bar. Makavejev follows with a cut to a quarry, where a truck driver (Boris Dvornik) is speaking with another driver. Then Makavejev takes the viewer to the bland hairdressing shop where Raika is at work shaving a man.

Typical of Makavejev, none of these sequences is prepared for; each appears as an unrelated narrative element. Yet it is the interweaving of these strands that will occupy the rest of the film, as the lives of the engineer, the worker, the truck driver, the hairdresser, and the hypnotist intersect, contrast, run parallel, and separate.

Jan and Raika, though of differing ages and backgrounds (Jan's education and position are contrasted to Raika's working-class situation), became casual lovers. Before they are shown together, Makavejev interconnects the disparate lives of the characters introduced in the opening sequences. At an open-air market, Raika, for example, sees Barbulović's mistreated wife (Eva Ras, a talented Hungarian-Yugoslav actress who became the lead actress of *Love Affair: Or, The Case of the Missing Switchboard Operator*) chasing a Gipsy woman who stole her handbag and becomes a witness afterward. Later, as Raika walks along a street, the truck driver calls to her and begins a long but interrupted flirtation. Later still, Raika and Barbulović's wife become friends and attend the hypnotist's show, where they join others onstage to be hypnotized and told to become birds.

The lovers, Jan and Raika, are shown together briefly at this point, in a bed covered with a black wool blanket. Most of their lives, however, are taken up with their separate worlds, as Jan carries on his work at the factory and Raika spends time at work and with others.

The story develops in its second half by way of crosscutting between preparations for a special event at the factory to honor Jan and Raika's growing interest in the truck driver. The climax of the film is a highly dramatic one that is often cited as a prime example of Makavejev's craft. At the factory, a number of local dignitaries, dressed in their finest, are seated at the awards ceremony (a scene that is striking in and of itself as the impersonal unattractiveness of the factory as a setting contrasts with the formality of the people at the ceremony). The local orchestra strikes up a rendition of Ludwig van Beethoven's Choral Symphony and the ceremony honoring Jan begins. In sudden crosscuts, Raika is shown with the truck driver in the countryside, in the back of his truck. At the very moment that Jan receives the award as a good manager, engineer, and Communist, Raika and the truck driver make love, reaching their sexual climax at the very instant that the Beethoven piece builds to its crescendo.

Though Jan and Raika later embrace one last time, it is clear that their brief encounter has ended. Raika runs through a desolate landscape as a band begins to play gypsy music. At the circus, the magician throws knives at a woman standing against a door as gypsy music continues to play. Finally, one sees that both Raika and Jan are alone, each going his or her own way once again.

More important for Makavejev than story is narrative discourse, the way in which the story is told. The film's loose, fragmented structure demands that the audience make connections that are suggestive and suggested, but not stated directly or didactically. The film shows a brief affair that does not last. While a Hollywood film might concentrate on the rise and fall of romance, keeping a clear focus on the individuals, Makavejev does exactly the opposite. The individual story is muted in favor of showing a number of fragments which make up the characters' environment: the factory, the shop, the town, the landscape. What unites all these images is an overwhelming sense of drabness. What this suggests to the audience is at least a double perspective on the affair. On the one hand, an affair—that is, a pure, sexual experience between two individuals—is a kind of celebration of life in the midst of so much grinding boredom. On the other hand, the environment itself and the vast differences in class, education, and age between Jan and Raika work against them from the start. Makavejev creates a purposeful ambiguity which, as several critics have noted, is the mark of a poet rather than a logician.

Makavejev's approach is thus antipsychological. Because he denies the viewer the usual formulas of cinematic storytelling and film language, he opens up film and its audiences to fresh insights gained from his unusual and disparate juxtapositions of images. In the opening sequences, he moves from the magician-hypnotist through the introduction of the three male characters and finishes with Raika's first scene in the hairdressing shop, all presented as jarring cuts without any transition. The immediate effect of watching such a film for the first time is one of a kind of exhilarating freshness and disorientation. Because so many contrasting strands are thrown at the viewer so quickly, the viewer must actively participate in keeping up with and "completing" the film in his own mind. Later reflection on the opening segments brings to mind a number of possible readings. It seems important, for example, that the whole film is framed by the image of a small-town circus and a magician. Like every image in Makavejev, this too is open to multiple possibilities. One can say that the depressing reality of common lives presented in the body of the film is framed by a world of imagination and fantasy (the circus). Yet that world is paltry itself: Man would like to soar like the birds, but the sad volunteers flap their arms onstage, able to fly only in their minds under hypnosis.

What seems, on first viewing Makavejev's work, to be almost entirely impressionistic appears on closer examination to be carefully constructed. Note that the opening segments move from a sequence with Jan, who is the representative of the ruling class in a Communist society such as that of Yugoslavia, on to two working-class men—the truck driver and Barbulović, who works in Jan's factory—on to Raika, the female interest, presented as the last of the series. Such a structuring of the film's beginning clearly frames Raika as woman at the bottom of the social structure in Yugoslav society, which is highly patriarchal. Furthermore, that Makavejev ends the film focused on Raika seen alone suggests that he has gone beyond a presentation of Yugoslav reality—the patriarchal structure of the opening—to a critique of that reality: Who is Raika? How can a woman, especially an attractive young woman, function in such a male-dominated structure? In part, Makavejev's next two films go further to attempt an answer to that question. In both *Love Affair: Or, the Case of the Missing Switchboard Operator* and *WR—Mysteries of the Organism*, the female protagonists are murdered by their male lovers. Makavejev, who is greatly influenced by the writings of Wilhelm Reich, clearly implies that political ideology underlies society, both East and West, that politics is controlled by men, and that such phallicism leads to repression and violence rather than to the female principle of freedom, sexuality, and caring.

Perhaps the most memorable expression of this contrast is in the climactic cross editing between the awards ceremony in the factory and the lovemaking in the truck. By traditional values, Raika should be viewed as being unfaithful to her man, but the liberating effect of Makavejev's juxtaposing of sex and politics is to make the viewer consider also the possibility that Jan is guilty of being unfaithful to the pure joy of living with someone by playing political power games. Either way, Makavejev draws no easy moral from his tale. Like Luis Buñuel, whom Makavejev admires, Makavejev sees the world with an ironic double vision that invites the viewer to question the underpinnings of the discreet and the not-so-discreet bourgeoisie.

Other imaginative manipulations of film language abound in *Man Is Not a Bird*. Music is often used in a jarring way to comment on the image; the use of Beethoven for the lovemaking scene is merely one example. The use of Yugoslav gypsy music at various points throughout the film, including the closing scene, is also significant. In Yugoslav society, the more than one million gypsies represent the bottom of the social structure in influence, power, and opportunity. The coupling of Raika's image with gypsy music in the end, therefore, underscores her isolation and helplessness as a woman alone in Yugoslavia in 1965.

Makavejev's collage technique is also seen in his use of double exposure. One scene begins with Jan and Raika together in a long-shot on the muddy bank of a river. The shot is the antithesis of the usual riverbank romantic scene. Then Makavejev unexpectedly creates a double exposure of Jan and Raika in bed together with a close-up of the cracked riverbank mud imposed upon them, creating an eerie effect, as if the mud were cracked skin or the map of veins on some enlarged body.

Finally, it is Makavejev's sly playfulness that triumphs over the limitations of environment. The juxtaposition of Beethoven, healthy sex, and the solemnity of a factory awards ceremony makes the audience laugh, and laughter is liberating. Makavejev's healthy irreverence is not obscenity; it is rather a joyous celebration of both the power of the cinematic image when liberated from the psychological realism of the Hollywood tradition and a joyous and serious plea for individual freedom from the oppression of tradition and politics of all forms. While such themes and techniques have won for Makavejev worldwide recognition, critics in Yugoslavia branded his films and those of other filmmakers of his generation, such as Živogin Pavlović and Aleksandar Petković, as "Black Cinema" for their seemingly unflattering portraits of Yugoslav life. Yet filmmakers and audiences alike recognize that a strong indication of the health of a society is its ability to tolerate and encourage a diversity of self-criticism in the arts as well as in politics.

Makavejev's accomplishments viewed in the decades after the making of *Man Is Not a Bird* are still fresh, impressive, and enduring. Rather than Black Cinema, the film finally settles in the memory as an "Off-White Cinema."

Andrew Horton

MAN OF IRON
(CZŁOWIEK Z ŻELEZA)

Origin: Poland
Released: 1981
Released in U.S.: 1981
Production: Polish Corporation for Film Production Zespoly Filmowe,
  Unit "X"
Direction: Andrzej Wajda
Screenplay: Aleksander Ścibor-Rylski
Cinematography: Edward Kłosiński and Janusz Kalicinski
Editing: Halina Prugar
Art direction: Allan Starski
Costume design: Wiesława Starska
Music: Andrzej Korzyński
MPAA rating: PG
Running time: 140 minutes

Principal characters:
Mateusz Birkut/
Maciej (Maciek) Tomczyk ......Jerzy Radziwilowicz
Agnieszka........................Krystyna Janda
Winkiel ....Marian Opania
Kryszka........................Krzysztof Janczar
Anna Hulewicz ....Wiesława Kosmalska
Anna's mother......................Irena Byrska
Captain Wirski..................Andrzej Seweryn
Lech Wałęsa ....Himself

On one level, Andrzej Wajda's *Man of Iron* is a sequel to his earlier
Czlowiek z marmuru (1977; *Man of Marble*), for *Man of Iron* completes the
two parallel plots developed but left unconcluded in *Man of Marble*. On
another level, however, *Man of Iron* is different from its predecessor. The
earlier film was meant to paint a general picture of political realities in
Wajda's Poland. The later film, in contrast, explains something quite specific: the backgrounds to the successful strikes and the foundation of an
independent trade union in the summer of 1980.

Both films incorporate documentary material into their stories; *Man of
Iron*, however, contains substantial footage of authentic documentary,
whereas *Man of Marble* relies on far more pseudodocumentary film, tailor-
made for Wajda's 1977 feature. As a result, the earlier film is a smooth
blend of documentary and pseudodocumentary materials used to "authenticate" the fictional story. The later film emphasizes the real-life events, and

the fictional story serves primarily as a backdrop for what actually happened.

Nearly all of Wajda's films convey political arguments, but *Man of Iron* does so the most bluntly, for it eschews the variously translucent metaphors that characterize the preeminent Polish director's previous oeuvre, from *Pokolenie* (1955; *Generation*) to *Bez znieczulenia* (1978; *Without Anesthesia*). In *Man of Iron* one sees a direct and literal account of crucial events in Poland from 1968 to the Gdańsk agreement of August, 1980. Wajda's version of that history is fictionalized and selective, but in its explicit portrayal of contemporary political realities, *Man of Iron* is unique among East European feature films.

Like *Man of Marble*, *Man of Iron* contains a story-within-the-story. The "outer" story concerns Winkiel (Marian Opania), a Warsaw television reporter who is sent to Gdańsk, the center of the newly formed *Solidarność* (Solidarity) trade union. His task is to dig up something unpleasant about Maciej Tomczyk (Jerzy Radziwilowicz), a second-rung leader of the workers' movement, in an effort to discredit the new union. Winkiel is a pathetic character; once a sympathizer of the dissidents, he is now a stooge for the authorities, who are confident of his reliability because the police once dropped charges against him for having killed a pedestrian while driving drunkenly. Threatened by this blackmail and bribed with booze in a city with Solidarity-enforced prohibition, Winkiel ambivalently sets about his task. In the course of his investigations, during which he gains admittance to the strike negotiations, he finds himself wavering. He delays his report until it is too late; the workers cause the government to back down, extracting an agreement from the authorities which, among other points, acknowledges the workers' right to have their own independent union. Winkiel's assignment is now irrelevant, and he shares in jubilation of the victorious workers who, however, treat him as the untrustworthy outsider that he is.

Maciej Tomczyk, also known as Maciek, is the son of Mateusz Birkut (also played by Jerzy Radziwilowicz), the central figure in the "inner" story of *Man of Marble*. Continuing the "outer" story of that film, the heroine Agnieszka (Krystyna Janda) has been forced by her superiors to abandon her documentary about the rise and fall of Maciek's father, the onetime Stakhanovite bricklayer. Having met Maciek during her investigations, she transfers her fascination with Birkut to his son, falls in love with Maciek, and marries him. Maciek is a shipyard worker and political activist. Agnieszka joins him in his dangerous extracurricular activities, and their story follows the two dissenters through encounters with the police, beatings, loss of job, and incarcerations—accurately reflecting the fortunes of Poland's semiorganized opposition in the late 1970's.

By the time the narrative of the "inner" story brings the viewer to the summer of 1980, Maciek is a prominent figure in the workers' struggle. He is close to Lech Wałęsa, the real-life Solidarity chief, who in fact makes two appearances in *Man of Iron*: one in a cameo role in which he attends the wedding of Maciek and Agnieszka, the other in real documentary sequences as the primary spokesman for the workers in their negotiations with state authorities.

Early in the film, Winkiel meets a former friend, Kryszka (Krzysztof Janczar), who reminds Winkiel of his liberal past as he shows him films of the 1970 worker-police confrontation. This documentary sequence is a remarkable set of clips that were in fact locked away in an official archive for ten years. With them begins the first of several flashback narratives within Wajda's film. These flashbacks explore the "inner" story of Birkut and Maciek, a father and son whose roles personify the dialectical progress of the Polish opposition between 1968 and 1980. In 1968, Maciek was a student caught up in a major scuffle between the government and the intellectuals resulting in violence; unable to persuade the workers to join them in their protest, the students and intellectuals were quickly suppressed. In 1970, the tables were turned; intellectuals and students were asked to support workers' strikes but stayed out and instead watched from their windows as the demonstrators were brutally crushed. During this heartrending episode, Maciek learns from another student, Anna Hulewicz (Wiesława Kosmalska), that his father has been killed by the police. Birkut's death is the culmination of an ongoing conflict between himself and Maciek, worker and student, and it leaves Maciek with a sense of guilt and a burning desire to recompense his father's sacrifice. This he does, years later, by engaging tirelessly in the organizational work that results in the agreement of August, 1980. At the end of the film, Maciek lights a candle on the spot where his father died—*in memoriam* and in celebration.

Thus, one of Wajda's favorite themes, the dialectic of generations, is carried through from *Man of Marble* into *Man of Iron*. Moreover, the theme is brought into deeper focus by the addition of two generations: The grandparents are represented by Anna Hulewicz's mother (Irena Byrska), an elderly sympathizer of the opposition, while the next generation is represented by the infant son of Maciek and Agnieszka. This little person, one must surmise, will be as profoundly affected by the actions of his parents as Maciek was.

A more abstract approach to the linking of past and present is the visual presence of Roman Catholicism. In Polish society the Church plays a special role; it is an extraconstitutional participant in the Polish power structure, capable at times of tilting the balance when regime and society are in conflict. The Church is intricately woven into the nation's tradition, and its function as a source of communal identity antedates that of the modern state; Christianity came to Poland almost a thousand years before the arrival of Communism.

It is interesting to compare Wajda's treatment of Roman Catholicism in *Man of Iron* to some of his earlier films, especially *Popiół i diament* (1958; *Ashes and Diamonds*). In *Ashes and Diamonds*, the Church is linked to a bygone era that has been swept away by the horror of war and fratricide; it is the scene of death and destruction, and its symbols—the charnel house, the bombed-out crypt with its upside-down crucifix, the meaningless martyrdom of its two central characters, and so on—are those of death without hope of resurrection. In *Man of Iron*, the Church is very much alive; Maciek and Agnieszka are wed in a religious ceremony, priests prepare a Mass for the striking workers before the gates (an ironic touch) of the Lenin Shipyard, and votive candles blink a message of hope even as they commemorate the victims of 1970. Since the filming of *Ashes and Diamonds*, the Church has been reborn, and Wajda takes note of this reality by accurately associating the Church with the "renewal" process depicted in his timely film.

Wajda's new attitude toward religion is neither commendatory nor critical. He has merely recorded its significance as an objective fact of life in the Poland of 1980. His acknowledgment of the Church's importance sets *Man of Iron* apart from previous films in which he might have made explicit reference to Catholicism but did not—for example, in *Man of Marble* (where the only reference is Birkut's crossing himself before his bricklaying performance, a gesture angrily cut by the Stalinists who were filming the event)—or, more to the point, in the otherwise authentically traditional setting of the nuptial celebration in *Wesele* (1972; *The Wedding*).

The power of the Church to buttress the workers' movement is shown to be one of several elements in a momentous political conflict. On the one side are the workers and the oppositionists, who grew increasingly wise and self-confident following each successive setback. These are the men of iron, they who have endured and, unlike the men of marble, proven themselves not to be the brittle showpieces of a decidedly nonproletarian regime. Wajda shows their quotidian quality: They are mortal, they are average, yet, when united, they are capable of uncommon heroism. It is from the workers themselves that Wajda drew both the inspiration and the title for his film; a shipyard worker reportedly asked the filmmaker when he was going to make a picture about them, the men of iron.

On the other side of the conflict is the State. The authorities are shadowy figures, almost never given names. They are referred to, as the "deputy boss" of Winkiel's television studio, as *góra* (the top), or simply as "they." At times "they" are not even accorded the use of active verb tenses in the dialogue; Winkiel, for example, learns that he has "been selected" (*wybrano*—a most impersonal verbal form in Polish) for the dirty work in Gdańsk. Yet "they" sit astride the formal power structure, and however much their authority lacks social underpinnings, the political stalemate is not broken until "they" back down and grant the concessions demanded by the strikers. In the end, one of "them" appears to have the last word: A man sitting in the back seat of a black limousine tells Winkiel that the government's agreement is only a scrap of paper signed under duress—an ominous foreshadowing of Poland's future.

Two exceptions should be noted. In a documentary clip, the Gdańsk party secretary, Tadeusz Fiszbach, is interviewed and named. Fiszbach, a liberal within the ruling party, has often been credited with preventing violence in his city during the crucial weeks of 1980, so his direct portrayal should be taken as an argument to the effect that conciliation was possible given the prevalence of reasonable men. Fiszbach's opposite number is Captain Wirski (Andrzej Seweryn), a security police officer in the fictional sequences. Wirski is a cold and sinister character, who works out in a police gymnasium by attacking lifelike dummies with his truncheon. Wirski's icy cynicism reflects the ugly side of power and reveals the true source of the regime's authority.

Like all of Wajda's films, *Man of Iron* is filled with visual metaphors which enhance the effect of the film's surface realism. A bust of Lenin broods over the hall in which government officials, ruling in his name, have acceded to the workers' demands; does the old Bolshevik applaud or weep for what has just transpired? On a more subtle level, Winkiel, servant of the besieged power elite, accidentally breaks his precious bottle of vodka in the hotel bathroom and desperately sops it up with a towel. As he wrings what he can of it into a glass, one wonders if this is an attempt to salvage the false comforts of a shattered social order.

Man of Iron, completed in haste and threatened with censorship by the weakened Polish government in the spring of 1981, won the Gold Palm at that year's Cannes International Film Festival. Elsewhere, *Man of Iron* was accepted with rather mixed accolades. Its flashback sequences can confuse those who are unfamiliar with Poland's recent history, yet anyone with a slight knowledge of the events would find the film immensely educational. The romance of Maciek and Agnieszka introduces a note of sentimentality which has offended some critics, but it serves adequately to bind together the complex story of Birkut, Agnieszka, Maciek, and the worker's movement. In their haste to finish the film while it was still politically feasible to do so—and, some say, in time for the competition at Cannes—Wajda and his editors satisfied themselves with roughly spliced segments of documentary film and awkwardly staged confrontations between Maciek and his father. The haste with which the film was made spills over into the tempo of the film, however, continuing the rapid pace set in *Man of Marble* and giving *Man of Iron* in particular a nervous energy that is quite in keeping with the subject matter: The progress of the Polish opposition was not smooth, it developed in fits and starts, and there were many jagged edges to its evolving form. Father-son confrontations are inherently awkward; had Wajda "perfected" the staging of the Birkut-Maciek conflict, perhaps the scenes would have lost some of their persuasiveness.

The contrast between the two major documentary sequences adds yet another aesthetic dimension to the film. The soundless clips from Gdańsk in 1970, with their rough-cut, black-and-white textures, portray a ragtag strike action being put down matter-of-factly by security forces equipped with tanks, water hoses, truncheons, and guns. Ten years later, the ascendant workers and their spokesmen were filmed in vibrant color as they stood firm before the shipyard gates and in the tough negotiating sessions. For the 1980 sequences, Wajda borrowed clips from *Robotniczy '80* (1980; *Workers '80*), an impressive documentary of the "renewal," made by Andrzej Chodakowski and Andrzej Zajączkowski. The comparative professionalism with which the 1980 film was made symbolizes the distance that the workers' movement had come since the pitiful effort of ten years earlier.

Man of Iron was produced under conditions politically more favorable than those that prevailed during the making of *Man of Marble*. Even in the relative openness of 1981, however, Wajda was obliged to cut two scenes from the original version. One was a portion of the 1970 documentary in which the then party secretary of Gdańsk, Stanisław Kociołek, was visible. Apparently the censors did not wish to see a real-life party official portrayed in a bad light. The second cut was made in the version of the film that went into foreign distribution; it showed Maciek recovering the body of a drowned dissident, the victim of a secret-police murder.

Like *Man of Marble*, *Man of Iron* tells a uniquely Polish story, but its message transcends that of a narrowly nationalistic context. The conflict between ordinary people and established power has a universal relevance. One recalls the origins of Western trade unionism amid hostile corporations and governments, but beyond that, one thinks of human beings everywhere struggling to break out of oppression, injustice, and alienation. In addition, the theme of the mass media, central to *Man of Marble*, receives a further twist in *Man of Iron*. Winkiel's task, after all, is the inverse of Agnieszka's; he is out to falsify the record, not to uncover the truth. In the end he fails his assignment but, in failing, he accepts and embraces the truth.

Yet the ironic ending of the "outer" story leaves the viewer with an ominous uneasiness. The agreement which the workers wrung from the government in August of 1980 did, in real life, turn out to be merely a scrap of paper. Wajda's disconcerting conclusion became a horrifying prediction. Seven months after Wajda's triumph at Cannes, Solidarity was snuffed out by martial law.

David W. Paul

MAN OF MARBLE
(CZŁOWIEK Z MARMURU)

Origin: Poland
Released: 1977
Released in U.S.: 1981
Production: Andrzej Wajda for PRF Zespoly Filmowe, Unit "X"; released by
   Film Polski
Direction: Andrzej Wajda
Screenplay: Aleksander Ścibor-Rylski
Cinematography: Edward Kosiński
Editing: Halina Prugar
Art direction: Allan Starski
Music: Andrzej Korzyński
MPAA rating: no listing
Running time: 165 minutes

> *Principal characters:*
> Agnieszka . . . . Krystyna Janda
> Mateusz Birkut . . . . Jerzy Radziwilowicz
> Jerzy Burski, older . . . . Tadeusz Łomnicki
> Jerzy Burski, younger . . . . Jacek Łomnicki
> Wincenty Witek . . . . Michał Tarkowski
> Michalak . . . . Piotr Cieslak
> Hanka Tomczyk . . . . Krystyna Zachwatowicz
> Maciek Tomczyk . . . . Jerzy Radziwilowicz

Man of Marble is, without a doubt, one of the finest products of the Polish cinema in the 1970's. The film projects a complex vision that its director, Andrzej Wajda, had long hoped to convey to his audiences: a reconsideration of the Stalinist era in Poland, together with a study of workers and intellectuals from two generations. The subject matter was a political "hot potato," and it took years for Wajda to secure the necessary production resources to shoot it. Filmed in 1976, *Man of Marble* immediately provoked the censor's ire, and it was withheld from circulation. Wajda, who was head of the Polish Filmmakers' Association and widely known abroad, fought for the release of his film until a compromise was achieved. The film was released in 1977, but it was shown only in limited engagements and with little publicity. Moreover, several scenes occurring toward the end of the film, referring to the real-life massacre of Polish workers by state police forces in Gdańsk in 1970, were edited out. Abroad, *Man of Marble* was not seen until late 1978 and early 1979, when it began playing the festivals. Continued official reluctance at home, together with an apparent lack of interest in the

West, caused a further delay in its foreign commercial distribution. Finally, the uprising among Polish workers in 1980 kindled international interest in things Polish, and the weakened Polish government allowed the film's distribution in the outside world. United Artists released it to North American audiences in January, 1981.

The script for *Man of Marble* was written by the late Aleksander Ścibor-Rylski, but it bears the mark of director Wajda throughout. Wajda's career began in the early 1950's, when he worked on documentary productions before serving as assistant director of Aleksander Ford's *Piątka z ulicy Barskiej* (1954; *Five Boys from Barska Street*). Wajda's debut as director came with *Pokolenie* (1955; *Generation*), the first in his well-known trilogy which included *Kanał* (1957; *Canal*) and *Popiół i diament* (1958; *Ashes and Diamonds*). *Ashes and Diamonds* in particular established Wajda as a filmmaker of international repute, but, curiously enough, the development of his style during the 1960's and early 1970's went almost unheralded outside Poland. Especially in the United States, where the commercial market for Wajda's films has always been uncertain, Wajda was for nearly twenty years identified with *Ashes and Diamonds*, while his subsequent work remained unknown. Such important films as his *Popioły* (1965; *Ashes*), *Krajobraz po bitwie* (1970; *Landscape After Battle*), and *Wesele* (1972; *The Wedding*) either waited years for international distribution or were never generally circulated.

Thus, when *Man of Marble* reached the United States, it was met by filmgoers who, for the most part, remembered only the stylized expressionism of *Ashes and Diamonds* and were therefore astonished by the subtleties and complexities of *Man of Marble*. In fact, Wajda's style had evolved steadily in the meantime; the elements of this maturing style are visible in the realistic detail of *Landscape After Battle* and the fantastical textures of *The Wedding*. In *Man of Marble*, Wajda's emphasis is on realism, albeit a realism that is laden with symbolism throughout. This style was repeated in his subsequent *Bez znieczulenia* (1978; *Without Anesthesia*) and expanded in *Człowiek z żeleza* (1981; *Man of Iron*).

Three interwoven themes dominate the films of Andrzej Wajda, from *Generation* to his later works. The first concerns the individual caught up in the tragedy of history; the second speaks to specific cultural issues defining the history and present-day reality of Wajda's homeland, exploring the essence of "Polishness"; and the third deals with what Polish critic Bolesław Michałek has called the dialectic of generations—the recurring sameness of basic social and philosophic dilemmas played out in an ongoing conflict of sons against fathers. All three of these themes are present in *Man of Marble*, and they are expanded by the addition of a fourth theme, that of moral integrity. The question of moral integrity is repeated in most of Wajda's subsequent films as well, including *Dyrygent* (1978; *The Conductor*) and *Man of*

Iron, and it becomes the main theme of *Without Anesthesia*.

Man of Marble has two plots, a contemporary one and a "historical" one. The contemporary story follows the efforts of Agnieszka (Krystyna Janda), a young film student, as she struggles to complete her diploma film. Under the sponsorship of a television studio, she has chosen to make a documentary about the Stalinist 1950's entitled "Fallen Stars." Her research focuses on Mateusz Birkut (Jerzy Radziwilowicz), a bricklayer whose supervisors made him into a much-publicized hero in the drive to construct the new workers' society. The "man of marble" in Wajda's title refers to the marble statue of Birkut that was once sculpted for the entrance to a proletarian museum but has long since been relegated to a storage bin, where Agnieszka finds it. Birkut's meteoric rise to fame, followed by his total plunge into ignominy, unfold under Agnieszka's painstaking investigation and become the central elements of the "historical" plot within *Man of Marble*.

As Wajda reveals Birkut's story through flashbacks and simulated documentary clips, his audience becomes privy to a nasty reality which Polish officialdom would have preferred to keep under wraps. Agnieszka, the contemporary heroine, is told by her producer that nobody has touched the 1950's, and she should therefore tread cautiously or, preferably, choose another topic. Wajda was in the same position in the real world of 1976, and his problems with the authorities stemmed from the very truths unmasked by the telling of Birkut's tale: that the heroes of the Stalinist era were largely the creation of the official media, that the everyday workers who were theoretically the masters of their state were in fact manipulated by a cynical elite who could dispense with them at will, and that, contrary to the governing ideology, the motivating values of loyalty and honesty and collectivism were systematically profaned by those in power for their own selfish ends. As Wajda's heroine probes ever more deeply into this unseemly past, she stirs up a hornet's nest and finds herself battling her producer for the resources needed to complete her project.

Birkut, the subject of her story, was an ordinary man whose honesty and simplicity were easily exploited. The key to Birkut's rise is discovered during Agnieszka's interview with Jerzy Burski (Tadeusz Łomnicki), a celebrated film director who cut his teeth on Stalin-era documentaries. Burski (played in the flashback sequences by Jacek Łomnicki) conceived the idea of casting Birkut as the leader of an exemplary five-man construction team. Birkut's team of "Stakhanovites" set incredible new records for speed of bricklaying, but it was Burski, the opportunistic young filmmaker, who gained the most from the carefully staged "performances" of Birkut's crew. Once Birkut's exploits were duly filmed and the heavily edited results were circulated as official propaganda pieces, Burski forgot about his prodigy and went on to greater filmmaking achievements.

The key to Birkut's fall reveals itself in the testimony of Michalak (Piotr Cieslak), a sinister character who constantly shadowed Birkut during his glory days. Agnieszka's interview with Michalak, now the manager of a striptease bar, leads into a flashback sequence that describes how Birkut got into political trouble by attempting to investigate the disappearance of his friend and coworker Wincenty Witek (Michał Tarkowski). Witek's mysterious internment is explained in a (simulated) documentary clip unearthed by Agnieszka, in which Birkut is asked before a court of law to verify Witek's role in an alleged political conspiracy. Unlike Witek, who had passively confessed to the false charges, Birkut fabricates a confession of his own complicity so outrageous as to ridicule the prosecution's case. This seals Birkut's fate, and the audience is led to understand that he, too, was then imprisoned.

Ironically, Witek reemerges amid the political rehabilitations surrounding the "Polish October" (1956) and becomes an important man in the new social establishment. Birkut, who is amnestied at this time, modestly retreats from public life once again and, after learning that his wife, Hanka Tomczyk (Krystyna Zachwatowicz), has denounced and deserted him, fades rapidly into obscurity. Witek, on the other hand, rises eventually to the directorship of a giant industrial concern in Nowa Huta, the city where he and Birkut had begun as bricklayers. It is to this exalted position that Agnieszka traces Witek, whom she finds preoccupied and evasive when she asks about his onetime close friend.

Agnieszka's persistent investigation turns up a broken and alcoholic Hanka, living in unhappy luxury in the resort town of Zakopane. It is painful for her to reminisce about Birkut, and the hard-driving Agnieszka exhibits a rare moment of compassion while questioning her. Neither Hanka nor anyone else to this point can tell Agnieszka what has become of Birkut, but from Hanka the young filmmaker learns the whereabouts of Birkut's son, who took his mother's name but was reared by his father. Journeying to Gdańsk, Agnieszka finds young Maciek Tomczyk (Jerzy Radziwiłowicz) in the highly symbolic setting of the Lenin Shipyards. In the film's final take, Agnieszka is proudly striding down the corridor of the television studios with Maciek at her side, evidently having discovered the missing keystone for the completion of her story.

Thus in the final version of Wajda's film the audience is not explicitly told what happened to Mateusz Birkut, the man of marble turned fallen star. Polish audiences caught a hint, however: The Gdańsk sequence was shot in the very location where some of the striking shipyard workers were mowed down by police in December, 1970. (It has been reported that some Polish audiences cheered when they saw these scenes, aware that Wajda was purposefully alluding to an agonizing subject forbidden to public discussion.) The censors excised more direct suggestions that Birkut had fallen victim to political violence, cutting out, for example, a scene shot in a Gdańsk grave-yard. The graveyard scene was subsequently included in *Man of Iron*, when the conclusion to the story of Mateusz Birkut was at last revealed in detail. Similarly left to the sequel is the final outcome of Agnieszka's project; the ending of *Man of Marble* ambiguously suggests that she might finish her project now that she has the final piece of evidence, but, in *Man of Iron*, one is shown that her cause is hopeless. Her producer can never approve the completion of such a politically sensitive story.

The authorities' opposition to Wajda's film was provoked by several things in it. First, as mentioned, digging up the Stalinist past was breaking a long-established taboo. Second, referring back to the nearer past, the 1970 ship-yard violence, was mining public memories too close to the surface for the regime's comfort. Third, the contemporary plot—Agnieszka's struggle with her producers—exposed the persistence of censorship in Wajda's country, a censorship no less pervasive for its lack of clear-cut dos and don'ts. This, combined with the human characters who link Birkut's story to Agnie-szka's—Witek, Michalak, Burski, and others—clearly reminds Wajda's audience of the connections between past and present. Agnieszka's bold at-tempt to reconstruct the truth about Birkut, whose story was enshrouded in lies, runs smack into contemporary power elite that evinces no greater con-cern for honesty than the Stalinists showed.

Amid this commentary on moral integrity, one is shown a fascinating self-criticism. Wajda, like Burski, began his filmmaking career in the Stalinist era, and one of Burski's "documentaries," a piece about the construction of Nowa Huta entitled "Architects of Our Happiness," bears a credit to one A. Wajda as assistant director. Burski, an award-winning celebrity living in the lap of luxury, is perhaps Wajda's alter ego. When Burski comments on the lightness of Agnieszka's personal baggage, she replies that her lack of possessions helps her in making films; he admits that she may be right.

Yet whatever guilt Wajda might have felt about his own career, *Man of Marble* emerges as a courageous work even for a director as well established as he. In retrospect, it is clear that only someone of Wajda's stature could have made *Man of Marble* in the persistingly tense cultural atmosphere of Poland in the mid-1970's.

Nor is *Man of Marble* "merely" a political film. It is, in every sense, a fine piece of cinema. It is studded with superlative performances, including that of Krystyna Janda in her film debut. Janda's portrayal of the hungry, in-defatigable Agnieszka is the nucleus of this rapidly paced film. The back-ground music accompanying her as she scrambles all around Poland trying to make her film is frenetically displeasing, and her insolent self-confidence contrasts strikingly with the cowardly reserve of her elders in the profession.

Agnieszka's energy propels her through many obstacles. Running parallel to the obstacles of bureaucracy and closemouthed witnesses throughout the film are spatial and architectural obstacles: long corridors and open high-ways that seemingly lead to nowhere, boundless construction projects and sprawling factory complexes, doors opening into places that fail to live up to their promise (for example, the montage of doors in an old Burski documentary about the construction of workers' flats in Nowa Huta), other doors opening onto bitter realities (such as the door Birkut opens upon his return from prison, to find that Hanka has left him), and the ramps, stairs, and overhead walkways of the Gdańsk shipyards, with their ominous symbolism. Nowa Huta, the ugly proletarian city built from scratch on the outskirts of Krakow, harbors many of the secrets that Agnieszka must uncover, but so, too, does the picturesque and opulent Zakopane, to which Hanka has fled from her past.

Wajda and Ścibor-Rylski made many brilliant choices in their effort to create a richly symbolic image system. The miserable little fish served to construction workers as their lunch provokes a food riot—something not unfamiliar in the recent history of Poland's workers—but when the modest Birkut is force-fed ten thousand calories a day to strengthen him for his record-setting construction effort, he complains that a man should not be fattened up as if he were a prize goose. A gigantic picture of Birkut over a public square is torn down, showing that he has fallen from grace. Michalak, seen in his younger days as an informant lurking around corners and behind doors, shows up years later as the purveyor of another kind of sleaze in Warsaw's entertainment district. The colorless, modern buildings of Nowa Huta—"ghastly," says Agnieszka—contrast meaningfully with the ancient, dreamlike setting of Krakow, where Birkut, having been made a "non-person," smashes the window of an official building with the brick awarded him earlier for his exploits on the construction team. The latter scene is reminiscent of another ironic twist on the bricklaying motif: Earlier, Birkut was seriously burned when he picked up a sizzling-hot brick slipped into his supply, presumably, by a worker resentful of Birkut's superhuman example.

Most interesting is the carefully crafted mixture of actual documentary footage from the 1950's and contemporary film made to look like the original material. Made like the originals in black and white, the pseudodocumentary sequences are so convincing that virtually the only thing that distinguishes them from the real period pieces is in the presence of actor Radziwilowicz and company.

Man of Marble was made at a crucial time in the recent history of Poland. The date Agnieszka gives as she signs off one of her filmed interviews is June 18, 1976—exactly one week before the outbreak of labor unrest in numerous Polish cities. Soon thereafter, dissident intellectuals and workers formed the coalition that would underlie the revolutionary events of August, 1980. The rerelease of *Man of Marble* was reportedly among the demands made by workers in Nowa Huta during the August strikes.

The significance of Wajda's film, however, is by no means limited to Poland. True, the story is a specifically Polish one told sometimes through cultural and political references that are obscure to non-Poles. Yet at the same time, *Man of Marble* is a statement of universal relevance about the power of the mass media to manipulate reality, to make or break heroes, and ultimately to fabricate a version of "truth" that distorts the actual truth. It is a lesson germane to all modern societies.

David W. Paul

MAN ON THE ROOF
(MANNEN PA TAGET)

Origin: Sweden
Released: 1976
Released in U.S.: 1977
Production: Svensk Filmindustri and Svenska Institutet
Direction: Bo Widerberg
Screenplay: Bo Widerberg; based on a novel by Maj Sjöwall and Per Wahlöö
Cinematography: Odd Geir Saether
Editing: Bo Widerberg
Art direction: no listing
Music: Björn Jason Lindh
MPAA rating: R
Running time: 110 minutes

Principal characters:
Martin Beck . . . . Carl-Gustav Lindstedt
Lennart Kollberg . . . . Sven Wollter
Gunvald Larsson . . . . Thomas Hellberg
Mrs. Nyman . . . . Birgitta Valberg
Palmon Hult . . . . Carl Axel Heiknert
Ake Eriksson . . . . Ingvar Hirdvall

Swedish director Bo Widerberg's route to becoming a film director was an uncommon but not a surprising one—he began as a film critic. Only during the period of the French New Wave has any significant number of film critics become directors. Widerberg wrote newspaper film criticism and in 1962 published a book, *The Vision of Swedish Cinema*, that strongly denounced the state of Swedish cinema. The next year he began directing his own films, and with *Elvira Madigan* (1967), he became an international success. Although that film was popular chiefly because of its romanticism and beautiful imagery, Widerberg has always been concerned with social issues. In *Ådalen 31* (1969), he portrayed the effects of a strike in Sweden in 1931. In 1971, he came to the United States to direct *Joe Hill* (1971), the story of a Swedish singer who came to the United States, became involved in union organizing, and was executed in 1915.

It was therefore natural that Widerberg would turn to the detective fiction of Per Wahlöö and Maj Sjöwall. A husband-and-wife team, they wrote a series of ten thrillers, featuring the character Inspector Martin Beck, in which a critique of Swedish society is an important part. Widerberg chose one of the later books, *The Abominable Man* (1972), which includes some criticism of the police and a definitely cynical attitude in that the victim of the chief crime is at least as villainous as is his killer. As is his custom, Widerberg wrote the script himself and kept it true to the spirit of the original book. There are no glamorous policemen, automobile chases, or sudden solutions to difficult problems. The policework is mainly quiet and methodical and is carried out mostly by men who are middle-aged and cynical.

The film opens with a dark, quiet scene in which the viewer cannot quite see what is happening and certainly cannot tell the significance of the room or of the man within it. In the last part of the film, however, one again sees that room and recognizes its significance. Indeed, a basic technique used in this film is to show something that the audience cannot understand in order to provoke suspense or interest or to set up a later action. At times, however, this technique conflicts with another technique that Widerberg uses—concentrating the viewer's attention upon an unimportant detail in a scene, such as a teabag or a newspaper. Occasionally this tactic leads the viewer to expect the teabag to be important to the case, although Widerberg's intention may have been merely to stress the ordinariness of the scene or actions—a policeman may spend more time manipulating a teabag than using a gun.

After the first scene of the man in the room, one sees a man in a hospital bed. The audience does not know who he is, but Widerberg subtly makes it clear that something is going to happen to him, and then the man himself notices something. Suddenly, he is killed in a short scene of a flashing blade and much blood. Only when the police are called in does the audience learn that the victim was a policeman, Inspector Stig Nyman. Then, as the police begin investigating the case, it is revealed that Nyman was despised and hated by many of his fellow policemen; in fact, he was called "The Abominable Man" because of the way that he treated both suspects and his subordinates. There are many people with a motive to kill him.

Three policemen take charge of the investigation of this murder, which one policeman describes as by far the worst scene of butchery that he has seen in more than twenty years of police work. Martin Beck (Carl-Gustav Lindstedt) is probably in his late fifties, rather heavy, and definitely world-weary. As he begins work on the case, it is apparent that his years have not dulled his mind or his ability to work. Lennart Kollberg (Sven Wollter) is younger and more energetic than Beck, but he has no illusions about the police or society. The audience first sees Kollberg with his wife and young child early in the morning, and one does not know who he is until he gets the telephone call that tells him about the Nyman case. Another younger police detective is Gunvald Larsson (Thomas Hellberg), who has little respect for authority and dislikes the bureaucracy of the police department.

As the police detectives investigate the murder, they are led to suspect Ake Eriksson (Ingvar Hirdvall), a onetime policeman who has made complaints against Nyman. Eriksson blames Nyman for the death of his wife, who died because she could not get insulin while she was locked in a cell under Nyman's orders. Earlier, Beck has remarked that they must find the killer quickly because the combination of careful planning and extreme violence in the crime makes it likely that the killer will strike again. Indeed, while Beck is talking to Eriksson's parents and looking at his room (the same room shown at the beginning of the film), Eriksson takes up a position on a rooftop and begins shooting at policemen. As the audience and the detectives have learned, he hates all policemen, not only Nyman.

The balance of the film then consists of the efforts of the police to get the sniper down from the roof. This is in many ways the least satisfying portion of the film. Most of the methods used by the police seem ill-advised and do not work. One man is shot as he dangles from a line below a helicopter; another helicopter is shot down, and even the usually sensible Beck is severely wounded when he tries to approach the sniper by himself. There is an excellent, chilling sequence in which Kollberg rescues Beck and lowers his nearly lifeless body on a rope. Finally, the sniper is killed, and for the first time the audience sees his face; then it immediately turns into a black-and-white newspaperlike photograph, and the film ends.

The strengths of *Man on the Roof* are not those of the usual thriller. Except for the last part, there is no conventional suspense or excitement. Instead, this film relies on an accumulation of small, everyday details and on superb acting performances. Most reviewers who were familiar with the Martin Beck novels said that Carl-Gustav Lindstedt portrayed Beck exactly as they had envisioned him. Lindstedt is well supported by all the other actors and actresses, from the smallest roles to the larger ones. Particularly noteworthy are Carl Axel Heiknert as Palmon Hult, a loyal subordinate of Nyman, and Birgitta Valberg as Nyman's widow. In a long monologue to Beck, Hult reveals what police work has done to him without actually admitting any acts of brutality toward citizens. Mrs. Nyman has to cope with both her husband's death and the investigation that reveals a side of him that she has never known.

Bo Widerberg has, in short, faithfully transferred this Swedish mystery thriller to the screen in a film that is, in the words of mystery writer Ross Macdonald, "carefully and prosaically built." It uses almost no theme music until the end, relying on its other strengths to make powerful its depiction of crime, police, and society.

Timothy W. Johnson

MANDABI

Origin: Senegal and France
Released: 1968
Released in U.S.: 1969
Production: Jean Maumy for Comptoir Français du Film and Films Domirev
    Production
Direction: Ousmane Sembène
Screenplay: Ousmane Sembène; based on his novel
Cinematography: Paul Soulignac
Editing: Gilou Kikoine and Bernard Lefèbre
Art direction: no listing
Sound: Henri Moline
Music: Ousmane Sembène and Traditional
MPAA rating: no listing
Running time: 90 minutes
Also known as: Le Mandat and *The Money Order*

> *Principal characters:*
> Ibrahima Dieng .... Makhourédia Gueye
>   (Mamadou Gueye)
> First wife..................... Younousse N'Diaye
> Second wife .... Issa Niang
> Imam .... Serigne Sow
> Shopkeeper .... Moustapha Touré
> Mailman .... Medoune Faye
> Ibrahima Dieng's nephew .... Moussa Diouf
> Ibrahima Dieng's sister .... Thérèse Bass
> Waterseller........ Colomb (Christophe N'Doulabia)
> Businessman......................... Farba Sarr

Until the end of colonial days, Senegal was French territory. Dakar, its capital city, was considered to be the Paris of Africa, a highly cultured, sophisticated, and urbane place. Director Ousmane Sembène was born in rural Senegal in 1923. He is a product of French imperial times but has also witnessed his country's transition to independence. He is one of many filmmakers from Africa, Asia, and Latin America who have noted that the impact of Western values and life-styles did not cease with the breaking of formal political and economic ties to the Western world. Sembène was one of the first African artists to decry the domination of Western culture, in the form of films, music, and television, over traditional values and art forms. He has argued that political imperialism merely was replaced by "cultural imperialism"—that foreign values, attitudes, and life-styles have been made to seem better and more appealing through mass media, which continue to be dominated by foreign powers. Sembène's commitment as a filmmaker is to correct and counterbalance the intrusive images that are exported to his country from the Western world.

Sembène believes that cinema has the power to transcend mere entertainment and to communicate a vast array of feelings, attitudes, and values about how life is and should be lived. His films emanate from his own experiences and are aimed directly at Senegalese people. Although he is the most prolific and most decorated black filmmaker, many of his films have had limited exhibition in his own continent. Sembène's caustic and penetrating depictions of Senegalese experiences are fervent and lucid cries for change. Film distribution in Senegal, however—as in most French-speaking African countries—has traditionally been dominated by French distribution systems. Theatrical screenings of Sembène's works have therefore been less frequent than their quality warrants.

Although he was reared in a rural village, Sembène admits to being very much a product of Western culture. His youthful trips to Dakar meant more to him than mere eye-opening trips to the big city. It was in Dakar that he discovered the thrilling, larger-than-life worlds of the films of Buster Keaton, Charlie Chaplin, and Shirley Temple. With mixed feelings, he was conscripted to fight for the French Army in World War II, and later he worked as a dockhand and union organizer in Marseilles. These encounters with European culture led Sembène to publish a series of stories and novels. Eventually, he received film training under Mark Donskoy at the Gorky Film Studios in Moscow.

With his first films, Sembène established a filmic interest in cultural conflicts and the impact of Western experiences on Senegalese sensibilities. The emotional and sociological remnants of colonial life resonate throughout his films. As enthusiastically as his characters try to live their lives, they repeatedly find their choices defined and their opportunities limited by a value system which is not African.

La Noire de . . . (1966; *Black Girl*) was Sembène's first short film. It concerned a Senegalese maid, Diouana, who is taken to the Riviera by her French employer. Diouana discovers what it means to be an African in Europe: to be depersonalized as "the black girl" and never to be called by her real name. *Emitaï* (1971) is a tragicomedy which takes place at the end of World War II, when French soldiers come to confiscate a village's precious rice harvest and the people refuse to cooperate. *Xala* (1974) is a wry comedy about a self-satisfied businessman who is happily coping with a Westernized life-style until he is stricken with *xala*, the curse of impotence, and must seek a traditional cure. *Ceddo* (1976; *The Outsiders*) is a historical epic about the kidnaping of a princess in order to prevent Moslem expansion into Africa in the nineteenth century.

Sembène's film style is simple and low-key. It is reminiscent of the work of Vittorio De Sica and the products of Italian neorealism. Sembène develops stories out of contemporary situations and historical events. His pace is leisurely and gentle. His performers are usually nonprofessionals. The female star of *Black Girl*, Thérèse N'Bissine Diop, was a seamstress when she was picked for the film. Afterward, she resumed that career. Makhourédia Gueye, the male star of *Mandabi*, was an airline clerk and likewise returned to that post.

Sembène also takes personal responsibility for seeing that his films are exhibited. While he always shoots in a thirty-five-millimeter format, he prints his films in a sixteen-millimeter format so that they can be shown in a nontheatrical circuit of churches, schools, and meeting halls throughout Africa. Sembène's films are thus made for a specific audience. As a result, his stories reflect uncommon warmth, honesty, and beauty. His are works of the heart which speak to the souls of African people.

Mandabi was Sembène's second feature film and is possibly his best film. At once poignantly humorous and wryly cynical, it is also a touching portrait of an ordinary man's fight to maintain his sense of self-worth. It is the story of a poor but genuinely happy man of Africa who believes that his gods have smiled on him when he receives a money order from a nephew who has gone to work in the mysterious, foreign place called France.

When the viewer first meets Ibrahima Dieng (Makhourédia Gueye), he is at the barber's, having the hairs in his nostrils trimmed. He is a big man, but he moves with the bracing air and countenance of a king. A Moslem, he has two wives and seven children. He has been unable to find a job in four years, but although he is poor, he is not a victim of poverty. He is content with life, has food on his table, and maintains a firm sense of self-worth.

Ibrahima's homecoming from a day of mundane and probably trivial tasks is fascinating. He sits on his bed while one wife removes his sandals and washes his feet. He reclines on the bed as the second wife massages his legs. Some audiences might respond to this tender and elaborate ritual as a form of male chauvinism. They would, however, be applying their own standards to the culture of other people. Ibrahima's wives act out of custom, duty, and love, not necessarily in that order. Ibrahima feels and acts like a very important person because he is treated that way.

Soon, the mailman (Medoune Faye) arrives with a "mandabi," a mailgram informing Ibrahima that his nephew has sent a money order from Paris and that he must go to the bank to claim it. Ibrahima is overjoyed, but he knows nothing about banks, checkbooks, or passbooks—financial paraphernalia that is totally unfamiliar to him. The moment he walks into the bank, the weight of 390 years of capitalism and colonialism falls squarely upon his shoulders.

At the bank, Ibrahima reluctantly hands his mailgram to a young black man who sits at a counter; the viewer realizes that Ibrahima cannot read. As the translator dictates, the audience first hears and then sees Ibrahima's nephew (Moussa Diouf), who is sweeping the streets of Paris with a broom, swearing obedience to his Moslem faith, sharing his isolation and loneliness, and asking his uncle to distribute the money he has saved to some family members.

The young man who translates the letter has obviously translated similar letters before. He is the first of many black men presented in the film who represent those who took over the colonial system when the French left. *Mandabi* is an African story; it portrays a world populated by black skins and black feelings. Nevertheless, whites remain a very large part of that world. The translator probably has been educated in France. He certainly reads and writes in more than one European language. Though his skin is no less dark than Ibrahima's, he is far removed from him emotionally. He is unable to perceive and appreciate Ibrahima's innate dignity and importance. To the young man, Ibrahima is merely another uneducated person who will pay to have meaningless lines of print turned into words.

Ibrahima proceeds to the teller's cage, only to discover that without proper identification he cannot get his money. The bureaucratic merry-go-round begins to spin. Even the name of the missing document—*carte d'identité*—helps explain why Ibrahima cannot understand what to do; it is in French, a significant remnant of earlier times.

At the next government office, Ibrahima meets other young men in Western clothes, who regard him with boredom. The bureaucrats are shown as universal types in their rudeness, scorn, and disregard for the people they are supposed to help. In this situation, their behavior is even crueler than usual. They are young blacks reading French magazines and behaving like the French bureaucrats whose chairs they now fill. Sembène seems to speculate here about whether "home rule" ever really came home to this part of the world.

Ibrahima is finally confronted with the entire illogical and infuriating dilemma: In order to receive his mandabi, he must have an identity card. In order to receive an identity card, he must produce a birth certificate. Since it is likely that he was born in a field rather than in a hospital, and since he was received as an addition to his family rather than as another statistic for a census keeper, Ibrahima is in serious trouble.

When a bureaucrat tells Ibrahima that the mandabi will be returned to France in two weeks if it is not claimed, the nightmare is complete. The deadline makes Ibrahima's struggle both finite and infinitely complicated. He must now confront and overcome an incomprehensible world. While the clock is ticking, he suffers through a series of lawyers and businessmen who add layers to his nightmare. He borrows money that he cannot repay for photographs that are never developed. He signs documents giving an attorney the power to cash his money order, but he may also have sold the man his house. It makes little difference. Even if the house is safe, he will probably lose it, because he had to borrow money in order to claim the money that he is never going to receive.

After a while, it makes no difference whether the mandabi will be cashed, for Ibrahima's life has been irrevocably changed. He is no longer a poor person like all the other poor people in his neighborhood. Instead, he is a fairy-tale rich man who is assaulted by friends and strangers alike, all hoping to benefit from his good fortune. Ibrahima becomes a walking symbol of money. His personal dignity, which was his most telling feature at the beginning of the story, is lost in the crowd.

Near the end of the film, Ibrahima begins to accept the truth about his mandabi: that it will never be his. He confronts the corrupt lawyer, crying and begging on his hands and knees for money that he knows he will never see. Even in this scene, however, Ibrahima retains his dignity. He has been cheated, but he has not been beaten. He will survive.

At the end of *Mandabi*, the mailman who had brought Ibrahima glad tidings at the beginning of the film returns. He says that things do not have to be so unfair and that people should fight to control their own lives. Ibrahima and his wives are aghast and incredulous: The man is using concepts which do not exist in their emotional vocabularies. That Ibrahima listens is a sign of hope.

By using a letter carrier as his agent of change, Sembène creates a fascinating metaphor for the revolutionary process. The mailman is an intermediary, a connector of people, and a collector of information about people. He is a man who has daily contact both with the bourgeoisie and with the poor. Ibrahima and the bank translator represent opposite ends of the black experience in Senegal and in other African states as well. Ibrahima is an old man who knows everything about traditions and little about the changing world. The translator is a young man who has abandoned his culture in a feverish attempt to catch up with that changing world. The mailman asserts from firsthand experience that Senegal did not change when French rule ended. He believes that real change occurs not when governments crumble but when people alter the ways in which they look at other people. To Ousmane Sembène, the mailman represents the solid core of African potential. If the translator's awareness of the future can be united with Ibrahima's appreciation for the past, the process of true revolutionary change will have begun.

Ted Siminoski

MARÍA CANDELARIA

Origin: Mexico
Released: 1943
Released in U.S.: 1945
Production: Armando Espinoso for Films Mundiales
Direction: Emilio Fernández
Screenplay: Emilio Fernández and Mauricio Magdaleno; based on an original
  story by Emilio Fernández
Cinematography: Gabriel Figueroa
Editing: Gloria Schoemann
Art direction: no listing
Music: Francisco Domínguez
Running time: 102 minutes
Also known as: Portrait of Maria and *Xochimilco*

> *Principal characters:*
> María Candelaria..................Dolores del Río
> Lorenzo Rafael ....Pedro Armendáriz
> Lupe...........................Margarita Cortés
> Artist.............................Alberto Galan
> Reporter ....Beatriz Ramos
> Don Damian ....Manuel Inclán
> Priest ....Rafael Icardo
> José Alfonso ....Julio Ahuet
> Healer ....Guadalupe del Castillo

Dolores del Río, star of *María Candelaria*, made her first Hollywood film
in 1925; by 1926, she was a star and remained one until 1942, when a series
of setbacks forced her to leave Hollywood. First, her picture *Journey into
Fear* (1943), which she made for Orson Welles, suffered such drastic cutting
that her role was no more than of featured importance. Welles and she were
going to become man and wife, but he met Rita Hayworth, and their acquaintance flamed into marriage. Del Río promptly packed her belongings
and returned to Mexico City, issuing a dignified statement to the press: "I
wish to choose my own stories, my own director, and cameraman. I can
accomplish this better in Mexico."

For her first Mexican-made film, *Flor silvestre* (1943), she selected Emilio
Fernández as director-writer, Gabriel Figueroa as cameraman, and Pedro
Armendáriz as leading man. Backed by this trio, del Río's career was reborn, and she won the Arieles, the Mexican equivalent to Hollywood's Oscar, for best performance in a leading role.

That same year, 1943, saw the release of del Río's second Mexican feature, *María Candelaria*, for which she was backed again by the three she had initially chosen—Fernández, Figueroa, and Armendáriz. It was an enormously popular feature and was subsequently dubbed into English for release in the United States by Metro-Goldwyn-Mayer and retitled *Portrait of Maria*. Del Río had cinched her claim as the leading actress of the Mexican cinema, and she was the first of the big international stars of the 1940's.

María Candelaria (also known in Mexico as *Xochimilco*) is a tragic romance of the lakes, telling the love story of María (Dolores del Río) and Lorenzo Rafael (Pedro Armendáriz). It is told in retrospect by a famous artist (Alberto Galan), who is being interviewed by a number of reporters in his studio. One particular woman (Beatriz Ramos) inquires about the history of a certain painting of an Indian woman whose majestic features reveal all the finer qualities of a vanished race. The painter, disturbed, breaks off the interview, and all the reporters leave the studio save the woman, who now apologizes for her impertinence. She is able to convince the painter that she is sincere, and he relents and tells her the story of the woman in the portrait, María Candelaria.

María is at work in her small garden tract near Xochimilco on the lakes when José Alfonso (Julio Ahuet), messenger for Don Damian (Manuel Inclán), the shopkeeper, comes to collect a debt that she owes his master. Since María has no cash, she says she will pay the debt in flowers, but José tells her that Don Damian will accept only money. María piles flowers in her canoe and goes out on the lakes to sell them. There follows a lyric passage of the flower-laden canoes drifting down the lakes.

María has been ostracized by all the other women in her village because they have regarded her mother as an impure witch and have stoned her to death. María lives in isolation, apart from all of them; she sees only Lorenzo Rafael, to whom she is betrothed. She now seeks Lorenzo out to accompany her to the marketplace, since the people of her town hinder her from selling flowers as she moves along the canal. Lorenzo succeeds in selling the flowers for her, but in the marketplace, she is seen by an artist who tries to persuade her to pose for him. Lorenzo distrusts the painter and does not like his proposition, so he and María return to Xochimilco, where María has only her garden and a pig given to her by Lorenzo to care for until it has given birth to its piglets. María intends to sell the piglets she will get and buy a wedding dress for her marriage to Lorenzo.

Don Damian lusts for María and is angry when she is able to pay her debt to him from the money she has acquired from selling the flowers. Lupe (Margarita Cortés) is secretly in love with Lorenzo, who ignores her because he is faithful to María. Lupe suggests that Don Damian kill the pregnant pig during the fiesta, which will make the wedding of María and Lorenzo impossible.

All the animals are blessed before the fiesta opens, and in the midst of the blessing ceremony, a shot rings out. The pig has been killed.

María is so shocked by the killing that she grows very ill, knowing that all of her hopes and plans now count for nothing. Don Damian is in charge of distributing quinine to the villagers, but he refuses to give up any for María. There is a heavy rain falling by nightfall, and Lorenzo breaks a window in Don Damian's shop and steals some of the precious quinine. He also steals a beautiful wedding dress for his beloved María.

She has barely recovered from her sickness when she learns that Don Damian has gone to the police, charging Lorenzo with theft, and Lorenzo has been thrown into prison. María pleads for his release, but it is to no avail. She remembers the painter who was obsessed with painting her, and she goes to him, agreeing to pose for the picture he wants to paint. When he finishes painting the head, he asks her to disrobe so that he can paint her body. María refuses and runs from the studio. The painter is forced to use another model when he paints the nude picture of her.

After seeing the completed picture, the ignorant and superstitious women of the village decide that María's disgrace is as great as her mother's had been, and she must die as her mother did. María's hut is set afire, but she escapes, running from the vengeful women, led by Lupe. She tries to reach Lorenzo in prison, and he, alarmed by her plight, succeeds in breaking down the prison door and runs to help her. Nevertheless, he is too late. She is dying from having been stoned to death, and her last words are "Lorenzo Rafael, I am innocent."

Shortly thereafter, a bell begins to toll, and María Candelaria's corpse floats down the current of the canal. Her body is covered by fresh flowers cut from his garden by Lorenzo. He watches in quiet sorrow as the body of the beautiful girl he had loved is borne out of sight.

At first, del Río performed in films exclusively produced in Mexico, playing later in *The Fugitive* (1947), made by John Ford in Mexico with Henry Fonda in the leading role. The del Río Mexican credits are then interspersed with those from many other lands. In Argentina, she filmed *Historia de una mala mujer* (1948), adapted from Oscar Wilde's play *Lady Windermere's Fan* (1892). She came back to Hollywood for a stunning role as Elvis Presley's mother in the stark tragedy *Flaming Star* (1960), and she did another role for John Ford as "Spanish Woman" in *Cheyenne Autumn* (1964). Twice she went to Spain and made pictures—*Señora ama* (1954) and *La dama de alba* (1966). Once she went to Italy to appear in a Carlo Ponti film starring Sophia Loren—*C'era una volta* (1967), known popularly in the United States as *More Than a Miracle*.

In 1959, del Río married an American theater producer, Lewis A. Riley, Jr., who encouraged her to appear on the stage, and she began to alternate her theatrical engagements with those in film. She won three more Arieles awards for her roles in Mexican films—*Las abandonadas* (1944), *Doña*

Perfecta (1950), and *El niño y la niebla* (1953). She played in a series of plays produced by her husband, for whom she first appeared in Buenos Aires in a production of Robert E. Sherwood's *The Road to Rome* (1927). Long known as Mexico's "First Lady of the Cinema," she also won acclaim as the "First Lady of the Mexican Theater," starring on the stage in plays as diverse as *The Little Foxes* (1939), *Camille* (1937), and *Auntie Mame* (1956). In addition, del Río starred in specials for television, largely in the United States.

DeWitt Bodeen

MARIUS

Origin: France
Released: 1931
Released in U.S.: 1933
Production: Marcel Pagnol for Paramount Publix Corporation
Direction: Alexander Korda
Screenplay: Marcel Pagnol; based on his play
Cinematography: Ted Pahle
Editing: Roger Spiri-Mercanton
Art direction: no listing
Music: Francis Gromon
Running time: 125 minutes

> *Principal characters:*
> César Olivier............................Raimu
> Marius ....Pierre Fresnay
> Fanny ....Orane Demazis
> Honoré Panisse ....Fernand Charpin
> Honorine Cabanis...................Alida Rouffe
> M. Brun ....Robert Vattier
> Félix Escartefigue ....Paul Dullac
> Piquoiseau ....Alexandre Mihalesco
> Quartier-Maître ....Édouard Delmont
> Chauffeur...............................Maupi

FANNY

Origin: France
Released: 1932
Released in U.S.: 1948
Production: Marcel Pagnol for Siritsky-International and Les Establissements
  Braunberger-Richebé
Direction: Marc Allégret
Assistant direction: Yves Allégret, Pierre Prévert, and Eli Lotar
Screenplay: Marcel Pagnol; based on his play
Cinematography: Nicolas Toporkoff, André Dantan, Roger Hubert, Georges
  Benoît, and Coutelain
Editing: Raymond Lamy
Art direction: no listing
Music: Vincent Scotto
Running time: 125 minutes

Principal characters:
César Olivier............................Raimu
Fanny ....Orane Demazis
Marius ....Pierre Fresnay
Honoré Panisse ....Fernand Charpin
Honorine Cabanis....................Alida Rouffe
M. Brun ....Robert Vattier
Félix Escartefigue ....Auguste Mouries
Tante Claudine Foulon................Milly Mathis
Chauffeur................................Maupi
Dr. Félicien Venelle..............Édouard Delmont

CÉSAR

Origin: France
Released: 1936
Released in U.S.: 1949
Production: Marcel Pagnol for Siritsky-International and La Société des Films Marcel Pagnol
Direction: Marcel Pagnol
Assistant direction: Pierre Méré
Screenplay: Marcel Pagnol
Cinematography: Willy
Editing: Suzanne de Troye and Jeanette Ginestet
Art direction: no listing
Music: Vincent Scotto
Running time: 120 minutes
　　Principal characters:
　　César Olivier............................Raimu
　　Marius ....Pierre Fresnay
　　Fanny ....Orane Demazis
　　Honoré Panisse ....Fernand Charpin
　　Césariot ....André Fouché
　　Honorine Cabanis....................Alida Rouffe
　　Tante Claudine Foulon................Milly Mathis
　　M. Brun ....Robert Vattier
　　Félix Escartefigue ....Paul Dullac
　　Chauffeur................................Maupi
　　Dr. Félicien Venelle..............Édouard Delmont
　　Fernand................................Doumel
　　Elzéar ....Thommeray
　　Pierre Dromard ....Robert Bassac

The 1930's is one of the richest and most interesting periods in French cinema history. Since films cannot be separated from their cultural surroundings, it is important first to remark upon the fertility of the other French arts. From 1920 to 1940, during that period called *entre deux guerres* (between two wars), painters, writers, and creators of all kinds were drawn to the artistically stimulating atmosphere of Paris. In the field of cinema itself, the advent of sound proved inspirational to filmmakers such as René Clair, who used the new technique to create such masterpieces as *Le Million* (1931) and *À nous la liberté* (1931). It was also in the 1930's that directors, such as Julien Duvivier and the much lamented Jean Vigo began to experiment with new storytelling techniques.

Compared to the achievements of Jean Renoir or Vigo, those of Marcel Pagnol, a playwright turned filmmaker, seem rather modest. In fact, Pagnol was denounced by the critics of his time for doing little more than filming his plays. Yet Pagnol's films live on and are possibly better remembered than those of the great directors mentioned above, or at least, better remembered by the general public, which was always more dear to Pagnol's heart than were the critics.

Of all Pagnol's work, the films dubbed the "Marseilles Trilogy" are perhaps the most widely known, although his *La Femme du boulanger* (1938; *The Baker's Wife*) and *Topaze* (1936) equally conjure up warm and instant recognition. Yet one must concede that few other Pagnol films rival the trilogy in its international and timeless appeal. It is quite likely that, even in a hundred years, the Marseilles Trilogy will still be applauded and loved by audiences worldwide.

The films that constitute the Marseilles Trilogy are *Marius*, *Fanny*, and *César*, named after three of the saga's main characters. Although Pagnol directed only the third picture, his hand is evident through the entire cycle. In typical Pagnol fashion, the trilogy started on the theater boards. When Pagnol wrote the original *Marius* stage play in 1928, (it was produced a year later) he was thirty-three and already a flourishing playwright, because of the considerable success garnered by his earlier play, *Topaze*. *Marius*, too, quickly became a popular favorite. It is therefore not surprising that Paramount, which had financial assets frozen in France, decided to acquire the film rights to both plays.

The film adaptation of *Marius* was shot in 1931, with the direction being entrusted to Hungarian director Alexander Korda, who had already acquired a reputation for his skill with actors. Pagnol himself was able to keep a large amount of creative control in the adaptation of *Marius*; indeed, he insisted that the roles in the motion picture be played by the same actors that had brought them to life on the stage.

The story of *Marius* takes place almost entirely in the Bar de la Marine, a Marseilles dock café owned by César Olivier (Raimu), who is aided by his son Marius (Pierre Fresnay). The Bar de la Marine seems to be patronized mostly by César's friends: Félix Escartefigue (Paul Dullac), captain of the local ferryboat; the widowed sailmaker, Honoré Panisse (Fernand Charpin); and M. Brun (Robert Vattier), a customs inspector from Lyons, a city often ridiculed in Marseilles.

Marius, at age twenty-two, is the victim of wanderlust. He watches eagerly as ships sail from Marseilles to distant, exotic locations. Yet he is also in love with, and loved by, his childhood sweetheart, Fanny (Orane Demazis), the daughter of Honorine Cabanis (Alida Rouffe), a local fishmonger.

In order to force Marius to admit that he loves her, Fanny pretends that she is going to marry the much older Panisse, who has asked for her hand. This ploy succeeds, and the two become lovers. Eventually, they are found out and become formally engaged. Yet Fanny realizes that Marius still suffers from his wanderlust and will not be happy as long as he stays in Marseilles. Preferring that her beloved be happy away from her rather than miserable with her, Fanny tricks him into taking a berth on a departing ship.

From a commercial standpoint, *Marius* was as successful on film as it had been as a play. Therefore, although it originally had been conceived as a single story, Pagnol decided that he would write a sequel. This second part of the trilogy, entitled *Fanny*, was first performed onstage in Paris in 1931 and was dedicated to Orane Demazis, who had created the role for *Marius*. (It is perhaps only partially coincidental that Pagnol had since fallen in love and married Demazis.)

Fanny continues the saga only a few months after the ending of *Marius*. The audience learns that Fanny is pregnant. In order to save her family's reputation, her mother, Honorine, persuades her to marry Panisse. The old sailmaker, who had always desperately wanted an heir, is more than delighted to have an entire family in one fell swoop. César, who is at first devastated to learn that Fanny will have Marius' child under another family's name, eventually agrees that the marriage with Panisse is better for both the mother and the unborn infant.

A year later, Marius unexpectedly returns and eventually discovers what he has left behind. He tries to persuade Fanny to take her baby, leave Panisse, and go with him, but Panisse's honest love for the little boy has made Fanny and César understand that the old man is the *real* father of the child. They join together to force Marius to leave.

Again, the success of the play naturally led to the decision to turn *Fanny* into a film. In the meantime, however, Pagnol had had a falling out with Paramount over the film adaptation of *Topaze*. That experience convinced the writer that, in order to retain control of his work, he should produce the film himself, which he did, in association with a distributor. For director, Pagnol chose Marc Allégret, who had been assistant to Robert Florey and Augusto Genina for several years. The cast from the original picture was reassembled, with the exception of Paul Dullac, who had played Escartefigue. This time, the role was played by Auguste Mouries.

The popularity of *Fanny* at the box office persuaded Pagnol to launch his own film production company, La Société des Films, Marcel Pagnol and try his hand at direction. Before he decided to create the third and final chapter of his story, *César*, Pagnol directed or produced several other films, including *Angèle* (1934) and his own version of *Topaze*. Although these films did not share the characters of the Marseilles Trilogy, one thing that they all had in common was the use of the attitudes and life-style of the author's native Provence (Southern France).

In 1936, Pagnol at last decided to write a happy ending to the Marseilles Trilogy and once more reassembled his now familiar cast for *César*, which he himself directed. Although the film was written directly for the screen and included some location scenes at sea and in Toulon (a city located about thirty miles from Marseilles, where Marius now lived), *César* was eventually performed onstage in 1946.

César opens with Panisse on the verge of death. Before the old sailmaker dies, however, the family priest Elzéar (Thommeray) makes him swear that the now twenty-year-old Césariot (André Fouché), the son of Marius and Fanny, will be told the truth about his birth. Yet Panisse wishes to die with the boy still believing him to be his father, so it falls to Fanny, after Panisse's death, to tell the truth to Césariot, who is understandably shaken.

Later, Césariot secretly decides to go and meet his natural father. As a result of a cruel joke, he returns to Marseilles convinced that Marius is a criminal, but fortunately, the truth is quickly revealed, and Césariot gives his blessings for Marius and Fanny to marry at last.

The Marseilles Trilogy is a remarkable filmic achievement. It is said that the best playwrights are able to play their audiences like violins. They know how to reach into their hearts, manipulate their feelings, and move them in accordance with their own designs. The most successful plays are those that elicit both tears and laughter from the public and leave them with a moral or a lesson to ponder after the curtain falls. In that respect, the warm popular response to the trilogy, over the years and throughout the world, is indeed a testimony of the films' success and attests Pagnol's considerable abilities as a playwright.

There are several reasons for this success. First, the trilogy is able to reach and move almost any audience, no matter their age or country. Pagnol shares with other great playwrights, from Aristophanes to William Shakespeare, the gift of being able to express a natural and almost universal understanding of what life is all about. Second and even more important, Pagnol is never heavy-handed about such expression. Instead, he succeeds in conveying this understanding through the use of humor, as well as through characters and scenes that can be both moving and entertaining at the same time.

Pagnol is an old hand at knowing how to amuse his public. He uses crisp and witty dialogue to craft some memorable scenes that poke gentle fun at the idiosyncracies of the natives of Southern France, whom he loved so much. There is, for example, the famous card game scene in *Marius*, in which César attempts to tell Escartefigue which card to play; there is César's stern refusal to let his sorrow show, even to his friends, in *Fanny*; and there is Panisse's moving, yet amusing, confession before his death in *César*. Those scenes are hilarious and give the trilogy a unique comedic flavor.

Yet is must be noted that Pagnol never allowed his characters to become caricatures. In fact, in a short scene in the stage version of *Fanny* (not incorporated into the film version), he spoofs the caricature of the Marseilles Everyman, as seen from the perspective of a Parisian. He brought his cast to life in such a way that, despite being separated from them by time and space, the viewer learns to love and respect each and every patron of the Bar de la Marine.

The trilogy's recurring theme is the conflict that can exist between different types of love. *Marius*, for example, shows its young protagonist torn between his wanderlust and his love for Fanny. In *Fanny*, it is the heroine who must choose between her strong love for Marius, and that for her baby, her family, her husband, and her place in society. In *César*, it is Césariot who must learn to accept that his love for his mother must be subordinated to her love for Marius.

There is argument over parental love: Is Panisse or Marius more worthy of Césariot's love? There is a study in marital love: Fanny still loves Marius, even after her marriage to the kind Panisse; Last, dominating the entire trilogy, is César's overpowering, yet shyly hidden, love for his son Marius. This love, more than any of the others, is torn between conflicting passions and emotions.

These passions are shaped by duty and society, the modern equivalents of the gods of the Greek dramas, who force unhappy choices on the characters. Indeed, one could easily portray the gods weaving the fates of the trilogy's inhabitants. (If Marius' wanderlust is not a curse of the gods, what then is it?) The comparison with classical drama even extends to the presence of the ever important chorus, whose role it is to comment on the meaning of the action; that role is assumed in Pagnol's trilogy by the patrons of the Bar de la Marine.

To handle such powerful themes, the trilogy required first-class actors. In that respect, Pagnol was extremely fortunate. The original cast members all exhibit deep knowledge and understanding of their characters. In fact, they *are* their characters. Raimu, who had originally requested Pagnol to expand his part in *Marius*, towers over the ensemble. He manages to be both amusing and moving at the same time. Orane Demazis, Fernand Charpin, and

Pierre Fresnay (the only member of the cast not actually from the South of France), too, bring exactly the right touch of bittersweet reality to their roles.

Compared to these remarkable achievements, all other traditional cinematic values can only be subordinated, thus explaining the accusation of "canned theater," often raised against Pagnol's works. Indeed, the trilogy does not exhibit the filmic inventiveness of Vigo or Renoir. In fact, direction, music, and even art direction do not intrude on the films, to the point of passing almost without notice. Pagnol's personality eclipses that of his directors. To some extent, Alexander Korda highlighted the atmosphere of inescapable doom that hangs over the star-crossed lovers of *Marius*, and Marc Allégret brought a personal touch of light comedy to *Fanny*, in spite of the otherwise rather gloomy plot. Yet it is still Pagnol's story, Pagnol's style, and, if one can say so, Pagnol's actors that dominate the films.

Pagnol himself fell victim to this criticism in *César*. He attempted to answer his detractors by taking the film on location and interweaving several quick cuts from one place to another in the story to give an air of simultaneity. The result is, however, simply too self-consciously cinematic and seems neither natural nor necessary.

Whatever flaws may exist in the three films, their assets are far greater. It would be difficult to find films with better dialogue. The story is natural, yet, at the same time, moving and entertaining. The actors not only play their roles, but they have also become a wonderful family of friends. If there be a viewer who can watch the trilogy and not be moved, it is someone with a cold heart indeed.

R. J. M. Lofficier

THE MARQUISE OF O...
(DIE MARQUISE VON O...)

Origin: France and West Germany
Released: 1976
Released in U.S.: 1976
Production: Les Films du Losange, Janus Film, and Hessischer Rundfunk
Direction: Eric Rohmer
Screenplay: Eric Rohmer; based on the story "Phoebus," by Heinrich von Kleist
Cinematography: Nestor Almendros
Editing: Cécile Decugis
Art direction: Roger von Möllendorff
Music: based on military music of the seventeenth century
MPAA rating: PG
Running time: 102 minutes

Principal characters:

Marquise of O	Edith Clever
Count	Bruno Ganz
Father	Peter Lühr
Mother	Edda Seippel
Brother	Otto Sander
Leopardo	Bernard Frey
Doctor	Eduard Linkers
Midwife	Ruth Drexel
Porter	Hesso Huber
Russian general	Erich Schachinger
Russian officer	Richard Rogner
Courier	Thomas Straus
Priest	Volker Prächtel

Eric Rohmer, born Jean-Marie Maurice Scherer in 1920, is often linked with the French New Wave because of his associations with Jean-Luc Godard and Jacques Rivette during the 1950's (he founded the short-lived *La Gazette du cinéma* with them in 1950, for example) and his editorship of *Cahiers du cinéma* from 1957 to 1963. Ordinarily less flamboyant stylistically, however, than other New Wave talents, most of his films seem far more conventional by comparison, particularly those that constitute his cycle "Six Contes moraux" ("Six Moral Tales"). Rohmer was also at least a decade older than the other New Wave *auteurs* and trained in literary studies as a classical philologist, later to become a professor of film studies. Rohmer joined the staff at *Cahiers du cinéma* in 1951, after having taught literature at the lycée in Nancy for eight years; he had published a novel in 1946, entitled *Elizabeth*, under another pseudonym, Gilbert Cordier. Doubtless for these reasons, his films that are literary adaptations are meticulously executed and discerningly faithful to the text and spirit of the original works that stand behind them. Indeed, Rohmer has maintained a fidelity to his literary sources that is unusual among filmmakers.

Rohmer's source for *The Marquise of O . . .* , a story written by Heinrich von Kleist, is a sort of fairy tale and detective story, transformed into a comedy of manners built upon the mysterious pregnancy of an apparently virtuous young widow, Giulietta (Edith Clever), the Marquise of the title. During the siege of a citadel in northern Italy, she is separated from her family and is discovered by a band of soldiers, who attempt to molest her. She is rescued by a handsome, aristocratic Russian count (Bruno Ganz), who seems to her "an angel sent from heaven." As a consequence of the excitement, she faints, and the bold Russian, momentarily overcome by her beauty and his own passion, takes advantage of her sexually.

The Russian count, an honorable man who is shamed by his behavior, soon proposes marriage to the marquise, but since she had vowed not to remarry after the death of her husband, her father (Peter Lühr) refuses to give his immediate consent to what seems to be the count's impetuous proposal, believing the man not to have his wits entirely under control. The count is highly agitated, since he is determined to marry the marquise before his military duties require him to travel to Naples. Not understanding his motives, the family is astonished and amused by his unexpected proposal.

During the count's absence, the fact that the marquise is pregnant comes obviously to light, and, though she claims to have a "clear conscience," this complication leads to a melodramatic break between the marquise and her family, especially her puritanical father, Giulietta protesting her innocence, and her father expressing his moral outrage over the way she has besmirched the family honor. In his rage, the father banishes her to a country estate. Puzzled and hurt, the marquise finally places a notice in a local paper requesting that the father of the child she bears reveal himself: This published notice, concerning a marquise who has "become pregnant without her knowing how," occasions some mirth; it ends with the promise that she will marry the father of the child she carries "for family reasons, if he will present himself." Thereafter, the count appears and takes the responsibility. To satisfy her parents, she marries him, but she will have nothing to do with him after the ceremony, so disappointed is she to learn that the man whom she had honored and respected above all others as her savior has in fact violated her. The count is duly penitent and devoted, however, and at last a reconciliation is effected.

There is a remarkable authenticity of atmosphere reflected in Rohmer's film, which was filmed in Germany with a French crew, utilizing German actors from Peter Stein's Theater an der Halleschen Ufer in Berlin, with the dialogue in the original German. The treatment is extremely sensual, and the sensuality is heightened by exquisite lighting effects—as when, for example, the count bursts forth to save the marquise from her would-be rapists, and in later scenes showing her in repose during her pregnancy. Cinematographer Nestor Almendros' lighting has been compared in its effect to the paintings of Caspar David Friedrich, Gottlieb Schick, and Jacques Louis David, whose *Mme Recamier* (1979) Vincent Canby believes may have influenced Almendros. The total effect of the lighting, costume, and decor is to create a memorable impression, as Molly Haskell has noted, of Biedermeier Germany. Rohmer's talent is formidable and has earned for him the reputation of being one of the most original and intellectual directors of the European cinema. Aside from its value as a finely realized cinematic adaptation, the film is a visual treat.

The story of the marquise is mythic (a woman mysteriously impregnated without her knowledge), melodramatic (impassioned protestations of innocence, overwhelmed by the rage of her ranting and unforgiving father), and satiric (the decorous and extremely tactful attempts by the count to set right the confusion caused by his own churlish lust). Rohmer displays a discerning sense of fidelity to his source (which he even adapts in the German language of the original) and carefully attempts to preserve the nuances and tone of his original, exploiting the meticulous irony of the situation, and making a moral point as truth is disclosed and the dilemma finally resolved.

In the Kleist story, the count is first reconciled to the parents when he bequeaths twenty thousand roubles to the infant son that the marquise bears him and prepares a will making her heiress to his entire fortune in the event of his death. Kleist describes in a few sentences the count's "second wooing of the Countess, his wife," which lasted for a year before she gave her "second consent" for a "second wedding." Rohmer takes the time in his film to dramatize the second wooing, to provide ample dramatic preparation for the romantic reconciliation at the end.

The Marquise of O... marked a departure for Eric Rohmer in that it was the first time that he had adapted a story from another writer to cinema. The "Six Moral Tales" upon which his reputation rested to that point were all based upon original scripts. *The Marquise of O...* was later to be followed by another adaptation (1978) of an even more difficult and intractable source, a twelfth century medieval romance by Chrétien de Troyes, *Perceval: Ou, Le Conte du Graal* (c. 1180; *Perceval: Or, The Story of the Grail*). In both cases, the director was at pains to shape the style of the picture to the substance of the source. Just as he extends the action of the "second wooing" of the marquise to prepare for the emotional reaction of the final reconciliation, so in *Perceval* he takes the notion that Perceval finally reaches knightly perfection when he realizes that he had forgotten God and seeks to develop his spirituality, described in a few sentences by Chrétien, and dramatizes the process by presenting a medieval Passion Play with Perceval impersonating Christ—a perfect metaphor to end the film.

The worldview of Kleist in *The Marquise of O...* is perhaps best captured in Rohmer's film by Bruno Ganz's long-suffering, conscience-smitten Russian count, who becomes the very embodiment of what Kleist called *die gebrechliche Einrichtung der Welt*, the flaw in the nature of things, the imperfect fragility of the moral order, a man who first appears *gross und heilig* (great and holy), but succumbs to base temptations that are coarse, vulgar, and indecent. Deceived by appearances, the marquise has great difficulty adjusting herself to the ambiguity of truth and reality. Like a true comedy, the tale ends in romantic reconciliation and the promise of an awkwardly delayed consummation of a marriage. The final mood is decidedly festive as virtue is rewarded after the satirically overstated melodramatic gloom that dominates the central portion of the film. The count has been properly humble and repentant for his transgression and is rewarded for his dedicated patience. The marquise is vindicated as well.

In an interview given at the Cannes Film Festival in 1976 when *The Marquise of O...* won the Special Jury Prize, Rohmer stated that in cinema "the imagination of the director precedes that of the spectator. When one leaves the theater, one must still be hungry—a good film is one which entices you to think after having seen it. This is why a film has in common with the novel something open and unachieved. It is an invitation to dream, but it is not a definitive dream."

Rohmer sees the cinema as a means of revelation. With reference to *Claire's Knee* (1970), one of his earlier films, he has noted that he wanted "to show the essential moments, while I noticed that in many films the reverse is done." Asked about his use of the fade-out to terminate each scene in *The Marquise of O...*, Rohmer explained that he was seeking a cinematic means of capturing Kleist's temporal transitions, suggesting by the phrase "a little later" that frequently appeared in his source. The director's stated intention was "to use all the processes of narration in cinema ever since the silent film to show that Kleist had almost written a script himself." The story, therefore, "could be brought to the screen without any changes but only by applying the cinematic process."

In working out this adaptation, the text was of primary importance. The actors were instructed to deliver their lines more slowly and deliberately than they would ordinarily have done, for the sake of clarity and concentration. Music was kept to an absolute minimum so it would not prove to be distracting: "When I listen to it" (music), Rohmer explained, "I close my eyes and concentrate. I give myself entirely to music."

For this reason, musical effects are kept to an absolute minimum in the film, which achieves a conscious balance between the real and the theatrical, between the rational and the emotional, and between the dramatic and the cinematic. Pauline Kael, whose characterization of an ironic narrative as merely a fairy tale is a bit simplistic, criticized the treatment of the film's central dilemma because, she believed, it "precludes animal passion." If so, this was surely a conscious directorial decision intended to keep the careful objectivity of presentation faithful to the narrative style of the Kleist story. The action of the film is mediated through the narrative method in such a way that the audience will sense the solution of the mystery, as the marquise herself cannot because of her lasting first impression of the count as her savior, creating the effect of dramatic irony for the film audience.

The complete success of *The Marquise of O . . .* as a splendidly realized cinematic adaptation, then, is a consequence of Rohmer's discerning sense of clarity and fidelity to his source and his absolute concentration upon the text, the characters, the social and physical atmosphere, and the tonal nuances suggested by Kleist. The task was not simply to tell the story, which is as tightly structured as a play, but also to find imaginative cinematic equivalents, and, in the words of Stanley Kauffmann, "to recreate a masterwork of one art in another" by carefully and imaginatively following the design of the original.

James M. Welsh

THE MARRIAGE OF MARIA BRAUN
(DIE EHE DER MARIA BRAUN)

Origin: West Germany
Released: 1978
Released in U.S.: 1979
Production: Michael Fengler for Albatros Film/Trio Film/Westdeutscher
   Rundfunk
Direction: Rainer Werner Fassbinder
Screenplay: Peter Märthesheimer and Pea Fröhlich; additional dialogue by
   Rainer Werner Fassbinder
Cinematography: Michael Ballhaus
Editing: Juliane Lorenz
Art direction: Norbert Scherer
Costume design: Barbara Baum, Susi Reichel, George Kuhn, and Ingeborg
   Pröller
Music: Peer Raben
MPAA rating: R
Running time: 120 minutes

> *Principal characters:*
> Maria Braun . . . . Hanna Schygulla
> Hermann Braun . . . . Klaus Löwitsch
> Karl Oswald . . . . Ivan Desny
> Bill. . . . . George Byrd
> Maria's mother . . . . Gisela Uhlen
> Maria's grandfather. . . . . Anton Schirsner
> Betti Klenze . . . . Elisabeth Trissenaar
> Willi Klenze . . . . Gottfried John

The Marriage of Maria Braun presents the late Rainer Werner Fassbinder's sardonic view of the "Economic Miracle" of postwar Germany, as
dramatized by the life of fictional character Maria Braun (Hanna Schygulla). The evolution of Maria's character from 1945 through 1954 mirrors
that of her country—a shattered dream replaced by hard-nosed pragmatism
which turns out to mask a soul-destroying cynicism. Although politics is seldom at the surface of the film, Fassbinder reinforces the political context of
The Marriage of Maria Braun by framing his film with photographs of German leaders from Adolf Hitler to Chancellor Helmut Schmidt.

The film opens with a shot of a poster of the face of Hitler, after which
the image and the wall upon which the poster hangs explode to reveal a
wedding ceremony taking place. It is the final days of the Third Reich, and
the Allied bombardment of Berlin is so fierce that the bride, groom, and

justice of the peace are forced to finish the ceremony flat on their faces. The husband is Hermann Braun (Klaus Löwitsch), who is sent to the Russian front the next day. The wife is Maria Braun, Fassbinder's metaphor for postwar Germany.

Maria's Germany is a nation in ruins; Fassbinder spends the first third of the film showing the viewer the massive physical and psychological devastation that the war brought to Berlin. The physical ruin is bad enough—bombed-out buildings and cratered streets abound—but the psychological havoc is worse. Families trade their heirlooms for sticks of firewood; wives gather forlornly at the train depot, hoping for some word of their missing husbands; and some of the women sell their bodies in order to survive.

In the early part of the film, Maria is a relentless optimist, certain that each succeeding train will be the one to bring Hermann back. She lives with her mother (Gisela Uhlen), grandfather (Anton Schirsner), and sister Betti Klenze (Elisabeth Trissenaar), whose husband, Willi Klenze (Gottfried John), was serving with Hermann on the Eastern front. The radio is on constantly as the announcer calmly reads an endless list of dead and missing soldiers.

Gradually, the viewer sees Maria begin to harden. First she bargains with her mother, trading two packs of cigarettes for a valuable brooch. Then she trades the brooch on the black market for a sexy dress. She makes her first compromise with her ideals when she takes a job as a hostess in a bar that caters to American soldiers. Her boss orders her not to wear her wedding ring to work.

A portly, genial black American sergeant known only as Bill (George Byrd) is smitten by Maria, and when Betti's husband, Willi, returns home and announces that Hermann is dead, Maria immediately goes to him for comfort, and they become lovers. She spurns his offer of marriage, however, because her fondness for him does not override her belief that she is still married, even if Hermann is dead.

Thus Fassbinder reveals Maria's strategic moral compromise: So long as her primary commitment is to her husband, nothing she does with another man really constitutes infidelity. This is a simple enough rationalization when she believes that her husband is dead, but when Hermann turns up alive, matters become more complex.

Hermann walks in as Maria and Bill are making love. The two men struggle, and Maria tries to stop the fight by smashing a bottle over Bill's head, accidentally killing him. The stoical Hermann takes the blame for the crime and is sent to prison, where Maria visits him and outlines her plans for the future: She will work hard, accumulate wealth, and take her pleasure where she finds it. Hermann, meanwhile, will live vicariously through her happiness while he is in prison. Hermann, bemused, accepts her scheme.

At first, Maria's plans are interrupted by pregnancy, but after the death at birth of Bill's child, she begins her quest with unrestrained fervor. Her business and pleasure come together in the person of Karl Oswald (Ivan Desny), a French textiles magnate with a factory in Germany. They become lovers (her way of gaining leverage over him) and business partners almost immediately; Maria proves adept at both pursuits.

Just as Maria builds her life, Germany rebuilds itself, as represented by the constant rattle of construction machinery on the sound track. Maria, however, finds that this growth is accompanied by pain; even as her career prospers, her personal life begins to unravel. Her troubles begin with an estrangement from her family. Despite her belief that her own succession of lovers has no effect on the purity of her relationship with her husband, she refuses to accept her mother's boyfriend. When her sister's marriage to Willi breaks up, she has little to offer in the way of encouragement.

Maria is also losing control of her uncomplicated relationship with Oswald, who has fallen desperately in love with her. He proposes marriage, but she counters by forcing him to call her "Frau Braun" as they make love. She inflicts a similar pain on her husband by frankly admitting her affair with Oswald, in effect cuckolding both men simultaneously.

Oswald, who is dying of a liver ailment, visits Hermann in prison and, unknown to the audience, bribes him to leave the country upon his release from prison. Thus, Oswald will have Maria to himself for what little time he has left.

That time, however, is not spent happily. Hermann's unexplained desertion breaks Maria's spirit as nothing else has been able to do. She becomes first cynical and finally cruel. She builds a luxurious new home but isolates herself in it, and Oswald dies as much from a broken heart as from his liver ailment.

Maria's spirits are revived briefly when Hermann, his exile ended by Oswald's death, returns to her. The scene appears to be building toward a final vindication of Maria's efforts. The radio broadcast in the background echoes the theme: Germany is on the verge of winning soccer's prestigious World Cup; indeed, it was this sports victory in 1954 that came to symbolize Germany's full recovery from the trauma of World War II.

Just as a life with her husband has been denied Maria twice before, though, so it is denied her now. The film ends, as it began, with an explosion. Maria carelessly blows out the flame on her gas stove rather than turning off the burner. Gas fills the room, and, minutes later, when she strikes a match to light a cigarette, both she and her new house—a monument to her amoral life and at the same time a symbol of the new postwar Germany— are destroyed. The film's final shots, photographs of Germany's postwar chancellors through the 1970's, mirror its opening: Germany can change its politics, Fassbinder seems to be saying, but it cannot save its soul.

By the time he released *The Marriage of Maria Braun* in 1978, Fassbinder had directed more than thirty feature-length films; at the age of thirty-three, he had proved himself to be Germany's most prolific filmmaker, as well as one of its best. The film's screenplay, by Peter Märthesheimer and Pea Fröhlich, with additional dialogue by Fassbinder, is a superb mix of high-class soap opera and black comedy. Only the ending is less than satisfactory. In its initial stages, the script had Maria killing both Hermann and herself when she learned of his deal with Karl Oswald. The ending Fassbinder substituted is much more ambiguous as to whether Maria's death was deliberate or accidental, and it left many critics dissatisfied.

Otherwise, Fassbinder's direction is especially sure-handed. There are many memorable scenes; the opening shot of the Hitler poster exploding to reveal a wedding ceremony is often cited as a classic. Fassbinder's use of background noise—artillery fire, the rumble of construction, and the ever-present radio—to tie Maria's personal life to that of her country is particularly effective.

The cast was outstanding. In one of the principal roles, Ivan Desny gave an affecting performance as Karl Oswald, Maria's devoted but perplexed employer/suitor. Klaus Löwitsch, as Hermann, had the difficult task of portraying a man who seems to have a greater influence on events when he is absent than when he is present. Hermann is a man both haunted and toughened by his ordeals. Löwitsch's portrayal of this enigmatic character creates a brooding presence throughout the film.

Hanna Schygulla appeared in more than half of Fassbinder's feature films, and as Maria Braun, she gives one of her most memorable performances. Schygulla manages to be hard and vulnerable, appealing and repellant, at the same time. Her ability to embody Maria's contradictions persuasively is the cornerstone of the film's success, and her performance is all the more remarkable for its subtlety.

The Marriage of Maria Braun won the 1978 Academy Award for Best Foreign-Language Film, and it was a financial as well as an artistic success. It proved to be a breakthrough film for Fassbinder in Germany, introducing him to a mass audience in his own country for the first time, and the film has been immensely popular with American audiences as well.

Robert Mitchell

THE MARRIED WOMAN
(LA FEMME MARIÉE)

Origin: France
Released: 1964
Released in U.S.: 1965
Production: Anouchka Films/Orsay Films
Direction: Jean-Luc Godard
Assistant direction: Claude Othnin-Girard, Jean-Pierre Léaud, and Hélène Kalouguine
Screenplay: Jean-Luc Godard
Cinematography: Raoul Coutard
Editing: Agnès Guillemot and Françoise Collin
Art direction: Henri Nogaret
Sound: Antoine Bonfanti, René Levert, and Jacques Maumont
Music: Ludwig van Beethoven and Claude Nougaro
Song: J. D. Laudermilk, G. Auber, and L. Morisse, "Quand le film est triste"; sung by Sylvie Vartan
Running time: 95 minutes

> *Principal characters:*
> Charlotte Giraud.....................Macha Méril
> Robert............................Bernard Noël
> Pierre............................Philippe Leroy
> Roger Leenhardt ....Himself
> Madame Céline ....Rita Maiden
> Nicolas ....Chris Tophe
> Girls in swimming-pool bar ....Margaret Le-Van/
> Véronique Duval

Of all the directors to emerge from the French New Wave, Jean-Luc Godard is, with Jacques Rivette, perhaps the most important, certainly the most controversial. Worshiped by his advocates, vilified by his detractors, Godard is very much a man of his times, a conscientious intellectual grappling with a rapidly changing French society and influenced not only by his *Zeitgeist* but also by the history of cinema itself. Godard is an innovator in film form in much the same way that James Joyce broke down the traditional parameters of literature, Robert Rauschenberg revolutionized the visual arts, and John Cage reinterpreted the very nature of music. Although critical and popular taste have been relatively quick to absorb and accept radical changes in literature and art, film, because of its commercial economic base, has remained problematical. Godard has thus remained an *enfant terrible*, despite a concomitant public willingness to accept formal developments in critical theory and philosophy as radical as the structuralism of Roland Barthes and Michel Foucault, or the deconstruction of Jacques Derrida. Many critics seem to be unable to accept Godard's cinematic appropriation of the same influence.

Part of the reason may lie in Godard's uncompromising fusion of French philosophy—in his case a personalized hybrid of existentialism, semiotics, and Saussurian linguistics—with Marxism, in particular his commitment to a Brechtian dismantling of traditional modes of representation as well as an adamant refusal to bow to bourgeois narrative codes. From the dislocating jump-cuts of *À bout de souffle* (1960; *Breathless*) to the analytic breakdown of language in *Le Gai Savoir* (1969), Godard's oeuvre has followed a logical evolution, an attempt not only to re-create cinema, to "return to zero," but also to create a truly revolutionary, nonbourgeois film structure. It is this mixture of ideology and sociology within a traditionally populist medium that alienates many critics, largely because they see, rightly or wrongly, Godard as an intellectual dilettante who is playacting the revolution through elitist means.

The Married Woman is a key film in Godard's evolution, insofar as it marks his first obvious break with clear, linear narrative and introduces his first use of collage (as opposed to montage) in addition to the Brechtian distancing devices employed so effectively in *Vivre sa vie* (1962; *My Life to Live*). The film also represents a concise summary of each of Godard's aesthetic concerns of the period, realizing his ambiguous juxtapositions of illusion and reality, of fiction and documentary forms, experience and imagination, and the conflict between objective "truth" and subjectivity. In short, Godard examines theater both as an extension of, and illusory alternative to, lived reality.

The film's plot, when divorced from Godard's formal experimentation, is actually quite simple, depicting twenty-four hours in the life of Charlotte Giraud (Macha Méril), an attractive young editor on a Paris women's magazine. The film opens as she makes her daily rendezvous with her actor lover, Robert (Bernard Noël), who urges her to leave her husband so that they can live together and possibly have a child. Charlotte is confused, finding it easier to lie and assure Robert that she has discussed their affair with her spouse and is committed to a divorce.

After Robert drops Charlotte off at the Printemps-Nation department store, she takes a roundabout route via several taxis to pick up her schoolboy son, Nicolas (Chris Tophe). Charlotte, it seems, is afraid of being followed by both her lover and Pierre (Philippe Leroy), her husband. Mother and son then take yet another taxi to an airfield, where they meet Pierre, a pilot who has just flown in from Germany with Roger Leenhardt (who plays himself), the veteran critic and filmmaker, Leenhardt is promptly invited to dinner.

At home, Pierre questions his wife's fidelity, but Charlotte denies any affair, seeming more concerned with measuring her bust to see if her breasts conform to a magazine's idea of perfection. When Leenhardt arrives for dinner, he is given a tour of the apartment, and the group settles down to a series of discourses in the style of *cinéma vérité*. After Leenhardt has left, Charlotte and Pierre argue over playing some records before making love.

The next day, Charlotte sets up an appointment with her doctor and then listens to her maid, Madame Céline (Rita Maiden), extol her own husband's virtues as a lover. Robert has meanwhile called to set up a rendezvous that afternoon in the Orly Airport cinema. He is flying to the provinces to play Titus in Jean Racine's *Bérènice* (1670).

Charlotte attends a photography session for her magazine at a swimming pool, and while drinking coffee in the pool bar, she overhears two teenage girls (Margaret Le-Van and Véronique Duval) discussing fashions and love. Charlotte then visits her doctor, and she discovers that she is three months pregnant. She has no idea who the father is. After meeting Robert at Orly, they both go to the airport hotel and make love. Charlotte is still unable to reach a decision about leaving Pierre, and Robert suggests that they end the affair. Charlotte seems to agree but cannot prevent herself from crying.

The film's subtitle, "Fragments of a Film Made in 1964," suggests that it is intended to present a dislocated vision of Charlotte, who is herself unable to piece together the splintered elements of her life. In this respect, Godard's use of collage is a perfect formal complement to his main thesis—that Charlotte, within the socioeconomic conditions of conspicuous consumption, has become a mere object, a prostitute to both her husband and lover and, by extension, a rabid consumer who helps to propagate the system that oppresses her.

In this case, collage has little to do with the associative montage of Sergei Eisenstein, who, using two juxtaposed shots, of varying duration, would create a dialectical juxtaposition that developed a synthesis which was more than the mere sum of the parts. With collage, the shots in a given sequence collide with one another not to expound a new thesis but rather exist independently as autonomous shots. Stylistically, this illustrates Charlotte's state of mind, that of a woman who lives entirely in the present, whose life is a staccato series of ups and downs, where each new experience completely supersedes the one before. As a result, a rational choice between Robert and Pierre is impossible: Charlotte is incapable of drawing conclusions from cause-and-effect situations.

Within the film itself, Godard heightens this formal breakdown through a series of disruptive, distancing devices, echoing the *Verfremdungseffekt* of Brecht. Godard achieves this on both macro and micro levels, within and between individual scenes. On a broader level, Godard disrupts the narrative by interjecting references that draw attention to filmic artifice and obvious appropriations from literature, particularly the love affair between Titus and Bérènice in Racine's play. A typical example is Charlotte's meeting with Robert in the Orly cinema, where Alfred Hitchcock's *Spellbound* (1945) is playing in an unlikely double bill with Alain Resnais' *Nuit et brouillard* (1956; *Night and Fog*). The Hitchcock references underline the clandestine nature of the tryst, reinforced by Robert's deliberately dropping his keys outside so that Charlotte can pick them up and discover the number of his hotel room. Godard accentuates the artifice by shooting the scene with a typically Hitchcockian tracking shot.

The Resnais reference is more psychologically motivated, in that it expresses Charlotte's absorption in the moment, her inability to draw moral or political correlations between her pregnancy, her affair, conspicuous consumption, or even the horrors of the concentration camp (in Resnais' film, reduced in part to a commercial "entertainment"). At one point, the Resnais film announces that even a church steeple might lead to a concentration camp, yet in Charlotte's unquestioned slavery to received information, anything might legitimately lead to anything else.

Godard's overall narrative structure is deliberately fractured, designed to counteract any charges of forced didacticism in his own film. The "plot" essentially consists of three set pieces, in which Charlotte makes love to Robert, Pierre, and then to her lover once more. These are interrupted by seven interviews, in which the actors define their relationship to their roles, as well as their characters' relationship to their filmic situation. Pierre discourses on memory, revealing his ability to cross-reference information and remember the slightest detail, while Charlotte proclaims her dependence on the present, on living for the moment. Leenhardt follows with his views on intelligence, urging Charlotte to inject some rational understanding into her actions—an absurd, blinkered notion given Charlotte's passive status as object for the whims of a male-dominated world. Nicolas gives his thoughts on childhood, although his account is essentially a very fragmented series of notes on how to paint a painting. The final interludes consist of Madame Céline's description of sex with her husband—lifted almost directly from Louis-Ferdinand Céline's novel *Mort à crédit* (1936; *Death on the Installment Plan*)—and Charlotte's discussions with her doctor on pleasure and science, the theater and love.

The interviews seem at first to be completely gratuitous digressions from the main narrative, but they in fact serve an important Brechtian role of investigating the ambiguous relationship between theater and real life. The viewer becomes aware that he is watching a film, that these are mere actors reading from a prepared script, albeit an often improvised one. Godard does not want his audience to be drawn into the deceit but rather to distance themselves from it, to enter the cerebral space that he has opened up and ask questions, to look at societal context rather than an emotional illusion. This, however, has wider connotations within the story itself, because the character Robert is also an actor. If one is encouraged to mistrust the film itself, one becomes doubly aware of Charlotte's own unease with her lover within the plot. Is Robert making love to her or only acting? What does "I love you" really mean? Is everything tied to the vagaries of language? By extension, can one give any credence to the "truth" of cinema itself?

Aside from the titles that Godard repeatedly interjects between scenes, the collage effect is most pronounced within seemingly self-contained sequences, such as the lovemaking between Charlotte and her husband and lover. Godard fragments the scenes into a series of abstract close-ups—a section of calf here, a thigh there, an arm, Charlotte's midriff, clasped hands—not only to drain the situations of any eroticism, but also to express formally the disjointed, hermetic nature of Charlotte's emotional life. As she lives entirely in the present, it is appropriate that her sex life is treated with cool detachment, as flesh turned into pure object rather than a coupling of two personalities. The respective sequences with Robert and Pierre are quite similar, suggesting that to both men, Charlotte is merely an object of desire. Robert, for example, asks Charlotte not to shave under her arms, so that she will be like the women in Italian films. Instead of asserting her individuality, Charlotte merely inserts her own, secondhand fantasy, that of preferring Hollywood heroines, who are prettier.

It is such channeling of ideas through media communication that provides the key to Godard's thesis. The married woman's existence consists of a series of received ideas based on consumption. Charlotte works for a fashion magazine so that she participates economically in the process (in a sense, she is her own pimp) and perpetuates her own imprisonment by the consumer society. Godard intercuts shots of advertising media throughout the film—from magazines, billboards, and posters—urging Charlotte to buy brassieres, girdles, pantyhose to develop the perfect body—in short, to become a slave to the economy of secondhand images. Charlotte is an object because she is pressured by modern life to see herself as others want to see her. Yet she is also an object that consumes, and the bombardment of signs tells her how to increase her value in the marketplace, much as if she were a whore on a course of financial self-improvement. Godard underlines the irony of the situation by refusing to deconstruct it visually. His collage cuts randomly from Charlotte to consumer objects and back again, completely disrupting any ongoing point of view and serving to tie the fragments together as "normality."

The Married Woman is not as formally radical as *Le Gai Savoir* or *La Chinoise* (1967), largely because Godard unifies the visual dislocation through medium (black-and-white film stock) and also a linear sound track. It was not until the latter films that he began to separate sound from visual to create a definitive, nonbourgeois cinema. His Marxism was still in its formative stages at the time of *The Married Woman*, and it is the film's sociological elements and Brechtian aesthetic rather than dialectical structure which define Godard's semiotic concerns with image as image, where direct experience is tied in with the commerce of signs.

Colin Gardner

MASCULIN-FÉMININ

Origin: France
Released: 1966
Released in U.S.: 1966
Production: Anouchka Films, Argos Films, Svensk Filmindustri, and
  Sandrews
Direction: Jean-Luc Godard
Screenplay: Jean-Luc Godard; based on the novels *La Femme de Paul* and *Le
  Signe*, by Guy de Maupassant, the play *Dutchman, The Slave*, by Amiri
  Baraka, and the play *Les Prodiges*, by Jean Vauthier
Cinematography: Willy Kurant
Editing: Agnès Guillemot and Marguerite Renoir
Art direction: no listing
Music: Francis J. J. Debout and Wolfgang Amadeus Mozart
Running time: 110 minutes
Also known as: Masculine-Feminine

> *Principal characters:*
> Paul .... Jean-Pierre Léaud
> Madeleine .... Chantal Goya
> Élisabeth .... Marlène Jobert
> Robert......................... Michel Debord
> Catherine-Isabelle .... Catherine-Isabelle Duport
> She.......................... Eva Britt Strandbert
> He............................ Birger Malmsten
> Elsa................................. Elsa Leroy

Director Jean-Luc Godard made some of the most eclectic, idiosyncratic, and artistically significant films of the 1960's. *Masculin-féminin* is one such film. Released in the middle of that turbulent decade, it marks the growing politicization of the always controversial Godard—continuing also his investigation into personal relationships.

Godard's association with the cinema began as an obsessive film viewer rather than maker. He shared this trait with many of the young directors of the French New Wave of the late 1950's and the 1960's. Several of them, Godard included, wrote for the influential film journal, *Cahiers du cinéma*, but they were all eager to put down the pen and assume what one critic called the *caméra stylo* (camera-as-pen). Indeed, New Wave directors scored huge international successes in 1958 through 1962 with films such as *Hiroshima mon amour* (1959), *Jules et Jim* (1962; *Jules and Jim*), and Godard's own *À bout de souffle* (1960; *Breathless*).

The New Wave directors' common fascination with the cinema united them in a rebellion against what they saw to be a stodgy "tradition of quality" in French films of the 1950's. They much preferred the more kinetic and less consciously intellectual work of American directors such as Alfred Hitchcock, Howard Hawks, and Jerry Lewis (the latter preference has frequently puzzled English-speaking critics). Their writing would come to establish what is now known as the "auteur theory"—a methodology for arranging cinema history that considers the director as the "author" of a film. In both written and film work the New Wave directors were advocating a more personal style of filmmaking than was customary in Hollywood.

Godard's affection for the American cinema reveals itself in his films as well as his articles. He frequently quotes from other films—putting old, familiar dialogue in his characters' mouths or even quoting a favorite director's visual style (shooting a scene in the style of Hitchcock, for example). His detractors have chided him for self-indulgence, but the many quotations and homages to other directors and films are merely the most playful manifestation of his films' reflexivity. He makes films about filmmaking. For many, Godard is the cinema's first modernist artist (working in feature-length films). He has taken the conventions of filmmaking and consciously, mercilessly, twisted and broken them. For example, *Breathless*, Godard's first feature, startled the film community with brazen jump cuts (cuts in which a jump in action is noticeable) that effectively communicated the helter-skelter world of the punk protagonist. At the same time, by radically breaking the convention of match cutting, Godard draws attention to the conventionality of cinematic forms.

Masculin-féminin was Godard's eleventh feature-length film. Reportedly, he himself considers it to be his first attempt at a specifically political film—an exegesis of societal structures and the personal relationships they promote. The main characters are described by a title in the film as the "children of Marx and Coca-Cola"; they comprise a group of young men and women, some more radical than others, who seem to belong equally to the "Pepsi Generation" and 1960's-style leftist politics.

The protagonist is Paul, an impulsive young man played by Jean-Pierre Léaud. Léaud literally grew up acting in New Wave films. He began as an adolescent, fifteen-year-old Antoine Doinel in François Truffaut's *Les Quatre Cents Coups* (1959; *The 400 Blows*) and then reprised that role at age twenty-four with *Baisers volés* (1968; *Stolen Kisses*) and at age twenty-six with *Domicile conjugal* (1970; *Bed and Board*). One of the many homages in *Masculin-féminin* occurs when Paul orders a military car under the name of General Doinel. For Godard, Léaud is as much an icon of 1960's French filmmaking as he is an actor.

The opening credits announce that *Masculin-féminin* will be a film in fifteen precise acts. This pronouncement is highly ironic, however, for even though the film dutifully counts from one to fifteen (the numbers appear on the screen, frequently accompanied by gunshots), the "precision" of the acts is doubtful. The film's narrative structure owes more to the unpredictable peripeteia of everyday life than to any sense of accuracy: Scenes begin and end seemingly at random; some sequences continue over more than one number; and so on. The effect is to make the viewer more aware of the arbitrariness of conventional scene construction and to engage the viewer more actively in narrative production.

The film begins, characteristically, with Paul reading in a café. As with most of Godard's films of this period, *Masculin-féminin's* story unfolds in the streets and cafés of Paris. Shot on location, the film has an ambience that has been compared to *cinéma vérité*. Paul strikes up an acquaintance with the film's other principal character, Madeleine (Chantal Goya), an aspiring singer who works for a magazine. While Paul speaks of being in the army and begins a philosophical discourse on relative freedom, one of the film's many acts of incidental violence transpires: A man and woman argue in the café. When he pulls her child outside, she follows and shoots him with a pistol. In conventional narrative terms, there is absolutely no motivation for this action. This is the woman's first appearance in the film and, although she will appear briefly later, her story is not pursued. The shooting is never explained. Here, as elsewhere, conventional narrative structure is eschewed in favor of a disjointed form that better reflects what Godard feels to be the fragmented, alienated quality of contemporary life, in which violence has no rational motivation and reason is seldom rewarded.

After contacting Madeleine, Paul goes to another café to see his radical friend Robert (Michel Debord). They talk about sex and make a pass at a woman in the café, pretending to reach for a bowl of sugar in order to rub her breasts. Although Paul and Robert are committed to social revolution, their behavior toward women—as exemplified in this scene—is frequently abusive.

Having introduced the five main characters of *Masculin-féminin*, the remainder of the film consists of vignettes of their activities. This form of narrative construction stems from Godard's interest in German playwright and drama theorist, Bertolt Brecht. Much of Brecht's work was translated into French during the 1950's, fueling a Brecht revival. From Brecht's antitraditional "epic theater," Godard draws the notion of alienating the viewer by breaking the narrative into tableaux and laying bare film technique. Identification with the protagonist is thereby blocked. Rather than empathizing with the characters, Godard (after Brecht) makes the viewer stand back and analyze the characters' positions within society. Moreover, that society is represented in terms of social class—as originally conceptualized by Karl Marx.

Robert distracts an army chauffeur so that Paul can paint "Peace in Vietnam" on the side of his car. Later, in a subway train, they watch an argument between two black men and a white woman—a scene that is excerpted from Amiri Baraka's *Dutchman, The Slave* (1964). As happens so frequently in Godard, characters quote—with or without acknowledgment—from a variety of sources: films, books, plays, poems, and so on. This wealth of quotation creates a thick, sometimes impenetrable, texture of allusions. Complicated by many puns and other wordplay, Godard's films are difficult to translate and inevitably suffer when seen dubbed or with subtitles.

The tentative romance between Paul and Madeleine continues. Once again in a café, they talk about her recording career. Their discussion is interrupted by a man reading pornography out loud to a popular song on the jukebox. While Paul accompanies Madeleine to the door, he proposes marriage, but she leaves without responding.

Paul speaks with Madeleine and Catherine-Isabelle (Catherine-Isabelle Duport), Madeleine's roommate, at an outdoor bar. The two women leave and Paul pays a young woman to show him her breasts in a photography booth. He then records a plea to Madeleine in a recording booth next door. Suddenly and unexpectedly, a young man emerges from a bowling alley carrying a knife and threatens Paul with it. He turns the knife on himself, however, stabbing his stomach and falling into Paul's arms. Once again, incidental violence has interrupted the narrative progression.

Robert and Paul meet in a laundromat and discuss a magazine article about Bob Dylan. They then proceed to joke about advertisements for brassieres, and Paul tells an obscene joke about the literary character, Camille. After this rather adolescent conversation, an ironic title appears on the screen: "Purity is not of this world." This is followed by: the number seven (of the fifteen precise acts); the sole word, "but"; the number eight; and, "every ten years there is a glimmer, a flash." Clearly, Robert and Paul's conversation is not the purity to which Godard alludes. This segment also illustrates the arbitrariness of Godard's numbering system.

Catherine and Paul, alone in their apartment, speak about birth control. She tells him that Madeleine fears becoming pregnant and for that reason has refused sexual relations with Paul. Madeleine herself and Élisabeth (Marlène Jobert), another roommate, soon enter with the news that Madeleine's record, "If You Win at Pinball" is doing well on the music charts in Japan. Madeleine has also brought a magazine featuring an article on her. Paul, in a somewhat mocking tone, reads aloud the fan-magazine hyperbole while the camera rests on Madeleine's face. She is becoming a popular culture icon and losing her personal identity. Madeleine, Élisabeth, and Paul eventually retire to one bed.

Interviews are a frequent occurrence in Godard's films. The camera often becomes an investigatory tool, probing into a character/actor's essence. *Masculin-féminin* features several discussions between characters that are closer to question-and-answer interviews than idle chatting (for example,

Robert and Catherine quiz each other on their sexual attitudes). The film also contains a segment that is titled, "An interview with a consumer product," in which Paul interviews Miss Nineteen-Year-Old (Elsa Leroy) for the French Public Opinion Institute. Actually, the interview is more of an interrogation as Paul asks the young woman questions designed to embarrass her. He queries her on socialism, birth control, the term "reactionary," and other matters she does not understand. Godard's motivations are a bit unclear at this point. Does he mean to ridicule this "consumer product," a woman who is at worst simply a victim of a consumer society? If so, it seems that Godard has chosen an easy target and one which does not deserve the hostility that generates Paul's questions.

In several Godard films the characters go to films—which is hardly surprising, considering Godard's cinephile background. In the present film Paul, Madeleine, and Catherine attend a film that appears to be a parody of pornography. Paul goes to the restroom, where he stumbles upon two men kissing and then writes graffiti insulting the French government. Returning to his seat he notes that the film is not being shown in the proper aspect ratio and leaves to find the projection booth, which is reached through an exterior door. While running through the alley, Paul pauses to spray paint more graffiti (against Charles de Gaulle), but the viewer does not see him complete it. After instructing the projectionist, Paul returns to his seat once again, but is not pleased with the film and suggests that they leave. They remain, nevertheless, and the sequence ends with a voice-over by Paul complaining that although they often go to films, they are usually disappointed. The films never live up to their expectations, to the films they had dreamed.

As Paul and Catherine walk down the street a man borrows matches from Paul and runs off-frame. Paul follows him to retrieve his matches. When he returns to Catherine, he tells her that a man has burned himself alive, crying "Peace in Vietnam." The recurrent references to Vietnam, de Gaulle, and the French Republic are but one manifestation of the politics of *Masculin-féminin*. Clearly, Godard has adopted the rhetoric of 1960's Left politics, but his politicization goes further than that to include sexual politics and what might be called the politics of language (that is, the relationship of language to social power structures).

Masculin-féminin, as the title indicates, is a film about men, women, and the relationship between the two. In the final analysis, it is not very optimistic about the chances for an armistice in the war between the sexes. The film confronts issues such as the reification of women in contemporary society and the mass media, but it does not offer many solutions. Moreover, the male characters are mostly distrustful of women, constantly interrogating them or using them for sexual gratification. Neither sex seems to obtain much comfort or solace from the other. Consequently, *Masculin-féminin* is at heart a deeply pessimistic film.

Godard's interest in the politics of language is especially evident in some of *Masculin-féminin*'s final sequences. Over shots of street scenes, Paul speaks a long voice-over, discussing the politics of interviewing. All questions, all language, he comments, convey an ideology. There is no neutral language. For Godard, language is not simply an objective tool for communicating ideas; rather, it is already inscribed with a specific (bourgeois) ideology. Godard here echoes the work of contemporary linguists and semioticians such as Roland Barthes, who struggle with the relationship of language and ideology. Godard extends their work into the realm of the cinema, investigating how film "language" (technique) is governed by ideology. This concern with film language has made Godard one of the most discussed directors of the contemporary cinema. Few other filmmakers are as intellectually challenging.

Masculin-féminin concludes with still another interview. This time it is the police taking statements from Catherine and Madeleine about Paul's unexpected death (which is not presented in the film). As in many of Godard's films, total narrative closure eludes the viewer. The cause of death remains vague and uncertain. As Catherine describes it, Paul was taking photographs and stepped too far back, falling out of a window—or committing suicide. The viewer will never know. The last shots of the film are of Madeleine. She talks indefinitely about her future (she is carrying Paul's baby) and as the camera continues to focus on her the camera cuts to the title, "FEMININ." A gunshot rings out and four letters disappear, leaving "F . . . IN" (the end).

Godard's work continued to become more and more political as the 1960's progressed. The French civil riots in 1968 radicalized him even further and he formed a Marxist film collective, the Dziga Vertov Group. From 1968 to 1972, this group produced radical films that dealt with social, sexual, and linguistic politics. Since 1972, Godard has spent the majority of his time developing video projects instead of producing films. His work, which is little seen outside France, has returned to more personal themes of the relationships between men and women, territory he originally charted in films such as *Masculin-féminin*.

Jeremy G. Butler

MAX HAVELAAR

Origin: The Netherlands
Released: 1978
Released in U.S.: 1979
Production: Fons Rademakers for Fons Rademakers Productie and P. T.
 Mondial Motion Pictures
Direction: Fons Rademakers
Screenplay: Gerard Soeteman; based on the novel by Multatuli (Eduard
 Douwes Dekker)
Cinematography: Jan de Bont
Editing: Pieter Bergeman and Victorine Habets
Art direction: Fred Wetik and Frank Raven
Sound: Peter Vink, Kees Linthorst, and Erik Langhout
Music: no listing
MPAA rating: no listing
Running time: 170 minutes

> *Principal characters:*
> Max Havelaar .... Peter Faber
> Tine .... Sacha Bulthuis
> Saidjah .... Lerry Iantho
> Regent...... Elang Mohamad Adenan Soesilaningrat
> Havelaar's predecessor .... Joop Admiraal
> Regiment commander .... Rutger Hauer
> Adinda.......................... Henny Zulaini
> Resident .... Carl Van Der Plas

In the Dutch cinema, Fons Rademakers is a special director. Since World
War II, he has managed to build a career in feature films spanning a period
of twenty-five years, during which time most Dutch filmmakers worked in
the field of documentary film. At first, he studied acting in Paris, and consequently, he worked as a stage actor in various countries; later, he switched
to cinema and was an assistant on films with Federico Fellini, Vittorio De
Sica, David Lean, and Jean Renoir. His first feature was *Dorp aan de rivier*
(1958; *Village on the River*), revealing a highly individual style, reminiscent
of Ingmar Bergman and Leopoldo Torre Nilsson. His international background succeeded in raising his productions to a superior level in comparison with the often easygoing, provincial character of most Dutch films. *Max
Havelaar*, his eighth feature, is considered a chef d'oeuvre and shows the
wide range of Rademakers' abilities. It was awarded prizes at Naples and at
the Teheran festival.
    Eduard Douwes Dekker, under the pseudonym, "Multatuli," a Latin com-

pound meaning "much have I suffered," wrote *Max Havelaar* in 1859 as a protest against the corruption among the native princes and the Dutch colonial rulers in the Dutch East Indies, which is now Indonesia. The modern stylistic devices which Multatuli used—alternating dramatic moments with comments on the state of the coffee market in Amsterdam and essays on emancipation, prostitution, and education; shifting from lyric exaltation to satiric acuteness—as well as his swift, pleasant tone, made the book a classic, and it has been translated into several languages. Gerard Soeteman, who wrote the scripts of *Turks Fruit* (1972; *Turkish Delight*) and *Keetje Tippel* (1975), adapted Multatuli's novel and transformed its complex, collagelike structure into a quasi-linear one, which retains two central stories—that of Max Havelaar, the writer in search of a publisher, and that of the character Max Havelaar in the book. The prospective publisher, Droogstoppel, is Havelaar's old classmate and a coffee merchant whom Havelaar (Peter Faber) encounters by chance. Droogstoppel agrees to read the manuscript, and the film flashes back to the adventures recounted. Moreover, the script accords the inner story of a native rebel couple much more space than does the novel, in which it is only meant as a short, romantic illustration of the state of affairs. In the film, an important parallel plot that involves Saidjah (Lerry Iantho) and Adinda (Henny Zulaini) counterbalances the Havelaar story and is interwoven with it. This plot represents the misery of the ordinary native people, who are practically slaves and who are oppressed by the native regents. Not only is the structure altered, but also the epic style affects the original tone. The heat and passion of Multatuli's attack on Dutch colonialism is exchanged for a more meditative, smooth approach, with occasional bursts of intensity.

Most of the film, lasting almost three hours, is set in Lebak, Java. The story of Havelaar is framed by sequences in Amsterdam, although the prologue takes place in Java as well. In this sense, the metaphor becomes structural, with the lush tropics hemmed in by the cold, dark atmosphere of the northern city.

The film opens at a leisurely pace, with some beautiful tracks of the Indonesian landscape. A group of Dutch soldiers marches through the fields where rice is cultivated. The little village where Saidjah and Adinda live offers an idyllic picture of Saidjah washing his much-beloved buffalo in the river. Suddenly, the peaceful mood is disturbed: A tiger assaults the buffalo. After a terrible fight, the tiger is killed, and the men return home in triumph. This feeling, however, does not last: The Regent (Elang Mohamad Adenan Soesilaningrat) demands homage, and the buffalo is taken away. A boy who dares to oppose this demand is shot. While the camera zooms out over his dead body, the singing of a psalm gradually swells, and the story switches to Amsterdam, in 1860. A preacher in church justifies government policies with regard to the East Indies.

Havelaar is now introduced, as he encounters Droogstoppel downtown and gives him his manuscript. Suddenly the film flashes back to Java in 1855. Havelaar's predecessor (Joop Admiraal), an assistant resident in Java, is poisoned at a banquet given by the local regent, because the man is preparing corruption charges against the regent. The murder is covered up by a falsified medical report. The depiction of his death struggle is horrifying. For the colonial administrators, the virulence of the jungle lies always in wait: The tiger, the poison, the night, the forest, the snakes. In short, nature is a menacing physical presence in the film. Nevertheless, Havelaar does not shrink from his "mission," as he calls it, when he is asked to replace the assistant resident, and accepts the challenge. He believes that nothing can happen to him, and on his way to his new post in Lebak he jumps overboard into shark-infested waters to save a puppy. Havelaar is an unprejudiced man, a strong-willed idealist who believes in the justice and rightness of the colonial system. He is happy with his promotion, precisely because of its poverty: There will be all the more for him to do. Unconscious of the insidious system of abuse, he confronts the regent, giving him the benefit of the doubt. He ascribes the regent's behavior to insufficient financial means and offers him money in order to mend his ways. As he gradually learns the real magnitude of the regent's misdeed, Havelaar appeals both to the native population and to his superiors for help. The people, however, are too afraid to testify for him, and the colonialists' interests appear to coincide with those of the regent, so Havelaar receives no help from either group. Desperately, he takes his campaign to the highest authorities of the Dutch bureaucracy, but the governor refuses to receive him. Havelaar finds himself actually locked up in an antechamber, alone with a painting of King William III, to whom he adresses himself. In his agony, Havelaar reminds one of the tiger or of his late predecessor: His defeat is a moral one. He resigns from the civil service and returns to Holland.

Saidjah, who, after the theft of his second buffalo, has tried to complain to the assistant resident, is consequently chased through the forest by the regent's riders and decides to join the rebels in an adjacent district. Later on he finds, among other women and children, his girlfriend, Adinda, slaughtered by regiment troops, and he chooses death as well. The film comes to a close as a painting dissolves to the face of Droogstoppel and others at worship in the Grote Kerk in Amsterdam. Once again, the hymn singing grows louder and louder, drowning Havelaar's complaints. The camera tracks in accusation along row after row of pious faces. The idea of the alliance between religious zeal and colonial exploitation is thus reinforced.

The characterization of Havelaar is significantly commented on by the frequent close-ups and medium-shots where Havelaar, as the agent of imperialism, is framed in the center of the screen, for example, against the wide blue skies of Indonesia: He defines and controls the space, but he is limited, and likewise framed. In his geometrical appearance, his isolation ironically becomes clear. Havelaar finds himself on the borderline between two worlds: His righteousness arouses the resentment of his fellows, while it leaves untouched the lives of the oppressed.

The contrast between European civilization and natural, primitive life is emphasized by the methodical and reserved shooting of the landscapes: Tracks along the rows of trees carefully planted in the European mode are juxtaposed to more fluid shots of the lush, unspoiled nature. The palace of the governor and the residence of Havelaar are small, civilized islands in a hostile environment. The ball, the reception of guests at the government palace, and the regent's feast in honor of the visit of his relatives contrast sharply with the poverty of the natives, who, after all, provide the work and money for the regent's festivities. Nevertheless, the Havelaar family cannot afford to live a luxurious life: Havelaar's income depends on the yield of his district. This system explains the extent of corruption that he discovers in the administration.

The various oppositions are skillfully confirmed by careful lighting: the dark, gloomy streets of Amsterdam; the unreal candlelight in church, deforming the burghers' faces; the pitch-darkness lying ominously over the Havelaar residence; the filtered sunbeams in the forest, twisting, playing capriciously, or scaring, as, for example, in the case of the pursuit of Saidjah and Adinda. Lighting is an essential ingredient of the setting.

In this film, Rademakers makes sparing use of music or sound effects. The silence practically becomes metaphorical: No one wishes to speak up or dares to testify, and Havelaar is entangled in silence. It is no accident that he shouts, in an empty reception hall, at the portrait of the king, or that he begs Droogstoppel to read his manuscript: He wishes to be heard. The silence also helps Rademakers to maintain an emotional distance from his subject in general and to restrain himself from pathos or sentiment when dealing with the story of Saidjah and Adinda.

The character of Max Havelaar is interpreted by Peter Faber in a bright and graceful manner. Yet his naïve and credulous attitude sometimes seems slightly overdone and hardly credible. As Havelaar becomes aware of the real situation, and as he enters the ring to fight against it, the acting helps to create the dramatic tension. His opponents form an interesting soundboard to his personage: The cowardly and cringing controller, bewildered by the incomprehensible ardor of his superior; the inscrutable regent with his enigmatic smile; Adinda, having no choice but to rely on the assistant resident, although she has doubts about him succeeding; Havelaar's adoring and anxious wife, Tine (Sacha Bulthuis), trying to console and to restrain him; the cynical commander of the district regiment (Rutger Hauer); the hypocritical resident (Carl Van Der Plas); they all wait and see how things will turn out.

Critics often point out that acting as well as dialogue in Dutch cinema is inferior in comparison with cinema from other countries. There has always been a number of talented directors and skillful cameramen, but few outstanding actors: The tradition is mainly in the documentary, animation, and experimental fields. With *Max Havelaar*, Rademakers made a film that was coproduced by the Indonesian company, P. T. Mondial Motion Pictures, thus incorporating a large number of Indonesian actors. The language constantly switches from Dutch to Malay (Bahasa), and the dialogue makes a supple and fresh impression. The unusual location and the introverted acting of the Malay people helps to compensate for the theatrical digressions of some of the actors, which, as a rule, annoy the Dutch public. *Max Havelaar* is not an ordinary anticolonialist film. It may not offer a faithful reproduction of historical reality, particularly the systematic horrors of Dutch colonialism, since, in the film, the cruel native regents are blamed and the Dutch are portrayed as mere accessories. The actual spirit of resistance among the Javanese is also slighted. In this respect, the idyll of Saidjah and Adinda is meager and ridiculous. Yet Rademakers' interpretation stresses a philosophical point of view: He assigns guilt to no individual or country. Corruption and prejudice are rooted in every human being and are to be found at every level of society. Rademakers' film thus adds an extra dimension to Multatuli's nineteenth century novel, and by erecting this monument, Rademakers pays tribute to the memory of Multatuli.

Arjen Uijterlinde

MAYERLING

Origin: France
Released: 1936
Released in U.S.: 1937
Production: S. Nebenzahl for Nero Film
Direction: Anatole Litvak
Screenplay: Joseph Kessel and J. V. Cube; based on the novel *Idyl's End*, by
 Claude Anet
Cinematography: Armand Thirard
Editing: no listing
Art direction: no listing
Music: Arthur Honegger
Running time: 90 minutes

Principal characters:
Archduke Rudolph of Austria . . . . Charles Boyer
Baroness Marie Vetsera . . . . Danielle Darrieux
Chief of police . . . . Vladimir Sokoloff
Countess Larisch . . . . Suzy Prim
Emperor Franz Joseph. . . . . Jean Dax
Empress Elizabeth . . . . Gabrielle Dorziat
Count Taafe. . . . . Debucourt
Baroness Vetsera (Hélène) . . . . Marthe Régnier
Loschek . . . . André Dubosc

From the time when Anatole Litvak's *Mayerling* had its premiere at the Marignan Theater in Paris in 1936, its story has been a popular addition to the list of moving love stories produced on film. It tells the tragic, factually based story of the love affair between Archduke Rudolph of Austria (Charles Boyer) and the young Baroness Marie Vetsera (Danielle Darrieux), who died on January 30, 1889, in a suicide pact made at the royal hunting lodge, Mayerling. French novelist Claude Anet used the Rudolph-Vetsera incident as the background for his moving and sensitive novel *Idyl's End*, which formed the basis for Litvak's film. American playwright Maxwell Anderson also dramatized the story, in a verse play, *The Masque of Kings*, which was produced by the Theatre Guild on Broadway in 1937.

A remake of the Litvak film, also called *Mayerling*, was done in 1969, directed by Terence Young and starring Omar Sharif and Catherine Deneuve. Litvak himself reworked the material for a live television version on American television in 1957, starring Audrey Hepburn and Mel Ferrer. A fresh approach to the story was made by Max Ophüls in 1940 in his film *De Mayerling à Sarajevo* (*Mayerling to Sarajevo*), in which it was shown that all the royal houses of Europe were doomed on the night that Rudolph and Vetsera died. After that event, the veneer of European royalty seemed to flake off bit by bit, until June 28, 1914, at Sarajevo, when revolutionaries assassinated the Austrian Archduke Francis Ferdinand and his wife, thus triggering World War I.

The most moving and popular of all versions of the Mayerling story, however, was this first Litvak feature film. Perhaps in real life, as some historians have insisted, the prince was a jaded debauchee and his mistress a half-witted girl, but in Litvak's film, the young lovers are extraordinarily appealing. *Mayerling* begins, like many popular film romances of the 1930's, in Vienna in the springtime. It is 1888, and Crown Prince Rudolph (Charles Boyer) is thirty years old, "the most seductive of men and the unhappiest of princes." Rudolph is married, but he and his wife are totally at odds; he married the Archduchess Stephanie only because it was the will of his father, the Emperor Franz Joseph (Jean Dax), the last of the despots. Rudolph, who is a true liberal, hates his father. He feels persecuted and trusts no one, seeking release in loveless affairs with countless women.

One spring day, while Rudolph is walking incognito in the Prater amusement park, he sees the beautiful sixteen-year-old Marie Vetsera (Danielle Darrieux). She is alone, and a stranger accosts her; he gets nowhere, however, because Rudolph intercedes. Marie is the kind of companion Rudolph has always wanted—innocent, unafraid, and excited by everything she sees in the Prater: the puppets, the carousel with its calliope music, and the swans gliding across the mirrorlike lake.

Marie is drawn to Rudolph, and that night she dreams about the beautiful, mournful young gentleman of whom she knows so little. She goes to the opera the next evening and is captivated by the people in the other boxes. Her attention is called to the imperial box, where Rudolph sits with his wife and his father. Marie recognizes Rudolph at once as the stranger she had encountered in the Prater. Rudolph catches her face in the crowd, and his interest is at once piqued. The Countess Larisch (Suzy Prim), a witty but foolish courtesan, knows Rudolph and is the catalyst for his meeting with Marie. The countess is very pleased when the crown prince is so delighted on meeting Marie. She counsels Marie that the two look like ideal lovers, but lets Marie know that they can have only a casual affair, for the prince is already married. Marie ignores the warning, for she is already in love, unable to think of anything but the captivating charm of the prince.

Soon the Countess Larisch is arranging a series of rendezvous for them. Rudolph is completely enamored of this beautiful girl, who in turn worships him. The clandestine meetings, however, are doomed. When Marie's mother (Marthe Régnier) receives an anonymous note hinting that Marie has a lover, she demands to know the name of the man who is showing so possessive an interest in her daughter. When Marie refuses to divulge the name of her secret lover, her mother sends her off to Trieste for six weeks to visit with friends of the family.

Marie is desolate, but Rudolph is bored when he cannot see her. He starts drinking in an effort to forget, but his old life of debauchery is no consolation for the loss of Marie. He writes secretly to the pope in Rome, hoping to have his marriage annulled, but when the emperor is advised of what is going on, he tells Rudolph to forget Marie, advising him of his duty as crown prince and future ruler of the Austrian Empire.

That night, there is a brilliant court ball. Rudolph manages to get word to Marie that he wants her to leave the ball and go with him secretly to Mayerling. They are together happily there for the entire next day and night. Marie goes to sleep blissfully in the arms of her lover. Rudolph watches over her, and when the day begins to brighten with the first light of dawn, he reaches for his pistol nearby. For the last time, he looks at her; then he fires the pistol. Marie never opens her eyes again; she has died content. Rudolph raises the pistol again, and a moment later, the film ends as a second shot is heard.

After the actual incident took place, the scandal was at first suppressed. Rudolph's death was reported but was attributed to a hunting accident. Marie's body was quickly taken to a cemetery reserved for paupers and suicides, where she was buried in unconsecrated ground in an unmarked grave; her mother was paid to leave Vienna. The court went into mourning, and Franz Joseph was bowed with grief. His empress (who had not spoken to him since he had arranged for the quiet murder of the one man she loved), veiled in black crepe, went to the isle of Corfu. She died ten years later, the victim of an assassination. Franz Joseph lived on alone in the Hofburg while his empire crumbled and fell around him. He finally died in 1916. Whispers of the scandal of Marie and the crown prince eventually were heard, and all Austria soon knew the truth of what had happened at Mayerling.

Charles Boyer was already enjoying stardom in American films when he went back to France and played Prince Rudolph for Anatole Litvak. He had come to Hollywood in 1931 and played small but important parts with Ruth Chatterton in *The Magnificent Lie* (1931) and as Jean Harlow's lover in *Red-Headed Woman* (1932). He returned to France for more leads in *La Bataille* (1934) and *Liliom* (1934), then signed a contract for American films with Walter Wanger, who featured him in *Private Worlds* (1935). Boyer had the right to make films abroad, and it was at this time that he made *Mayerling* for Litvak in France. His Hollywood roles were brilliant then, and he was a magnificent Napoleon to Greta Garbo's Maria Walewska in *Conquest* (1937), one of the few occasions when Garbo did not dwarf her male support. He gained his first Academy Award nomination as Best Actor for his portrayal of Napoleon and was later nominated as Best Actor for *Algiers* (1938) and *Gaslight* (1944) as well; for *Fanny* (1961), he was nominated as

Best Supporting Actor. Despite these nominations, Boyer never won the coveted Oscar.

Danielle Darrieux, who was only twenty-one when she made *Mayerling*, was both beautiful and warm. She was at her best in this film and was again impressive with Boyer in the French *Madame de . . .* (1953; *The Earrings of Madame de . . .*), directed by Max Ophüls. Universal Studios brought her to Hollywood, where she made one starring picture for them, *The Rage of Paris* (1938), but it was not a success. Darrieux returned to Hollywood on several occasions, most notably with James Mason in *Five Fingers* (1952), but she was at her best and most beautiful in French-speaking roles.

Director Anatole Litvak was born in Kiev, Russia, in 1902. A philosophy student in St. Petersburg, he turned to filmmaking and made *Tatiana* (1925; *Hearts and Dollars*) when he was only in his early twenties. He directed films in Germany and England as well as in Russia. His first picture after *Mayerling* brought him to the United States, where he made *The Woman I Love* (1937) and was briefly married to its star, Miriam Hopkins. *Tovarich* (1937), with Claudette Colbert and Charles Boyer, brought him a contract with Warner Bros., where he made such pictures as *The Sisters* (1938), *Confessions of a Nazi Spy* (1939), and *All This and Heaven Too* (1940). He served in the United States Army for the *Why We Fight* series, directing many films with Frank Capra. After the war, some of his most notable films were *Sorry, Wrong Number* (1948), *The Snake Pit* (1948), *Anastasia* (1956), and *The Night of the Generals* (1967). Of all Litvak's films, however, *Mayerling* was probably his most successful, both critically and popularly, throughout Europe and the United States.

DeWitt Bodeen

MAYNILA
In the Claws of Neon
(MAYNILA, SA MGA KUKO NG LIWANAG)

Origin: Philippines
Released: 1975
Released in U.S.: 1980
Production: Severino Manotok, Jr., and Miguel de Leon for Cinema Artists
Direction: Lino Brocka
Screenplay: Clodualdo del Mundo, Jr.; based on the novel by Ramon Reyes
Cinematography: Miguel de Leon
Editing: Edgardo Jarlego, Jr., and Ike Jarlego, Jr.
Art direction: Socrates Topacio
Music: Max Jocson
MPAA rating: no listing
Running time: 125 minutes
Also known as: Manila: In the Claws of Darkness

Principal characters:
Julio Madiaga	Rafael Roco
Ligaya Paraiso	Hilda Koronel
Atong	Lou Salvador, Jr.
Pol	Tommy Abuel
Omeng	Joonee Gamboa
Imo	Pio de Castro III
Benny	Danilo Posadas
Mr. Balajadia	Pancho Pelagio
Perla	Lily Gamboa-Mendoza
Father	Abelardo Reyes
Ah Teck	Tommy Yap
Mrs. Cruz	Juling Bagabaldo
Bobby Reyes	Jojo Abella
Cesar	Chiqui Xeres-Burgos
Rikki	Rikki Jiménez

Lino Brocka's *Maynila: In the Claws of Neon* depicts the search of a young man from the provinces for his childhood sweetheart, as he descends into the unknown depths of the city that has swallowed her up. As a work of great originality, social commitment, and harsh cinematic beauty, *Maynila: In the Claws of Neon* is the pivotal film of contemporary Philippine cinema and a turning point in the career of its most prominent filmmaker.

If much of Brocka's work perhaps lacks the smooth professionalism of the films of Gerardo de Leon, the fun-loving epic sweep of Manuel Conde's *Genghis Khan* (1950), the competent artistry of the best of Lamberto V. Avellana, the popularity of Cesár Gallardo's *Geron Busabos* (1964; *Geron the Tramp*), or the simple pathos of Manuel Silos' *Biyaya ng Lupa* (1959; *Blessings of the Land*), with *Maynila* Brocka has nevertheless gone a step beyond these masters of the so-called Golden Age of Filipino films by successfully blending the artistry of a true cineast's vision with the committed concern of an astute observer of the social reality of his country.

Maynila appeared at a time when these prominent predecessors had all but been forgotten, and the film industry was churning out something like two hundred films a year aimed at the lowest common denominator of the *bakya* crowd, the vast masses of uneducated film consumers (named after the wooden sandals they often wear)—the taste of these people having been formed by *komiks* (Tagalog comic books), kung fu, and third-rate Hollywood horse operas.

Politically, the Philippines were three years into the martial law proclaimed by President Ferdinand Marcos in 1972, and censorship had never been more strict. It must be recognized as a feat of no little courage and of considerable artistic cunning to propose and carry through to production a film so blatantly critical of the social injustice rampant in that country.

Brocka's aims and methods are indirect, didactically motivated, and divergent to the point of sometimes appearing self-contradictory. *Maynila* is not outright revolutionary in its message. Instead, Brocka attempts to educate his audience in a twofold way: cinematically, to appreciate the complexities of an artistically constructed film, and sociopolitically, appealing in particular to students, intellectuals, and members of the more privileged classes, to throw light on the suffering and humiliation of a large segment of the population so that his viewers can identify with the characters. At no time, however, does Brocka disdain the use of the traditional elements of popular cinema, thrills, sex, and blood, and one can indeed detect a considerable fascination on Brocka's part with violence, sordid conditions, and crimes of passion.

Maynila is the story of a boy in search of a dream, and of the city that transforms this dream into a nightmare. It is based on a partly autobiographical novelette by Ramon Reyes that appeared in the popular magazine *Liwayway* toward the end of the 1960's. Clodualdo del Mundo's screenplay kept quite close to the story's documentary naturalism. Lino Brocka introduced a number of important changes into the original script in order to create greater poetic reality and to add a tragic dimension to the main character, the young fisherman Julio Madiaga (Rafael Roco), a *provinciano* exposed to the corruptive influence of the city.

Brocka added the word "Maynila" to the title, thus indicating his intention to make the city itself a central character of the film. Maynila is the original Tagalog name for Manila, the word that a boy from the provinces would use. "Sa mga kuko ng liwanag" has been translated in many different ways and caused great confusion in foreign titles of the film. The trade magazine *Variety* originally offered the title "The Nail of Brightness," a bit of a misunderstanding. In 1979, the Edinburgh Film Festival presented the film as *Manila: In the Claws of Darkness*, corresponding to an early French translation *Manille dans les griffes des ténèbres* or the German *Manila—in den Fängen der Nacht*. Later translations, however, give a rendition nearer to the original meaning: *Maynila: In the Claws of Neon*. The film is almost universally referred to as *Maynila* or sometimes *Manila* or *Manille*, the original old form being preferable, since Maynila is symbolic of the depravity of all big cities.

Brocka has explained that the Tagalog word "liwanag" means light, for example the light of day, but refers specifically to the neon lights that attract provincials to the city like night moths drawn to the glow of lamps. In Manila, they are in the claws of neon, victims of their own petty pleasures, the lure of the jaded nightlife, the hoped-for riches, glitter, and glamor of the big city that originally enticed them away from their provincial homes. To be sure, the film provided a satiric commentary on the First Lady's campaign to make Manila the "City of Light."

Julio Madiaga comes to the city in search of Ligaya Paraiso (Hilda Koronel), an ephemeral being who can be understood allegorically as well as literally. Her name means happiness and paradise. She has been taken to the capital by a certain Mrs. Cruz (Juling Bagabaldo) with the promise of education and a job, but has subsequently disappeared, accused of having stolen Mrs. Cruz's earrings. Julio has only a single precious letter and the memories of his lost sweetheart, fleeting glimpses of the past flashed across the screen: Julio and Ligaya as children in a boat, her sudden departure at the insistence of her mother, who looks down on the poor fisherman, but most of all Ligaya's angelic face, strongly reminiscent of the iconographic images of Spanish Catholicism. The beautiful expanses of beach and countryside contrast sharply with the filth and closeness of the city streets.

The story is told in the form of a flashback, starting chronologically just before the film's final scenes. As it opens, Julio lurks outside the apartment house of Ah Teck (Tommy Yap), on the all-too-uncompassionate street called Misericordia, preparing to take his revenge on the Chinaman who held Ligaya captive as his common-law wife and has now strangled her after she tried to escape with her baby in order to join Julio. In the background a palmist's sign asks: "May problema ka ba?" (Do you have a problem?), and a handwritten scrawl on the wall to Julio's left seems to offer a solution: "Makibaka" (Join the Struggle), one of the slogans during the student protests of the late 1960's and early 1970's.

Julio must pass through a series of quasi-initiation rites before he is able to "join the struggle," which in his case is entirely apolitical. As a typical *provinciano* from the countryside he is at first uncertain, bashful, and reserved. He is a living example of the Filipino proverb that Brocka places at the end of his film, in essence: The first time you kick a dog he is surprised; the second time, he looks at you; the third, he begins to bark; and the fourth time, you better watch out or he will kill you. Like Insiang, Bona, and "Jaguar" in other Brocka films, Julio must be humiliated and broken before he can rise up and strike back in an act of crazed vengeance.

On his odyssey through the back alleyways of Manila, a kind of descent into Dante's Inferno in search of his Beatrice, Julio is accompanied by three principal guides. Atong (Lou Salvador, Jr.) is his mentor at the construction site, the man who helps him to get work, gives him refuge, and warns him about the corrupt foreman, Mr. Balajadia (Pancho Palagio), who takes his cut from the workers' pay and forces them to take their meals at his wife's cantina. Atong's fate echoes that of his father and presages Julio's own presumed death at the hands of the mob. Atong's father was driven off his land by a rich hacienda owner and is paralyzed from injuries sustained while attempting to defend his property. In a Manila slum, he is killed when the squatters' huts are gutted by fire. Atong is a constant victim of the construction bosses and is eventually assassinated by them because they believe he will lead a strike of the workers.

When Julio is laid off from work at the construction site and thrown out of the barracks, he tries to sleep in the park, apparently oblivious to the fact that it is a favorite rendezvous for homosexuals. Here he meets his second guide Bobby Reyes (Jojo Abella), who allows him to stay in his flat and later introduces him to the world of male prostitution. For Bobby, who says that he is not gay himself, the only thing that counts is money. He persuades Julio to earn some easy cash as a male prostitute at Cesár's Club, but Julio's attempts end in a fiasco. Brocka's portrait of homosexuals is strangely stereotyped—although perhaps individually authentic—particularly in the character of Julio's first customer Rikki (Rikki Jiménez), an affected queen with a jealous Pekingese dog. The whole lengthy incident has the function of allowing Julio to understand better his beloved Ligaya, who has been put in a brothel by the evil Mrs. Cruz, has been drugged, abused, and humiliated by the customers, and finally forced to live with Ah Teck.

Julio's third guide is Pol (Tommy Abuel), his faithful companion throughout his year-long ordeal in Manila. Pol's weakness is his timidity and hesitation, once again characteristic of *provincianos*. He falls in love with Perla (Lily Gamboa-Mendoza), Atong's sister, whom he meets after Atong's death. Believing that Julio also loves her and not wanting to offend him, Pol never broaches the subject with Julio until it is too late. He later learns that the only course left to Perla was prostitution, a fate that parallels that of Julio and Ligaya. Pol's empathy with Julio, his inner strength, and his feelings of the guilt of omission are expressed in the powerful scene in which he tells Julio of Ligaya's death: Before he can bear to say that she is dead, he puts out a lighted cigarette on the palm of his own hand.

Brocka introduces a number of other figures who embody different aspects of the Filipino character. Benny (Danilo Posadas), for example, is the prototype of the dreamer who hopes to be discovered like the famous singer Nora Aunor (an unprecedented rags-to-riches story in the Philippines and a singer and actress very much admired by Brocka—even though her talents are most often exploited in mindless films for the *bakya* crowd). Benny's hopes are literally dashed when he falls to his death after a self-indulgent rendition of "The Impossible Dream" from *Man of La Mancha* (1972). The camera focuses in on his Nora Aunor Songbook as it is buried under the dust and debris of the building site.

After a year of dreaming, searching, and thorough disillusionment, Julio finally sees Ligaya quite accidentally as she enters a church. To be alone they go to a motion-picture theater, where significantly the scene of Christ bearing the Cross in Nicholas Ray's *King of Kings* (1961) is being projected. From there they move on to a squalid hotel room where in a long and tender love scene Ligaya relates the story of her imprisonment in the brothel and her life with Ah Teck. She begs him to help her, and he persuades her to flee. At night he waits for her in vain.

Julio's final act of revenge on Ligaya's murderer, Ah Teck, is reminiscent of Samuel Fuller's *Forty Guns* (1957). As Julio stalks through the city toward Ah Teck's house, the camera cuts rather melodramatically back and forth between his determined expression and his marching feet. At the apartment, he hesitates, only to confirm Ah Teck's identity and then plunges an ice pick into his heart. A wild chase ensues, and Julio is cornered by the enraged mob in a dead-end street. The saintly image of his lost love, Ligaya, is superimposed over Julio's distorted features, a face brutish and yet vulnerable, scarred by his tribulations, a mask reflecting the ills, corruption, and violence of Manila.

Maynila is rightly considered Lino Brocka's most important work, a rough diamond among a few smoother pearls. Of his prolific production, *Maynila* is the film that most clearly bears his own personal stamp. In Miguel de Leon, Brocka was fortunate to have one of the most sensitive cameramen of the Philippines as well as an extremely progressive producer, willing to allow Brocka to improvise and experiment as he had never before been able to do. The film remains uneven, like the city it depicts, sometimes overly melodramatic, confused, and unpolished, yet always vital, always alive with the passion, the hurt, and the violence of the characters and city it portrays, real, old-fashioned, gut cinema in a modern guise.

Stephen Locke

O MEGALÉXANDROS

Origin: Greece
Released: 1980
Released in U.S.: 1983
Production: Radiotelevisione Italiana-Zweites Deutsches Fernsehen-
  Angelopoulos Productions
Direction: Theodoros Angelopoulos
Screenplay: Theodoros Angelopoulos
Cinematography: Ghiorgios Arvanitis
Editing: G. Triandafillidis
Art direction: Mikis Karapiperis
Music: Christodulos Halaris
MPAA rating: no listing
Running time: 210 minutes
Also known as: Alexander the Great

> *Principal characters:*
> Alexander..................... Omero Antonutti
> Stepdaughter................... Eva Kotamanidou
> Schoolteacher................ Grigoris Evanghelatos
> Guide........................ Michalis Yannatos
> Italian anarchists........ Laura De Marchi/Francesco
>   Carnelutti/Brizio Montinaro/
>   Norman Mozzato/Claude Betan
> Woman of the village............. Tula Stahopoulou
> Man of the village .... Thanos Grammenos
> Alexander the boy .... Ilia Zafiropoulos

O Megaléxandros is the most controversial of the films of Theodoros Angelopoulos, the most celebrated Greek director of the 1970's and 1980's. Although the film continues the cinematic approach that Angelopoulos established in his earlier work, Greek critics held that the director had fallen into a mannerism that was a parody of his style in the way that Ernest Hemingway's *Across the River and into the Trees* (1950) had been a parody of that author's best work. Political critics were distressed at what they saw as a repudiation of the guerrilla revolutionary that Angelopoulos had previously extolled. The film fared poorly with the public, which seemed confounded by the theme and weary of the director's demanding style.

On the surface, the story of *O Megaléxandros* is much simpler than the plot lines of other Angelopoulos films. In spite of this time/plot simplicity, the film is actually the director's most poetic and surrealistic film, deliberately dealing with cultural myth rather than historic reality. The time is

1900, and the major *persona* is not the Macedonian who conquered the known world of his time but a figure from Greek folklore. The legend of this Alexander originated in the 1400's during the struggles with the Turks. Kept alive in oral tradition, the Alexander legend centers on the national yearning for a liberator. For the film, Angelopoulos used some of the Alexander lore collected in *The Book of Megaléxandros*. Grafted on to this material are incidents based on an event in 1870, during which a group of English gentlemen was kidnaped by Greek brigands at Marathon. The foreign tourists were held for ransom and an amnesty. Unfortunately, the government bungled the negotiations. The captives were subsequently killed, and the British military intervened.

In the Angelopoulos film, the story begins on New Year's Eve, with a magnificent ball at the royal palace juxtaposed to a prison escape by Alexander (Omero Antonutti) and his cohorts. Later in the morning at Cape Sounion, Alexander and his men capture a group of English lords who are out sightseeing. Alexander announces that he will not free the Englishmen until his band is granted an amnesty and the major landowners of his district deed their land to the peasants. While this ultimatum is being studied by the palace, the bandit-patriots proceed to their village stronghold in the mountains. En route they encounter five foreigners who wave red and black flags from a bridge. These turn out to be Italian anarchists who have come to take refuge in Greece, more specifically in the very village from which Alexander operates.

When the enlarged group arrives at its destination, the village is found to have undergone fundamental changes since Alexander and his men were incarcerated. All the old property values have been abolished in favor of an anarcho-communism in which everyone shares equally. As the warriors return to their old homes and tend to their prisoners, the schoolteacher (Grigoris Evanghelatos) and peasants from the commune speak at length with the anarchists. The Italians learn that in the village, everyone, even the women, has a vote and that everything is owned in common. To be part of the community, the Italians must swear an oath of allegiance to the egalitarian principles that the peasants have drawn up. The Italians do so with joy and are accepted into the commune.

A feast ensues in which the Greek peasants regale their new Italian comrades with food and song. The Italians begins to respond with their own lively songs, but the festive mood is shattered when a group of warriors enters the room. Dressed in forbidding black robes and carrying rifles, they dance a warrior's dance, the anger of which seems as much directed at the commune as at their mutual enemies. The peasants discover that the bandit-patriots are not pleased with the new values of the village. They want to own their own land and their own animals. They want to rule their wives as they have always ruled them. They believe that by risking their lives in combat for the village, they have earned privileges.

As the tension between the peasants and the warriors grows, the royal army moves up the mountainside and puts the village under siege. All that prevents the army from crossing a key river is that the English hostages will be killed. The army draws Alexander into secret negotiations during which he is promised preferred treatment should the affair end satisfactorily for the monarchy. Within the village, ideological antagonism turns into bloody conflict. The Italians are killed, key leaders of the commune are killed, and the schoolteacher is imprisoned. The government, however, also proves treacherous. An enraged Alexander responds by killing the English nobles. The army then moves forward to crush the rebellion.

Interwoven into this political schema is a complex portrait of Alexander. Details of his birth are unknown, so he has adopted a village woman (Tula Stahopoulou) as his mother. Later he marries this woman, which makes his stepsister his stepdaughter (Eva Kotamanidou). Other sequences show this sister-daughter as his mistress. A small boy, who is the son of the adopted mother, is also depicted as being the young Alexander (Ilia Zafiropoulos), even though he sometimes appears in the same sequence as the elder Alexander. The web of relations becomes so complex and ambiguous that the viewer understands that Alexander is not a real person at all. The film will conclude with the young Alexander riding a mule into the city. As Angelopoulos himself has stated, "This is a modern city—present-day Athens, in fact—in contrast to the rural turn-of-the-century world of the rest of the film. When the little Alexander enters the city, he brings all the experience of the century with him. He has gained a total experience of life, sex, and death, and he comes into the city at sunset, and over it there is a great question mark. How long will the night last, and when will a new day break?"

The symbolic nature of Alexander is most clearly demonstrated in the scene in which he appears to be killed. The revolt has been lost, the dream of the anarchist commune has been crushed, and the army is riding upon the village plaza. In a sequence shot from directly above the participants, the peasants surround Alexander, swirling ever closer to him until their bodies smother him completely. When they move back, there is only an empty place where Alexander stood, for Alexander, as one has guessed all along, is not separate from the peasants, but part of them. The army clatters into the plaza a few minutes later to find a ceremonial bust of Alexander's head in a place of honor.

Certainly one reason that Greeks reacted negatively to the film is that Angelopoulos has gone out of his way to remind his nation that most Greeks are only a single generation removed from villages, the values of which have not changed significantly in four hundred years. Part of the village ethos was celebration of the bandit-patriots who had traditionally fought local oppressors and foreign occupiers. Angelopoulos' early films advanced the idea that the Greek partisans of World War II and even the Communist insurgents of the Civil War belonged to this pantheon of heroes. In *O Megaléxandros*, while still accepting the heroism and essential honesty of the bandit-patriot, Angelopoulos rejects the notion that the military captain literally sitting on a white horse should be a role model. The liberator who is not accepting of democratic controls will surely turn into a new oppressor. This refers not only to modern Greek history but also to the historic brawls between the military captains who led the Greek struggle for freedom in the nineteenth century.

Leftist critics claimed that *O Megaléxandros* was wrong for the times. At a time when the Greek people had finally won the right to honor the Resistance fighter of World War II and put to rest the passions of civil war, Angelopoulos seemed to be resurrecting charges of leftist cruelty. That his Alexander bore a striking physical resemblence to Aris Velouhiotis, the major guerrilla leader, was no help, and talk of anarcho-communism evoked traditions that the organized Left, still very much under the influence of Stalinism, considered anathema. For the Right, Angelopoulos' continued commitment to political revolution was sin enough. If Alexander on his horse looked like Aris to the Left, he looked very much like a mockery of Saint George to the Right. The English lords allied with the palace in the film were very much like the American allies of contemporary conservatives just as the Italian anarchists were a parallel to the extraparliamentary groups disrupting normalcy in Europe and elsewhere.

As far as Angelopoulos was concerned, *O Megaléxandros* simply deepened his analysis of revolution begun in films such as *I Kynighi* (1977; *The Hunters*) and *O Thiassos* (1975; *The Traveling Players*). The time for greater sophistication seemed appropriate precisely because the guerrillas of the 1940's were being idolized uncritically and precisely because the Left was again showing a strong taste for charismatic leaders. During the dictatorship of the colonels (1967-74), Angelopoulos had made reclaiming the revolutionary tradition one of his priorities. Now, during a time when parliamentary socialism was on the rise, he turned from the simple advocacy of democracy and socialism to the question of what kind of democracy and what kind of socialism were appropriate for Greece.

The stylistic peculiarities of Angelopoulos, having lost their novelty, seemed to work against the film with many viewers. His trademarks had always been the tracking shot, the circular shot, and the long-distance shot. His pace, as usual, was deliberately slow, with some tableaux almost as motionless as a painting. The film has few close-ups of any characters, no montage, many scenes related secondhand, and no development of individual characters. These factors were meant to express the anonymous nature of the historical process and to counter romantic emphasis on individual personality and the extraordinary event. Dead spaces in the narrative were provided to allow the viewer to think as well as to feel. These distancing devices succeeded so well that many found the film passionless and arid. The opening sequence of escape from prison and the journey to the mountains is clearly overly long. If the character of Alexander needed to be seen from afar, the lack of other strong personalities with individual destinies robbed the film of a certain energy.

Whatever their misgivings about the film, the Greek critics recognized *O Megaléxandros* as a major work by a major Greek artist. At the annual Thessaloniki Film Festival, *O Megaléxandros* won in the categories of Best Film, Best Photography, and Best Sets and Costumes. Later the film won the Golden Lion Award at the Venice International Film Festival. While able to gain some international visibility on the basis of Angelopoulos' critical reputation, the film did not do as well at the box office as did *The Hunters*, which in turn had been only mildly successful compared to the triumph of *The Traveling Players*. In the United States, *O Megaléxandros* was shown at some festivals but was not immediately officially released and did not draw significant critical attention.

Dan Georgakas

THE MELODY HAUNTS MY MEMORY (SAMO JEDNOM SE LJUBI)

Origin: Yugoslavia
Released: 1980
Released in U.S.: 1983
Production: Jadran Film
Direction: Rajko Grlić
Screenplay: Rajko Grlić, Branko Šömen, and Srdjan Karanović
Cinematography: Tomislav Pinter
Editing: Živka Toplak
Art direction: Stanislav Dobrina
Music: Branislav Živković
Song: "You Love Only Once"
MPAA rating: no listing
Running time: 103 minutes
Also known as: The Melody Haunts My Reverie and *You Love Only Once*

Principal characters:

Tomislav	Predrag Manojlović
Baby	Vladica Milosavljević
Mirko	Zijah Sokolović
Vule	Mladen Budiščak
Mali	Dragoljub Lazarov
Baby's father	Erland Josephson

The Melody Haunts My Memory, Rajko Grlić's third feature film, was shown in the section "Un Certain Regard" at Cannes in 1981, won several awards, including the Grand Prize at the Valencia Film Festival in 1981, and, among other Yugoslav honors, was voted, in 1983, by ninety Yugoslav critics, the ninth best Yugoslav film ever made.

The film derives its title—which, in the original means "you love only once"—from a romantic Yugoslav song that was popular in the early 1950's. In this carefully controlled, stylish story of a passionate marriage between an idealistic Partisan hero and a bourgeois dancer in a small town near Zagreb just after World War II, Grlić explores the downfall of a Communist idealist undone by his obsessive passion, while also subtly suggesting the overall contradictions of Yugoslav society after the war, when the "new society" had to be constructed from an uneasy partnership between the·enthusiastic Partisans and the less appreciative remnants of the middle class.

Rajko Grlić is a member of a new generation of Yugoslav filmmakers known as "The Prague School," who studied at the FAMU school in Czechoslovakia during the early 1970's and who then returned to Yugoslavia to begin making imaginative and popular films beginning in 1974. Born in Zagreb in 1947, Grlić began writing, directing, and acting in amateur films as a teenager. In 1971, he was graduated from the FAMU school and returned to Zagreb, where, like many of his generation, he worked in television as well as feature film production. The unusual degree of cooperation between members of this new movement in Yugoslav cinema can be seen in the cooperation between Grlić and fellow filmmaker Srdjan Karanović. Besides writing and directing his own projects, Grlić has coscripted Karanović's first three features, including the well-respected *Miris poljskog sveća* (1977; *The Fragrance of Wild Flowers*), while Karanović has reciprocated by participating in Grlić's first three features. The result is that Grlić, like Karanović, has shown a strong interest in a creative use of film language and an increasing concern for capturing the complexity and contradictions that lie below the surface of Yugoslav society.

Grlić's first feature, *Kud puko da puklo* (1974; *Whichever Way the Ball Bounces*), demonstrated both his debt to the innovative Yugoslav auteurs of the 1960's and his own determination to start a new direction for his own career. A reflexive film about an actor who is starring in the film being filmed, Grlić's first feature echoed similar works made by such directors as Dušan Makavejev and Želimir Žilnik during the late 1960's—works which mixed political-social commentary with fresh approaches to film technique and style. Unlike the characteristic films of the so-called Black Cinema, however, Grlić's opening film is less blatantly political and more strongly interested in personality and character as they develop through social relationships.

Bravo Maestro (1978), his next film, showed Grlić as a strong stylist who was able to depict the corruption of a talented young composer (the "maestro") by the lure of wealth, privilege, and power, filmed with razor-sharp insight and irony. Seen as a prelude to *The Melody Haunts My Memory*, this work also focuses on an idealistic young male who is a volatile mixture of ambition, arrogance, and sensitivity bordering on deep insecurities. If Grlić's first film was a generally playful search for both a subject and a style, his second film is an accomplished tale told with an excellent sense of pacing as the composer's life is revealed in a series of brief moments which ironically comment on one another. Furthermore, Grlić proves himself particularly successful at capturing emotional intensity through understated scenes in which his well-directed actors suggest but do not overstate the powerful tensions within.

The Melody Haunts My Memory also demonstrates Grlić's talent for portraying social complexity through personal crises. Popular throughout Yugoslavia, the film suggests the importance of Grlić and the directors of the The Prague School, who have managed to capture large audiences with films that concern serious social problems presented through a sophisticated cinematic style and technique.

The first three scenes foreshadow the themes and rhythm of the rest of the film. Opening on a dark night, the first sequence shows a long-shot of a prisoner being chased by some men in a car (the next two scenes reveal who these men are). The scene is one of action, confusion, darkness. In the next scene, shot in broad daylight, the viewer is introduced to the intense Tomislav (popular stage actor Predrag Manojlović), a local Communist hero and leader in a small town in Croatia soon after World War II. This lean, nervous, yet attractive man, who resembles a Yugoslav Anthony Perkins, never seems to stand still. Activities and celebrations are in progress, and it is clear that Tomislav is at the center of everything. He appears on a balcony with his comrades and friends, including Mirko (Zijah Sokolović), Vule (Mladen Budiščak), and Mali (Dragoljub Lazarov), to mouth the slogans of the new society being formed in Yugoslavia after the war and before the break with Joseph Stalin and the Soviet Union in 1948. After participating in a partisan *kolo* (dance), the four friends leave to take an afternoon swim in a nearby river. This third scene reveals the pure male friendship of these men, who romp in the water and devour watermelon while sitting under a small waterfall.

Though the remainder of the film centers on the tempestuous relationship between Tomislav and a blatantly middle-class dancer named Baby (Vladica Milosavljević), these opening scenes portray the environment in which Tomislav has been created. The "my" of the title refers to Tomislav; it is through his eyes that the viewer follows the birth, development, and destruction of this relationship. Shot in dark and deep yellow-brown hues by one of Yugoslavia's best-known cinematographers, Tomislav Pinter, the opening scenes establish an interplay between dark and light, private and public life, pain (the chasing and shooting of the prisoner) and pleasure (most purely expressed in the swimming scene, in which politics and duty can be forgotten). Furthermore, all three scenes involve constant action, movement, activity. Tomislav, the viewer realizes immediately, is a man of action rather than reflection.

After speaking to a group of actors, Tomislav meets Baby, a ballerina with a quiet, sultry beauty. While they speak about her need for an apartment, Grlić shoots them in separate frames with their faces only half-lit. No music plays. The viewer is made to sense the intensity of their glances during this first encounter. Then Grlić, with his crisp, elliptical style, abruptly moves his story ahead, bypassing many scenes that would occur in a more traditional film and showing Baby being given a small apartment above a pharmacy.

Tomislav wants Baby, and he goes after her with all of the intensity, naïveté, foolhardiness, and male chauvinism of a spoiled child or a war hero who is accustomed to making direct choices rather than considering subtle questions. Against the advice of his friends, he abuses his power and position by forcing himself upon Baby: He announces that he is moving in with her and will share her bed. Telling himself that Baby can be "reeducated," Tomislav fights off criticism from his comrades that she is not a Communist Party member and that he should not mix business and pleasure. Without fanfare, courtship, or tenderness, he soon declares that he will marry Baby. With his friends as witnesses and officials, Tomislav and Baby legally become man and wife against her protests and in a dark room, which, like most of the film, is only partially lit.

Baby is portrayed as Tomislav's opposite in every way. She matches his agressiveness with a placid passivity, his one-dimensional emotions with a vague, impenetrable face, and his intense idealism and puritanical didacticism with a bland, traditional outlook. For example, though she verbally protests each of his moves, Baby quickly and quietly falls into bourgeois patterns of accepted wifely functions: She cooks, sews, worries about her man. Even though he has dragged her from a dance studio where she has been trying to revive her career, she becomes his housebound wife, often kept locked in her room while he is gone.

The Melody Haunts My Memory is a devastatingly cunning film which draws the audience into what appears to be a love story, only to reveal, subtly, a chilling tale of obsession and abuse of power. Love by most definitions exists nowhere in the film; instead, Grlić documents but does not explain Tomislav's blinding need to possess and control Baby. Tomislav never seems to realize that he is treating her as object rather than as a human being who is a woman. His downfall is that he is impotent to love, share, or understand. Conversely, Grlić depicts Baby as a shallow, bland person who is obviously attracted to Tomislav's destructive recklessness, which is a kind of abandon she lacks. On their wedding night, for example, as they first make love, the camera remains fixed on her face, which shows no sign of joy. It is as if she, like the weak middle class which produced her, has accepted a stronger force because she is incapable of conceiving of a healthier or more beneficial alternative.

That such a marriage is impossible for Tomislav soon becomes apparent. Baby quietly sets about subverting his simple Communist values by selecting his clothes (she substitutes stylish civilian clothes for his old uniforms), influencing him to move into an expensive house when he would prefer an austere apartment, and then bringing her parents from Zagreb to live with them. Her father is played with properly stiff professionalism by Ingmar Bergman's popular actor, Erland Josephson). Tomislav's compromises finally become a difficult thorn for his friends. Based on a foolish bet that he has made with Baby, Tomislav frees a dangerous man from prison, who then proceeds to murder his wife, Tomislav's maid.

Grlić balances the deepening marital problems with the widening rifts between the friends as each goes his separate way (suggesting the various directions taken by those in power after the war). Mirko, who has become a factory manager, is shamelessly decadent, misusing funds and power as he pads expense accounts, takes "business" trips for pleasure, and treats friends to elaborate parties. Vule remains the conscience of the group, trying to warn his friends of the dangers of their actions and reminding them of the ideology to which they should adhere.

Tomislav's increasingly erratic behavior becomes a public problem when he drunkenly fires his pistol in the town square while ordering musicians to entertain him. (He never *requests* anything; it is not in his nature to do so.) He is thrown in prison but leaves to make passionate love to his wife. Grlić's control of the film is clear from the building and dramatic sense of obsession that unfolds. The use of music, supervised by Branislav Živković, is particularly important. In the early scenes, there is often no music at all; Grlić allows the viewer to concentrate on the swiftly developing emotional chemistry between Tomislav and Baby, as well as the nature of male friendship as it exists among Tomislav, Vule, Mirko, and Mali, without the influence of "movie music" to suggest the emotions that "should" be felt. These early scenes are thus almost documentary in feeling. As Tomislav's obsession grows, a stronger, richer use of the music, which is constructed around the theme song "You Love Only Once," complements Grlić's stylish yet graphic portrayal of sexual passion. Many scenes of female nudity help confirm Baby's status as sex object rather than a person, in contrast to Tomislav, who is never seen nude.

Predrag Manojlović proves to be an excellent interpreter of Tomislav's self-destructive desire. Beginning with his boyish playfulness in the opening scenes, Manojlović convincingly portrays Tomislav descending to the lowest depths of obsession as the film progresses. In and out of prison and finally confined to a mental hospital, where his hair is cropped down to stubble and his face remains unshaved, Tomislav, by the last section of the film, has truly left the "new society"—and, in fact, any society—far behind.

Vule remains his one good friend. Freeing him from the hospital and finding him a new apartment, he gives Tomislav one last chance. The strong sound of violins plucking on the sound track, almost cutting off the dialogue, signifies Tomislav's growing isolation from the real world. A violent encounter with Baby leads to yet another lockup in a mental ward. When Tomislav finds Baby in Zagreb, their passion explodes in a lovemaking scene in an elevator. At this point, however, their roles are reversed: Baby, going off to a dancing job, locks the sleeping Tomislav in her apartment.

The end swiftly follows. Tomislav awakes, breaks out of the apartment, and finds the nightclub where Baby dances. A clarinet plays as he walks down an empty street at night. In the club, the theme song, sung by Ivo Robić, is in progress, backed up by a full band. Richly romantic, the words proclaim that love is the only truth. Tomislav sits in Baby's dressing room, where Baby has left him, claiming that she will return in five minutes. He looks in the mirror, smiles, listens to the music, puts his pistol barrel in his mouth, and pulls the trigger. Onstage, a magician pulls a dove out of his hat, and freeze-frame captures the dove in flight.

Eroticism has been frankly portrayed in Yugoslav cinema since the 1960's. Part of the popularity of *The Melody Haunts My Memory* with Yugoslav audiences was the result of Grlić's complex linking of sexual passion with personal obsession and, furthermore, both of these elements with the complex Stalinist period between 1945 and 1948. Tomislav's inflexible personality and politics are ultimately self-consuming. Yet Yugoslav audiences are aware that the fate of Yugoslavia, though no less complicated, has been a happier one: Marshal Tito's break with Stalin opened the path for a new form of nonaligned socialism. On an international level, the film succeeds also as a nondidactic exploration of the darker side of passion in male-female relationships. In this sense, Grlić's work can be viewed as the male counterpart to the study of female obsession and passion in François Truffaut's *L'Histoire d'Adèle H.* (1975; *The Story of Adèle H.*).

The dove caught in freeze-frame is an appropriately elusive image with which to conclude the film. While the film is intensely personal in its focus on two individuals, Grlić manages (by forgoing the use of music in the opening scenes, for example) to keep the audience sufficiently distanced from the action to enable it to consider the wider implications of the story. Similarly, the dove is neither an affirmation of freedom (Tomislav's escaping spirit) nor a condemnation of his suicide—life must continue, and Tomislav's personal anguish is of little significance. Rather, the closing shot is both and more, for the magician, like the filmmaker Grlić himself, is able to manipulate appearances for his audience. Grlić thus pulls his viewers away from the emotional intensity of an individual death, leaving them to ponder the entire experience he has produced from his cinematic hat.

Andrew Horton